James Clark Ross

Jane Franklin

John Franklin

Eleanor Franklin

Akaitcho

Greenstockings

William Scoresby

Robert McClure

Johann August Miertsching

Thomas Simpson

Leopold McClintock

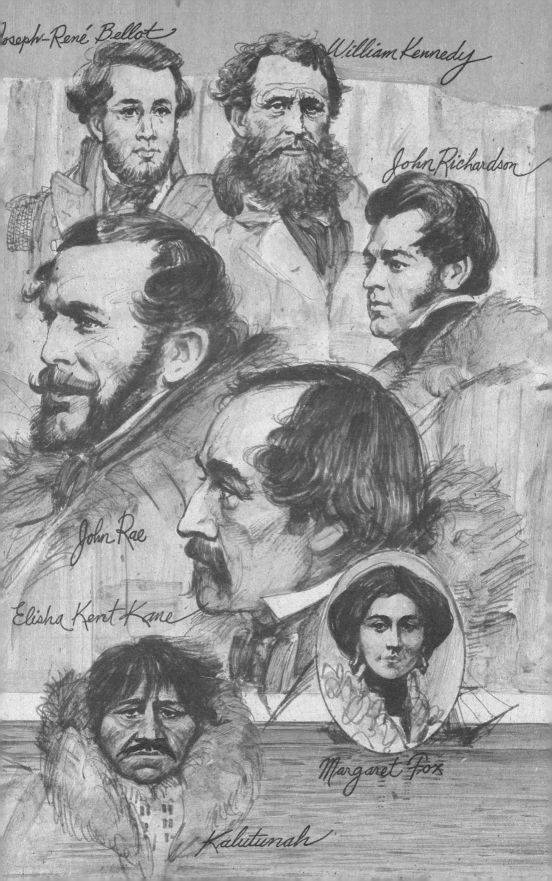

Joseph-René Bellot

William Kennedy

John Richardson

John Rae

Elisha Kent Kane

Margaret Fox

Kalutunah

The Arctic Grail

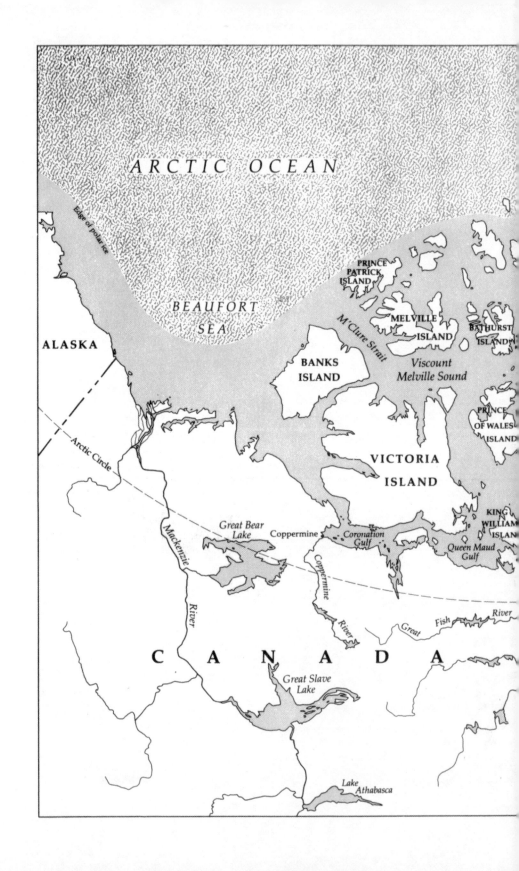

ARCTIC OCEAN

Edge of polar ice

BEAUFORT
SEA

ALASKA

PRINCE
PATRICK
ISLAND

MELVILLE
ISLAND

BATHURST
ISLAND

M'Clure Strait

BANKS
ISLAND

Viscount
Melville Sound

PRINCE
OF WALES
ISLAND

Arctic Circle

VICTORIA

ISLAND

Mackenzie

Great Bear
Lake

Coppermine

Coronation
Gulf

KING
WILLIAM
ISLAND

Queen Maud
Gulf

Coppermine

River

River

Great

Fish

River

C   A   N   A   D   A

Great Slave
Lake

Lake
Athabasca

The Arctic

On every side of us are men who
hunt perpetually for their personal
Northwest Passage, too often
sacrificing health, strength, and life
itself to the search; and who shall say
they are not happier in their vain but
hopeful quest than wiser, duller folks
who sit at home, venturing nothing
and, with sour laughs, deriding the
seekers for that fabled thoroughfare?
— *Kenneth Roberts*

The Arctic trails have their secret
tales that would make your blood
run cold.
— *Robert W. Service*

The quest
for the North West Passage
and the North Pole, 1818-1909

Grail

By Pierre Berton

Viking

VIKING
Published by the Penguin Group
Viking Penguin Inc., 40 West 23rd Street, New York, New York 10010, U.S.A.
Penguin Books Ltd, 27 Wrights Lane, London W8 5TZ, England
Penguin Books Australia Ltd, Ringwood, Victoria, Australia
Penguin Books Canada Ltd, 2801 John Street,
Markham, Ontario, Canada L3R 1B4
Penguin Books (N.Z.) Ltd, 182–190 Wairau Road,
Auckland 10, New Zealand

Penguin Books Ltd, Registered Offices:
Harmondsworth, Middlesex, England

First American Edition
Published in 1988 by Viking Penguin Inc.

10   9   8   7   6   5   4   3

For illustrations used in this book, grateful acknowledgment is made to their sources as follows: The Metropolitan Toronto Library for "First communication with the natives of Prince Regent's Bay," page 14; "*Victory* crew saved by the *Isabella*," page 106; The *Investigator* trapped off Banks Island, page 200; Belcher's ships in winter quarters, page 234; "Life in the brig," by Elisha Kent Kane, page 272; "Sighting of the *Ravenscraig*," page 344. The National Archives of Canada for "Boats in a swell amongst the ice," C–94116, page 62. The *Illustrated London News* (13 Oct. 1849) for The Arctic aurora, page 156. The National Maritime Museum, London, for "The Death of Franklin," page 310, and "A sledge from the *Alert* making a push for the Pole," page 410. The National Archives, Washington, for Rescue of Greely survivors, 200 (S) 2F B71, page 434. Andreemuseet, Gränna, Sweden, for Andrée's balloon after foundering, page 488. The National Geographic Society ©, for Peary's North Pole expedition, page 550.

LIBRARY OF CONGRESS CATALOGING IN PUBLICATION DATA
Berton, Pierre, 1920–
The Arctic grail.
Bibliography: p.
Includes index.
1. Northwest Passage.   2. North Pole.
I. Title.
G640.B47   1988   910'.091632   88–40063
ISBN 0–670–82491–7

Printed in the United States of America
Set in Times Roman
Endpaper art by Tom McNeely

Contents

Illustrations

Maps

Chapter One

FIRST COMMUNICATION with the NATIVES of PRINCE REGENTS BAY, as Drawn by JOHN SACKHOUSE and Presented to CAPT ROSS. Aug 10.1818.

Ross and Parry encounter the Etah Eskimos (as drawn by John Sacheuse)

In the published memoirs of that stubborn and often maddening *John* Arctic explorer Sir John Ross, there is a remarkable illustration of *Barrow's* an encounter that took place on August 10, 1818, between two Brit- *obsession* ish naval officers and a band of Greenland Eskimos.

The most striking thing about this drawing is the contrast of cultures it depicts. The Eskimos are dressed, as one might expect, in jackets, trousers, and boots made from fur and sealskin, perfectly adapted for the harsh climate of ultima Thule. The two men who greet them are attired exactly as they would be had they been envoys to some palm-fringed island in the South Pacific or off the coast of Africa. There they stand, resplendent in cocked hats, tailcoats, and white gloves, swords dangling from their waists, the points of their buckled shoes that once trod the parquet floors of Mayfair sinking into the soft snow – costumed actors in a savage land.

Behind them, against a magnificent backdrop of chiselled mountains, their two ships float at anchor – square-rigged vessels of the kind that defeated the French at Trafalgar but that will prove hopelessly unfit for Arctic channels. The seamen aboard are shivering in regulation wool and broadcloth, since no exploring nation has yet recognized the need for special Arctic clothing.

Officers and natives are equally startled by this unexpected encounter. The two peoples view the world in ways as different as their appearance. Almost a century will pass before either recognizes the need to understand or learn from the other.

The British officers have until now met only one Eskimo, the Anglicized interpreter John Sacheuse, whom they call Sackhouse. The Eskimos here, on the rim of Melville Bay on the western shore of Greenland, have never before seen a white man. To the naval officers, who stand peering at these strange, squat creatures, muffled in furs, the moon itself could scarcely seem more remote than this bleak, treeless shore. To the Eskimos, their astonishing visitors must be celestial beings. In a dialect Sacheuse can hardly understand they ask, "Where do you come from, the sun or the moon?"

The picture is all the more remarkable because it was sketched by Sacheuse himself. A young Christianized native from southern Greenland, he had stowed away two years earlier on a whaling ship and eventually reached England, where he studied drawing under one of the Nasmyth family of landscape and portrait artists.

Sacheuse has here recorded a historic moment, for this is the first Arctic expedition of the nineteenth century, the new beginning of a long quest, first for the North West Passage, later for the North Pole. That quest, pursued for most of the century, will foster a golden age of exploration. Ship after ship – British at the outset and later American, Scandinavian, Austrian, and Italian – will sail off through the ice-clogged northern seas on the most romantic of voyages, seeking a Passage that may not exist and has no commercial value and an almost unidentifiable pinpoint at the top of the world that has very little scientific significance.

The two naval officers in Sacheuse's illustration are Commander John Ross, captain of the *Isabella* and leader of the expedition, and his second-in-command, Lieutenant William Edward Parry of the *Alexander*. Both men have an appointment with history, but history will not treat them equally. Ross's reputation will be clouded by the events of this first journey. He will never quite recover from the resulting wave of sarcasm and vituperation. Parry, the taller of the two, will go on to acquire a towering reputation as "the beau ideal of the Arctic officer." History, like life, is not always fair. Ross did not deserve the extremes of criticism levelled against him; Parry did not merit the excessive adulation he received. In the tangled web of Arctic channels, luck was often as important as skill; in the hierarchy of the Royal Navy, class and cronyism often outweighed ability. Parry had luck and class. John Ross had neither.

Ross's assignment was to try to fill up some of the blank spaces on the map of the Arctic. There were so many of them, so much to discover! Was Greenland an island, for instance, or was it connected to North America? Nobody knew; Ross was asked to find out. Did Baffin Bay exist or was it a figment of an earlier explorer's imagination? Nobody was quite sure. Another of Ross's tasks was to determine its existence. But the most important of all his instructions was "to endeavour to ascertain the practicability of a Passage from the Atlantic to the Pacific Ocean along the Northern Coast of America."

That was the real quest – to find the elusive transcontinental channel that had obsessed and frustrated English mariners and explorers from Elizabethan days. As Martin Frobisher had declared, "it is *still* the only thing left undone, whereby a notable mind might be made famous and remarkable."

The swashbuckling Frobisher, friend of Drake and Hawkins, was the first to seek the Passage in three voyages between 1576 and 1578. He was as optimistic as he was naïve. He was sure that Frobisher "Strait" led westward to the Pacific and that a fortune in gold lay on an island near its mouth. His backers were more interested in the gold, which turned out to be iron pyrites, so that Frobisher never managed to explore the strait, which we now know to be only a bay.

Seven years later, a more hard-headed Elizabethan, John Davis, a friend of Walter Raleigh, tried again. He rediscovered Greenland, which had been forgotten after the failure of the Norse colonies three centuries before. Then he crossed the ice-choked strait that bears his name to chart the east coast of a new land (Baffin Island). He was convinced the mysterious Passage existed but was frustrated in his attempts to sail farther north by an implacable barrier of ice.

Like Frobisher before him, Davis had noted a broad stretch of water north of Ungava. As every schoolchild knows, Henry Hudson sailed through this strait – it is named for him – in 1610. On bursting out into a seemingly limitless sea he thought he had reached the Pacific. It was, in fact, Hudson Bay, and it was there, after a dreadful winter, that he met his death at the hands of a mutinous crew, four of whom were later murdered in a skirmish with the natives.

Those who survived were brought home by Hudson's first mate, Robert Bylot, whose pardon was ensured through that feat of seamanship. Bylot made two more mercantile voyages to the great bay and concluded there was no navigable passage leading to the Pacific from its western shores.

The next year, 1616, the indefatigable Bylot made a fourth Arctic voyage with the brilliant William Baffin as his pilot. They managed to get through the ice that had stopped Davis, travelling three hundred miles farther north than he had – a record that stood for more than two centuries – and mapped the entire bay that now bears Baffin's name. They also found three broad openings, any one of which might lead to lands unknown and which they named for their patrons, Sir James Lancaster, "Alderman Jones," and Sir Thomas Smith. These deep, navigable sounds were to play their part in the nineteenth-century exploration of the frozen world. Two led to the North West Passage. The third – Smith Sound – was the gateway to the North Pole.

After that, interest in the Passage dwindled. When Luke Foxe returned in 1631 after exploring the Foxe Channel and Foxe Basin north of Hudson Bay, he reported that there could be no route to the Orient south of the Arctic Circle. That killed all hope of a commercially practical Passage. There was a brief flurry a century later when Christopher Middleton explored the west coast of Southampton Island in Hudson Bay. He thought the channel known as Roes Welcome Sound might lead to the Passage, but all it led to was a cul-de-sac, which he ruefully named Repulse Bay. Such is the resilience of the questing spirit that a century later Repulse Bay again became a target for those aiming at the secret of the North West Passage. Once again, Repulse Bay repulsed them.

For, just as the Elizabethans had forgotten about the existence of Greenland, so the British of the Regency period had forgotten the whereabouts of Frobisher's discoveries and, even more astonishing, had disputed whether there really was a Baffin Bay at all. In spite of the fact that whaling ships had been operating in Davis Strait for two centuries and had undoubtedly penetrated the bay, Baffin's discoveries became suspect. Finally, the bay was removed from the maps of the time.

Indeed, except for Hudson Bay and part of Baffin Island, the Arctic region was a blank on the map. Even the northern continental coastline remained an enigma. Only two overland explorers had managed to reach the Arctic waters: Samuel Hearne at the Coppermine's mouth in 1771, Alexander Mackenzie at the Mackenzie delta in 1789. From the tip of Russian Alaska to the shores of Hudson Bay, everything, save for these two pinpoints, was uncharted and mysterious. It was quite possible, for all anyone knew, that a chunk of North America could reach as far as the Pole itself. But one thing *was* certain: if somewhere in that fog-shrouded realm a Passage linking the oceans was found to exist, it couldn't be much more than a curiosity.

Why, then, was the British Admiralty dispatching two shiploads of seamen in a new search for a navigable channel through the unknown Arctic? The answer is that the Navy had to find something for its ships, its men, and, most important, its officers to do now that Europe was at peace. Britain controlled the seas. Napoleon had been packed off to exile in 1815. There were no wars left for the Royal Navy to fight. Its new enemy would be the elements themselves.

By 1817, when the idea of a renewed search for the North West Passage was first proposed, 90 per cent of all naval officers were unemployed, eking out a miserable existence on half pay, which was not much above starvation scale, and yearning for an opportunity – *any* opportunity – that would restore them to service and bring them promotion. Most of the able seamen had been discharged after the defeat of France; their numbers had dropped from 140,000 to 19,000. But the officers, who belonged to a different class, were kept on; in fact, their strength was actually increased to 6,000. This time-honoured custom led to a ridiculous disproportion. In the British Navy there was an officer for every three men.

Under such conditions promotion was impossible. To reach high rank, a young lieutenant like Edward Parry would have to have some miraculous feat to perform. No wonder, then, that men who had never seen a palm tree or an iceberg were desperate to go to the ends of the earth – literally – if not for the glory of King and Empire at least to serve their own ambitions. The Navy was eager to send them. What matter if the ships were too big and cumbersome and the crews too large for effective Arctic service? What matter if the Passage was commercially impractical? England was about to embark on a new age of discovery in which it was the exploit itself that counted. Like the headwaters of the Nile and the mysterious Congo, the Passage was there, waiting to be conquered, and so was the North Pole. The race to succeed took on some of the aspects of an international sporting event. How humiliating it would be for England if a mariner from another nation – a Russian, perhaps, or an upstart American – should get there first and seize the prize!

The moving spirit behind this new attitude was an Admiralty bureaucrat named John Barrow, Jr., a moon-faced man with short-cropped hair, bristling black brows, and the tenacious temperament of a bull terrier. He came from humble farming stock in North Lancashire, and the position he held for the best part of forty years – second secretary to the Admiralty – sounds humble enough; but he was a powerful figure in the service. John Ross, who didn't care for him, said that Barrow gave the impression that he was *first* secretary, and, in fact, there were some then and later who thought he was.

Certainly Barrow's career was remarkable. He had left school at thirteen and risen to his position through a combination of hard work, energy, and administrative ability, as well as an instinct for getting to know the right people and choosing the most influential patrons. In his job he took all the latitude allowed. He was responsible for the internal operations of the Admiralty, but in that role he could be highly selective. If you wanted to get on in the Navy it was

19

useful to be on the right side of the second secretary – and it helped if you were a member of the upper crust. Barrow, the dirt farmer's son, had some of the snobbery of the British working class.

He has been called the father of modern Arctic exploration. He wasn't imaginative, but he was curious. He shared with his contemporaries that passion for charts and statistics that was the mark of the English adventurer. The "most honourable and useful" employment for the Navy in peacetime, Barrow felt, was to complete the geographical and hydrographical surveys that had been launched in the previous century by such seamen as Cook and Vancouver. Napoleon was no sooner locked up in St. Helena (Barrow's suggestion) than the Admiralty dispatched an expedition to the Congo, the first for which Barrow was responsible.

But it was not the fetid jungles of the Dark Continent that caught Barrow's fancy; it was the Arctic. Although he had travelled in both Africa and China, he had been drawn to the polar regions ever since he had made a youthful voyage to Greenland on a whaler. A little learning had made Barrow an expert. He hadn't even seen an iceberg, but he had fallen in love with the *idea* of the Arctic. His understanding of that mysterious realm was, to put it charitably, imperfect. Its known terrors failed to dampen his enthusiasm or smother his optimism. Barrow always overestimated the ability of nineteenth-century expeditions to bull their way through the appalling pressures of the shifting ice pack. To him, the discovery of the Passage was a kind of joyride – a romantic excursion into the Unknown.

Barrow himself didn't believe there was a Baffin Bay. In his optimism he was convinced of the presence of an "Open Polar Sea" – a temperate ocean, free of ice, surrounding the Pole and walled off from the rest of the world by a frozen barrier. He was wrong on both counts, but then who knew what really lay in the uncharted North? Was there really open water hidden beyond the fog? Were there islands, peninsulas, channels? Or, as many believed, was there a clear, easily navigable route that would link Europe with Asia?

The North West Passage had glamour. There was a good deal of talk, then and later, about the advancement of science, but it was the elusive Passage that caught the imagination. Certainly science would be advanced – seas charted, coastlines mapped, thousands of minute observations recorded, the flora and fauna of the new land meticulously noted, geological specimens collected, the habits of the natives

20

exhaustively studied. The keeping of records of every kind was a British obsession. But all this was incidental to the Great Quest. Nobody gave out handsome prizes for scientific discoveries, but there would be a sultan's ransom for the first man who could thread his way through the Arctic labyrinth. National honour was at stake. As Barrow put it, "it would be somewhat mortifying if a naval power but of yesterday should complete a discovery in the nineteenth century, which was so happily commenced by Englishmen in the sixteenth." He meant Russia.

To the Royal Navy, anything seemed possible in those heady post-Napoleonic days. The frustrations and failures of the Elizabethan and Jacobean explorers were forgotten or minimized. Had not Nelson triumphed over the French Navy? Every Englishman was convinced that the nineteenth century belonged to Britain. It was inconceivable that a couple of stout ships could not sweep through the Arctic in a single winter to the greater glory of the Empire. As Barrow, the super-optimist, put it in his convoluted prose, "from the zeal and abilities of the persons employed in the arduous enterprise everything may be expected to be done within the scope of possibility."

Whoever discovered the answer to this puzzle would be rich beyond his wildest dreams. Nudged by Barrow, the Royal Society persuaded parliament to offer a series of prizes to anyone who could solve the mystery – or even part of it. The first explorer to reach a longitude of 110 degrees west would get five thousand pounds. Twenty degrees farther west, to the meridian of the Mackenzie, the ante was doubled. At 150 degrees west, the prize reached fifteen thousand pounds; and if the Pacific were attained, it would be twenty thousand – an enormous sum in those tax-free days, equal to well over a million dollars in 1988.

But there was another prize to be captured, as elusive as the North West Passage and even more difficult to attain. The North Pole represented the ultimate in geographical discovery. Like that of the Passage, its value was symbolic rather than commercial. Whoever managed to reach it would gain lasting renown, not only for himself but also for his country.

As the leading maritime nation, Great Britain could not afford to ignore this trophy. Thus Barrow planned two expeditions for the spring of 1818. He was convinced, as many were (though without a shred of evidence), that a belt of temperate water, free of ice, surrounded the Pole. If a ship could force its way through the intervening pack, the rest of the voyage would be simple. Of course it wasn't simple, as Captain David Buchan quickly learned. Buchan was in command of two ships, *Dorothea* and *Trent*, assigned to navigate the seas north of Spitzbergen. There he got an object lesson in the power of moving ice. At one point his frustrated crews, dragging the two ships through the pack with anchors and ropes, found after three days of struggle that they had actually been pushed *back* two miles.

The savage storm that soon followed all but wrecked both vessels. Nipped by the great bergs, hurled from floe to jagged floe (the *Trent*'s bell tolling mournfully as she rolled from side to side), they were fortunate to limp back to Spitzbergen, where the attempt on the Pole was called off. Both ships returned to England in October. The expedition is notable only because Buchan's second-in-command, the commander of the *Trent*, was Lieutenant John Franklin, making the first of four journeys into the frozen world that would, in the end, claim him and thus immortalize his name.

The second expedition that Barrow planned was to seek the North West Passage by sailing up through the dubious Baffin Bay. Somewhere along its western side, Barrow felt sure, there must be an entrance that would lead, presumably, to Russia. The Navy searched diligently for an officer who had experience with ice conditions and found none. Finally, it hit on Commander John Ross, who had spent two seasons in the Baltic, which, though not very frigid, was as close as any naval officer had come to polar conditions. At that time, there were seven hundred officers with the same rank as Ross. He was one of only forty-six who were actively employed. Naturally he jumped at the chance; it was his only hope of being promoted to post captain.

This stocky red-haired Scot, around whom so much controversy was to swirl, seemed the best choice for an Arctic adventure. Not yet forty-one, he had three decades of sea experience. He was undeniably brave, having been wounded no fewer than thirteen times in battle – "scarred from head to foot," in the words of a future polar explorer, Elisha Kane. Ross boasted of his injuries, claiming that few other naval officers in his condition "could perform those services which require strength and manual labour." Modesty was never Ross's strong suit. But Parry, his second-in-command, liked him on sight and found him breezy, good tempered, affable, and clever at surveys. It was an assessment that Parry would later revise.

Ross *was* good at surveys. He was also inventive. He had an inquiring mind and shared with his fellow Britons the growing pre-occupation with science that was to distinguish the century. He had several ingenious inventions to his credit, including a new sextant known as the Royal William. He was also a firm disciple of phrenology, which had invaded England from the continent in 1814 and captivated the literati. Belief in this curious pseudo-science did not make John Ross an eccentric. Many leading figures of the day, including Jane Griffin, the future Lady Franklin, were convinced that character and ability could be determined by examining the shape of a person's skull. Using drawings of the cranium, subdivided by dotted lines like those on butchers' charts, the phrenologists identified bumps of knowledge, passion, and greed. Ross, in fact, called himself a phrenologist and would later write a paper on the subject, analysing the bumps on the heads of various acquaintances from Lady Elizabeth Yorke to the Countess of Hardwicke.

Ross was the choice of Sir George Hope, one of the Lords of the Admiralty, and there was nothing Barrow could do about that. The second secretary, who was ambitious for recognition, would have preferred the polished and more pliant Parry to the rough-hewn and independent Scotsman. He was never Ross's friend; he would soon become his enemy.

Like Barrow, Ross was of relatively humble stock, a son of the manse; Parry ranked higher on the social scale. His father was a fashionable doctor in Bath, a governor of the Bath hospital, and a fellow of the Royal Society. He had influential friends: his practice included members of the nobility. Young Parry was enrolled in one of the best grammar schools in England before going off to sea at thirteen. (Ross had gone to sea at eleven.) His cultured family had wide interests in art, music, and literature, and he got into the Navy through the influence of Admiral Cornwallis, the commander of the Channel fleet, whose niece was one of Dr. Parry's patients. In the nineteenth-century navy, as Parry well understood, connections counted.

He believed in "the incalculable advantage of being on the spot." When he returned from the West Indies in 1817, he wangled an introduction to the venerable Sir Joseph Banks, president of the Royal Society – a man to whom the Navy listened. He cultivated both Banks and Barrow, presenting each with a slim volume he'd written on nautical astronomy, carefully dedicated to the admiral under whom he'd served in the West Indies. He wrote gleefully to his parents about these important contacts. "Independently of the immediate advantages to be derived from such introductions I feel that it must be the means of future advantage in every possible way," he exclaimed. "I feel already that I begin to stand upon higher ground than before. . . ."

Barrow, the farmer's son who liked to hobnob with members of the upper classes, took to him at once, for he saw him as an ally. He became Parry's patron; Parry became his loyal disciple. Parry would be the means by which Barrow achieved recognition for launching an era of Arctic exploration; Barrow would be the instrument that would give Parry an Arctic command of his own.

But in 1818 Parry was no better qualified for Arctic exploration than Ross, whose Baltic stint had scarcely prepared him for the rigours of the white world. There was one man who *was* qualified – the most experienced sea captain in England at that time. William Scoresby was quite prepared to go. But neither the Admiralty nor John Barrow had any intention of sending him. For William Scoresby wasn't Navy. He was a member of that despised commercial band of Greenland whalers who had been pushing farther and farther north without recognition for decades. A whaling captain in charge of one of His Majesty's ships? The prospect was unthinkable.

In the annals of Arctic exploration, Scoresby has rarely been given his due. John Barrow, among others, saw to that. Barrow took most of the kudos for persuading the Admiralty, through Banks, to seek out the Passage on Scoresby's evidence that a miraculous change in the Arctic climate had increased the possibility of channels open to the west. In fact, Scoresby had been making meticulous observations in this area and communicating them to Sir Joseph Banks long before Barrow entered the fray.

Scoresby was an extraordinary man, perhaps the most remarkable Arctic expert of his era. A whaler like his father, he had been eighteen years at sea, seven of them as a master. He had been given his first command at the age of twenty-one and was soon known as the most courageous and skilful of the Greenland whalers. But he was more than that. In the winters, when the whaling season ended, he had taken classes in philosophy and science at Edinburgh. Like Ross, he was inventive. He had devised a new "marine diver" to take the temperature of deep-sea waters (and discovered that the water on the ocean floor was warmer than that at the surface). He had invented a pair of "ice shoes" for walking more easily across the pack. He had

24

produced a paper on polar ice conditions and in 1818 was completing his monumental work, which has since been called "one of the most remarkable books in the English language" as well as "the foundation stone of Arctic science."

This was the man the British Navy snubbed when it planned its first expedition. Scoresby did not have Ross's bulldog stubbornness or Parry's natural charm and good looks. His face was weathered by the elements, and his nose and cheekbones were a little too prominent. He was unassuming, even shy, and a devout Christian who forbade his crews to go after whales on the Lord's Day. Years later he would be ordained a minister.

For the past decade, Scoresby had been in regular communication with the ailing Joseph Banks, describing his scientific investigations in the chemical composition of sea water and polar ice, in the movements of the Arctic currents, in the infinitely diverse forms of snowflakes, and in the new botanical species he had discovered on the Greenland shore. In 1817, he found the coast of Greenland clear of ice for the first time in anyone's memory. At Banks's request he sent him details; the sea, he said, was "perfectly devoid of ice" as far north as the 80th parallel. Conditions were perfect for a voyage of discovery, and he, William Scoresby, was eager to command it.

Scoresby was no romantic. He had no illusions about the Passage. In a prescient letter to Banks, he forecast that it would "be found only at intervals of some years" because the Arctic climate and the Arctic ice were ever shifting and changing, a fact that the British naval explorers never fully comprehended. Even if someone accomplished a voyage through the unknown Arctic fastness to the Pacific "it might not again be practical in ten or twenty years." That was an assessment that holds true today.

Scoresby in 1817 knew what the Navy took decades to learn. He scorned the proponents of the Open Polar Sea theory, a fantasy that Barrow for one would never relinquish. (Another delusion was that land extended all the way to the Pole, joining the continents of Asia and America.) The idea that beyond an intervening wall of ice lay a warmer ocean, free of impediment, was one no Greenland whaler could accept. The barrier was there; all could see it. Why should it suddenly vanish in a colder clime? To believe that required an excess of optimism and wishful thinking. But in post-war Britain there was no lack of those.

Banks would have liked to see Scoresby in charge, if not of the expedition itself, at least of one of the pair of ships being fitted out for Arctic service. In December 1817, he urged the whaler to come to London to meet Barrow. The encounter that followed was, to put it mildly, not propitious. Barrow was more than evasive; he was alarmingly rude when the two met for the first time in Banks's drawing room. When Scoresby tried to approach him, Barrow edged away. Scoresby persisted, finally managed to corner him, and asked, bluntly, what his expectations were. Barrow responded coldly that if he really wanted to go he should call next day at the Navy Board and make his proposals. With that he turned sharply and left the room.

Banks then told Scoresby as gently as possible that all his efforts to get him a command had failed. The Admiralty could not or would not employ anybody but its own officers. He might, perhaps, be taken on as a pilot, but an officer of the line would be in command. Banks, who wasn't Navy himself, knew something of naval snubs from his exploring years in the South Seas aboard British ships. He was both disappointed and sympathetic, but he did not have the energy to circumvent Barrow. He was old and sick with gout, confined to a wheelchair, and approaching his death. Scoresby decided to have nothing more to do with the expedition. He had come to London at his own expense – all for nothing. Barrow never again mentioned him by name or gave him further credit for helping to launch a new era in Arctic exploration.

2

The Croker On April 21, 1818, the expedition to seek the Passage set off for
Mountains Baffin Bay with Ross in the *Isabella* (385 tons) and Parry commanding the smaller *Alexander* (252 tons). These were transports. Ross didn't think either was suitable for Arctic exploration and said so in his brusque fashion, whereupon he was told, equally brusquely, that he didn't have to go if he didn't like the conditions. He knuckled under. In fact, Parry's vessel had difficulty keeping up with the *Isabella*, a deficiency that limited its usefulness. But the Navy had no intention of building special vessels for Arctic service. In six decades of polar exploration it never did so. After all, its main task was the defence of the realm. Exploration was no more than a peacetime diversion. The Navy's refitters did their best to brace and strengthen

the converted ships for their coming battle with the ice; but if war came they would be expected to perform a different and, to the Navy, more important service.

By mid-June, the expedition had crossed the Atlantic and entered Davis Strait, and the officers and their crews had their first view of the icebound sea in all its splendour and all its menace. Here was a crystalline world of azure and emerald, indigo and alabaster – dazzling to the eye, disturbing to the soul. No explorer who passed through this maze of drifting, misshapen bergs ever failed to record the feelings and sensations that engulfed him when he first encountered the glittering metropolis of moving ice. To some the great frozen mountains that whirled past seemed to have been sculptured by a celestial architect, for here were cathedrals and palaces, statues and castles, all of brilliant white, coruscating in the sun's rays, each one slightly out of focus as in a dream. Some reminded Parry of the slabs at Stonehenge; there were actually some upright pieces supporting a third resting horizontally on top. Ross was confounded by the intensity of the colours – the greens and blues and the blazing whites. "It is hardly possible," he scribbled in his journal, "to imagine anything more exquisite . . . by night as well as by day they glitter with a vividness of colour beyond the power of art to represent. . . ."

Both men were awed by the strangeness of the savage realm they'd invaded. Soon they would enter unknown waters. Meanwhile, it was comforting to encounter the whaling fleet – some three dozen ships flying the British red ensign – and to hear the cheers of the whalers as they passed through. It was, Parry thought, rather like coming upon a flourishing European seaport. But he also knew that this was where civilization ended.

From the whalers Parry and Ross got their first warning of the vagaries of the Arctic climate. The warm-up, it seemed, had ended. The ice was far more formidable than expected. The previous winter had been terrible – the worst in a decade. The whaling fleet was hard put to find a clear passage north.

The following day Parry climbed one of Greenland's mountains to take some observations and was moved by the spectacle below. It made him shudder at his own insignificance, he said, and taught him to reflect "upon the immensity of the creator who could call these stupendous mountains and those enormous masses of ice into being."

No more devout explorer ever entered the Arctic. The evangelical movement, with its emphasis on prayer and Sunday observance, was then sweeping Great Britain. It did not attract the apparently godless lower classes, but it did have a marked influence on middle-class Anglicans such as Parry. The movement emphasized the need to spread the gospel among the lower orders, and these, of course, included British seamen, who by and large could scarcely be called fervent churchgoers. Almost forty years later, when Parry was an admiral, he would address these seamen in an inspirational pamphlet. "I want to see every man among you," he wrote, ". . . sailing under the British flag, a religious man, having the fear of God before his eyes and the love of God glowing in his heart."

To Parry, a man without religion was like a clock without weights or mainspring. He himself prayed constantly, day and night. His sense of the infinite, already well developed, was certainly deepened and strengthened by the Arctic. In a later remarkable declaration Parry announced that he would give up his wife before he would give up his God.

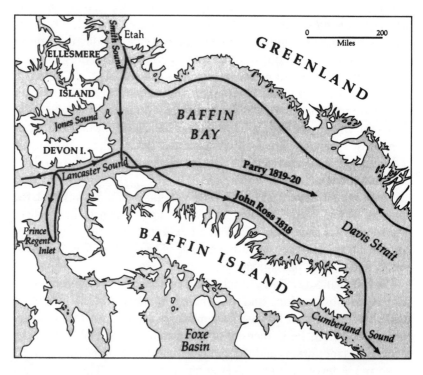

The start of the quest

By July 2, Parry saw another manifestation of the Creator's power. The two ships entered a dismaying labyrinth of icebergs. Parry set himself the task of counting them and gave up when he reached one thousand. For the next month the expedition moved sluggishly north along the Greenland coast, beset by ice, blinded by fog, and almost crushed by the pressure of the encroaching pack during one screeching gale. It was a close call. The sterns of the two vessels collided violently. Spars, rigging, lifeboats were torn apart. Even the hardened whalers were shaken by the near catastrophe; their own boats, they said, could not have stood such a hammering.

A day or so later, not far from the aboriginal village of Etah, Ross and Parry came face to face with an unknown Eskimo culture – the encounter recorded in the illustration by John Sacheuse, their native interpreter from South Greenland. Even Sacheuse had never heard of, much less encountered, this strange race of polar Eskimos whom Ross dubbed "Arctic Highlanders." He could understand their dialect only with great difficulty.

The scene that followed was pure farce. The natives on the shore hung back, obviously terrified at the strange apparitions on the ships. It was decided that one of Parry's officers should go forward bearing a white flag on which was painted the civilized emblem for peace – a hand holding an olive branch. The natives, of course, had no idea what an olive branch was, or what it was supposed to mean. On these bleak shores no olive trees grew – actually, no trees at all. Yet none of the white men seemed to appreciate the absurdity of the gesture. Ross made a more practical move. He put up a flag on a pole and tied a bag full of presents to it. That worked marvellously.

These Eskimos had had no contact with the world beyond their desolate domain. They were astonished at the presence of Sacheuse, for it had not occurred to them that there might be others like themselves in the world. As for the men with sickly looking skins, they were convinced they had come from the sky. They knew nothing of boats – had never seen one; even the native word "kayak" had no meaning for them. They spoke to the ships as if they were living things. "We have seen them move their wings," they said. When Sacheuse tried to explain that ships were floating houses, they had difficulty believing him.

They were startled by their first glimpse of a mirror and tried to discover the monster they believed was hiding behind it. They laughed at the metal frames of the eye-glasses worn by some of the

29

seamen, spit out in disgust the biscuit that was offered, wondered what kind of ice the window panes were made of and what kind of animal produced the strange "skins" the officers were wearing. They were shown a watch, thought it was alive, and asked if it was good to eat. The sight of a little pig terrified them; a demonstration of hammer and nails charmed them; the ships' furniture baffled them, for the only wood they'd ever known came from a dwarf shrub whose stem was no thicker than a finger.

Between these naïve people and the English mariners there was a gap that would not be bridged until each learned from the other. Sacheuse made them take off their caps in the presence of the officers, a gesture that suggests how quickly he had absorbed the white way of life. It was the first small attempt – one of many that would be made in the years to come – to "civilize" the natives. They obeyed cheerfully enough but must have been as mystified by the ritual as the English were to find that human beings actually lived in this uninviting land. Yet nobody on this so-called scientific expedition thought to investigate how a band of people who couldn't count past ten had managed to adapt to their formidable homeland – an omission, repeated through the century, that would cost many future explorers their lives.

The expedition had now reached the top of Baffin Bay, rediscovering it after two centuries. (Baffin's charts turned out to be surprisingly accurate.) Ross sailed west to the southern tip of what is now Ellesmere Island, then south, seeking a channel that might lead him to the North West Passage. At the end of August a possibility loomed up – a long inlet leading westward that William Baffin had named for his patron Sir James Lancaster, one of the founders of the East India Company.

Was this the way to the Orient? Or was it simply a dead end, a bay rather than a strait? Nobody knew. Baffin himself had given up hope at this point and failed to trace it to its end. But Parry, for one, was full of optimism. Surely this was the route that could lead, if not directly to the Russian coast, at least into the heart of the Arctic to connect with other lanes of water!

Ross was less sure. As the two ships moved up the sound he became convinced that no passage existed. That suspicion was confirmed on a foggy afternoon at the end of August when they reached the thirty-mile point. Ross hove to, waiting for Parry to catch up and the weather to clear. The officer of the watch roused him from his cabin to announce the fog was lifting. Squinting into the ten-minute gap that appeared in the murk, Ross saw, or thought he saw, a chain of mountains blocking all access to the west. He was apparently the only man who glimpsed that mysterious range, which he charted as the Croker Mountains, named after the *first* secretary of the Admiralty. That was the story he told Parry and the others. Later, in his published account, he changed it and insisted that two of his crew had also seen the mountains. Few believed him.

To the stunned surprise and anger of Parry and the others, Ross, without a word of explanation, turned about and headed for home, skimming down the sound past the *Alexander* "as if some mischief was behind him."

William Hooper, purser of the *Alexander*, expressed in his journal that day the frustration and disappointment felt aboard Parry's ship: "Thus vanished our golden dreams, our brilliant hopes, our high expectations! – and without the satisfaction of proving those dreams to be visionary, these hopes to be fallacious, those expectations to be delusive! To describe our mortification and disappointment would be impossible, at thus having our increasing hopes annihilated in a moment, without the shadow of reasoning appearing. . . ." It wasn't until the next day, when the expedition put in to shore near the mouth of Lancaster Sound, that Parry was given any explanation by Ross. Parry held his tongue; Ross, he indicated later, was beyond argument. (But Parry, who had other fish to fry, was also remarkably silent about the episode in his private journal.)

Ross's actions were nonetheless inexplicable. He seems to have misinterpreted his instructions, claiming his main task was to explore Baffin Bay. Yet his orders were quite clear: the principal object of the voyage was to see if there was a passage leading toward the Pacific. It was almost as if the doughty seaman didn't believe in the existence of the North West Passage and had seized the first opportunity to confirm that opinion.

But why the haste? Why this sudden scramble to return home? Parry had expected to winter on the shores of Baffin Bay; so had most of the crew. "Do not expect us back this year," a young artilleryman named Captain Edward Sabine, the astronomer of the voyage, wrote to his brother. ". . . Ross will not return if he can possibly find an excuse for waiting on the northern coast of America." But Ross had found an excuse to hightail it for home, even though the expedition was supplied with winter clothing and provisions for another season. Thus were sown the seeds of dissension that pitted Parry, Sabine, and, of course, John Barrow, against the commander.

There were suggestions later that all had not been well on the expedition. Ross was convinced that "a serious conspiracy existed during the voyage and still existed against him." The conspirators included Parry, Sabine, and possibly his own nephew, a young midshipman and future polar hero, James Clark Ross. No doubt Ross felt he had reason for the charge. At one point, he had managed to sneak a look at one of Sabine's letters to his sister in which the astronomer had called Ross "a stupid fellow." Thus, on the very first voyage of discovery, there was a hint of the terrible tensions that marked so many later forays, when men found themselves crammed together under trying conditions for long months in a forbidding climate. There was much worse to come.

The expedition returned to England on November 11, 1818. John Wilson Croker, whose name was on a range of mountains that most of Ross's officers believed imaginary, invited the commander to dine on the sixteenth. Ross was about to accept the invitation when he received a heartbreaking letter from his wife. Their only child was dead.

"I am not fit to go into company," he told Croker. "I must write to my wife."

To which Croker replied, "Damn the child. You'll get more children, come and dine with me."

This appalling response shook Ross, who responded with anger, "Mr. Croker, you have an only child of your own. If it please God to take him from you I hope you will be better supported under the calamity than I am, but I cannot and will not dine with you."

Croker was "very much displeased." Barrow was already furious at what he considered the failure of both his expeditions, in spite of the solid contributions each had made to science. The attempt at the Pole might be excused; nature had clearly conspired against Buchan and Franklin on that first abortive expedition in 1818. But Ross's dereliction in not examining Lancaster Sound could not be forgiven. Ross had restored Baffin Bay to the map, encountered a new race of Eskimos, made a series of scientific observations, and collected new botanical specimens. But to Barrow, it was the Passage that really counted.

Parry certainly believed a passage existed and undoubtedly said so to Barrow. But publicly he kept quiet, as he had on board the *Alexander*. There would certainly be a new expedition in the spring, and

Parry badly wanted to lead it. So did Ross, who had been promoted to post captain and who applied for the command on December 29.

Parry was ahead of him by almost a fortnight. He had nothing to gain by a controversy with his old commander. It certainly wouldn't help his naval career. Besides, what if Ross was right about the Croker Mountains? Parry would look a fool if he disputed that discovery. He whispered his opinions to his family but swore them to silence. "Every future prospect of mine depends on it being kept secret," he explained. Let the "blundering Ross," as Parry called him, blunder further.

Ross did. In January 1819, he published his account of the voyage. This contained not only the author's own engraving of the mysterious mountains but also a further explanation of his reasons for turning back. The sound, he declared, had been blocked by ice. That was news to Parry and Sabine.

Ross's work was scarcely off the presses of John Murray's publishing house before Barrow pounced. In a savage article in the *Quarterly Review*, he tore Ross's book to shreds. The article ran to fifty pages and was unsigned, but everybody knew who had written it.

In his review Barrow came close to calling Ross a coward. He talked of his "indifference and want of perseverance." He hammered away at what he called Ross's "habitual inaccuracy and looseness of description." He sneered at his chapter on the new-found band of Greenland Eskimos and made fun of the term "Arctic Highlanders." ("He has transferred half of Scotland to the shores of this bay.") He attacked the "absurdity and inconsistency of the plates," especially those dealing with the Croker Mountains. No paragraph, however minor, escaped his scrutiny – even Ross's description of the icebergs at night. "Icebergs display no colour at night," Barrow scoffed.

There was worse to come. Young Edward Sabine now entered the lists. He had been hired, on Joseph Banks's recommendation, to make scientific observations during the voyage. He'd had little scientific training but spent several months diligently studying the variations of the compass and the vibrations of the pendulum. He was outraged that Ross in his book downgraded his efforts, gave another officer credit for certain observations, and criticized Sabine's qualities as a naturalist, which he'd never claimed to be.

Sabine fought back with a pamphlet, accusing Ross of plagiarism. He said that the commander had stolen material from one of his papers on the Eskimos and made extensive use of other material without giving him credit. Ross replied with another pamphlet claiming he hadn't trusted Sabine's work and so had made his own observations.

The Navy could not ignore this unseemly sniping. The Admiralty Board held a court of inquiry and decided that John Ross's actions were not becoming to an officer and a gentleman. He was retired on half pay and never again given a naval command. Ross would be heard from again, but in the meantime, Edward Parry would lead the next expedition to seek the North West Passage.

3

Winter Even the most cursory study of the annals of Arctic exploration
Harbour makes one thing clear: many a reputation rests on luck as much as skill. The shifting Arctic climate doomed some men to frustration and even to death while it made heroes out of others. Parry was luckier than most. He sailed north at the right moment, when the Arctic channels were clearer of ice than they had been in a decade. In fact, he almost got through the North West Passage. More than thirty years would go by before any other vessel got as far; and no other sailing ship entering from the east ever got farther.

If Parry had tried in the previous year or if in 1819 he had met with the violent winds and ice conditions encountered by later explorers, he would not have achieved his place in history. In his day the shifting nature of the polar winds and currents and the implacable movements of the great ice streams were not understood. Parry himself was never able to repeat his triumph. Everything after 1819 was anticlimax. His real achievement lies not in his passage through the Arctic archipelago; other experienced officers in the British Navy could have made it through to Melville Island in that salubrious summer. His greater accomplishment was his understanding of his crew and his determination to keep them healthy in mind as well as body.

The greatest peril of wintering in the Arctic was not the cold; it was boredom. For eight, sometimes ten months nothing moved. Ships became prisons. Masts and superstructure were taken down, hatches hermetically sealed, the ships smothered in blankets of insulating snow. Hived together in these wooden cockleshells with little

34

to do, the best-disciplined seamen could break down. Small irritations could be magnified into raging quarrels. Fancied insults could lead to mutinous talk and even mutiny, as Bligh in the South Seas and Hudson in the North had discovered.

Parry was determined to cope with the monotony of the Arctic winter, and it is a tribute to his careful planning, which the more intelligent of his successors copied, that the British Navy was comparatively free of the friction that marred many of the later private Arctic expeditions from the United States.

Parry's background fitted him for the role. Since childhood he had loved music; he had a good ear and at the age of four could repeat any tune after hearing it once. At school he threw himself into competitive sport and amateur theatricals. As a young naval officer he practised the violin three or four hours a day (though never, of course, on Sundays). He would, he said, sacrifice almost anything to become a tolerable player – anything, that is, except his duties. There would be plenty of music aboard Parry's ships (he even brought a barrel organ along) and there would be sports, amateur theatricals, and a newspaper, all designed to maintain a happy ship.

Parry belonged to a new generation of explorers as Ross had belonged to the old. He was the model by which those who followed would be judged, the touchstone for the British in the Arctic. He personified those public school values for which Thomas Arnold was soon to make Rugby famous. He had an unquestioning faith in the British ability to surmount any obstacle. In his observations of the Eskimos his measures were invariably Anglo-Saxon; their failings, strengths, and morals were judged by British standards. Devout, steadfast, and loyal, he believed in hard work and team spirit, was meticulous in collecting every kind of specimen and recording every scintilla of data, and saw the absolute necessity of keeping the lower orders occupied. A beau ideal, indeed.

A handsome officer, tall, slightly stooped, with curly chestnut hair and soft grey eyes, he was amiable, well spoken, and eager to please, but never too eager – just the sort of man to appeal to John Barrow. There was that certain studied diffidence about Parry that would become a hallmark of the Victorian Englishman. His journals are rarely exclamatory; he doesn't go overboard with excitement, nor does he make too much of hardship. That would be indecent, although, of course, it would be equally indecent if you did anything less than your best.

He worried about scurvy, the nemesis of every Arctic traveller, and urged that the Navy's favourite antiscorbutic, lemon juice (wrongly referred to as lime juice), should be prepared from fresh fruit. Along with this he carried pickles, spices, herbs, and sauerkraut. The new era of Arctic exploration coincided with the invention of tinned food. Parry was convinced that canned soups, vegetables, and meats would help stave off the disease and at least vary the traditional diet of salt meat. He ordered quantities of tinned food, which was so new that nobody had yet invented the can opener. Parry's cooks used an axe.

He could scarcely believe his good fortune at having been given such a senior command. He was only twenty-eight, but at that he was the oldest officer on the expedition. Sabine, who had again signed on as supernumerary, was thirty, but all the others, including Lieutenant Matthew Liddon, commander of Parry's second ship, *Griper*, and John Ross's nephew, James, were under twenty-three. Parry's ship, *Hecla*, was a bomb vessel built at the close of the Napoleonic Wars and therefore of exceptionally sturdy construction, "a charming ship" in contrast to Liddon's *Griper*, one of "these paltry Gun-brigs . . . utterly unfit for this service!"

By April 1819 the ships – resplendent in a fresh coating of black and yellow paint – were ready to go. The British public was agog, its appetite whetted by the controversy over the Croker Mountains, its imagination fired by the prospect of a solution to the perennial puzzle of the Passage. The Navy had never stood higher in public esteem. A companion voyage to Parry's, led by another officer, John Franklin, newly returned from his failed attempt to reach the Pole, would trek overland to explore the Arctic coastline of North America. (Few questioned the incongruity of a naval man leading a land exploration.) Together, Franklin and Parry would conquer the Arctic for the glory of England and Empire!

Down to the docks at Greenwich the well-wishers flocked. In Parry's view, no other official expedition had ever attracted "a more hearty feeling of national interest." The multitudes that scrambled aboard the decks included Edward Sabine's niece, a Miss Browne, with whom, it was understood, Parry had an understanding. A flirtatious little incident followed when Parry amused his party by encircling the girl with a life preserver and making her inflate it.

At last the wind was right, and the ships were towed down the sunlit Thames as crowds cheered and handkerchiefs fluttered. Parry's instructions, on leaving the Nore on May 11 and crossing the Atlantic, were to head directly up Davis Strait to Lancaster Sound and attempt the passage. If the Croker Mountains should bar the way, he was to continue north to those other inlets with the plebeian names, Jones and Smith sounds, in hopes that one might lead into the heart of the Arctic. Once again the Admiralty instructions made it clear that the search for the Passage was his primary object. Scientific work was secondary. He was not to stop to examine or chart the coastline. He was to get through as quickly as possible and deliver his documents to the Russian governor at Kamchatka, sail on to the Sandwich Islands (Hawaii), and then return home. Optimism ran high; Parry had forecast the possibility of getting through to China although that was "perhaps too much to hope for."

It certainly was. It was as well that Parry did not realize how slim his chances were of forcing his way through. In a bad season, when the ice was heavy, the odds were about one in a hundred, in a light season about fifty-fifty. Even in an exceptional season – and this *was* an exceptional season – there was a 25-per-cent chance of failure.

Parry's first setback came when he ran into the great river of ice that detaches itself from the polar pack and pours down the centre of Davis Strait. Boldly, he had decided to force his way directly through it to the west – a short cut that would save weeks of detours – using the *Hecla* as a battering ram to clear the way for the weaker *Griper*. But by June 25 he was trapped, and a week went by before he could extricate both ships. Unable to penetrate that chill barrier, he sailed north for three weeks, crossing the Arctic Circle into Baffin Bay before attempting once more to bull his way through by brute force.

Now his crews experienced for the first time the exhausting drudgery that would plague Arctic exploration for all of the century. Straining at the oars in small boats, they attempted to tow the big vessels through the ice-choked channels. Winding and sweating at the capstans, with cables attached to anchors in the bergs, they warped their ships westward, foot by foot. Trudging along the floes, clinging to hawsers like tug-of-war teams, they manhauled them in the direction of Lancaster Sound. On one long day they toiled for eleven hours and moved no more than four miles. Once, when the *Hecla* was trapped, the crews worked for seven hours with ice saws to cut her free, only to find her frozen in again at day's end. Parry urged them on with extra rations of rum and meat.

On July 28, with his men wet and played out, Parry broke out of the eighty-mile barrier and reached open water off the western coast of Baffin Bay. Soon the ears of the exhausted seamen were assailed by the music of the great black whales – eighty-two of them counted in a single day – a shrill, ringing sound, rather like hundreds of musical glasses badly played.

The broad entrance to Lancaster Sound lay directly ahead, the towering mountains of Bylot Island crowning its southern gatepost. Parry viewed the spectacle with mingled apprehension and excitement. The next few days would make his reputation or break it. He could not wait for the slower *Griper*. As soon as the wind was favourable, he signalled a rendezvous with Liddon and, on August 1, headed up the sound under full sail.

The weather was clear; the mysterious channel lay open. As the wind increased to a gale Parry could notice the "breathless anxiety . . . now visible in every countenance." Nobody had sailed up this broad lane of water since the days of the Iceland fishermen who almost certainly had explored it six centuries before. Everything was new: long inlets – or were they only bays? – leading south and north from both shores; serrated hills on the south rising one above the other to the snow-clad peaks above, contrasting with the smoother outline of the north shore, only flecked with snow. Was there land ahead? Was the route to the North West Passage blocked, as Ross believed? William Hooper, who had been Parry's purser on the previous voyage with Ross and who was now purser of the *Hecla*, wrote in his journal, "I never remember to have spent a day of so much fearful anxiety." Ever since entering the sound he had been overcome by "an agony of feeling . . . gradually winding itself up."

But the lookout, high in the crow's-nest – a barrel tied to the top mast – could see no hint of any barrier. Here, the sound, clear of ice, was eighty miles wide. Two days went by and all hands began to feel a sense of relief. The optimists who had figured the distance and bearing to the west began to believe that the Passage could be mastered.

Then, at six on the evening of August 4, hopes were dashed when the lookout reported land ahead. "Vexation and anxiety" were seen on every countenance until it turned out to be a small island. At last the question was answered: the channel ahead was clear. Ross's failing eyesight had played him false, or perhaps he was deceived by one of the mirages caused by the refraction of light that were to become familiar to future explorers. Parry was careful not to gloat, but the ship's surgeon, Alexander Fisher, confided to his diary that none could "avoid feeling a secret satisfaction that their opinions have turned out to be true. . . ."

The *Griper* joined Parry's ship, passing under her stern and raising a shout of congratulation at what Hooper called "our escape from Croker's Mountains." The purser was ecstatic: "There was something peculiarly animating in the joy which lighted every countenance. . . . We had arrived in a sea which had never before been navigated, we were gazing on land that European eyes had never before beheld . . . and before us was the prospect of realizing all our wishes, and of exalting the honor of our country. . . ."

The Croker Mountains vanished from the map. Where Ross had insisted he had seen land there was only water ahead – a broad strait that Parry named, not for Croker, but for his patron, John Barrow. The first secretary would have to be content to have his name on a small bay on the north shore of Lancaster Sound.

The water highway stretched straight as a bowsprit directly into the heart of the unknown Arctic archipelago. Parry was like a man travelling through a long tunnel, able only to guess at the mysteries that lay to the north and south. On the north shore of the sound he could see precipices, cut by chasms and fiords, rising sheer for five hundred feet above the rubbled beach; to the south, the tableland was interrupted by broad channels, one of them (which he named Prince Regent Inlet) more than forty miles wide. Was this the route to the Bering Sea?

Blocked by ice ahead, Parry, joined now by the *Griper*, turned into the inlet and sailed southwest for more than one hundred miles past the snow-choked ravines and vertical rock walls of the great island (Somerset) on his starboard. More ice barred his way, facing him with a new dilemma. Perhaps this was only a bay after all! Back he went into Lancaster Sound, finding open water along the north shore. Snow, sleet, and rain held him up, but then, on August 12, the weather cleared and he headed west into the very heart of the archipelago.

Island masses loomed up, bisected by more broad channels to which he gave names. He left the Precambrian cliffs and glacially ravaged peaks that rose above the notched coastline of Devon Island, crossed the thirty-mile mouth of the broad channel that led into the northern mists and which he named for the Duke of Wellington, and swept on – past the terraced rock hills of Cornwallis Island, past the tattered fringes and wriggling fiords of Bathurst Island, and finally

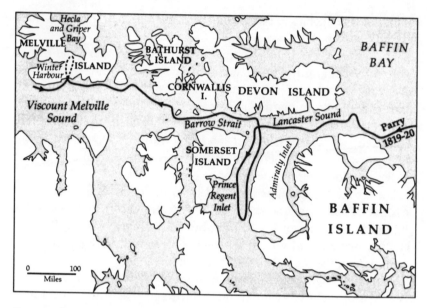

Parry's first voyage, 1819-20

---

into the immense inland sea that he named Viscount Melville Sound
after the First Lord of the Admiralty.

On September 4 the two ships crossed the meridian of 110 degrees
west and the following day, after divine service, Parry broke the news
to his ecstatic crew that they had gained the five-thousand-pound
parliamentary bounty. His own portion would be one thousand
pounds, a small fortune at that time. It was well earned; in one
remarkable five-week sweep, he had explored some eight hundred
miles of new coastline.

To the north of the sound Parry could see the twelve-hundred-foot
cliffs and the rugged highlands of another great island, which he also
named for Viscount Melville. Eighteen days later, with the weather
worsening and more ice forming, he gave up the struggle and went
into winter quarters in a small bay on the island's south shore. It was
an exacting task. The crew worked for nineteen hours without a
break in the ghostly light of the aurora sawing a channel, square by
square, in the bay ice, which seemed to reform before their eyes.
After three days, a channel 2⅓ miles long had been cut and the
ships safely warped through. They would remain here for more than

40

eight months, protected from the fury of the sea by a reef of rocks. Parry named it Winter Harbour.

Parry and his men were now marooned at the very heart of the darkest and most desolate realm in all the northern hemisphere. The nearest permanent civilized community lay twelve hundred miles to the east at the wretched little hamlet of Godhavn on an island on Greenland's west coast. The nearest white men were the fur traders at Fort Providence on Great Slave Lake, seven hundred miles to the south. Another twelve hundred miles to the southwest were the uninhabited shores of Russian Alaska and beyond that Siberia. To the north, a frozen world stretched stark and empty to the Pole. Thus for hundreds of miles in every direction the land was devoid of human life; the nearest Eskimos were close to five hundred miles away. Soon any surrounding wildlife would vanish, including exotic quadrupeds yet to be identified – muskoxen, caribou, lemmings – as well as new species of gulls and terns. A few guttering candles, rationed carefully to one inch a day, flickered wanly in the polar night to mark the one point of civilization that existed in a frozen realm almost as large as Europe.

These were the first white men to winter in the Arctic archipelago. Under such conditions Parry realized men could become half crazed. His regime, foreshadowing Dr. Arnold, had one purpose: to keep his crews so busy that no man would have a moment to consider his situation. There would be plenty of daily exercise, regular inspections of men and their quarters, and afternoons crammed with makework. The emphasis was on physical health, cleanliness, and "business." The men were up at 5:45 scrubbing the decks with warm sand. They breakfasted at 8 a.m., were inspected right down to their fingernails at 9:15, and then set about running round the deck, or, in good weather, on the shore. They were kept occupied all afternoon, drawing, knotting yarn, making points and gaskets. After supper ("tea" for the officers) they were allowed to play games or sing and dance until bedtime at nine. The officers' evening occupations were, to use Parry's words, of "a more rational kind." They read books, wrote letters, played chess or musical instruments.

Around them in the gathering gloom, the land stretched off, desolate and dreary, deathlike in its stillness, offering no interest for the eye or amusement for the mind. Parry noted that if he spotted a stone of more than usual size on one of the short walks he took from the ship, his eyes were hypnotically drawn to it and he found himself pulled in its direction. So deceptive was the unvarying surface of the snow that objects apparently half a mile away could be reached after a minute's stroll. In such a landscape it was easy for a man to lose his bearings. Parry found it necessary to forbid anyone to wander far from the ships. When the darkness fell their isolation was complete. In mid-season one could, with difficulty, read a newspaper by daylight only at noon.

He had not reckoned with the intensity of the cold. The slightest touch of an unmittened hand on a metal object tore off the skin. A telescope placed against the eye burned like a red-hot brand. The men's leather boots were totally impractical; they froze hard and brought on frostbite. Parry devised more flexible footwear of canvas and green hide. Sores refused to heal. Lemon juice and vinegar froze solid and broke their containers; so did mercury in the thermometers. When doors were opened, a thick fog poured down the hatchways, condensing on the walls and turning to ice. Damp bedding froze, forcing the men into hammocks. Steam rising from the bake ovens congealed and froze, forcing a reduction in the bread allowance. There wasn't enough fuel to heat the ships. The crews were never warm. The officers played chess bundled up in scarves and greatcoats.

In spite of all this, the expedition produced and printed a weekly newspaper to which Parry himself contributed and put on fortnightly theatricals (the female impersonators shivering gamely in their thin garments). It was almost too cold, Parry admitted, for actors or audience to enjoy the shows. In his own cabin the temperature dropped in February to just seven degrees Fahrenheit.

By mid-March, with Liddon and more than twenty men sick – half from scurvy – Parry began to look to the future. When would the thaw come? How long must they remain imprisoned? A month later it was still bitingly cold. Parry had not reckoned on that; he began to have doubts about completing the passage to the west.

Another fortnight dragged by. The sun now shone at midnight. The temperature nudged back up to the freezing point. Game began to appear – a few ptarmigan and, a month later, caribou. The fresh meat reduced the danger of scurvy but too late for one seaman, William Scott, who died at the end of June.

That month Parry travelled north across Melville Island on a fortnight's journey with four officers and eight men to a great indentation on the coast that he named Hecla and Griper Bay. They dragged eight hundred pounds of equipment with them on a two-wheeled cart – the first example of manhauling by naval personnel in the North. Although Parry knew the Eskimos used dogs for hauling sledges and would later make some use of them himself, the tradition he established – of men in harness, like draught animals – would continue into the new century to the days of Robert Falcon Scott in the Antarctic. The British Navy was never comfortable with dogs.

July was the only really bearable month on Melville Island, but the ice still choked the harbour. As Parry's surgeon, Fisher, whiled away the hours carving the names of the ships on a huge sandstone boulder on the beach – a famous monument in the years to follow – Parry chafed to be off, his sails in readiness for an immediate start. He knew how little time he had: nine weeks at the most, a painful truth he could not conceal from the crew.

The delays that followed in late July and early August were maddening. The ice melted; they moved forward. The ice blocked their way; they anchored. The ice shifted; they moved again. The wind changed; the ice moved back. On August 4 they were able at last to set off into the west. Again the ice – the implacable ice! – frustrated them. The following day the floes closed in on the *Griper*, hoisting her two feet out of the water before retreating. Parry sent an officer ashore to climb a promontory and examine the state of the frozen sea to the west. He reported land some fifty miles distant, but the sea itself was covered with floes as far as the eye could reach, so closely joined that no gleam of water shone through. Parry named the new land Banks Land after the president of the Royal Society whose death, unknown to Parry, had occurred the previous month.

His optimism was fading. The previous summer the Passage had seemed within his grasp. All winter he had planned to break out of Winter Harbour and sail blithely on to the Bering Sea. Now the Arctic was showing its real face. The ice held him in thrall for five days. When it cleared he veered north-northwest. Again it stopped him. He ran east looking for a southern gap and once more found himself beset. Like a rodent in a trap he was scurrying this way and that, vainly seeking escape. On August 23, his ships battered by heavy blows, he managed to reach Cape Providence after performing "six miles of the most difficult navigation I have ever known among ice." He had no way of knowing then that he was facing the dreaded ice stream that flows down from the Beaufort Sea, where the ice is

43

fifty feet thick, its growth unimpeded by the presence of islands. This polar pack, squeezing down past Banks Land into Melville Sound and on through the channels that lead south and east toward the North American coast, is all but impenetrable, as John Franklin would one day discover. One hundred and twenty-four years would pass before the motors of the tough little RCMP schooner *St. Roch* finally pushed it through the barrier on the eastern side of the present Banks Island.

By now heartsick and disillusioned, Parry had to admit that any further attempt was fruitless. He could not know, nor would it have been much comfort to him if he had known, that no sailing vessel would ever conquer the Passage – and no other vessel, either, in his century. A decision had to be made. By careful rationing he might stretch his food and fuel for another winter, but he could not answer for his crew's health. Reluctantly he turned his ships eastward, hoping to find an alternate passage to the south. None appeared. At the end of August he set off for England and was home by the end of October with all but one of the ninety-four men who had gone north with him.

Parry had been bamboozled by the vagaries of Arctic weather. He hadn't reckoned on the severity of the climate or the shortness of the summer. He was convinced, rightly, that his chosen route was impractical. If the Passage was to be conquered another way must be found. Future explorers would have to hug the continental coastline, which his colleague Franklin was charting.

He remained an optimist. Promoted to commander, buoyed up by the applause of the politicians, the congratulations of the Navy, and the cheers of the public, he could be pardoned for believing that next time he'd make it. But almost nine decades would pass before any white explorer travelled from Atlantic to Pacific by way of the cold Arctic seas.

4

Fame, fortune, and frustration William Edward Parry was the nineteenth century's first hero-explorer. He stood at the head of a long line of celebrated Britons that would include Franklin and M'Clintock, Burton and Speke, Livingstone and Stanley, Scott and Shackleton. These were folk figures, larger than life, their failings, flaws, and human frailties ignored by a public and a press that saw in them the personification of Imperial expansion.

Fortune accompanied fame. Parry had one thousand pounds from parliament; now he accepted another thousand from the British publisher John Murray for the rights to his journal. He agonized briefly over whether he should take the money; but when he learned, to his annoyance, that Dr. Fisher was about to publish an account of his own, he swallowed his scruples and rushed into print without bothering to add the appendices that were planned to make up half the book.

Letters of congratulation poured in. Parry might not have discovered the Passage, but he had, in his phrase, "made a large hole in it." Equally important, he and his crew had *"done our duty."* Surprisingly, one of the first fan letters came from the maligned John Ross. Parry had to admit that it was also among the most ardent and sincere. What a curiosity! "I propose having it framed and glazed and then to put it into the British Museum," he wrote to his parents. What was his old adversary up to? Was Ross trying to curry favour? Parry would have none of that. He proposed in his own good time to pen a civil response but in such a way as "to prevent the possibility of his bringing on a correspondence, which is the game he now wants to play."

Meanwhile, his time was occupied by a round of social events that might have turned the head of a less phlegmatic officer. His portrait was painted by a member of the Royal Academy. He was given the freedom of his native city, Bath. He was presented at court; the new king, George IV, offered congratulations. London hostesses vied for his presence; exclusive clubs sought his membership, "which many noblemen would be glad to accept if they could get it" – a slight touch of snobbishness there, but one can hardly condemn Parry for revelling in his new-found glory, purchased at considerable cost and hardship. The first of the Arctic heroes was setting a pattern that others would seek to emulate. Considering the spoils, who would not dare to brave the Arctic blasts?

Certainly Parry was eager to be off again. His main business that winter of 1820-21 was to prepare for a second voyage to conquer the Passage. Nothing less, as he told Barrow, would satisfy the British public. The quest had taken on some of the characteristics of a race. Parry's main fear was that the Russians would beat the English to it.

The decision was made before the year was out. Once again, as in all British naval expeditions, there would be two ships (if one foundered the other would succour the beleaguered crew), the *Hecla* again and the *Fury*, which was the *Hecla*'s sister, all its working parts interchangeable. Parry would command the *Fury*. The *Hecla*'s commander would be a dashing young lieutenant, George Lyon, "a most gentlemanly clever fellow," so Parry had been told, whose drawings "are the most beautiful I ever saw." Lyon was used to hardship; he had barely survived a mission to the desert interior of North Africa on which a companion had died. Some of Parry's shipmates from earlier voyages, including James Clark Ross, would also join the new expedition, whose commander was so optimistic that he urged Barrow to send a supply ship to meet him in the Bering Strait. The Navy declined.

This time trunks of theatrical costumes were packed aboard along with the mandatory printing press, the magic lantern, and a full library of books that would be used in the schoolroom Parry intended to establish. In that long Arctic night he was determined that his unlettered crew would learn to read their Bibles.

He expected this time to spend at least two winters in the Arctic; he was, in fact, provisioned for three. To help fend off scurvy he proposed to grow great quantities of mustard and cress and ordered stacks of hot frames for the purpose. As for the cold and the dreadful dampness, he would thwart that with the newly designed "Sylvester stove," named for its inventor. It would carry warm air to every part of the ship (hermetically sealed this time with a cork lining) and, thanks to a more abundant supply of fuel, would burn day and night. Although the Navy was still sticking to wool, flannel, and leather, Parry improved on his improvised footgear, using flexible canvas tops and insulating cork soles and even made a small concession to aboriginal culture by supplying deerskin jackets for his men. He himself took along a fur coat to wear over his uniform.

Thus equipped, the expedition was ready to sail. "Oh, how I long to be among the ice!" exclaimed Parry, with all the zest of a schoolboy. This time his route would be different. The only other known avenue leading into the Arctic was Henry Hudson's original route. Was it possible that despite earlier disappointments a passage still might be found leading westward from Hudson Bay? The most likely opening was Repulse Bay, which had certainly repulsed Christopher Middleton in the previous century. Still, it had been only partially explored. Was it really a bay or, like Lancaster Sound, might it prove to be a strait? This was Parry's initial goal. Perhaps he might be able to link up with John Franklin, still exploring the Arctic coast of North America to the west.

Again, his instructions ordered him to give the Passage priority. Everything else including the mapping of the continental coastline was to be secondary. In retrospect, the Navy seems to have got its priorities backward. The Elizabethan idea that the Passage would provide a practical route to the fabled wealth of the Orient had long been discarded. But the collection of botanical and geological specimens, the recording of the folkways of the aborigines, the magnetic and environmental observations – all these made sense. So did the mapping of the islands and the charting of the coastline. Yet everybody remained obsessed by the puzzle of the Passage, even though it was the least important of the Arctic mysteries. It fired the imagination of the most hard-headed. The search was akin to other quests that whispered to Englishmen of romance, brave deeds, daring sacrifice. England was about to enter a new age – another Arthurian period, perhaps – with a new Grail to be sought and new glory to be won.

At Deptford, crowds sought to swarm aboard the *Hecla*, to walk decks and touch railings that had once been encased in ice, to bask vicariously in her ordeal. So many demanded admission that Parry mounted a grand ball on the *Fury*, which was especially decked out for the occasion. As the band played on the upper deck, the glittering company danced on and on into the night under a rising moon, each celebrant convinced that he was in the presence of adventure.

Ten days later – April 27, 1821 – both vessels were ready to sail. On May 8, they reached the Nore. Six weeks later they were off Hudson Strait. Here Parry sent one final letter home, invoking the Deity and recording his own humility in the presence of his Maker. "I never felt so strongly the vanity, uncertainty, and comparative unimportance of everything this world can give," he wrote, "and the paramount necessity of preparation for another and a better life than this."

The only known route to Repulse Bay was to circle round the western shores of Southampton Island at the top of Hudson Bay. But Parry decided to gamble by taking a short cut through the mysterious Frozen Strait, which lay to the northeast. This was unknown territory. Some, indeed, believed the strait didn't exist; half

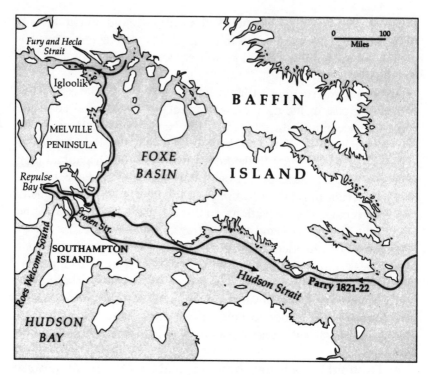

Parry's second voyage, 1821-22

the available maps didn't show it. Parry wasn't even sure that he had reached the entrance and so pushed blindly on in a thick fog and a fierce blizzard to find, to his surprise, that he had come through the strait, which wasn't frozen, and entered Repulse Bay without knowing it. Alas, a quick survey disclosed that the bay was land locked. This was not the route to the Passage. If one was to be found it must be farther north.

For the next six weeks he searched for a promising inlet but found nothing. At last, on October 8, he gave up, found an anchorage off the east coast of the Melville Peninsula (the name of the First Lord was becoming ubiquitous), and anchored at a point he called Winter Island. This would be his resting place until the following July.

It was a long winter, but it passed more comfortably than the one Parry had endured on his earlier voyage. The new Sylvester stove kept the ships warm and dry, and scurvy was not a problem, thanks partly to the hundred pounds of mustard and cress that Parry man-

48

aged to grow. Nor was the crew affected by the melancholy brought on by the long night, for in these southern latitudes the sun did not completely vanish.

Lyon, who was used to the garish hues of the Mediterranean, was charmed by the pastels of the northern skies. The delicacy and the pureness of the tinting, he thought, excelled anything he'd seen in Italy, while the pink blush that accompanied a hard frost was "far more pleasing than the glittering borders which are so profusely seen on the clouds of warmer climates."

In the clear nights, devoid of haze, the moon and the stars shone with such lustre that Lyon was almost persuaded the surrounding desolation was pleasing. As for the aurora, he, like every other new-comer to the North, was dazzled and awed. When it first appeared, he noted a shower of falling rays "like those thrown from a rocket," trickling and pulsating down the great well of the sky. This was followed by a series of massive illuminations, some as faint as the glow of the Milky Way and others like "wondrous showers of fire," streaming and shooting in all directions. He could almost fancy that he heard a rushing sound because of the sudden glare and the rapid bursts of light, but that, he was convinced, was an illusion: the aurora was as silent as the land itself.

There were diversions. The officers shaved off their whiskers to play female roles in the theatre. (Parry played Sir Anthony Absolute in Sheridan's *The Rivals*.) The school was a success; by year's end, every man had learned to read. But the greatest event was the arrival on February 1 of a band of sixty Eskimos "as desirous of pleasing us as we were ready to be pleased." Soon there was fiddling and dancing on the decks as the newcomers made repeated visits to the ships.

As Parry noted, in his restrained way, the natives "served in no small degree to enliven us at this season." There were undoubtedly other pleasures. The Eskimo women were remarkably accommodating, as later explorers discovered. (Both Peary and Stefansson took native mistresses.) It is hard to believe, though there is little supporting evidence, that fleeting alliances were not formed by the officers and men of the Parry expedition. That, after all, had been the pattern in the South Seas since the days of the *Bounty*. The only recorded hint comes from a private diary kept by the American explorer Charles Francis Hall, who visited the area more than forty years later. An old Eskimo woman named Erktua told Hall that

49

Parry was her first lover and Lyon her second and that Parry had been jealous of Lyon. She added that Lyon, after abandoning her, had left two Eskimo sisters pregnant. Hall believed her story but later questioned it when he learned that Erktua was claiming that *he* had tried to seduce her. Parry noted that the Eskimo men were accustomed to exchanging wives and that it was not uncommon for the men to offer their spouses freely for sale. The women, he noted, were modest enough when their husbands were with them, but in their absence "evinced . . . their utter disregard of connubial fidelity." The departure of the men was usually a signal for throwing aside restraint. Lyon, who noticed many young Eskimo couples showing affection by the traditional method of rubbing noses, also noted that "they have no scruples on the score of mutual infidelity. . . . It is considered extremely friendly for two men to exchange wives for a day or two, and the request is sometimes made by the women themselves. These extraordinary civilities, although known, are never talked of, and are contrived as secretly as possible." Small wonder then that Parry wrote of the natives' presence enlivening the season.

Were these winters in Foxe Basin as placid and as pleasant as the official journals of the two commanders indicate? The British were notoriously tight lipped in these matters, but here and there a hint of darker passions emerges. In the light of what is now known about the tensions and dissensions that existed on so many later voyages, it is not reasonable to believe that even under Parry everything was congenial. Two months after Parry returned to England, Douglas Clavering, an old naval hand who had just returned from a scientific voyage to Greenland and Spitzbergen on the *Griper*, wrote to a friend that Parry, who was already planning a third expedition, had declined to take *any* of his former officers (with one exception, James Clark Ross) on the voyage, "in consequence of quarrels, misbehaviour and insubordination." Besides the expedition to Foxe Basin being a complete failure, Clavering wrote, "from one acquainted with the facts . . . I know enough to say . . . it is also thought most disgraceful." Clavering's gossip seems to have come from James Ross himself, through his friend Edward Sabine.

In the official journals, of course, there is no suspicion of discord. In May, Parry sent Lyon off on a fortnight's sledge trip up the Melville Peninsula to seek an opening to the west – a journey that left the travellers badly frostbitten. Lyon did not find a passage but thought there might be a route around the peninsula to the north,

50

and Parry, desperate to get his ships free of the ice, kept his crews toiling for three weeks to saw a channel out to open water. Although two men died, perhaps from the effects of the work, Parry was able on July 2 to set his course north.

At Igloolik, the native village at the top of Foxe Basin, he again encountered an impenetrable barrier. But thanks to the Eskimos, who turned out to be astonishingly expert map makers, he was pretty sure a passage existed to the west between the head of the peninsula and the west coast of Baffin Island.

Once again Lyon was dispatched across the ice with a band of Eskimos to pick up fresh fish and assess the chances of getting through. He lived with the natives and clearly enjoyed the experience. He learned to eat their food (including an Eskimo delicacy, *nerooka*, the contents of the entrails and stomachs of slaughtered deer) "on the principle that no man who wishes to conciliate or inquire into the manners of savages should refuse to fare as they do." He danced with the Eskimo women, taught them to play leapfrog, even allowed himself to be tattooed in the native style. Waking one midnight in a tent from a feeling of great warmth, he discovered he was sharing a large deerskin coverlet with his Eskimo host, his two wives, and their favourite puppy, "all fast asleep and stark naked."

But Lyon found no open water. The ice, though decaying, was still as thick as three feet while the land was obscured by fog. Parry's patience was wearing thin. He was convinced he was at the threshold of the Passage, yet he couldn't move. On their maps, the Eskimos had indicated the presence of a narrow fiord. Did it actually lead to the open sea? Parry determined to find out for himself. On August 18, 1822, he stood on the north point of the Melville Peninsula overlooking the narrowest part of the inlet the Eskimos had shown. Toward the west, where the water widened, he could see no land and was certain he had discovered the polar sea. He was convinced he could force his way by this narrow strait, which he named for his ships – Fury and Hecla. Now all he could do was to wait for the ice to clear.

But the ice did not clear. The weather grew almost balmy. An eastern breeze sprang up. But the ice refused to budge. By late September, with a bitter gale blowing in from the northwest, Parry gave up. In his later, matter-of-fact account, one can sense the bitterness of his disappointment. He had waited until the last moment, cherishing the belief that a miracle might occur, but there was no miracle. When he called his officers together, all agreed they should remain at Igloolik for another winter and try again the following summer. They could not know that it would be eleven months to the day before they could once more break free of the encircling bonds of ice.

5

Innuee and For the next ten months, Parry and his crews were in almost daily
kabloonas contact with the band of two hundred Eskimos who spent the winter at Igloolik. A strong case can be made, though few thought to make it at the time, that the only important results of this abortive and largely negative expedition were the accounts that Parry and Lyon brought back of the natives' customs and society. Lyon's work especially provided the underpinnings for later anthropological studies of the Melville Peninsula natives.

Both officers had been privileged to observe an aboriginal society in its untouched state, before the onset of white civilization – a society that had managed to exist and even to thrive in one of the harshest environments on the globe. Parry produced a long essay on Eskimo culture in an appendix to his published journal. Lyon devoted most of his published account to describing his adventures among the natives and his observations of their habits.

They were, of course, amateurs, not anthropologists. Anthropology, in fact, hadn't yet become a discipline and wouldn't do so until mid-century. But both were keen observers. They liked the Eskimos, and in that long and monotonous confinement they had the time to examine a culture that both found foreign and fascinating. If they judged the Eskimos in terms of their own moral standards it is not surprising. After all, they were English officers; it did not occur to them, nor would it have occurred to any other Englishman in that age, that differing conditions require differing codes of conduct. Parry's attitude was similar to that expressed by naval colleagues who followed in his footsteps. The cheerful natives, he discovered, "maintain a degree of harmony among themselves which is scarcely ever disturbed." That being the case, they could only benefit from Christian evangelism. "On a disposition thus naturally charitable what might not a Christian education and Christian principles effect!"

Parry's assessment here makes curious reading in the context of an

52

earlier passage. He had seen and commented on the effect that a century of Christian civilization had produced among the Eskimos of Hudson Strait, whom he compared unfavourably with those of Igloolik. These "civilized" Eskimos were thieves, pilferers, and pickpockets, so greedy that one even offered to sell his two children for some trade goods – but only after removing their clothes, which weren't part of the bargain! Parry couldn't abide them, but he failed to link cause and effect.

By contrast, the uncivilized natives of Southampton Island and the Melville Peninsula were honest to a fault. If you dropped a handkerchief or a glove, they ran after you to return it. Sledges could be left unguarded without fear of loss. Lyon once purposely left a stock of knives, scissors, looking-glasses, and other coveted objects in an Eskimo hut, then wandered off, leaving a dozen natives behind. When he returned, he found his possessions intact and carefully covered with a skin.

There were some minor cases of pilfering. Parry, in an act of singular insensitivity, tied up one thief and threatened to have him flogged. But, as Lyon said, where objects of iron were involved, "it is scarcely to be wondered that such a temptation should prove irresistible; had small golden bars been thrown in the streets of London, how would they have fared?"

To Parry and Lyon, the most unusual aspect of the Eskimo character was its lack of passion. They were not a warlike or quarrelsome people. Those human emotions, so much a part of the European psychological profile, were curiously lacking or, at the very least, sublimated. Love and jealousy were apparently unknown – a fact that Lyon divined from his study of "the deplorable state of morals and common decency" among the women, who, though remarkably modest in public (even sitting apart from the men at a dance), thought nothing of bestowing their favours in private "without shame and without complaint from their husbands."

In Lyon's view, the Eskimos did not possess much of the milk of human kindness. Sympathy, compassion, gratitude – these qualities did not appear on the surface. Death was so much a part of Eskimo life that they had become inured to it. In a pitiless land, there was no room for pity. Three days of lamentation were allowed after a death, and the mourners all cried real tears – but only for about a minute. They seemed indifferent to the presence of death. Nobody bothered to cover corpses. Bodies were dug up and gnawed by the dogs. Lyon once saw a plate of meat placed on the body of a dead child that lay wrapped in his cabin. The British thought the Eskimos callous, but in the Arctic, where exposure, starvation, and disease killed so many so young, no other attitude was possible if sanity were to be maintained.

Parry remarked on what he called "the selfishness of the savage"; he thought it one of their greatest failings. The British, who showered presents on the natives and fed them when they were near starvation, were annoyed that none said thank you or showed gratitude. Obviously, it never occurred to any Eskimo to acknowledge a gift or a service. In their own world, they were forced to depend on one another. You helped a man out one day; he helped you out the next. That was the way the Arctic world worked; no one was expected to acknowledge kindness. The Eskimos cheerfully helped the British, hauling water on sledges, showing them how to build a snow wall around the *Fury*, drawing maps of the coastline, bringing in fresh fish. In return they expected presents, but to say thank you would have been redundant. Their own doors were always open and their food shared with strangers without hope or expectation of payment.

They accepted tragedy as they accepted death, with fatalistic indifference or, on occasion, with laughter and high spirits. A man could leave his dying wife, not caring who looked after her in his absence. A sister could laugh at the sufferings of a dying brother. A sick woman could be blockaded inside a snow hut without anybody bothering to discover when she died. Old people with no dependants were simply left to eke out a living or expire. This "brutal insensitivity," as Lyon called it, was appalling to his English readers, who could not comprehend the savage conditions faced by the people of Igloolik.

If they discarded pity they also discarded the harsher emotions. Revenge was unknown to them, as was war. They did not quarrel among themselves; an exchange of blows was a rarity. They could not afford the luxury of high passion; they needed to husband their feelings in the daily battle with the environment. They had learned to laugh at adversity, and they laughed and grinned a great deal, even when life was hard for them, as it usually was.

The Eskimos lived for the day – for any day might be their last. Parry thought them improvident, and so they were in his terms. Life for them was feast or famine. When food was available, they ate it all; when there was none, they went without, uncomplaining. The British thought them gluttons, but gluttony in that spare land was one of the few luxuries they knew. They were always thirsty and, when they could, drank copious quantities of water and other fluids. For thirst – raging thirst – was as common in the Arctic as in the desert. To eat snow was tabooed for whites and natives alike, for the resultant loss of body heat could kill a man. But snow could only rarely be melted because fuel was as precious a commodity as food; water was a luxury to be obtained at its expense.

Parry once conducted an experiment by offering a young Eskimo, Tooloak, as much food and drink as he could consume overnight. In just twenty-one hours, eight of which were passed in sleep, Tooloak tucked away ten and a quarter pounds of bread and meat and drank almost two gallons of liquids, including soup and raw spirits. This native gourmandizing was turned into a contest by the irrepressible Lyon, who decided to pit his man, Kangara, against Tooloak. Kangara managed to devour in nineteen hours just under ten pounds of meat, bread, and candles and six quarts of soup and water. Lyon insisted that if Kangara had been given Tooloak's extra two hours, he would have "beaten him hollow."

Parry found the Eskimo diet "horrible and disgusting." The odor of blubber, which the natives crammed into their mouths raw, "was to us almost insufferable." Some of his crew who first encountered the spectacle in Hudson Strait turned away from the sight in order to avoid being sick, whereupon the mischievous Eskimos ran after them, gleefully holding up pieces of raw blubber, inviting them to eat. Lyon, who had nibbled on sheep's eyes with the bedouin of the Western desert, was less fastidious. He found the *nerooka* "acid and rather pungent, resembling as near as I could judge a mixture of sorrel and radish leaves." Apparently, he concluded, "the acidity recommends it to these people," but he didn't ask why nor did he seem to connect the half-digested vegetable diet with the Eskimos' remarkable freedom from scurvy.

The natives were just as repelled by British food. They couldn't abide sugar; even the smallest children disliked it. They spat out rum. When one was offered a cup of coffee and a plate of gingerbread, he made a wry face and acted as if he were taking medicine. One miserable woman who had been left to starve after her husband's death was brought aboard the *Hecla* and offered bread, jelly, and biscuit. Lyon noticed that she threw the food away after pretending to eat it.

If the Eskimos mystified the British with their customs and attitudes, they, in turn, were confused and baffled by the strange men aboard the big ships. They couldn't understand, for instance, why these strangers hadn't brought their wives with them, and when told that some had no wives, they were astonished. Surely every man in the world had at least one wife! Nor could they comprehend a community whose members were not related. In their tight-knit society, *everybody* was related by blood or adoption. To solve the problem, Lyon told them that he was father to the whole crew. That did not satisfy some of the women, who noted that certain of his "sons" seemed older than he. Nor could they understand the British caste system. It was clear that Parry and Lyon were important men; the Eskimos were convinced they owned their ships. But the gradations of rank confused them; in their society, everyone was equal.

In spite of the clash of cultures, the two peoples got along famously. As Parry put it, "If . . . they are deficient in some of the higher virtues, as they are called, of savage life, they are certainly free, also, of some of its blackest vices. . . ." They were immensely helpful to Parry and his men, who, in turn, were generous with them. If the Britons thought of themselves as the Eskimos' superiors, there is evidence that the Eskimos thought the opposite. Parry noted that "they certainly looked on us in many respects with profound contempt; maintaining the idea of self sufficiency which has induced them . . . to call themselves, by way of distinction *Innuee*, or mankind." There is a telling little anecdote in Parry's published account of an Eskimo, Okotook, trying to tie some gear onto a sledge by means of a white navy cord. It broke in his hand, whereupon he gave a contemptuous sneer and spat out the word for white man: "*Kabloona!*" To him, the material was clearly inferior, but then, what could one expect from a *kabloona*?

To the British, the Eskimos were like children – untutored savages who could only benefit from the white man's ways. This paternalism was quite unjustified. In the decades that followed, the real children in the Arctic would be the white explorers. Without the Eskimos to care for them, hunt for them, and guide them through that chill, inhospitable realm, scores more would have died of starvation, scurvy, exhaustion, or exposure. Without the Eskimos, the journeys to seek out the Pole and the Passage would not have been possible. Yet their contribution has been noted only obliquely. It was the British Navy's loss that it learned so little from the natives. Had it paid attention, the tragedies that followed might have been averted.

Here was a nation obsessed by science, whose explorers were

charged with collecting everything from skins of the Arctic tern to the shells that lay on the beaches. Here were men of intelligence with a mania for figures, charts, and statistics, recording everything from the water temperatures to the magnetic forces that surround the Pole. Yet few thought it necessary to inquire into the reasons why another set of fellow humans could survive, year after year, winter after winter, in an environment that taxed and often broke the white man's spirit.

The British felt for the Eskimos, lamented their wretched condition, and couldn't understand why, on being offered a trip to civilization – as Tooloak was by Parry – they flatly and vociferously refused the proposal. (Parry, to his credit, was relieved. "Not the smallest public advantage could be derived from it," he declared.) Actually, in most instances, the white men were far worse off and much more wretched than the natives who were the objects of their sympathy. The Eskimos were clothed more practically and housed more efficiently in winter, and enjoyed much better health than the white explorers who were to attempt arduous overland expeditions that brought exhaustion and even death.

The Eskimos wore loose parkas of fur or sealskin, but the British Navy stuck to the more confining wool, flannel, and broadcloth uniforms, with no protective hoods. The Eskimos kept their feet warm in sealskin mukluks; even Parry rejected Navy leather. The Eskimo sleds were light and flexible, the Navy's heavy and cumbersome – and hauled by men, not dogs. No naval man ever learned the difficult technique of dog driving or the art of building a snow house on the trail. Fifty years after Parry's experiences, naval ratings were still dragging impossible loads and carrying extra weight in the form of tents that were generally either sodden or frozen.

Most puzzling of all, and most damning, is that in an age of science Europeans were unable to understand how the Eskimos escaped the great Arctic scourge that struck almost every white expedition to the North. The seeds of scurvy were already in Parry's men, in spite of the lemon juice and marmalade, but no one connected the Eskimos' diet with the state of their health. Though the effects of vitamins were unknown, the explorers sensed that scurvy was linked to diet and that fresh meat and vegetables helped ward it off. Nobody caught on to the truth that raw meat and blubber are effective antiscorbutics. For another half century, the Navy sent ship after ship into the North loaded down with barrels of salt meat while Navy cooks boiled or roasted away all the vitamins from the fresh provisions that were sometimes available.

Why this apparent blindness? Part of it, no doubt, was the conservatism of the senior service and part the arrogance of the nineteenth-century English upper classes, who considered themselves superior to most other peoples, whether they were Americans, Hottentots, or Eskimos. But another part of it, surely, was fear: the fear of *going native*. Could any proper Englishman traipse about in ragged seal fur, eating raw blubber and living in hovels built of snow? Those who had done such things in some of the world's distant corners had been despised as misfits who had thrown away the standards of civilization to become wild animals. Besides, it was considered rather like cheating to do things the easy way. The real triumph consisted of pressing forward against all odds without ever stooping to adopt the native style. To the very proper officers who still donned formal jackets and polished buttons for mess dinners in the Arctic wastes, that idea was unthinkable. They enjoyed these strange, childlike, wayward people, but they didn't want to copy them.

And yet, when the Eskimos began to leave in the spring in April of 1823, the English missed their company and perhaps even envied their flexibility. The natives were on the move; the white men were still closeted in ships caught fast in the ice.

Parry was determined to send one ship home and carry on alone and had already shifted the *Hecla*'s stores to the *Fury* for that purpose. But the winter had been appallingly cold, the ice showed no signs of budging, and the tell-tale signs of scurvy – blackened gums, loose teeth, sore joints – were making their appearance. Parry believed that cleanliness and exercise would help forestall the disease. Of course, he was wrong.

August came; no release. Once again the crews toiled to saw a channel through the pack towards open water. Weakened by illness, debilitated in mind and body by eleven months of being cooped up, they could not apply themselves with the same vigour. When Parry climbed the masthead of the *Fury* and gazed off to the westward, his heart sank. As far as he could see, the ice stretched off unbroken. There was no help for it. He would have to return home.

On August 12, he bade good-bye to Igloolik. For thirteen months he had hovered off the mouth of the narrow strait to the north, tantalized by the conviction that this was the entrance to the Passage

– that the open sea lay less than a hundred miles to the west. Once more he had to admit defeat; the ice master of the *Hecla* was already dying of scurvy; others would follow unless he could get back to civilization.

It was not easy. Even when he escaped from the ice-locked harbour and fought his way through the pack, there were hold-ups. In one period of twenty-six days, he was beset for twenty-four. The scurvy patient died before he could get home. Finally, on October 10, he anchored off Lerwick in the Shetland Islands, to the ringing of bells and the cheers of the inhabitants, who rushed to the wharfside to greet the ships, "the first race of civilized men we had seen in seven and twenty months." That night the little town was illuminated as tar barrels blazed in every street.

Parry must have faced this enthusiasm with mixed feelings. His discoveries had been negative: there was no route to the Passage by Hudson Bay, for he was convinced that no ship could squeeze through the ice that clogged Fury and Hecla Strait. On the earlier expedition he had ventured briefly down the long fiord he had named for the Prince Regent – perhaps *that* would point the way! John Franklin had returned from his survey of the continental coastline to report the discovery of a navigable channel running west. Did the bottom of Prince Regent Inlet connect with that passage? Parry was convinced that it did. All that was left was to mount another expedition to explore it. With his usual optimism he declared that he "had never felt more sanguine of ultimate success." He was confident that England might yet be destined "to succeed in an attempt which has for centuries engaged her attention, and interested the whole civilized world."

Parry, in short, had not given up. He was scarcely home before he was lobbying for a third chance to seize the prize. The mystery of the Passage obsessed him, as it obsessed all literate England. No hardship was too unbearable, no years of isolation too stifling, no experience too horrifying to deter the naval explorers from trying again. The most ghastly horrors of all – death by starvation, marked by one act of cannibalism – had been visited on Parry's friend and colleague John Franklin, in his overland journey to the Arctic. One might expect both men to have shaken the snows of the Arctic from their boots forever to enjoy a more comfortable existence. But even as Parry pushed for another try at the Passage so Franklin pleaded for a second chance to invade the dark interior that had claimed the lives of eleven of his men.

Chapter Two

John Franklin

Franklin's second overland expedition off the Alaskan Coast

John Franklin got back to England in October 1822, just as Parry *Franklin's* was settling down for his long winter at Igloolik. Franklin had man- *folly* aged to map 550 miles of the North American coast east of the mouth of the Coppermine, a remarkable accomplishment in the cir- cumstances, for in every other respect the expedition had been a disaster – probably the most harrowing overland journey in Arctic history.

When Parry returned, Franklin was still being pointed out as "the man who ate his shoes," a jocular yet Gothic phrase that masked the horror of an odyssey riven by disputes, starvation, cannibalism, and murder. Franklin himself was only days, perhaps hours, from death when he was saved by a band of Indians. Eleven of his party were not so fortunate.

Yet within two years he was desperate to be off again on a second expedition, so eager, in fact, that he was prepared to leave his bride of seventeen months, even though he knew she was dying of tubercu- losis. It was this reckless ambition, this hunger for fame and promo- tion that had been Franklin's undoing in that first expedition when, with little preparation and no experience, he had set off blindly across the Barren Ground of British North America. It would be his undoing again a quarter of a century in the future, when he and 129 men vanished forever into an unexplored corner of the Arctic.

Back in 1819 he had seemed an unlikely choice to lead that first expedition across the tundra north to the mouth of the Coppermine. He was then thirty-three years old – plump, unaccustomed to hard exercise, and inexperienced in land travel. As a child he had been weak and ailing, not expected to live past the age of three. For a naval officer, he was uncommonly sensitive. His nephew, who served as a midshipman under him, noticed that when a flogging was or- dered, Franklin trembled from head to foot. Years later, his son-in- law wrote that "chicanery made him ill, and so paralysed him that when he had to deal with it he was scarcely himself."

He had little humour and not much imagination, but he was dogged and certainly brave – calm when danger threatened, coura- geous in battle. He'd gone to sea at twelve, joined the Navy at fifteen, and had taken part in three of the most important battles of the Napoleonic Wars – Copenhagen, Trafalgar, and New Orleans, where he was wounded. He seemed blessed by Providence. He was once shipwrecked off the Australian coast and marooned for weeks on the Great Barrier Reef. Rescued at last, he barely escaped capture and imprisonment by the French. He had seen his best friend shot to death as he chatted on the poopdeck of one of Nelson's ships and had survived when thirty-three out of forty officers were wounded or slain. The bombardment left him partially deaf.

He had gone with Buchan on the failed North Pole expedition because he frankly sought promotion. He would be a fool, he told a friend, to embark on such an adventure "without some grounds of sanguine expectation."

He had friends aplenty and virtually no enemies. What was it about this simple, plodding, run-of-the-mill naval officer that commended him to so many, including two of the least typical women in England? His writings, so tedious, so formal, give little hint of the Franklin charm, which, by all accounts, was his greatest asset. Everybody liked John Franklin – liked his humility, liked his "cheerful buoyancy of mind," to quote his friend and trailmate John Richardson, liked his affectionate, easy disposition (a trifle too easy, perhaps, for a man destined to command an unruly pack of Canadian voyageurs).

Franklin literally wouldn't kill a fly. "The world is wide enough for both," he'd say as he blew the offending insect off his hand while taking observations. Like Parry, he was excessively religious – he wouldn't even write a letter on the Lord's Day – but he lacked Parry's evangelical zeal. He read his Bible daily and prayed morning and night, but his prayers, to quote his future son-in-law, Philip Gell, "were those of a child." He was fond of small children and (Gell again) "seemed to follow their innocency."

After his death, a memorandum to himself containing twelve rules for self-examination and entitled "Have I this day walked with God?" was discovered among his papers. It is possible to believe that this introspection, this quest for the Infinite, derived at least partially from those ghastly days in the fall and winter of 1821 when, with all hope abandoned, he quietly prepared himself for death.

Franklin's assignment in 1819 was to book passage through the Hudson's Bay Company to York Factory on the western shore of the great inland sea. From there he was to proceed across the face of Rupert's Land, following the fur traders' route via Cumberland House to Fort Chipewyan on Lake Athabasca. He was to move north to Great Slave Lake and then strike out onto the tundra to the headwaters of the Coppermine River, which Samuel Hearne had explored in 1771. The expedition would then follow the Coppermine to its mouth and proceed eastward in small boats to map the unexplored Arctic coast.

He set off in May, the same month that saw Parry weigh anchor on his first expedition. Franklin was accompanied by John Richardson, surgeon and naturalist, and two young midshipmen, George Back and Robert Hood, map makers and artists, necessary companions in that pre-photographic era. There was also a tough Scottish seaman, John Hepburn. Later there would be a considerable party of Orkney boatmen, Indian guides and hunters, interpreters, and French-Canadian voyageurs. Although Franklin's main task was to survey the coastline, there would also be time to collect plants and observe bird life (Richardson's forte), and to study natural phenomena and the natives. The Navy, as usual, was too optimistic. It expected this party to travel through eight hundred miles of virtually unexplored territory either to link up with Parry's ships (wherever they were) or to reach Repulse Bay, then the northernmost mapped site on the west coast of Hudson Bay. It is a measure of Franklin's own naïveté that he confidently expected to get to either the goal or the rendezvous. He might as well have contemplated a voyage to the moon. His insistence on exceeding the limits of his capabilities was to cost the party dearly.

The disasters that awaited him were not entirely his fault. Barrow had picked him because of his experience on the North Pole journey the previous year, and also, no doubt, because he came from a well-placed family: a niece would later marry the poet laureate, Alfred Tennyson. But it was an odd choice. There was very little about the earlier polar trip that could prepare Franklin for the swift rivers of the tundra. He had no canoeing experience, no hunting experience, no back-packing experience. But then, neither did any other naval officer of the time. The hard muscles and stamina required of Canadian voyageurs and traders were disdained by those who trod the quarterdeck of a ship of the line. The Navy simply assumed that its officers were capable of any demand, and it sent Franklin and his companions off to the wilds with little preparation and a minimum of equipment, expecting them to cover five thousand miles by foot and canoe and to pick up what they needed from fur-trading posts along the way. The Navy, in short, was pinching pennies.

At the outset Franklin learned that he would not be able to engage Orkney boatmen at York Factory; he would have to hire them on their own ground. The islanders showed a marked reluctance to go off on what they clearly considered a wild-goose chase. Franklin was both nettled and amused by their caution, which "forms a singular contrast with the ready and thoughtless manner in which an English seaman enters upon any enterprise, however hazardous, without inquiring or desiring to know where he is going, or what he is going about" – an assessment that says more for the Orkneymen than it does for the others. Franklin, indeed, might easily have been speaking of himself.

In the end, four Orkneymen signed on but only to go as far as Fort Chipewyan on the rocky shore of Lake Athabasca, which Franklin did not reach until the end of March 1820, after wintering at Cumberland House in the Saskatchewan country. (Parry, at the time, was still frozen in at Winter Harbour.)

He could not have arrived at a worse time. The Hudson's Bay Company and its Montreal rival, the North West Company, were locked in a mercantile contest that had four years before even erupted into bloody warfare. As a result, Franklin could buy only a fraction of the food supplies on which he had counted because the beleaguered traders had eaten the rest. He was forced to pitch his tent in a no man's land between two opposing posts, bargain for goods, and pay a premium for the voyageurs he needed; so much for the Navy's cheese-paring.

The Franklin party, deserted by the Orkneymen but supported by voyageurs, left Fort Chipewyan in July 1820. Franklin was undoubtedly glad to get away. He had arrived in considerable pain brought on by his inability to master snowshoeing, but he was equally pained by being forced to witness "the wanton and unnecessary cruelty of the men to their dogs, especially of those Canadians who . . . vent on them the most dreadful and disgusting imprecations."

Franklin had scarcely enough provisions to feed his party of sixteen for one day. By the time he headed out of Fort Providence, the last outpost of civilization on the north shore of Great Slave Lake, and into unexplored country, he was depending entirely on a group of newly hired Copper Indians under their leader, Akaitcho, to feed the party. The voyageurs were soon in open revolt; they couldn't handle loads of 120 to 180 pounds on short rations. The Indians saved the situation by bringing in seventeen deer.

In spite of all this, Franklin insisted on trying that fall to reach the mouth of the Coppermine, which no white man had seen since Samuel Hearne's day. Akaitcho wisely refused to go so late in the season, and after a long argument Franklin finally gave in. On August 19 the party went into winter quarters on a small lake 250 miles north of Fort Providence and named their camp Fort Enterprise. It was their home for ten months. Most of the winter was spent shuttling goods by sledge from posts as far away as Fort Chipewyan to build up a cache for the following year's journey.

No doubt the hard-nosed traders were baffled and even amused by the spectacle of four young British naval officers – green amateurs – setting off by canoe, sledge, and foot for the unknown shores of the Arctic Ocean. They themselves had little interest in the quest for a Passage that had no mercantile value. A skit produced a few years later at York Factory appeared to satirize Franklin's published journal. Certainly George Simpson, the head of the Athabasca district and the future "Little Emperor" of the Hudson's Bay Company, had no faith in the expedition's success. He later confided his scepticism to his journal:

". . . it appears to me that the mission was projected and entered into without mature consideration and the necessary previous arrangements totally neglected; moreover, Lieut. Franklin, the Officer who commands the party has not the physical powers required for the labor of moderate Voyaging in this country; he must have three meals p diem, Tea is indispensible [sic], and with the utmost exertion he cannot walk *Eight* miles in one day. . . ."

It was a harsh and unjust assessment, influenced in part by his conversations with young George Back, who travelled twelve hundred miles that winter seeking supplies for the party, but who appears to have been out of sympathy with his leader, for Simpson also wrote of "a want of unanimity amongst themselves," to which Back had referred.

Simpson did not much care for Back, who was blunt and overbearing in his repeated calls for supplies. "That Gentleman seems to think that every thing must give way to his demands," Simpson wrote, in upbraiding one of his traders for letting Back have too much, thus sacrificing the primary interest of the Company. Simpson had more important issues on his mind – the struggle with the rival Nor'westers – and was clearly irritated by Back's incessant nagging and his "impertinent interference in our affairs."

Back's long trek that year was as opportune as it was remarkable, for it kept him from clashing with his fellow midshipman and artist, the delicate and romantic Robert Hood. Hood, who fathered one child during his months at Fort Enterprise, had fallen in love with a second native woman – a remarkably attractive fifteen-year-old Copper Indian girl known as Greenstockings. Back, who was a bit of a dandy and was later to gain a reputation as an inveterate womanizer, was equally smitten. The two men were prepared to fight a duel at dawn over Greenstockings, but Hepburn, the Scottish seaman, forestalled it by removing the charges from their pistols. Franklin was undoubtedly relieved to be able to send Back away for most of the winter.

Nominally, Franklin was leader of the party. Actually, he was a prisoner of the voyageurs. Without them he could not move, and they knew it. Franklin was unable to maintain discipline. When some got drunk on rum and others pilfered meat, he could do no more than urge them to mend their ways. He suspected that one of his interpreters, Pierre St. Germain, was doing his best to dampen the Indians' enthusiasm in order to abort the spring journey. But he could only threaten the man with a trial in England at some future date. St. Germain didn't give a hoot. "It is immaterial to me," he said, "where I lose my life." He was convinced the whole party would perish after reaching the sea.

Then there were the Indians, irked because the presents they expected were in short supply. Thinking he could get all he needed from the trading companies, Franklin hadn't brought enough from England. As the packers shuttled back and forth from Fort Providence, the Hudson's Bay post on Great Slave Lake, the trader there told their leader, Akaitcho, that the naval men were "merely a set of dependent wretches" who wouldn't bother to reward them once they'd reached their goal.

The Indians were also in deadly fear of the Eskimos, whose forefathers *their* forefathers had murdered in a famous encounter at Bloody Falls on the Coppermine during Hearne's journey down the river. Franklin's expedition set off on June 14, 1821, but as soon as it entered Eskimo country, the Crees departed in a body. That left only two hunters, the recalcitrant interpreters Pierre St. Germain and Jean Baptiste Adam. Franklin, in effect, made the pair captives. They pleaded to be allowed to leave; he refused. They planned an escape; he put a watch on their movements. After all, the safety of the entire party depended on their hunting skills. The naval men wouldn't stoop to hunt and didn't know how, anyway. But Franklin realized that once the Indians were at a distance, fear of the Eskimos would keep the two Métis clinging to the expedition.

The fifteen voyageurs who had come this far weren't afraid of the Eskimos, but they dreaded the sea voyage in fragile birchbark canoes. Well they might; these cockleshells, already battered by the raging rapids and frequent portages along the Coppermine, were totally unfit for Arctic navigation. Franklin sent four voyageurs back with his guide, the North West Company trader Willard-Ferdinand Wentzel. Somebody, he realized, would be needed to look to the provisions at Fort Enterprise and to keep an eye on the Indians.

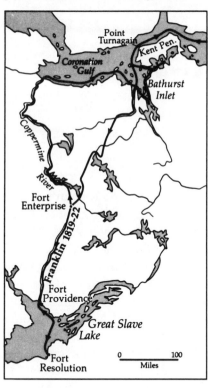

Franklin's first North American Expedition with Back and Richardson, 1819-22

Rugged though they were, the Canadians were exhausted. Every one had made at least one winter journey back to Fort Providence (near the modern town of Yellowknife), 150 miles from the winter camp. Most had gone on for supplies as far as Fort Resolution – another 75 miles. One had gone as far as Fort Chipewyan, a further 200 miles, making a total return journey of 850 miles. Before reaching the navigable waters of the Coppermine they had been forced by fatigue to abandon one of their canoes. They had successfully manoeuvred the other two, each loaded with two tons of baggage and supplies, down the white water of the river to its mouth, the first white men since Samuel Hearne to achieve that goal. Now they were played out and hungry. The naval officers didn't paddle, of course; nor did they drag sledges or carry packs – only their personal belongings.

The party of twenty, including eleven voyageurs, that now set out to explore the coastline was far too large for the hunters to feed. Yet Franklin, who had only fifteen days' supplies left, still pushed on. By August 8 he was down to two bags of pemmican and a meal of dried meat. The Indians saved him temporarily by bringing in three deer and a bear.

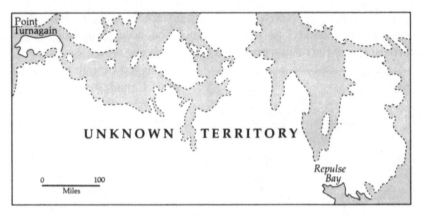

The unexplored Arctic coastline, 1821

By this time the paddlers were close to panic. As Richardson said later, it was madness to continue. Shipwreck and starvation faced them. But Franklin, eager to go on, ignored common sense. At last, on August 18, he reached a point where the coastline, which had been trending almost due north, turned eastward. Here, at Point Turnagain (a goal of sorts), he gave up. There was not a moment to lose. A more incisive leader would have turned back immediately; but Franklin dallied, and that dalliance doomed his party. Winter was coming on, the winds were rising, the canoes were falling apart, the sea was a maelstrom. But Franklin, in his zeal to complete the Passage, wasted five days on the Kent Peninsula vainly seeking an Eskimo settlement where he hoped the expedition could winter.

At last, early in the morning of August 23 the party took to the canoes to head back. After battling mountainous waves for twenty-five miles they abandoned the water route. To get back to their base at Fort Enterprise they would have to travel overland for three hundred and twenty miles.

The trip that followed was a horror. Franklin, who had exerted himself least, was the first to faint from lack of food; a few swallows of precious soup brought him round. But by September 15, the men were reduced to eating singed hide and a few lichens scraped from the rocks. Five days later Franklin found he couldn't keep up. The starving voyageurs were in open revolt, threatening to throw away their baggage and quit. Luckily, they didn't know which way to go. One canoe had already been jettisoned. Now they insisted on abandoning the remaining one. That put the leader in a frenzy of anguish. The Coppermine blocked their way; how would they be able to cross it? They were surviving on old shoes and scraps of untanned leather, fortified by the occasional meal of deer meat. The voyageurs stole some of the officers' portions, but there was nothing Franklin could do.

They reached the Coppermine and tried vainly to cross it on a raft of willows. Richardson attempted to swim over with a line and failed – emerging paralysed and speechless. After an agonizing week, they managed to get across in a makeshift canoe fashioned from bits of painted canvas in which the bedding had been wrapped. At this point one of the Eskimo interpreters wandered off and was never seen again.

The party split into three groups. George Back was dispatched with the three strongest voyageurs to try to locate the Indians. He reached Fort Enterprise to find it deserted. Akaitcho was convinced the crazy white men had already been lost. He and his nomads were off somewhere, following the caribou; Back and his men set off to find them. One of his party, Gabriel Beauparlant, died during this journey.

The second split occurred on October 6, two days after the Back group left. By then the party was in a bad way. Two of Franklin's voyageurs died, weakened by diarrhea. Hood by this time was too fragile to continue and urged the others to go on without him. Dr. Richardson and Hepburn offered to stay with him, an act of considerable sacrifice. Franklin and the others stumbled on toward Fort Enterprise, but this attempt was too much for four of the remaining voyageurs. Unable to continue, they gave up one by one and tried to make it back to the Richardson camp.

Only one arrived, a young Iroquois, Michel Teroahauté. At this point the harrowing tale of the Franklin débâcle grows darker. Two days after his arrival, Michel brought some fresh meat into camp. The others fell on it with relief and gratitude but remarked on its strange taste. Michel claimed it was part of a wolf that had been gored by a caribou. At first Richardson believed this odd story; later he became convinced that they had eaten human flesh – part of the body of one of the voyageurs who had turned back but never arrived. Had Michel killed him, or had he simply looted one of the corpses? Richardson had no way of knowing, but he was convinced from the Indian's evasive words and suspicious actions that his guess was correct. As the days dragged by, Michel became surly, refusing to hunt or even carry a log to the fire – which none of the others had the strength to do.

The smell of death, and something worse, was in the air. Hood was barely breathing. The party was existing on handfuls of *tripe-de-roche*. On Sunday, October 20, after reading the morning service, Richardson crawled off to gather some of this lichen, leaving the dying Hood sitting before his tent, arguing with Michel. Then, to his horror, he heard a shot and an anguished shout from Hepburn, who had been trying to cut down a tree a short distance from the others. Richardson hurried back to find Hood dead with a ball in his forehead, a copy of Edward Bickersteth's *A Scripture Help* in his hand. Was it suicide? Michel said it was. But Richardson concluded from the dead man's position that it was impossible for him to have shot himself. There were no witnesses, for Hepburn's view had been screened by a copse of willows.

Both Hepburn and Richardson were now thoroughly alarmed. Michel became even more erratic and hostile, uttering threats, saying he hated white men, claiming they'd killed some of his relatives. He was heavily armed with a gun, two pistols, a bayonet, and a knife. Hepburn had a gun, Richardson a small pistol. Neither was in any condition to resist an open attack, which Richardson was convinced was coming.

At thirty-three, John Richardson was on the threshold of a long and distinguished career as a surgeon and a scientist. A man of great stamina and strong resolve, he would have made a better leader for the expedition than the indecisive Franklin. Son of a prosperous Scottish brewer, the eldest of twelve children, a friend of the poet Robbie Burns, a graduate of Edinburgh, then the most distinguished medical school in Britain, he was a broad-gauge scientist whose interests included botany, natural history, and geology as well as medicine. He knew Greek and was able to read certain texts on lichens in the original Latin. On this voyage he collected everything – rocks, plants, lichens, birds, fish – a contribution to natural history that gave some meaning to an otherwise tragic mission.

Now he proceeded to act with a resolution that contrasted sharply with Franklin's wobbly leadership. With Hood no longer in need of them, the three men, sustained by eating part of their dead comrade's buffalo robe, set out for Fort Enterprise on October 23. During a halt that afternoon, while Michel was out gathering *tripe-de-roche*, Richardson, with Hepburn's agreement, came to a terrible decision. He was certain the Iroquois was only waiting for an excuse to attack them, and so when Michel returned, Richardson shot him through the head with his pistol.

The two survivors reached Fort Enterprise on October 29 to find Franklin and three voyageurs near death. Two others had been sent off the week before to try to find Back's party and the missing Indians. Richardson was horrified by Franklin's condition, as Franklin was by his. "No words can convey any idea of the filth and wretchedness that met our eyes," Richardson wrote, ". . . the ghastly countenances, dilated eyeballs and sepulchral voices . . . were more than we could at first bear." Tragically, the weakened men had weakened themselves further by burning most of the nourishment out of the hides and bones that were their only fare.

On November 1, one of the voyageurs, François Semandrè, lay down, apparently to sleep. Two hours later the others heard the death rattle in his throat. His comrade, Joseph Peltier, followed a few hours later. The others were too weak to remove the bodies from the hut. The limbs of the survivors began to swell, but their bodies were so reduced in flesh that it became painful for them to turn over, as they lay stretched out on the hard floor. As their strength decreased, Franklin noticed that he and the others were overcome by fits of pettiness, fretful arguments over small matters followed by apologies, then more recriminations. "If we are spared to return to England I wonder if we shall recover our understandings," muttered the stolid Hepburn.

Then, on November 7, a gunshot was heard. The Indians had been found! George Back had sent a small advance party speeding toward the dying men. At the first sight of the emaciated figures, the usually stoic natives burst into tears. Over the next several days, they nursed the starving white men, in Richardson's words, "with the same tenderness they would have bestowed on their own infants." Akaitcho, who had never stooped to cook for himself, prepared venison soup with his own hands and personally nursed Franklin back to life.

All of the Englishmen except Hood lived. But one Eskimo and nine of the white men who had paddled Franklin's canoes along the Arctic coast were dead from starvation and the exhausting travail of hauling heavy sledges and crushing weights and paddling frail, overloaded craft through rapids and ocean while the officers sat at their ease. As Douglas Clavering asked, in a letter to a friend, "Was the undertaking worth the suffering his party endured?"

It was another year before Franklin returned home to an enthralled public who gobbled up his Gothic tale of adventure, starvation, cannibalism, and murder in a harsh and brooding land. His own account brought him six hundred pounds in royalties and made an even thousand for John Murray, the Navy's favourite publisher.

The man who had eaten his shoes was now a glamorous hero – one who had faced death and conquered it, who had, against fearful odds, helped to unlock part of the mystery of the Passage, and who had actually navigated part of it in two flimsy canoes. By capturing the imagination of the British public, John Franklin unwittingly laid the groundwork for his future role as tragic hero, the kind the English preferred above all others. Would the great Franklin search that dominated the Arctic saga in mid-century have captured the nation's imagination in the way it did without these preliminaries? Would the Admiralty have sent him north in his fifty-ninth year if he hadn't, in the Navy's view, proved his mettle on that ghastly journey in 1821?

Franklin's triumph was achieved on the backs of eleven dead men, but nobody cared about that. He owed his life and that of his fellow officers not to his own abilities but to those of his Indian hunters. But more than a century would pass before a different kind of explorer, Vilhjalmur Stefansson, would, in a book that still excites controversy, question the Franklin myth.

Why, Stefansson asked, were the Englishmen a dead weight on the party? Why was all the hunting done by voyageurs and natives? "Was it beneath their dignity to co-operate in securing food? Was helping the workers, in their minds, detrimental to discipline? Whatever the reason, there is no sign either that they tried to assist in the hunting, or that they studied the methods of the hunt so as to be able to use them later."

There has always been an element of mystery surrounding the climactic days of the first Franklin expedition. Tantalizing little scraps float down through the years. What really went on in the final bloody days in Richardson's camp? All that exists is Richardson's word and Hepburn's silent witness to those violent events; and, as Richardson himself made clear, the evidence of cannibalism and murder on Michel's part, though plausible and perhaps damning, was entirely circumstantial. All four men in the party were half out of their minds from hunger. Wentzel, Franklin's erstwhile adviser and guide, called Richardson a murderer and wanted to see him tried. But Wentzel did not care for any of the Englishmen, who, he said, acted "imprudently, injudiciously and showed in one particular instance an unpardonable want of conduct." George Back, who gossiped a lot, talked again, this time to Wentzel, of dissensions among the Franklin party and added, "To tell the truth, Wentzel, things have taken place, which must not be known."

Nor will they ever be known. Back's remark was probably, though not necessarily, a guarded reference to cannibalism, which Richardson had yet to make public; and cannibalism in Franklin's day was perhaps the most horrifying and dreadful crime of all. As for Franklin's many follies, they were quickly glossed over and forgotten. His achievements brought him promotion to post captain. But that was not enough. Surely other glories must lie ahead. It is hard to believe that a man who had come within days of death by starvation would be willing to chance a second trip to the Arctic. But the lure of the Passage was too much. John Franklin could hardly wait to return.

2

Not the least remarkable aspect of John Franklin's career is his successive marriages to two spirited and strong-minded women who were, in many ways, his exact opposites in temperament and outlook.

What did they see in him? On the face of it, no more than a plodding, earnest, and rather ordinary naval officer – a hero, cer-

Miss Porden's core of steel

tainly, in everybody's eyes, but that wasn't enough to dazzle either of the pair, given her own strong character. He was reserved in public; perhaps that shyness was part of his charm. No doubt they saw him as a cuddly teddy bear of a man – even-tempered, affectionate in private, and, perhaps most important, pliable.

Franklin did not fit the nineteenth-century role of the stern, dominating husband; both Eleanor Porden, his first wife, and her friend Jane Griffin, his second, had known enough of these. One cannot imagine either one submitting to any man who would act as her lord and master, bully his wife, keep her in the background, or treat her as a chattel. When Eleanor overheard somebody at the Royal Institution for the Advancement of Learning remark that "the young ladies had far better stay at home and make a pudding," she made a sharp reply. "We did that," she said, "before we came out."

The contrasts between Miss Porden and Captain Franklin were striking. She was well known and respected, a poetess who had, in his absence, published a prodigious epic, *Coeur de Lion*, a two-volume tome in sixteen cantos. Her work is forgotten now, but in her day it moved the Bishop of Carlyle to call her "the Sappho or perhaps the Clio of her time." She was tiny, frail, and sickly but, as Franklin was to discover, she had a core of steel. Her father was a notable architect who sprang from a long line of architects; one of his commissions had come from the future George IV. She had been brought up with a taste for poetry, literature, and art. In London, she presided over a regular salon where the conversation was bright, gossipy, and opinionated. Jane Griffin, who dined at the Pordens' house, remarked on her "universal talents – she makes all her own clothes, preserves & pickles, dances quadrilles *con amore*, belongs to a poetical bookclub, pays morning visits, sees all the sights, never denies herself to any body at any hour, & lies in bed or is not dressed till 9 o'clock in the morning."

The lie-abed had a lively, inquiring mind, a good sense of humour, and a considerable ego where her poetry was concerned. Like other members of her class, she was a devout Anglican, but the evangelistic fervour of those times had not touched her. Unlike Parry and Franklin, she wore her religion lightly and refused to enter into ecclesiastical controversy, which, she said, was "the bane of society . . . almost inconsistent with Christ's humility." "I should be inclined to say," she told John Franklin after they were betrothed, "that my religion like my character was of a gayer nature than yours," and *that* was an understatement.

Franklin had met her and, indeed, been attracted to her before his expedition to North America. When he returned in 1818 from his abortive voyage to the North Pole, he had been intrigued by a set of hortatory verses she had produced for the occasion:

> *Sail, sail, adventurous barks! go fearless forth*
> *Storm on his Glacier-seat, the Misty North –*
> *Give to Mankind the inhospitable zone*
> *And Britain's trident plant in seas unknown. . .*

He asked to meet her. They were clearly attracted to one another from the outset. But Franklin forbore to propose before leaving on a journey he knew would take more than two years. Nor did he believe that his feelings (which she only sensed, since he never mentioned them) would survive the journey.

The courtship, if it can be called that, was frustrated by impossible distances. She wrote him one letter in May of 1821 and a second a year later. He did not receive either until he reached York Factory on Hudson Bay in August of 1822. He was not able to reply until October when he was returning home aboard the Hudson's Bay Company ship *Prince of Wales*, six hundred miles off the Orkneys. The course of true love moved with a more deliberate pace in those gentler times. When Franklin reached England, the popular Miss Porden was still not spoken for.

He called on her a few days after his arrival. Shortly after that he proposed – and botched it. The hero of the Arctic was alarmingly formal and almost as cold as the tundra itself – so distant that she found their meeting "exquisitely" painful. She wrote to him immediately in some alarm, for she found it easier to set down her feelings on paper than to express them aloud. "I looked several times in your countenance," she wrote, "for a gleam which might encourage me to return to our former style of pleasant and familiar conversation, but in vain."

She felt that he distrusted her in some way; certainly he seemed to have mistaken her character. Perhaps she herself was no longer "quite the same in feelings or dispositions that I was four years ago." She did not accept his proposal, but she didn't reject it, either. She left the door ajar by explaining that "no one else in all my acquaintance . . . could have spoken to me on the subject you have done, without meeting an instant and positive denial." That was something, for she was much sought after; there were, it was said, no fewer than ten aspirants for her hand.

He hastened to write a mollifying letter, explaining that his apparent coldness was only the result of his apprehension that she would decline his offer. More letters followed. She was plainly reassured. "You have unsettled all my plans and put my head in the most amiable confusion," she told him in December. They were betrothed; but it can hardly be said that he swept her off her feet.

In the eight months or so that lay between engagement and marriage, they saw each other only sporadically. He was in Lincolnshire, secure in the bosom of his family, preparing his book for publication. She was in London with her literary friends, preparing to write a biography of her architect father, who had died the month before Franklin's return. Parent and daughter had been very close, and his death was for her a shattering experience. Now, at the one time when she needed the comfort of a warm and loving helpmate, she was denied it.

Franklin seemed disinclined to tear himself away from familiar surroundings. Five months passed before he invited her to Lincolnshire to meet his relatives. By this time she was ailing with a chronic cough that often kept her confined. Though nobody dared speak the name, she was suffering from tuberculosis, the scourge of the day, as fatal then as lung cancer.

They corresponded by post. Her letters were long and graceful; his shorter, blunter, and less frequent. They can in no sense be called love-letters, even by the less expressive standards of that day, for the word "love" was never mentioned. The closest Franklin could come in revealing his feelings was to write of his "sincere esteem" for his future bride. She addressed him as "Dear Sir" and signed herself "your sincere and affectionate Eleanor Anne Porden." He addressed her as "my dearest friend" until late May, 1823, when she asked a little plaintively: "Why can't you call me by my name? . . . With my friends I am always Eleanor."

After five months Franklin broke the news of his betrothal to his father and sisters and was prompted at last to tell her something about his family. Until that time she had not even known how many sisters he had. He added: "I should now be glad to hear of your

78

relatives, if you do not find any other subject to occupy your next letter."

But Eleanor Porden was not short of subjects. What her correspondence lacked in intimacy it made up for in erudition. In these last months before their marriage there were no protestations of undying affection, no coquettish references to coming nuptials, no cries from the heart. But there *was* a long reference to a Mr. Millington who was about to give a lecture on Electro-Magnetism, the wonder of the day. Miss Porden announced that she would attend and take notes for her next letter so she might "hope to be indulged by your remarks upon the new discoveries." Franklin, however, declined "to venture . . . on so intricate a subject."

It was not an easy engagement. It foundered more than once because John Franklin and his fiancée could not agree on matters as diverse as religious observance and a woman's place in the society of the day. Their correspondence that spring of 1823 took on the aspect of a contest, in which Eleanor Porden won every round.

In March she discovered suddenly that Franklin disapproved of her literary career. She had not expected this, for he had previously given no hint of it. But now he demurred when she mentioned in passing that she expected "full indulgence of my literary pursuits both as to writing or publication." He told her at once that he had an objection almost amounting to horror to publication of anyone connected with his name – an odd statement for a man who was about to publish his own work. He might alter his feelings, he added, but could not pledge himself to anything.

She was devastated. "I have seldom received so severe a shock," she told him when she had composed herself sufficiently to write. It confirmed, she said, her suspicions that everything literary was anathema to him. In a three-thousand-word letter, she threw down the gauntlet: ". . . you must not expect me to change my nature. I am seven and twenty, an age after which woman alters little." *Nothing* must be allowed to interfere with her literary career; she was asking no favours, claiming no concessions; it was hers by right. If Franklin now felt the betrothal was rash he must tell her so; it was up to him to break it off. And that was that; she heard no more objections.

Then there was the question of the Lord's Day. To Franklin, Sunday was a sombre day on which one read the Bible, but never "a light or trifling book," and certainly not a novel by Walter Scott or a play by Shakespeare. He wouldn't travel, he wouldn't write a letter, he wouldn't entertain on the Sabbath. He was appalled that his Eleanor should go so far as to hold her salon on the sacred day. She, in her turn, was appalled at his being appalled.

She told him bluntly that he must not expect perfect conformity in their religious opinions. "I presume," she wrote, "you are not bound to consider me as eternally condemned if it should turn out that we differ on some point of faith. . . . The simpler our Religion is, the better." She had little use for books of Moral Instruction – the kind Franklin believed should be the Lord's Day's sole reading; they weren't more than "dilutions of the Sacred Text." The time was better spent, she thought, learning from history or the classics.

"Still less do I agree with you in any idea of seclusion on a Sunday. . . . Pardon me if I say that I almost consider the wish of seclusion on that day as partaking of the same aberration of religious zeal which drove many of the early Christians to the deserts of Syria and Egypt. . . ."

A month later they were still at it. The engagement was in jeopardy. She would not fix a date for the wedding. Franklin tried to bring her around by sending her some letters written by an evangelistic Anglican friend, Lady Lucy Barry, a woman of markedly narrow religious views who clearly disapproved of Miss Porden's light-hearted attitude to religion in general and Sunday in particular. That drove Eleanor Porden into a mild fury and almost ended the engagement.

In a spirited letter she told John Franklin, in effect, to choose between Lady Lucy and herself: "Should I find you to be really tainted with that species of fanaticism which characterizes Lady Lucy Barry's letters, it would be the severest shock I could receive. With such a woman I could not and would not associate . . . whether I am ever anything to you or not, I conjure you to fly from her acquaintance and from those whose religious feelings resemble hers."

She was convinced that the malevolent Lady Lucy was about to convert Franklin to the dreadful conformity of Methodism. If so, she said, his greatest act of kindness would be "to bid me farewell."

In the face of this ultimatum, Franklin backtracked. He didn't intend to become a Methodist, he declared, and he agreed that Eleanor was a good, practising Christian. He went to some lengths to insist that he hadn't shunned her literary circle, as she had charged, and "though I cannot join in a quadrille, it would give me great

80

pleasure to see you and your friends doing so. . . ." That was enough for her; a month later, on August 19, 1823, they were married. They would have less than twenty months of married life together (during which time she would present him with a daughter) before he left her on her deathbed to return to the Arctic, which was his first and perhaps his only love.

3

The new bridegroom was eager to be off again, and so was Edward *Fury Beach* Parry, who returned to England two months after the nuptials. He had first met Franklin in 1818 when the two were outfitting their respective vessels at Deptford and had found him "the most clever man of our cloth, as far as I can judge, with whom I have conversed for some time."

When Parry had reached the Shetland Islands on his route home that fall of 1823, following his winter at Igloolik, he received a letter of congratulation from Franklin. "I need not be ashamed to say that I cried over it like a child," Parry told him that October. The tears were of pride and pleasure, especially "in seeing the virtues of the Christian adding their first and highest charm to the unconquerable perseverance and splendid talents of the officer and the man."

Franklin came down to London the following month expressly to see Parry. There the two explorers talked of their respective plans – Parry to attempt the Passage again by way of Prince Regent Inlet, Franklin to explore the country west and east of the Mackenzie delta, perhaps with the backing of the Hudson's Bay Company, which was anxious to forestall Russian commercial interests in that area.

But Parry himself was at a low point. On his return, he learned that his father had died the previous spring. He was inconsolable – so depressed that he would not take food or even speak. His sister rushed to his London hotel to find him delirious with a high fever. His condition was kept from his mother until the crisis passed.

If this were not enough, he soon learned that the delectable Miss Browne, Sabine's niece, with whom he had an understanding, had lost interest in him. One can scarcely blame her; after all, she hadn't seen him since that spring two and a half years before when he had flirtatiously fiddled with her life preserver. But now her mother was going about claiming that he had jilted her in the most dishonourable fashion. Parry was miserable, but his dejection turned to wounded pride when he learned from friends that Miss Browne had not been constant during his absence. All that meant, in those strait-laced days, was that she had been seen in the company of other men. But Miss Browne went one step further in breaking the social taboos of the time: she actually got engaged to somebody else. Her mother was trying to nudge her back into the embrace of the Arctic hero, but Parry was having none of that. The knowledge of Miss Browne's shocking conduct cured his melancholia and helped him shake off "the more bitter and less remediable feelings by which I had first been agitated." Parry's prose style was as serpentine as some of the Arctic inlets.

The incident came close to estranging him from his friend and shipmate Edward Sabine, the fickle Miss Browne's uncle. There was a painful meeting at the Royal Society – they were both Fellows – in which they pointedly avoided mentioning "*the* subject." But even though Sabine "behaved very well," there was a distance between them, doubtless aggravated by a new jingle making the rounds of London and Bath:

> *Parry, why this dejected air?*
> *Why are your looks so much cast down?*
> *None but the Brave deserve the Fair*
> *Any one may have the Brown!*

That, of course, was the price of fame. But if Parry was taunted by catty whispers, he was also being lionized by the best and brightest in the realm, from Sir Humphrey Davy, Britain's leading scientist, and Sir Thomas Lawrence, the society portraitist, to Robert Peel, home secretary and future prime minister. Peers of the realm – the Duke of Buckingham, the Marquis of Chandos – entertained him, not to mention those Parry rather boastfully referred to as "numerous other individuals of high respectability." It was all dreadfully expensive, of course, for Parry, who was not yet a wealthy man, had "*worked* hard to return their civilities." But, he said, "I believe it is *worth the money*" (his emphasis). He had long since learned the value of friends in high places. Now he needed them again.

He had been plagued during these gloomy months by uncertainties about his future. He had been forced to admit, if only to his mother, that he had not been very successful, "indeed rather to the contrary." The Navy had offered him a sinecure as a hydrographer, and he worried that those duties might prevent him from following his main obsession. To his elation, Lord Melville, whose name Parry had made sure to immortalize during his explorations, indicated that one job need not interfere with the other. "I know I stand on very high ground indeed," a jubilant Parry told his brother, pledging him to silence.

The decision was made in the first week of January 1824. Once again *Hecla* and *Fury* would sail north under Parry's command. He thought at first of quitting his post as hydrographer, but John Barrow, who had plainly been working for him behind the scenes, persuaded him not to. "It is," Barrow pointed out, "your *sheet anchor*."

He saw Franklin daily. Both men were busy that winter planning their respective expeditions, though Franklin's wasn't yet officially set and wouldn't be for another year. But Franklin was dogged; ". . . the steadiness with which [he] pursues his object is very admirable," Parry noted. The more he saw of Franklin, the more he liked him. Franklin presented him with his portrait, which Parry had framed and placed in his ship's cabin opposite a likeness of the King.

Meanwhile, he had fallen in love again, with the nearest available candidate, a young woman named Jemima Symes, who was conveniently living at his mother's house in Bath. She was very ill with one of those unspecified nineteenth-century ailments that no one seemed able to name. Her condition was not helped by the fact that Parry was anxious to be off once more for the frozen ocean. But for the moment, at least, she fitted the role of future partner for whom the explorer clearly longed.

At Deptford, the *Hecla* again drew crowds. She was now the most famous ship in the Navy; in the three months before Parry sailed some three thousand persons signed the visitors' register. They came from all over the British Isles and as far away as Vienna, and they included Prince Leopold of Saxe Cobourg, the uncle of the future Prince Consort, two royal duchesses, and on the last day the family of Sir John Stanley of Alderley, whose daughter, Isabella, would one day be Lady Parry.

On April 27, 1824, another future Arctic wife, Jane Griffin, and her sister Fanny were invited to dine at the home of the Franklins to meet Parry. Eleanor Franklin was pregnant and her health was failing, otherwise the meeting might have taken place earlier, for Parry was about to sail. Now she was forced to curtail her guest list to those to whom she most wanted to pay respect. There were sixteen at dinner, an imposing assemblage that included Parry's old Arctic colleague Lyon, Sir John Barrow (who sat at the top of the table), Captain Beechey, who had been with Franklin on the abortive North Pole expedition, and Isaac Disraeli, the father of a future prime minister. The perceptive Jane Griffin was accustomed to painting word pictures of everybody in her journal. Lyon had "heavy eyelids & good teeth & is altogether very pleasing." Barrow "is said to be humorous & obstinate & exhibited both propensities." Beechey was a "prim looking little man and was very silent."

But it was Parry who interested her most, "a fine looking man of commanding appearance, but possessing nothing of the fine gentleman . . . his figure is rather slouching, his face full & round, his hair dark & rather curling." To her he seemed "far from light hearted & exhibits traces of heartfelt & recent suffering, in spite of which he occasionally bursts into hearty laughs & seems to enjoy a joke."

Miss Griffin thought Parry was returning north rather against his inclination, complaining to her that he'd seen nothing of the rest of the world. But this peculiar English reluctance was a mask for Parry's inner eagerness. He was raring to go but wasn't going to show it publicly. One mustn't appear too keen; it just wasn't done.

His priorities were clear. He was to sail down Prince Regent Inlet, which he had briefly and only partially explored on his first voyage, and look for a channel west that would connect with the coastline examined by Franklin in 1821. If that could be done, the Passage was as good as conquered.

The Passage, as always, was the chief goal. He was not to stop to examine or chart the coastline. He wasn't to make scientific observations or collect specimens unless he was blocked by ice. With his ships fully provisioned and the lemon juice ration increased by one third, he set off on May 8, optimistic as always, certain that this time he would achieve his purpose.

Again he reckoned without the perversity of the Arctic weather. To his astonishment and chagrin he found that the belt of ice in Baffin Bay was twice as broad as it had been on his earlier voyage. He was faced with an additional hundred and fifty miles of jostling bergs, all jammed together, holding both his vessels in thrall and threatening at times to crush them like eggshells. He had confidently expected to work his way through in a month, as he had in 1819. It took him more than two.

When at last he reached Lancaster Sound on September 10, he was a month behind schedule. Three days later, only twenty-one miles from the entrance to Prince Regent Inlet, his ships were again beset. The season was almost over. Should he try to make an ignominious retreat to England? The commander of the *Fury*, Lieutenant Henry Parkyns Hoppner, agreed that this was unthinkable. They should try to push on west as far as possible and attempt the Passage the following year.

It seemed, however, that the Arctic was making Parry's decisions for him. A gale blew up that drove him back down the sound and into Baffin Bay. The wind changed and another gale blew him back again. At last he was able to find a wintering place on the northwestern shore of Baffin Island, in a small bay off Prince Regent Inlet. For the next ten months this forbidding shore would be their home.

Parry had never encountered a bleaker landscape. No cheerful Eskimos arrived to while away the dreary hours. No animal was seen. The gulls and dovekies that had fluttered around the ship were gone. The white plain was as devoid of life as it was of colour. In his journal Parry wrote of "the inanimate stillness" and "the motionless torpor" of his surroundings.

He had, of course, prepared for it. There would be costume parties and grand balls, in which men and officers frolicked together in fancy dress. Discipline was relaxed but never abandoned: "masquerades without licentiousness," in Parry's words, "carnivals without excess!"

Everyone waited breathlessly to see what the captain would wear during the Grand Venetian Carnival that Lieutenant Hoppner had proposed for November 1, aboard the *Fury*. Parry kept them guessing, climbing down the *Hecla*'s side enveloped in a large cloak that he did not throw off until all were assembled on the *Fury*'s deck. To the delight of the company, he stood revealed as an old marine with a wooden leg whom the sailors recognized as a man who played the fiddle for ha'pennies on a road near Chatham. Parry, the amateur thespian, maintained the role, scraping on his fiddle and crying out, "Give a copper to poor Joe, your honour, who's lost his timbers in defence of his King and country!"

Not to be outdone, Hoppner appeared as a lady of rank, fashionably dressed, with a black footman in livery, who was revealed to be Francis Crozier, a midshipman aboard the *Hecla*, then starting out on a career that would end tragically a quarter-century later with the lost Franklin expedition.

And so they capered to the music of their captain's fiddle – monks in cowls, Turkish dancers, chimney sweeps, ribbon girls and ragmen, Highland warriors, dandies, Jews and infidels, bricklayers and farmers, tropical princesses and match girls, whirling about in quadrilles, waltzes, and country dances, a bright pinpoint of revelry in the sullen Arctic night.

On July 20, 1825, they were freed at last from their winter harbour and set sail for the western shore of Prince Regent Inlet. Parry felt that the real voyage had only now commenced. They were passing land that had never been explored, and the prospect of a speedy passage seemed bright.

Once more the Arctic would thwart them. Hugging the shore of Somerset Island, whose crumbling, perpendicular cliffs sent masses of limestone tumbling onto a mounting pile of rubble at their base, they ran into a stiff gale, which on July 30 grounded the *Fury* on an exposed and narrow beach. She was scarcely hauled free when both ships were trapped. A huge berg forced the *Fury* against a mass of grounded ice, threatening to tear her to pieces. She trembled violently. Beams and timbers cracked. A crash like a gunshot was heard on the larboard quarter. Her rudder was half torn away; she began to leak badly, yet there was no landing place safe enough to make repairs. All her crew could do was to fight to keep her from grounding again and to work the four pumps in shifts until their hands were raw and bleeding.

For a fortnight, the officer and crews of both ships sought to save her. They tried to fasten her to an iceberg; but the icebergs were wasted by weather, and the cables snapped. They tried to raise her to examine her battered keel, but a blizzard frustrated them. Both ships were in peril of being smashed against the rubbled headland. Nothing seemed to work. The crews had reached the breaking point, so exhausted that some fell into a stupor, unable to comprehend an order. On August 21, Parry was forced to cast off the *Hecla* to save her from being driven aground. The same gale drove the *Fury* onto the beach and blocked her exit with huge bergs. It quickly became obvious that she would have to be abandoned.

The decision gave Parry great pain. Everything about this expedition had been fraught with failure. He hadn't found the Passage – hadn't got near it – and had explored no more than a few miles of new land. Worse, he had lost a ship, the one catastrophe the Navy would find it hard to forgive.

Off he sailed, the *Hecla* crammed to suffocation with the double complement of officers and men. He left her sister ship and most of its stores on the beach – Fury Beach, it would be called; perhaps these provisions might succour some future expedition. Parry himself was home on October 16, 1825, with nothing to show for sixteen months of cold and exertion.

A court martial followed – nominally Hoppner's, but, as Parry said, "virtually mine as he acted . . . under my immediate inspection and orders." Hoppner was acquitted and all the officers praised and flattered for their exertions. Parry was relieved, but the fact remained that he had lost a ship.

Jemima Symes was happy to see him back safe. She was still sick but had written him a cheerful letter. "Everybody tells me that she will *now* get well," Parry informed his brother. "My sisters are of the opinion that my absence and her extreme and constant anxiety respecting me have done much towards keeping her ill."

But his relationship with Miss Symes soon languished for reasons that can only be guessed at – her frail health, or her own diminishing ardour for a suitor wedded to the Arctic and to his religion, or possibly his own desire for a wife with a hardier constitution and higher social standing. The day after he wrote to his brother about her continuing illness, Parry was bemoaning his susceptibility to attachments of the kind that had foundered so grievously in the case of Miss Browne. "I have always felt a desire to be *attached somewhere*," he confided. "I have never been easy without it, and with less disposition I will venture to say, than 99 in 100 of my own profession, to *vicious* propensities, either in this or in other ways. I have always contrived to fancy myself in love with some virtuous woman. There is some romance in this, but I have it still in full force within me, and never, till I am married, shall I, I believe, cease to entertain it."

His general loneliness, his hunger for love and the stability of marriage, and the knowledge of his failure brought on depression. He suffered from headaches and took drugs to try to alleviate them. He had been confirmed in his post of hydrographer and was now determined never again to seek the elusive Passage. After eight years of "continual harassing both bodily and mental" he wanted to be quiet and free of complications. But he did not expect to be: "London is *not* quiet."

He produced another polar narrative, a single volume this time and thinner in comparison with the hefty and detailed tomes of earlier voyages. Reading these excerpts from his journal – so much sparser than in previous years – one gets the impression that Parry was growing weary of it all. "I am persuaded," he wrote, ". . . that I shall be excused in sparing the dulness [*sic*] of another winter's diary."

The published result did not meet with the chorus of huzzahs that had greeted Parry's earlier works. The *Gentleman's Quarterly* wrote that "the last two expeditions undertaken by Captain Parry have been peculiarly unfortunate. Literally nothing has been accomplished with the primary object of these Expeditions. . . ." And Barrow, in the *Quarterly Review*, was markedly unenthusiastic about Parry's expedition, which he pointed out had left the question of the Passage "precisely where it was at the conclusion of his first voyage. . . . It has added little or nothing to our stock of geographical knowledge." Barrow hastened to add that no blame should be attached to the gallant captain; but all the same, the truth of those words from a man who had always espoused Parry's causes must have been galling.

He had said he would never go north again, that he was through with the Arctic. But those were hasty sentiments, uttered at the end of a long and dispiriting battle with the ice. It began to dawn on him that there was one way to restore his bruised reputation, by another daring attempt – if not to seek the fabled Passage, then why not the North Pole itself?

4

The silken flag Long before Parry returned from the North, John Franklin was ready to leave on another expedition by land and sea to explore the Arctic coastline. He was faced, however, with an agonizing decision. His wife, Eleanor, was in the final stages of tuberculosis, growing weaker by the day. She had drawn up and signed her will, set her personal affairs in order, even chosen a chapter from Corinthians for her funeral service. Franklin's departure date was set for February 16, 1825; it could scarcely be postponed without aborting the expedition for another year; in fact, seamen and stores had already been sent off to North America the previous fall to await the expedition's arrival.

Eleanor herself urged him not to delay. "It would be better for me," she said, "that you were gone." In his misery, he could only pray that her sufferings would end before he took off; but that was not to be. She rallied. He allowed himself the luxury of hope that she might recover, for the doctors "saw symptoms of amendment." Of course, that was all wishful thinking; the disease was clearly terminal, and they both knew it. He sailed on the appointed day, carrying the silken Union Jack she had embroidered for him to raise on the Arctic shore. He continued to write to her, letter after letter, from New York City, from Albany, from the British naval station at Penetanguishene on Georgian Bay. And there, on April 22, he finally learned that his solicitude was in vain. She had succumbed just six days after his departure. Even though he must have expected the worst, it was a devastating blow.

For him there was no ritual to numb the finality of her passing – no funeral, no graveside farewell, no memorial service. That would not come until he planted her flag on the treeless tundra by the Arctic's rim.

His plan was to travel overland to Great Slave Lake and on down the Mackenzie to explore the coastline westward as far as Kotzebue Sound off Russian Alaska, where a naval vessel, the *Blossom*, under Captain William Beechey, would pick him up. Two of the officers from his earlier expedition, John Richardson and George Back, were again with him.

Richardson, a tireless and prodigious traveller, was Franklin's intellectual superior as well as his greatest supporter and perhaps his closest friend, a skilled cartographer as well as a surgeon and naturalist. Franklin was delighted to have him. The same could not be said of George Back, whom Franklin had first met on the original failed attempt to reach the North Pole in 1818. Franklin's enthusiasm for Back cooled after the first North American journey; in fact, he didn't want him on the second. "You know I could have no desire for his company," he told Richardson, "but do not see how I can decline it, if the Admiralty press the matter, without being of great disservice to him, and publicly making an exposure of his incapacity in many respects. . . ."

Something had obviously gone wrong on that previous and tragic expedition, although there isn't a whisper of it in either Franklin's or Richardson's accounts. There Back comes through as a steadfast companion and an extraordinary traveller. After all, he had made that twelve-hundred-mile snowshoe trip in the winter of 1820-21 to bring provisions from Fort Chipewyan to Fort Enterprise, proudly recording that he had succeeded beyond Franklin's most optimistic expectations. More, he had saved his starving leader's life by pushing Akaitcho and his Indians to bring help to the beleaguered party. At the time of Franklin's second expedition he was twenty-nine years old, with two Arctic endeavours behind him and a strong war record. (He had been a prisoner of the French for five years.)

But he did not fit the Franklin pattern of the even-tempered, morally upright explorer. He was a boaster; he was vain; he could be rude and peremptory; and he had an eye for the native women – there was that nasty contretemps with young Hood over the beguiling Greenstockings. That alone would have been enough to offend his pious leader. Back was also indiscreet; he talked too much, and Franklin would not have cared for that.

Yet Franklin had no intention of making a public issue over what he considered George Back's failings. One of the reasons why the British expeditions into the Arctic appear so tranquil when compared with the stormy American attempts was that the Americans told all, or almost all, while the British closed ranks and kept any hint of trouble out of their journals. Back got the job only because Franklin's first choice died unexpectedly. He remained a controversial figure. Franklin's niece, Sophia Cracroft, later referred to him as "selfish, sly and sycophantic." John Hepburn, reminiscing in his old-age years, recalled that he was not very brave "but charming to those from who he hopes to gain something."

Given these assessments and the divergent temperaments of the two officers, who were thrown together on this second expedition for four months under conditions that were often trying, it's hard to believe that there was no clash of personalities. But Franklin never mentioned it.

He had learned something from the previous disaster. Well-disciplined British seamen would replace French-Canadian voyageurs on the new expedition. The boats would be constructed of mahogany and ash, not flimsy birchbark, but would be light enough to be carried on the shoulders of half a dozen men. With memories of that ghastly coastal voyage, Franklin ordered waterproof clothing. And he made sure that enough supplies were shipped ahead from England this time, besides presents for the Indians, who would still do all the big-game hunting since neither Franklin nor his officers knew how.

Perhaps this did not matter, for conditions had changed in the North West. The two warring fur companies had amalgamated, and George Simpson, the new governor of the Hudson's Bay Company, had declared there wasn't a man in the service, including himself, "who would not be happy to form a member of the Expedition and share your danger." No doubt there were mercantile considerations in Simpson's effusive remarks; on the far side of the Mackenzie Mountains, his Russian rivals were making inroads into the fur trade.

In that first summer of 1825, John Franklin and his companions travelled 5,083 miles from New York. Their former Indian comrades greeted them with enthusiasm when they arrived at Great Slave Lake. From that point it was an easy passage north down the Mackenzie, a placid waterway free of rapids.

Franklin reached the delta on August 16, a glorious autumn day, with the channels free of ice and the waters alive with seals and whales frolicking in the waves. He was elated at the spectacle. There were no obstacles to his ambitions in sight. This time his expedition seemed to be crowned with success.

Then his mood darkened. On a small island in the skeinwork of the great delta, he unfurled his dead wife's silk flag, true to his promise that it would not be produced until the Arctic was reached. Now, as he planted it in the half-frozen soil, he felt a surge of grief, difficult to control. But control it he did, for he had no desire to cloud this moment of triumph for his companions. This was only the third occasion on which a white expedition had reached the Mackenzie's mouth. With the best grace he could muster, he maintained a cheerful countenance and accepted the congratulations of the company.

They returned to a wintering spot on Great Bear Lake, which they named Fort Franklin. There they spent a cheerful nine months. The officers taught the men to read and figure. Richardson gave the

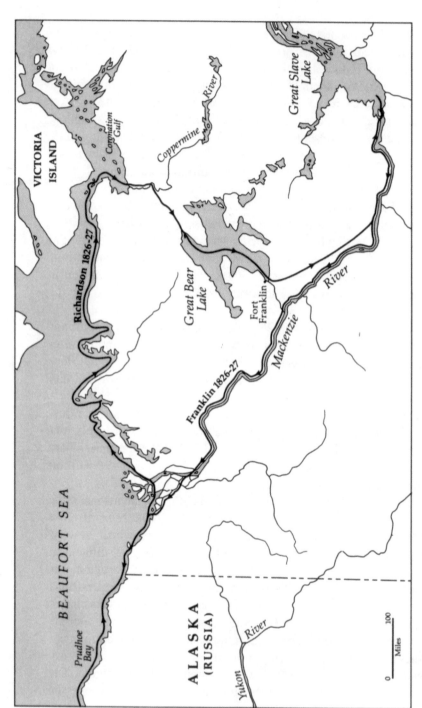

Franklin's second expedition with Back and Richardson, 1825–27

officers lectures on the flora, fauna, and geology of the region. Franklin read Dante and Milton. There were games of shinny and blind-man's buff. And nobody went hungry.

In late June, 1826, they were ready to set off again. Franklin and Back would take two boats and fourteen men and trace the unknown coastline from the Mackenzie westward, expecting to link up with the British vessel on the Alaskan coast. Richardson would explore the uncharted coast between the mouths of the Mackenzie and the Coppermine.

The Eskimos, whom Franklin shortly encountered, were a little baffled by the white man's method of travel. Why, they asked, didn't the explorers use dogs and sleds as they did? The ice conditions along the coast made water travel difficult. But these were naval men with no training in dog driving.

An Eskimo interpreter, Augustus, an old friend from the previous expedition, accompanied Franklin. He explained to the first Eskimos they met – a band of two hundred – that Franklin's explorations might lead to the opening of trading relations that could only benefit the natives. A wild scene followed. The Eskimos became excited and tried to steal everything from the party, even cutting the buttons from their naval jackets. The women howled, the men clamoured as they seized canteens, kettles, tents, bales of blankets, shoes, even a jib sail. Franklin remained cool. Ordering his men not to provoke the natives, he managed to get them all away in the boats. The Eskimos, warned by Augustus that the white men would use their rifles if necessary, did not give chase.

The next day they all apologized, explaining that they'd never before seen white men and couldn't resist seizing items that seemed incredibly valuable. As a sign of friendship they agreed to return a large kettle and a tent. Franklin was convinced that his forbearance had prevented bloodshed; the man who wouldn't hurt a fly had forestalled the probable massacre of his party.

On July 27, 1826, the party reached the most westerly river of the British dominions near the border of Russian Alaska. Franklin named it the Clarence River after the Lord High Admiral. Up went another flag to the accompaniment of the inevitable three hearty cheers from the members of the party. This schoolboy enthusiasm was a mark of British naval forays into the Arctic. No expedition was launched, no sledge trip mounted, no returning party welcomed, no discovery made without seamen and officers alike waving their caps and shouting triple hoorahs.

Franklin now had no doubt he could round the northwest corner of the continent, reach his ultimate goal of Icy Cape, rendezvous with the British ship that would come up from Kotzebue Sound to meet him, and return in triumph to England. Like Parry, he reckoned without the unaccommodating Arctic. Ice, fog, sleet, and gales hampered his movements. The boats were trapped on a bleak headland, which he ruefully named Foggy Island. On August 16, a year to the day after he'd planted his wife's flag at the Mackenzie's mouth, he was forced into a painful decision. He had reached the point "beyond which perseverance would be rashness." He was only half way to his goal, but this time he recognized that he had "higher duties to perform than the gratification of my own feelings." Franklin had learned something from that previous savage journey. His fatal dallying on the Kent Peninsula had taught him the tragedy of indecision.

The wind was already rising. They struggled back through mountainous waves and a sea churned white with foam, constantly bathed in spray and bailing for their lives. They made camp at last to wait until the gale died down. A party of Eskimos met them, astonished that any had survived.

Two days later, a pair of young natives dashed breathlessly into the camp to announce that a band of fierce Indians planned to attack the boats and kill every man. They were furious because they felt that these white men were ruining their trade with the Eskimos – a trade based on Russian goods. The Eskimos told Franklin he must embark at once and make for the Mackenzie with all speed, not stopping to rest unless they could find an island out of gunshot. Franklin took this advice seriously – it turned out to be accurate – and made for the delta with the Indians somewhere behind him. He reached it on the thirtieth in safety and by the end of September was back in winter quarters at Fort Franklin. His summer had covered 2,048 miles, 610 of them through unexplored territory. Richardson, when he returned to Fort Franklin, had done equally well, covering 1,980 miles of which 1,015 were previously undescribed.

What Franklin did not know was that the naval vessel *Blossom* was only 150 miles to the west when he turned back. Had he realized that he would certainly have pressed on to a triumphant rendezvous. As it was, he and Richardson had opened up most of the Arctic coastline of North America, leaving a gap of only 150 miles between Point Turnagain and Icy Cape. It was a remarkable achievement that would eventually win both men knighthoods.

But there was still another blank on the map. The area between Point Turnagain and Repulse Bay also remained unexplored. Franklin was convinced that the coastline ran east in that direction without impediment and that there were no insurmountable obstacles in the way. In short, he thought the main work of exploration had been completed. All that was required was to link up his discoveries with those of Parry and the Passage was a *fait accompli*.

It would not be that easy. Twenty-five years were to pass before another expedition would make an effective link. That expedition would be led by none other than John Franklin – *Sir* John by that time; but Franklin himself would not live to bask in the glory of that achievement.

5

In the spring of 1826, while John Franklin was preparing to leave his winter quarters to explore the coastline, the course of William Edward Parry's life was changing. Not only had he fallen in love again but he had also reversed his decision to abandon Arctic exploration. Now it was the North Pole that beckoned; ever the optimist, Parry was sure he could reach it in a single season. He wrote two letters that spring, one to Lord Melville in April putting his polar proposal on paper, the other to Sir John Stanley of Alderley, asking for his daughter's hand in marriage. Neither bore immediate fruit.

Parry had first met Isabella Stanley when she came aboard the *Hecla* before that last ineffective voyage. Now, through his friend Edward Stanley, Isabella's brother, he renewed acquaintance with the family. He was clearly seeking a wife, and Isabella, a zesty twenty-four-year-old, fragile looking in the style of the period but undeniably beautiful – perhaps the most beautiful of all the lively Stanley daughters – was available. By May he was in love and sure enough of her agreement to approach her father. Of course he did not use the word "love" to Sir John. It would, perhaps, have been considered unseemly in those formal days to admit to something as

Treadmill to the Pole

unrefined as passion. He merely said he was "irresistibly drawn towards . . . Isabella by sentiments much warmer than those of common esteem and regard. . . ."

The real obstacle was not the gouty Sir John; it was his wife, Maria Josepha, mother of nine living children, an intelligent, liberal, and tough-minded woman who couldn't abide Parry's obsessive religious beliefs. There might also have been some objection to Parry's station in life, for the Stanleys were not above snobbery; they sneered at the wealthy cotton magnates from Manchester as "cottontots." Lady Stanley and the Arctic hero had what he called "a long and not very agreeable conversation" in which she tried "to scold me out of my religious sentiments." Isabella sided with Parry, despite her less ardent piety. But she admired his consistency even though, as he put it, "I see a storm brewing in the distant horizon."

Parry was adamant: "I trust in God, that *whatever happens*, I may never give *Him* up, – no, not even if I have to give up Isabella herself!"

An ominous two-month silence followed in which the lovebirds were kept from each other. There was an equally ominous silence from Lord Melville, who was, as he later said, not "sanguine" about the success of Parry's North Pole proposal. But behind Parry stood the formidable figure of John Barrow, advising, suggesting, nudging, and, with the help of the Royal Society, pressuring the Admiralty. Although the assault on the Pole (by way of Norway this time) had originally been John Franklin's idea, Barrow, who knew his man, had seen to it that Parry got a copy of Franklin's plan; Parry quickly seized the idea.

In July, Lord Melville gave in and so did the Stanleys. "Mama is changed and not unkind," is the way Isabella put it. (One senses the residue of a certain coolness.) The two were married in October. Isabella's first gift to her husband was a Bible and prayer book. On their honeymoon night, he read aloud from the 107th Psalm. "I required comforting this evening," she confided to her diary, "and dearly indeed did he comfort me."

For her, any separation was an agony. The first occurred in March 1827, when he was called to Deptford to preside at a court martial. She was wretched: "Never have I passed a more truly miserable day than this. The utter loneliness of it. The feeling of desolation. The first Sunday since we married that we have been separated. I could only feel that he was gone. . . ."

96

She knew that a longer and more agonizing parting was to come. Parry's plans to reach the Pole were well developed. He expected to leave England in the *Hecla* that April for weeks, months – who knew? – perhaps even years.

As usual he was the incurable optimist; ". . . few enterprises are so easily practicable," he wrote. But he ignored the experts. The best advice for would-be polar travellers – and it was to stand the test of time – had been laid out by the whaling captain William Scoresby in an address to the Wernerian Society eleven years before. Scoresby made several important points. First, he said, the best mode of travel was by light, flexible sledges built on slender wood frames and covered with waterproof skins – the kind the Eskimos used. Second, the sledges should be pulled by either reindeer or dogs; Scoresby preferred dogs. These, he explained, would have to come from the area being explored and would require trained drivers, for the handling of Eskimo dogs was a specialized art. Third, he said, any expedition seeking the Pole must be prepared to set out on the ice when it was frozen hard and relatively flat, in late April or early May. Later on, higher temperatures created grave problems as pools formed, hummocks appeared, slush covered the surface, and rains made travel difficult.

Scoresby knew what he was talking about. He'd had sixty thousand miles of experience travelling on and through the ice. His book, *An Account of the Arctic Regions*, published in 1820, had shown him to be the foremost authority on the physical geography of the Arctic. All of this, together with the fact that he was now a minister of the cloth, ought to have recommended him to Parry. But Parry paid no attention to all his common-sense proposals, for Scoresby was only a whaling captain. Whaling captains were often used as "ice masters" on naval vessels in the North, but they were never placed in charge.

Yet Scoresby had been farther north than any other white explorer – to a latitude of 82°30′. It was an unofficial record, not one that Scoresby himself appeared to care about; on that occasion he and his father had been after whales, not fame.

So Parry went ahead building two cumbersome amphibious boat sleds, each seventy feet long with a twenty-foot beam, weighing three quarters of a ton and equipped with steel runners so that they could be dragged over the ice. He did not take dogs, and the eight domestic reindeer he purchased were never used. Again, he ignored Scoresby's advice about making an early start. He didn't propose to head off across the ice until June 1, and even that late deadline was missed. Beset off Spitzbergen, he spent ten precious days seeking a safe harbour for the *Hecla* and did not get away until June 21. His optimism was undiminished. "The main object of our exercise appeared almost within our grasp," he wrote.

Parry was deeply in love. It had been a wrench to part with Isabella and even more wrenching for her, since she found herself pregnant. Unable to write to him, she confided her feelings to her diary, longing for the moment when he would return. By that time, she hoped, he would find that she had attained "more truly the real spirit of religion, more strength to resist temptation and to bear the trials to which he may be exposed."

Here was nothing resembling the spirited ripostes of Eleanor Franklin, who, sick or not, had insisted on worshipping her God in her own fashion. In spite of her mother's misgivings, Isabella Parry had given herself to her husband heart and soul, without a murmur of complaint. "How truly, how *earnestly* will I strive that my beloved husband may find me thus improved," she wrote. ". . . I know there are times when I shall fail when my natural evil inclination will get the better of me, but I know also that if I try *earnestly* to do what is right, if I pray fervently for help, He who knows all weaknesses will help me. . . ." She yearned for her husband's presence that spring and spoke to him through her diary: ". . . I would not recall you, your path leads to glory and honour and never would I turn you from that path when I feel and know it is the path you ought to go. . . ."

But the path that Parry had chosen was rough. He had expected to find the smooth, flat expanse of ice that some whalers had reported. It did not occur to him that, as Scoresby had made clear, this condition only existed at an earlier time of year before the weather changed and the ice grew rougher. It is inconceivable that Parry was unaware of Scoresby's thesis. Why didn't he take him seriously? The answer must be that his old mentor, John Barrow, had no use for the whaler. Sometime after he snubbed Scoresby at Sir Joseph Banks's home, he had penned an anonymous article in the *Quarterly Review* sneering at Scoresby's "idle and thoughtless project of travelling over the ice of the sea to the North Pole." That clashed with Barrow's conviction that an "Open Polar Sea" existed – one reason, doubtless, why Parry built heavy boats rather than the light sledges Scoresby suggested. Scoresby, like most whalers, scoffed at the theory of an

98

Open Polar Sea. When he heard it discussed at the home of his friends the Stanleys, he flatly predicted that Parry would never reach the Pole.

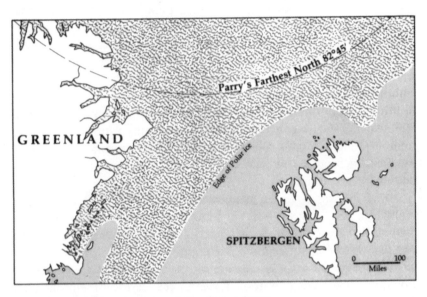

Parry's last voyage: toward the Pole, 1827

Parry and his second-in-command, James Clark Ross, set off, each in charge of a boat-sledge with twelve men. Once again, they were unlucky with the weather. The season, now well advanced, was the most unfavourable he could have encountered. Parry had never seen such rain; twenty times as much fell that summer as had fallen in any of the seven previous summers he had spent in the Arctic. It came down in torrents, once for a steady thirty hours. But when the sun came out it shone so fiercely that the tar ran out of the seams of the boats.

The weather played havoc with the ice. A turbulent expanse of broken cakes, piled one atop the other, stretched to the horizon – high, sharp, angular masses that impeded every step of the men dragging the boat-sledges. It was like trying to haul a cart through a stonemason's yard, with stones ten times their normal dimensions. And there was worse: "pen knife ice" – needle-like crystals that tore at the soles of the boots – and slush, knee deep, that caused the men to revert to all fours. When there wasn't rain there was fog, so thick it caused the party to grope blindly, yard by yard, from one hummock of ice to the next, trying to avoid the thousands of ponds that formed between the blocks.

The need to launch and land the boats, to load, unload, and reload them, to make long circuits round ponds too shallow to navigate, slowed the expedition to a turtle's pace. Parry had figured to make more than thirteen miles a day; he made scarcely half a mile. On one occasion it took two hours to move a hundred yards.

He kept expecting to meet what he called "the main ice," the smooth continuous plain the whalers had described. He couldn't get it into his head that in summer it didn't exist. His men were wet and exhausted, their fatigue aggravated by the scanty rations. Parry had underestimated greatly, allowing no more than a pound and a quarter of solid food a day, scarcely enough for men performing hard labour for ten hours.

But there was a worse problem, which made the struggle even more heartbreaking. A stiff wind blowing down from the Pole was driving the ice before it. At last Parry understood what every one of the despised whaling captains knew, that even as his party plodded grimly north, the ice was moving south. They were on a treadmill. For every two steps they took forward, the ice took them one step back. On July 26, Parry recognized that although they seemed to have pushed ten or eleven miles north, they were actually three miles *south* of their starting point that day. He kept that knowledge from his men, who still believed they were pressing close to the 83rd parallel, at which point the company would receive the thousand-pound reward that parliament had offered to anyone who could get that far.

Two days later Parry gave up. Even that goal was unattainable. He had managed to reach the hitherto unattainable latitude of 82º45′ – one quarter of a degree farther than Scoresby's unofficial record. It was a considerable achievement, given the circumstances, and it would stand for fifty years, adding to Parry's towering reputation as the greatest of the Arctic explorers.

But, had he taken Scoresby's advice, he would certainly have achieved more. The statistics of his journey are sobering. He and his party had clocked 978 miles of polar travel, but because of the circuitous route, the constant need to shuffle supplies back and forth, and the southward movement of the ice, it was discovered that when Parry reached his farthest point, he was only 178 miles north of the harbour where he'd anchored the *Hecla*.

He could not have continued. His men were suffering from chilblains, snow blindness, and incipient scurvy. By the time they reached the first solid land – no more than a rock in the sea – they had been fifty-six hours without rest, were unable to comprehend orders, and, as Parry noted, had "a wildness in their looks." They recovered and reached the *Hecla* on August 21, 1827, after an absence of sixty-one days.

Once again, Parry had missed his target. It would have been easier if the Admiralty, buoyed up by his optimism, hadn't felt it necessary to announce that he was going to the Pole. "I wish I could say we have been successful but this we have not," he wrote ruefully to his Isabella. He was crazy with desire to "clasp my dear girl to my heart." All the reserve found in his journals vanished when he poured out his soul to her in these letters from shipboard. "How can I express the anxiety of my fond heart, my beloved Isabella, as I approach the English shores! . . . Daily, almost hourly, I have prayed for you my love. . . ."

She had already received one letter from Hammerfest. It all but prostrated her. "I *could* not open it my hands trembled and my heart beat too violently but in a few moments I calmed. . . ."

As he approached London, Parry grew more ardent. He landed at Inverness but was held up at Durham for lack of horses; the Duke of Wellington, travelling the same road, had commandeered all the available transport. He used the delay to express "the unspeakable joy and comfort" her letter, received at Edinburgh the previous night, had given him. All the frustrations of the polar trip were dissipated when he learned for the first time that he was to become a father. He was ecstatic: "Oh, my darling wife, how can I ever be thankful enough for all God's mercies to me? . . . You well know, sweet girl, all your Edward feels on such an occasion, for you know every inmost feeling of my heart. . . . Tell me when you write more particularly about yourself. You cannot, dearest girl, write on any subject one ten-thousandth part so interesting to your Edward. . . . You are quite right, love; success in my enterprize is by no means essential to our joy, tho' it might have added something to it; but we cannot, ought not to have *everything* we wish. . . ."

He and Franklin arrived home from their respective expeditions about the same time and, by coincidence, walked into the Admiralty with their reports within fifteen minutes of one another. Both would soon be knighted. Parry stubbornly insisted that although the Pole would be more difficult to reach than anybody had previously believed, he himself could not "recommend any material improvement in the plan lately adopted."

This arrogant and egotistical assessment flew in the face of all reason and experience. It was too much for William Scoresby, who publicly recorded his disagreement. The whaler pointed out that the Eskimos invariably used dogs and light sledges and that their *umiak*, a light boat only thirty feet long, carried as many passengers as Parry's large, heavy craft but could be hoisted on the backs of six or eight men. The boat should weigh no more than four or five hundred pounds, said Scoresby. Parry's had weighed 1,450. The Russians, too, had used light sledges and dogs and had managed to make direct distances on the ice much longer than Parry had, some of them travelling "*many leagues a day* without difficulty."

"Why was it," Scoresby asked, "that *our* expedition assisted by all that natural ardour so peculiar to British seamen, could seldom complete more than four or five miles a day . . . ? Surely it was not that our adventurers were less capable, less hardy, less enterprizing than others?" He listed three reasons: the boat-sledges were too heavy, the season too far advanced, and Parry had chosen the wrong meridian to ascend. He was too far east, though, of course, he had no way of knowing that. But Scoresby was convinced from a study of Parry's narrative that the Pole could be gained only by an approach from the west. In that he would again be proven right, but not until long after his death.

Many years later, a very different kind of explorer, John Rae of the Hudson's Bay Company, writing to Governor George Simpson, was to make his own assessment of official Arctic travel. The way to get credit, Rae wrote sarcastically, ". . . is to plan some . . . scheme . . . and after having signally failed, return with a lot of . . . reasons – sufficiently good to gull John Bull – for your failure."

The two newest knights were both heroes in the public eye, but, it seemed, their Arctic exploits were behind them. Parry, safe in his sinecure as naval hydrographer, would never again be sent on an expedition. Franklin would soon be counted too old to attempt a fourth. For the moment the public was satiated by tales of polar ice, and the Navy, too, had grown weary of the Arctic. It seemed as if the great adventure, on which Barrow and "the Parry school" (as it came to be called) had embarked with such enthusiasm, was at an end.

But no one, at that point, had reckoned on that much-despised explorer John Ross, the scarred veteran of half a dozen battles not only with Napoleon's navy but also with Barrow and his disciples. Ross was determined to go north again, and, like those of so many other explorers, his motives were mixed. It was not just that he wanted to find the North West Passage for the honour and glory of Great Britain. Having made himself a laughing stock over the illusory Croker Mountains, he was determined to regain his honour – a word much used by all explorers of that period – by succeeding where his enemies had failed.

The Navy, of course, had no intention of sending him anywhere. He needed private funds, and who better to supply him than the country's leading distiller and philanthropist, Sheriff Felix Booth, who required nothing more than that his name be permanently attached to some barren piece of rock extending into the forbidding Arctic seas.

Thus it came about that the longest peninsula in the Arctic and also its biggest gulf both bear today the name of a popular brand of British gin. In one way or another, Ross got his revenge.

Chapter Three

John Ross's crew saved by the Isabella

For most of the decade, John Ross had nursed his wounded pride at *Endless* his Scottish home – North West Castle, he called it – at Stranraer. A *winter* prodigious writer with a voluminous correspondence, he addressed his roving intellect to a variety of inquiries, ranging all the way from the "science" of phrenology to the principles of steam propulsion. It was Ross's *Treatise on Navigation by Steam* that showed him to be ahead of his time and also ahead of the British Navy, which was strongly committed to sail. Lord Melville, for one, was convinced that "the introduction of steam was calculated to strike a fatal blow to the naval supremacy of the Empire."

Ross felt hard done by. In exploding the myth of the Croker Mountains, Parry had made him a laughing stock. His own boasts hadn't helped. In some quarters those who exhibited an excess of vanity were now said to be afflicted with "Ross-ism." The Navy had promoted him and Lord Melville had assured him that the service held him in high esteem, but Ross was not taken in by that hollow accolade. When other expeditions were mounted, he was passed over. Parry and Franklin were heroes, but Ross was ignored. That rankled.

But now, in 1827, the Passage beckoned once more. Parry was back after another failure; he and Franklin had not been able to link their separate explorations. Ross saw a chance to regain his lost honour – and at Parry's expense. All he had to do was cruise down Prince Regent Inlet beyond Parry's last point of discovery and continue on to Franklin's Point Turnagain, and the laurel would be his. He went to Melville with a proposal to send a steam vessel to the Arctic in one final, victorious sweep. But the Admiralty wasn't planning any further expeditions, especially one led by John Ross in a steam-powered ship.

Ross didn't give up. If the government wouldn't support an expedition, other patrons might. He went to see his old friend Felix Booth, the distiller, and sheriff of London, who was sympathetic. He felt that Ross had been slighted through anonymous rumours. There was also some suggestion that an American expedition was being formed to seek the Passage. That would never do!

Booth was prepared to advance seven thousand pounds to Ross's three thousand to make up the total amount the explorer had calculated the expedition would cost. There was, however, a hitch: the government award of twenty thousand pounds promised to the first expedition to sail through to the Pacific. Booth didn't want anyone to think he was after private gain.

The events that followed were twisted into an ironic, indeed a ludicrous, sequence. With Booth retiring from the plan, Ross was forced to go back to the government with a new Arctic scheme. The government, of course, turned it down, and, being unaware of Booth's position, persuaded parliament to cancel the reward, apparently to discourage all Arctic schemes in general and John Ross's in particular. This had the opposite effect from the one intended, for it brought the scrupulous Felix Booth back into the picture. In the end he committed more than seventeen thousand pounds to the venture.

Ross's second-in-command would be his nephew James, now an experienced Arctic traveller. John Ross believed that Parry's ships and crews had been far too large. His company would total no more than twenty-three. His ship would be an eighty-five-ton Liverpool steam packet, the *Victory*, its tonnage increased to one hundred and sixty-five by a series of improvements but still less than half the tonnage and draught of the *Hecla* or the *Fury*. A sixteen-ton tender, the *Krusenstern*, accompanied the expedition, which reached Disco Island off the west coast of Greenland on July 28, 1829.

Now it was John Ross who was lucky, for this was the mildest season in the memory of Greenland's oldest inhabitants. Steaming northwest across Baffin Bay, Ross expected at any hour to encounter the ice that had trapped Parry. To his astonishment and delight, the ocean was clear. "But for one iceberg . . . we might have imagined ourselves in the summer seas of England." At six on the morning of August 4, he found his men scrubbing the decks barefoot – a remarkable spectacle. Two days later, he entered Lancaster Sound. He had crossed Baffin Bay in nine days; Parry on his second voyage had taken two months.

In the sound, some disagreeable memories returned to haunt him. He couldn't resist a crack at Parry in his journal. Sir Edward had not uttered so much as a whisper at the time to support his later belief that Lancaster Sound was a strait. Even if he had done so, Ross felt he had been justified in turning back. Now, it was his turn to solve the problem that had stumped Parry. If he ever returned to England, Ross told himself, he would be received in a very different manner.

His luck continued to hold. He breezed down the sound and into

Prince Regent Inlet in thirty-six hours, again outdoing Parry. The only difficulty was the steam engine, which hadn't worked properly since the start of the voyage. Ross seemed to be spending half his time in the engine room helping the men fix boiler leaks and faulty pumps. The engine was soon abandoned in favour of sail, a circumstance that was to provoke a lively, choleric, but ultimately ineffective pamphlet war between Ross and the builder, Braithwaite, each of whom blamed the other for the problem.

On August 12, the expedition passed Fury Beach. There was no sign of Parry's vessel, but the tent poles of the previous expedition were clearly visible in the shadow of the glowering limestone cliffs. It had always been Ross's plan to replenish his own stores from those left by Parry, but to his mortification, he found that the current and the tide made it impossible to land.

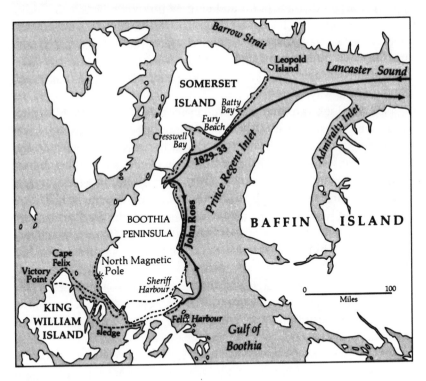

John Ross and James Clark Ross, 1829-33

On he went. Cresswell Bay, named by Parry, seemed on first inspection to be a passage to the west – an apparent victory over his rival and hailed as such by some of Ross's supporters on board. Ross, however, took no joy in this revelation, or later claimed he didn't. "I would rather find a passage anywhere else," he told his nephew, because, as he said later, "I am quite sure that those who have suffered as I have from a cruelly misled Public Opinion will never wish to transfer such misery to a fellow creature if their hearts are in the right place." As it eventually turned out, Cresswell Bay was an inlet that led nowhere.

The *Victory* returned north and this time found an anchorage off Fury Beach, strewn with Parry's supplies, all in good condition. The crew stowed as much as they could on board. "God bless Fury Beach," they cried as they rowed back to the ship. At least they weren't going to starve.

Ross again pushed south down into the inlet. On August 16 he passed Parry's farthest point and entered unknown waters, breaking out some bottles of his sponsor's gin in celebration. By the end of September he had gone three hundred miles farther than Parry and was only two hundred and eighty miles from the point where Franklin had turned back in 1821. But, of course, there was a land mass blocking the way.

Now his luck ran out. The Arctic turned fickle. Buffeted by gales and raging seas, almost crushed by jostling icebergs, he gave up. Like the others, he had failed, and, like the others, he was tormented by that failure. Could he have got through the Passage if the engine hadn't given out? Could he have achieved his ambitions in a bigger ship? The answer, though he didn't know it, was no, for Prince Regent Inlet was virtually a dead end. There was one narrow channel leading through the great mass of land to the west (later to be named Bellot Strait), but it was so constricted that Ross had missed it on his voyage south.

Now, in October, he struggled through the encroaching ice of the great gulf that lay at the bottom of Prince Regent Inlet. Ross, whose powers of description were considerable, pictured it later for his readers.

Let them remember, he wrote, that "ice is stone – a floating rock in a stream." Then "imagine, if they can, these mountains of crystal hurled through a narrow strait by a rapid tide; meeting, as mountains might meet, with a noise of thunder, breaking from each other's precipices huge fragments, or rending each other asunder, till, losing their former equilibrium, they fall over headlong, lifting the sea

110

around in breakers, and whirling it into eddies while the flatter fields of ice, formed against these masses . . . by the wind and the stream, rise out of the sea until they fall back on themselves, adding to the indescribable commotion and noise. . . ."

At last Ross found a suitable harbour, which he named Felix Harbour after his patron. The land off which they anchored the *Victory* would be called Boothia Felix (it is now Boothia Peninsula) and the gulf, the Gulf of Boothia. No bottled stimulant ever received greater recognition.

It was as well for Ross's sanity that he had no idea in that late autumn of 1829 that he would be forced to spend *four* winters in the Arctic. No other explorer had spent more than two. The remarkable aspect of Ross's long imprisonment is that he was able to bring his crew home virtually free of the scurvy that weakened other expeditions. This was no accident. Ross had divined what others had ignored and would continue to ignore for the next half century. He had learned from studying the Eskimos that "the large use of oil and fats is the true secret of life in these frozen countries, and that the natives cannot subsist without it, becoming diseased and dying under a more meagre diet." Ross was convinced that if others had followed "the usage and experience of the natives," fewer would have perished.

He was on the right track: seal blubber is rich in Vitamin C. Of course, he was in an area where game and fish abounded, yet he had to depend on the Eskimos not only to hunt for fresh meat and fish but also to provide furs to replace the Navy issue of wool. Without the natives, the story of Ross's four-year ordeal would have ended tragically.

The *Victory* and its little tender were frozen in for eleven months. On July 24, 1830, the bay was free of ice, but to Ross's dismay there was no way out of the harbour; it was too shallow, the tides were too low. He had chosen the worst possible wintering place. The crews struggled for two months but succeeded in moving the ships no more than three miles. Ross named his new anchorage Sheriff Harbour (after Sheriff Felix Booth, of course) and resigned himself to another winter in the ice.

The following summer – 1831 – he waited again for the ice to set him free. Again he waited in vain. "To us," Ross said, "the sight of ice was a plague, a vexation, a torment, an evil, a matter of despair." Once more the *Victory* managed to make about three miles, to be stopped by an impenetrable ridge of ice. The new harbour was named for the ship but changed later to Victoria Harbour to honour the young princess who would shortly be queen.

Again, the worst aspect of these three winters was boredom. The usual schools, lectures, and small entertainments soon palled. There was nothing to do, nothing to gaze out on, for the landscape and sky never changed. To Ross, even the storms lacked variety "amid this eternal sameness of snow and ice." Some men were able to sleep through most of the winter. Others "dozed away their time in the waking stupefaction, which such a state of things produced."

It was not a happy ship; perhaps no ship could have been under the circumstances, although Parry had gone a long way to lighten the dark season for his crews. But Ross was not Parry, as William Light, a steward on the expedition, made clear in his published reminiscences of the voyage. Parry, Light recalled, knew how to bend, "but with Capt. Ross the case was different, he was trebly steeped in the starch of official dignity, the maintenance of which he considered to consist in abstracting himself as much as possible from familiar intercourse with those beneath and suffering no opportunity to escape him, by which he could shew to them that he was their superior and commander. The men were conscious that they owed him obedience; they were not equally convinced that they owed him their respect and esteem."

Light's memoir, published with the aid of a ghost writer, draws aside the curtain of naval imperturbability that conceals so much. In no other instance was the English public allowed a peek at the lower deck, given an insight into the real feelings of the ordinary seamen or a hint at the tensions that often marred relations aboard crowded vessels trapped in the ice.

Light was very hard on John Ross – sometimes, out of ignorance or prejudice, too hard. At one point, for instance, he complained of being fed on a diet of salmon instead of salt meat. "In this unpardonable manner did Capt. Ross persevere in forcing upon his men a kind of food which . . . was injurious to their health and totally unfit to support the physical strength. . . ." But Ross knew better. He recognized the signs of incipient scurvy that first spring of 1830 and moved when he could to stamp it out. As he wrote in his diary: ". . . the first salmon of the summer were a medicine which all the drugs in the ship could not replace."

Light was undoubtedly closer to reality in his assessment of Ross as a haughty, unsociable, and almost hermit-like officer who treated

112

his men with iron authority but little compassion and kept to his cabin, sustaining himself on his sponsor's gin. He was the oldest man on the voyage – he passed his fifty-fifth year on this Arctic trip – and he hadn't been to sea for a decade. He belonged to another, tougher era. As Light put it, "the quarterdeck of a British man of war is not the one best adapted to teach a man urbanity and civility toward his inferior!"

Ross also possessed a towering ego. He took nobody's advice and grew angry or stubborn when any was offered. The men blamed him for getting them into such a pickle by choosing the wrong harbour. There were times, according to Light, when they came close to mutiny. Ross himself alluded to one such incident during his evidence to the select committee that examined him after his return.

To the crew, it seemed he lacked both energy and enthusiasm – qualities that distinguished James Clark Ross, his nephew. In fact, many of the expedition's most notable discoveries were made by the younger man, though his uncle tried to grab as much of the credit as he could. This was John Ross's great failing as an explorer; he lacked magnanimity, as Sabine had discovered over a decade before.

James Clark Ross was more popular than his uncle and far more energetic, "the life and soul of all the schemes and plans," to quote Light. In times of stress, the men came to him for advice. He was by far the most experienced Arctic hand on board, a veteran of five previous expeditions. Only four others had had any Arctic experience, and these were limited to two years or less.

During the first two winters the ship was frozen into the ice, James Ross roved along the Boothia coastline by dogsled and small boat. Of the six hundred miles of new territory charted by the expedition, two thirds were his. It was he who discovered that Prince Regent Inlet came to a dead end in the Gulf of Boothia, he who collected most of the specimens, and he who paid daily visits in good weather and bad to the observatory that had been set up on the shore.

In the spring of 1830 he crossed a body of water (later named for him) to a bald and forbidding land later named for King William IV of England. It was actually an island, but Ross didn't realize that – a mistake that would help to doom the lost Franklin expedition seventeen years later. He and his sledging crew followed the coast northwest to its northern point, which he named Cape Felix – a fourth nod toward his uncle's sponsor. Here he was astonished at the spectacle of vast masses of ice blocks hurled up on the shore, as far as half a mile above the high-tide mark. What had caused this amazing pressure? Ross could not know that this was the work of the great ice stream pouring down from the Beaufort Sea – the same ice that would eventually trap Franklin's ships.

The coastline turned toward the southwest, and Ross proceeded twenty-five miles in that direction to a promontory he named Victory Point. To the southwest open sea stretched off in the distance toward Point Turnagain. The unexplored gap was only about two hundred miles, as the crow flies, but Ross didn't have the supplies to go farther.

His crowning achievement – the one for which he is remembered – came in the spring of 1831, when he located the North Magnetic Pole, then on the western coast of Boothia Felix. This was the great object of his ambition. "It almost seemed as if we had accomplished every thing that we had come so far to see and to do," he declared, "as if our voyage and all its labours were at an end and that nothing now remained for us but to return home and be happy for the rest of our days." His uncle tried to seize part of the glory for that, too, a claim that deepened the rift between them.

For the *Victory*, in Light's phrase, was "a house divided." Uncle and nephew were often at loggerheads, and the crew tended to take sides. There were times when the two Rosses, who shared the same small cabin, scarcely spoke to one another. At one point in the early spring of the second winter, when nerves were frayed and tempers undoubtedly ran high, "the fire which had been concentrating for some time in their breasts, like the lava in the craters of Vesuvius and Etna, burst forth with an explosion, which terrified the other inmates of the cabin" – in the overheated prose of Light's collaborator, Robert Huish. The argument, whatever it was about, was settled when John Ross sent for a magnum of Booth's gin. But two months later, the two were at such odds that James Ross refused to attend divine service and went for a walk on the shore. If Light is to be believed, he didn't miss much. The elder Ross didn't have Parry's evangelism; he babbled through the prayer book so fast that Light, for one, scarcely understood a word he said.

The tensions and monotony of this two-year confinement were alleviated from time to time in the winter by the presence of the Eskimos. The seamen taught them to play football and leapfrog, to the natives' obvious enjoyment, and, with the permission of the husbands, borrowed the women for their sexual pleasure. John Ross

114

liked them, too, in a fatherly, stand-offish kind of way. They were, he declared, "among the most worthy of all the rude tribes yet known to our voyagers, in whatever part of the world." But, although they kept his people warm, well fed, and free of the sexual tensions that often threaten the sanity of active men in an isolated environment, they remained barbarians to Ross.

"We were weary for want of occupation, for want of variety, for want of the means of mental exertion, for want of thought, and (why should I not say it?) for want of society. . . . Is it wonderful that even the visits of barbarians were welcome, or can any thing more strongly show the nature of our pleasures than the confession that these visits were as delightful; even as the society of London might be. . . ?"

Nonetheless, their gluttony repelled him. "Disgusting brutes!" he wrote in his journal. They were uncivilized, in his definition of the word, and therefore lesser beings. "Is it not the fate of the savage and the uncivilized on this earth to give way to the more cunning and the better informed, to knowledge and civilization? It is the order of the world; and the right one. . . ."

The crew felt closer to the Eskimos than Ross did; but then, they *were* closer, in more ways than one. The steward felt that Ross was interested only in what he could get from the natives. As long as they had geographical information that he needed, he received them well, but once he got from them everything they knew, his attitude changed and they were no longer permitted aboard ship. "There was scarcely a sailor who did not draw a comparison between the treatment which they received from the savage and untutored Esquimaux in their snow built huts, and that which the Esquimaux received from the tutored and civilized Europeans in the comparatively splendid cabin of the *Victory*. . . ."

Ross made a vain attempt to move one Eskimo family who had built their snow hut close to the ship – too close to suit the captain. A hilarious confrontation followed. Ross had claimed the land in the name of the King, but neither he nor his nephew could make the Eskimos understand that the land they had lived on for centuries was no longer theirs. The white men explained the purpose of their visit, or tried to. The Eskimos in reply offered them a slice of seal blubber. The white men asked how long the family intended to stay. The Eskimos asked if they had any fish-hooks with them. The white men explained they'd taken possession of the land in the King's name. The Eskimos remarked, chattily, that the seals were becoming very

115

scarce. It had not occurred to them that anybody owned the land any more than anybody owned the sea or the air. They were planning an immediate trip inland in search of caribou. The naval officers, seeing their snow huts, had come to the wrong conclusion: to a white man, a house meant permanence, but the Eskimos could build one in a couple of hours. They could pack a light sled in half an hour with all their worldly possessions. No landlord or tax collector ever came to their door. The concept of permanence, of real estate, of tithe, title, and deed, was foreign to them.

All over the globe at this time, the British were attempting to foist their own concept of morality on totally different cultures. John Ross was no exception. He needed an Eskimo interpreter such as John Sacheuse, who had been on his first expedition and died shortly afterward. On Boothia Felix he found a likely candidate, a young man named Poowutyuk, whom he took aboard the *Victory* and endeavoured to train. But neither one had the slightest understanding of the other's culture.

Poowutyuk thought of the ship's crew as one big Eskimo-style family, where each individual foraged for himself. The best foraging, he quickly discovered, was in the steward's cabin, where the food was kept. One night he appropriated a variety of foodstuffs, including a jugged hare and a roast grouse, both intended for the captain's table. These he stuffed into his baggy sealskin trousers while he searched about for a comfortable place in which to consume them.

His eye settled on a tub, half full of flour – to him a warm sort of snow. He climbed inside in his wet furs and proceeded to demolish his trove of delicacies. Ross, deprived of his dinner, set up a hue and cry to uncover the thief, who to the astonishment of the search party eventually rose from the tub "like a ghost from the tomb," covered from head to foot in flour.

Poowutyuk was proud that he had been able to look after himself. The idea of theft was unknown to him. As the steward said, he believed that "as the hare was every man's property before it was killed, it was equally so afterward." Ross didn't see it that way. He ordered the Eskimo youth to suffer a dozen blows on the back with a stick. Poowutyuk was more puzzled than pained by this treatment. It didn't occur to him that he was being punished. But what was going on? Was it some sort of ritual or custom? A ceremony, perhaps? At last he had it figured out. Since it was too cold for him to disrobe, and since his garments were thick with flour, and since he couldn't reach his own back, the accommodating *kabloonas* were beating the flour out of him, as he had seen them beating rugs. He submitted quite cheerfully while Ross, uncomprehending, drew up a code of punishment for any more immoral acts that might occur in the future, oblivious to the fact that no one had yet been able to teach the Eskimos what, in the white man's view, an immoral act was.

Thus passed three winters. Ross had come to the melancholy conclusion that the *Victory* would never escape from the ice and that they would have to sink her in the spring, hike overland to Fury Beach, subsist on Parry's stores, and then make their way out of the inlet and into Lancaster Sound in small boats. There, he hoped, the whaling fleet would succour them.

He realized that this would be a race against time, for he had calculated his rations would run out in June. In April 1832, the crews began the exhausting drudgery of sledging supplies forward to set up a series of depots for the march north. It was a tedious business. That month they were able to move forward eighteen miles, no more, yet they had covered a total of one hundred and ten. The distance to Fury Beach – a twisting, switchback route that curled around bays, capes, and inlets – was three hundred.

On May 29, they beached the tender and moored the *Victory* so that she would sink in ten fathoms of water. It was a dismal moment for Ross, who had sailed on thirty-six different vessels and until this moment had never abandoned one.

Now the struggle began to get to Fury Beach before the supplies ran out. Ross put his men on two thirds of the normal rations. They slept each night in trenches dug in the snow, huddled together in their blanket bags. Ross, in Light's phrase, was a "featherbed traveller" who rode for most of the journey on a sledge with a blind man, a cripple, and three invalids. The small size of the party was an asset; a larger one might easily have perished.

By the time they reached Fury Beach on July 1, they were weak from hunger. Boxes of Parry's foodstuffs lay scattered along the beach, and the ravenous men rushed at them. To their anger, Ross stopped them. Up stepped Thomas, the carpenter – Ross's one indispensable man and therefore bolder than the others – crying out that this action was "shameful and scandalous." Light, too, was angered and disgusted by the action and said so in his memoirs, but again he was far too harsh on his captain. Ross knew that half-starved men can make themselves ill by sudden gluttony. He distributed small portions, but after he retired, his crew pilfered the rest, hiding it under their blankets. In Ross's words, they "suffered severely from eating too much."

Three of the *Fury*'s boats lay on the beach, but it was a month before the channel was clear enough to allow them to get away. They proceeded up the coast in fits and starts until, at last, relief seemed at hand. It was all illusion. On September 1, standing on a high promontory above Cape Clarence at the northern tip of Somerset Island, Ross looked out on Barrow Strait and Lancaster Sound and saw a solid mass of ice. The inlet, too, was closed. There was no help for it; they must leave the boats behind and return by sledge to Fury Beach.

They now faced a fourth Arctic winter – a dreadful prospect, for they had lost the warmth of the ship and would be forced to exist on reduced rations in a makeshift shelter – no more than a hovel of spars and canvas, banked high with a nine-foot wall of snow.

That winter, Thomas, the outspoken carpenter, died. Several more were too sick to work. Ross was left with thirteen men strong enough to shuttle provisions in seven long journeys through the snow from Fury Beach to Batty Bay, where he had cached the boats. On July 8, 1833, they set off once more, reached the boats in six days, and waited a month before a gale cleared the ice in Prince Regent Inlet. They embarked at last, rowing and sailing, three tiny dots on the grey expanse of Lancaster Sound, dwarfed by the Precambrian cliffs of Devon Island and the cloud-plumed glaciers of Baffin. To Ross, the change was magical. For the first time in four years he felt like a sailor; he had almost forgotten what it was like "to float at freedom on the seas."

They passed the mouth of the great fiord – the longest in the world – that Parry had named Admiralty Inlet; on August 25, they reached its companion, Navy Board Inlet. Then, at four in the morning of the following day, the lookout thought he saw a sail and woke James Clark Ross, who, peering through his telescope, saw that it was indeed a ship. Everyone was awake in an instant, firing rockets; but the wind was against them, and the sail vanished over the horizon. Another sail was spotted; it too seemed to diminish. But now John Ross's luck returned. The wind calmed; the crew rowed like madmen; at last they saw the ship heave to.

Ross was astonished when he identified the rescue vessel. She was the *Isabella*, the very ship that he had commanded on his first voyage in 1818. The whaling captain was equally astonished. He couldn't believe his eyes as he told Ross that he had been dead for two years. Ross drily denied it. Now he learned that all England had long since given him up and that a rescue party under George Back was even then heading across the Canadian tundra searching for his remains.

And so they climbed on board, a scarecrow gang, unshaven, filthy, starved down to their bones, half-clothed in tattered skins. It was four years since John Ross had left the west coast of Greenland with a complement of twenty-three men; of these, all but one had managed to survive.

It was a remarkable feat. Ross's understanding of scurvy had helped; so had the presence of the Eskimos, who were indispensable hunters. Parry's discarded supplies were also a factor. And the very modesty of the expedition, strapped as it was for funds, contributed to its survival. In the Arctic, the Navy had indulged in a form of overkill: big ships, big crews. On his third voyage, Parry had 122 officers and men, more than five times the size of Ross's crew. It's doubtful that the Eskimo hunters could have kept that number alive and healthy for four winters. It was difficult enough for Ross's party to travel north by stages, sleeping in snow trenches and tempting the buffeting seas in three small boats; a larger party could not have done it.

The tragedy is that the Navy learned nothing from Ross – nothing of the benefits of freshly killed meat, nothing of the advantages of small exploratory parties. The next major expedition to invade the heart of the Arctic archipelago would be larger than ever, and its members would die from hunger and from the scurvy that Ross and his hunters had kept at bay.

Ross returned to England to find himself a popular hero and a social lion. He dined with royalty. Hostesses scrambled to have him as a dinner guest. Four thousand fan letters clogged his post box. When he visited the continent, he was showered with medals and awards by foreign governments. A committee of parliament voted him five thousand pounds to cover his losses. Another eighteen thousand went to Felix Booth to cover his expenses, while the crew members received double pay. Booth was made a baronet, Ross a Knight Commander of the Bath.

The expedition's accomplishments were considerable, especially the discoveries and charts of James Ross, whose map of Boothia, for instance, was standard for the rest of the century. As for the North West Passage, John Ross hadn't found it and was prepared to dismiss it. When a parliamentary committee asked him if its discovery would be of public benefit, he responded bluntly, "I believe it would be utterly useless."

Ross might be a public hero, but he was still a pariah among his peers. In the Navy's view he had not behaved like a gentleman. He had tried to seize too much credit for the explorations and discoveries of his nephew. He had seemed too eager for monetary gain, while his nephew, appearing before the select committee, made a point of showing his disinterestedness. "Ross will do himself harm by the eagerness he has shown on this matter," John Franklin wrote to his new wife, Jane, "and no one is more annoyed at it than young Ross, of whom the uncle is very jealous."

Ross published his journal himself, without the help of John Murray, and proceeded, to the undoubted horror of his fellow officers, to use high-pressure methods to market it. He opened a subscription office in Regent Street and even engaged agents to peddle it from door to door, a most unseemly procedure in naval etiquette and one that caused Barrow to attack him for his "lust for lucre." Another naval author, Captain Beaufort, made a point of telling the parliamentary committee that he had received no money from the publication of his own book because "I did not think that materials acquired in the King's service ought to be sold."

The harshest blast, predictably, came from Barrow. In a long essay in the *Quarterly Review* he attacked the narrative as "ponderous," called Ross a "vain and jealous man," and railed against "the cold and heartless manner in which the bulk of narrative is drawn up – the unwillingness to give praise or make acknowledgement even to him [Ross's nephew] on whom the safety of the expedition mainly depended."

These criticisms were well taken, but Barrow showed his own vanity and jealousy when he attacked the expedition as an "ill-prepared, ill-conceived . . . and ill-executed undertaking," castigated Ross as "utterly incompetent to conduct an arduous naval enterprise for discovery to a successful termination," and declared that the results of his four-year odyssey "are next to nothing." The same, of course, might have been said of Parry's later voyages, and with more truth. But Parry was Barrow's man and a gentleman; Ross was not. The Navy's failure to analyse the very real strengths of his expedition was to cost it dear in the years to come.

2

In John Ross's absence the world had moved on. The railway loco- *The* motive had come into its own – a harbinger of the age of steam. *indomitable* Michael Faraday had discovered the principle of electricity, and two *Jane* scientists had separately invented chloroform. The first sewing machine had been patented. The Empire had abolished slavery. George IV was dead, and John Franklin had left the Arctic wastes and the London drawing-rooms for the salubrious waters of the Mediterranean.

Within a year of his return from the North, the widowed explorer had renewed his acquaintance with his wife's friend Jane Griffin and proposed marriage. As he put it to his future father-in-law, a wealthy silk weaver, "The various interchanges of ideas and sentiments which have recently taken place between Miss Jane and myself have assured us not only of entertaining the warmest affection for each other, but likewise there exists between us the closest congeniality of mind, thought and feeling. . . ."

In short, they were in love. They were married on December 5, 1828, and spent their honeymoon in Paris, where it was remarked that Franklin seemed remarkably plump and comfortable for a man who had once starved almost to the point of death.

Jane Griffin was then thirty-six years old. In her younger days, she had had a host of suitors, for she was an elegant and lovely woman, a little shy but also highly intelligent. There were those who would come to think of her as "a tall, commanding looking person, perhaps with a loud voice too!" She was not flattered by this "visionary Lady Franklin" as she termed it, for she was small, slight, and soft spoken. Her reputation was at odds with her physical presence.

Before she met John Franklin she had turned down all aspirants for her hand, an act she came to regret in the case of at least two. One of these rejected suitors was Peter Mark Roget, who later distinguished himself by creating the thesaurus that still bears his name. When he married someone else, Jane Griffin confided to her diary,

". . . the romance of my life is gone – my dreams are vanishing & I am awakening to sober realities & to newly-acquired wisdom."

She was a confirmed, indeed a prodigious, diarist and correspondent and a voracious reader who thirsted after wisdom. She devoured books (295 in one three-year period) – books on every subject: travel, education, religion, social problems, but never novels, for novels in that day were considered frivolous, especially for a serious-minded young woman.

She was incurably restless and had travelled a great deal with her father before her marriage. In her voluminous journal she conscientiously noted everything in her cramped, spidery hand – every plaque, every historic tablet, every monument, every church, the chief products and industries of every town, even the distances covered. She believed in self-improvement. At nineteen, she had worked out a plan to organize her time and enrich her mind, with every moment given over to some form of study.

Jane Griffin belies the stereotype of the Victorian woman of means, languid at her needlework, simpering fetchingly at the society balls. A description of her multitude of activities leaves one slightly out of breath, for she indulged herself in a kaleidoscope of worthy interests. She was a member of the Book Society. She took lectures at the Royal Institution. She visited Newgate Prison and the Vauxhall Gardens. She attended meetings of the British and Foreign School Society. Nor did she take a back seat at fashionable dinner parties. She took on the redoubtable Dr. Arnold on the subject of fagging (of which she disapproved) and reprimanded the family of Benjamin Disraeli when they repeated some gossip about John Franklin's last parting from his dying wife. Her voice trembled with anger as she "replied to all this unfeeling nonsense." She did not know Franklin well at this point; but they had met on occasion, and she felt it proper to give him a going-away present of a silver pencil and a pair of fur-lined gloves.

She was a shrewd observer of the human species and described almost everyone she met. John Ross, for instance, was "short, stout, sailor-looking & not very gentlemanly in his person, but his manners & his language are perfectly so; his features are coarse & thick, his eyes grey, his complexion ruddy & his hair of a reddish, sandy hue. Yet notwithstanding his lack of beauty, he has a great deal of intelligence, benevolence & good humour in his countenance." She would revise that opinion in her later years and even ban Ross's portrait

122

from her gallery, but her assessments, while sharp, were reasonably benign. Franklin's friend John Richardson "was not well dressed – & looks like a Scotchman as he is – he has broad & high cheek bones, a widish mouth, grey eyes & brown hair – upon the whole rather plain, but the countenance thoughtful, mild & pleasing. . . ."

In the months before her marriage, the peripatetic woman set off with her father on another trip, this time to Russia. Her fiancé would have liked to accompany her on the same ship, but she did not feel it proper and, in her peremptory way, put him off. Her objection, she told him, arose "from a strong sense of impropriety in the arrangement, as well as from a conviction that we should all be placed in a number of awkward and disagreeable situations during long and rough voyages and journeys which it would be extremely unpleasant for me to partake in and impossible to avoid. . . ." He joined her in St. Petersburg, where she did her best to note down not only everything she saw but also everything she *didn't* see. They were married immediately after their return.

In many ways, Jane Griffin was the exact opposite of her complacent, easy-going, humourless husband. "What an irritable, impatient creature I am by comparison," she told him. In that odd partnership, hers was the stronger will, but she was clever enough not to show it. "You are of a much more easy disposition than myself," she had written before their marriage. ". . . It must be my province, therefore, . . . to combat those things that excite my more sensitive temper; while it must be and shall be yours . . . to control even this disposition whenever you think it improperly excited and to exert over me . . . the authority which it will be your privilege to use and my duty to yield to. But do I speak of *duty*? You are of too manly, too generous, too affectionate a disposition to like the word and God forbid I should ever be the wretched wife who obeyed her husband from a sense of duty alone." Her wedding ring, she told him, would not be "the badge of slavery, but the cherished link of the purest affection."

She loved him and she was fiercely ambitious for him. He became an extension of her. "I never *can* be a happy person," she once wrote, "because I live too much in others." Certainly she lived in her husband, and, when it was necessary, pushed and prodded him along in her subtle fashion.

After two years of idleness, in which he was offered and turned down a commercial job in Australia, Franklin was at last given command of a twenty-six-gun frigate in the Mediterranean. He left early in 1830. Jane was not allowed to travel with him but had no intention of staying home. She joined him the following autumn and almost immediately plunged into a whirlwind of Middle Eastern travel through Greece, Egypt, Turkey, Syria, Asia Minor, and the Holy Land. Franklin hastened to explain that she travelled "not out of vulgar curiosity . . . but in order to inform herself and broaden her mind so she can be more interesting to others. . . ."

When Sir John returned to England in 1833 after his Mediterranean service, Lady Franklin was in Alexandria, preparing for a trip up the Nile. That did not stop her from directing his career by long distance. At her suggestion, he went, rather diffidently, to see the new First Lord of the Admiralty, Sir James Graham, to ask for further employment. Sir James, besieged by scores of other half-pay officers demanding the same thing, told him there was nothing available.

"You will fancy, my dearest, that your shy, timid husband must have gathered some brass on his way home," he wrote to his wife, describing his attempt, "or you will be at loss to account for his extraordinary courage." He had done it, he said, "because I knew you would have wished me to do so. . . ."

He had been planning to join her at Naples, but she would have none of it. Only by staying in England, close to the Admiralty, could he be sure of getting a posting. "Your credit and reputation," she declared, "are dearer to me than the selfish enjoyment of your society."

Now she pushed him further. A ship or a station were not comparable, she told him, to an expedition, preferably another Arctic exploration. "The character and position you possess in society and the interest – I may, say celebrity – attached to your name, belong to expeditions and would never have been acquired in the ordinary line of your profession." An expedition by ship this time, she felt, would be best. She would not want him to ruin his health "if you should feel to be unequal to any of your former exertions." On the other hand, "a freezing climate seems to have a wonderful power of bracing your nerves and making you stronger."

She badly wanted him to go after the ultimate prize: the North West Passage. There was talk, she said, of reviving the search. She made it sound like a contest, a prizefight, perhaps. James Clark Ross was a contender, for either the Passage or the Antarctic. He could take only one; somebody else would surely step in and undertake the other. Sir Edward Parry was on his way back from Australia (he had

124

taken the job that Franklin had turned down), "and he will be working hard for the vacancy or perhaps Richardson. I wish him well and young Ross also. . . . I grudge them nothing of their well-earned fame. But if yours is still dearer to me. . . . You must not think I undervalue your *military* career. I feel it is not that, but the other, which has made you what you are. . . ."

In spite of what she said, the Navy had, for the time at least, given up all intention of seeking the Passage. Public excitement over Arctic heroism was flagging. The *Edinburgh Review* captured the general sentiment in 1835 when it declared that the effort and funds expended on the search might be better applied to other purposes: "It may doubtless gratify the national vanity to plant the standard of England even upon the sterile regions . . . but . . . if no advantage can be gained by revisiting such inhospitable regions, it must be admitted that the mere knowledge of their existence, and of the indentations of their shores, is *comparatively* useless, and utterly unworthy of that sacrifice or risk of life and resources by which it may have been acquired."

The British government clearly agreed. After a second stint of idleness, Franklin was offered a post as governor of Antigua, a tiny palm-fringed speck in the Caribbean. That was too much for Lady Franklin – an almost insulting comedown for an Arctic hero. To her it was a minor post, no more important than that of first lieutenant on a ship of the line. When a better offer came, the Franklins accepted it. At least it *sounded* better: governor of Van Diemen's Land (Tasmania), a penal colony off the south coast of Australia. The day would come when both would bitterly regret the decision.

3

In June 1833, when Franklin was preparing to leave his Mediterranean command and return to England, George Back arrived at Fort Alexander on Lake Winnipeg to launch a rescue operation for John Ross, who had been missing for four years. Here, a twenty-five-year-old Hudson's Bay clerk, Thomas Simpson, wrote down his first impression of the explorer, a generally favourable assessment, tinctured with a touch of the fur trader's suspicion of all naval men. "He seems a very easy, affable man," Simpson wrote, "deficient, I should

Enter the Honourable Company

125

say, in that commanding manner with the people so necessary in this savage country. From my soul I wish them every success in the generous and humane objects of the expedition. . . ."

Five years later, the same Thomas Simpson had revised his opinion. He attacked Back's account of the expedition as "a painted bauble, all ornament and conceit, and no substance." As for the explorer himself: "Back, I believe to be not only a vain but a *bad* man."

These remarks, written to his favourite brother, Alexander (the two enjoyed "a Damon and Pythias relationship"), tell as much about Thomas Simpson as they do about George Back. The romantic young clerk, frustrated in a routine job in a backwater trading post, was burning with ambition to match the deeds of Parry and Franklin. Back must have appealed to him as a glamorous figure, right out of history. The following spring, when news arrived of Back's discovery and successful exploration of the Great Fish River, Simpson bubbled with praise. It was "greater than any of us in the North anticipated." Back, he felt, deserved and would get a knighthood.

That was before Simpson himself became an explorer. A highly emotional man, unstable at times, immoderately ambitious, he would reach the point where his own craving for fame would make him jealous of Back – afraid that the older explorer might outdo him in bold deeds and discoveries. The time would also come when Back himself would fail and Simpson would rejoice, but that was in the future. In 1833, Back was a rescuing angel.

Concern over John Ross's long absence had reached a peak in England the previous year. His brother George, the father of James Clark Ross, worried about his relatives' fate, had petitioned the King to launch a rescue operation. That the government declined to do; the unfortunate Ross was not the Admiralty's favourite explorer, and the general feeling at that level was that he had blundered and died. John Barrow was convinced that the entire expedition had perished the first winter. Would Parry, in a similar case, have been regarded so carelessly – or Franklin? Certainly not Franklin, as events were to prove.

But the government in the end could not resist public pressure. It finally pledged two thousand pounds toward a rescue operation, but only if the Hudson's Bay Company would provide supplies and equipment. The rest of the cost – three thousand pounds – was raised by public subscription.

Back's party numbered only twenty. He brought three men from England, picked up four soldiers in Montreal, and recruited the others at Norway House. His only fellow officer was a medical man, Dr. Richard King, a sardonic travelling companion who was to bear the brunt of the expedition. King's experience with Back turned him into a blunt critic of both the Royal Navy, for its exploring methods, and the Hudson's Bay Company, for its treatment of the native population, an attitude that pitted him against two Arctic Establishments and rendered all his criticisms ineffective.

King became an exponent of land-based travel as opposed to exploration by naval vessels. He thought it would be much easier to trace the course of the North West Passage by moving along the coastline on foot or by dogteam rather than trying to bull cumbersome ships through masses of shifting ice. He believed fervently that small parties living off the land were preferable to large ones dragging heavy equipment or heavy vessels trying to manoeuvre in ice-blocked channels.

He had the maddening quality of being shown to be right after the fact, but at the time few were prepared to listen. He was prickly, abusive, and ungentlemanly enough to take his cause to the public rather than to pursue it quietly in the back rooms of the Admiralty. For twenty-two years he ranted on, vainly attempting to mount various expeditions to explore along the continental edge, with himself as leader. And he was a good leader; while Back headed off in a light canoe as a one-man advance guard, King was in charge of organizing the supplies and the main party.

The fur traders were convinced that the pair were off on a wild-goose chase. On his first northern trek with Franklin in 1820, Back had heard from an old Indian warrior named Black Meat of a mysterious river, known as the Great Fish, that was supposed to wriggle through the Precambrian schists of the naked tundra northeastward to the Arctic Ocean. It was his plan to find this river, follow it to its mouth, cross over by land to Prince Regent Inlet, and look for Ross's party.

The company men were sceptical that any such river existed, a scepticism supported by the tension that existed between the fur trade and the Navy. The naval officers were seen as interlopers and amateurs, blundering about in a hostile land and writing romantic accounts of supposed hazards that voyageurs considered to be part of everyday life.

As one Hudson's Bay man, William Mactavish, wrote to his family during Back's absence in 1834: "You'll hear what a fine story they'll make out of this bungle, they will you may be sure take none of the blame themselves. . . . They will return next summer and like all the other Expeditions will do little and speak a great deal." Mactavish didn't like Back. He thought him heartless and snobbish. Back, he said, despised those who helped him because of their lack of formal manners.

But Back persisted in his search and early in 1834 found the headwaters of the mysterious river. In April a dispatch caught up with him reporting that Ross had been found alive. That left him free to devote himself to the expedition's secondary purpose: to explore the northeast corner of the continent.

That summer, Back and King headed down the Great Fish River into unexplored territory, "a violent and tortuous course of five hundred and thirty geographical miles, running through an iron ribbed country without a single tree on the whole line of its banks. . . ." The river expanded into large lakes with clear horizons, then narrowed again into a frothing maelstrom "most embarrassing to the navigator." Back counted no fewer than eighty-three falls, cascades, and rapids before it poured its waters into Chantrey Inlet.

To the north and to the east, Back could see land in the distance – Boothia Felix, in fact. He wrongly suspected a water passage led through it, but it was too late in the season to contemplate an attempt at such a North West Passage, nor did his instructions allow it. King disagreed with his leader; he was convinced that Boothia was a peninsula, not an island; again he turned out to be right. John Ross had already learned it from the Eskimos.

King William Land could also be seen to the north, though neither man knew what it was. King wanted Back to move out of Chantrey Inlet and explore the coastline eastward. Had he done so he would probably have discovered that King William Land was an island, separated from Boothia Felix by a channel. Years later it was discovered that this was the only practical route through the North West Passage, but that information came too late to prevent the greatest of all Arctic tragedies.

Back did not continue beyond Chantrey Inlet. With no fuel and

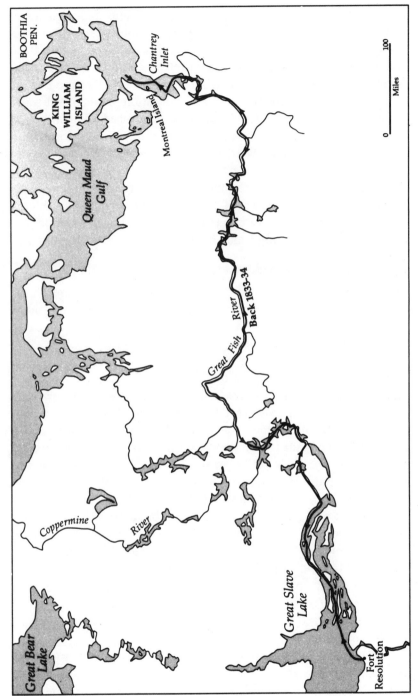

George Back explores the Great Fish River, 1833–34

only a little water, the expedition retraced its steps and returned to England the following year, 1835. King was not happy. He and his leader were not on the best of terms, and he clearly felt that Back could have done better. In 1836 he proposed that he lead an expedition with no more than six men down the Great Fish River to explore Boothia Felix and settle for all time the question of whether it was a peninsula or an island. Until that was established, "I consider it would be highly impolitic to send out an expedition on a large scale." A small expedition could be mounted for a thousand pounds; Back's had cost five times that. There were precedents in the journeys of both Mackenzie and Hearne. But King was, as usual, undiplomatic in the proposal he made to the Geographical Society and in the book that followed: "The question has been asked, how can I anticipate success in an undertaking which has baffled a Parry, a Franklin, and a Back? . . . if I were to pursue the plan adopted by [them] . . . of fixing upon a wintering ground so situated as to oblige me to drag a boat and baggage over some two hundred miles of ice to reach the stream that is to carry me to the scene of discovery, and, when there, to embark in a vessel that I knew my whole force to be incapable of carrying . . . I very much question if I could effect so much."

This gratuitous slur on the reputations of the three naval officers who occupied the pinnacle of the pantheon of Arctic explorers was enough to doom King's plan. Besides, Back – who had now been promoted to captain and earned the Society's gold medal – had plans of his own. At his urging, the Navy did exactly what the waspish doctor advised against. It mounted another large and expensive expedition. George Back set off in the 340-ton *Terror* with orders to winter at Repulse Bay and then to drag boats across the isthmus at the base of the Melville Peninsula to explore the far shore.

The result was an unmitigated disaster. Back, who failed to reach his first objective, was trapped in the ice for ten months, most of them fraught with terrible dangers and hairbreadth escapes. The ice captured him and played with him, and once hurled his battered vessel forty feet up the side of a cliff. In the spring, when the pack broke up, the *Terror* was attacked – there is no other word for it – by a great submerged berg that set her on her beam-ends and almost destroyed her before the sea again grew calm.

The splintered ship, leaking, waterlogged, and almost impossible to steer, had no chance of getting back to England. Back headed for the Irish coast and, with only hours to spare, managed to ground his sinking craft on an Irish beach. This was his last expedition. Knighted by the new queen, he passes from the Arctic picture. His critic, Richard King, fared no better. Vindicated by history, he was shunned by the Arctic Establishment.

Meanwhile, the Hudson's Bay Company was bestirring itself, suddenly mindful of a clause in its original charter charging it with the task of discovering a North West Passage. Since such a Passage had no commercial value, the company had generally ignored that obligation, but now its licence to trade beyond its original territorial boundaries was about to expire. It was time to take action.

It certainly didn't want King. It wanted one of its own – two, in this case. Peter Warren Dease, an old company hand who had been with Franklin on his second expedition would supply the stability. Thomas Simpson, the ambitious young cousin of the governor, would supply the energy. Their first task would be to map the unexplored western section of the Arctic coastline, from Prudhoe Bay, Alaska – Franklin's farthest point – to Point Barrow at the very northern tip of the Alaskan peninsula.

Young Simpson was not happy with the idea of a divided leadership. He wanted all the glory for himself. Raised in poverty, a sickly youth tending to consumption, he had managed to overcome both obstacles. He graduated from King's College, University of Aberdeen, with honours and by 1836 was as tough as any of the Canadian voyageurs. But he also suffered from an intellectual pride that came close to snobbery and from a suspicious nature that bordered on paranoia.

Simpson was one of those men who believe themselves to be surrounded by dark forces conspiring against them. Although he owed his position to his cousin George Simpson, the "Little Emperor" of the Hudson's Bay Company, he was convinced his powerful relative was inhibiting his advancement. He had been brought to Canada seven years before as Simpson's personal secretary. By accompanying the governor on his journeys he had himself become a seasoned northern traveller. But he described the Little Emperor as "a severe and most repulsive master" who, he was convinced, was leaning over backward in his treatment of him to frustrate any charges of nepotism. Young Simpson tended to be hot-headed and intolerant. In 1834, at Red River, he had managed to provoke the Métis population, which he held in contempt, even going to the point of engaging in fisticuffs with one young mixed-blood, touching off a fracas that was calmed only by the diplomacy of the governor himself. He did not like mixed-bloods, a failing that would one day destroy him.

In spite of his youth, Thomas Simpson was convinced that he should be the sole leader of the party exploring the northern coast of Alaska. He blamed the jealousy of senior company officers and the intransigence of his cousin for failing to get what he felt was his due. In fact, George Simpson had a high opinion of his young relative, who, he had noted, "promises [to be] one of the most complete men of business in the country." But the governor was also aware of Thomas's deficiencies. Peter Dease may have been "rather indolent [and] wanting in ambition," but "his judgement is sound, his manners are more pleasing and easy than many of his colleagues," and he was also steady in business and "a man of very correct character and conduct" – in short, just the man to act as a steadying influence on the impetuous and mercurial Thomas.

Thomas Simpson was undeniably industrious. A stubby, burly figure, he was bursting with energy. To prepare himself for the expedition, he spent the late fall of 1836 at Fort Garry, toughening his body and studying astronomy, surveying, and mathematics. He even worked on his literary style (since he would be required to keep a journal) by reading the works of Sir Walter Scott. He left Fort Garry on December 1, 1836, and joined Dease, a chief factor of the company in the Athabasca region, sixty-two days later after a journey of 1,277 miles. He had now reached the zenith of his ambitions, for he was about to realize "some, at least, of the romantic aspirations which first led me to the New World."

A lesser man – or a less ambitious one – would never have reached Point Barrow that summer. By July 31, 1837, the party was only halfway between Franklin's Farthest West and its objective. The men were played out. Dease wanted to turn back. But Simpson persuaded him to stay behind while he and five others made a dash to the point.

They plunged off into the fog, travelling light and fording their way through a tangle of icy rivulets until, to Simpson's "inexpressible joy," they met a group of Eskimos. Without their help they would never have made it. In the natives' skin boats, which would float in half a foot of water, they battled ice and tides until, early on the morning of August 4, Simpson, with "indescribable emotions," saw in the distance the long spit of gravel hummocks that was Point Barrow.

As he wrote to his brother that fall in immodest triumph, "I and I *alone*, have the well-earned honour of uniting the Arctic to the great Western Ocean. . . ." He wanted a promotion and wrote to the governor asking for a chief tradership, pointing out that he had "the *exclusive* honour of unfurling the Company's flag on Point Barrow" and begging his cousin not to "reject my just claims, although I am one of your own relatives."

The absence of any reply confirmed Simpson in his dark suspicions. "Had I been in His Majesty's Service," he wrote to a friend, "I should have expected some brilliant reward, but the poor fur trade has none such to bestow." After his return, he spent the winter at Fort Confidence on Great Bear Lake on what he called "the happiest terms" with the good-natured Dease and his family. But, he added, "it is no vanity to say that everything which requires either planning or execution devolves upon me." Dease, he told his brother, was "a worthy, indolent, illiterate soul and moves just as I give the impulse."

He occupied those long, dark days reading Plutarch, Hume, Gibbon, Shakespeare, Smollett, and "dear Sir Walter." A rumour reached him that William IV was dead and the Empire had a new young queen, but nothing official came from the company's council, which appeared to ignore him. "They do not deserve such servants as we are, as they do not know how to treat us," he wrote to his friend Donald Ross. "Have we been sent to the Arctic regions that our means & lives should be the sport of a tyrrannical [*sic*] Council?"

Their task the following summer was to try to fill in some of the unexplored territory to the east, beyond Point Turnagain, the farthest spot that Franklin had been able to reach in 1820. In this they were not successful. Once again, the energetic Simpson persuaded the easy-going Dease to let him go a little farther on foot beyond the point where the boats gave up. Again he travelled light, with a handful of companions, but this time it didn't work out. His men grew lame, and there were no Eskimos to help out. Simpson saw a vast bulk of land across the sea to the north, which he named Victoria Land after the new queen. He also saw open water farther to the east but had no idea where it led. Again he blamed Dease for not pushing forward with sufficient vigour to complete the job. "All that has been done is the fruit of my own personal exertions," he told his cousin. He liked Dease for his upright character but considered him and his followers a dead weight. "My excellent senior is so much engrossed with family affairs," he wrote, "that he is disposed to risk nothing;

133

and is, therefore, the last man in the world for a discoverer."

What Thomas Simpson wanted, and what he never achieved, was to risk everything – but only as sole commander of an expedition. If he could only go a little farther and explore the rest of that unknown section of coastline; if he could only link it with the explorations that had been made from the east! Then, he was certain, he would win the accolade. He knew he must be patient. If he could accomplish something more the following summer, then, surely, Dease would be recalled and he would be put in sole charge.

When the two set off again in 1839, Simpson found, to his surprise and delight, that Coronation Gulf, which had been a solid sheet of ice the year before, was partially open. So was the grand strait between the continent and Victoria Land, soon to be named for Dease. On they went across Queen Maud Gulf, expecting the coastline to lead them north along King William Land to its northernmost point at Cape Felix, named by James Clark Ross nine years before. But now a narrow strait, soon to be named for Simpson, beckoned to the east. They followed it and, to Simpson's joy and excitement, found that it led to Chantrey Inlet and on to the mouth of Back's Great Fish River. Three days later they arrived at Montreal Island in the estuary and discovered Back's cache of pemmican, chocolate, and gunpowder.

Now Simpson indulged in an orgy of exploration. He pushed eastward another forty miles to the mouth of the Castor and Pollux River, then doubled back to explore the south shores of both King William and Victoria lands. In just three years he had filled in most of the blank spaces on the coastal map. He had closed the western gap, connected Franklin's explorations with Back's, and come within an ace of discovering the whole of the North West Passage, though he did not recognize it. He had actually come in sight of Rae Strait (yet unnamed), which separates King William Island from Boothia Peninsula. Who knows what he might have accomplished if he had made a fourth foray into that unknown realm?

As it was, he had made two errors. He thought Boothia was an island and that a strait of water led directly into Ross's Gulf of Boothia. If that were true, there were only about a hundred miles left unexplored. Actually there was no strait. Boothia *was* a peninsula, and there were seven hundred miles of coastline awaiting exploration to the only gap in Boothia – the still unknown Bellot Strait. More seriously, he also made the mistake of believing that King William

134

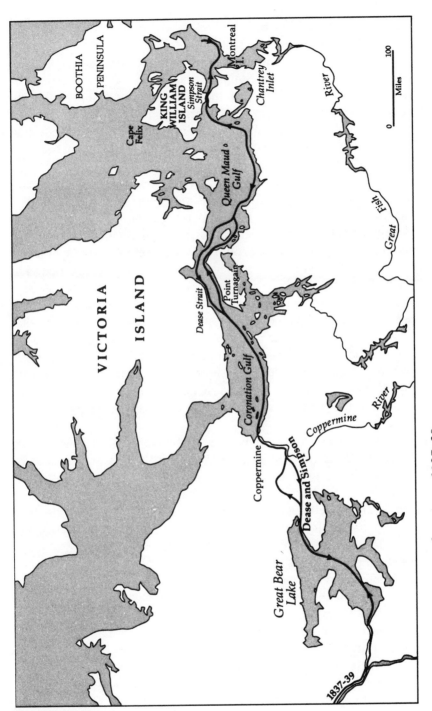

Dease and Simpson's explorations, 1837–39

Land was connected to Boothia and that there was no passage leading south along its eastern coastline.

He didn't want to share another expedition with Dease. "Fame I will have," he told George Simpson that fall of 1839, "but it must be *alone*. My worthy colleague on the late expedition frankly acknowledges his having been a perfect supernumerary." Then he added a sentence that takes on a significance in the light of the tragedy that was to follow. "To the extravagant and profligate habits of the half-breed families," he wrote, "I have an insuperable aversion."

The attainment of all his ambitions was within his grasp. Peter Warren Dease had gracefully bowed out. Simpson proposed a daring plan to the directors of the company in London. He would take a dozen men down the treacherous Great Fish River and from its mouth sail on through the supposed water passage he thought led to the Gulf of Boothia; from there he would push on through Fury and Hecla Strait to York Factory on the western shores of Hudson Bay. He was prepared to spread the task over two seasons and finance it with five hundred pounds of his own money, a small fortune at that time. Had he done so he would almost certainly have discovered his errors, learned that King William Land was an island, and that a safe channel existed off its eastern shore – a piece of information that would have saved the doomed Franklin expedition from being caught in the great ice stream that clogs the alternate route on the western side.

Simpson was convinced he was on the verge of conquering the Passage. "I feel an irresistible presentiment that I am destined to bear the Honourable Company's flag fairly through and out of the Polar Sea," he wrote to his cousin. But the Little Emperor did not reply. The impetuous young explorer fidgeted all through the long winter, waiting for some praise or gratitude. None came. By June of 1840 he could stand it no longer. That summer he decided to go to England to press his case.

What he did not know – what he would never know – was that even as he planned that trip to London, the Governor and Committee of the company were dispatching a congratulatory letter to him approving his plan. He was to be given sole command of the new expedition and everything he needed to accomplish his goal.

The letter never reached him. That summer, while he was riding through the country of the Dakota Sioux with four heavily armed mixed-bloods, tragedy struck. The details are murky. The two survi-

136

vors swore that Simpson had been taken sick, accused two of the party of plotting to kill him, and shot them dead. The witnesses fled, returning later with a larger party to find Simpson himself dead of gunshot wounds, his rifle beside him. The authorities brought in a verdict of suicide.

Since that day, Thomas Simpson's death has been a matter of mystery and controversy. His brother Alexander, to whom he had poured out his soul so often by letter in those sunless days at Fort Confidence, was convinced he had been murdered. The half-breed assailants, Alexander claimed, were planning to steal the secret of the North West Passage, which was among Thomas's papers. That is a little too melodramatic and far-fetched to hold water. What secret? The Passage was not a gold mine to be pounced upon in the dark of the night and looted. In any case, Simpson's theories were wrong.

Undoubtedly there was a quarrel, and that is understandable in the light of Simpson's known dislike of mixed-bloods, whom he termed "worthless and depraved." There is also Simpson's own mercurial character to be considered, especially in the light of the fancied slights, the frustrations, and the long tensions of an Arctic winter. He had talked of the Métis and "the uncontrollable passions of [their] Indian blood." He himself was subject to similar passions. Was it murder or suicide? And what was the cause? No one will ever know. The irony is that his considerable triumphs had not been ignored, as he believed. In England the gold medal of the Geographical Society as well as a pension of one hundred pounds a year awaited him. He did not live to receive either but went to his grave a victim of impossible distances, leisurely communication, and his own paranoia.

4

Van Diemen's Land in 1836 was nothing more than a vast and horrible prison, and John Franklin was its warden. The colony harboured 17,592 convicts and 24,000 "free citizens," some of them former convicts themselves. And each year another 3,000 convicts arrived.

It was a long way from the clean, cold air of the Arctic, and the living conditions for almost half the population were far more appalling than those suffered by the Eskimos, shivering on the barren

Prison warden

137

windswept islands of northern Canada. To Franklin, there were worse horrors than besetment among the floebergs. The man who would not hurt a fly was so distressed by the lot of the convicts that, according to his future son-in-law, Philip Gell, "more than once his health was shaken under the burden." Gell added that "he found another source of hopeless sorrow in the fate of the perishing Aborigines." There were but ninety-seven left in the colony.

Franklin's six years in Van Diemen's Land were the most painful of his life. Early in his tenure he set down his impressions of the colonists, who, he found, displayed "a lack of neighbourly feelings and a deplorable deficiency in public spirit." The Franklins, especially Lady Franklin, didn't fit into the snobbish, ultra-conservative, and generally unsophisticated upper-class clique, whose members thought him a weakling and saw her as a meddler. To the bureaucrats who ran the government, the new governor appeared inept, inexperienced, and dangerously liberal-minded. He worked hard. He took his job seriously. But he was no match for the Byzantine manoeuvrings of a tightly knit colonial service.

The real problem was Lady Franklin. She did not act the role of the conventional governor's wife, whose duties had historically consisted of dressing smartly, making and receiving calls, and entertaining in public. Her contemporaries found her lofty and a trifle preachy. Jane Franklin had little use for the brittle chit-chat of the drawing-room; she wanted to discuss philosophy, art, and science. Her own room at Government House was described by one visitor as "more like a museum or a menagerie than the boudoir of a lady," being cluttered with stuffed birds, aboriginal weapons, geological specimens, and fossils.

She flung herself into her usual round of activity, visiting museums, prisons, and educational institutions, which brought down a hail of criticism. She formed a committee to look into the conditions endured by women convicts, but the governess she chose to run it defected after a newspaper article claimed it wasn't suitable work for unmarried ladies. When she showed an interest in the aborigines, another paper attacked her as "unwomanly." She tried to start a college at New Norfolk but was frustrated when the colony's insidious colonial secretary, Captain John Montagu, insisted that public money could not be squandered on such a project. "A more troublesome interfering woman I never saw," Montagu said privately. She hated snakes and tried to rid the island of them by offering a bounty of a shilling a head out of her own pocket. That sort of gesture prompted one critic to remark that she was "puffed up with the love of fame and the desire of acquiring a name by doing what no one else does." The project petered out; there were just too many snakes. No doubt Lady Franklin felt that the worst ones were to be found in the Colonial Office itself.

In her travels, which were extensive and exhausting – she was away for as long as four months at a time – she went where no woman had gone before: to the top of Mount Wellington in Australia, across the wild country to the west coast of Van Diemen's Land, overland from Melbourne to Sydney by spring cart and horseback, careless of hardship, ever curious, always questioning, and compiling statistics in her voluminous journals on everything from the price of sheep in Yass to the flight patterns of the white macaw.

It was inevitable that she should be considered the power behind the throne in Van Diemen's Land. One hostile newspaper went so far as to call her husband "a man in petticoats." In the smouldering antipathy between Franklin and his colonial secretary, Montagu, she was the tinderbox. Matters came to a head in the winter of 1841-42 when Franklin, on Montagu's advice, dismissed a popular surgeon for dereliction of duty. The doctor's friends got up a petition charging that the dismissal was unjust. Lady Franklin evidently agreed. After much thought and no little vacillation, the governor recanted, to the fury of Montagu, who was convinced that Jane Franklin was behind the move. From then on the two were at odds.

Franklin was no match for the powerful and wily civil servant, who had a section of the press on his side. Montagu engaged in a campaign of obstruction that could have one ending only. After receiving a pompous note in which the colonial secretary came very close to calling him a liar and a weakling, Franklin sacked him. It was actually only a suspension; the Secretary of State for the Colonies in London, Lord Stanley, would have the final word. Unfortunately for John Franklin, the same ship that carried to England his report on Montagu also carried Montagu himself, burning for revenge, armed with a thick sheaf of documents and memos, and crying out, "I'll sweat him. I'll persecute him as long as I live."

Montagu's friends in the Tasmanian press backed him. The Cornwall *Chronicle* published an article entitled "The Imbecile Reign of the Polar Hero," while the *Colonial Times* put the blame squarely on the shoulders of the Arctic Hero's wife: "If ladies will mix in politics they throw from themselves the mantle of protection which as females they are fully entitled to. Can any person doubt that Lady Franklin has cast away that shield – can anyone for a moment believe that she and her clique do not reign paramount here?"

There was worse to come. Lord Stanley backed Montagu, offered him another job, and issued a stinging rebuke to Franklin – a public horsewhipping, in one observer's words. As if that were not humiliation enough, he let Montagu have a copy of his reproof, which Montagu rushed to Tasmania by immediate post before Lord Stanley got around to sending it officially. Thus several copies were passed about in pro-Montagu circles, with many a nudge and snigger, several months before the explorer received the dispatch himself.

Montagu went further. He also shipped out a three-hundred-page packet of the dispatches, letters, and documents he had used to shore up his case. This arrived in April 1843 and was held in a bank in Hobart, the capital, where favoured customers were allowed to peruse it in secret. Franklin was never able to see the packet, in which Montagu called him a "perfect imbecile"; but he knew it was there, as did everybody else in town, and he also knew through hearsay what it contained.

By this time Jane Franklin was in a state of nervous prostration and Franklin himself, trying to appear outwardly cool, was inwardly in turmoil and close to a breakdown. The press was predicting his imminent recall, and on June 18, the *Colonial Times* announced it under the headline "GLORIOUS NEWS!" A newspaper had arrived from England reporting the gazetting of the explorer's replacement, but so glacial was the speed of the official post that Franklin himself had no official word for another two months. In fact, his replacement arrived three days before he was formally told – in a six-month-old dispatch – that his term of duty was ended. After all this humiliation, it was a relief to be out of Government House.

In spite of the controversy, Franklin remained personally popular. Two thousand cheered him off when, on January 12, 1844, he sailed for England. More than ten thousand signed an address of farewell. And when, a decade later, Lady Franklin appealed for funds for the search for her lost husband, the Tasmanian people contributed seventeen hundred pounds.

But in 1844, Franklin had reached the nadir of his career. He felt that his honour had been stained and did his best to seek redress.

When that was not forthcoming, he insisted, against his friends' advice, on publishing a pamphlet outlining his side of the story. Did he really believe the British public was eager to gobble up his dry, factual account of an obscure bureaucratic squabble on an unknown island on the other side of the world? Probably not; but he had to do *something* – or so he thought. In truth, his name scarcely needed clearing. His closest friends and Arctic cronies had always been on his side. No pamphleteering was required to retain their loyalty. As for the general public, who never read the pamphlet, the man who ate his boots was still an Arctic hero.

For Sir John Franklin, that was not good enough. Something more was needed, some daring public adventure that would remove the stain of Montagu's perfidy. He would soon reach his sixtieth year; his career was almost at an end. But he could not – *would* not – rest until he regained what he considered his honour through some great new feat of exploration – or, more likely, some great *old* feat.

Once again, the North West Passage beckoned.

5

"They cannot help it, these Arctic fellows," Lord Brougham, the former Lord Chancellor, remarked when he heard that John Franklin was off again to seek the North West Passage. "It is in the blood." Yet it is improbable that Franklin would have pushed so hard to lead another expedition – or that his friends would have pushed so hard – if his reputation had not been at stake. Van Diemen's Land was the key. "If you don't let him go the man will die of disappointment" was the way his friend Parry put it to the Navy. It was as if Franklin was being chosen for reasons that had nothing to do with his abilities, out of sympathy for his despondency.

The logical choice to lead a new expedition, if there was one, was not Franklin but that most seasoned of all explorers, James Clark Ross. Nonetheless Ross, who had just married, bowed out on the grounds that he had promised his wife's parents not to go to sea again. It seems a thin excuse. Parry and Franklin, his two heroes, had thought nothing of deserting their brides in favour of Arctic exploration; that was Navy tradition.

It is more likely that Ross also felt sorry for Franklin, possibly nudged by the indomitable Jane, who wrote to him: ". . . if you . . . do not go, I should wish Sir John to have it . . . and not to be put aside for his age. . . . I think he will be deeply sensitive if his own department should neglect him. . . . I dread exceedingly the effect on his mind. . . ."

Others rallied to the cause. John Richardson told Franklin that he would be happy to sign a certificate stating that his constitution was perfectly sound and that his strength was sufficient for any journey through the frozen seas. There were objections, of course. Both Back and Sabine felt Franklin was too old, pointing out that he had suffered greatly from cold on previous expeditions. Lord Haddington, the new First Lord, also worried about the explorer's age and constitution. "You're fifty-nine," he pointed out.

"Not quite," said Franklin stoutly. He was still two months short of a birthday.

Haddington remained doubtful, realizing that he'd be blamed if Franklin succumbed during the voyage; but the eager explorer brought him round. Although he agreed he was too plump for another overland expedition, he pointed out that life on shipboard would not tax him. Lord Haddington sympathized. He was, the explorer told his wife, exceedingly kind, almost to the point of tenderness. In short, the most ambitious Arctic expedition yet mounted by the British was to be led by a man who got the job because everybody felt sorry for him.

All this took place in February 1845. By that time events were moving at high speed – the expedition was expected to leave in three months – and England was again caught up in North West Passage fever.

The pot had begun to simmer in the fall of 1843 with the return of James Clark Ross and Lieutenant Francis Rawdon Moira Crozier after four years in Antarctic waters. This had been a highly successful expedition. Ross, who was knighted for his work, had got farther south than any man. He had actually seen the edge of the Antarctic coast, until then unknown, and had added to the knowledge of terrestrial magnetism. As Admiral Beechey pointed out, Ross's two ships, *Erebus* and *Terror*, had already been fitted for the ice and could easily be equipped with engines and the new screw propellers the Navy had finally adopted.

This was all John Barrow needed. By December 1844, he was ready with a detailed proposal for a new attempt to discover the

Passage. He was convinced that this time it would be successful. Barrow sounded the proper note: English pride demanded it. If some other power seized the opportunity, then England, "after having opened the East and West doors, would be laughed at by all the world for having hesitated to cross the threshold."

He saw few problems. "It is remarkable," he wrote, "that neither sickness nor death occurred in most of the voyages made into the Arctic regions." What he didn't say, for he didn't realize it, was that in the second year of almost every voyage, and sometimes in the first (John Ross's was an exception), the seeds of scurvy had been sown, and only a swift return to civilization had prevented mass tragedy. Nor, of course, did he point out that every previous naval attempt to seek the Passage had met with failure because of the unpredictable ice conditions.

Barrow was sure he knew where the Passage could be found. Dease and Simpson had explored the narrow channel that ran along the North American coastline between the Beaufort Sea and King William Land. Parry had navigated a parallel channel, three hundred and fifty miles to the north, that led from Baffin Bay to Viscount Melville Sound. In between lay an unknown labyrinth of land and water. Barrow, with his usual optimism, believed that a connection could be made between the two channels and the Passage conquered in a single two-month season. At the age of eighty-two, he was ready to retire; the successful voyage would be his crowning achievement. Franklin was more cautious. He thought it might be necessary to spend two winters in the Arctic and use the three summer seasons to get through the Passage.

His orders were to follow Parry's route through Lancaster Sound and Barrow Strait, ignoring Prince Regent Inlet – apparently a dead end – but stopping short of the great ice barrier that had frustrated Parry in 1819. When he reached Cape Walker, at the entrance to Melville Sound, he was to turn south or southwest and into unknown waters to try to find the channel that Dease and Simpson had explored. Having done that, he could proceed west, unimpeded, along a fairly familiar coastline all the way to the Bering Sea.

Nobody, of course, could be sure of what lay in the heart of the Canadian Arctic. Here was a great blank space on the map – a quadrilateral seventy thousand square miles in size through which Franklin was ordered to proceed. Nobody knew what it contained. It might be a vast expanse of open ocean. It might be a large land mass,

143

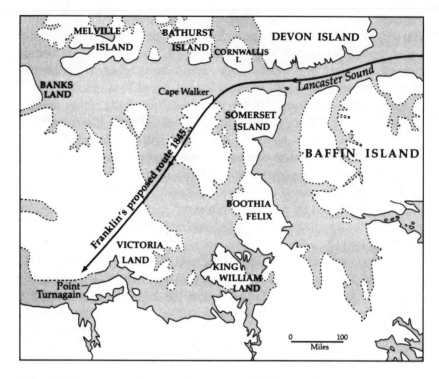

Franklin's proposed route from Cape Walker, 1845

or perhaps two or three; no one knew, for only the peripheries had been explored. Franklin's instructions also contained an after-thought. If he couldn't get through to the south, then he was given permission to try an alternative route north through the unexplored Wellington Channel, which some (Barrow was one) supposed led to the "Open Polar Sea." This unfortunate clause would be responsible for years of fruitless search in the wrong direction.

Franklin was given three months to organize his expedition. It would be the largest yet – 134 men on two barque-rigged sailing ships with twenty-horsepower auxiliary engines and screw propellers. Nobody except old John Ross asked why so many men were needed to trace the Passage. Ross felt that a smaller steam vessel would be more efficient and less expensive. The new engines, one of which came from a railway locomotive, were a problem because their fuel took up a great deal of room that might otherwise have been used for

144

provisions, while their weight weakened the stern frame and after-posts of the ships.

At 340 and 370 tons respectively, the *Erebus* and the refitted *Terror* were even larger than Parry's ships. Their draft of water – nineteen feet – was greater than that of any previous Arctic vessel; but, in spite of the known Arctic shallows, the Navy ignored earlier setbacks. Ross's *Victory*, with a draft of only nine feet, hadn't been able to get over the bar of her winter harbour; Parry's *Fury* had run aground and been abandoned; Back had almost lost the *Terror* after a terrible buffeting in the ice.

John Ross seems to have been the only naval explorer concerned about the possibility of failure. He had several conversations with Franklin, urging him to leave depots of provisions at various points in case he should be wrecked or trapped in the ice and also, if possible, to leave a boat or two. His own party had been saved by Parry's abandoned boats and provisions. But Franklin replied that he had no boats to spare. Later he described Ross's suggestion regarding food depots as "an absurdity."

"Has anyone volunteered to follow you?" Ross asked.

"No. None," said Franklin.

Incredibly, no one had given a second's thought to the possibility that the expedition might encounter trouble. Optimism reigned. Success, it was felt, was all but certain. As Barrow had written in his original proposal: "There can be no objection with regard to any apprehension of the loss of ships or men." No plans were made for a relief expedition; indeed, if one had been thought necessary, the whole project would have collapsed because of the extra cost. Franklin, desperate to get away, kept silent, fearing cancellation.

"Then," Ross told him, "I shall volunteer to look for you, if you are not heard of in February, 1847, but pray put a notice in the cairn where you winter, if you do proceed, which of the routes you take." This advice, too, was ignored. By February of 1847, Franklin would still have another year of provisions stowed aboard his ships. His menus, however, depended heavily on salt meat. The crew would receive twice as much of it as they would of tinned meat. British sailors loved it, preferring it over other forms of diet. Even the small birds – dovekies – that they shot for sport would be preserved in salt, which made them useless as antiscorbutics.

None of these men was a big-game hunter. Perhaps they expected the natives to supply them with fresh meat – an enormous task for such a complement. More probably Franklin intended to live solely on his own stock of provisions, keeping down scurvy with the classic Navy ration of an ounce of lemon juice a day – an inadequate dosage.

He stocked his ships with twelve hundred books, including John Ross's account of his four-year entrapment with its shrewd comment on the need for fresh meat to combat scurvy. But who listened to the discredited Ross? Parry had more clout, and Parry still harboured the naïve belief that scurvy could be held at bay by morale-building entertainment and lots of exercise – which actually accelerates the onslaught of the disease.

Although recent research suggests that lead poisoning from badly soldered tins may have been a factor in the Franklin tragedy, the main cause of death was clearly scurvy. Franklin himself would succumb earlier than most of the others, perhaps as a result of the infirmities of age. But the remaining crew, almost to a man, dropped in their tracks, their gums blackened, their teeth rattling loosely in their heads, their flesh spongy and sunken from internal bleeding – weakened, debilitated, and only half comprehending the truth that the disease, growing within them for months, had at last brought them down.

John Ross was also concerned about the inexperience of Franklin's officers, none of whom except Crozier and the two Greenland ice masters had any polar background. Franklin chose Crozier to command the *Terror* because he had been James Ross's second-in-command in the Antarctic and had also been on three of Parry's expeditions. Some of the most pleasant weeks in Van Diemen's Land had been spent with Crozier and Ross when the two stayed with the Franklins before and again after their explorations. The forty-eight-year-old Crozier, a relatively untutored Irishman, had fallen in love with John Franklin's niece, Sophia Cracroft; but Sophia, who was to become Lady Franklin's lifelong (and unmarried) companion, preferred Ross, who was already spoken for. Now, with Ross married, Crozier resumed his suit in England without success and was understandably gloomy when the expedition departed. If one Navy wife, Lady Belcher, is to be believed, Crozier told a fellow officer that he didn't expect to come back. "Look at the state our commander's ship is in, everything in confusion," he is said to have told a friend; "he is very decided in his own views but has not good judgement."

The most strident criticism of all came not from a naval man but

146

from a civilian, the wiry and waspish surgeon-naturalist Richard King, who didn't believe in sea expeditions. He was still convinced, after his journey with George Back, that the best way to find the Passage was by taking an overland route from the mouth of the Great Fish River and north along the west coast of Boothia. Moreover, his experience with the natives and fur traders had convinced him of the superiority of small parties of no more than six men, all hunters, led by seasoned Arctic travellers. Franklin had a copy of King's book with him, giving King's reasons for believing that Boothia was actually a peninsula and King William Land an island. But few took much account of King. If his theories had been accepted, Franklin's ships might have been spared their tragic ordeal in the ice and the Passage discovered and even navigated in mid-century. At the very least, the search for the missing expedition would have been shortened.

But the Admiralty, which controlled Arctic exploration, leaned towards expensive sea voyages, and so did the Geographical Society, whose board was dominated by senior naval officers. Worse, King was impetuous, self-confident to the point of arrogance, and never reticent about pushing his views in the bluntest possible manner – views that differed radically from the Navy's. He was convinced, again rightly, that the unexplored Arctic quadrilateral contained large land masses separated by narrow, ice-blocked channels. But the Establishment of aging Arctic hands, led by Barrow, allowed themselves to believe that most of it was open water. King wanted to send a second overland party to explore Victoria Land and Wollaston Land before any sea expedition was launched. Had that course been followed, it would have been discovered that both areas were part of the great mass now known as Victoria Island. In short, there was no wide open ocean between Cape Walker and Banks Land, through which Franklin was ordered to sail. His vessels were not designed for the kind of coastal manoeuvring they were to encounter.

But King had no friends in the hierarchy. His shrill attacks had made him a powerful enemy. As he himself later wrote, "Sir John Barrow hated me at once and for ever for thus having pointed out the manifest incompleteness of his polar scheme. He vowed he would smash the impudent fellow who presumed to differ with him on a subject he flattered himself was exclusively his own."

Yet one can't help sympathizing with Barrow, who was publicly attacked in two issues of the *Athenaeum* magazine in January and

February of 1845, before Franklin set off. King not only published his letters to the second secretary – in itself a breach of ethics as far as the naval establishment was concerned – but he also expressed himself in the most insulting fashion. "Had you advocated in favour of polar land journeys with a tithe of the zeal that you have the Polar Sea Expeditions, the North West Passage would have long since ceased to be a problem and instead of a baronetcy you would have received a peerage for the country would have saved at least £200,000 . . . if you are really in earnest upon this subject, you have but one cause to pursue, search for the truth and value it when you find it. . . ." Noting that seven of ten polar expeditions had failed since Barrow entered the field, King predicted the next one would be "a lasting blot in the annals of our voyages of discovery."

He even wrote to Franklin's old nemesis Lord Stanley (and published that letter, too), predicting that Franklin would "have to 'take the ice,' as the pushing through an ice blocked sea is termed." Stanley made no reply.

Nobody listened to King, who in addition to hitting the naval establishment below the belt had also managed to antagonize the fur-trading establishment. He had already angered the Hudson's Bay Company, whose ideas of Arctic travel paralleled his own, by denouncing the fur traders as destroyers of the native population. King sympathized with the Indians and Eskimos, saw the value of learning from them, and in fact had helped found the British Ethnological Society. But he could expect no backing for his ideas from the one powerful interest that might have been expected to sympathize with him. In his second published letter to Barrow, the irascible doctor announced that any leader of a land expedition who co-operated with the fur-trade monopoly was "wholly unfit to command."

King's strictures were brushed aside in the rising chorus of enthusiasm sweeping across Great Britain. As Sir Roderick Murchison, president of the Geographical Society, exulted shortly after the *Erebus* and the *Terror* left their Thames berths in May, "I have the fullest confidence that everything will be done for the promotion of science, and for the honour of the British name and Navy, that human efforts can accomplish. The name of Franklin alone is, indeed, a national guarantee. . . ."

Lieutenant James Fitzjames, soon to be gazetted a captain and Franklin's second-in-command on the *Erebus*, was especially enthusiastic. "We are very happy. Never was more so in my life. . . . You

148

have no idea how happy we all feel – how determined we all are to be frozen and how anxious to be among the ice. I never left England with less regret. . . ." Fitzjames, who found Franklin "really a most delightful person," was all for mounting an expedition to the Pole on his return. Parry had told him it was perfectly possible.

In the days before the expedition sailed, Franklin appeared haggard, wan, and nervous. He was suffering from influenza and one night before the departure was so tired that he fell asleep on a sofa. His wife sat beside him, embroidering the traditional flag for him to take to the Arctic, but he looked so chilly she covered his feet with the Union Jack. He felt its touch, woke, and started up in alarm. "Why," he said, "there's a flag thrown over me. Don't you know they lay the Union Jack over a corpse!"

By the time the expedition was ready to leave, Lady Franklin was, according to Crozier, "in a sad state." She had spent those final days in her husband's cabin aboard the *Erebus*. Now, with her stepdaughter, Eleanor, she travelled down the Thames as the two ships were towed to a small village near Gravesend. A week later, on May 19, 1845, the ships sailed. Eleanor noticed that a dove had settled on one of the masts and remained there for some time – a good omen. They watched for two hours. "Dear Papa left in excellent spirits," Eleanor reported to her Aunt Sophie, "– he puts his trust in God His only Refuge & Strength, and believing on Him he surely will be established and, I trust, preserved. . . ."

Franklin watched them standing on the pier as the *Erebus* moved off – two dwindling figures on the shore. He pulled out his pocket handkerchief and waved it repeatedly, hoping they could still see it.

Aboard ship, the mood was jovial. When the expedition left the Orkneys and the tugboats departed, there was a lively demonstration. Charles Hamilton Osmer, purser on the *Erebus*, described it to his wife: "Never, no never shall I forget the emotions called forth by the deafening cheering . . . the suffocating sob of delight mingled with the fearful anticipation of the dreary void . . . could not but impress on every mind the importance and magnitude of the voyage we have entered upon. There is something so thrilling in the true, hearty British cheer. . . ."

Crozier, in the *Terror*, was not so effusive. In a last letter to his closest friend, James Clark Ross, written from Disco Island in Greenland, he poured out his heart: "In truth I am sadly lonely and when I look back to the last voyage I can see the cause and therefore no prospect of having a more joyous feeling." He was still pining for Sophia Cracroft, whom he had last seen aboard Franklin's ship as they were towed down the Thames. His gloom was increased by the lateness of the season. Crozier, who had been with Parry, remembered ruefully how the ice had blocked their progress. He feared the ships would "blunder into the ice and make a second 1824 out of it," a reference to Parry's third abortive voyage when the *Fury* was lost.

These were the last letters that could be sent that summer of 1845. The next mail to friends and loved ones, they hoped, would be posted from Russia, after the Passage had been navigated. The company now numbered 129, five men having been invalided home from Greenland.

And so they set off across Baffin Bay, two stubby ships, gleaming in their fresh black and yellow paint, to be glimpsed by some Greenland whalers and then never seen by Europeans again, each loaded down with mountains of provisions and fuel and all the accoutrements of nineteenth-century naval travel: fine china and cut glass, heavy Victorian silver, testaments and prayer books, copies of *Punch*, dress uniforms with brass buttons and button polishers to keep them shiny, mahogany desks, slates, arithmetic books, lead lining for sturdy boats and heavy oak for cumbersome sledges, most of them to be found years later – bits and pieces of European civilization, tarnished and rotting on the cold shores of an unmapped Arctic island.

6

The Arctic In the tangled chronicle of Arctic exploration, the Franklin saga *puzzle* stands as the centrepiece. The flurry of polar inquiry touched off by John Barrow and the Royal Navy in 1818 provided the curtain raisers for the drama that followed, a drama that exhausted the British and stimulated the Americans. Before the mystery of the expedition's whereabouts was solved, the emphasis had been on the search for the Passage. In the years that followed, the eyes of the world were turned to the North Pole.

John Franklin was last seen by a whaling ship on June 25, 1845, his two vessels tethered to an iceberg. Neither he nor any of his 128 officers and crew were ever seen again by white men. No one knows how he died or what it was that killed him. His body was never found. Men and ships combed the Arctic for twelve years before the fate of his expedition was finally unravelled. For all of that time Englishmen waited in suspense, devouring each chapter of the Gothic mystery as it unfolded in the popular prints.

Between 1848 and 1859 more than fifty expeditions were mounted to search for the aging explorer. Untold funds were squandered. Ships foundered, were lost or abandoned. Men died of mishap and scurvy. When the great search finally came to an end (if it ever did, for Franklin relics are still turning up in the Arctic), the white curtain of uncertainty had been drawn aside, the great archipelago of islands and channels had been mapped and charted, and the secret of the North West Passage – or, as it turned out, *passages* – had been unlocked. Yet a new century would dawn before anybody was able to take a ship through the Arctic labyrinth from ocean to ocean.

Franklin in death succeeded where he had failed in life. The mystery of his disappearance elevated him from minor Arctic hero to near sainthood. He became, unwittingly, the symbol of nineteenth-century Arctic exploration. Even today when one thinks of the North West Passage, one thinks of Franklin. Had he failed in his quest and retreated, as others did, his name would be half forgotten. Today every schoolchild knows it, but how many have heard of Ross, Parry, Back, or Richardson?

Of all the Arctic odysseys, the tale of the Franklin search is the most complicated, the most frustrating, and the most ambiguous. It needn't have taken twelve years. It didn't have to cost a sultan's ransom. The Arctic Establishment in Great Britain was singularly myopic; for a decade it dispatched ships to every corner of the Arctic but the right one. It moved with maddening slowness, refusing to heed the Cassandras who urged that speed was essential if Franklin was to be saved. Its early optimism, which knew no bounds, turned to pessimism in the final years of the search. It was not the British Navy that discovered the final truth about the lost ships. It was a private expedition, launched and paid for by the dead explorer's indomitable widow.

If the Establishment had listened to its critics in the first years of the search, Franklin's fate would have been known by 1847 or 1848 and some of his men rescued alive. But the Arctic puzzle would have remained, most of the seventy-thousand-square-mile quadrilateral still a blank space on the map to be explored and claimed by any other nation with the will or the funds to conduct a probe. By the time the British era of exploration gave way to the American, the British had established title to most of the North American Arctic. In short, all this bumbling about in the ice streams seeking the lost Franklin party made it possible for Canada to claim the Arctic as its own. Ironically, Canada's insistence on its sovereignty rests on a strong historical base made possible by the singular intransigence of what is known as the Parry school of Arctic explorers.

John Ross, the perennial outsider, was the first to challenge the complacency of these greying experts early in 1847. Actually Ross, then in his seventieth year, was older than any of them except Barrow. His nephew was forty-seven, Parry was fifty-seven, Sabine was fifty-nine, Richardson was turning sixty. Mindful of his promise to Franklin, Ross began to worry about the expedition's safety. In late January and again in February and March he pointed out to the Admiralty and to anyone else who would listen that the coming year would be Franklin's third winter in the Arctic and that supplies would be running low.

There was no word from Bering Strait. Nobody on the northern coast of Russian Alaska had any evidence of his passing. He must, then, be beset somewhere in that maze of frozen channels he had been sent to explore. If Franklin was to be relieved, he must be found that summer and he, Ross, was prepared to lead a rescue party. In fact, he had declined to take retirement, with the prospect of a fatter pension, in order to stay on the Navy's active list for just that purpose.

The Admiralty, however, preferred to listen to the advice of what came to be known as the Arctic Council – Parry, Barrow, James Ross, Sabine, Richardson – and turned him down. As James Ross remarked to Parry, there was "not the smallest reason of apprehension or anxiety for the safety and success of the expedition. . . ."

John Ross was mortified, especially perhaps because it was his own example that had caused the complacency. He had spent four winters in the Arctic and lost three men only. If the much-maligned John Ross could do it, why not the popular Franklin? Everybody ignored the fact that Ross's much smaller crew had survived because they had the help of Eskimo hunters and the use of the boats and supplies left behind by Parry. Here was a further irony: Parry's disaster had contributed to Ross's survival; but Ross's survival had laid the groundwork for Franklin's tragedy.

152

Jane Franklin, meanwhile, was having her own qualms. She had spent the summer of 1846 in another whirl of travel, extending from the West Indies to the United States. As usual she had climbed mountains, visited and inspected factories, hospitals, and schools, and engaged in some lively conversations with public officials. In a sharp-tongued encounter with the mayor of Boston she castigated "the ferocity and folly of 4th July orations" and went on to remark that if the English "did not think quite so highly as deserved of the Americans, it was owing to their own bragging."

She returned that fall, dismayed by the lack of news from the Bering Strait, from which everyone had confidently assumed her husband would be dispatching letters home. She began to prepare herself for the worst and wrote to her friend James Clark Ross that it was perhaps better to remain in "happy ignorance" of any disaster than to know the truth. But she wouldn't listen to his uncle. Her husband's Arctic friends persuaded her that Sir John Ross was a pessimist – after all, he had been the only one to question the probability of success. "Sir John Ross's plans are all absurd," she was told.

Sir John persisted. Twice he collared the Marquis of Nottingham, president of the Royal Society, who told him stiffly, "You will go and get frozen in like Franklin, and we shall have to send after you!" Ross was appalled by this callous response; but when the Royal Society asked the Arctic Council for advice, it got the same answer.

Once again, the difficult Dr. King entered the fray with a plan of his own, which was as usual prescient. He urged the government to plant food caches in the area of Barrow Strait while he would lead a party down the Great Fish River to its mouth and then north between King William Land and Victoria Land, for he was convinced (again rightly) that the missing ships were caught in an ice-clogged channel somewhere north of the estuary. The Great Fish River, he insisted, was the best point from which to succour them, but both Parry and the younger Ross, when asked their opinion, pooh-poohed the idea. Ross said he couldn't imagine any position in which the ships could be placed that would lead them to make for the Great Fish. Lady Franklin, like everybody else, was cool to Dr. King. "I do not desire that he shd be the person employed," she said, in her forthright way. But she did hope that somebody would ask the Hudson's Bay Company to explore the area in the hopes of finding some clue to her husband's party.

Both Dr. King and John Ross kept pressing, each for his own

expedition – King by land, Ross by sea – without any success. In November 1847, with still no news from Franklin and a third winter looming, a meeting was held at Lady Franklin's home, without John Ross's knowledge. A friend told him the details: "All my proposals were sneered at and my opinions scouted, while I was represented to be too old and infirm to undertake such a service."

To Ross's annoyance, Lady Franklin chose his nephew to lead any expedition to which the Admiralty might agree; and it was clear, at last, that the Admiralty would agree if James Clark Ross was in charge. John Ross had suggested four small ships; his nephew opted for two large ones. Sir John, incensed by "the frigid treatment of the Admiralty," convinced himself, if nobody else, that his nephew's real purpose was not to seek the lost ships at all. "He knows better than to trust himself in such ships to follow the track of Franklin," he told the new First Lord of the Admiralty, Auckland. "His object is the north-west Passage."

The elder Ross, indeed, was convinced that his old enemy Barrow was using the Franklin search as a cover for the realization of an old obsession: the North West Passage. It was a characteristically mean-spirited assessment, but there may well have been truth in it. After all, the two objectives were not incompatible: whoever found Franklin would almost certainly discover the route of the Passage also.

Thus did the year fade out. In spite of the Admiralty's tardy preparations for relief, optimism remained high. At the end of November, the *Athenaeum* interviewed a number of Arctic officers who purported to believe that Franklin had succeeded so well that he had already *passed* Bering Strait, "in which case they look for tidings, either by Russia or by the Isthmus of Panama by February next." But by then Franklin had been dead for nearly half a year, and his hungry crews, weakened by scurvy, were planning to abandon their ice-bound vessels and attempt to drag their sledges overland, south toward the very region that the sharp-tongued Dr. King had vainly suggested searching.

Chapter Four

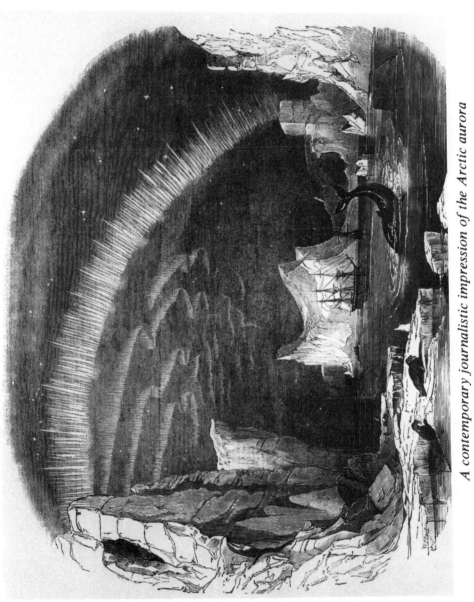

A contemporary journalistic impression of the Arctic aurora

The Great Search began early in 1848, a year of turmoil in Europe. *The lost ships* France and Italy were in revolt. Louis Philippe, the Citizen King, was forced to abdicate and flee Paris for the safety of London, while Giuseppe Mazzini, the Italian patriot, left London to return in triumph to the newly liberated city of Milan.

In England, too, where men of property had long enjoyed a form of democracy, change was in the wind, albeit peaceful change. The reform movement known as Chartism, organized by the new working class, had reached its zenith, paving the way for its successors, the Christian Socialists and the Fabian Society.

By now the country and its government were beginning to show concern over the fate of the Franklin expedition. In March, in reply to a question in the House of Commons, the First Lord of the Admiralty announced that a stupendous sum – twenty thousand pounds – would be paid to anybody who "might render efficient assistance in saving the lives of Sir John Franklin and his squadron." A later amendment offered half that sum to anyone who could merely discover what had happened to the lost ships.

The government had already moved to comb the entire Arctic for the lost expedition – at least, it thought it had. It determined now to mount a complicated and ambitious three-pronged attack that would see four ships and an overland party as well explore the maze of islands and channels from three directions – east, west, and south. James Clark Ross's two ships would enter the archipelago from the east by way of Lancaster Sound and Barrow Strait, move west to Melville Island and Banks Land, and then proceed south. Two more ships would sail round Cape Horn hoping to rendezvous that July in the Bering Strait to scour the Western Arctic. The land expedition under Sir John Richardson, Franklin's friend and trail mate, would travel to the Canadian North West and follow the Mackenzie River to the Arctic coastline, to search eastward along the rim of Wollaston Land and Victoria Land (King's suggestion without King as leader). The government, with an optimism bordering on naïveté, confidently expected that both of the naval expeditions would link up with Richardson. It was widely assumed that the fate of the expedition would be known by the end of the year.

Lady Franklin herself was tempted to join Richardson. In one of the many letters she wrote to her missing husband – to be carried by one or other of the search parties – she told him, "It would have been a less trial to me to come after you . . . but I thought it my duty & my interest to remain, for might I not have missed you, & wd it have been right to leave Eleanor – yet if I had thought you to be ill, nothing should have stopped me. . . ." Like all those other cries from the heart, this letter was returned to her unopened.

Once again, everybody, including the most seasoned Arctic hands, reckoned without the vagaries of the Arctic weather, the sluggishness of sea travel in an era of sail, and the presence of the daunting ice streams pouring down from the permanent polar pack.

Richardson had had no lack of enthusiastic volunteers when he organized his party in the late winter of 1847-48. These included two clergymen, a Welsh justice of the peace, several country gentlemen, and some scientific foreigners. He rejected them all in favour of the best-qualified man available, John Rae, who had just been promoted Chief Trader in the Hudson's Bay Company and given grudging permission to go on the search by Governor George Simpson.

A seasoned Arctic hand with an unsurpassed record for northern travel, Rae was surprised and flattered to be selected. He knew Richardson by reputation and liked what he'd heard, especially "his disregard of self in volunteering to remain behind with the feeble and sick [during the first Franklin expedition] the nobleness of which few men unless placed under similar circumstances can realize."

Rae knew whereof he spoke, for he himself had tramped over much of the same country, though with better success than Franklin. Indeed, his long snowshoe journeys were prodigious. In one two-month trek in the winter of 1844-45, he had travelled on foot a circuitous twelve hundred miles from the Red River Colony to Sault Ste Marie and thrived on it. His one companion, who was admittedly rather fat, lost twenty-six pounds; Rae *gained* two.

To the gold-braided bluecoats of Arctic exploration, John Rae was an outsider and, in spite of his many accomplishments, would always be one. He did not fit the pattern set by Parry, Ross, and Franklin. Like most Hudson's Bay men, he didn't consider it a stigma to go native. Indeed, he brought his adaptation of Indian and Eskimo methods to a fine art. He copied the native way of life, adopted native dress, native shelter, native food, and native travelling methods. He wore deerskin clothing, built snow houses, drove dogteams, slept under caribou blankets, and used Arctic peat and reindeer moss for

158

fuel north of the timber line. And no party in which Rae acted as leader ever suffered from scurvy.

He preferred to travel light, by small boat, snowshoes, or light dogsled. He was not only a crack shot with a rifle but had also made himself an expert on animal habits. Unlike Franklin and Richardson, who would not stoop to hunt – and didn't know how anyway – Rae insisted on personally providing his small band of companions with fresh meat.

He was a lean, tireless man with a handsome angular face, deep-set intelligent eyes, and black side-whiskers, "muscular and active, full of animal spirits," in the words of the author R.M. Ballantyne, who met him in 1846. Like many of his colleagues, he cared as little for the Navy as the Navy cared for him. The pious young officers were shocked, as their journals show, because the fur traders had little interest in either Christianizing or civilizing the Eskimos. The fur traders, for their part, considered the naval men to be bumbling amateurs. That, generally, was Rae's assessment.

Rae had been assigned by the Hudson's Bay Company to follow in Thomas Simpson's trail and complete the mapping of the northern coastline of North America. His explorations in 1846 and 1847 were prodigious. He had studied the art of surveying as he studied everything else. Unencumbered by heavy sledge-loads of provisions, tents, or equipment, by large numbers of followers, or by the umbilical cord of an ice-locked vessel, he was able to cover the coastline at record speeds.

When Richardson engaged him, Rae had just completed that successful exploration for the company. He had arrived at Repulse Bay in August 1846, after a nine-hundred-mile journey from York Factory by boat. Finding it impossible to complete his survey of Melville Peninsula that year, he resolved "with a boldness and confidence in his resources that has never been surpassed" (to quote Richardson) to spend the winter on its inhospitable shores. No other land party had ever wintered on the Arctic coast. All others had carried enough provisions with them to see them through a summer journey. Rae was different. He settled down at Repulse Bay, which Parry had rediscovered a quarter of a century before. Unlike Parry, snug aboard the *Hecla* and warmed by his Sylvester stove, Rae and his men lived on shore. Parry had plenty of provisions. So did John Ross who followed him. Rae had nothing.

The shores of the bay were devoid of wood or even shrubs for fuel.

Rae taught his men to gather the withered stems of the *Andromeda tetragona*, a small herb that grew in the rocks, and to pile it up in cocks, like hay, for fuel. Others used rocks, earth, and snow to build a house that would shelter the party of sixteen. Rae killed enough deer, with the help of his Eskimo interpreter, to keep the party well fed and free of scurvy until spring.

The following summer he completed his survey of the unexplored section of the Gulf of Boothia, giving it the name of Committee Bay. To chart the 625 miles of new coastline, he travelled 1,200 miles on foot, living entirely off the land, before recrossing the isthmus to Repulse Bay and embarking for York Factory. On September 6, 1847, fifteen months after

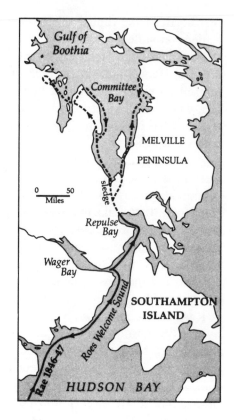

John Rae crosses Melville Peninsula, 1846-47

setting out, he was back with all of his men healthy, a remarkable achievement regarded as a near miracle. Only then did he learn that John Franklin was missing and that anxiety was being felt for him in England.

He had proved that there was no western exit from the Gulf of Boothia. He was also convinced that John Ross was right and Thomas Simpson wrong: Boothia Felix was not an island but a peninsula: there was no Passage there. But the Navy, which ignored so much, ignored that, too. It puzzled Rae. Why had John Barrow taken up Simpson's view without question "in opposition to that of their own officers although the latter had the testimony of the Eskimos in their favour?" The answer, of course, was that Barrow trusted

160

neither John Ross nor the heathen natives. The open-minded Rae was not privy to Admiralty politics.

Rae reached London in the winter of 1847-48, where Richardson made him his second-in-command. They embarked from Liverpool for North America at the end of March. The plan was to take four boats down to the mouth of the Mackenzie and try to probe the unknown lands across the channel. No one knew exactly what lay between the mainland and Parry's discoveries to the north. The only clues were two bald and forbidding shorelines on the far side of the narrow strait north of the Coppermine country that Thomas Simpson had briefly explored. One was called Wollaston Land, the other Victoria Land. Both were actually part of the same vast island, 135,000 square miles in size, but nobody realized that. And it was into this mysterious and unmapped realm that Franklin's instructions were supposed to take him.

Richardson hoped to reach the Mackenzie delta by the end of August to launch his coastal search. That was perilously late: Thomas Simpson had turned back from Point Barrow as early as August 4, Franklin from Point Turnagain on August 23. But Richardson left England at a time when the official public attitude to the Franklin expedition was one of sublime complacency. *The Times* remarked that same week that "although these precautions are most proper . . . we do not ourselves feel any unnecessary anxiety as to the fate of the ships. . . . We place great hope in the *materiel* as well as the *personnel* of the expedition, for ships better adapted for the service, better equipped in all respects, or better officered and manned, never left the shores of England. . . ."

The exploring party consisted of five British seamen and fifteen British soldiers – sappers and miners who joined Richardson in Montreal. Rae was later to write that during the summer's operations he had "work enough and suffered more petty annoyance (the most disagreeable of all) than I was ever subjected to before." He would not, he said, engage on another such expedition for double the pay.

He admired Richardson, but the doctor had now reached the age of sixty and lost some of his spryness. He tired easily and had to turn his load over to a younger seaman. He tended to be irritable, and George Simpson's admonition to Rae to "make every allowance for any little testiness he may shew & ascribe it to his great anxiety to accomplish the object of his mission creditably" suggests that Rae had reported minor quarrels to the governor. Rae, who was used to travelling in all kinds of weather, was undoubtedly frustrated at times by the slower pace of the older man, who had difficulty divesting himself, in Simpson's phrase, of "recent habits of personal ease & comfort." Nonetheless, the two got on remarkably well. Richardson, an even-tempered and pious man (he prayed for his daughters three times a day), had nothing but praise for Rae in his letters home. In 1856, in a letter to Richardson, Rae made an apologetic reference to the journey, remarking that "very, very often I showed a very ill temper and a hastiness that was not right."

Rae had a heavier cross to bear in the men that Richardson had engaged. These military people, with no previous Arctic experience, caused George Simpson "some degree of alarm and apprehension." It was injudicious, he thought, not to have taken more experienced men, and he was right. None was used to carrying the heavy loads the Hudson's Bay men were hardened to. At York Factory, the chief factor, John Bell, complained to Richardson about this, whereupon the doctor drew Rae's attention to several of the Britishers trotting past, each with 180 pounds on his back. Rae was puzzled, for Bell wasn't the kind of man to make such a complaint without evidence. Then he realized that they had seen the men cover only about twenty yards of trail before vanishing around a curve. He followed another track to discover that as soon as they were out of sight, they threw off half their load, which they had toted for only about fifty yards.

Rae went to some pains to relate this anecdote because the army and navy boasted that their people, untrained in portage work, could do it as efficiently as Hudson's Bay men. "I have never found it so," he wrote. He considered that the men Richardson brought from England were "in every respect inferior for this kind of duty to the men I had with me in Repulse Bay, both as to strength, activity, willingness to do and knowledge of their work." They grumbled continually, in direct contrast to the voyageurs of mixed blood, who would travel for months without uttering a word "that could offend a refined or sensitive woman."

"Had they been alone and starving they could not have killed anything, however abundant the game might have been," he wrote in his unpublished autobiography. Rae, who believed that the leader of any expedition should be prepared to hunt for it, suited his own actions to this credo. Richardson's journal is replete with references to Rae's ability with a rifle ("A skilful hunter like Mr. Rae could supply the whole party with venison without any loss of time. . . .").

Rae had learned to shoot with an old flintlock as a boy in the Orkneys, where his sole amusements were boating, shooting, fishing, and writing. Cut off from the world – it took three weeks for the packet boat to get to Leith and back – he had led a solitary childhood. Educated by a tutor until he was sixteen (he taught himself natural history), he preferred lonely walks with his Newfoundland dog as his only companion. Later, he studied medicine in Edinburgh and graduated in 1833 before joining the Hudson's Bay Company.

In northern Canada the young doctor continued to be a loner, believing in the efficiency of small parties over large ones, a preference that apparently caused some raised eyebrows among his contemporaries. "Na, na, doctor," the Governor of the Red River colony had said to him sarcastically in 1844. "Take as few men as possible, for none of ye will ever be seen back again."

Rae met "severe and hostile criticism" from his fellow fur traders when he introduced oars instead of the traditional paddles in canoes. His critics were stifled when he took part in a race – oars against paddles – and won.

Now, in 1848, Rae, the loner, was travelling with a set of men whose training and outlook were totally different, "the most awkward, lazy, careless set I had anything to do with." The expedition covered no new ground and found no trace of Franklin. It was, in Rae's report to Simpson, "very expensive, very troublesome and far from satisfactory." Simpson himself, who had supplied Rae's services grudgingly, was under no illusions. He was convinced that Franklin and his company would never be heard of again.

Richardson and Rae wintered at Fort Confidence. The following spring Richardson returned to London, leaving Rae to attempt an exploration of the two mysterious land masses to the north – Victoria and Wollaston lands. But Rae's passage was blocked by the ice, and he returned empty-handed to winter at Fort Simpson on the Mackenzie.

The other expeditions fared no better. Through a series of delays and mix-ups, the two ships, *Plover* and *Herald*, that were supposed to act as supply depots for the western search didn't make their rendezvous off Alaska until July 1849, a year later than expected. The exploring party, under Lieutenant W.J.S. Pullen, made a remarkable seven-hundred-mile journey in small boats along the northern Alaska coast as far as the Mackenzie delta and found nothing. Pullen wintered with Rae at Fort Simpson, tried unsuccessfully to reach Banks Land the following spring, and finally returned to London via Canada in October 1851, having established beyond doubt that Franklin hadn't got west of the Mackenzie.

The third of the 1848 expeditions was that of James Clark Ross. Abandoning his promise never again to go north, Ross headed off in May, two months after John Richardson, in command of two big vessels, the *Enterprise* (450 tons) and the *Investigator* (400 tons), carrying three years' provisions for his crews and another year's provisions for the Franklin party.

Ross was at the end of his career; this expedition would be his last. Still handsome at forty-eight, short, stout, and hawk-faced, with the most piercing black eyes his contemporaries had ever seen, he was no longer the energetic officer who had enlivened the crew of his uncle's *Victory*. Clements Markham, the naval historian, who knew him, later wrote that he was "somewhat shaken by his Antarctic work, and lacked those qualities in a commander which are needed to keep his followers in high spirits and good humour." But he could not leave his friend and former shipmate Crozier to an unknown fate; besides, it was generally held that he knew more about Crozier's and Franklin's intentions than any living man.

His two senior officers, Leopold M'Clintock and Robert McClure, were destined to become Arctic heroes. As active and energetic as Ross had once been, they were first and foremost among the new generation of nineteenth-century explorers. McClure had gained his experience with George Back on the disastrous voyage of the *Terror* in 1836. M'Clintock, who had been in the Navy for seventeen years, seized the chance to go north; it would prove the turning point of his career.

It was Ross's task to follow Franklin's route through Barrow Strait and then south or southwest, but he found his way through the strait blocked by impassable ice north of Somerset Island. The ships were frozen in for eleven months at Port Leopold on the northeast tip of the island. From this anchor point Ross carried out an unhurried exploration of the eastern shoreline of Peel Sound, using manpower to haul the heavy sledge-loads of tents, equipment, and provisions across the ice. Here M'Clintock began to develop the theories of Arctic sledging that he would refine in later excursions in search of Franklin. In thirty-nine days the party travelled five hundred miles, but at heavy cost to the men. Four broke down from hunger, exposure, and exhaustion; one had to be carried back to the ships; all were on the sick list for an average of ten days. Even Ross was forced to take to his bed. Only M'Clintock stayed healthy, but then M'Clintock, as an officer, walked ahead searching out the route; he didn't have to suffer the drudgery of hauling in the traces. As he himself put it: "One gradually becomes more of an *animal*, under this system of constant exposure and unremitting labour." But it didn't occur to him, apparently, to use dogs as Ross himself had done on his earlier exploration of Boothia and King William Land.

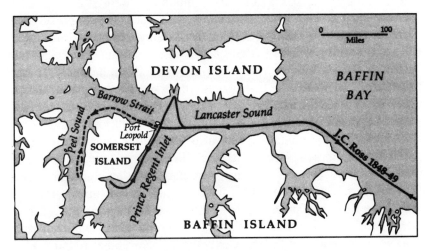

James Clark Ross's fruitless search for Franklin, 1848-49

If the party had had dogs and light sledges they might have succeeded in their quest, for at one point Ross was only 180 miles from the lost ships. But he couldn't believe that Franklin had gone south through Peel Sound; all he could see for fifty miles was an unbroken sheet of ice. Astonishingly, in spite of all his Arctic experience, Ross didn't appear to realize that a channel could be frozen one year, open the next.

In fact, the *Erebus* and the *Terror* had sailed down this very stretch of water three years before, in the summer of 1846. But Ross was convinced that Franklin, faced with the ice, had followed the Admiralty's second plan, which Ross himself had advised as an alternative to Franklin's original instructions. According to this theory, Franklin had gone north by way of Wellington Channel to the so-called Open Polar Sea. It was this conviction by the most seasoned of all Arctic explorers that confused the Admiralty, changed the direction of the search, and helped prolong it for another decade.

2

Arctic fever For eighteen months, while the three search expeditions were out of touch with the world, Lady Franklin waited in hope, persisting in the belief that her husband and his companions were still alive. Her letters to him had been dispatched with each search party. Her friends, who also wrote letters to the missing explorer, were urged "to say nothing whatever that can distress his mind – who can tell whether they will be in a state of mind or body to bear it?" To her husband, she wrote: "I try to prepare myself for every trial which may be in store for me, but dearest, if you ever open this, it will be I trust because I have been spared the greatest of all. . . ."

Outwardly, she continued her various activities – distributing anti-Chartist pamphlets, discussing everything from popery to mesmerism (this last with F.D. Maurice of the Christian Socialist movement). Inwardly she was in as much turmoil as the unruly states of Europe. Ross had promised her that he would be back in October, 1848, with Franklin and his ships, but October came and went with no word from any of the three expeditions. November found her, in her niece's words, "much out of health & in deep despondency." That despondency could only deepen, for the silence – the unbearable silence – continued. There was a creeping sense of finality that culminated in the death that year of Sir John Barrow. An era in Arctic exploration had ended.

In January 1849, public prayers were being said in sixty churches for the safety of the expedition; fifty thousand friends, relatives, and well-wishers joined in the supplication. Jane Franklin was now committed heart and soul to the task of finding her missing husband, an obsession that did not sit well with her twenty-four-year-old stepdaughter, Eleanor. She was planning to marry the Reverend Philip Gell that year and resented her stepmother's insistence on committing every penny of her private resources – and more – to the search. Franklin had left without making any arrangements for Eleanor, since he fully expected to return. In the end, Jane Franklin settled

166

five hundred pounds a year on the couple, who were married in June. It made it harder for her to finance an expedition of her own, but the Gells didn't think it was enough.

She was by now employing every means to speed the search. She went to Hull and other ports with William Scoresby to interview whalers heading out for Davis Strait and Baffin Bay, urging them to carry extra provisions in case they encountered the lost ships. In the apartments she had taken in Spring Garden, London, with her faithful niece, she received a steady stream of callers – anyone and everyone who had anything to tell her about the expedition or any suggestions to make about a search. She even visited a clairvoyant, who gave her the usual optimistic but inconclusive reading.

She launched into a campaign of eloquent letter writing that would have no end until the dénouement, ten years later. In April she wrote to Zachary Taylor, the new American president, dangling before him the carrot of the twenty-thousand-pound prize but also appealing to his humanitarian and patriotic instincts. "I am not without hope that you will deem it not unworthy of a great and kindred nation, to take up the cause of humanity . . . and thus generously make it your own," she wrote. There was also the puzzle of the North West Passage; American seamen might wrest from Britain the glory of solving that problem, and if they did, "I should rejoice that it was to America we owe our restored happiness." Faced with what one British parliamentarian, Sir Robert Inglis, called "the most admirable letter ever addressed *by* man or woman *to* man or woman," the president pledged he would do what he could.

The Admiralty, to whom she addressed another letter, was less forthcoming. She wanted to borrow two ships and fit them out at her own expense. "It will not be, I trust, and ought not be a reproach to me, that I use every means and argument I can think of, that is upright and true, to move you to the consideration of my request," she declared. But the Admiralty was unmoved. It had sent a supply ship, the *North Star*, out after James Ross; that ought to be enough. She wanted to go with it, but was refused and had to be content with sending another letter to her husband, who by this time had been dead for almost two years.

She was, in the words of a friend, in a "restless, excited state of feeling." She could not be still. She had to do *something*. With her niece she decided to travel that summer of 1849 to the Shetlands and Orkneys to interview more whalers who might have some news of the missing men. She went to the house where her husband had stayed before setting off. She took cake and cherry brandy with the seventy-five-year-old mother of John Rae ("the most beautiful old lady we have ever beheld," wrote Sophia). In August, she was heartened to learn that the Tsar of Russia, touched by one of her appeals, was offering to send a search expedition to the Siberian coast. In September her hopes soared when a bottle was retrieved from the sea with news of Franklin; it was, alas, old news dropped off in 1845 when the ships were scarcely under way. Then a whaling seaman turned up to claim he'd talked to some Eskimos who had seen Franklin and his men that March. For a brief time she felt the thrill of released emotions. It was premature; the story was quickly discredited.

In November, within a week of each other, both Richardson and Ross returned to England to report failure. Ross, with six of his company of sixty-four dead and another twelve sick, had managed at last to escape from the ice, which pushed him out of Lancaster Sound and into Baffin Bay. Ross's own health was broken. *The Times* correspondent reported from Portsmouth that "the opinion in naval circles in this port is decidedly against any further waste of money and sacrifice of life and comfort in such an adventure, which, it is believed, will yield nothing but repeated disappointments." That provoked a chorus of protest in the paper's letters column, but Leopold M'Clintock had been equally sour in his journal that fall when for twenty-four days they had been "utterly helpless, fearful lest every breeze should drift us upon the land and dash our ships to pieces." It struck M'Clintock then that "our situation and final release should be a salutary rebuke to those who advocate attempting a North West Passage. . . . Surely this ought to be the last polar expedition."

But, of course, it wasn't. In a little more than a year, M'Clintock, the acknowledged sledging expert, would be at it again, trudging across the snow-covered granites of the wrong island, heading, like everybody else, in the wrong direction.

With the return of Richardson and Ross, a kind of Arctic fever swept England. Books about polar journeys, dioramas showing Arctic vistas, newspaper and magazine articles about northern adventure, complete with engravings, all combined to whet public interest and pique curiosity. Where was Franklin? Why hadn't he been found? How could two ships and 129 men vanish from sight, without a word, without a hint for almost five years?

And where was John Rae? Had he found anything? Nobody knew. The problem of communication bedevilled the searchers and frustrated the search. Letters took six months to reach their destination, whether they moved by ship round Cape Horn or travelled through the northern interior by York boat, canoe, toboggan, or dogsled. Rae was operating blindly, with no idea of what was going on in the rest of the Arctic. Richardson sent him a dispatch when he reached Lake Winnipeg in August 1849. Rae didn't get it until the following spring. At that, Richardson's news was already several months old. He told Rae that James Clark Ross would probably make contact with him on Great Bear Lake. Even as he wrote those words, Ross's ship was being driven back into Baffin Bay. Yet in April of 1850, Rae still believed Ross's sledge teams were combing the western Arctic.

In November 1849, the Admiralty bestirred itself to seek some further help from the Hudson's Bay Company. The correspondence moved as ponderously as the great Arctic ice streams, as ships crossed and re-crossed the Atlantic with messages between the company's London and Montreal headquarters. Sir George Simpson was totally in the dark. He had no idea that Rae's attempt to explore Victoria Land had failed. He told Rae to go west from the Mackenzie delta to Point Barrow, not knowing that Lieutenant Pullen of the supply ship *Plover* in Bering Strait had already covered that ground. Rae didn't get Simpson's message until June 25, 1850. He sensibly ignored it and postponed further search until 1851, when he would again travel east to Wollaston and Victoria lands.

Long before that, in the fall of 1849, with James Ross reporting impassable ice conditions in Barrow Strait, the Admiralty had turned its attention to the west. If ships couldn't pierce the unknown Arctic core from the east, perhaps they could enter the Arctic Ocean from Bering Strait and proceed eastward.

Fortunately, Ross's two ships, *Enterprise* and *Investigator*, were now available and were quickly refitted. Captain Richard Collinson in the *Enterprise* would lead the expedition. Lieutenant Robert McClure, Ross's former second-in-command, would command the *Investigator*. The two ships left Plymouth on January 20. This was only the first of *six* expeditions that would be sent off in 1850 to search for John Franklin.

The assumption at the time was that Franklin had somehow gone farther west. There was no basis for this belief, and it didn't sit well with Lady Franklin. Besides, it was all very well to send two ships off to the Bering Sea, but it would be winter before they reached Alaska; that could delay their search for another year. She resolved to fit out her own expedition – the ships would have to be small to be within her means – but she was confident she could raise funds in America. She was determined that her husband be found, alive or dead. "There is no trial," she declared, "that I am not prepared to go through if it become necessary." But she kept up the pressure on the Admiralty with the aid of such powerful friends as Richard Cobden, the free trader, who pushed her cause in parliament.

Meanwhile, she considered the vast areas in the eastern Arctic that had not been examined. What about Boothia Felix and the coastline from the mouth of the Coppermine to the Great Fish River? She had even sent off a letter to John Rae, suggesting, with considerable prescience, that he might consider examining the mouth of the Great Fish.

The ever-troublesome Dr. Richard King entered the fray, urging that he be allowed to lead a government expedition to the mouth of the same river. The Navy wanted nothing to do with Dr. King, or the Great Fish River either, for that matter. But it had to do *something*, for the pressure was mounting. Thousands of dollars were pouring in, much of it from the United States, to underwrite the private expedition Lady Franklin was proposing. Thousands more were going to Sir John Ross for another private expedition. The Navy could not afford to be left behind.

As a result, the Admiralty announced its own official expedition to the eastern Arctic – the most ambitious yet. It would dispatch no fewer than *four* big ships under Captain Horatio Austin to scour the Arctic for Franklin. James Ross's views had become the official theory. Franklin had either gone west, following Parry's old route to Melville Island or beyond, or he had gone north through the unexplored Wellington Channel. The Navy would concentrate on these areas.

It is a measure of the Navy's belated alarm that it was prepared to underwrite *another* expedition to be commanded, not by one of its own, but by a whaling captain, William Penny. Penny was no ordinary seadog; at forty-one, he was the acknowledged leader of the Davis Strait whalers. He had been in the Arctic since the age of eleven and had commanded a whaling ship for sixteen years. His opinions and advice were sought and accepted without question. His surgeon, Peter Sutherland, who accompanied him on the Franklin search, wrote that no words were more familiar to him than "What does Penny think of it?" Sutherland described him as "vigorous and full of energy and zeal in the Franklin cause." Indeed, no more dedicated explorer set out in search of Franklin. Bluff, outspoken, unsophisticated, often difficult and quick to take offence, Penny attacked any project with a directness that commanded respect if not always affection. As one naval officer put it, "his enthusiasm blinds him."

Penny, the whaler, was certainly not the Admiralty's choice; he was Jane Franklin's. Her behind-the-scenes manoeuvring eventually confirmed him in his post, but it wasn't easy. The Lords Commissioner of the Admiralty worried that discipline could not be maintained in the Arctic without Navy regulations. It was to them, in Sutherland's phrase, "an experiment fraught with danger." And what if it all worked? The results "would prove inimical to the strict rules of government service."

But the Navy reckoned without the artifice of Lady Franklin, who, supported by public opinion, made the selection of Penny virtually a *fait accompli* before the Admiralty realized what was happening. The expedition began as a private search to be financed by Lady Franklin herself. In the fall of 1849 she offered Penny the command, which he accepted, refusing any fee for his services. Then she urged him to apply to the Admiralty for permission to take a ship to the Arctic. At the same time, she convinced the Admiralty to underwrite the cost of the expedition that she had conceived for Penny. The Admiralty had to give in. Already the country was clamouring for more government effort in the Franklin search. "Let 1850 be the year to redeem our tottering honour, and let not the United States snatch from us the glory of rescuing the lost expedition," read one letter to *The Times*. "A cry for help from 130 gallant men comes to us on the northern gale now blowing," read another. "Oh! let them not cry in vain." The idea of Franklin's lady squandering her last penny on a private quest did not sit well with the English public, to whom she had become a heroine. The Navy capitulated.

But a whaling captain commanding two government vessels? Penny himself knew that would not be an easy mouthful to swallow. January passed and so did February while the Admiralty dawdled.

Penny himself was certain the Navy wouldn't accept him. He wanted out, but Lady Franklin asked him to wait. In March, she got her way at last. Penny sailed in April in command of two relatively small ships, the *Lady Franklin* (200 tons) and the *Sophia* (100 tons), but not before he had what his friend Sherard Osborn called "a disagreeable conversation" with Austin, Osborn's "hot headed" superior. The acrimony was papered over once the ships forgathered in the Arctic but was to break out later in a manner that again frustrated and delayed the Franklin search. Osborn's note to his friend Penny saying "I feel certain . . . that the year 1851 will see Franklin's expedition saved and on their road home" was symptomatic of the misplaced optimism of the time.

Lady Franklin was equally hopeful – at least on the surface. But the letter that Penny carried to her lost husband suggested the depth of her fears. "I desire nothing," she wrote, "but to cherish the remainder of your days, however injured & broken your health may be . . . I live in you my dearest – I pray for you at all hours. . . ."

She and her niece Sophia were on the dock at Aberdeen on April 13 when the namesake ships set off for the frozen world. One week later Sir John Ross's own expedition headed for Lancaster Sound. The two little ships under Ross's command, *Felix* and *Mary*, had been bought with funds raised from the Hudson's Bay Company and by public subscription. Thus did the oldest of all naval commanders keep the promise he had made to his friend in 1845.

All the previous year, the seventy-two-year-old Ross had been urging an expedition using small, manoeuvrable vessels, manned by experienced whalers, and carrying Eskimo dogs and sleds to probe the hinterland. But when he offered to command it himself, the Arctic Council advised against it. Once again the Navy opted for large vessels and sledges that would be hauled by men and not animals. Only William Penny used dogs on the Franklin search.

The official expedition, consisting of two sailing vessels and two steam cruisers, all under the command of Captain Austin, got under way in May 1850, provisioned for three years. This was the most ambitious and costly expedition ever sent north. The government was now committed to spending sixty thousand pounds on the eastern section of the search, and great things were expected from both Austin and Penny. Leopold M'Clintock, one of Austin's officers, his gloom of the previous autumn long since swept away in the fervour of the new adventure, wrote that "success in our present expedition is

172

the summit of all my waking dreams." He carried a letter from Francis Crozier's uncle that he determined to keep with him at all times in case he "should be the fortunate one to find our missing countrymen." But Crozier's bones had long since found their final resting place.

At this point there were ten British ships heading for the Arctic, searching for John Franklin. That same month two American naval vessels left New York, bringing the number of search vessels to an even dozen. This, too, was Lady Franklin's doing. For some time she had been corresponding with Henry Grinnell, a New York philanthropist and shipping merchant, who had been moved by her letter to the U.S. president. Since that time, the Franklin search had obsessed Grinnell. "It occupies all my thoughts," he wrote her, "too much so perhaps for a man with a wife & six children." Grinnell had underwritten the cost of the ships that an American naval officer, Edwin De Haven, would take to the Arctic. "Should they be so fortunate as to rescue your husband & his companions," he wrote, "I shall feel as though my work was done on this earth." For Henry Grinnell this was the beginning of his long fascination with the Arctic and the first of several expeditions he would cheerfully sponsor.

Yet in spite of these ambitious projects Lady Franklin remained uneasy. She was no longer a tyro where the Arctic was concerned. She had seen everybody, read everything, digested it all. Before the decade was out she would know more about the North than any armchair expert. Suppose her husband's ships had been beset in the ice in, say, James Ross Strait off King William Land, and, having abandoned their vessels, the men had made for the Great Fish River? That was very close to what had actually happened, but she could convince nobody of the soundness of this possibility.

Expedition after expedition was setting off for the Arctic, but all were concentrating on the far North. The two American ships were heading for Smith Sound at the very top of Baffin Bay. The Navy had ordered Penny to explore Jones Sound, north of Lancaster Sound. But nobody, apparently, had considered looking at the coast to the south. There was no help for it: she herself would have to see to that. As she wrote to her friend Sir James Ross, "if everything else fails, the search will be deemed incomplete till this coast has been explored & it will be impossible for me to resign myself to its abandonment."

On June 5, her own modest expedition was ready to set off for that purpose in the ninety-ton *Prince Albert*, a former pilot boat lent by a friend and outfitted with funds from other friends and Lady Franklin's own dwindling fortune. The commander would be Lieutenant Charles Codrington Forsyth, a man with no Arctic experience whom she had known in Van Diemen's Land. The first officer was a civilian, W. Parker Snow, one of the several eccentric figures who enliven the tale of the Franklin search. Snow had volunteered for the mission because of a dream, which he thought showed him exactly where Franklin was – somewhere in the region of the North Magnetic Pole. As a dreamer, the quixotic Snow was closer to the mark than the practical naval men, who refused to take him seriously. His career, to put it mildly, had been checkered and a little unsavoury. After four years at sea as a youth he had landed up in the Australian bush leading a wild, perhaps criminal existence. The rest of his forty-one years had been equally turbulent. Arrested while on naval service, released when he saved a man attacked by a shark, robbed of all his possessions, temporarily blind, weak, and destitute, he had in his later years become a reasonably successful writer. One of the several schemes he proposed for the succour of the Franklin crews was that convicts should be employed in the search on the grounds that they were mentally resourceful. Snow would have known, for he had mingled with such people, but the notion was not one that would recommend Snow to the Admiralty as a level-headed explorer.

Nonetheless Lady Franklin chose him, perhaps because of his enthusiasm for Prince Regent Inlet and Boothia Felix. She herself drafted the orders. Forsyth was to proceed down the inlet to the narrowest point of Somerset Island and then, with Snow, sledge south, past the farthest point reached by James Ross.

Had they been able to do so, they might have unlocked the riddle of the lost party, for of all the thirteen ships searching the Arctic from the Bering Sea to Lancaster Sound, only this one was headed in the right direction. Sir John Franklin was a stubborn man, with the reputation of following his orders to the letter. Those orders had been explicit. He was to head west to Cape Walker and then he was to head south. Only if ice blocked the way was he to attempt an alternative route through the Wellington Channel. Lady Franklin was one of the few who believed it was more than possible that Franklin had found a way to stick to his original instructions. But then, she knew her husband better than any of her naval friends did.

Of the nine ships that left England in 1850 to probe the Arctic *The American* channels from the east, only one got back that year. All through the *presence* dark Arctic winter the other eight were imprisoned in the ice of Barrow Strait and Wellington Channel. From this central point sledging parties searching for Franklin fanned out in every direction except the right one.

This was the most remarkable winter yet in the annals of Arctic exploration. Scores of men, dragging heavy sledges, were crawling and sliding over insular land masses that had scarcely been noted on earlier maps. The Arctic had never seen such activity and would not see it again in that century. At last the mysterious contours of that drab and silent realm were being unlocked.

As usual, the official naval accounts tended toward the prosaic. The journals kept by the new generation of British polar explorers were no more revealing than those of the earlier ones. Wide-eyed expressions of enthusiasm, gloomy premonitions of doom were subdued by the British tendency to understatement. Hardships were minimized, human foibles went unreported, personal philosophies were omitted. The British were rarely introspective; Arctic exploration was old stuff to them. The stiff upper lip prevailed.

But now a very different presence had insinuated itself into the frozen world. For the first time, two American naval vessels had entered the mysterious archipelago. For a time they were within hailing distance of the British ships clustered in the frozen channel just west of Lancaster Sound.

These were the two little vessels (*Advance*, 144 tons, and *Rescue*, 81 tons) that Henry Grinnell, the New York shipping magnate, had bought for thirty thousand dollars at Lady Franklin's behest and then turned over to the U.S. government so that they might be placed under naval discipline. The expedition is notable, not so much for its commander, Lieutenant Edwin De Haven (who discovered Grinnell Land), but for its chief medical officer, a sickly, twenty-nine-year-old surgeon named Elisha Kent Kane. This was the expedition that launched Kane into an orgy of Arctic exploration, that made him the best-known explorer of his day, and provided, through his own colourful accounts, the stimulus for future expeditions. Both Roald Amundsen, the conqueror of the North West Passage, and Robert

Peary, the polar explorer, were reared on Kane's version of his Arctic exploits. His Arctic journal and his subsequent published account of that first memorable winter in the ice, with its extravagant descriptions, romantic overtones, and lively portrayal of the harsh polar conditions, contrasted sharply with the phlegmatic accounts of the British.

On the face of it, this restless, driven man had no business being in the Arctic. He had a damaged heart and, in fact, would die before the decade was out. When he was a medical student suffering from rheumatic fever, he had gone to his bed each night never knowing whether he would wake the next morning. He was slender and fragile but comely. A housemaid in the residents' dormitory at the Blockley Hospital in Philadelphia described him then as "so pretty, with his sweet young face, and complexion like a girl's and his curly hair. . . . There was never so fine a gentleman came to Blockley with his pretty, gentle manners."

He was both sensitive and rebellious. At school he had courted expulsion. As for the navy, he detested its harsh discipline and its authoritarianism. Heavy weather made him seasick. When the Grinnell Expedition, as it was called, reached the Whalefish Islands off Greenland, he was so ill that De Haven tried to send him home. Kane stubbornly refused. Why? What was this delicate young semi-invalid thinking of to traipse off to a chill, forbidding realm at the top of the world, far from hospitals and creature comforts, far from medical attention and a loving family?

There was another side to Elisha Kent Kane's temperament that belied his apparent fragility. He was an irrepressible adventurer. This was by no means the first time he had gone to the ends of the earth – literally. Much of his young life had been crammed with romance in the far corners of the world – Mexico, Egypt, the Mediterranean, Brazil, the African coast, the interiors of India and China. He had explored the catacombs of Thebes, stood at the entrance to the pass at Thermopylae, walked across the Peloponnesus, and once hung suspended from a bamboo rope attached to a two-hundred-foot crag over a volcanic crater in the Philippines.

For much of that time he was ill. He had contracted "tic fever" in Macao, "coast fever" in Africa, and "congestive typhus" during the Mexican War, in which he was also wounded in the abdomen by a lance during hand-to-hand combat as the head of a guerrilla company. Yet he kept on. Indeed, a fellow medical student had long been convinced that his chronic heart problem led him to court reckless escapades for, as he himself put it, he groaned "with the miserable tediousness of small adventures." Doomed to an early grave, he had nothing to lose. There was, perhaps, more to it than that. His journal entries suggest that Kane was out to prove something, not just to himself but also to his family and especially to his father, who tended to think of him (at least in young Kane's view) as a bit of a scapegrace.

Kane was the eldest of seven children born to parents who were pillars of the Philadelphia upper class, as austere as the Arctic itself. His mother was a society beauty, his father a prominent judge who had been attorney general of Pennsylvania. They did not want him to go to the Arctic. Kane, ever the rebel, went anyway, his resolve no doubt stiffened by parental opposition. He *couldn't* quit. To have left the ship before the voyage proper had begun would have been to endure a humiliation worse than all the ailments and infirmities that the Arctic might visit upon him.

Kane exhibited an almost childlike enthusiasm that July for the strange new world that surrounded him. The icebergs fascinated him as they fascinated every Arctic traveller. He saw them in metaphysical terms. They seemed to him the material for a dream. "An iceberg," he wrote, "is one of God's own buildings, preaching its lessons of humility to the miniature structures of man. . . ."

They crossed Melville Bay, a half moon bitten out of the western coast of Greenland, which Kane saw as a "mysterious region of terrors" – never still, never silent. The vast floes, some a mile across and estimated to weigh more than two million tons, converged irresistibly upon each other at the rate of a mile an hour, crumpling like corrugated cardboard before the enormous pressure – grinding, cracking, crumbling in the dynamic process the seamen called "hummocking." The sound and the fury of the restless pack never ceased. "Tables of white marble were thrust into the air, as if by invisible machinery." A floe would heave up ten feet, then fling itself atop another with a rasping crunch. A second would slide on top and then a third, causing the others to break away, "and then, just as you were expecting to see the whole pile disappear, up comes a fourth, larger than any of the rest, and converts all its predecessors into a chaotic mass of crushed marble."

The refraction of the pale Arctic light played tricks with his eyes, as it had years before when John Ross saw his non-existent range of mountains. Icebergs seemed to float in the air with other icebergs upside down on top of them and even, sometimes, a third layer of icebergs on top of that. Kane's imagination caused him to see strange objects floating in the heavens: "There is a black globe floating in the air about 3⁰ north of the sun. . . . Is it a bird or a balloon? . . . on a sudden it changes shape. . . . It is a grand piano . . . you had hardly named it before it was an anvil . . . *presto* it has made itself duplicate – a pair of colossal dumbbells. A moment! and it is the black globe again."

At one point the entire horizon became distorted. Great bergs were suspended in the sky. His ship, the *Advance*, seemed to float "in the concave of a vast sphere." Its consort, the *Rescue*, lay not far away "in mid-space, duplicated by her secondary image."

He missed "the soothing darkness of which twilight should have been the precursor." There was no relief from "the perpetual light garish and unfluctuating." He felt stimulated, could not sleep, his meal hours confused. For the first time he understood the disciplining value of alternate night and day.

Smith Sound was their objective, but Smith Sound was clogged with ice. They headed for Lancaster Sound instead. On August 19, Captain Penny, the whaler, came alongside in the *Lady Franklin*. He had tried to reconnoitre Jones Sound, but that, too, was blocked.

Two days later, at three in the morning, with the wind at gale force, another sail was reported ahead, a little schooner under a single reefed topsail and towing what appeared to be a yacht, "fluttering over the waves like a crippled bird." This was John Ross's *Felix*, towing the little *Mary*. Soon the *Advance* was alongside. The sailing master appeared with a cloak thrown over his night gear. "You and I are ahead of them all," he cried in a stentorian voice. Ross came on deck shortly after, "apparently very little stricken in years and well able to bear his part in the toils and hazards of life." Kane could not contain his admiration for the scarred Arctic veteran. It was on this very spot, off Admiralty Inlet, that Ross had been rescued seventeen years before and now "here he is again, in a flimsy cockle-shell, after contributing his purse and his influence, embarked himself in the crusade of search for a lost comrade."

Every one of the search ships was now concentrated in the Lancaster Sound area. Crowding on all possible sail, De Haven's *Advance*, with the smaller *Rescue* struggling behind, made for the harbour at Port Leopold at the entrance to Barrow Strait where James Ross had

178

spent the winter of 1848-49, only to find the entrance blocked by ice. Late that evening another topsail schooner worked its way through the pack, and two officers came aboard the *Advance*. These were Captain Forsyth of the tiny *Prince Albert*, Lady Franklin's own vessel, and his eccentric and egotistical second, Parker Snow. Snow and Kane hit it off immediately, sitting up long into the Arctic night, swapping tales of travel and adventure over glasses of champagne. "To me," Snow wrote, "it was a true feast for the mind; and I revelled in it to my heart's content."

But Snow's heart was not really content, for the *Prince Albert* had signally failed in her attempt to explore Prince Regent Inlet. Forsyth had got as far as Fury Beach, and there, faced by what he considered impenetrable ice conditions, had turned about and, to Snow's irritation, decided to return to England. In vain Snow pleaded with him to stay – at least to let him take a boat to Fury Beach and perhaps to explore the coastline by sledge. But Forsyth's mind was made up, and Snow, the amateur, didn't know enough about ice conditions to argue. "The mantle of gloom spread itself abroad, in fog and despondency of spirits, over our little vessel, so joyous but a short time back." Lady Franklin had squandered thousands of pounds for nothing.

Snow played one last card: he suggested that Forsyth proceed to Port Leopold and attempt to use the harbour as a base for further exploration. But, as the Americans had discovered, the harbour was blocked. Forsyth decided to make a brief excursion to the mouth of Wellington Channel to pick up dispatches for England and then make haste for home.

The *Prince Albert* followed the *Advance* across the ice-choked waters of Barrow Strait and then westward in the lee of tall, broken cliffs to a long, projecting tongue of limestone known as Cape Riley. Two cairns could be seen on the shore, and here, for the first time, the Franklin searchers got a tantalizing series of clues to the lost expedition. Two ships of Austin's flotilla, the *Assistance* and *Intrepid*, had reached the spot two days before and left a note reporting they'd found traces of what seemed to be a Royal Navy encampment. Other traces had been found ten miles away on Beechey Island – a peninsula, really – up Wellington Channel.

Kane was eager to inspect these early traces. Here were circular mounds of limestone, marking, probably, the position of tents, along with other clues: a crude fireplace, the foundations of a larger, triangular enclosure, some bird bones, the rusting top of a food canister, a few scraps of canvas, some fragments of what appeared to be a boat. No other white man had been in the area since Parry, and Parry had not camped on this spot. Every sign pointed to the lost party.

De Haven pressed on to Beechey Island. He was not alone. By August 27, through a series of happenstances, six vessels under three different commanders – De Haven, Penny, and Ross – were clustered within a quarter of a mile of each other off Beechey. The Arctic had conspired to thwart their plans: the Americans couldn't get through the ice that blocked Smith Sound, nor could Penny penetrate Jones Sound. So here they all were, the officers gathered for a conference on the shore. Suddenly, Elisha Kane looked up and spotted one of Penny's sailors dashing across the ice and crying out: "Graves, Captain Penny! Graves! Franklin's winter quarters." There was an immediate scramble over the loose shale and rough ice to the crest of the narrow isthmus connecting Beechey to the mainland, and there "amid the sterile uniformity of snow and slate," Kane cast his eyes over a mournful spectacle.

Three mounds, supporting three weathered headboards, marked the last resting place of a trio of Franklin's seamen, who had died in the winter and early spring of 1846 of natural causes (their bodies were exhumed 138 years later). There was no doubt now, as the party encountered more and more relics, that this had been the main shore encampment for the two wintering ships. Rope fragments, sailcloth, tarpaulins, casks, clothing, blankets, and scraps of paper were strewn about, not to mention a small mountain of six hundred empty preserved-meat tins, each filled with pebbles to form some sort of ballast. There was even a pair of officer's gloves, laid out to dry on a rock and never recovered.

This discovery only deepened the mystery. Franklin had departed so hurriedly, apparently, he had failed to leave any kind of memorandum on paper suggesting the condition of the party or the direction it had taken. They might have gone anywhere. Beechey, Gibraltar-like in its contours, stood at the crossroads of the Arctic. Channels stretched off in every direction: Wellington Channel to the north, Barrow Strait to the west, Lancaster Sound to the east, Prince Regent Inlet and Peel Sound to the south. It was all incredibly puzzling. Franklin had certainly left a cairn, but the cairn contained no message. The party dug around it in every direction and found nothing. To Kane, as to the others, it was "an incomprehensible omission."

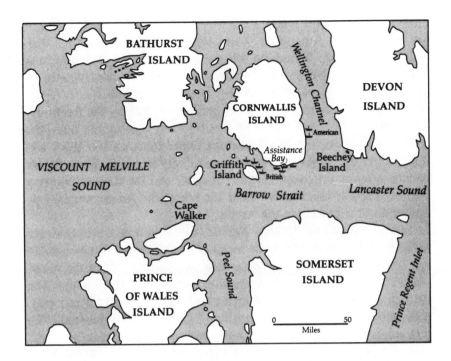

Area of the Franklin search, 1850-51

A few hints began to appear. Sledge tracks pointed north along the east coast of Wellington Channel. Lieutenant Griffin of the *Rescue* traced them at intervals for forty miles. It looked as if Franklin had reconnoitred the upper waters of the channel, preparing to explore it more thoroughly when spring came.

The following day, August 28, Austin arrived with his flagship and steam tender; his other two vessels were a few miles to the west. Forsyth, in Lady Franklin's own little ship, had already left for England before the Beechey Island find, convinced that the route to the south was impassable. And so the great search that was supposed to sweep the whole of the Arctic was concentrated now in one tight little area off Barrow Strait.

Kane made a round of all the ships. He saw John Ross once more; the "manly old seaman," as Kane called him, felt that Franklin had probably gone farther west. Unlike Kane, the other British officers did not much care for Ross. To Penny, he was "an utterly selfish man . . . his manner is proverbial for false statements." Indeed, Ross, badly undersupplied, was a drag on the company that winter and of little use as far as the search itself was concerned. But the British got on well with the Americans. Kane, when he boarded Austin's flag-ship, the *Resolute*, found the officers "a gentlemanly, well-educated set of men." All this neighbourly comradeship caused Austin to name the sheltering cove at Beechey Point, Union Bay.

The flotilla moved out to avoid getting trapped by the freeze-up. With masses of new ice groaning and grating against her sides, the *Advance* cast off, struggling past ice tables fourteen feet thick and hummocks like cones of crushed sugar, forty feet high. Soon the ice stream covered the entire expanse of water and De Haven, following orders, knew it was time to head for home; the Americans had no intention of wintering in the Arctic.

First, however, the smaller *Rescue*, which had become separated from her sister ship, had to be located – and quickly, if they were to get free of the ice. It was now so cold that coffee froze in the mugs. Kane, in spite of all his Arctic reading, was not prepared for this. The British capacity for understatement had made it seem all too easy. "We are literally running for our lives," he wrote in his journal. "We are staggering along under all sail, forcing our way while we can." The English vessels followed in their wake, a compliment, Kane thought, to his commander's seamanship.

The *Rescue* was found far to the west, sheltered by the cliffs of Griffith Island in Barrow Strait. De Haven took her in tow. The two little vessels headed eastward in a race with time and ice, leaving four ships of the British squadron lost in the mist. Kane felt a wave of disappointment. He had hoped to winter in the company of his new English friends; now he realized that if they became beset, they would be at least fifty miles from the nearest ship. That interval, "in these inhospitable deserts, was as complete a separation as an entire continent."

He could hear the sounds of the *Advance* crunching through the new ice like a "rasping noise of close-grained sugar." His own limbs had stiffened and as he tried to warm them in his tiny cabin, De Haven came down to tell him that the worst had happened: the ice had caught them; they were frozen in for the winter – "glued up," in Kane's phrase, in the mouth of Wellington Channel.

The ice pushed them helplessly north up these unexplored waters for more than two months, without a sail fluttering from the frozen spars. They passed the highest latitude attained in the channel until that time and were then capriciously borne back again past their

182

starting point. All around them, in their icy cradle, the uproar of the surging pack rang in their ears. Kane tried to describe it: "a wild yet not unmusical chorus." It was almost as if the ice were alive, he thought, issuing animal-like shrieks or plaintive cries, like those of a nighthawk.

Would the Grinnell Expedition suffer the fate of Franklin? He thought it likely. He kept a portrait of Sir John in his cabin in a gutta-percha frame, and sometimes, in the dark of the Arctic night, he spoke to it, "a good, genuine hearty representative of English flesh and blood." In his imagination he saw himself shaking hands with the missing explorer. How, he wondered; and where? There was no sign of the lost expedition anywhere along the Wellington Channel.

The American vessels were not equipped to ward off the stinging cold, which grew fiercer as the winter advanced. Food congealed. Barrels of fruit had to be chopped apart with an axe. Sauerkraut resembled mica or slate. Butter and lard had to be carved with a cold chisel and mallet. When one seaman tried to bite into an icicle, a piece of it froze to his tongue. Two others lost all the skin on their lips. Facial hair turned to cardboard, and if a man stuck out his tongue it froze to his beard; contact with the metal of a gun penetrated two layers of wool mittens with a sensation of scalding water.

It was dangerous to walk too far from the ship over the rumpled ice. The frost, Kane found, seemed to extend to the brain. An inertia crept over the system; the desire to sit down and rest was almost uncontrollable; drowsiness and death could easily follow.

The British were stubbornly sticking to woollens – broadcloth and felt boots – but the Americans wore furs: boots of dogskin, breeches of sealskin, jumpers of reindeer hide, and caps and masks of wolfskin – all of which helped to hide the ghastly pallor of their features, starved for sun. By Christmas their faces were bleached to a waxy paleness. One man told Kane he was the palest of the party. Since there were no mirrors on board he was unconscious of his own ghostly appearance, "as white as a cut potato," Kane said.

In these pitch-dark conditions, morale began to drop. Men moped and grew testy. It required an effort to wash. At Christmas there was an attempt at play-acting. Never in his life had Kane enjoyed "the tawdry quackery of the stage" so much. The activities that followed seemed exhausting. A foot race knocked out all the officers except Griffin of the *Rescue*; one of Kane's messmates actually fainted. The tell-tale signs of scurvy were clearly apparent. Simply climbing a ladder caused the strongest man to pant for breath. Most of the crew sank into indolence and apathy in the everlasting dark. Kane, who had once carped at the eternal light of Arctic summer, now cursed the Stygian gloom of winter: "I long for the light. Dear, dear sun, no wonder you are worshipped!"

The *Rescue*, badly battered by the ice, had to be temporarily abandoned. Her crew crowded aboard the *Advance*. Kane was now one of thirty-three men all jammed together in a room no bigger than his father's library in Philadelphia. There were no partitions, no privacy.

The symptoms of scurvy increased daily. Kane, as medical officer, had his men kick a football about on the ice until their legs ached and slide down icy slopes until they could slide no more, then tramp across the ice. Like Parry, Kane believed that exercise was an antiscorbutic. In fact, it increased the symptoms of the disease.

The sun returned on January 29 after eighty-six days of total darkness. It was arranged that all hands give three hearty cheers when the orb appeared briefly on the eastern horizon, but Kane did not take part. Instead he found a solitary hummock of ice, a mile from the ship, where he could drink in the rosy light of dawn in solitary tribute. "Never, till the grave-sod or the ice cover me, may I forgo this blessing of blessings again!" he wrote dramatically.

By February 10, the two ships – one crammed with thirty-three men, the other, empty, drifting beside it – had been carried more than three hundred miles. Kane could feel the scurvy in his limbs – it was as if he had taken a bad beating. Nineteen men, including De Haven, now suffered from ulcerated gums and blotched limbs. The worst off were those who preferred salt meat, hardtack, and beef to vegetable foods. Kane got the idea of treating olive oil, lime juice, potatoes, and sauerkraut as medicine rather than food. The men took it in a spirit of martyrdom and began to get well.

By March the *Advance* was still locked in its cradle of ice, partially suspended on two frozen hummocks. Men were sent across to the *Rescue* to dig an eight-foot pit around her hull so she might be repaired. This novel dry-dock worked. That same month the first open leads of water appeared. In April, the *Rescue*'s crew returned to their ship. On June 5, the break-up came so suddenly that the men had to scramble to reload the vessels with the accumulation of eight months – supplies and equipment – for ice as solid as rock was quickly becoming part of the ocean again.

184

Seated on the deck of the *Advance*, Kane saw a spectacle before him, strange but sublime, as a series of frozen waves rippled across the white expanse "as if our ice was a carpet shaken by Titans." This astonishing spectacle – a seemingly solid surface swelling, rising, and falling – produced in him a feeling of nausea. Soon the white world became a mosaic, the "calves" of bergs, of every shape and thickness – honey-combed, cellular, water-sodden – broke away, shifting and rising to form a granular stream.

The *Advance* was still attached to a submerged mattress of ice. De Haven anchored a cable to a berg on the starboard bow and let the swell drive the block against the ship like a great battering ram. At last, after eight months and twenty-four days, they were free. By early July they were back among the whalers of Baffin Bay and within a week picked up letters and mail sent to them by a vessel from New London. Kane spent twenty-four hours devouring the news from home. His scurvy had long since vanished and he had never felt healthier, probably because the Arctic was so free from communicable diseases.

On July 12 they spied another sail and heard across the waters the faint sound of a hand-organ grinding out "The Garb of Old Gael." To their surprise and delight it was a familiar ship – Lady Franklin's own *Prince Albert*, heading back to the Arctic on a second expedition and under the command of a new master, a Canadian, Captain William Kennedy.

Another year had gone by. New expeditions were being planned. But the fate of John Franklin remained as dark and mysterious as the Arctic night. After a futile quest in Baffin Bay, the two American ships returned to New York on September 7 to report defeat.

4

While the Americans were locked in the drifting pack up Wellington *The crusaders* Channel, their British counterparts were preparing an ambitious series of sledge journeys for the spring of 1851. William Penny and Sir John Ross managed to get their small vessels into Assistance Bay, a snug cove on the south coast of Cornwallis Island. Austin's four-vessel squadron was beset in the ice some fifteen miles to the west in a narrow channel (now Resolute Passage) just off Griffith Island.

Austin had left all sledging arrangements to Leopold M'Clintock, who had studied these techniques under James Clark Ross three years before. On that trip, he and Ross had managed, not without considerable suffering, to stay away from their ships for forty days. This time, M'Clintock planned a sledging trip of eighty days. He had learned a good deal from his earlier experience and had spent the intervening months experimenting with sledge design, cooking gear, and provisions. When the expedition set out from England, he was two months short of thirty-one – a lithe, wiry, muscular Irishman with a lean, intelligent face and a small body, who seemed to have been built for sledging.

He came from an impoverished branch of the Anglo-Irish aristocracy. One of twelve children, he had gone to sea at the age of eleven, so small that it was said to find him in his midshipman's berth was like searching for a flea in a blanket. Promotion came slowly because he was not from a naval family. Without a patron he was forced to rely on sheer ability, and in that he was not deficient. Clements Markham later wrote that he was "quite unrivalled as an Arctic first lieutenant." He served as second-in-command aboard the *Assistance*, which, Markham said, was "the happiest, the healthiest, the cleanest, the dryest, and the most efficient ship that ever wintered in the Arctic regions."

This was M'Clintock's big chance, and he intended to make the most of it – not, one suspects, through any thrust of naked ambition but simply because he had that curious, roving, disciplined mind that caused him to apply himself to the problem at hand and try to solve it. Like so many of his fellow Britons, he was an avid collector: everything from the skins of Arctic birds to the eggs of gulls. Indeed, everything was the object of M'Clintock's curiosity. On one occasion he even measured the astonishingly broad grin of an Eskimo: it came to a remarkable four and a half inches.

Yet few knew M'Clintock's inner thoughts. His journal reveals little; his conversations were terse. He was reserved – unruffled to the point of muteness, an odd characteristic in an Irishman. "I could not have conceived so much calmness to have been the property of only one man," Charles Parry, the explorer's brother, wrote of him. "In the greatest difficulties, and under the most aggravating circumstances, his face would not alter a muscle. . . . No outward show of anxiety, no nervous irritability, no unnecessary noise, ever betokened an anxious mind." M'Clintock rarely raised his voice, gave orders softly, and never appeared to show the least anxiety when the Arctic gales screamed in the rigging or the ponderous floes threatened to crush his ship.

He had applied himself rigorously to the problems of Arctic land travel. His meticulous attention to detail and his inventiveness would give him his place in history as "the Father of Arctic Sledging." That was an overstatement, a simplification at the very least. M'Clintock was the father of *naval* sledging only. Much was made by naval historians such as Sir Clements Markham of M'Clintock's record sledge journeys during the Franklin search. But Hudson's Bay traders, using dogs, snowshoes, and lighter, more flexible sleds, had made much longer ones with less resultant fatigue. The Navy, however, didn't recognize any records but its own, and to this day M'Clintock is regarded as the undisputed king of the sledgers.

Certainly he improved the Navy's own sledging practice, building on his experiences with Ross. One of his techniques in the fall of 1850 was to establish a series of depots thirty miles apart in order to stretch out the travelling time. Another was to use auxiliary sledges that would start off with the main party, later transferring their loads to the sledges pressing on before returning to base. M'Clintock even thought of equipping his heavily loaded sledges with sails, but it apparently did not occur to him that the loads could be lighter if the crews were trained as hunters to shoot their own food, especially on Melville Island, which abounded in muskoxen.

Nor did he consider the use of Eskimo dogs and trained dog drivers. Penny's expedition was the only one that had brought dogs along, a bit of foresight that allowed Penny to travel easily from ship to ship; but then, he wasn't Navy. M'Clintock was to use dogs occasionally in future years, but he preferred the naval tradition of manhauling. There seems to have been a feeling that it was a form of cheating to use animals for transport. As for the idea of using dogs for food – that was too repulsive! This tradition persisted into the next century with the tragic journey of Robert Falcon Scott to the South Pole. Scott and his men, dragging their heavy sledges on foot, died of hunger and exhaustion. Roald Amundsen, the Norwegian, beat them to the Pole, ate his dogs, and lived.

Strangely, to the English there was something noble, something romantic, about strong young men marching in harness through the Arctic wastes, enduring incredible hardships with a smile on their lips and a song in their hearts. They were like the knights of old, breaking new paths, facing unknown perils in their search for the Grail. The parallel is by no means inexact, for M'Clintock had given his sledges the names that suggested knightly virtues – Inflexible, Hotspur, Perseverance, Resolute. Each sledge proudly carried a banner of heraldic design and each had its own motto (*Never Despair . . . Faithful and Firm*), some even in Latin.

The sledge crews trained daily beneath the frowning cliffs of Griffith Island on the ice of the strait in which Austin's ships were beset. It must have been a stirring if incongruous spectacle to see them drawn up in line – fifteen sledges in two long rows, their crews in white cotton jumpers, their pennants flapping briskly in the polar wind. Off they went, loping across the ice like so many schoolboys, each six-man crew dragging a load of more than a ton.

At six o'clock on the evening of April 15, their training completed, they set out with the inevitable three hearty cheers of their comrades ringing in their ears. But it was not romantic. Within a fortnight, M'Clintock had to send back a third of his men, suffering from exhaustion, rheumatism, and frostbite. A week later, more returned to the ship. M'Clintock could write, as he did later, about creating a new age of chivalry ("we are made to feel as did the crusaders of old"), but the reality was grimmer. One Arctic veteran, Captain Henry Kellett, was to write that sledge travelling was far more dreadful than battle. "I have been a long time at sea," he declared, "and seen varying trying services, but never have seen such labour, and such misery after. No amount of money is an equivalent. . . . Men require much more heart and stamina to undertake an extended travelling party than to go into action. The travellers have their enemy chilling them to the very heart, and paralyzing their very limbs; the others the very contrary."

The sledges set off in eight directions. M'Clintock's own party of four sledges and an auxiliary was given the longest and most difficult task: to probe westward down Barrow Strait to Parry's farthest point on Melville Island. M'Clintock went seventy miles past Parry's western limit. There at Cape Dundas, as he stood atop a high sandstone cliff, he could see, looming out of the fog to the southwest, the barren expanse of Banks Land. But there was no sign of Franklin.

Had the missing ships gone up Wellington Channel, as the clues suggested and so many believed, and then worked their way west to become beset north of Melville Island? If so, it was likely that the lost party would try to make its way overland, probably to the head of

188

Busnan Cove, which Parry had described as "one of the pleasantest and most habitable spots we have yet seen in the Arctic region." M'Clintock headed in that direction and found evidence of Parry's passing – the wheels of his cart and even the bleached bones of a ptarmigan his men had eaten more than three decades before. But no evidence of Franklin.

They continued on, dragging their sledges to Parry's Winter Harbour. There they encountered the great block of sandstone, ten feet high, twenty feet across, on which Parry's surgeon, Fisher, had carved an inscription. Again there was no hint that Franklin had been there – nor the missing Robert McClure, who was thought to be in the area. That June, wading through newly formed pools of water and slush, they headed back to the ship. As M'Clintock had planned, they had been absent for eighty days and travelled 875 statute miles – a journey that was called "unprecedented." But John Rae easily outstripped M'Clintock's record. That same year, 1851, he and two others travelled 1,060 miles in thirty-nine days, "a feat never equalled in Arctic travel" in the view of the Geographical Society's Sir Roderick Murchison.

Other sledge parties headed for Cape Walker, the point at which Franklin had been ordered to turn south. Here was a mighty pile of conglomerate sandstone towering a thousand feet above the sea on an islet at the tip of an undiscovered land mass now named for the Prince of Wales – but not a clue to the lost ships, not a scrap of paper, not a cairn, not a trace. One party tried to follow Franklin's intended route to the southwest from Cape Walker but found the pack so dense and heavy they were certain Franklin couldn't have gone that way. Another party headed down the western shores of Peel Sound, whose eastern limits had been explored by Ross and M'Clintock in 1849. Faced with a dreadful blizzard, they had to turn back, agreeing with the previous investigators that Peel Sound was impassable, frozen solid to the bottom and rarely if ever open to navigation. That was wrong. In 1846 Franklin had found it clear of ice. But by now, all the Navy men were convinced that every route to the south was permanently blocked. Franklin *must* be somewhere to the north.

None of the other sledge expeditions turned up a single clue to Franklin's fate. In total, they had covered 7,025 miles on foot and explored 1,225 miles of new land. Bathurst Island, which Parry had seen only in the distance from his ship, was now on the map. So was the northern tip of Prince of Wales Land. Penny had been up Wellington Channel and beyond by sledge and boat and had seen, in the distance, the strait separating Devon and Bathurst islands that now bears his name. For more than fifty miles ahead all he could see was open water. Was Franklin somewhere beyond? He had picked up a piece of English elm, which he disregarded at the time. It was almost certainly from one of the missing ships.

Now there occurred one of those odd contretemps involving two disparate personalities that affected and prolonged the Franklin search. Penny was convinced that Franklin had gone up Wellington Channel and beyond into the Arctic Ocean. He could not follow his instincts, being forced to turn back for lack of provisions, but he was certain he was on the right track. The channel was still a mass of floating ice. His own little ships couldn't force their way through to continue the exploration, but a steamer probably could. And so he asked Austin to lend him one of the steam tenders for that purpose. Austin refused, either through sheer stubbornness, as Penny claimed, or through a misunderstanding, as Austin claimed.

Whatever took place on August 11, it was not a propitious meeting. It was, in fact, the culmination of a series of acrimonious encounters between two men of opposite temperament who struck sparks off each other whenever they met. Penny's first interview with Austin – a blunt-spoken whaler meeting a crusty naval veteran – had not been pleasant. Austin had the reputation of being difficult, even rude, and often unpredictable. During their meetings that season – happily infrequent – they had done their best to get along, but frequent apologies were often followed by later recriminations.

Penny, aboard Austin's vessel, brusquely outlined his explorations past Wellington Channel.

"You say we have been acting in concert," he told Austin. "Let us prove the sincerity of that concert. Give me a steamer and with the little *Sophia* I will go miles further."

Austin drew himself up but did not reply, whereupon Penny declared, "Then I know the truth of your sincerity and will have nothing more to do with you."

This teapot tempest, which was witnessed by the *Sophia*'s captain, Alexander Stewart, had considerable significance. For if Penny had got through the ice of Wellington Channel with steam power and explored the country farther to the north, he could have killed all speculation that Franklin had gone that way and thus have changed the course of the search. As it was, the vast majority of Arctic experts, not to mention the English press and public, remained convinced that Franklin was to be found somewhere beyond Wellington Channel.

If Penny had been a naval officer, if Austin had been less officious, it's possible, even likely, that events would have taken a different turn. But in the labyrinthine saga of the Franklin search, personality and temperament were as significant as seamanship. Although Austin had provisions for three years – enough to allow Penny to winter north of Wellington Channel – the naval commander decided to abandon the search in the area of Lancaster Sound. He was convinced that Franklin had entered the Arctic by way of Jones Sound, to the north, but his exploration in that direction was also fruitless. Blocked by ice, his ships saved at the last moment, he limped back to England, as did the others. A committee of naval officers studied the Penny-Austin dispute and found no fault with their colleague. The Admiralty never again employed Penny. Even Lady Franklin couldn't get him a ship in the continuing search for her husband.

Meanwhile, the great quadrilateral to the south remained unexplored. More than six years had passed since the *Erebus* and the *Terror* had left England, and in spite of the tantalizing clues from Beechey, no one yet knew their fate. Public interest by this time had been whipped to a frenzy. The quest for the missing ships had been transformed into something more exalted than a mere search. As Leopold M'Clintock had divined, it had taken on the trappings of a crusade. "Since the zealous attempts to rescue the Holy Sepulchre in the middle ages," one writer of the day declared, "the Christian world has not so unanimously agreed on anything as the desire to recover Sir John Franklin, dead or alive, from the dread solitude of death into which he has so fearlessly ventured."

5

For most of 1850 England waited for news. It came first with Lady Franklin's own ship, the little *Prince Albert*, which returned in October, within a few days of the transport *North Star*, which had been sent out in 1849 to supply James Ross's fruitless expedition. But the

The dutiful warmth of a son

two pieces of information that she brought – one incomplete, the other dubious – only served to tease and torment an already inflamed public.

Something had been discovered at last, but what? Parker Snow had gone ashore at Cape Riley and had seen the remains of five or six tents and one or two artifacts, including a piece of British rope and canvas. Could these have come from the lost party? He could not be certain, for his superior, Forsyth, eager to get home before the weather closed in, had declined to follow the others up the channel to Beechey Island.

But Snow had a more sensational story, which he proceeded to rush into print. It took up a full chapter in his own account of the voyage – a book that scooped all the other would-be scribes trapped in the ice of Barrow Strait.

Snow reported that John Ross's Eskimo interpreter, Adam Beck, had encountered a group of Eskimos during the outward voyage of the *Felix* who insisted that Franklin and his men had been murdered by Greenland natives near Cape York in 1846. Few of the others believed this tale. Penny, the most experienced of all, bluntly rejected it. His own interpreter, Carl Petersen, a Greenlander who spoke the language well – probably better than Beck – had talked to the same Eskimos and got nothing from them. But Beck, when interrogated by several other officers, stuck to his story. John Ross, with his usual stubbornness, backed his interpreter and insisted the story was true (though he continued on to Beechey Island). Actually, it was poppycock, a distorted rumour based on the death of a single member of the crew of the transport *North Star*, which had been forced to winter in the vicinity the previous year. But Snow made the most of it in his book, even though he was sceptical about its truth. It was, for a budding writer, too good a tale to ignore. "I am extremely doubtful whether I should put it down or not," he began, but "I think it my duty to narrate it strictly as it came to hand." And so he did, with the crocodile tears flowing freely.

Jane Franklin, already close to a breakdown, was infuriated by Snow's report of Ross's stand. She had contributed a hundred pounds to his expedition; now, she said, she wished she could have added to the gift the phrase "with a deep sense of gratitude to Sir John Ross for murdering her husband."

Equally maddening and frustrating was the failure of the inexperienced Forsyth, whose two ice masters had quarrelled and contra-

192

dicted each other about the state of Prince Regent Inlet. There was no help for it; she would have to draw on her funds to send the *Prince Albert* back out again under a different captain to do what Forsyth had failed to do. For she still believed it possible that her husband and his men were somewhere to the south of Prince Regent Inlet.

The two men she chose for the task were as unlikely a pair as had ever been sent to the Arctic. The new captain, William Kennedy, was a tough Canadian fur trader, the son of a Cree woman and a Hudson's Bay factor. He had never been to sea in his life. The second-in-command would be Joseph-René Bellot, a twenty-five-year-old sub-lieutenant on leave from the French Navy, who knew nothing of the Arctic except what he had read in books.

They were a study in contrasts. Years of hard travel by canoe and dogsled across the Labrador wilderness had weathered Kennedy. His broad, flat face with its distinctive cheekbones indicated his mixed blood. With his craggy features and his vast tangled beard, he looked older than his thirty-seven years. The diminutive Bellot was barely twenty-five, a cheery, round-faced youth, introspective but bursting with that *élan* that is said to characterize his race.

Kennedy knew little about the sea but was a seasoned wilderness traveller. Bellot, who had never pulled a sledge or slept in the snow, was a good navigator. They were poles apart in blood, background, upbringing, outlook, and temperament, but they got along famously, perhaps because they were united in what they considered to be a sacred cause. Unsullied by personal ambition, they volunteered their services to embark on a long and dangerous mission without pay. They were not out to prove a point, to advance themselves politically, to gain fame or fortune, or to redress a personal slight. Kennedy made it clear that he would be quite prepared to serve under Bellot, if Lady Franklin so chose. Both men came to London of their own accord to answer her heartbreaking call for help – two outsiders from alien worlds with no link to any of the several British establishments involved in the search for her husband.

Jane Franklin had by now become an international heroine. Because of the sympathy her cause had engendered, Kennedy was able to travel from the fishery he managed on the Saugeen River in Canada West to London at no personal cost. The mayor of Hamilton helped get him a free ride to New York. Henry Grinnell, Lady Franklin's American supporter, got him free passage across the Atlantic. Aboard the Cunard steam packet he met another future Franklin searcher, the pompous Sir Edward Belcher, who was so impressed he got him a British railway pass. (Belcher, who did not care for many of his colleagues, was later heard to remark that "Kennedy is better than any of your Backs or Raes.") The proprietor of the Adelphi Hotel, sympathetic to Kennedy's mission, refused to charge him for food or lodging.

Lady Franklin was also impressed, if not by Kennedy's credentials, at least by his natural simplicity, his integrity, and his good humour. He had, after all, abandoned his business and, over the protests of his family, hurried to her side. This was a man who had crisscrossed North American forests, prairies, and mountains by canoe, York boat, Red River cart, or toboggan from Fort Chimo in Ungava to the Oregon Territory.

And he had known her husband! His earliest memories went back to the summer of 1819, when John Franklin had arrived at Cumberland House by canoe. Kennedy was only five at the time, but he would always remember Franklin teaching him his ABCs and preaching in the local church – the first religious ceremony the young Kennedy could remember. A strict teetotaller – the *Prince Albert* was alarmingly dry – he had quit the Hudson's Bay Company after a fruitful thirteen-year association because he disapproved of the company selling liquor to his mother's people. His earnest idealism charmed Lady Franklin, while Bellot's bubbling enthusiasm delighted her.

In Joseph-René Bellot, Jane Franklin saw something of the son she never had. His almost childlike eagerness to be of service was touching, his shyness and modesty enchanting. Of all the various adventurers who tested themselves in the chilling gloom of an Arctic winter, this slight young Frenchman with the dark eyes, the sensitive nostrils, and the full lips of a poet is surely the most attractive.

He came from a poor working-class family, one of seven children sired by a blacksmith, but his intelligence was such that his home town paid for his education. He never forgot the sacrifices his parents had made for him. As a naval cadet he sent home part of his meagre pay and peppered his journals with expressions of gratitude to them and reproaches to himself for neglecting to write home often enough. He was impetuously brave. He had saved one comrade from drowning at the risk of his own life and was severely wounded by a lance during a skirmish in Madagascar – an injury he described as no more

194

than a scratch. For that he was made a Chevalier of the Legion of Honour; he was not yet twenty.

Bellot's youthful ardour, like Kennedy's, was stimulated by the nobility of Lady Franklin's cause. He was convinced that France should play her part in the great crusade and asked for leave so that he could personally represent the French Navy in the search. How could France resist such a chivalrous request? The Minister of Marine cheerfully gave his assent.

Bellot in the meantime had shot off a letter to Kennedy, asking for a berth on the expedition and remarking that Franklin's "glory and success have made him a citizen of the world, and it is but justice that all seamen should take the most lively interest in his fate." Though he was ardently patriotic, his views had been broadened internationally by the idea of the Great Exhibition of 1851 – history's first world's fair, which was about to open in London, with its gargantuan greenhouse, known as the Crystal Palace. As Bellot later put it to Lady Franklin: "If any credit is given to me for my zeal in a foreign cause, it only originated after the universal exhibition was ordered, which blotted out all narrow-minded prejudices of nationality." After he met her, these high-minded principles became more personal: ". . . it is with all my feelings, with all the dutiful warmth of a son, I have embarked in that cause."

The Admiralty was not so enthusiastic. A naval officer from a foreign command serving under an untutored mixed-blood from the wilds of subarctic America? It was madness; the pair couldn't possibly get along; the crew would mutiny! In the end Lady Franklin prevailed, as she usually did. After all, it was she and her supporters, not the Navy, who were paying for the voyage. The Navy need not have worried. The mixed crew of Shetland Islanders and Canadians took to the young first mate immediately, and the voyage that followed, though arduous, was one of the happiest in Arctic annals.

The expedition left Stromness in June 1851 to the strain of the time-worn sailor's ditty, "The Girl I Left Behind Me." It was an emotional parting. Both Jane Franklin and her "French son," as she now called him, were moved to tears. "I must supply your mother's place," she had told him, but now she could scarcely speak. "Take care of yourself," was all she was able to say. The spirited young man, who had danced the schottische a few nights before, now sobbed like a child. "We are really *very* fond of him," Sophia

Cracroft wrote, "– his sweetness & simplicity & earnestness are most endearing." It was some time, she noted, before he could screw up his courage to say a last good-bye to her aunt.

"Poor woman!" he wrote in his journal, after the ship got under way. "If you could read my heart you would have seen how much the somewhat egotistical desire of making an extraordinary voyage has been succeeded in me by a real ardour and genuine passion for the end we aim at." A short time later, as the little sloop rolled and pitched, he was violently seasick and badly bruised by being thrown about his cabin. "O shame! O despair," he scratched on the page. But he bore the misery without flinching. He had tried to harden himself to such conditions before leaving France and insisted on sleeping under a single blanket on a mattress three inches thick, "just enough to say I do not sleep on the boards." He might be frail in appearance but he was convinced that "will and moral energy can always take the place of physical strength."

In another marked act of chivalry, John Hepburn, who had almost starved with Franklin in 1820, insisted on joining the ship. Now fifty-seven, he had vivid memories of those early days. Bellot was as fascinated by these tales as he was by the voyageur songs that Kennedy sang. He insisted on transcribing some of them in his journal. Kennedy, he wrote, was his kind of man. "Dear Mr. Kennedy! how kind and conscientious he is! . . ." The admiration was mutual. "I am a man of his heart, he says, and he really wins my heart by his simple straight forwardness. Poor man! He does not belong to our time, and his perfectly primitive education has made him too good to lead the men of our day!"

Bellot, a Catholic, was impressed by Kennedy's profoundly Protestant faith "and the piety . . . with which he entreated the great God of Jacob to inspire our resolutions and direct our understandings. . . . What limit can there be to the daring of a man who is not only persuaded, but convinced, that whatever he does is at the suggestion and by the permission of God?"

The veteran trader's French, Bellot realized, was more than a century out of date – "some of those old expressions have a perfume quite peculiar to themselves." This quaint form of the language so pleased Bellot that he made the mistake of remarking on it, only to discover, to his embarrassment, that Kennedy considered it a defect that he wanted Bellot to help him correct. "God forbid that I should think of spoiling him," wrote Bellot. "I am too selfish to . . . divest his language of its charming originality."

Early in July they came upon the two American ships, which having reached Greenland after their long winter in the ice, were now heading back for Beechey Island. Elisha Kane came on board and looked with astonishment at Bellot. "I have seen many things here to surprise me," he declared, "but what I least expected to find here was a French officer." The two romantics got along famously, visiting back and forth as the three ships struggled together across the ice-choked waters of Davis Strait. Bellot, with his usual enthusiasm, took to the Americans. "Go a-head! is their captain's maxim," he wrote. "With stout ships and bold resolution they have triumphed over everything. . . . Such are the daring pioneers of civilisation amidst the vast plains of America . . . the word impossible is not in their dictionary."

But he also noted that the American sailors were fed up and planning to desert at the first opportunity. Under no circumstances, they declared, would they endure another winter in the Arctic. They did not get the double pay of their English counterparts, and they had no intention of doing anything to help the expedition continue north. Their officers were powerless, their captain, De Haven, badly shaken. After some weeks, the two expeditions parted, Kennedy heading for the mouth of Lancaster Sound and the Americans eventually turning toward home.

The *Prince Albert* was less than ninety tons, "a small, fairy-looking craft" in Kennedy's words, originally designed for the fruit trade in the Azores and now the tiniest vessel ever to enter the Arctic archipelago. She was, however, far more manoeuvrable than the Navy's heavy ships. By September 9, having failed once again to get past Fury Beach in Prince Regent Inlet, she stood off the harbour at Port Leopold, as others had done before.

The way was clear to the harbour, but it was difficult to tell whether or not the harbour itself was open. The supplies cached by James Clark Ross in 1848 lay at Port Leopold and also, probably, a message from Austin. There was no thought of turning back as Forsyth had done. As Bellot declared, "it would be a disgrace for an expedition like ours not to press forward, when we think of what Parry and Ross did, who had neither provisions at Fury Beach nor a steam vessel at Port Leopold." Kennedy agreed. "Like Cortez," he said, "I have burned my ships, and there is too much ice behind for us to dream of returning."

Kennedy determined to scout the ice-choked harbour in a small gutta-percha boat with four of his men. All they took with them were signal rockets and lanterns. While the others waited aboard ship for their return, the young Frenchman snatched a few hours' sleep. He was awakened at eight; the news was bad: the ice was closing in. From the yardarm he could see that the passage Kennedy had taken was blocked. He could not get back to the ship. Had he been able, Bellot wondered, to reach the cache of provisions that Ross had left at Port Leopold? Was there no way he could rejoin the *Prince Albert*?

Bellot was distraught. "May God help us!" he cried to his journal. "I no longer think of success; all my prayers are for the safety of my companions. Dear parents! Dear friends! may the thought of you sustain and preserve me from temptations to which I may yield."

He decided that he would, if necessary, push forward through the ice toward the harbour and lose the ship. Lady Franklin had told him that the *Prince Albert* was not as important as men's lives. At the very worst they could exist on Ross's stores. He took the watch that night, let off signal rockets, and waited. There was no reply. When morning came he was shaken to discover that the *Prince Albert* was no longer off Port Leopold. The ice stream had made his decision for him, driving his ship back miles down Prince Regent Inlet.

His ice master, John Leask, pointed toward the stern with tears in his eyes. A solid wall of new ice barred the way to the north, cutting off all hope of rescuing Kennedy by sea.

Leask turned toward Bellot. "What is to be done?" he asked. "What is your opinion?"

Now, for the first time, the realization sank in that he, Joseph-René Bellot, aged twenty-five, was in sole command of the ship and in control of the expedition – that the crew must follow his orders, that he must make the decisions, that his captain was marooned somewhere to the northwest, and that the lives of five missing men now depended entirely upon his judgement and resolve. And the murderous Arctic winter was already closing in.

Chapter Five

Robert McClure

The Investigator trapped off Banks Island

By the fall of 1851, with only one ship – Kennedy's – somewhere in *Grasping at* the eastern Arctic and all the others home, Jane Franklin was once *straws* more in despair. Austin's reports had confirmed the general belief that her husband had spent his first winter at Beechey Island. But where on earth had he gone the following spring of 1846? Had both vessels sunk with all hands? In all the history of Arctic exploration that had never happened. Had he been forced to change his original route? If so, why hadn't he left cairns to mark his passage? And what had become of the cylinders he had been instructed to throw overboard when he left Lancaster Sound? None had been recovered. Not so much as a pile of stones, a post, or a fragment of equipment had been discovered by the sledge crews that had explored the middle Arctic for a thousand miles or more.

Every effort had been made to communicate with the missing expedition. Sailors had painted or chalked gigantic messages on the cliffs. Ships had left caches of food and clothing. Foxes had been trapped and released wearing collars carrying messages in the unlikely event that some of Franklin's men might shoot them for food. Balloons were sent off with papers carrying information about the location of the rescue ships. Blue lights were flashed, guns fired, rockets exploded in the Arctic night. But the Arctic remained silent.

Apart from the unexplained scrap of British elm found by Penny off Wellington Channel, only one other clue had appeared, and it, too, was not identified. The indefatigable John Rae, on his third Arctic journey, exploring the south coasts of Wollaston and Victoria lands (which he proved, at last, to be one and the same) had picked up on August 21, 1851, two fragments of wood that had clearly been part of a Royal Navy vessel. But years would pass before anyone realized they were almost certainly from one of the Franklin ships. Rae had stood on the east coast of those desolate shores and gazed across Victoria Strait toward King William Land. He had wanted to cross over, but the state of the ice made that impossible. Franklin Point, as it came to be called, was only fifty miles to the east, and it held the clue to the riddle. But Rae could not reach it.

The country grasped at straws, clinging to the belief that the lost crews might still be alive, and so did Lady Franklin. She and Sophia Cracroft bombarded the press with anonymous letters and the Admiralty with signed petitions urging more action. William Penny belatedly discovered a whaling captain who had been the last to board the *Erebus* in Baffin Bay; he claimed that Franklin had told him he had rations for five years and could easily stretch that to seven. A yachtsman named Donald Beatson was convinced Franklin was alive in the polar sea north of Alaska; with Jane Franklin's encouragement, he proposed to take a schooner east from Bering Strait, where two other naval vessels, *Investigator* and *Enterprise*, had also apparently vanished. Beatson's plans fell through, so nothing came of that. An adventurous young naval lieutenant, Bedford Pim, thought Franklin might be in Russia and got the government's permission to hike across Siberia to find him. Lady Franklin gave him five hundred pounds, but nothing came of that, either.

If all this were not enough, Lady Franklin was persuaded to open her husband's will in the presence of her stepdaughter, Eleanor, and Eleanor's husband, the Reverend Philip Gell. She did not want to do so; it would be an admission, she felt, that the family had given him up for lost. That would certainly dampen the public's ardour for the search and perhaps dry up the flow of public money that was supporting her private expeditions. Her outward posture was a defiant insistence that John Franklin was still alive. If, in her secret heart, she had doubts, she quenched them. Her considerable energies were devoted to the one overriding purpose. Did she really believe her aging spouse could have sustained himself in the Arctic after six years? Perhaps not. Like the quest for the Passage, the search had for her become an end in itself; it was the sheet anchor in her life's unquiet channel. Equally important – perhaps more important to her than the question of life or death – was John Franklin's reputation. She had once told him that it took precedence over "the selfish enjoyment of your society." That reputation, bruised in his Tasmanian years, could be restored only if it could be proved decisively that he, ahead of all others, had located the North West Passage. That was her goal: to give to him the gift of immortality, and she pursued it with an awesome tenacity.

The will caused another estrangement with the Gells. Made out in 1829, a year after Franklin's second marriage, it left all the property that his first wife had brought to their marriage to Eleanor. Jane Franklin would get the income from her husband's estate, which included the ten thousand pounds that was Jane's at the time of her marriage. But there was a problem. She had her missing husband's power of attorney and had been using up all the proceeds from the full estate on the search. Now the Gells insisted that she pay back every penny of their portion, if and when his death was finally admitted – with no allowance being made for the money she had already diverted to them. This left her even more dependent on public support for her cause.

In this gloomy autumn, with Captain Austin's ambitious expedition branded a failure and the Navy reluctant to mount another, there was one bright spot: public opinion was still on her side. *The Times* summed it up in an editorial immediately after Austin's return in October 1851. The paper called for a complete review of the Franklin search as well as the government's plans for the future: ". . . though we do not think the geographical importance of these expeditions commensurable with the cost or exposure of a single sloop's crew, we unhesitatingly admit that our obligation to rescue those who have been dispatched on the enterprise is of a very different magnitude. It signifies supremely little whether Boothia Felix is a peninsula, an island, or a gulf . . . but it does impinge most emphatically to our national honour that we should ascertain the fate of our missing countrymen, and redeem them, if living, from the dangers to which they have been consigned."

The Times went on to urge "a little more continuous perseverance." Why, it asked, must ships return home with eighteen months' provisions instead of spending another winter in the ice? "We shall never attain our end by sailing up to the ice and then sailing back again." Lady Franklin's campaign was bearing fruit.

Now Sherard Osborn, the most prolific and also the most enthusiastic of the literary explorers – he had been captain of the steam tender *Pioneer* under Austin – entered the fray. In February 1852, he published *Stray Leaves from an Arctic Journal* in which he pleaded, in the purplest of passages, for a renewed search up Wellington Channel: "Franklin and his matchless followers need no eulogy from me; the sufferings they must have undergone, the mystery that hangs over them, are on every tongue in every civilized land.

"The blooming child lisps Franklin's name, as with glistening eye and greedy ear it hears of the wonders of the North, and the brave deeds there done. Youth's bosom glows with generous emotion to emulate the fame of him who has gone where none as yet have followed. And who amongst us does not feel his heart throb faster in recalling to recollection the calm heroism of the veteran leader, who, when about to enter the unknown regions of which Wellington Channel is the portal, addressed his crews in those solemn and emphatic words of Holy Writ – his motto, doubtless – 'Choose ye this day whom ye will serve'; and found in that blissful choice his strength and his endurance."

Like Osborn, the old Arctic hands were convinced, as were the public and press, that Franklin had vanished somewhere up the Wellington Channel. Seven of the ten leading experts consulted agreed with that assessment. In a speech to the Geographical Society in late November, 1851, Osborn captured the prevailing optimism. "The instructions of Sir John Franklin were to proceed to the northward of Wellington Channel if possible," he declared, conveniently forgetting that Franklin's instructions were to go that way only if the route to the southwest were blocked. Osborn swallowed whole the tale that the expedition was equipped for six or seven years. To cries of "Hear! Hear!" he asked his audience if they believed that Franklin and his officers were the kind of men likely to turn their backs on their duty after being absent for only eighteen months. He said he had once opposed the theory of an Open Polar Sea, but more recent observations had convinced him that the water was clear above Wellington Channel and that Franklin could have forced his way up the channel and on to the Bering Sea. Thus did the naval establishment also grasp at straws.

Penny, in a letter read to the meeting, declared that there was no doubt as to the route Franklin had taken. The whaler used negative evidence to support his theory: the fact that he had found no traces of the expedition along the Wellington Channel, he explained, proved that Franklin had gone on to points yet unexplored without stopping.

In the spring of 1852, the Navy gave in to the pressure. This time it proposed to send *five* ships on the search under the crusty Sir Edward Belcher, a Nova Scotia-born veteran of the War of 1812 and perhaps the least desirable officer to put in charge of a complicated search. Belcher's orders were to look for the lost explorer somewhere to the north of Beechey Island.

But then there was heard another cry from the heart. To the importunings of a wife were added the pleadings of a parent. The father of Lieutenant Samuel Gurney Cresswell, second mate aboard Robert McClure's *Investigator*, reminded the Admiralty and the public that another expedition besides Franklin's was lost in the Arctic. McClure's ship, separated from its consort, had last been seen in

204

Bering Strait in the summer of 1850, heading east. Almost two years had passed and nothing more had been heard from it. The Navy, which had acted tardily when Franklin went missing, could not afford more foot-dragging. One lost expedition was bad enough. Two would be disastrous.

Francis Cresswell pointed out that if McClure was in trouble, he would undoubtedly head for Parry's old Winter Harbour on Melville Island; the massive sandstone block made an obvious post box. Hastily, the Navy split Belcher's squadron in two. One sailing vessel, accompanied by a steam tender, would move west to Melville Island to search for McClure. Two other ships would move up the Wellington Channel to search for Franklin. A fifth would anchor off Beechey Island to act as a supply vessel, thus allowing the expedition to increase the length of its stay, as *The Times* had urged.

This was still not enough for Lady Franklin. Every nook and cranny of that wrinkled and treeless realm must be scoured for her missing husband. There were still some corners that had not been looked at, some rumours that had not been laid to rest. And so with the help of funds lavished upon her by a sympathetic public, she bought Donald Beatson's steam yacht, *Isabel*, and got permission from the Navy to employ a young, firm-jawed officer, Edward Inglefield, to take it north along the east coast of Baffin Bay and thence on to Lancaster Sound and Beechey Island with supplies for Belcher's naval squadron.

The ambitious young man had additional ideas. He didn't want to be a mere transport captain; he wanted to be an explorer. In spite of the clear evidence that Franklin had entered Lancaster Sound and wintered at Beechey Island, he insisted that both Jones and Smith sounds also be examined – an area, he claimed, "to which it is well known that Sir John Franklin's attention had been sometimes directed."

Had Franklin gone up Wellington Channel into the Open Polar Sea and then sailed east through Jones or Smith sounds to emerge into Baffin Bay, there to be murdered by Eskimos, as Adam Beck, John Ross's native interpreter, had claimed? Or, having reached the polar sea, had he sailed west toward Bering Strait as many believed? In short, did one of these other entrances hold the clue to the puzzle? It was unlikely but possible. Previous expeditions had found both inlets blocked by ice, but if open they could well lead westward into the uncharted webwork of Arctic islands. Inglefield, of course, was also using the Franklin search to do a little exploring on his own. His other purpose was to solve "the much vexed question of the entrance into the Great Polar Basin." In short, for Inglefield, it was the Pole, not the Passage, that beckoned. Meanwhile, on his roundabout route to Beechey Island he ought at least to be able to lay to rest Adam Beck's dark pronouncement about John Franklin's murder.

Now at last, it seemed to Lady Franklin in that spring of 1852, every corner of the great archipelago would be scrutinized. Nine ships were in the Arctic. Inglefield was well to the north. Belcher's five ships patrolled the centre. McClure in the *Investigator* and Collinson in the *Enterprise*, having reached Alaska, were somewhere to the west. And her own sloop, the *Prince Albert*, under William Kennedy was presumably searching the southern maze of channels. Everything that could be done had been done, or so it seemed. Surely before another year was out, the mystery would be solved.

2

For all of the winter of 1851-52, Jane Franklin was out of touch with the *Prince Albert*. Kennedy and Bellot had sailed from Stromness in the Orkneys on June 3, 1851. She could not know that on September 9 the pair had become separated, with Kennedy marooned and perhaps dead from exposure in a small boat at Port Leopold while Bellot in the schooner was helpless to save his captain, having been forced by wind and current back down Prince Regent Inlet.

Bellot found a sheltered harbour at Batty Bay, a tiny indentation on the inlet's western coastline, and there on those bleak and rubbled shores he pondered the responsibilities that had been thrown on his young shoulders. Kennedy was some fifty miles to the north. Bellot could only hope that he had landed safely in his flimsy gutta-percha craft and had found James Ross's cache of provisions.

He was frantic to reach him, but the treacherous weather had made a sea voyage unpredictable. He decided instead to move north by land, following the coastline, naïvely expecting to achieve his goal in three days. He left on foot on September 10 with three men. Lacking snowshoes and thus unable to take dogs or sledges, the quartet laboured through the heavy drifts, never quite sure where they were.

206

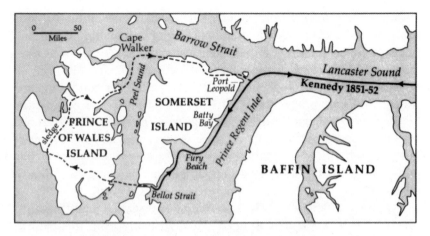

Kennedy and Bellot search for Franklin, 1851-52

Bellot's seamen ministered to him affectionately, as if he were their little brother. He had insisted on travelling light, rationing them to a pound of pemmican a day, and no biscuit. But they hid some biscuits in their pockets anyway – not for themselves but because they feared an unadulterated diet of pemmican might affect their young leader's stomach. At night when he was asleep they tucked him snugly in his buffalo-hide blanket.

But after two nights of hard struggle, they were forced to give up. In fact, it was touch and go whether they would get back to the ship alive. They threw their baggage aside and just managed to stumble aboard, played out and bitterly disappointed. All agreed that had they gone ten more miles they would never have returned.

Bellot saw that a land journey was impossible: the ground was too rugged, the snow too deep. He would have to wait until the sea ice would bear his weight and then travel along the coast by dogsled. He realized there was no further point in scrambling to save Kennedy. By this time his captain had either found James Ross's cache at Port Leopold or was dead of exposure.

He had been too impulsive; he must plan more carefully. His men must fashion snowshoes, sew moccasins, adapt the sledges. "We must not go like a parcel of thoughtless children," he admonished himself – following that with another rueful realization, "command invests one with a terrible moral responsibility."

The winter closed in. The ptarmigan and Arctic hares shed their summer coats and turned as white as the falling snow. The crew

207

swathed the ship in a woollen tent. The ice that froze in the bay was broken up by fierce squalls, making sledging impossible. Bellot and his crew were in a torment over their lost captain. "Every wind that blows makes us think of the mental suffering of our friends. . . ."

Out of deference to Kennedy, Bellot insisted on continuing the regular calls to prayer that had been a feature of life aboard the *Prince Albert*. He noticed that during these rituals some of the crew members had tears in their eyes. One seaman who so forgot himself as to indulge in mild profanity received a sharp rebuke from the young lieutenant. Had not the captain banned bad language aboard his ship?

At last, on October 13, he set off with two seamen and the ship's doctor, for he knew that Kennedy suffered badly from rheumatism and might need medical aid. They took food for nine persons and four dogs, extra clothing, shoes, medical supplies, buffalo robes, and a portable kitchen – and lost almost all of it a few hours later when one of the sledges broke through the ice. Back they went to the ship, empty handed, downcast. Bellot made immediate plans to set out again. "I must harden myself also to the most vexatious disappointments," he said. "With God's help, I promise myself that I will not return from a third attempt without having reached Port Leopold."

Two days later, with nine men in a small boat, he set off again to retrieve the lost baggage. Steering the craft through open leads of water, they recovered most of it, frozen up in the ice. But the sledge was broken. To return to the ship, repair it, and make preparations for a fourth voyage would take a week.

Bellot made a bold decision. Underequipped as it was, the party would make a dash for Port Leopold, hoping the good weather would hold. He dispatched one man to the *Prince Albert* to report the change of plan and then set off.

They camped that night in a sheltered ravine. Bellot slept uneasily, worrying over his decision and musing about his odd situation. He couldn't help smiling a little at the contrasts that had distinguished his brief career. Here he was, many thousands of miles from his native land, commanding men of a foreign nation, a French commissioned officer among men bound solely by civil engagement. A Catholic, he was doing his best to keep alive in their minds a different religion, the precepts of which he delivered in a tongue that was not his own. Yet he was comforted by his awareness that there was not one of these men who did not regard him as a fellow countryman and was prepared to obey him as if that were really the case. The reason, Bellot recognized, was that all were united in a common crusade. He asked himself, as he tossed in his buffalo blanket, "What is there to prevent nations from forming a similar union of efforts directed towards a common end?"

The following afternoon they reached Cape Seppings near Port Leopold. In the distance, Bellot could see a tent left by James Clark Ross. The party began to fire their rifles. Through his telescope Bellot could see something black: a moving object? He dashed off ahead of his companions and was soon greeting his five missing comrades, all sporting ragged beards. Kennedy had supposed the ship had been forced out into the Atlantic and had returned to England. Unruffled, he had planned to winter at Port Leopold and continue the search for Franklin on foot, his greatest privation being the lack of a Bible. He had finished building an Eskimo sledge and was making shoes from canvas when Bellot reached him. Had the ship's party arrived a day later he would have been gone. They sat up for most of the night, swapping stories, singing songs, and drinking hot chocolate taken from James Ross's stores. The entire company was reunited aboard the *Prince Albert* on October 26.

Kennedy intended leaving on his overland journey far earlier than M'Clintock's naval crews had done the previous year; he was, after all, accustomed to overland travel in the dark of winter. His men would not haul heavy sledges; they would use dogteams and live in snow houses. Bellot asked himself why the British government had not asked the Hudson's Bay Company about the native mode of travel. "Not one of its naval expeditions," he noted, "has possessed the means of travelling by land." Bellot's approach to the Eskimos – it was Kennedy's approach, of course – differed from the official attitude that they were a poor, sad race from whom the white man could learn little. "It is impossible," he noted, "not to reflect on the question of the relative happiness enjoyed by the savages, compared with the so-called misfortunes produced by their intercourse with Europeans."

Undoubtedly Kennedy, the mixed-blood Cree, influenced Bellot in these musings. The former fur trader liked to tell the story of a Cree chief who refused to give his daughter in marriage to a Hudson's Bay officer. "My daughter to you? You do not even know how to hunt!"

But if Kennedy helped to broaden Bellot's mind on the subject of aboriginal superiority, Bellot could not budge Kennedy's belief in the literal truth of the Bible. After one sharp religious discussion that left them both in bad humour, he gave up. Bellot the liberal Catholic didn't believe in predestination any more than he believed in the Holy Ghost; to him, the only real freedom was "the omnipotence of free will." But he wasn't going to get into any more arguments.

At the beginning of January 1852, Kennedy set off on a preliminary sled trip to Fury Beach to see if Franklin had been there. He hadn't. Some of the crew had tried to get out of the journey by pleading illness, but Bellot, who was eager to prove "that a French officer will never hang back but . . . is always eager to be foremost," shamed them. The main sledge journey began on February 25, almost six weeks before M'Clintock's crews had dared to face the elements. It was one of the longest in Arctic history – 1,265 statute miles in ninety-five days compared to M'Clintock's "record" of 875 miles in eighty days. But it found no trace of Franklin.

Kennedy and Bellot described a great clockwise circle from Batty Bay, down Prince Regent Inlet, west across Somerset Island and Peel Sound to cross and recross Prince of Wales Island before sledging north to Cape Walker and then east along Barrow Strait to Port Leopold and back to the ship at Batty Bay.

But they did not go as far south as the region of the North Magnetic Pole, as Kennedy had originally planned and as Lady Franklin had ordered, perhaps because Kennedy was suffering from snow blindness and also because, in the haze of winter, both men thought they saw a land barrier blocking Peel Sound – the same mirage-like phenomenon that had bedevilled John Ross thirty-four years before. Thus they also assumed that Franklin couldn't have come that way. It would have been more profitable had Kennedy listened to Bellot, who at the outset wanted to go to the bottom of Prince Regent Inlet and talk to the Eskimos that John Ross had encountered on his trip to Boothia Felix. Bellot reasoned that if more than a hundred men were lost in the area, the Eskimos would at least have heard of it. He was right, but he deferred to Kennedy.

This three-month journey, which was abruptly ended when scurvy began to strike the party, had one positive result. They had seen a narrow gorge leading westward across Boothia from Prince Regent Inlet. Kennedy became convinced that this was not an inlet but a strait, cutting Boothia in two and separating it from Somerset Island.

This time he was right, and Bellot, who was dubious about it, was wrong. Thus they had become the first white men to stand at the northernmost point of the American continent and had also discovered another route leading to the North West Passage, though not a navigable one. Lady Franklin had urged Bellot to name some of the new features after some of his friends, a suggestion that Bellot refused, believing such honours should be reserved for the English. But now Kennedy, the most modest of explorers, insisted on naming the new strait for Bellot, and Bellot Strait it remains on the maps.

By the time the journey ended and the *Prince Albert* returned home, Joseph-René Bellot felt that he had acquitted himself well. "I was afraid on two occasions that my courage would fail," he wrote, "but, fortunately, at the critical moment I recollected my position and my character. Thanks to Heaven for it!"

He returned to France, eager to be out again, unaware that the Arctic, which had already seduced his soul, would within two years also claim his body.

3

Where *was* Robert McClure? To the Admiralty his whereabouts *The ambitions* remained a mystery. He was supposed to have entered the Arctic *of Robert* with his ship, the *Investigator*, from the west in the company of his *McClure* superior, Richard Collinson, in the *Enterprise*. Somehow the two had become separated. McClure had last been seen in August 1850 off Cape Lisburne on the northwest coast of Alaska. Collinson, arriving too late that year to follow, had turned back to Hong Kong for the winter and did not return to the search until the following August. But McClure was provisioned only until the following spring of 1852. If he were not found by then it was more than possible that he and his crew would share the fate of Franklin. The Cresswell family had every reason to be alarmed.

McClure had spent twenty-six years in the Navy. This was his first command, and he intended to make the most of it. If he could find Franklin, or discover the North West Passage – or both! – he would be the most famous man in England, as well as the richest naval officer of his day. Most of the Arctic explorers were understandably ambitious, but in McClure, ambition was more naked and less admirable. M'Clintock, for instance, liked to attack and solve a problem such as Arctic sledging for its own sake. But one gets the distinct impression that McClure was out for McClure.

He made important discoveries, but like old John Ross, he was ungenerous to the point of selfishness in his refusal to share his triumphs with others. Nonetheless, one must admire his daring. He took big chances and won, though he imperilled his crews as well as himself. He had more than his share of luck, too, and he knew how to make the most of it. But he was also unstable, subject to spasms of uncontrollable fury if the progress of his expedition – and thus his personal aspirations – was threatened.

He had waited a long time for a command of his own. Like M'Clintock, McClure came from an army, not a navy, background. Educated at Eton and Sandhurst, he joined the Navy at the comparatively late age of seventeen. His Arctic career began when he served as mate of the *Terror* during George Back's attempt to reach Repulse Bay in 1836. This disastrous expedition – he was sick for much of it – gained him no kudos. He did better in 1848, when he served as first lieutenant aboard the *Enterprise* during James Clark Ross's failed attempt to find Franklin. In January 1850, three months after Ross returned, the new expedition set off. Collinson would be the leader. McClure was rewarded with command of the sister ship.

Reserved and aloof, he was not comfortable in command. He did not have the easy confidence of a Parry or the cheerful buoyancy of a Franklin. He didn't care much for his officers, who were young, inexperienced, and in some instances incompetent and slovenly. His crew was unruly and often sullen. In his dealings with them, McClure swung to extremes. On the one hand he flogged his men unmercifully for trifling breaches of discipline – his cook, for instance, got forty-eight lashes for blasphemy and profanity (a prerogative of cooks from time immemorial). That was unusual in an Arctic commander. Collinson, not the easiest of leaders, ordered only two floggings in five years of Arctic service. On the other hand, in moments of peril or privation McClure had the ability to gather his men together and rally them with a few words.

He made little provision to while away the boredom of an Arctic winter as Parry had done; his crews were left largely to their own devices. On more than one occasion he put his fierce ambitions ahead of the safety of his people. Yet he managed to survive through four winters – from 1850 to 1854 – with a minimum of the discords that

212

marked so many other northern voyages, partly through tough discipline but also because he was able in a tight spot to rouse his men to superhuman effort.

It was not in Robert McClure's make-up to be on familiar terms with his officers. The only man with whom he might be said to have had a warm relationship was a civilian supernumerary, Johann August Miertsching, a Moravian missionary from Labrador who had been brought along because he spoke the Eskimo tongue and could act as an interpreter. With Miertsching, McClure could, in a sense, relax the formality he thought proper to his command.

The pious young evangelist – he was then thirty-two – was a favourite with all hands, strong, cheerful, and never out of sorts, probably because he had long been accustomed to exacting conditions in Labrador. Unlike the British sailors, dressed in their customary wool, the more practical missionary wore Eskimo clothing.

Miertsching got on well with McClure, but he was not blind to his flaws. It is his account of four winters spent with the *Investigator*'s crew that provides a more rounded picture of the commander than McClure's own journals, sandpapered, adapted, and rewritten by the uncritical Sherard Osborn (he of the purple phrases), or the sour memoirs of Alexander Armstrong, the ship's doctor, who did not care for his commander.

After they reached the Straits of Magellan, it became obvious that the two ships could not stay together in the mist and fog, nor did they need to until they took to the ice. Collinson accordingly set a rendezvous point at Cape Lisburne off Alaska. McClure was on his own until then, his first port of call being Honolulu.

The voyage to Honolulu in these early months of 1850 was not a happy one. Miertsching noted that "a devil of discord seems to have fixed his abode amongst us." The young German had not experienced life aboard a man-of-war before and was shocked by the impiety of the brawling crew. "I have met insolent and Godless men, yet were they angels compared to these brazen sinners," he wrote. "I feel as if my lot had been cast among half a hundred devils. The harsh rules of naval discipline are barely enough to keep them under control."

The California gold rush was then at its height. Ships loaded with adventurers were racing for the West Coast. But the *Investigator*, having rounded Cape Horn, was heading directly for Hawaii. The weather was dreadful. Seventeen of the crew were ill. And then, on

May 15, 1850, the ship was almost lost because of the negligence of the officer of the watch, McClure's first officer, William Haswell.

Haswell had left the deck for a few minutes and in that brief time a squall struck the *Investigator* a dreadful blow, smashing all three masts. "The fury of the captain was terrible, positively inhuman," Miertsching wrote. He kept out of the way on that and the following day, "the most unpleasant that I have yet experienced on board." Haswell was placed under arrest, guarded in his cabin by two armed marines. Then McClure's anger subsided as quickly as it had risen.

When the missionary himself fell ill, McClure took him into his own cabin and poured out his apologies. He seemed to regret the fact "that he had so forgotten himself on that day and had not handled the affair as a sincere Christian should have done." But then, Robert McClure had none of Parry's religious passion, or Franklin's. In one of his long discussions with Miertsching, he declared that no one at sea could hold to the form of Christianity as it was observed on land.

"At sea," he explained, "a man must have spirit and not hang his head." The missionary, he declared, was not yet a true seaman. McClure said he'd known one naval officer who had tried to practise "land Christianity" aboard a man-of-war. "He learned by experience that it did not serve on board a ship; so he gave up the sea, and became a parson and writes tracts for old wives."

McClure was amused by Miertsching's practice of handing out gospel leaflets to the crew. He'd do better, the commander said, giving them to "lost women," who would receive them with more thanks than his sailors did. But the Arctic would shake McClure out of his cynicism, as it shook so many others.

When the *Investigator* reached Honolulu harbour on July 1, 1850, McClure discovered to his alarm that Collinson, having waited four days, had set sail the previous morning for Bering Strait. If McClure didn't catch him, so he was told, Collinson planned to take to the ice at once; the supply ship *Plover*, which had been anchored in the strait since 1849, would act as his consort. That was too much. Was McClure to be denied his chance at fame and fortune? He had planned to get rid of some of his officers in Honolulu, especially Haswell, who was still under arrest. But now every hour counted. He was persuaded by the officers of two Royal Navy vessels in the harbour to change his mind after Haswell made a suitable apology. McClure was reluctant to do that, but there was little time to argue.

He was in a frenzy to be off, working around the clock to provision

214

his ship and then to round up those crew members who had indulged too freely on their shore leave and were lodged in jail. McClure paid their fines but found them unfit for duty. Two weeks later Miertsching noted that several were still on the sick list, not yet recovered from "the frightful excesses in Honolulu." Two, in fact, took another month to recover, a tribute of sorts to the robust life on what were then known as the Sandwich Islands.

The *Investigator* left port at six in the evening of July 4. McClure, who offered the missionary a celebratory glass of wine, "showed a composure which was forced." He had decided upon a daring but dangerous gamble not just to catch up with Collinson, but also to beat him to the rendezvous point at Cape Lisburne, north of Kotzebue Sound – and then, if possible, to get ahead of him in what now appeared to be a race for the western Arctic.

The expedition's orders were to swing round the outer islands of the Aleutian chain in a western sweep that would take it close to the Kamchatka Peninsula of Asia. That was Collinson's route. But McClure proposed instead to sail directly north and cut through the fog-bound and uncharted Aleutian archipelago at its eastern end. In spite of thick mists, violent tides, shoals, and reefs, he managed it. The *Investigator* entered Kotzebue Sound on July 29, in half the time the trip round the Aleutians would have taken.

Anchored in the sound at the northern limits of Bering Strait was the depot ship *Plover*. There was no sign of Collinson. McClure sailed on toward his rendezvous point at Cape Lisburne. En route, he was hailed by another Royal Navy vessel, the frigate *Herald*, commanded by Captain Henry Kellett, a genial Tipperary Irishman whose surveys of the Central American coastline had for three summers been interrupted by the Franklin search. Kellett's current task was to keep the *Plover* supplied.

Now McClure engaged in a deception that fooled nobody, certainly not the perceptive and experienced Kellett, who came aboard to discuss plans. McClure pretended to believe that Collinson in the *Enterprise* was ahead of him. That was manifestly impossible because Collinson had not taken McClure's short cut through the Aleutians. Kellett knew this. He himself, in a much faster ship, had taken fifty days to reach this spot from the Sandwich Islands. Collinson, who had followed Kellett's advice to take the long way round, was at this point still only thirty days out of Honolulu.

McClure was proposing to enter the Arctic unaccompanied, which the Royal Navy considered too dangerous to allow. The orders had been unequivocal: the two ships were to stick together. McClure ignored this, using the fiction that he was actually trying to follow the Navy's instructions and catch up to his superior.

Kellett, as post captain, outranked him and could have stopped him. He tried everything short of a direct order to hold him back. McClure kept up the pretence, even to the point of hanging on to some personal mail for Collinson, which he said he would deliver when they met. Kellett later urged him by signal to wait at least forty-eight hours. McClure signalled back: "Important service. Cannot on my own responsibility." In short, he dared his senior to halt him by direct order. This Kellett declined to do. The Admiralty hadn't counted on such an impasse; there were no specific instructions as to what should be done if the ships failed to rendezvous off Alaska. So Kellett let McClure go.

Away he went, into the grinding confusion of the pack. A tongue of ice, solid as granite, blocked their way. With a strong following breeze blowing, McClure ordered every shred of canvas up and then boldly turned the ship's prow toward the very centre of the obstacle. The *Investigator* shuddered to a near standstill, the masts trembling so violently they seemed about to shake the ship to pieces. Then, suddenly, the ice split under the impact and they were through into open water.

It required forty men in five boats to tow the *Investigator* around Point Barrow, an exhausting haul. Now they entered uncharted waters. Soon McClure could see the permanent polar pack ninety miles to the north, a stupendous, glittering wall of white, the growth of ages. He had never seen anything like it in Baffin Bay or in the straits of the eastern Arctic.

By fits and starts, by luck and happenstance, sometimes beset, sometimes frustrated by blind channels, the *Investigator* groped her way along the northern coast of Alaska and then past the Mackenzie delta, seeking Banks Land, the distant mass spotted years before by Parry. All along the route they encountered Eskimos, many of whom had never before seen a white man. Like their predecessors, McClure and his officers were worried about the natives' immortal souls and their lack of civilization. The commander who had dismissed the idea of Christianity aboard ship wrote in his journal: "Would that some practically Christian body . . . could send a few of their brethren amongst the tribes . . . to carry to them the arts and advantages of

216

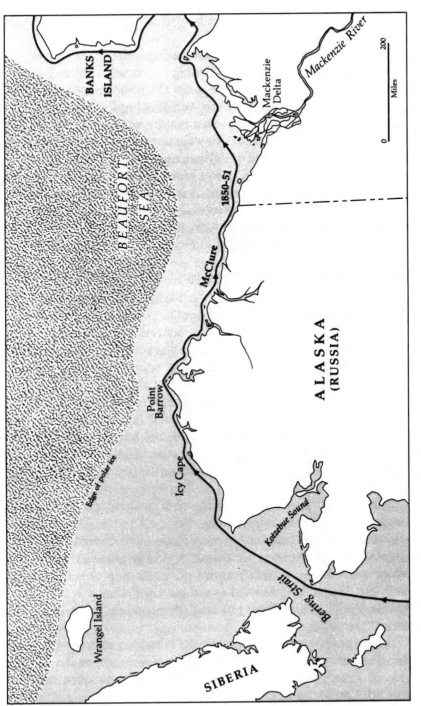

McClure rounds the tip of Alaska, 1850

civilized life, and trust to God, in his own good time, showing them the way of eternal life."

Dr. Armstrong thought the Eskimos "the most filthy race on the face of the globe . . . thieving, cunning . . . treacherous and deceitful. . . ." He trusted that "the day is not far distant when the light of civilization will dawn on this poor, benighted but intelligent race of human beings." Like so many other naval men, Armstrong thought it deplorable that the Hudson's Bay Company had made no effort to remove them from "a state of heathen darkness."

Equally bewildered, the Eskimos were convinced that the ship had been carved out of a single enormous tree and asked where such trees grew. Since community property was part of their way of life, they thought nothing of pilfering any object they wanted. One enterprising man even went so far as to slip his hand into McClure's pocket, and a woman tried to conceal a large anvil by hiding it under her, like a hen sitting on an egg. This misunderstanding of the natives' views confirmed the British belief that the Eskimos were an immoral lot desperately in need of divine guidance.

The natives at Cape Bathurst were enchanted by Miertsching, who spoke their language, wore their dress, and told them wonderful and exciting tales about a great good Spirit who had created the sun, moon, stars, rocks, and water. They accepted it all with amazement and wonder. They had their own concept of Heaven and Hell – remarkably like the Christian one – a good land with a good spirit who looked after the animals so that they did not disappear from the land, and a bad land with a bad spirit who did great harm. They believed that each person who died would be sent to the destination he had earned in life.

Miertsching, who was beginning to love these simple, cheerful people, was reluctant to leave them. Their chief pleaded with him to stay and tell them more of his marvellous stories, even offering his sixteen-year-old daughter as a lure. A throng followed him to the beach where fifteen kayaks paddled off to the ship to bid him farewell. But Miertsching worried too about the Eskimos' souls. "Why has the Lord banished these folk here where no missionary can reach them?" he wondered.

As the *Investigator* sailed slowly east between gathering masses of ice, the land on its starboard bow began to rise until, on the western side of Franklin Bay, the mainland cliffs soared to seven hundred feet. McClure tried to continue, but the ice blocked him and he was shouldered northward in a zigzag course toward a lofty, mountainous land of dizzy scarps backed by two-thousand-foot peaks. Here, on August 7, under a towering promontory that he named Lord Nelson Head, he planted a flag and took possession of the territory, naming his discovery Baring Land, after the first lord of the Admiralty. He did not yet know that he had landed on Banks Land – actually Banks Island – which he had been trying to reach ever since leaving Point Barrow.

Like every other successful explorer in the frozen seas, McClure had luck on his side. Caught in the grip of the moving ice, unable to round the southern shore of the new land, no longer master of his own fortunes, he found himself driven steadily northward up a narrow channel that followed the eastern shore of Baring (or Banks) Land. Was this a bay, a dead end? If it was a strait, he could scarcely bring himself to contemplate the possibilities – which included the discovery of the North West Passage.

On September 9 he was only sixty miles from the western stretch of Barrow Strait (actually Viscount Melville Sound) – only another sixty miles from territory already explored, the final gap to connect the East and the West.

"I cannot describe my anxious feelings," he wrote. "Can it be possible that this water communicates with Barrow's Strait, and shall be the long sought North west Passage? Can it be that so humble a creature as I am will be permitted to perform what has baffled the talented and wise for hundreds of years!" He was aware that Providence was on his side: ". . . all praise be ascribed unto Him who hath conducted us so far in safety." Of John Franklin there was no mention.

Then, on September 17, young ice frustrated his passage. He had come as far as possible that season. Should he try to find an anchorage farther south in some sheltered bay or should he allow his ship to become frozen into the pack? The next day he sent his ice mate aloft. From the crow's-nest the lookout could see for twenty miles. In the distance the land veered off to the northeast and northwest, leaving a clear expanse of water beyond. There could be no uncertainty now. Barrow Strait lay dead ahead and beyond that Melville Island, which Parry had reached thirty years before. The last link in the Passage was in sight.

McClure was determined to stay in the pack ice. It was dangerous; but he had not come this far to turn back, and he had no intention of

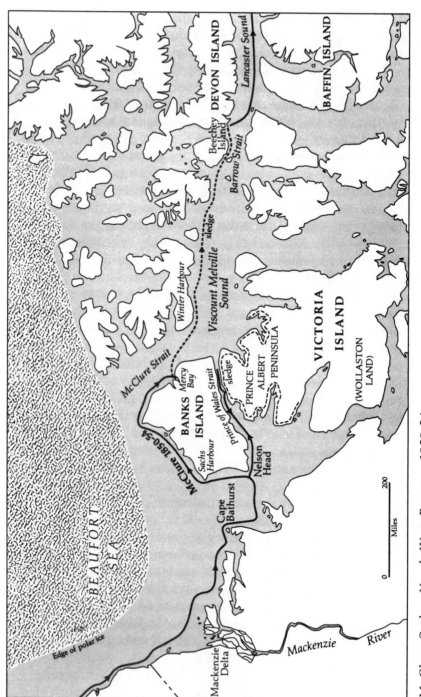

McClure finds a North West Passage, 1850-54

relinquishing the ground gained. He reckoned on being trapped in the ice; instead, he was caught in the moving pack. A dreadful gale, blowing down the channel, forced the ice south and with it his ship, anchored to a vast floe. Like an unhorsed rider in a cattle stampede, McClure was helpless. The *Investigator* was borne remorselessly back the way she had come. For more than a week she was in daily peril. Swept thirty miles south, she was whirled about and once again forced north, in danger of being crushed against the cliffs of the newly discovered Princess Royal Islands in the middle of the channel.

On September 26, McClure prepared to abandon ship. A year's provisions were stacked on deck, ready to be thrown into the boats if the *Investigator* went down. The men stood by with bundles of warm clothes, their pockets stuffed with ammunition and biscuit, prepared if necessary to leap from the foundering ship and try to struggle to shore across the grinding pack.

The following night was worse – a seventeen-hour vigil in which huge bergs, three times as big as the ship, crashed against its sides until the oakum squeezed from the distended seams. Unable to flee, convinced they were doomed, the crew abandoned all discipline, broke open casks of liquor on deck, and soon became roaring drunk. As the ship was flung over broadside, an enormous heap of crushed ice threatened to bury her and all the sixty-six men aboard. Then, miraculously, the commotion died and the ship righted herself. The bitter cold had bound the rampaging ice into a solid, unmoving sheet.

Exhausted and limp, shocked into silence, the drenched and inebriated sailors tried to snatch some rest. So great had been the pressure that nine-inch hawsers had snapped like threads, tearing all six ice anchors away.

With the storm over and two feet of water pumped out of the hold, McClure, who had scarcely spoken a word since the turmoil, mustered his crew and coldly read out the Articles of War regarding ship's discipline. He followed this with a savage tongue-lashing in which he called them a band of thieves, unworthy of the name of Englishmen. He was ashamed, he said, that such a rabble should walk the decks of a British ship. He promised that those who had opened the casks of liquor would be punished. Then he relented and reminded his men of the miracle that had saved them. Human strength had been ineffective; almighty Providence had preserved them from certain death. His words brought tears to the eyes of the most hardened seamen, who cheered their captain and promised to mend their ways.

The terrible trial that all had gone through had sobered both the men and the officers, and McClure was now the commander of a happier ship. He himself took to reading the Bible, morning and night. As Miertsching put it, "he seems now to realize that he is not the good exemplary Christian which he used to think himself."

4

The Passage It was now October 1850. In a radius of five hundred miles to the
at last northeast, eight British ships were frozen into the ice of Barrow Strait and two American vessels were caught in the moving pack in Wellington Channel, but McClure had no way of knowing that. With the *Investigator* sealed, covered, and protected by a vast wall of ice, he turned his attention again to the North West Passage.

He *must* be sure that the water his lookout had seen in the distance actually was a continuation of Barrow Strait. On October 10, he led a sledge party across the ice to the land on the east side of the channel. He named it Prince Albert Land, but actually it was a peninsula of the vast Victoria Island. With Dr. Armstrong and a few companions he struggled up a fifteen-hundred-foot mountain, panting from the unaccustomed exercise, and from that vantage point saw in the distance the termination of the ice-packed channel, which he had named Prince of Wales Strait. Armstrong was convinced that "the highway to England from ocean to ocean lay before us," but that wasn't good enough for McClure. Nothing would do but that he himself set foot on the shore of the Passage.

Eleven days later he led a sledge party on an exhausting five-day journey along the eastern shore of Banks Island to the end of the channel. There, at dawn on October 26, 1850, a fine, cloudless day, Robert McClure, standing on a six-hundred-foot promontory, confirmed the presence of a water route from Atlantic to Pacific. "Thank God!" a crew member muttered, as the copper sunrise brightened to reveal the land ahead curving off to the north toward the strait that would be named for McClure and to the southeast toward Melville Sound.

It did not matter that Prince of Wales Strait was blocked and that

222

no ship was ever likely to force its way through the ice stream by this route. It did not matter that they had seen the Passage from afar but had not conquered it. McClure knew now that his name would go down in the history books as the man who had made the greatest maritime discovery of the age. It was as well that he didn't know that some of Franklin's men had found another North West Passage two years earlier and that sentiment would favour the dead explorer. Nobody could take away from Robert McClure this moment of triumph.

The discovery brought a surge of patriotic emotion to the heart of the often captious Dr. Armstrong. He confessed to "an indescribable feeling of pride and pleasure" at the thought that "the maritime greatness and glory of our country were still further elevated above all nations of the earth; the solution of this great enigma leaving nothing undone to confirm Great Britain's Queen – Empress of the Sea. . . ."

McClure arrived back at the ship on October 31, thin and exhausted, having rushed on ahead of his crew, lost his way, and wandered about without sleep for the whole of one freezing Arctic night. By the time he found the *Investigator* and was taken aboard, unable to speak, his limbs stiff with cold, he looked more like a corpse than a living human being.

Two days later he made a formal announcement of his discovery to the ship's crew, who would share in the reward, and told them that he hoped they would be home with their families the following year. They cheered him for that: three hearty cheers for the Queen, three more for the discovery of the Passage, three for their commander, three for the rest of the officers, three for sweethearts and wives, and a tiger, after which there was grog for all and extra bread and meat for supper.

McClure, in victory, was uncharacteristically humble. He surprised his second officer, Samuel Gurney Cresswell, a gifted watercolourist, by declaring that "the world may speak of me or the ship as having done this but a higher power than me has directed us." Cresswell, whose father, a close friend of Parry, would soon force a new search for the *Investigator*, didn't expect such modesty, though, as he later remarked, the voyage "ought to make anyone a wiser and a better man." But the sledge journey, together with the excitement of the discovery, had exhausted the captain, who was not a robust man. For the next month he was confined to his cot.

He had not entirely forgotten the main object of the expedition – the search for Franklin. He dispatched three ambitious sledge journeys the following spring. These would have the dual purpose of solving several geographical puzzles while maintaining the hunt for the lost ships. Was Wollaston Land part of the newly discovered Prince Albert Land? Was Banks Land insular or was it part of Melville Island?

The hundred-odd sledgers didn't get away until April 1851. They lacked the enthusiasm of M'Clintock's crews, who, unknown to them, were fanning out over the islands and channels to the east and north. The *Investigator* lay not in a sheltered harbour but in a perilous position in the middle of the newly discovered Prince of Wales Strait, and most of the men who left her thought themselves doomed, for they did not expect to find her in one piece when they returned. McClure himself expected a terrible upheaval when the ice broke up. He had prepared for that by placing a depot on one of the Princess Royal Islands containing three months' provisions in case the ship should be crushed. If that happened, he hoped they might be able to reach the Mackenzie delta by small boat or sledge and then travel up the river to the nearest trading post. It was a long shot at best.

With the threat of shipwreck hanging over the parties, the tensions that had abated the previous fall now returned. Robert Wynniatt, whose sledge party was ordered to follow the south shore of Melville Sound toward Cape Walker, broke his chronometer a week after his departure. He used that as an excuse to return to the ship, prodded, perhaps, by his reluctant crew. McClure, who thought he'd come back with word of Franklin, flew into a rage, turned him about, and sent him off again without a new instrument – an absurd and senseless act.

Lieutenant Cresswell's party, sent to explore the northeast coast of Banks Land, also came back a week early. Two of the men were suffering badly from frostbite, and another had to have part of his foot amputated. Those of the party who weren't disabled were sent out again after only two days' rest to chart the south shore of Banks, another harsh decision by McClure, who was bitterly grieved that none of the three parties had managed either to find Franklin or to fulfil their secondary assignments. He would undoubtedly have been even angrier had he known that Wynniatt's party was, at one point, no more than sixty miles from one of M'Clintock's questing sledges.

The one journey that might have been providential was not undertaken. Parry's Winter Harbour, on Melville Island, was only a hundred miles away. Dr. Armstrong felt it was derelict of McClure not to leave a message giving his position there, as it was more than likely that somebody would find it. In fact, M'Clintock did visit it, seeking just such a message, and found nothing. McClure's neglect doomed him to spend three more winters in the Arctic.

McClure had one slim hope of salvaging something from the three sledge journeys. One hundred miles south on the shores of Prince Albert Land, the party under Lieutenant Haswell had discovered a new band of Eskimos. McClure determined to seek them out: perhaps they could tell him something about Franklin's lost expedition or at least help to fill in the geographical gaps. He took Miertsching and six men and, setting a cracking pace, in just four days reached the tents of the natives on June 2.

Here, to his astonishment, an Eskimo woman drew an almost perfect chart of the area on the paper he supplied, showing the coastline of North America (which none of the natives had ever visited) and filling up blanks on the existing maps, making it clear that Wollaston Land was not an island but a peninsula on the southwest coast of Victoria Land. Of Franklin, however, there was no word.

The Eskimos were astonished to learn from Miertsching that there were other lands inhabited by human beings. McClure was much taken with them, for he found them both amiable and intelligent. Their simple habits brought out in him an unexpected tenderness, and when it came time to depart, Miertsching noted that "the captain was so grieved at leaving these loving people helpless in this frightful region of ice that he could not refrain from tears."

A touching little scene was then enacted. In an impetuous gesture, McClure took off his thick red shawl and wound it round the neck of a young Eskimo woman who was standing nearby with a child on her back. She was startled and embarrassed because the idea of unreciprocated gift-giving was foreign to these Eskimos; it was part of their code always to offer something of equal value in return, and she had nothing to give him. To his great discomfiture she took the baby out from under her hood, covered it with kisses, and in a remarkable gesture, offered it to McClure in exchange. Miertsching had difficulty explaining that his captain was not proposing a barter. At last she understood and, laughing, accepted the shawl, which till then she had refused to touch. What animal was it that had a red skin? she asked. But there was no time to explain. One of McClure's men was suffering badly from frostbite and he wanted to get back to the ship.

Six weeks later, on July 14, the ice in Prince of Wales Strait broke up without incident. McClure started back north, hoping to skip through the North West Passage and thus complete his circumnavigation of the Americas. It was not possible. The same ice stream that had frustrated Parry blocked his way. On August 16 he made a sudden decision, to turn about, sail south again and then west to try to circle Baring (or Banks) Land. If it *was* an island, he could enter waters connected to Barrow Strait (this portion would shortly be named for him) from the far side and still make his way through the Passage.

It was another daring decision, some would say a foolhardy gamble. The season was late. He knew nothing of the fogbound, ice-choked channels he was proposing to enter. He was chancing an encounter with "the frightful polar pack," as Miertsching correctly termed it. He was risking his ship and the lives of his crew. Having discovered the Passage and vainly scoured the western Arctic for John Franklin, it would have been prudent to have returned the way he had come. Yet McClure was a man obsessed. He had seen the Passage, but he had not sailed through it. He didn't want half the glory; he wanted it all.

To his astonishment, the channel to the south was free of ice. He sped down it in a single day, rounded Nelson Head with a fresh breeze spurring him on, and by August 18 had covered three hundred miles without a check. The white world had come alive. Polar bears lumbered over the shore ice. Caribou pounded across the barren slopes. Seals basked in the sunshine. Geese, wild swans, and ducks rose in flocks from the water. At a landing on the southwest corner of Banks Land (Sachs Harbour), he left a note in a cairn for his erstwhile commander, Richard Collinson, who found it three weeks later. Collinson had already found an earlier note that McClure had left in the cache on one of the Princess Royal Islands near the entrance to Prince of Wales Strait.

McClure's luck continued to hold. He rounded the southwest cape of Banks Land and scudded north at speeds as high as seven knots. For a day he travelled up a broad lane of water created by the polar pack on his left and the island on his right. Then the lane began to narrow; the land became precipitous; the pack drew closer until it seemed as if he were in a kind of canyon with the crystalline scarps of

226

ancient ice rising a hundred feet out of the sea on one side and the dizzier cliffs of sedimentary rock towering above him on the other. Soon the *Investigator* was so close to land that her boats had to be hauled up to prevent them from smashing against the serried rock walls on her starboard bow. By the time the ship stood off the cape that McClure named for Prince Alfred, the channel was no more than two hundred feet wide. The crews took to the boats and towed the ship past the promontory, blasting the projecting crags with black powder.

On August 20, with the ice pressing down from the northwest, the ship came to a halt. Shore parties, taking advantage of the lull, explored the barren headland and came upon an astonishing spectacle: masses of petrified trees lay piled up on the hills and in the gorges, some of them with trunks ten inches thick. Here was evidence that this frozen land had once been a temperate realm of thick forests and smiling meadows.

That discovery was scarcely made before the Arctic returned to the attack with all its fury. Once again, the men were ordered on deck with bundles of belongings, ready to leave at any instant, while the high spring tide and the west wind hurled masses of ice down upon the ship, throwing her broadside against the floe to which she was anchored. Beams cracked. Doors sprang open. "This is the end!" McClure cried out, "the ship is breaking up; in five minutes she will be sunk!" He was about to cut the cables when another miracle occurred. The ice suddenly became motionless, and the catastrophe was averted.

By now McClure was convinced that a Higher Power was shielding him, that no lives would be lost, that all would return safely to their homes. His pale and trembling followers were clinging to the bulwarks, too shaken to speak. He mustered them and promised that he would bring them to a safe winter harbour and would do his best to make life pleasant for them.

He was, apparently, a changed man, all the daring, all the gambling spirit sucked out of him by this last encounter with the elements. Before many days had passed the *Investigator* entered the main channel northeast of Banks Island that would later be called McClure Strait. Melville Island lay on the port side. Barrow Strait and Lancaster Sound lay ahead. For most of September the expedition moved southeastward, hugging the coast of Banks Island, a forbidding shore without a bay or a harbour that might offer shelter or protection – a passage, in Armstrong's words, that "should never be again attempted; and . . . I feel convinced . . . will never be made again."

At last the *Investigator* reached a large bay, which McClure chose as his winter harbour. He named it Mercy Bay, causing the astringent doctor to remark later that "some of us not inappropriately said it ought to have been so called, from the fact it would have been a *mercy had we never entered it*." For the bay was a cul-de-sac in which the crew would be confined for the next two years and from which the ship itself would never be freed.

The critical Dr. Armstrong felt, as did some of the others, that McClure should have taken his chances and gone on to Parry's Winter Harbour or even to a berth farther east, thus completing the transit of the North West Passage. It's more than possible that he might have accomplished that feat. A few days later, his sailing master, Stephen Court, found open water as far as the eye could see beyond Point Back, a promontory seven miles distant that had an unobstructed view of the channel.

What had happened to the daring captain, who once gambled on a fast shortcut through the Aleutians and a perilous dash past the Arctic pack off Banks Island? Was it a failure of nerve, as some would later say? Perhaps; but if so it was understandable. McClure and his crew had come through a frightful experience. Providence had smiled three times on them. It was late in the season – September 23, a full week later than the date in 1850 when the American ships off Wellington Channel to the east had become "glued up" by the ice, to use Elisha Kane's phrase. For once, McClure put the safety of his ship and the ship's company ahead of his personal ambitions. He could not know that this latest decision would come close to being the death of all of them.

5

Mercy Bay *October 1851.* Only three search ships remained in the Arctic. McClure in the *Investigator* was frozen in at Mercy Bay. Unknown to him, Collinson in the *Enterprise* was anchored off Victoria Land on the eastern shore of Prince of Wales Strait. Five hundred miles to the east, Bellot and Kennedy, having just been reunited, were snug aboard Lady Franklin's little *Prince Albert* at Batty Bay in Prince Regent Inlet. Austin's unproductive expedition had returned to England that same month. Press and public were urging the Admiralty to try again. Lieutenant Cresswell's father was demanding an additional search for the *Investigator*, and with good reason.

It was not an easy winter for Robert McClure and his men. In his haste to find a secluded harbour, McClure had chosen a trap – and he soon realized it. Suspecting that the ice in that sheltered backwater might not melt the following summer, he reduced rations. Dr. Armstrong insisted the diet wasn't enough to keep the crew healthy; by April 1852, the men were losing flesh at an alarming rate. But McClure stuck to his quota. When three half-starved men stole some meat, he had them flogged.

That April, when Sir Edward Belcher's five-ship squadron was setting out from England and while Kennedy and Bellot were completing their own luckless three-month search, McClure set off on a quest of his own. Travelling by sledge across the rough pack of the strait, he started for Parry's Winter Harbour on Melville Island – a journey that could have been made and should have been made the previous year. There, on the summit of Parry's sandstone block, he found a flat tin case containing M'Clintock's message and saw, to his dismay, that it had been left there the previous June.

Now, as he realized the depth of his negligence and the seriousness of his position, Robert McClure sat down and wept like a child. Austin's expedition, he realized, must have gone home. By now his would-be rescuers were all back in England. Everything he had worked for, the triumphs he had achieved, the charting of new lands as well as the crowning discovery of them all – the Passage – were as dust. There was little hope of succour; he would not live to bask in his success.

By the time he returned in May, scurvy was making insidious inroads among his crew. By July, sixteen men were ill with it. Dr. Armstrong urged a more liberal diet to help the sufferers regain their strength, but McClure, with his mind agitated by the prospect of another winter in Mercy Bay, turned him down. Freshly killed musk-oxen and a quantity of wild sorrel helped to stall the disease, but they were not enough to stop the hunger. One desperate man stole a loaf of bread, fresh from the oven, in spite of the sure knowledge that retribution would be swift. He received three dozen strokes of the cat on his bare back.

McClure meant to stretch out his provisions as long as possible because it became clear, as August arrived, that Mercy Bay would remain ice locked. The bay was shaped like a funnel, fifteen miles deep and seven miles broad at the entrance, where shoals caught the ice to form a barrier. The previous September the portals of this cul-de-sac had been free of ice. But the season of 1852 was a backward one. By August 27 the young ice was strong enough to allow the crews to skate to the shore.

Once again the land turned white. The men had nothing to occupy them – McClure was no Parry. One, Mark Bradbury, was clearly going mad. McClure gloomily climbed a nearby mountain to gaze out over the unbroken ice of the bay. He kept up a cheerful attitude in front of his company, but Miertsching could hear him praying and sighing alone in his cabin.

On September 9, he assembled his crew and told them what they had already sensed: they were stuck for another winter. He put the best face on it he could, promising that all would return safely home, but then he was forced to reveal that the half-rations they had been existing on for the past year would be cut back again. He himself had turned over his private stock of food for the use of all.

They were down now to one meal a day. Most ate their ration of half a pound of salt meat raw because it shrank so much in the cooking. In October, a delegation pleaded with the captain for an increase; the men were so hungry, they said, they couldn't sleep. Again, McClure refused. Sub-lieutenant Robert Wynniatt went mad, like Bradbury. And so the year ended in despondency, each man thirty-five pounds lighter and twenty now ill with scurvy.

As the winter of 1852-53 dragged on, the health of the men grew worse. The two mental cases howled all night, contributing to the pall of gloom. At one point the demented Wynniatt tried to kill his captain. A sailor coming on board stiff with cold fell and broke his leg. By the end of January, a clerk, Joseph Paine, and one of the mates, Herbert Sainsbury, were close to death.

The ship itself seemed to echo the sufferings of the men, the bolts and fastenings cracking in the -60^0 cold. Miertsching noted that the doctor's reports had reduced McClure to despair. "How it must affect our captain," he wrote, ". . . when he sees his once-strong, rugged and hearty crew wasted away and scarcely with the strength to hold themselves upright."

On March 2, McClure announced that he would put into opera-

230

tion a plan he had concocted the previous fall. Twenty of the strongest men would stay with the ship. Those who could not last another winter would attempt to reach civilization. One party would head for the depot and boat that he had cached at Princess Royal Island in Prince of Wales Strait. Thus supplied, it would try to reach the Mackenzie River. Another would travel to Port Leopold, where James Clark Ross had cached a boat, and attempt to reach the whaling grounds in Baffin Bay.

It was a reckless scheme, born of desperation. McClure was, in effect, sending the sick to their deaths. As Armstrong observed, there was no hope that in their weakened condition they could survive such arduous and lengthy journeys. Sixteen were hospitalized; the demented Wynniatt couldn't be made to understand that he was to leave the ship; Bradbury "must be handled like an idiot child."

Even healthy men in the prime of condition would be hard put to make those long journeys. On the other hand, McClure felt he had to take some action. If the forty weakest stayed, they would surely perish with the others. At least there was a chance that the twenty who remained might come through; for one thing, there would be fewer men to divide the provisions. And – such is the human condition – those detailed to leave expressed their delight at the prospect, while those who were chosen to stay with the ship were bitterly disappointed. It does not seem to have occurred to McClure that if by some miracle the ship was saved and he returned to England with the survivors, having abandoned the sick, he would never be able to raise his head again in civilized company.

On April 5, with the sledges ready and a slim store of provisions packed for the journeys, John Boyle, one of the men designated to leave, died of scurvy. McClure immediately called all hands to the quarterdeck and delivered another of those eloquent, morale-building addresses that seemed to rally his crew. He told them to be true to themselves and to the service, not to despair but to look forward to the future with determination, and to bear all vicissitudes with the fortitude of British seamen. In the gloomiest hour, he declared, relief might come.

The following day, he and Haswell walked the ice with Miertsching, discussing the problems of digging a grave for Boyle in the granite-hard ground and the slim possibilities of future survival.

"Sir," said McClure, addressing the missionary, "if next year in Europe you neither see nor hear of me, then you may be sure that

Captain McClure, along with his crew, has perished and lies unburied but wrapped in the fur coat which you gave me, enjoying a long and tranquil sleep until awakened on the Day of Resurrection by the Redeemer in Whom is all my hope and trust. . .”

At that point, the commander was interrupted by one of the seamen, who rushed up to announce that something black was moving on the heavy ice to the seaward – a muskox, perhaps.

But it was not a muskox. A second seaman came running up. “They are men,” he cried. “First a man, then a sledge with men.”

Apart from their fellows, they had not seen another human being for twenty-one months. Were these Eskimos, then? McClure and his companions held their breaths as one of the strangers drew nearer, his face, like an Eskimo’s, “as black as old Nick.”

“In the name of God,” cried McClure, “who are you?”

The stranger stepped forward and uttered a sentence that ran through them all like an electric shock.

“I am Lieutenant Pim, late of the *Herald*, now of the *Resolute*. Captain Kellett is with her at Dealy Island.”

This announcement must have momentarily confused McClure, for he had last encountered Kellett aboard the *Herald* in Kotzebue Sound. It did not matter, for one thing was clear. The miracle he had not dared to hope for had come to pass; the relief that he had promised his crew was at hand. Once again in his darkest hour, Providence had smiled on Robert John Le Mesurier McClure.

Chapter Six

Elisha Kent Kane

Margaret Fox

Belcher's ships in winter quarters

The year 1853 opened without a hint of Franklin's whereabouts. *The spirit* After more than seven years the unsolved mystery continued to tan- *rappers* talize the public, vying for space in the newspapers and illustrated periodicals with more recent events. France had a new emperor, Napoleon III. A steamship, the *Pacific*, had set a new Atlantic record from New York to Liverpool in just ten days. A sensational new novel, *Uncle Tom's Cabin*, was the talk of New York and London. The Duke of Wellington was dead at eighty-three; and Jane Franklin's old beau, Peter Mark Roget, had just published his *Thesaurus*, at seventy-two.

Jane Franklin, in her sixtieth year, was very much alive and as determined as ever to find her lost husband, in spite of two more setbacks. Both of her ships had returned to England with no news. Kennedy and Bellot had come back the previous October in the *Prince Albert*, eager to set out again. Bellot, who was back in France and newly promoted, was doing his best to persuade his government to join in the search. Commander Edward Inglefield had returned a month later in the *Isabel*, having probed the northern reaches of Baffin Bay without success.

Inglefield had wangled a leave of absence from the Navy in order to take the *Isabel* north. He was Lady Franklin's devoted admirer, a member of that dwindling congregation who remained convinced her husband was alive. An attractive, darkly handsome young man, Inglefield had considerable common sense and interests that ranged beyond the narrow confines of the quarterdeck. He was an inventor (the Inglefield anchor), a collector of old glass, an able watercolourist, and an active gardener. Aware of the smouldering discontent that could threaten any Arctic voyage, he had decided to dine at the same time as his crew and eat exactly the same food, bringing no extra delicacies for his officers' mess. Though he found no trace of Franklin, his discoveries on that brief summer voyage in 1852 were among the most significant made during the great search.

He quickly disposed of the tale of murder by the natives told by John Ross's interpreter, Adam Beck. Beck had claimed the bodies of the Franklin crew were buried beneath a cairn at North Omiak, Greenland. Inglefield took it apart and found only animal bones.

More important, he ventured into Smith Sound, at the head of Baffin Bay.

Inglefield was convinced he was on the threshold of the mysterious Open Polar Sea. After passing between the two glowering capes that mark the sound's entrance, he could see the grey waters stretching off through seven points of the compass, unobstructed by ice. He said later that "wild thoughts of getting to the Pole – of finding our way to Behring Strait – and most of all of reaching Franklin and giving him help, rushed rapidly through my brain." Before he turned back he had reached, by his own calculations, a latitude of $78^0 28' 21''$N, "one hundred and forty miles farther north than any previous navigator," a boast that ignored both Buchan and Parry, who had crossed the 80th parallel east of Greenland. The Pole was still 860 statute miles away, but Inglefield had discovered the only practical way to reach it – the "American route," as it came to be called. He named many of the landmarks, one for Lord Tennyson, the poet laureate, to gratify his wish that "there is nothing worth living for but to have one's name inscribed on the Arctic chart," and many more that would be closely associated with later explorers – Littleton Island and Cape Sabine in particular.

Then, having found no evidence of Franklin's passing, he turned south to examine Jones Sound, which also held no clue to the missing ships. He sailed into Lancaster Sound, by now the accepted highway to the western Arctic, picked up mail from Sir Edward Belcher's five-ship search party at Beechey Island, and returned to England, convinced that "nothing but the most improbable accident could have brought Sir John Franklin to these shores."

The *Illustrated London News* praised Inglefield's summer search as "a patriotic and humane act," and so it was, for he had made considerable personal sacrifice to outfit the expedition. Lady Franklin offered to sell the *Isabel* to pay his expenses, but Inglefield would have none of it. Instead, like Kennedy, he was prepared to go out again. It is a tribute to the force of Jane Franklin's personality that she inspired this kind of dedication.

By this time she had achieved near sainthood in her campaign to find her husband. She had the support of the public and the applause of the press. "Indomitable" was the adjective most often used to describe her. Because of her persistence, seven ships were frozen into the ice of the Arctic archipelago: McClure at Mercy Bay on Banks Island, Collinson at Cambridge Bay on Victoria Island, and Bel-

236

cher's five vessels in the Wellington Channel, at Beechey Island, and in Melville Sound.

That was not enough for the resolute and persevering widow. She had now passed her sixtieth year but had lost none of her energy or commitment. "We are all growing old & shattered, grey haired & half-toothless," she wrote in one of the letters she dispatched to her long-dead spouse. She still clung stubbornly to the belief that he or some of his men might still be alive. The handful of die-hards who shared this slim hope offered a variety of wistful theories. Perhaps he was living among the Eskimos in the High Arctic beyond the Wellington Channel. Perhaps he had managed to cross the polar sea to reach the coast of Siberia and was a prisoner or a guest of the aborigines. Or perhaps, as young Bellot believed, he was living on Boothia Peninsula, sustained by native hunters.

She could not give up. If the public imagination was captured by her tenacity, the officialdom of several countries must have been exasperated by her obstinacy. Her correspondence was voluminous. She wrote to everybody – long, graceful, pleading letters in a neat, minuscule hand, asking for help. She wrote to the new emperor of France. She wrote to the Tsar of Russia. She wrote again and again to the British Admiralty. She kept up her correspondence with Henry Grinnell, the New York philanthropist who had backed the first American expedition to the Arctic.

There she struck a chord. Elisha Kent Kane, the literary ship's doctor on that expedition, was determined to go north again, this time in full command of another Grinnell expedition. It was one of two obsessions to which the remarkable doctor was slave that season. The other was an extraordinary nineteen-year-old named Margaret Fox, as celebrated in her own way as Kane, the Arctic hero and popular lecturer. To some she was close to being a saint, to others a mystic, to a few the servant of the Devil, and, to a vociferous minority, a charlatan.

Margaret Fox was a medium, a "spirit rapper," who communicated, so it was said, with the souls of the dead. She wasn't just an ordinary medium. With her younger sister, Katharine, she was *the* medium, the original, copper-plated genuine article, the mould from which all future mediums were fashioned. The cult of spiritualism, with all its exotic paraphernalia, began with the Fox sisters in 1848. Before they made their startling claim, there were no such things as séances, tables that lifted, ectoplasm, voices from the void, or any of the trappings of the occult that to this day are to be found in those dark and curtained rooms where the bereaved and the curious gather hoping to hold converse with the dead.

By the time Elisha Kane discovered the Fox sisters, during their Philadelphia engagement in November 1852, spiritualism had swept the country. One million Americans believed in it. From a popular social fad it was developing into a religious movement. Famous figures of known probity – judges, senators, clerics, professionals, journalists – flocked to see the sisters perform or attended private séances to declare they were perfectly genuine. Some, like Charles Beecher Stowe (the son of Uncle Tom's creator), might call their gift "demonic," but others – the great editor Horace Greeley was one – were captivated by the "perfect integrity and good faith" of these innocent-looking children with their dark, lustrous eyes, their impassive features, and their remarkable translucent skin, which to many gave them an other-worldly look.

The efforts made to prove them fraudulent served only to enhance their appeal and their notoriety. The sisters sat at the séance tables with their hands and arms unconcealed while the spirits spelled out, in a series of sepulchral raps, the answers to questions thrown at them. It was all quite marvellous, rather like the tap-tapping of the new telegraph keys, using the code that Mr. Samuel Morse was in the process of patenting. The mixture of the scientific and the occult excited the imagination. If signals could transmit messages from the living, why not from the dead? Even when the sisters were stripped mother-naked, as they were during one investigative séance, the rappings continued.

The phenomenon was known as "the Rochester Rappings" because it had all begun at the Fox home near Rochester, New York, in 1848. The two girls – Katharine was then thirteen, Margaret sixteen – had scared their mother out of her wits when the mysterious sounds were heard, apparently out of nowhere. The two children had merely meant to tease their parent, but the impact was so startling that it got beyond control before they could reveal their secret. In fact, they did not confess it for forty years, although a few investigators caught on to it early in the game and even published their suspicions, without much effect.

It was simple enough: the two sisters had double-jointed toes, which they had learned to crack with very little effort. On this flimsy foundation was constructed the great edifice of modern spiritualism, and *that* was the work not of the two children but of Leah Fox Fisher, their older, widowed sister, who knew a good thing when she saw it and exploited both girls for most of their lives.

Elisha Kent Kane did not for an instant believe in spirit rappings. Out of sheer curiosity, he had dropped in on the sisters at the Union Hotel and, seeing Margaret – so innocent, so demure – reading by the window, thought he'd knocked on the wrong door. The contrast between his concept of a stage medium and this innocent child-woman captured the explorer's imagination, and his heart.

Margaret was to insist that Kane fell in love at first sight, and certainly that assessment accords with his known impetuosity. His letters to her, which she published after his death under the title of *The Love Life of Dr. Kane*, may have been edited or changed; there is no way of knowing. But to anyone who has read his original, unexpurgated journal (as distinct from the published version), the letters ring true. They sound like Kane: passionate, heartfelt, brooding, egotistical, and more than a little condescending:

". . . you write to me entirely as to a friend . . . I write as to a lover, overflowing with the feeling of the moment. . . ."

"Whatever may be my faults, I have at least loved you. Were you an empress, darling Maggie, instead of a little nameless girl, following an obscure and *ambiguous* profession, it would be the same. . . ."

"I am sick . . . sick with hard work, and with nobody to nurse or care for me . . . is it any wonder that I long to look – only to look – at that dear little deceitful mouth of yours; to feel your hair tumbling over my cheeks. . . ."

Kane may be the only lovesick swain in history who reversed the accepted mode of romantic entreaty and told the object of his affections that *she* was not worthy of him: "Maggie, dear, you have many traits which lift you above your calling. You are refined and lovable; and, with a different education would have been innocent and artless; but you are not worthy of a permanent regard from me. You could never lift yourself up to my thoughts. . . . Maggie, darling, don't care for me anymore. I love you too well to wish it. . . . I really am sold to different destinies . . . I have my own sad vanities to pursue. I am as devoted to my calling as you, poor child, can be to yours. Remember then, as a sort of dream, that Doctor Kane of the Arctic Seas loved Maggie Fox of the spirit rappings."

That was the problem – the spirit rappings. From the outset, Kane was convinced that Margaret was living a life of deception. All through the early months of 1853, as he planned his next assault on the Arctic, he tried to convince her to change her mode of life. They had one thing in common: they were both celebrities of the first order. Kane was mesmerizing thousands with his eloquent lectures about his Arctic odyssey, mingling with the "great men," as he told Margaret. She had given private sittings to such notables as James Fenimore Cooper, Horace Greeley, William Cullen Bryant, and George Bancroft.

"I speak for humanity and not for money," he told her during a successful lecture campaign in Boston. That wasn't entirely true, since he was raising funds for his next expedition – as much as fourteen hundred dollars for a single appearance. But "when I think of you dear darling, wasting your time and youth and conscience for a few paltry dollars and think of the crowds who come nightly to hear of the wild stories of the frozen north, I sometimes feel that we are not so far removed after all. My brain and your body are each the sources of attraction and I confess there is not so much difference."

But, of course, there were vast differences between them, in temperament, age, education, background, upbringing, and outlook. She was a placid, untutored teenager, one of six children from the poverty-stricken family of an alcoholic. She didn't really comprehend what she was doing. Others interpreted her spirit rappings; she herself made no claims. Kane, the educated, well-travelled, and snobbish scion of a prominent Philadelphia family, was a totally different human animal and knew it. Yet he loved her and gave every evidence that he longed to marry her. That is what gnawed at him.

His family was opposed to any such alliance, especially his father, whose approval Kane vainly sought all of his short life. His family had, apparently, picked out a well-to-do Philadelphia girl for him, but Kane was already enamoured of Margaret. There was a perverse streak in him, a kind of "I'll show them" attitude that had taken him to the distant corners of the globe and had manifested itself again when, a semi-invalid, he went north over their objections in 1850.

Now that he was an Arctic hero, who had emerged from the frozen seas in better health than when he had left, there was less resistance to a new venture. But, with equal recklessness, he had fastened on to the most unsuitable of all potential consorts. It was not only that Margaret Fox was a notorious stage performer; there was also the matter of her upbringing. Once when Kane brought his brother to the Fox home, he took Margaret's mother aside and urged her not to

240

mention the possibility of marriage in front of him. "My brother," he said, "feels like death about it."

There was only one solution: he must change Margaret, remould her. "No right minded gentleman," he told her, ". . . can regard your present life with approval." He would go off to the Arctic, she would give up spirit rapping and, at his expense, enter a boarding-school of his choosing, somewhere in a country backwater, far from the temptations of the big cities. It was not a scheme that was welcomed by Mrs. Fox or the eldest sister, Leah, for it meant that the money from the séances would dry up. But Kane was adamant: "Your life is worse than tedious, it is sinful, and that you have so long resisted its temptations shows me that you were born for better things than to entertain strangers at a dollar a head."

All during the winter months of this turbulent courtship Kane lived a frantic life, scribbling away against a deadline on a book about his Arctic adventures, flitting from city to city to deliver lectures, indulging in a voluminous correspondence with Arctic travellers, scientists, savants, and would-be adventurers, including Lady Franklin herself, in addition to planning every detail of his next expedition.

It is small wonder that in the middle of all this whirl he fell ill, first in February and again in April, when he was felled for a month by one of the worst attacks yet of the rheumatic fever that had weakened his heart. The planning went on without him.

Kane's ship was to be the *Advance*, from the previous expedition, but this would be a private venture; the U.S. government had concluded that the Franklin search should be left to the British. The U.S. Navy would supply only the seamen. Henry Grinnell would again provide the funds, and various scientific societies would contribute the necessary instruments. Kane was intending to head for Smith Sound to seek the Open Polar Sea, which Inglefield had reported lay beyond. Now he got news that Inglefield was planning a second expedition – to steal a march on him, in Kane's view ("Nothing is left to me but a competition with the odds against me"). What was billed as a humanitarian search for Franklin was looking more like a clash of ambitions – at least on Kane's part. As it turned out, Inglefield had no interest in racing the Americans to the polar sea; his task was more prosaic – simply to carry supplies to the Belcher expedition at Beechey Island.

Meanwhile the organization proceeded: boats and sledges, pemmican and pickles, books and biscuits were all ordered, the latter being "meat biscuits," perfected by the enterprising food processor Gail Borden, whose next experiments in the field of concentrated food would make his name a household word.

Kane arranged for a more personal item. He commissioned an Italian painter to prepare a portrait of Margaret to take with him on the voyage, which was set for May. That done, she was spirited away to a tiny village eighteen miles out of Philadelphia where she was to receive an education from the wife of the local miller, a situation that reduced her to tears until Kane, at the last moment, dashed by for a final hour of consolation.

He sent her one last letter: "The day will come – bright as sunshine on the waters – when I claim your hand and unrestrained by the trammels of our mutual dread, live with you in peace, tranquility and affection.

"Be good and pure. Restrain every thought which interferes with a guileless life, and live to prove your improvement, your love for

Ky. . . ."

Kane's main purpose, he insisted, was to search for Franklin. He had become convinced that somewhere beyond Smith Sound, walled off from the world by a barrier of ice, lay the famous Open Polar Sea, where the air was milder and the skies free of icy blasts, a kind of northern "mediterranean," to use Kane's own analogy. This curious piece of wishful thinking, which had persisted since John Barrow's time, had been reinforced by Inglefield's report. But unlike Inglefield, Kane affected to believe that Franklin and his lost crew were somewhere on the shores of that Elysian paradise, subsisting on its animal life, "unable to leave their hunting ground and cross the frozen Sahara which intervened between them and the world from which they are shut out." After entering Smith Sound, Kane proposed to advance into the unknown by dogsled until he reached the open sea, at which time, "if such reward awaits us, we launch our little boats, and bidding God speed us, embark upon its waters."

With crowds cheering, guns booming, and pleasure craft loaded with well-wishers alongside, the *Advance* left New York harbour on May 31 with a company of seventeen officers and men. "The object of my journey is the search for Sir John Franklin," he wrote in a farewell note to his brother Thomas. "Neither science nor the vain glory of attaining an unreached North shall divert me from this one conscientious aim. . . ."

242

It doesn't ring true. He knew perfectly well that Inglefield's careful search had not turned up any Franklin clues. It may be that he convinced himself that his motives were noble and self-sacrificing; he tended to view the world and himself through a romantic veil. But the evidence suggests that Dr. Kane of the Arctic Seas had another goal in mind. He was not the first explorer to use Franklin as an excuse to raise funds for geographical discovery. In pretending to look for the lost expedition, he gave every evidence of seeking something almost as illusory and even more unattainable – the North Pole itself.

2

That same spring of 1853, while Kane pursued his liaison with Margaret Fox and prepared for his own journey to the Arctic, British sledging parties were waiting impatiently for the weather to clear in order to continue to search for Franklin and also for Robert McClure, who was then in fact icebound at Mercy Bay.   *Searching for the searchers*

To search for the searchers – Collinson and McClure – had been as much a part of Sir Edward Belcher's given task as finding the original lost expedition. Wellington Channel must be probed for Franklin, Viscount Melville Sound and its environs for McClure and Collinson. Once these tasks were complete, the Admiralty was convinced that "every accessible part of the Polar Sea west of Lancaster Sound will have been visited." That done, Belcher and his five vessels might as well abandon all search attempts and come home.

In short, the Arctic Establishment in Great Britain had written off the entire area west of Somerset Island and south of Barrow Strait and Melville Sound. Peel Sound had been found to be blocked in 1851, therefore, the theory went, it must have been blocked five years before when Franklin had set off from Beechey. It apparently occurred to nobody on the so-called Arctic Council that this channel might have been clear one year and frozen the next. Parry had had experience with the shifting quality of the Arctic environment, yet he and James Ross and others concluded that the route that Franklin had actually used in 1846 was permanently impassable.

Since almost everybody believed that Franklin would be found somewhere north of the Wellington Channel, Belcher would take two of his ships to search that area. Two more of his vessels, *Resolute* and *Intrepid*, led by Henry Kellett – the same officer who had tried to hold McClure back at Cape Lisburne, Alaska – would sail west to Melville Island. The twenty-six-gun frigate *North Star* would remain at Beechey Island as a supply depot for both parties.

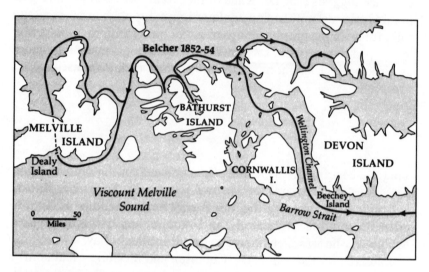

Belcher's search for Franklin, 1852-54

Leopold M'Clintock would command Kellett's sister ship. Even though he too was convinced that Franklin had gone north, he was delighted to have a command of his own, especially under the hearty, cheerful Kellett, a naval captain of thirty years' experience, whom he described as "kind, generous and open hearted." This was in striking contrast to the irritable, fifty-three-year-old Belcher. Then and later one of the most controversial and detested figures in the Royal Navy, Belcher was manifestly unsuitable for a job that would try the nerves of the best of men. But he had seniority and so, by the rigid standards of naval advancement, was given the overall command. The grandson of a Nova Scotia chief justice, he had gone to England at the age of twelve to join the Navy. Harsh, quarrelsome, hypercritical, and possessed of a towering ego, he had gained considerable notoriety in 1830 as the result of a messy and spiteful separation from his wife, who accused him of twice infecting her with venereal disease. One of his many failings was his refusal to listen to the advice of the more experienced officers who served under him, fifteen of whom

244

had been with Austin in 1850-51. In the end this would bring disaster to his expedition and personal humiliation to its leader.

Thus it is small wonder that M'Clintock was happy to get out from under Belcher's command and sail with Kellett to Melville Island. It was not an easy trip. These were the first ships that had attempted it since Parry's day. Barrow Strait was clogged with ice. Kellett's *Resolute* was more awkward than M'Clintock's steam-powered *Intrepid*. She grounded in the shallow channel, keeled over, and almost foundered, to be tugged afloat by the *Intrepid*, a striking example of the advantages of steam over sail.

Squeezing through a lane of water between land and frozen sea, the two vessels reached Melville Island on September 1, 1852, the second expedition in history to get that far. A few days later they were off Winter Harbour, but though they could see Parry's sand-stone block looming up on shore, six miles of solid ice barred their way. They could not know that McClure's note was there, waiting for them. With winter approaching, they made haste to retreat to winter quarters off Dealy Island, thirty-five miles east on the Melville coast.

Six land expeditions fanned out over Melville Island that fall, setting up depots for the real test that would come the following spring. One party turned aside on its return journey, curious to examine Parry's sandstone monument. There it discovered McClure's letter written the previous April and giving the news of his discovery of a North West Passage.

It was too late in the season to rescue the McClure expedition, frozen in and starving at Mercy Bay. Midwinter conditions made sledging impossible. Kellett could only mark time until the following spring, hoping that McClure and his men would somehow survive. His own ships were well provisioned. Fresh venison, bear, and musk-ox were available in abundance while soirées, vaudeville shows, and plays broke the monotony. M'Clintock had brought along a set of conjuring tricks to amuse his men, and the gregarious Kellett himself chaired the theatrical committee. On Christmas Day, while McClure's sailors eked out the Yuletide with a few scraps of salt meat, enhanced by a rare ration of raisins and cocoa, Kellett's people sat down to a feast of stuffed roast pig.

Meanwhile, M'Clintock was preparing for the greatest sledging journey of his life, one that the naval historian Clements Markham, with his usual hyperbole, was to call "the greatest Arctic effort that has ever been made or ever will be made." Convinced that Franklin had entered the open sea beyond Wellington Channel, M'Clintock decided to search for the lost crews by striking northwest across Melville Island to the unknown waters beyond.

But Kellett, since his sledges had found McClure's message at Winter Harbour, knew he must send relief to Mercy Bay as soon as possible. His party left on March 10, earlier than any spring journey yet made by the Navy in the Arctic and only a fortnight later than the 1852 spring departure of Kennedy and Bellot.

The man who volunteered to find McClure was a remarkable young naval lieutenant named Bedford Pim. He had served with Kellett aboard the *Herald* in 1850 and had been one of the last to see McClure before that expedition vanished into the western Arctic. He was not cut from regular Navy cloth but belonged to that small band of individualists who preferred to travel alone – a band that included John Rae and Richard King. Pim, too, was convinced that Franklin had gone up Wellington Channel and across the polar sea, perhaps to be beset in Bering Strait and cast up on the shores of Russian Siberia. Pim himself had visited Siberia, met the Russians, and lived with the natives on the Asiatic coast.

When he returned to England, Pim conceived a grandiose plan to cross Siberia in search of Franklin. He even went to Leningrad to ask for Russian aid. The Russians were enthusiastic but no more forthcoming with money than the English (save for Lady Franklin), and so the plan died. When Pim learned that Kellett was going north again he volunteered to join him. Now, in March of 1853, he was sledging west across the frozen expanse of Melville Sound on a rescue mission.

It was typical of Bedford Pim that he took a small party of ten men, with one manhauled sledge and one small dogsled. The manhauled sledge broke down. Pim sent all but two of his party back and, ever the loner, mushed on with his dogs in the –50° weather. It was slow going; twenty-eight days elapsed before he reached the cliffs of Mercy Bay.

Pim moved along the sullen coastline, seeking a cairn, unaware of the ship hidden from view by the hummocky ice. At last one of his men pointed to a black spot in the bay. Pim identified it through his telescope, left the sled behind, and pushed forward ahead of his men, throwing his hat in the air and screeching into the wind. All agreed that the scene that followed could not be properly described. When McClure finally identified his rescuer as the man he had last seen

246

near Bering Strait – his face "black as Erebus" from the smoke of the coal-oil lamp – the news that he sent back to his ship was at first treated as a joke. Then came pandemonium. The sick sprang from their beds. The artificers laid down their tools. All the men who could crawl poured from the hatchway. Some could not trust their eyes and began to touch and paw their rescuers. Pim was shocked by their wretched appearance and even more distressed to learn that their next meal consisted of a tiny piece of bread and a cup of weak cocoa. He sent immediately to his sledge for a package of bacon. His own men were so affected that tears rolled down their cheeks.

Next morning McClure mustered his crew to remind them that he had urged them to trust the mysterious workings of the Almighty. He could not resist adding a moral homily: he urged them when they returned home to remember that "there are *churches* in England as well as *public houses*."

Thus was averted a second grievous Arctic tragedy, one that could have matched that of John Franklin. But the miseries of the *Investigator* party were not yet ended, for now the disagreeable side of McClure's character showed itself. Kellett's man, Pim, had saved McClure. It followed that Kellett and his crew were eligible for part of the prize of £10,000 that parliament had voted for the discovery of the North West Passage. But McClure did not intend to share either the prize or the glory. He was determined to keep up the pretence that his men were all healthy enough to sail the *Investigator* out of the Arctic and home to England, unassisted by Kellett or anybody else. To achieve this, he rushed off immediately to persuade Kellett that he was perfectly able to continue his voyage.

To this end he left two instructions. The twenty-four members of the crew who were desperately ill were to leave on April 15 by sledge and make their way to Kellett's two vessels off Melville Island. The remainder were to stay with the ship and continue on the same rations that had brought them to a state of near starvation. This callous order was designed to show that the expedition could get along without help.

By the time the party of sick set off, three more of the ship's company were dead. It was a ghastly journey – half the men were so miserable and lame from scurvy they couldn't stand upright. Their stronger comrades had to tend their needs by day and even put them to bed at night. It was the spectacle of this scarecrow party of shrunken creatures, tottering forward, hollow-eyed, staring blankly ahead, that convinced Kellett that McClure could not carry on as he wished.

When Kellett suggested that McClure abandon his ship, he heard an echo of that previous encounter at Cape Lisburne three years before. Once again, the wily McClure was insisting he must obey his orders; he could not abandon the *Investigator* on his own responsibility. Kellett thought he was being noble, but McClure was looking forward to the future when he would be able to swear with a straight face before the inevitable inquiry that he had been quite prepared to go on without any help – in short, that he, and he alone, was the conqueror of the Passage.

Kellett suggested a compromise. If McClure would go back to the ship with Dr. Armstrong and if the men were fit and willing, he could carry on. McClure did not want his severest critic to force any decision and so insisted that Kellett's surgeon, Domville, accompany him. They reached the *Investigator* on May 19. To McClure's surprise and mortification, only four men out of twenty would volunteer to go on with him. Both doctors agreed that they should not. That was it. Kellett's order to McClure to abandon his ship was now in effect, and the *Investigator* was left to her fate.

Meanwhile, on April 4, M'Clintock's other sledging parties had gone off to explore the western Arctic and search for Franklin in the unlikely event that he'd managed to get that far. Struggling in harness like so many beasts of burden, dragging back-breaking loads as heavy as 280 pounds a man, sometimes trudging knee-deep in slush, they performed superhuman feats at enormous personal cost. M'Clintock's own crew actually walked and hauled more than a ton of supplies 1,328 miles in 106 days, a new record that established him, at least in the eyes of the Navy, as the acknowledged master of the craft. (Kennedy's and Bellot's similar journey – 1,265 miles in 95 days – was ignored, perhaps because they had used dogs.)

M'Clintock discovered a new island, which he named Prince Patrick Island, on the rim of the Beaufort Sea – empty of either vegetation or animal life on its bleak west coast – but he did it at the expense of most of his crew. One man, John Coombes, dropped dead in harness. Two more were deathly ill. The rest took a year to recover. As late as July 1854, two of the sledgers, George Green, ice master, and Henry Giddy, bosun's mate, were still badly shaken and weakened, while two others, Hiccles, a marine, and able seaman Richard Warne, were invalids. In spite of this, the Royal Navy continued to follow the gospel of manhauling according to M'Clintock, perhaps because it had so many available and idle seamen. But was it really necessary to send out big ten-man sledges loaded down with supplies when two or three dog drivers could cover the same ground? Nobody, apparently, bothered to consider the alternative.

By the time the sledge crews got back, the surviving members of the *Investigator*'s company were lodged aboard Kellett's two vessels. It seemed to them that their troubles were over. There was game aplenty: ten thousand pounds of muskox and caribou meat were taken that summer. With no sign of Franklin in the western Arctic, Kellett had planned to take his ships back to Beechey once the ice broke. On August 18, he was able to set sail, to the great joy of his frustrated passengers from the abandoned *Investigator*. Two transport ships, accompanied by the screw steamer *Phoenix*, were due to arrive from England with supplies and mail, and then return. Homeward bound at last! It seemed too good to be true – and it was.

Again, they reckoned without the Arctic weather. The two vessels had moved scarcely more than a hundred miles to the east before the ice closed in again. McClure's men, who had suffered through three dreadful Arctic winters, now faced a fourth.

But a small party got away, for McClure was eager to get the news of his discovery to England. He had earlier dispatched Cresswell to Beechey Island by sledge with the demented Wynniatt. There they encountered Edward Inglefield, now in command of the steamer *Phoenix*, who arrived in August with letters and dispatches for Belcher. The *Phoenix*'s steam power had allowed her to break through the pack and clear a passage for the transports that brought new supplies for Belcher's depot ship, *North Star*. In spite of this, one of the transports, the *Breadalbane*, was crushed in the ice as she lay anchored off Beechey Island. She sank in fifteen minutes, her crew rescued and crammed aboard Inglefield's vessel. (More than a century later, in 1981, Canadian divers found her in 340 feet of water.)

Toward the end of the month Inglefield again nosed into the pack and managed to get back to England with Cresswell and his news, "a triumph not for this age alone but for mankind," in the declamatory words of Franklin's old nemesis, Lord Stanley. (Lady Franklin was pointedly absent from the public reception.) Inglefield was promoted to captain for his feat, and Cresswell was reunited with his father to whom, as much as to anyone, he owed his life.

One man did not return to England – Inglefield's second-in-command, the French naval officer Joseph-René Bellot. This had been a last-minute posting, for Bellot had hoped to persuade the French to mount an expedition of their own. Jane Franklin had offered him command of Inglefield's old ship, the *Isabel*, which was being fitted out for another voyage by William Kennedy. With his usual humility, Kennedy offered to serve under his former mate. Bellot declined because he felt the promotion of a foreigner over a Briton might weaken English enthusiasm for the cause. "I was taught unselfish devotedness ever since I saw Lady Franklin," he said. It was just as well. Kennedy planned to take the *Isabel* to Bering Strait for another attempt at the western Arctic, but he got no farther than Valparaiso, where his crew mutinied, once again dashing the hopes of John Franklin's persistent widow.

With the French refusing to enter the picture, Bellot offered to join Inglefield. "Give me but a plank to lie on – but a corner for my clothes – and I will be content," he wrote. Inglefield was glad to have the attractive young Frenchman who was, in Sophia Cracroft's shrewd observation, "free from that common, almost invariable characteristic of little people – touchiness."

When the *Phoenix* reached Beechey Island, Bellot, with his usual enthusiasm, volunteered to carry the Admiralty dispatches to Belcher, whose two ships were farther north up the Wellington Channel. He set off on August 12 with four seamen, taking a gutta-percha boat and marching along the eastern shore. Two nights later, the party members were separated. Bellot and two others found themselves trapped on an ice floe. Drawing on Bellot's expertise, they set about building a snow hut. On the morning of August 18 Bellot left the hut to examine the state of the ice. Without warning, a great fissure fifteen feet wide opened up under him. He was gone in an instant.

The Eskimos wept when they heard the news. "Poor Bellot, poor Bellot," they cried. He was just twenty-seven years old.

3

The blue Elisha Kane had not entirely recovered from his bout of rheumatic
devils fever when the *Advance* set sail from New York on May 31, 1853.
Nor was his condition improved by violent bouts of seasickness as the

little 144-ton brig tossed and rolled in the Atlantic. The slightest swell made him ill. Amos Bonsall, one of the crew, later remarked that no one but Kane could have persevered in such a voyage, given the same accumulation of illnesses. Scarcely any of the seventeen crew members thought he could recover.

It was not a propitious beginning for one who had never before captained a ship, knew little of navigation, and wasn't used to leading men. Undisciplined himself (he had hated the strictures of the American Navy), rebellious and strong-willed, he had little shipboard experience, his previous duties having been confined to the care of the sick. Now he found himself in command of an ill-starred crew who had never worked together. Several, like Bonsall, a Pennsylvania farmer, were amateurs, and at least two were troublemakers.

During Kane's illness, Henry Grinnell's son, Cornelius, had taken on the job of preparing for the expedition. Unable to find enough volunteer seamen to fill his roster, he combed the New York wharfs and came up with two unruly characters: William Godfrey, a harbour boatman from the city's turbulent East Side, and John Blake, who went under the alias of John Hussey. Within a week this pair got into a quarrel with Henry Brooks, the first mate. In the British Navy that kind of insubordination would have brought an immediate flogging. Kane, who was opposed to corporal punishment, had both men tied up and confined for a day or two in the booby hatch between decks. Less than a week later, Godfrey caused such a disturbance in the mess that the crew approached Kane and asked that he be sent home from Newfoundland. But when Godfrey promised to reform, Kane, still uncertain of command, let him stay.

The *Advance* reached Upernavik, the farthest north of the West Greenland settlements, on July 20. Here Kane took on two more crew members, a plump and cheerful Eskimo youth of nineteen, Hans Christian Hendrik, and Carl Petersen, the Danish dog driver who had been with Penny in 1851. Petersen came reluctantly. He had not yet entirely recovered his health from the exhausting sledge journeys across Devon Island, and he was not impressed by the expedition itself. The ship was not well commanded, he noted. Kane would have to depend on his sailing master, John Wall Wilson, who came to loathe and despise him.

Wilson had already told Kane that he knew nothing about ice. Kane, with that breezy insouciance that characterizes the confident amateur, told him that he personally understood it very well and would help him through it. The crew was generally untrained; only the carpenter, Christian Ohlsen, had any real experience in polar navigation. The food, too, was inadequate – again because of Kane's confinement. There was salt meat, for example, but no fresh provisions. Petersen had a premonition that the *Advance* would never leave the Arctic. Nevertheless, he signed on.

Early on, Petersen had an example of Kane's recklessness and stubbornness. He noted that the captain didn't agree with the English navigators, who had learned to treat the ice with great respect. Instead of docking, when necessary, against a berg – the accepted method – he plunged ahead, trying always, in Petersen's phrase, "to bid defiance to the ice." It wasn't long before the *Advance* collided with a huge berg and lost a boat and a jib boom, an accident that caused an unpleasant argument between Kane and his first mate, Brooks, each of whom blamed the other for the encounter.

Kane blundered on through the Middle Ice of Baffin Bay until on August 6 he saw the two sombre fifteen-hundred-foot capes – Alexander and Isabella – that form the east and west portals of Smith Sound. Following the route that Edward Inglefield had pioneered, he reached Littleton Island off the Greenland coast and buried a lifeboat and some provisions in a small cove to the north in case of an emergency – a prescient move. Meanwhile, Godfrey and Blake continued to cause trouble. On August 11, Godfrey was back in the booby hatch for assaulting the sailing master, Wilson. But Kane couldn't keep him there for long; the two troublemakers were "bad fellows both but daring, energetic and strong"; he needed every available hand on deck.

Now Kane sailed into the great basin that today bears his name. He had gone farther north by this route than any other white explorer including Inglefield, whom he thought of as his rival. But winter was closing in, and the crew, weary of warping and tracking the brig through the encroaching ice, were uneasy, homesick, and exhausted. They wanted to turn back; Kane was all for plunging on. It was still August; Penny, he pointed out, hadn't wintered until September. Why should he let himself be outdone? (But that year, far to the west, the ice was already trapping Kellett and crushing the *Breadalbane*.) In Petersen's view, Kane wanted to winter farther north than any Englishman because he believed that "the Stars and Stripes ought to wave where no Union Jack had ever fluttered in the polar gale."

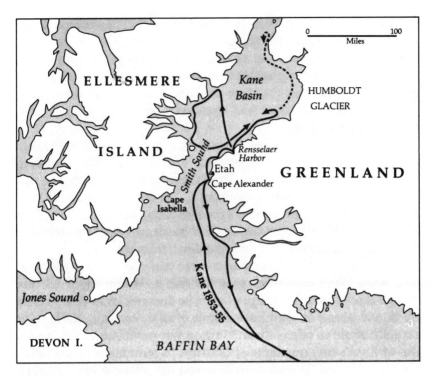

Kane's "search" for Franklin and the Pole, 1853-55

In the end, his officers persuaded him to stop. He could not turn back, for the ice was closing in. He found a sheltered bay on the Greenland shore, which he named Rensselaer Harbor after his father's country estate, and there he prepared to spend the gloomiest winter any of them had ever known.

Except for the people of Spitzbergen, warmed by a milder current, no white man had ever wintered this far north. Even the pugnacious Godfrey felt it: they were all, he said, "terribly afflicted by blue devils." It was impossible, Godfrey later declared, to describe the effect produced by the unchanging polar landscape. "The very soul of man seems to be suffocated by the oppressive gloom. . . ."

Hans, the Eskimo, was afflicted, too. "Never had I seen the dark season like this. . . . I was seized with fright, and fell a-weeping." Homesick for his native sweetheart, he packed his gear and prepared to leave for the south. Kane persuaded him to stay.

The polar darkness, however, was not entirely to blame for the pall cast over the ship's company. The men shivered in their quarters and

253

subsisted on cold food because Kane had vastly underestimated the amount of fuel needed for the journey. By the end of February they were out of oil, almost out of candles, and rapidly running out of coal. It was no longer possible to melt enough water to wash in; the men had to forgo their tea; there would be no more fresh bread, only hard tack; the galley stove was abandoned and all cooking done in the smoky main cabin.

This was serious enough. Kane's own personality made things worse. He was snobbish, overbearing, boastful, and quite unable to keep his unruly crew in order. To Wilson, his severest critic, he was "peevish, coarse, sometimes insulting . . . the most self-conceited man I ever saw [who] thinks no one knows anything but himself. . . ." By January the officers were taking their meals in silence to prevent a disagreeable argument or a dressing down from their captain.

If Kane abused his officers, he tried to curry favour with the men, who obeyed him only when they felt like it. Wilson observed that "Kane is not fit to take charge of men, he does not know how to treat them, and adopts his own ways in spite of all we can say. . . . He . . . is actually afraid to offend them." Wilson was particularly contemptuous of Kane's easy treatment of Godfrey, "a most audacious villain." If he had his way, Wilson said, he would have flogged him "until he could not stand and keep him at hard duty but I would make a good man of him."

By midwinter, several of the men were suffering from scurvy while a mysterious ailment had killed off all but six of the fifty dogs. That meant the men would have to manhaul the sledges, British fashion, when they struck north toward the fabled Open Polar Sea. Kane began his preparations in February against the advice of both Petersen and Ohlsen, who did not relish crossing that turbulent expanse of mountainous ice, jagged bergs, thick snow drifts, and howling winds so early in the season. There were other problems, too: Kane had to turn his cabin into a jail to confine the unruly Blake.

On March 19, he sent Henry Brooks and seven men to establish a shore depot for the polar dash. Petersen was right; it was far too early. In the forty-below weather, the snow was as sharp and dry as sand and the terrain unbelievably rough. The weather was so bad that on some days the party couldn't move their overloaded sledge. Unable to reach the shore, they turned back, Brooks and three others so frostbitten they could no longer walk. After eight miles they collapsed, realizing that unless they got relief they would freeze to death. Petersen, Ohlsen, and a young German scientific observer, August Sonntag, started for help. The brig was thirty miles away; they knew there was no time to stop for food, drink, or sleep if their comrades were to survive. They made the trip in thirteen hours, staggering aboard, delirious and haggard, their faces black, their limbs swollen, almost insensible from fatigue. Ohlsen, the only one able to speak, had his toes so badly frozen they had to be amputated.

Kane gathered up seven men and set off, the crippled Ohlsen lashed to the sledge. He would have to serve as guide, since Petersen and Sonntag were now powerless. In that dreadful tangle of broken ice, the sledge was useless. After twenty miles, the party left it and struggled forward on foot, with Ohlsen half fainting, supported between two men. They found the tent containing the missing men with difficulty, half expecting the occupants to be dead, grateful to discover them barely alive. The rescue party needed sleep, but the tent was too small to hold a dozen men. They dozed in two-hour shifts, those waiting outside leaping and stamping their feet to keep from freezing to death. Then the invalids were strapped into their sledge and the party set off for the brig.

It was a nightmare journey. Again and again the sledge had to be unloaded and lifted over a barrier while the sick lay groaning on the ice. After ten miles, even the healthy men, groggy with fatigue, began dropping in their tracks until only two were left – Kane and Godfrey – to raise the tent and cover up the sleepers. Kane was determined to go another nine miles to pick up the sledge abandoned on the outward journey. Godfrey offered to go with him. He may have been a trial, but he was tougher than the others; and on this journey he proved his worth.

Long before they reached their goal, Kane was delirious, babbling and swooning as Godfrey pushed him along. He thought Godfrey was a bear and called on his imaginary crew to shoot him. After they got the sledge, Kane's beard was so solidly frozen to his clothing that Godfrey had to hack off part of it with a jackknife before the captain could sleep.

By the time the others, rested and less weary, caught up, Kane and Godfrey had a pot of blubber heating on a fire. After a little rest they started forward again, at the rate of about a mile and a half an hour. By then all were demented, seized by a kind of frenzy, laughing frantically, gibbering, shouting oaths, mimicking the groans and

255

screams of the invalids – a company of madmen, subject to bursts of maniacal fury at one moment, only to turn into blubbering children the next. Godfrey said later that he had never before or since felt such a strong inclination to suicide, even searching about for a chasm into which he might fling himself before the longing passed.

The safety of the ship, and of the half-crazed men who reached her at last, devolved upon young Isaac Hayes, the ship's doctor. He was twenty-one, a green medical student just out of school when Kane took him aboard. Now he was staring at near corpses, covered from head to foot with frost, their beards lumpy with ice, their tread feeble, their eyes vacant and wild. They flung themselves, fully clothed, on their bunks and passed out. When they awoke to the fearful pain of thawing flesh, the ship, to Hayes, "presented all the appearances of a mad house." Astonishingly, Kane, the perennial invalid, was the last to collapse and the first to recover.

His ill-planned expedition had cost two lives. Jefferson Baker, a young hunting companion of Kane's, died of tetanus. Pierre Schubert, the cook, expired after his foot was amputated. Most of the others lost portions of their feet or toes.

As Kane sat by the bunk of the dying Baker in April, he heard a shout from the deck. A seaman had spotted eight people on the shore. These were Eskimos from the community of Etah, seventy miles away, the most northerly permanent human habitation in the world. They had never before seen white men, but their parents probably had, for these were descended from the same "Arctic Highlanders" John Ross had encountered thirty-six years earlier. They pointed at the crew and burst into peals of laughter, then cheerfully sold Kane four dogs to add to the three healthy animals left on the ship.

Kane was anxious to see for himself the massive glacier he had already named for Alexander von Humboldt, the noted natural scientist and explorer. Some of his men had reached it the previous August. On April 25, he sent off a party of six with some of the dogs and followed the next day with a smaller team. Godfrey was again his sole companion. Unruly as he was, he had saved Kane's life on the previous outing, was the fittest man and the best dog driver on the ship.

The scenery along the Greenland coast was spectacular: red sandstone cliffs rose a thousand feet from the frozen sea, riven by bays and fissures and sculptured by the frost and the wind into misshapen

256

pillars and columns. Ahead, the most massive glacier in the known world sprawled across Greenland, its glittering face looking down on them from four hundred feet. But they could not climb it. Three men went blind, another suffered chest pains, several were crippled by scurvy. On May 4 Kane himself fainted, and with one foot frozen was strapped into the sledge. When he reached the ship ten days later, he was in a stupor.

He had failed again. With two of his crew dead and most of the rest shattered, he had only three men healthy enough for duty. Of the officers, four, in Kane's phrase, were "knocked up." Almost a year had gone by with little to show. Kane had not found Franklin – indeed, had not made much effort to find him – and had seen no evidence of an Open Polar Sea. His only hope was to explore the Kane Basin to see whether there was an opening in that ravelled coastline. On May 20 he sent off Hayes and Godfrey in a light sledge with ten days' provisions. They returned on June 1, both completely snowblind, Hayes so badly afflicted he couldn't complete his report for another six weeks. The pair had managed to chart two hundred miles of the winding western coastline north of Inglefield's farthest. They hadn't found a passage west, nor had they been able to get far enough north to glimpse any open water. What Hayes didn't report was that Godfrey had gone half mad, tried to desert, and threatened Hayes with a gun, which the young doctor was able to wrest from him after a struggle.

In these conditions, Kane asked himself, could Franklin have survived? In the gloom of winter he would have said no, but after the arrival of the Eskimos, he was less certain. Here was "a savage people . . . destitute of any but the rudest appliances of the chase, who were fattening on the most wholesome diet of the region, only forty miles from our anchorage. . . ." It was quite possible, he thought, that the missing explorer or some of his men, divided into small parties, could be still living among the natives.

The hundred-mile blank on his crude map of the Kane Basin *must* be filled if he was to salvage anything from the expedition. He had but a handful of men healthy enough to do the job. He sent five off to explore the Humboldt Glacier and two more – William Morton, his steward, and Hans Hendrik, the Greenland Eskimo – to sledge north to the top of the basin. This time they *must* succeed. As Kane remarked, ". . . it is my last throw."

The glacier party returned with one man snowblind to report it could not scale the face of the ice sheet. Morton and Hans staggered back on July 10, their dogs limping – one animal, in fact, in such bad shape that he had to be carried on the sledge. Nonetheless, they had sensational news. They had found a new channel, thirty miles wide, leading north out of the basin (Kane named it Kennedy Channel after a friend) and followed it until they reached a massive cliff – Cape Constitution – jutting into the water. At that point they had come eighty miles farther north than had Inglefield.

Morton clawed his way for five hundred feet up the rocky promontory and there he beheld a marvellous sight: open water as far as he could see, lapping at the ridges of coastline that marched off in rows toward the horizon. The cliffs were aflutter with sea fowl and swallows, the glittering sea was free of ice. Morton and Kane were convinced that what he had seen was the Open Polar Sea. "The Polynya has been reached," he exulted. He was wrong, of course. The magical waters Morton saw in the distance were another mirage, the product of wind, waves, and wishful thinking. Kane, however, believed that Morton's discovery more than justified the trials he had gone through. "I can say that I have led an expedition whose results will be remembered for all time."

His elation was mixed with foreboding over the growing shortage of food and fuel and the unreliability of his officers and crew. Hans's absence with Morton had deprived them of the daily seal the Eskimo was used to bringing in. Everybody was sick and out of sorts. Kane's journal entries began to turn petulant. "Petersen mopes still. He has no native morale. . . ." "William Godfrey continues on the sick list. Malingering! [He] is a bad fellow." Henry Goodfellow, his brother Tom's young protégé, was "utterly ineffective." Brooks, the powerfully built first officer, was "not a reliable man." The two had words, whereupon Kane relieved Brooks of his duties, putting Ohlsen, the carpenter, in his place. "I have spoiled this man by kindness," Kane wrote, and then added a self-pitying sentence: ". . . it is very hard for a man like myself of a kindly, trusting nature to find that neither kindness nor trust will accord with the position of command."

He knew he must make further attempts to justify the expedition, especially to his family. On July 8 he spent most of the day on shore observing the action of the ice upon the land. "I hope, if I have the health to fill up my notes that I may advance myself in my father's eyes by a book on glaciers and glacial geology."

The dreadful possibility of a second winter in the Arctic faced him,

258

for the ice in the bay showed no signs of breaking up, "For there never was, and I trust never will be, a party worse armed for the encounter." He rejected any suggestion of abandoning the brig. Instead he decided to take Hans and six men in a whaleboat to try to reach the *North Star*, Belcher's supply ship at Beechey Island. There he hoped he could get enough provisions to tide him over the winter.

It was a mad scheme. The whaleboat, aptly named *Forlorn Hope*, made its way through alleys of pounding ice until it was stopped dead in Baffin Bay. The previous summer Kane had come this way through open water, as had Inglefield in 1852. Now he hiked across the pack to a towering berg and from its pinnacle, 120 feet above the surface, saw for a radius of thirty miles a daunting expanse of solid white.

It was now August 1854. On his return to the brig he did his best to keep up the crew's spirits – a difficult task; except for a little hot coffee and soup, the men were existing on cold salt pork. When they were unable to blast the *Advance* out of the harbour, Kane knew the worst: "It is *horrible* – yes, that is the word – to look forward to another year of disease and darkness to be met without fresh food and without fuel."

Was he also to suffer the fate of Franklin? As the winter closed in, remembering the problems facing those earlier searchers, he had the name of his ship painted in huge letters on a nearby cliff. In a cairn he left an account of his discoveries, encased in glass, and sealed up with melted lead. The coffins of his two dead crew members lay buried beneath. How many more graves would there be before the winter was out?

4

It was as well that Kane failed in his attempt to reach Beechey Island, *Ships* for the Belcher expedition was in disarray that August and preparing *abandoned* to abandon the search for Franklin. None of the five ships had spent a comfortable winter in spite of the usual theatricals and sports events. McClure's men, crowded aboard Kellett's two vessels off Dealy Island in Viscount Melville Sound, had only the single set of clothes they had been allowed to bring from the trapped *Investigator*. At night they shivered under inadequate bedclothes. Even though considerable game had been shot and frozen the previous fall, rations had to be cut by a third. Space was so cramped that McClure and Kellett, sharing a tiny cabin, found that one man had to stay in bed while the other washed and dressed; there wasn't room for two to stand upright. And when the steward came to tidy the room, both had to go out onto the cold deck.

The previous November, McClure's sub-lieutenant, Herbert Sainsbury, had died of tuberculosis. In January 1854, two members of M'Clintock's sledge crews had also died, worn out from their exertions three years before. By then the sick list had reached thirty-five.

Kellett was concerned about Collinson. In April, he sent off one sledge party to search Prince of Wales Strait for the missing explorer and another to bring back all the private journals from the *Investigator*.

Meanwhile, news arrived from Belcher that shocked and dismayed the normally even-tempered Kellett. In a curiously ambiguous letter, Belcher seemed to be telling his subordinate to abandon both his ships and head for Beechey Island. But he also appeared to be manoeuvring Kellett to make the decision on his own responsibility. Kellett, who had twice been manipulated by McClure, realized he was again being used as a scapegoat. The loss of a ship was taken seriously by the Admiralty. The loss of two ships would be a disaster. Did Belcher really mean what he seemed to mean?

In fact, Belcher was planning to abandon *four* ships, all in good condition, none in any real danger of being trapped for a second winter. But this aging and cranky commander, beset in Wellington Channel, had no intention of spending another season in the Arctic. The last one had been marked by dissension, backbiting, threats, charges, and countercharges, mostly his own fault. At fifty-five, in poor health, and with no previous Arctic experience, Belcher wanted no more of it. His tedious memoir of this voyage, based on his journal, reveals him as a man of shallow, incurious mind, who never cared for high command, accepted it with a kind of sour resignation, feared trouble from the beginning, and felt himself put upon. He was so insecure that he once said he didn't want any officers serving under him who had taken part in more than one Arctic expedition.

There is no exhilaration in Belcher's account of his Arctic experience as there is in Kane's or Bellot's, no hint of Lyon's feeling for the land or its people. "I shall proceed with our monotonous voyage," he wrote at the outset, "but really . . . I cannot flatter myself that bergs, floes, sailing ice, etc, will greatly interest anyone. . . ." As for the Eskimos, "our traffic with these people, who were filthy in the extreme, cannot prove interesting." Filthy they may have been, but no more so than the members of Belcher's own sledging parties, whose faces were black with smoke from oil lamps and who did not wash for weeks because the natural oil of their bodies helped to protect them from the cold. But none of that occurred to Belcher, who was more concerned with the dismaying responsibilities of Arctic command.

"Upon what a volcano do we stand! The sullen chief, if he be so, must chew the cud and vegetate year after year in sullenness and vexatiousness of spirit. No such purgatory could exist, better calculated for a man of narrow mind – none so dangerous to a sensible mind. . . . I proceed in charity to all . . . willing to overlook all faults in others, providing they do not, when I tell them of it, still continue to tread upon my corns."

He was unconsciously describing himself – a man of narrow mind, sitting on a volcano. Years before he'd had an acrimonious encounter with his admiral because he objected to being sent civilian help during a skirmish in Borneo. "You may be a skilful navigator and a clever seaman," his senior told him, "but a great officer you can never be with that narrow mind."

Belcher was not open enough to listen to the advice of those who'd had more polar experience. He believed himself a man of common sense and "what a very difficult position a man of common sense is placed in when he accepts such a command." Such a man, he declared, "is pestered by assertions that such was the course Captain H. pursued; and if he either doubts, opposes, or varies from these self-constituted Mentors, he must look for sulkiness, opposition, and the petty mutiny of petty minds." Those words aptly describe conditions on Belcher's two ships in the Wellington Channel: constant and bitter arguments between Belcher and his officers that led to more than one arrest.

He apparently expected trouble. Before leaving England he had tried to ward it off in a pompous letter to Kellett in which he urged that everyone should "strive to maintain the general happiness of our community – that they will see the necessity of avoiding any subjects which may cause irritation . . . and that they will use their utmost endeavours . . . to soften irritable remarks." Belcher went on to say that "all must pull together. . . . One failure, one dark spot on the record, may not at the moment be thought important – but remember that the eyes of the whole civilised world are upon us! . . . Let us strive to exhibit what can be achieved by discipline, good feeling and that untiring zeal which is ever conspicuous in our noble profession."

Belcher did not merely ignore his uncalled-for dictum. He jumped on it and stamped upon it. Kellett's ship that winter had been a model of good deportment, in spite of bitter cold and short rations. Belcher's was a disaster. He bullied one sensitive young officer, an artist named Walter May, to the point where May returned his profanity and was relieved of his duties. Belcher, often drunk, upbraided May for the most trifling indiscretions, such as forgetting to report that he had shot an Arctic hare. The wretched artist again felt the fury of Belcher's disapproval when he handed in a report on the wrong sized paper, and not the larger sheets "which your rank demands of you." Belcher insulted the family of one captain, Richards, and put another, Sherard Osborn, under arrest after a series of confrontations. When he heard that his officers were jeering at him behind his back, he threatened to cut off all communication between the ships. Now, in the summer of 1854, he wanted out.

Kellett could scarcely believe his eyes when he read Belcher's confidential dispatch. Anybody who forsook the ships at this point, Kellett thought, "would deserve to have their jackets taken off their backs." M'Clintock had become convinced at last that the search for Franklin – and for Collinson – should move south. But now he had to turn away from his plans because Kellett needed his best sledger to find Belcher and reason with him.

Kellett had no intention of abandoning his two ships without a direct order. He felt fairly sure that both vessels were in a position to get out. At the very worst they could let the ice stream carry them eastward to a point that would allow them to escape the following year. M'Clintock, travelling at top speed, reached Belcher in seven days (the distance was more than 250 miles). He argued for hours, but the adamant Belcher wouldn't budge; he insisted that every member of his expedition be crowded aboard the depot ship, *North Star*, at Beechey Island. This time his orders were unambiguous.

Meanwhile, two of Kellett's sledging parties had returned with interesting news. They had found a note from Collinson, McClure's senior, at the depot McClure had established on Princess Royal Island on August 16, 1851. It revealed that Collinson had reached that spot just fourteen days after McClure departed. His note said that he intended to take the *Enterprise* east. Obviously he was still somewhere to the south.

The second piece of news was disturbing – or should have been. There were *no* journals to be found aboard McClure's abandoned ship. Armstrong had managed somehow to squirrel his away (Miertsching's narrative would be written from memory), but what had happened to the others? The only plausible explanation is that McClure had made away with them because he didn't want any other version of his journey published that might conflict or compete with his own.

On June 15, Kellett reluctantly abandoned the *Resolute* and the *Intrepid* and, following Belcher's instructions, started for Beechey Island with his crews. A month later Belcher arrived at Beechey, sitting on his boat atop a sledge dragged by his men. His own ships had been abandoned in the Wellington Channel. At the last moment two more supply ships arrived to help take the men home, saving them from terrible overcrowding.

This, "the last of the Arctic voyages," as Belcher was to call it, was also, apart from the Franklin loss, the most disastrous. The mystery had not been solved; Collinson had been callously forsaken; four big ships, all in perfect condition, had been abandoned, or so it was thought. But the following year the whaling fleet found Kellett's *Resolute* floating about in the pack in Davis Strait. Without a captain, without a crew, without steam or sail, she had made her way miraculously from Viscount Melville Sound into the Atlantic. No human agency had propelled her. The ice – the inexorable, maddening, fickle ice – had done the job and in the process turned the unspeakable Sir Edward Belcher into the laughing stock of the Royal Navy.

5

The year 1854 was not a good one for Jane Franklin, but then none had been since her husband's disappearance. At the very outset, on January 12, with seven ships still known to be searching the Arctic, she got the first of several shocks. The Admiralty, without waiting for

Belcher, Collinson, or Kane to return, announced that as of March 31 the names of all the officers and crew members of the *Erebus* and the *Terror* would be struck from its books.

She was stunned. The previous October, Lieutenant Cresswell had brought back the first news of McClure's discovery of the North West Passage. Was that all that counted? Her husband's fate was still unknown. There were a few who held out the hope that he or some of his crew were still alive among the Eskimos. She was certainly one of these. Now it seemed to her as if the long quest for the Arctic hero had been a sham – an excuse to seek not human beings but the nebulous Passage.

It took her a week to compose herself. Then she dispatched to the Admiralty one of those exquisitely composed and fervently indignant letters that had become her hallmark. The Navy's decision was "presumptuous in the sight of God, as it will be felt to be indecorous, not to say indecent . . . in the eyes of men." In a bold act of defiance, as ludicrous as it was symbolic, she scorned Victorian convention by throwing off her widow's black mourning, "the habiliments of despair," and appeared in brilliant pink and green. "It would be acting falsehood, & a gross hypocrisy on my part," she declared, "to put on mourning when I have not yet given up all hope." Her stepdaughter, Eleanor, from whom she was partially estranged, donned black. She had surrendered any expectation that her father was alive and was opposed to the spending of her mother's dwindling fortune on further searches.

But Lady Franklin would not give up. The discovery of the Passage and the apparent abandonment of the Franklin quest were suspiciously coincident. "My Lords," she wrote, "I cannot but feel that there will be a stain on the page of the Naval Annals of England when these two events . . . are recorded in indissoluble association." Then, four days before her husband was officially declared dead, the Crimean War broke out. The Navy could no longer afford the luxury of an Arctic search for an expedition that had been missing for almost a decade. Every ship, every man would be needed in the struggle against the Russians.

With Belcher's return to England in the late fall, the Admiralty lost all stomach for polar exploration. In the space of two years, six ships had been lost or abandoned. Why squander any more money on a wild-goose chase? As *The Times* put it, "Surely enough has been done in favour of a sentiment rather than of rational calculation." Lady Franklin could argue that the fate of her husband and his crew was still unknown, but even that point was lost when that consummate Arctic traveller, John Rae, arrived in England with the first firm news.

It is one of the many ironies of the Great Search that this time Rae, the man who would eventually profit from these findings, wasn't searching for Franklin at all. He believed that the explorer had certainly gone south and not north, as almost everybody else believed, but he was convinced that he had been well to the west of Boothia Felix, which Rae now wished to examine on behalf of the Hudson's Bay Company. Rae wanted firm answers to two geological puzzles: Was Boothia a peninsula or an island? Was King William Land an island or a peninsula?

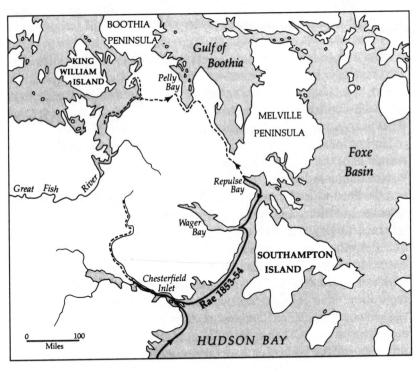

John Rae gets the first news of Franklin's fate, 1854

In August 1853, Rae reached Repulse Bay by boat from Churchill on the first leg of his quest. He and his six men again wintered in snow houses and the following April trekked west across the Boothia isthmus (it was indeed a peninsula) to link up with Thomas Simpson's farthest, thus completing on his return journey the exploration of the Arctic coastline and proving King William Land an island. Rae's methods differed radically from M'Clintock's. He travelled without a tent and very little bedding, keeping warm in snow houses built on the outward journey and used again on the return. When he reached his final destination – Pelly Bay – he cut off the ends of his flat sledges, used them for fuel, and headed back east with a lighter, more manoeuvrable conveyance.

At Pelly Bay, Rae met the first Eskimos he'd encountered since leaving Churchill, and there, on April 21, 1854, one of them, Innook-poo-zhee-jook, told a fascinating tale – one that would be worth ten thousand pounds to Rae and his men. He had heard stories from other natives of thirty-five or forty whites who had starved to death some years before, west of a large river, perhaps ten or twelve days' journey away.

Rae, who found him an intelligent man, noticed that his informant was wearing a golden cap band round his head. The Eskimo told him it had been obtained where the dead men were found. Rae bought the band and announced he would pay a good price for any other relics brought to him after he returned to Repulse Bay.

He had no idea at this point whether or not the dead men were members of the Franklin expedition, though he must have suspected it. Nor did he know exactly where the relics came from; the Eskimos had declined to lead him to the spot. That was Rae's story; it is open to some questions and was indeed treated with scepticism when he returned to England. Thirty-five dead men! Who else could they be *but* Franklin's crew members? Did Rae think the Eskimos were inventing corpses? Scarcely. He himself had championed the Eskimos as a truthful race and would do so again at some cost to his own reputation. Rae in his notes wrote that the information was "too vague to act upon, particularly at this season, when everything is covered with snow." Since his informant was reluctant to lead him to the spot where the bodies had been seen, Rae didn't pursue these clues. While his explanation is plausible enough, it must also be recognized that Rae's primary purpose was not to search for Franklin. His obsession was with the equally baffling problem of the North American coastline, which he was about to solve. He wanted to get on with it and so did not push or bribe his Eskimo companion to take him farther. If a Royal Navy explorer of the calibre of M'Clintock had been given the same information, the result might have been different.

It did not really matter, for Franklin was long dead. When Rae arrived back at Repulse Bay in the fall of 1854, a number of natives, lured by his promise of reward, gave him more details about the dead men. Rae was now able to conclude that the bodies had been found near the estuary of Back's Great Fish River. It was too late in the season for him to follow up that information, but there was no doubt now (if there had ever been) that the corpses the Eskimos had seen belonged to the Franklin party.

The natives brought to Repulse Bay a treasure trove of relics, easily identifiable as having belonged to Franklin and his men – silver forks and spoons marked with his officers' crests, one of Franklin's decorations, a small plate bearing his name, and other relics identifiable by names and initials – a gold watch, a fragment of embroidered undervest, and a quantity of smaller objects – including chains, coins, a surgeon's knife, a silver pencil case.

The Eskimos had no knowledge of the fate of either of Franklin's ships, nor was Rae able to tell from their accounts what route the lost explorer had taken when he left his winter quarters at Beechey Island. But he had learned enough to abandon his plans for another winter at Repulse Bay and get back to England as fast as possible with the news. He wanted, he said, to prevent further expense and possible loss of life in the now fruitless search for the explorer. Did he also want to be in a position to claim the parliamentary reward of ten thousand pounds? Certainly he was castigated for that in a spirited exchange of letters in *The Times*. Rae, however, insisted he'd never heard of the reward. That is hard to swallow. The original reward of twenty thousand pounds was posted in March 1848, just before Rae and Richardson set off to find Franklin. It is inconceivable that they hadn't known about it or discussed it. The later reward of ten thousand pounds for finding evidence of Franklin's fate was made in 1850. Rae had spent an entire year in England, from the spring of 1852 to the spring of 1853, at a time when Franklin fever was at its height. The news of the Beechey Island discovery was still fresh. Rae himself talked to some of the explorers assigned to the Belcher expedition. He visited the Admiralty and pointed out on a map what he considered to be the likeliest spot (southward and westward of Cape Walker) for discovering Franklin's fate. Although his biographer and others have accepted Rae's story, it passes all comprehension that he didn't know that whoever found the first Franklin relics would be rich for life.

But Rae had a more serious charge to defend. In his report to the Admiralty he had passed along, as required, stories told him by the Eskimos of acts of cannibalism among Franklin's starving men. Rae was still at sea when the Admiralty gave the report to *The Times*, which published it on October 23, 1854. Other publications picked it up. The British public was both horrified and sceptical. Englishmen eating Englishmen? It was beyond belief. The popular opinion was that the uncivilized natives had murdered Franklin's men.

Charles Dickens caught the public mood in *Household Words* when he described the Eskimos as "covetous, treacherous and cruel . . . with a domesticity of blood and blubber." It was impossible, he wrote, that "the flower of the trained adventurous spirit of the English Navy, raised by Parry, Franklin, Richardson and Back," could have descended to this, the most dreadful of crimes to the Victorian mind. ". . . it is in the highest degree improbable that such men would, or could, in any extremity of hunger, alleviate the pains of starvation by this horrible means."

Rae was excoriated, not because he had published the account in *The Times* – the Admiralty had done that – but because he stuck up for the Eskimos. He held his ground and insisted that their story was to be believed. At the same time, the combative Dr. King entered the lists to cast doubt not only on Rae's geographical discoveries but also on the means by which he had obtained the Franklin relics. Fortunately for Rae, no one paid much attention to King.

His reputation was not helped, however, by his long battle to claim the ten-thousand-pound reward. Lady Franklin was cool when he called on her, offended that anyone should be allowed the prize until a more detailed search was made. The Admiralty dallied, waiting for Collinson and for James Anderson, a Hudson's Bay factor who was sent down the Great Fish River to search for more evidence. Anderson found a few relics but no graves or skeletons. For Lady Franklin that was not enough.

In spite of her protests, Rae finally got his ten thousand pounds, two thousand of which were awarded to the men of his party. But there continued to be a feeling that there was something not quite gentlemanly about Rae, the man who lived like a native and insisted on taking the natives' part. His only accolade had been the Founder's Medal of the Geographical Society. Almost every other Arctic explorer – Parry, Back, Sabine, Richardson, Franklin, both Rosses, McClure, and M'Clintock – was knighted for his work. John Rae alone stood outside that charmed circle, a commoner to the end.

The Royal Navy's vain search for Franklin ended in a series of anticlimaxes. Belcher faced a court-martial for the loss of his ships and was grudgingly acquitted: his orders had allowed a latitude of decision. The court handed him back his sword in chilly silence. Two of the officers he'd arrested – Walter May and Sherard Osborn – weren't punished; they were promoted. Belcher himself was never given another command.

As for Robert McClure, he refused to give Kellett any credit for rescuing his crew. He stuck stubbornly to his story that he could have navigated the Passage without help and had only called it off when directly ordered to do so. To Lady Franklin's distress, he and his crew also received ten thousand pounds for his discovery and the glory of having succeeded where Franklin, presumably, had failed.

Thus the fate of Franklin lost some of its mystery and much of its lustre. In the fall of 1854 when Rae and Belcher returned to England, the public had already turned its attention elsewhere. People were now talking about the charge of the Light Brigade, immortalized in poetry by Alfred, Lord Tennyson, a member of the extended Franklin family. Only Lady Franklin continued her uphill battle to get at the truth; apart from Collinson, only one other man was still somewhere Out There, searching for her husband, or pretending to – the most romantic if not the most expert of all the polar explorers, Elisha Kent Kane.

Chapter Seven

Kalutunah

Kane's comrades in their cramped quarters aboard the Advance

August 1854. Elisha Kane had been cooped up for a year aboard the *Advance*, still seeking, after his fashion, a man who had been dead since 1847. Kane had no way of knowing that the Passage had been discovered and that John Rae had located the general area of the Franklin disaster almost a thousand miles to the southwest of Rensselaer Harbor. Dickens's *Bleak House* had become a best-seller in his absence and Verdi's *La Traviata* had had its disappointing première – not that Kane would have cared for either, since he had no ear for music and no time for novels. He would have been more interested to learn that Van Diemen's Land, which had proved Franklin's undoing, was now Tasmania, freed at last from any more convict ships; and that Gail Borden, who had made his biscuits and pemmican, had just invented Borden's Condensed Milk. But there was very little left of Borden's provender. The crew was subsisting on salt meat, the worst possible diet for those suffering from scurvy. And how were they to cook it? Only 750 pounds of coal remained. Before the winter was out, Kane knew he would have to start breaking up the ship for fuel.

He had other concerns. His relations with his crew, especially his officers, had continued to deteriorate. John Wilson, his sailing master, had felt for some time that Kane was trying to curry favour with the men while treating his officers "like a parcel of minions." The men grew insolent, refusing to attend evening prayers. One man who quit the service swore at his captain, using language "such as I never heard used by a sailorman except in this brig," but received no more than a tap on the wrist, being confined briefly to his quarters – "perfect child's play," in Wilson's scornful phrase.

As a result, the crew despised their captain. Wilson claimed that Kane couldn't go forward "without hearing his name used in the most insolent manner by the men in the forecastle." As for the officers, there wasn't one who would "trust one word he says or place a particle of confidence in him. He does nothing but quarrel from morning to night with those around him."

When Kane wasn't quarrelling he was boasting – about his narrow escapes, his exploits with women, his global adventures, his reception by foreign heads of state, and the expensive dinners at which he had been host. His table talk was embroidered with French and Latin phrases that irritated Wilson and the others: ". . . not one of the officers liked to be in the cabin, & all stay out as much as possible. He has not one friend in the ship left, save the lying scamp, Morton, whom he bribes, & who tells Mr. K. all he can hear us say. . . ."

The constant rows were too much for Ohlsen, the carpenter whom Kane had appointed to replace Henry Brooks as first mate. Ohlsen quit his post in June, shortly before Kane left on his vain attempt to reach Beechey Island for more supplies. When Kane returned on August 6, he received a cold reception from his officers – the coldest Wilson had ever seen in his life. The sailing master even felt a little sorry for him, "he seamed to take it so much to heart."

Now Kane became aware of secret meetings in Ohlsen's and Hayes's quarters. Men were gathering in groups, whispering together. Finally, William Morton came to him to report that several wanted to leave the ship rather than spend another winter in the High Arctic. They intended to try to make their way to Upernavik, the northernmost of the Greenland settlements, seven hundred miles to the south.

To Kane this was not only madness, it was also "a gross violation . . . of everything gallant and honorable." He saw these men as traitors. And yet, if he refused the dissidents permission to leave he would be faced with an appalling morale problem. "We are a set of scurvy-ridden, broken down men . . . a reluctant, brooding, disheartened spirit would sweep our decks like a pestilence. . . ."

He discussed the situation with Sonntag, the German scientist, who reassured him that not many would want to desert him and that the success of their proposed expedition was doubtful. On August 24 Kane called the company together to warn them of the dangers they faced. He gave them twenty-four hours to make up their minds.

The following day he got his answer, and it was a shocker. All but five opted to leave. Of these loyalists only Morton and "Irish Tom" Hickey, the cabin boy, were fit for duty aboard ship. Goodfellow, thoughtless and lazy, was useless. Brooks was flat on his back from amputated toes; Hans, the Eskimo, could only work outdoors and might take off at any time.

To Kane's dismay, four of his officers were determined to leave. Hayes he could understand – the party would need a doctor – and Hayes was convinced that if the crew did not split up, the entire brig would become a hospital. But Sonntag's defection was indefensible;

274

he had added deceit to treachery! Amos Bonsall, his old Pennsylvania neighbour, had also quit, and he couldn't talk him out of it, even though his arguments reduced the former farmer to tears. Wilson, who couldn't stand Kane, had second thoughts and returned to the fold, also in tears. James McGary also began to waver, couldn't make up his mind, but finally elected to stay. Nine of the ship's company of seventeen wanted to leave.

Kane refused to speak to the defectors, communicating with them through Ohlsen and in writing. He would give them provisions, equipment, and a boat to be built by Ohlsen, whom Kane called "the instigator of the whole concern, scheming and non-reliable but efficient." He advised them to elect a leader; they chose Ohlsen. But Ohlsen started to vacillate when Kane insisted that he and the others sign a statement making it clear that "from the moment of your leaving the brig you will be under your own control and your connection with the expedition will be regarded as closed."

In Kane's description, Ohlsen refused, "argued, urged, entreated, almost threatened, behaved like a madman." Kane then withdrew his permission for Ohlsen to leave; he would do so, he declared, at his peril. At the last minute the carpenter relented. If Kane would let him go, he said, he'd sign the waiver. Now Kane refused. If Ohlsen tried to leave, he said, he'd shoot him as a deserter. Ohlsen, "crying like a woman," had no choice but to remain.

The defectors took three days to organize themselves. On the surface the leave-taking was cordial; Kane even broke out his private stock of champagne. Later he would claim that "they carried with them a written assurance of a brother's welcome should they be driven back." Inwardly, he seethed with a black rage. They were deserters who had betrayed him by leaving their posts. He washed his hands of them. Their departure was, he thought, "a purgation, ridding me of condemned material worthy heretofore but rotten now." Those who had stayed were "natural gentlemen." He speared the malcontents with his pen: Bonsall, Hayes, and Sonntag "never had the associated gallantry or right mindedness of Goodfellow . . . or McGeary [sic] . . . Peterson [sic] was always a cold-blooded sneak, Ohlsen, double-faced, fawning and insincere."

He saw himself as a martyr, put upon by traitors. "I have made up my mind to act towards these miserable men without a thought of self . . . God will take care of us. I did not know before this awful prospect of a second winter that I had so much faith."

A few days later the pugnacious Blake and another of the crew, George Riley, returned crestfallen, complaining of a lack of order and discipline among the defectors. Actually, they had become panic-stricken when their small sledge went through the ice and almost drowned them. Blake rejoined the defectors, but Riley remained with Kane. On September 5, 1854, all connections were cut. The seven dissenters, led now by Petersen, vanished, presumably forever.

Outwardly calm, Kane that night poured out to his journal all his feelings of betrayal, his sense of personal injury, and his self-justification of the events of the previous weeks. It is an extraordinary passage, in which he began softly and then slowly worked himself into a vengeful rage against the men who had deserted him. He had sent them a larger sled, along with a letter to which they had not bothered to reply: ". . . neither written advice . . . nor thanks, nor goodbyes, nor words of any sort. So they go. From my very heart I can say a blessing go with them. Neither their ingratitude nor their selfishness shown in clear repulsiveness only after their departure can make me feel unkindly to these men.

". . . They are deserters, in act and in spirit – in all but the title. They leave their ship, abandon their sick comrades, fail to adhere to their commander, and are false to the implied trust which tells every true man to abide by the Expedition into which he has entered.

"When the first roll was called . . . I said not a word . . . all I exacted was a signed paper. . . . Since then, one by one – some from doubt, some from selfishness and some from fear – five strong men have come back to me. . . . So Providence favoured me in doing my duty. . . .

"One satisfaction I have – no slight one – that this misguided party have wanted for nothing – they have had the best of everything, even at self sacrifice. Their ingratitude is nothing. They should have had the same treatment had they spit in my face. I cannot but feel that some of them will return broken down and suffering to seek a refuge on board. They shall find it to the halving of our last chip – but – but – but – if I ever live to get home – *home*! . And should I meet *Dr. Hayes* or *Mr. Bonsall* or *Mister Sonntag* – let them look out for their skins. If I don't live to thrash them . . . why then, brother John, seek a solitary orchard and maull [*sic*] them for me. Don't honour them with a bullet and let the mauling be solitary save to the principals. It would hurt your Character to be wrestling with such low minded sneaks."

276

With that off his chest, Kane set about turning a portion of the ship into a reasonable facsimile of an Eskimo igloo. The crew tore the planking off the upper deck to use as winter firewood, sealed the quarterdeck with a padding of moss and turf, and prepared a living-space eighteen feet square. Ceiling and floors were lined with moss and the floor was caulked with two inches of oakum and plaster of Paris. The entrance, a long, narrow passage between decks, was also insulated. This would be winter quarters for the company of ten. Fortunately Ohlsen, who had been blubbering in his bunk, now recanted, shook hands with his captain, and reported for work.

Kane realized he would have to depend on the Eskimos for fresh seal and walrus meat to stave off scurvy and for dogs to pull sledges. But to his dismay he discovered that a band of natives with whom he had been dealing aboard ship had slipped away, taking a number of cooking utensils and buffalo robes with them. Something would have to be done – and quickly – to restore relations and stop any further pilfering.

He dispatched his two best walkers, Morton and Riley, to the tiny community of Anoatok, halfway between the ship and the main Eskimo village of Etah. There they found three of the culprits, a boy and two women, asleep with their loot. They sent the boy to Etah to report to the headman, Metek, and then kidnapped the two women, one of whom was Metek's wife. Held prisoner aboard the ship, wailing and singing doleful songs, the women were the bait that brought Metek posthaste back to the brig to return a sledgeload of pilfered objects. Then and there Kane concluded a formal treaty with the Eskimos. They promised to supply him with fresh meat and dogs and to refrain from further thefts. He on his part swore to give them presents and guns with which to hunt. The pact was solemnized and the bargain held to by both sides.

A worse irritant was an infestation of rats that quit the hold for the warmth of Kane's makeshift igloo. There were rats under the stove, rats in the cushions, rats in the lockers, rats in the bedding. They chewed away at furs, woollens, shoes, specimens – everything. When Kane put his hand into a mitten one day he was bitten by a mother rat that was raising her brood inside it. Before he could staunch the blood, the rat family had run off with the mitten! But Kane put the rats to good use. During his adventurous years around the globe he had eaten everything from bats to puppy-dogs. When travelling with the Eskimos he cheerfully ate the raw blubber that nauseated some of his crew. Now he simply cooked and ate the rats. By the end of October half his company was down with scurvy, but Kane scarcely suffered, thanks to the fresh meat.

As the weeks dragged on, the brig was slowly stripped of all available firewood. The upper deck, bulwark, fancy shelving, and bulkheads were all gone by early November. The oppressive Arctic night was shattering the crew's morale. McGary became so homesick one night that he walked the deck, disconsolate, refusing to eat anything. Wilson was tormented by thoughts of home and friends, especially one particular friend, Bessie Pierce, whose "dear image seems to float around me like a halo around the sun." A gloomy thought crossed his mind. Perhaps she had decided to marry! The prospect seemed "to cast a shadow over all my bright anticipations . . . and rush me back into the darkest recesses of seclusion. . . ."

Kane, too, confessed to moments of despair: "My thoughts, my diseased craving for love and caressment, everything that unbends, I crush, strangle, before they take shape. The Father – I cease to remember his years – the Mother – I will not count her tears – weeping on her wet pillow for her firstborn and her last."

He could not, as leader, allow these feelings to show. On the contrary, he continued the authoritarian style that added to the tensions aboard the *Advance* that winter. To Wilson, the cramped cabin was "the most perfect hell hole." Kane was venting his increasing rages on the youngest member of the crew, Tom Hickey. But none was exempt from the captain's temperamental outbursts. According to Wilson, "from the time he gets up in the morning until we are all turned in, he is incessantly quareling [sic] with someone or making use of his arbitary [sic] power." Kane's habit of going to bed at three or four in the morning but never rising until noon was another irritant. "He turns day into night," Wilson recorded, "but makes us all get up at 7 bells . . . and breakfast at 8."

To the crew, Kane was a martinet. Kane, of course, saw himself as the rock on which the others depended, the stern parent keeping his errant children in line. "Every energy of my nature – a vile foul nature too – is bent to bear myself and those who lean on me out of this great trial. If I let weakness come over me now – we, I mean all of us – are gone. But if – if the Lord does not blot me out and I will return as a man who has braved a hard temptation and abided by his trust, then those who live either with me, or after me . . . will give me credit for something more than a blind will & a groping material-ism. . . ."

His loneliness was accentuated by his estrangement from the one companion he thought of as a gentleman, and thus worthy of a certain intimacy. This was Henry Goodfellow, a feckless youth who had been taken on as a natural history observer as a favour to Kane's brother Tom. Goodfellow was worse than useless. Wilson found him "lazy, dirty, ragged and impudent to every one." To Kane, who continued to indulge him, he was "one of the most impracticable and helpless men I was ever connected with." Goodfellow grew more slovenly by the day, neglected his duty, refused to look after himself, and slowly withdrew from his shipmates, most of whom were no longer on speaking terms with him. When Kane lost his temper with him, Goodfellow cut him dead; to avoid further turmoil and discord, Kane relieved him of all duties and took them over himself. While the others toiled, Goodfellow lounged about, reading novels.

Kane could "never speak to him without disgust" but, martyrlike, still catered to him. "This is the man to whom I had looked for an interchange of home thoughts – for confidential copying – for relief from my heavy daily toil – yet for him – rather say for Tom – I'm keeping a double set of nightly watches, losing my scanty hours of sleep. He asks me for a glass of lime juice and water. 'Yes, Henry.' So off I go to get it and he now just awake and prepared for a new guzzle and a new nap. He has more cool impudence than any man I ever knew."

By early December, five of the crew were prostrate with scurvy. Morton's Achilles tendon was so badly perforated the bone was exposed, but Kane feared that an operation would bring on tetanus. The chief antiscorbutic consisted of gratings from raw potatoes. There were only twelve of these left, at least three years old – "poor old frozen memorials of the dear land they grew in."

The three healthy men were put to work tearing the oak ribbing off the ship for firewood. Kane had managed to collect more than a ton of fuel in this way, but that would scarcely last past January. For February and March, the worst of the winter months, he counted on the three inches of oak sheathing, nailed to the ship's side as protec-tion against the ice. Ohlsen was sure that its removal would not greatly affect the brig's seaworthiness if it were cut off no deeper than the waterline. That would provide an extra two and a half tons of firewood. "With this – God willing – I may get through this awful winter and *save the brig besides*!" Kane told himself.

But these wishful hopes were dashed at about three o'clock on the morning of December 7. Kane was wakened with the news that five sledges with six teams of dogs, each with strange drivers, were approaching the ship. A few minutes later, a group of Eskimos came aboard, supporting Bonsall and Petersen, both in dreadful condition. They had left the brig fourteen weeks before but, as Kane had prophesied, they had not been able to reach Upernavik. The other defectors, exhausted and starving, were crouching in a stone hovel some 150 miles to the south. The pair had managed to get back to the brig by bribing the southern Eskimos. Now they pleaded for help for their comrades.

Kane acted at once, gathering up a hundred pounds of provisions and dispatching them with the strange Eskimos. Petersen and Bonsall were too far gone to move. Kane and the able-bodied men couldn't desert the sick aboard the ship. Although he didn't trust the new natives to take the food back to the others, he had no choice. He gave them presents, sent them on their way, and hoped for the best.

2

Kalutunah The eight men who had left for the south the previous August were an oddly assorted lot – a German astronomer, a Baltimore seaman, a Pennsylvania farmer, a Greenland cooper, a Hull sailor, an East River boatman, an Irish patriot, and a Philadelphia medical student. Of these, only the Greenlander, Petersen, had any Arctic experience. But it can scarcely be said that Petersen was in charge. For the man on whom the party really depended for its life or its death was a cheerful and voluble Eskimo *angetok* (medicine man) from the village of Netlik. His name was Kalutunah.

They had encountered him during the first winter and met him again as they struggled with maddening slowness in their two small boats through an almost impenetrable wilderness of ice. By the time they reached Netlik on the coast near Northumberland Island, they were running short of food and fuel. Kalutunah's people gave them blubber to eat and moss for lamp wicks in return for needles and knives. Four days later on September 16 the ice closed in for good, and they realized they had no hope of reaching civilization before spring. They set to work in the freezing cold to build a shelter on the shore using boulders, chinked with moss, and tin and lumber from the two boats.

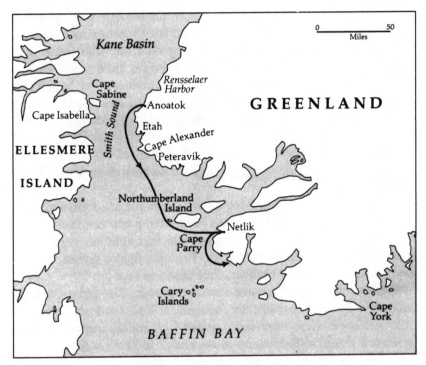

Southward route of Kane's defectors, autumn, 1854

On October 9, after more than three weeks of "unmitigated misery," to quote Dr. Hayes, they moved at last into this "cold, fireless, damp vault-like den." By the eighteenth their biscuit was gone and they were reduced to eating rock moss, which produced dreadful cramps and diarrhea. Exposure, starvation, and certain death faced them.

Two days later, they were reprieved when two of the most inhuman-looking creatures the men had ever seen crawled into the hut – "shapeless lumps of whiteness" in Hayes's description – covered from head to foot in a coating of ice and snow. Kalutunah and a companion had travelled for thirty-six hours without a break to bring frozen meat and blubber, which the destitute men fell upon like

281

wolves. Two years earlier, George McDougall, one of Kellett's officers aboard the Franklin search ship *Resolute*, had recorded his disgust at seeing "these degraded creatures," as he called the Eskimos, eating seals' intestines. To him they were an object of pity. Now, however, the mukluk was on the other foot.

It was obvious that the party could not survive without native help. The Arctic Highlanders were eager for the white men's goods, especially metal and wood. Petersen, the only one who spoke their language, carefully negotiated a treaty: food for knives, needles, and other treasures. It required considerable diplomacy, for he guessed that if the whites were seen to be starving, the natives might prefer to let them die in order to make off with everything. Petersen, accordingly, insisted to Kalutunah that with their magic sticks (guns) the whites were perfectly able to look after themselves. Kalutunah, however, wouldn't rent or sell them dogs or sledges. Clearly, he didn't want them to get away.

The two Eskimos left, leaving meat enough for one meal and some blubber for fuel. It was two weeks before the party saw them again. Unskilled in hunting, they survived the fortnight on rock moss, growing steadily weaker. When the Eskimos finally turned up with several days' supply of blubber, they began to recover.

It was a maddening, cat-and-mouse existence. The natives, in total control, appeared sporadically, bringing a little food and fuel, and then vanished. Here were eight civilized creatures, trapped in their wretched shack, scrabbling for moss, unable to bring in more than an occasional fox or ptarmigan in spite of their superior weapons, while the Eskimos came and went at will. Hayes was astonished at the natives' indifference to the elements. One day a young woman turned up with a six-month-old baby strapped to her back. She had travelled forty miles in -35^0 weather, often dismounting from the dogsled and walking because of the roughness of the route, her only motive being an insatiable curiosity to see the white strangers and their treasure.

They *must* get free of the Eskimos! The best chance was to send back to the ship for more supplies, hole up for the winter in the hut, and try to reach the whaling fleet in the spring. Petersen agreed to go with Kalutunah to his village and bargain for dogs and sleds for a flying trip to Rensselaer Harbor. Godfrey offered to go with him as far as Netlik.

They reached the village on November 3. At first they were well fed

282

and well treated, but as time passed, Petersen, a cautious Dane who had lived among the Eskimos for twenty years and was married to one, began to feel uneasy. Many strangers began to crowd into the village including a glowering dog driver named Sip-su, who boasted that he'd killed two members of his own tribe because they couldn't hunt. And Kalutunah seemed to be under Sip-su's spell.

Petersen was anxious to be on his way: the huts were crowded with people; a dozen sleds had been collected together, but now he was told with some surliness that nobody wished to go with him. When all the Eskimos laughed heartily at that announcement, he knew he was in danger. He quietly warned Godfrey in the next hut to be on his guard and told the crowd that if anything happened to him, his friends would arrive with their magic guns and kill them all. At those words, the Eskimos laughed all the more.

His suspicions were confirmed when he offered to buy a dogteam. The sombre Sip-su turned to Kalutunah and asked a sinister question: "Don't you think we can get his things in a cheaper way?"

Petersen's only security lay in the Eskimos' belief that he had a pistol in his pocket. The natives feared it, convinced it was a magic wand. Actually, he had no pistol and his rifle, which the natives also feared, was outside the hut. They crowded around him, urging him to have a nap, their duplicity transparent. Petersen closed his eyes, feigned sleep, and listened to them piecing together a plot to kill all the white men and capture their belongings. Sip-su was the instigator; he announced he would lead the attack with Kalutunah as his lieutenant.

Petersen opened his eyes just as Sip-su started to search for the non-existent pistol. Outside, a crowd had gathered around the rifle, afraid to touch it. Petersen managed to seize it and announced he was going off to hunt for bear. The Eskimos tried to persuade him to stay, insisting they meant no harm. But Petersen was determined to get back to the hut with Godfrey, in spite of the intense cold.

They had at least forty miles to go and had proceeded no more than two when the Eskimos gave chase. Petersen brandished the magic rifle, keeping them at a distance. But he could never be sure that they did not lurk in ambush behind one of the frozen hummocks. That forced the white men to lengthen their journey to avoid such dangers, while Petersen, his hands freezing, kept his weapon at the ready.

They could not stop to sleep. If the natives didn't get them the cold would. Drowsy, exhausted, starving, and mad with thirst, they stumbled into the hut after trudging for twenty-four hours and fell forward on their faces crying "Water! Water!" They had survived only because the Eskimos had fed them well during their three days at Netlik.

Now the party prepared for an attack. Instead, Kalutunah appeared, all smiles, with a large piece of walrus meat and some liver. To Hayes, "the Eskimos appear to us more as our good angels than as our enemies." He was convinced that they had been influenced by a bad leader and by extraordinary temptation: the miserable store of trade goods, which were to the natives like precious jewels.

Hayes was right. Another Eskimo, Kingiktok, appeared and explained that the sinister Sip-su had repeatedly said that if the white men died, those who followed him could get all the valuables. Kalutunah was opposed, arguing that the white men's magic weapons would keep them alive. But the band grew impatient; they could see that they themselves were keeping the white men alive – or at least Kalutunah was. The more treasures he brought back the more they wanted. When Petersen and Godfrey reached the village, Sip-su plotted against them, only to have his courage fail in the presence of the magic gun.

The party, having managed to get five dogs from the natives, decided to return en masse to the brig. It was not possible. After a few miles they turned back, stupefied by cold and exhaustion. The following morning the two strongest, Petersen and Bonsall, set off alone. Those left behind were again without food except for pieces of walrus hide; by the third day even that was gone.

In a moment of lightheadedness, Dr. Hayes walked out into the moonlight "with desolation and the silence of death everywhere before me," sat down on a rock facing the frozen sea, and "better than ever before, better probably than ever again . . . felt what it was to depend upon oneself and God."

In a demented act of determination he banished the cheerless vista from his view. He forgot his loneliness, forgot the cold moon, the dark cliffs, the desolate waste of white, and in his mind forced the bleak landscape into a pastoral mode. The sea became a fertile plain, the ice hummocks walls and hedges. The vapour rising from an open channel became smoke from cottages. Clusters of ice blocks suggested herds of cattle and flocks of sheep. Larger masses were converted into trees, while a wall of snow casting a dark shadow in the moonlight became the margin of a forest. A pinnacled berg in the distance appeared as a church, another became a ruined castle, and far to the southwest he thought he saw the outlines of a great fort under whose bristling guns lay a fleet of stately ships.

The vision brought back a flood of boyhood memories. He turned away, resolved to continue the struggle for existence, determined to live to view some day in the future the spectacle that his disordered mind had conjured up on the moonlit surface of that pitiless sea.

When Kalutunah and two others returned again, the desperate men became convinced that they meant to leave them to their fate. The Eskimos had food, but they had hidden it. They refused to take the party north or to rent them dogteams. It appeared that they were determined to let the men starve to death and then plunder the hut. Hayes, with his new resoluteness, had no intention of allowing that. The party must take matters into their own hands. He didn't want to murder the Eskimos; his plan was to put them to sleep with an opium derivative, laudanum, then steal their dogs and sledges and head for the brig.

The Eskimos allowed them two small pieces of meat. Hayes made a soup and offered some to Kalutunah and his friends, dropping the contents of a vial of laudanum into their bowls. While the whites watched and waited, the natives ate greedily. Soon they became drowsy. Hayes and the others helped them off with their coats and boots, and then moved quickly to don their own travelling clothes.

At this point Godfrey reached for a tin cup. The contents clattered to the ground. *Panic!* With a single sweep of his hand, Hayes doused the light. Kalutunah grunted and asked what was the matter. Hayes gave him a hug and muttered the Eskimo word for sleep. Kalutunah laughed and began to snore.

They knew they had no time to lose. They crawled out of the hut, taking the natives' boots, mittens, and coats, then barricaded the doorway as best they could. August Sonntag already had the sledges ready. Unaccustomed to these strange and inexperienced drivers, the dogs howled in terror and were off at the first crack of the whip.

It was a clumsy journey. None of them understood how to handle Eskimo dogs – an art that requires months of training. One sledge overturned and the dogs, squirming out of their traces, hightailed it back to the hut. With three men on each of the remaining two sledges, the party blundered on as far as Cape Parry, where they found shelter in a cave.

Their freedom was short-lived. The Eskimos had awoken quickly and, with their usual ingenuity, fashioned mukluks out of blankets, cut up other blankets as ponchos, retrieved the lost sled and the wandering dogs, and quickly picked up the party's trail. Since they knew how to handle the dogs, it was no trick to catch up with the white men. There they stood, silent accusers, their heads protruding from blankets – one red, one white, one blue – their feet wrapped in old cloths and, in one case, a discarded pair of boots, and their arms filled with the treasure they could not bear to abandon – tin cups, saucers, cutlery, even an old hat. The situation would have been ludicrous had it not been so threatening.

Hayes held them off with a rifle. The Eskimos pleaded with him not to shoot. Hayes managed to take two prisoners and, in sign language, offered a deal. If Kalutunah would drive the party north, the dogs, sledges, and clothes would be returned. Otherwise he would shoot them. Kalutunah cheerfully agreed, grateful that he was not to be killed with the magic weapon.

They were taken north through a series of tiny Eskimo settlements where they were treated with great hospitality, fed, and rested. The last stop was the larger village of Etah, but to reach it they must travel around Cape Alexander, "the blowing place," where they were forced to cling to a narrow shelf in the cliffside no more than fifteen inches wide, high above the sea. After five miles of terror they reached Etah to discover that Petersen's Eskimos had devoured all the food that Kane had sent back with them – and they still had seventy miles to go!

The natives helped them, but by the time they reached the brig one man was stupefied by cold and the others were at the breaking point. Hayes, in later life, could never remember their arrival; but Kane could! Hayes, he said, had managed to utter a few words: "We come here destitute and exhausted to claim your hospitality; we know we have no rights to your indulgence but we feel that with you we will have a welcome and a home."

Kane took one look at him – covered with snow, fainting from hunger – grasped his hand, and beckoned his companions to come aboard. The young doctor's feet were so badly frostbitten and gangrenous that Kane had to amputate several of his toes. Then he gave him his own bed to sleep in.

But he did not forgive him.

286

3

He forgave no one. The addition of eight men to his crowded ship *Retreat*
presented an embarrassing problem. They arrived with only the
clothes on their backs. All the equipment they had taken, including
the two boats, was lost. They didn't even have blankets. Kane had
hoped to eke out an existence through the winter with his small but
faithful company and then make a dash for the sea; now he had
almost double that number. They must share and share alike – he
was prepared for that – but the unfaithful could not be treated like
the faithful.

The loyal party was more than a little bitter at the returnees, who
had squandered their goodwill as well as their clothes, food, and
equipment. Well, he, Kane, had warned them! He had predicted
exactly what would happen and they hadn't listened to him – to *him*,
with his Arctic experience. They had leaned on him, trusted him,
"and like little children been taught by me their very walk," and yet
in their innocence and stupidity they had gone against his "drearily
earned experience of Arctic ice."

"God in Heaven," Kane wrote in his private journal, "it makes my
blood boil!"

He could not let go. In page after page he scribbled once again the
full story of his crew's defection. There is an air of self-justification
here, of self-pity and, above all, of disdain for these "eight weak or
timid or immoral men." At first, charity – "Poor devils, how they eat,
how they swilled coffee and meat-biscuit soup" – but also condescension: "Like the Eskimos they had unconsciously adopted their very
manners."

Soon this turned to fury, not unmixed with the snobbishness of
the well-bred Philadelphian. Bonsall was "a country boy of low bred
training and selfish instincts." Sonntag was "a weak, sycophantic
specialité student, a German Jew employed of a second-rate observatory." Hayes was "a vast extenuator of every abomination," Petersen
"a double faced mischief maker."

"These men can never be my associates again," Kane wrote. And
so, on that cramped little vessel with its one crowded room, he
ordered an incredible arrangement. The ship's company would be
divided into two groups: the faithful and the unfaithful. Each would

287

mess separately. The unfaithful would be forbidden any duties connected with the ship. They would contribute to their own daily routine, but they would be treated as guests aboard the *Advance*. The faithful would do all the work, but since most were down with scurvy or useless, that meant that Kane, ever the martyr, must take on most of the burden himself.

This extraordinary disposition was further complicated by Blake and Godfrey, the two malcontents, who were so unpopular that they were forced to mess apart from the others. An act of insubordination by this unruly pair finally forced Kane to violence. He seized a belaying pin, bashed in Blake's skull, and knocked Godfrey to the ground. A third man, George Whipple, "a poor weak unfortunate" in Kane's words, fell to his knees begging forgiveness and escaped with a cuffing. Blake suffered a concussion but recovered. Kane warned him that if it happened again he'd use a real weapon and if there was a third breach of discipline, he'd kill him. "This is what should have been done long since," John Wilson remarked. "Then we would all have been saved much trouble. . . ."

Christmas came without fresh food and only one bottle of champagne left to toast the Yuletide. Kane thought that night of his family in Philadelphia who must be worried sick about him. Some day, he confided to his journal, he would have their "approval" – a word that occurs more than once in Kane's nocturnal scribblings, supplying one key to his restless, impulsive nature. He was determined – almost pathetically so – to justify himself, the reckless wanderer, to the stern and proper jurist who had fathered him.

Now on this dark Christmas night, the man who had scoffed at Margaret Fox's séances, had a mystical experience of his own, one that he attributed to an "animal magnetism" he could not control. He saw his home as clearly as he saw the crowded room in which he and the company were quartered. It embarrassed him. "How I saw it," he wrote, "no journal shall ever record. I dread the non-practical, mystified atmosphere of the whole matter." He did not then, or later, mention the nineteen-year-old spirit rapper whom he had closeted in a Pennsylvania backwater. But he had her portrait and, it is said, carried it with him wherever he travelled.

As the winter wore on, tempers again began to fray. Goodfellow and Brooks came to blows. Wilson was convinced Kane's brain had become unhinged: "He must have someone to quarrel with all the time, first one, then another." Kane saw it differently: "My task is a hard and thankless one, totally unappreciated by my clients and made, thank Heaven, without care or regard for their appreciation or non-appreciation."

Fresh meat was scarce; even Hans the hunter was hard put to find anything; at Etah he found the Eskimos starving. The stalwart Brooks, peering at his own ravaged face in the mirror, burst into tears. Although the crew remained divided into the faithful and unfaithful, to use Kane's terms, he had to call upon the healthier of the former deserters to help with duties, making it clear that this in no way represented any kind of restoration to their posts. By March, fourteen men were flat on their backs with scurvy.

But now Kane faced a more serious problem. He learned that Godfrey and Blake were planning to steal dogs, sledge, and provisions and leave for the south; the date was set for March 20.

Kane rose that morning, armed himself, and ordered Godfrey to cook breakfast. Then he crawled through the narrow passageway between decks that led to the sleeping quarters, concealed himself, and waited. Blake appeared first, showing none of the previous signs of the illness he said had plagued him. Godfrey, dressed for travel, followed. Kane leaped out and thrust a pistol an inch from his nose. When Godfrey confessed to the plot, Kane knocked him down and hammered him with a piece of lead concealed inside his mitt. But now he faced a dilemma: he could not confine the malefactors, for he needed every able-bodied man. As a result, Godfrey managed to slip away. Kane was alarmed. He had sent Hans south with the sledges on March 18 on another attempt to get meat at Etah. If Godfrey caught up with him and took his team, there would be no escape for any of them, for the brig, looted for fuel, was no longer seaworthy.

To Kane's further alarm, Hans did not return. A week passed; nothing. A few ptarmigan, shot by Petersen, helped keep the invalids alive. Then on April 2, a man was seen a mile from the brig. Could it be Hans? No – it was William Godfrey with two dogs and a sled-load of walrus meat. He had made an incredible trip on foot seventy miles in -50^0 weather and reached Etah in thirty hours, something no one else had been able to do. Now he was back to report that Hans was ill and that he himself had decided to live with the natives.

Kane's version of what happened differs from Godfrey's account. Both were self-serving. To Kane, Godfrey was a deserter who must be clapped in irons. Godfrey thought of himself as the saviour of the ship's company. A verbal tussle ensued, with Kane ordering Godfrey aboard and Godfrey refusing, claiming he was going back to Etah for more supplies. Kane threatened to shoot Godfrey, who pointed out, reasonably enough, that he had returned of his own accord with meat for all. "Is this an offense that deserves capital punishment?" he asked.

Kane handed a pistol to Amos Bonsall and ordered him to shoot Godfrey if he tried to leave. Godfrey defiantly walked away. Bonsall's pistol misfired; Kane used his rifle, but it failed in the cold. A second attempt sent a bullet whistling over Godfrey's head. Not in the least disturbed, he continued to walk away. Incredibly, he reached Etah, staggering into one of the huts, where the Eskimos massaged his half-frozen limbs and let him sleep for fifteen hours.

The meat he'd brought to the brig was a godsend. Kane, however, was still suspicious. Godfrey was at large, and his crony, Blake, was aboard ship. What mischief were they planning? Certainly the sternest discipline would be needed if Godfrey's example was not to be followed. He called the men together and warned that anyone who deserted would be shot.

He couldn't let Godfrey get away with it; on April 10 he set off for Etah himself, and there he found Hans hunting seal, no longer ill but in love with the young Eskimo woman Merkut, who had nursed him. With Hans back on the brig, Kane again turned his attention to Godfrey. "Cost what it may I must have him back," he declared. He disguised himself as an Eskimo, took one of Hans's friends with him, armed himself with a six-shooter, packed a set of leg irons, found Godfrey in a hut at Etah, and forced him back at gunpoint. Godfrey came meekly enough. Either he was afraid of his captain (as Kane suggested) or the meeting was more amiable than Kane made out (as Godfrey suggested).

Kane still hoped to add some lustre to his expedition. Taking Hans, he went off on a bear hunt with some of the Etah Eskimos, hoping to get beyond the Humboldt Glacier. Perhaps, after all, Henry Grinnell's confidence in him would not be misplaced. To him, the philanthropist was a second father, and Kane longed to be able to take him by the hand and say, "I have not failed you or myself." At the same time, a mood of fatalism crept into his journal. "It may be that I, taxed beyond all corporeal existence, give way on the brink of consummating my hopes, crying: 'I have discovered a new land but I die.'"

Nothing so melodramatic took place, and Kane did indeed have the opportunity of sketching that colossal tableland broken by glittering white precipices, split by frozen water tunnels, and wrinkled by gargantuan crevices and dizzy ravines.

Hans went off towards Etah, ostensibly to get some walrus hide to make boots but actually to resume his liaison with Merkut. That was the last Kane saw of him. The two were married and went off to raise a family – a defection that was a blow to Kane, for he needed Hans's help in moving his ailing party south. He attempted one last exploration of the western side of the basin, hoping to find some trace, he said, of the lost Franklin party. It was a useless and exhausting journey that broke Morton down. Kane on his return wasn't much better.

The brig would have to be abandoned. She was a sorry-looking vessel that May, her upper spars, bulwarks, deck sheathing, stanchions, bulkheads, hatches, ice timbers, and railings all torn off for fuel. Every scrap of hemp, every tarred rope, everything burnable down to the last broomstick had been sacrificed to keep the crew from freezing to death. Now they would have to make their way to Upernavik by small boat. The healthier men were already fashioning runners to haul the two whaleboats and a smaller dinghy over the snows to open water.

The open water lay some eighty miles to the south at Naviliak, on the coast not far from Etah. Everything – three boats, fifteen hundred pounds of supplies, and four disabled invalids – would have to be shuttled, a mile or so between rests, by men weakened by scurvy and hunger. The sick were lodged at a halfway house at Anoatok, while the others toiled for thirty-one days to move everything to the open sea. In that time – May 17 to June 18 – the exhausted men, so weak they could pull only one boat at a time, each trudged a distance of 316 miles. Kane did more. Travelling constantly by dogsled – to Etah to get food, to Anoatok to minister to the invalids, back to the brig to help bake bread – he covered 1,100 miles.

On the final lap, as the last of the sick men were being brought forward, Christian Ohlsen came to grief. One of the runners of his boat had partially broken through the frozen surface and only his strength had kept it from swamping while the others pulled it back onto solid ice. But Ohlsen had ruptured his bladder. He lingered for a few days, then died – the third casualty of the Second Grinnell Expedition.

Without the Eskimos, as Kane himself acknowledged, they would

291

never have made it. The entire population of Etah turned out to wave farewell as the whaleboats *Faith* and *Hope* set off on June 19, around the curling waves of Cape Alexander. The air was turbulent with kittiwakes, ivory gulls, and jaegers, screaming and diving for fish, but Kane had other things on his mind. They were perilously late leaving – so late that "hours may measure our lives." But for the help of the natives they would have been held back another fortnight.

For the next forty-nine days they fought their way through blizzards, pack ice, and bergs, exhausted from the labour of tracking the boats and weak from lack of food. Kane insisted on a disciplined routine: the men must get their rest at night whether it meant lying under the ice-sheathed cliffs in their buffalo robes or sleeping aboard the boats. The routine extended to morning and evening prayers, a ritual he believed kept up his crew's morale. If there was grumbling, there is no hint of it in the various accounts that followed. No longer idle, the ill-starred company now knew their only hope of survival lay in working as a team.

The scenery was often spectacular: one night they beached their boats beneath a hanging glacier, eleven hundred feet high, which Kane likened to a vast cauldron of ice boiling over. Near Netlik, a huge pillar of granite – Clarence Rock – rose into the mists like a pyramid surmounted by an obelisk. By then their provisions were almost exhausted. Kane allowed each man only six ounces of bread dust a day, plus a walnut-sized lump of tallow. He himself took the helm for sixteen hours without a break. As his men tracked the boats through veins of water between distorted ice fields, he noted the slow loss of muscular power and realized they must find food quickly or die.

He fastened his little flotilla to a great floe from whose peak he could see in the distance the red, brassy face of Dalrymple Rock. Then, as if to emphasize his helplessness, a gale hit with sledge-hammer force. The floe was hurled and crushed against the base of the rock, amid a clamour like "the braying of a thousand trumpets." Somehow they survived, helplessly whirled about in the boats as the headland flashed past. They forced themselves with boat hooks into a stretch of open water and, when the tide rose, pulled their craft over an ice shelf and into a sheltering gorge where, too weak to unload their supplies, they simply dropped in their tracks and slept.

Here was game aplenty. As they waited for the storm to subside, they gathered ducks' eggs – twelve hundred in a single day – and shot

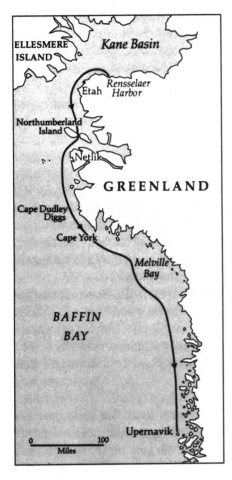

Kane's retreat from Rensselaer Harbor, 1855

sea fowl. By the time they quit their crystal retreat they had two hundred pounds of dried meat to sustain them on the next leg of the voyage.

At Cape Dudley Diggs, the tongue of a great glacier barred their way. Kane, climbing a berg, saw to his dismay that here the season was late. The ice was still impassable; they would have to wait for the tardy summer to open a lane. He could not bear to tell the others. They waited another week, crept forward in their battered craft to Cape York, and waited again. It was July 21. There was game but no fuel. To cook the meat, they were forced to burn oars, sledge runners, and, finally, the little dinghy, *Red Eric*. They set off again and found, after an exhausting journey, that they had mistakenly entered a cul-de-sac. The prospect of repairing the sledges and retracing their steps with the boats again on runners was so horrifying that even McGary, the toughest of the crew, was reduced to tears. It took three days of backbreaking toil.

By the time they crossed Melville Bay their food was gone. Only the fortuitous capture of a seal saved them from starving to death. Then, at last, on August 1 they sighted the famous landmark known as the Devil's Thumb, a huge bulbous pinnacle that told them they'd entered the whaling grounds of Baffin Bay.

Two days later, Petersen came upon the first native they'd seen since leaving Etah. To his joy, he recognized an old friend, paddling his kayak on the search for eider among the islands.

"Paul Zacharias," Petersen cried. "Don't you know me? I'm Carl Petersen."

The man stared at him in fright. "No," he said, "his wife says he's dead," and he paddled off as fast as he could.

Another two days, and a new sound was heard as the men rowed along. It wasn't the gulls; it wasn't the cry of a fox; it was the soft slapping of oars accompanied by a low "halloo!"

"What is it?" Kane asked.

Petersen listened for a moment and then in a trembling half-whisper exclaimed: "*Dannemarkers!*"

The cry echoed again from a nearby cape, then died. Both boats pulled toward it, scanning the shore. Had it all been a dream?

Half an hour passed. Then the single mast of a small shallop showed itself. Petersen began to sob and to cry out, half in English, half in Danish. It was, he said, an Upernavik oil boat. He knew it well: the *Fraulein Flairscher*. "Carlie Mossyn the assistant cooper must be on his road to Kingatok for blubber!"

Petersen was right; in a moment Carlie Mossyn himself appeared. Kane's crew was hungry for news of the outside world, which they had left two years before, and pleaded with Petersen to translate their questions.

"What of America? Eh, Petersen?"

"We don't know much of that country here, for they have no whalers on the coast," said Carlie, "but a steamer and a barque passed up a fortnight ago, and have gone out into the ice to seek your party."

And then he added, as if an afterthought, "Sebastopol ain't taken." That was gibberish to the men who hadn't heard of the Crimean War.

And only now did they learn that they had been searching for Franklin a thousand miles from the spot where Rae had discovered the first clues to his fate. Now Kane knew that his searches had been futile, that all his trials and sacrifices had been for nothing. Yet he could take heart in his discoveries. He had moved his ship farther north in the western Arctic than any other white man. He had explored much of the basin that immortalizes his name; he had discovered the largest glacier in the known world; and, he believed, he had "proved" the existence of an Open Polar Sea. More important than all of these satisfactions he had, through an exercise of will power,

294

careful planning, and discipline, managed to bring all but one of his bickering and insubordinate crew through some of the most treacherous waters in the world to a safe haven in a friendly Greenland port. The following night, August 6, 1855, he and his men slept under a civilized roof for the first time since leaving the *Advance*. Their rest was understandably fitful. After eighty-four days in the open air, they all were oppressed by a suffocating sense of claustrophobia.

4

In May 1855, while Elisha Kane was preparing to make his escape *The high cost* from Rensselaer Harbor, Captain Richard Collinson returned to *of dawdling* England with the *Enterprise* after an absence of five years and four months. He had spent five winters away from home; he had been out of touch with the civilized world for three years; he had circumnavigated the globe, returning home by way of the Cape of Good Hope. He had visited and explored all the mysterious "lands" that might or might not be islands – Banks, Baring, Wollaston, and Victoria. He had sailed up Prince of Wales Strait and had got as far east as Victoria Strait, directly across from King William Island. Yet his remarkable voyage was a failure because he had discovered nothing new. Wherever he went, he found that some other explorer had been there before him: the bold McClure, the indefatigable Rae, the ambitious Simpson.

It was maddening. Each time he thought he had made a new and significant discovery he came upon evidence that somebody else had preceded him. Had he been a year or two earlier he might have emerged as one of the greatest of the Arctic explorers. As it was, he returned to England with a reputation as a man who had simply covered old ground.

His reception was chilly, not because of these failures, which could be understandable, but because he was at odds with his officers. At one time or another all had been under arrest. Two were still confined – one, Francis Skead, for the past three years. Collinson, "a lean, spare, withered looking man with a vinegar countenance," in the description of Lieutenant Sharpe of the *Rattlesnake*, demanded that they be court-martialled. The Lords of the Admiralty declined. They were used to this sort of problem. It was understandable that after

295

more than four years cooped up on a crowded ship, even disciplined naval men would feel the tension.

History has excused Collinson on these grounds. As his brother Thomas, an army general who edited his journal, put it, "there appears to be something in that particular service . . . [Arctic exploration] that stirs up the bile and promotes bitter feelings comparatively unknown under the ordinary conditions of sea service." He suggested that "it might be supposed to be some form of that insidious Arctic enemy, the scurvy, which is known to affect the mind as well as the body of its victims."

This brotherly assessment scarcely absolves Collinson. For one thing, his bitterness did not dissipate on the return journey round Africa's southern tip, as might be expected, but lingered on after the completion of the voyage. For another, too many of his officers were at loggerheads with their commander. In fact, the trouble aboard the *Enterprise* began long before the Arctic night closed in, as the journal of the second ice master, Skead, makes clear. Through Skead's admittedly biased eyes, Collinson emerges as a super-cautious commander, hesitant to take the slightest chance, always prepared to retreat when he might have gone forward in triumph, lackadaisical in pressing the Franklin search, and sometimes too drunk to handle the ship. Skead felt so strongly that when Collinson's journal was published, he scribbled angry marginal notes throughout his copy: "*Bosh*" . . . "*not true*" . . . "*lies*" . . . "*absurd statement*" . . . "*what an excuse!*" . . . "*drunk.*"

Undoubtedly Skead overstated the case. From the outset he had been critical of his commander, who tried to post him to the supply ship *Plover* when they reached the Bering Sea. Nonetheless, Collinson was no McClure; indeed, the two commanders represented opposite sides of the same coin. Where McClure was impetuous, Collinson was prudent. Where McClure took a gamble, Collinson hung back. Had he possessed some of McClure's boldness, he might have reached King William Island and discovered the fate of Franklin. He might even have got through the North West Passage. It has been said that he was unlucky, but it was not just luck that dealt him an indifferent hand; it was also his own refusal to take chances.

He had another problem: he could not speak with the Eskimos because he had no interpreter. Johann Miertsching, the Moravian missionary, was supposed to have transferred to his ship at Honolulu, but Collinson had left before he arrived. As a result, if he had encountered natives who had some clue to Franklin's fate, he would not have been able to communicate with them.

According to Skead, the frustrations wrought by Collinson's caution began when he took the longer route to the Bering Strait. The winds weren't nearly as bad in the Aleutians as he'd been told – and as the more daring McClure discovered. Even before the Bering Sea was reached in mid-August, Collinson seemed wary of wintering in the Arctic and talked of returning to Hong Kong.

In sailing around the northern coast of Russian Alaska, Collinson made a serious error. He believed the coastal waters were so shallow it was dangerous to approach within fifteen miles of the mainland. His officers tried to reason with him, but he was obdurate. "I must have fifteen miles," he kept saying.

As it turned out, there was plenty of depth nearer the shore. It was the lurking permanent ice pack of the Arctic Ocean, fifteen miles from the coast, that posed a more serious threat to his passage. Collinson reached Point Barrow – standing twenty-five miles off the shore – and then turned back. He was convinced that an Open Polar Sea – the same fancy that had seduced Barrow and later lured Kane – lay to the northwest. "This cursed *polar basin* . . . is one of the phantoms which has led to our failure," Skead wrote. If it hadn't held them back, they might have found an open channel along the coastline. "We now end the season to continue to seek for what no one but the Captain believes has any existence." They were eighteen days behind McClure.

Having turned back, the *Enterprise* rounded the northwest corner of Alaska and headed south to Point Hope. On August 30, Collinson found what he had missed on the northward journey – a note in a cairn from Kellett, reporting that McClure was ahead of him. He was astounded and chagrined. If only he'd found that message earlier! Instead of retreating, he would certainly have pressed on and perhaps caught McClure. Yet there was still time to catch up; at least, Collinson's officers thought so.

"For God's sake, go back at once, it is not now too late," the surgeon, Robert Anderson, pleaded.

"No, no," Collinson replied. "I must seek Kellett."

Kellett in the *Herald* was farther south at Grantley Harbor; so was Thomas Moore in the *Plover*. Collinson reached them on September 1. According to Skead, Moore told him there was a good anchorage in a harbour off Point Barrow, and Kellett urged him to retrace his steps.

"If you make haste, Coll, you'll be able to winter at Point Barrow."

"No, no," said Collinson. "I'm not going to take *my* ship there."

Instead, he dawdled, deciding to seek winter quarters somewhere on the northwest coast of Alaska. Again according to Skead, Kellett remarked that "he would rather have seen us upon the rocks than looking for winter quarters at so early a part of the summer season."

Two weeks went by before Collinson moved north again. He got as far as Icy Cape on September 22, found no suitable harbour, and stopped. One of his officers, Lieutenant George Phayer, offered to go himself to Point Barrow to check the harbour there. Collinson, nettled, didn't deign to reply. He turned south and spent the winter at Hong Kong.

It was a costly decision. When he returned the following July and once again rounded the Alaskan peninsula, it became painfully clear that had he persevered and wintered at Point Barrow he would almost certainly have caught up with his junior ship. Together, he and McClure might have shared the honour of discovering a North West Passage.

Ignoring the advice of his ice master, Collinson allowed himself to become beset in the pack off Point Barrow. Here, it turned out, there *was* a lane of open water and none of the shoals he had feared. He tried to make for it but was borne helplessly westward. Skead, scarcely on speaking terms with his captain, who treated him "with as much indifference as if I had been the purser," noted that the so-called shoals had proved to be "nothing but bugbears."

By August 12, the sea was calm. Skead was impatient to move ahead. But instead of putting his men to work, warping and towing the ship through the lanes in the melting ice, Collinson insisted on waiting for fair winds. At this time in the season every mile counted, but there was no sense of urgency aboard the *Enterprise*. An ordinary yachtsman might have taken his craft east, Skead thought – "aye & his wife and daughters to boot." He had never seen men have it so easy aboard any ship on which he'd served. "As we make so little progress when there are so few obstacles to our advance, I am afraid to think of what we shall do if we meet with difficulty from ice. Poor Sir John! God help you – you'll get none from us."

On August 26, 1851, Collinson reached the southern promontory of Banks Land and took possession of it in the name of the Queen, not knowing that McClure had claimed it the year before and named it Nelson Head. At this point he gave Skead command of the *Enterprise*, "being in a condition which totally prevented him from attending the ship." Skead took her into Prince of Wales Strait the following day and there, at the Princess Royal Islands, they discovered that McClure had already been there – just six weeks before.

Collinson's frustrations continued. According to Skead, he was drunk again on September 1 and when asked for instructions replied simply, "Do what you think best." They sailed up Prince of Wales Strait, following unwittingly far in McClure's wake, and were stopped by the ice as McClure had been. They turned back and rounded Banks Land from the east. There, at Cape Kellett, they found that McClure had again preceded them. At this point, in fact, he was only a fortnight ahead.

Had Collinson gone forward he might easily have wintered with the *Investigator* at Mercy Bay and taken charge of the combined expedition. But again he turned back and on September 13, 1851, went into winter quarters on the eastern coastline of Prince of Wales Strait at Walker Bay, on what was then called Prince Albert Land, actually part of the massive Victoria Island, as Collinson was to discover. And there, once again, Collinson's sledge crews found that others had preceded them – in this instance Lieutenant Haswell of the *Investigator*.

The weather remained fine. Five weeks elapsed before the ocean began to ice up. In that time, Collinson could have found a wintering harbour farther south, putting himself in a better position for a thrust to the east the following spring. His ice master was beside himself with frustration. "How much we have lost, it is painful to contemplate," he noted. His captain's inactivity was "a marvellous proceeding considering Franklin was perishing for food and shelter." Relations between Skead and the captain became so strained that in April 1852, the ice master was put under permanent arrest.

That summer, the *Enterprise* squeezed through Dolphin and Union Strait and the island labyrinth of Coronation Gulf. This was a remarkable feat of navigation on Collinson's part and one that would bring high praise from Roald Amundsen, who travelled in the opposite direction in a much smaller craft more than half a century later. Unfortunately, Collinson was again covering ground already explored by Richardson, Rae, Dease, and Simpson. The

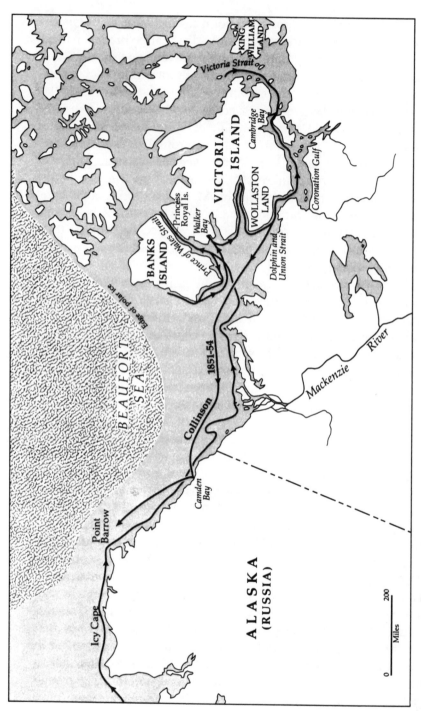

Collinson's expedition, 1851–54

expedition wintered at Cambridge Bay on the southeastern shore of Victoria Island no more than 120 miles from King William Island, which no one had yet explored.

Collinson was now in a position to solve both the secret of the North West Passage and the fate of Franklin, but he muffed it. He had no way of questioning the Eskimos who visited the ship that winter of 1852-53 and almost certainly had tales to tell of foundering ships and dying men a few score miles to the east. One of his officers persuaded some of the natives to draw a chart of the coastline to the east; it seemed to him that the Eskimo artists were indicating a ship in the area, but Collinson pooh-poohed that.

In April 1853, he led a sledging party up the west coast of Victoria Strait only to discover a note in a cairn that told him John Rae had covered the same ground two years before! If he had known earlier he could have opted for the east coast of the strait where, at Victory Point on King William Island, the clues to the Franklin mystery lay hidden. Victory Point was less than forty statute miles away, directly across the strait; but Collinson was worried about the roughness of the ice and so the opportunity passed him by. The frustrated Skead thought the whole area could and should have been investigated. "Two serving officers in good health & strong were under arrest on trifling charges," he wrote, adding that there were plenty of men available also to explore the estuary of the Great Fish River. But Collinson wasn't listening to Skead.

In July one of Collinson's crew came upon some wreckage not far from Cambridge Bay, including a fragment of a door frame that, in hindsight, almost certainly came from one of the Franklin ships, but Collinson saw nothing significant in that. With his fuel running low he left the area and turned west again to winter at Camden Bay on the north coast of Alaska.

When the *Enterprise* finally reached Port Clarence off the west coast of the Alaskan peninsula on August 24, 1854, the officers of the supply ship *Rattlesnake* were shocked at the state of anarchy that existed on board. At that juncture every one of Collinson's executive officers was under arrest. Skead had been confined for two years and eight months. "Fancy that in such a climate!" exclaimed Lieutenant Philip Sharpe of the *Rattlesnake*, who described the ice master as "wasted to nothing." The first, second, and third officers were also under arrest; none had been allowed off the ship for the previous fifteen months. The only officers free, Sharpe discovered, were the surgeon and assistant surgeon, "and these Captain Collinson dare not arrest." The ship was being handled by one of the ice mates, "a nobody."

The situation had reached the point "that all are determined to go to the utmost, lose their commissions, everything, to try Capt. Collinson by a Court Martial, for lying, drunkenness, tyranny and oppression and cowardice. . . . Oh! the accounts are horrible, we thought our own plight was bad enough, but it is nothing compared with theirs. . . . Never was there such an expedition set sail under such auspicious auspices; had such golden opportunities which were thrown away; and made such signal failures."

The story of Collinson's troubles with his officers spread quickly. John Rae, returning to England in 1855, was told that Lieutenant Charles Jago had threatened to knock Collinson down on his own quarterdeck. The same May the embattled captain returned home by way of Hong Kong and the Cape of Good Hope. He had one claim to fame: he had shown that the narrow passage along the North American coastline could be navigated by a large ship, which had not before been believed possible. It was this that caused Amundsen to praise him as "one of the most capable and enterprising sailors the world has ever produced." He was scarcely that.

He emerged from his long Arctic confinement a bitter man, outraged because the Admiralty refused to court-martial his officers and further affronted when the committee investigating claims to the discovery of the Passage passed him over. McClure and his crew got ten thousand pounds. Collinson got nothing more than an honourable mention. In 1858, the Geographical Society threw him a bone in the shape of its Founder's Medal. But Richard Collinson was so miffed with the Admiralty that he never again applied for a naval command. Nor did anybody rush to offer him one.

5

The polar idol Elisha Kent Kane returned to America in the fall of 1855 to find himself a popular hero. His journal of the First Grinnell Expedition, with its haunting descriptions of icebergs and its terrifying account of the besetment in Wellington Channel, had been published in his absence. Congress, after some vacillation and considerable debate, had finally, in March, voted $150,000 to send two ships to search for him. Some congressmen were concerned that the Franklin crusade was taking on unexpected dimensions. Kane, the searcher, was now being sought. Would a new search be required for Kane's searchers? How long could this go on?

Luckily, Kane was found at Godhavn after the two search ships, blocked by the ice in Smith Sound, returned to southern Greenland. Kane's younger brother, John, who accompanied the rescue expedition, didn't recognize the gaunt, bearded creature in the strange, wild costume when the two were reunited. But by the time the combined expeditions reached New York in October, with cannons roaring and crowds cheering, Kane was looking healthier than when he had left over two years before. His body had fleshed out, his face was bronzed, and his neatly trimmed black beard showed only a touch of grey.

With reporters and well-wishers swarming around him, he went straight to the home of his sponsor, Henry Grinnell.

"I have no *Advance* with me," were his first words.

"Never mind," Grinnell told him. "You are safe; that is all we care about. Come into the parlor and tell us the whole story."

Kane never told the whole story. His rooted bitterness over the defection of his crew, his physical encounters with Godfrey and Blake, his exasperation with Goodfellow and the others were either omitted or toned down in the accounts that followed. There was still enough, on the day after his arrival, for the *New York Times* to devote its entire front page to the adventure. The book, on which he worked at a driving pace that winter, sold sixty-five thousand copies, made him a small fortune, and turned him into a national icon.

Kane's reputation as a brilliant leader and a bold explorer rests almost entirely on his two books – a striking example of the power of the pen. The public and press, without access to his personal journal or that of his sailing master, John Wall Wilson, had no insight into his flawed leadership, his mercurial temperament, his erratic personality, or his towering ego. When Wilson set out to write a book of his own, Kane paid him $350 to suppress it. It was wasted money, for the manuscript, prepared with the help of a ghost writer, contains scarcely a word of the vituperation to be found in Wilson's original journal.

Kane's best-seller, though carefully sandpapered, did not sit well with some of his former associates, especially Hayes and Bonsall, who felt he had taken too much of the glory on himself and downgraded their part in the adventure. William Godfrey wrote a self-serving account of his own, again with a ghost writer's help, but it received little attention. Kane's literary style laid the foundation for his canonization as "the outstanding polar idol of the mid-century." He was a far better writer than explorer, and that is his real contribution to the history of Arctic discovery. For it was Kane's graphic tale, prominently displayed on the bookshelves of the nation, that fired the imagination of others and served as the impetus for the continuing polar quest.

If anything, the explorer's bizarre liaison with Margaret Fox increased his stature as an exotic and compelling adventurer. On the day he landed in New York, she had waited breathlessly for him to call. Apparently she waited in vain. She was not in Pennsylvania, where he had confined her. She was in New York, living with a friend during one of the many excursions in which she indulged herself, thanks to the leniency of Henry Grinnell's son Cornelius, whom Kane had put in charge of her educational program. She could hear the guns heralding the arrival of her lost love, but the night passed with no word from him. The following day young Grinnell arrived to explain that Kane was ill with rheumatism and also concerned about his family and friends, who disapproved of the alliance. He would come when he could.

Was this the same ardent adventurer who had showered her with love letters and confessed his undying passion before vanishing into the Arctic mists? What had happened to Kane, the creature of sudden impulse and reckless emotion, in that long polar night? There is no mention of Margaret in his private journal (and certainly none in his published work). In those sombre evenings when, in his despair and loneliness, he had poured out his innermost thoughts, writing longingly of his family in Philadelphia and his other "family," the Henry Grinnells of New York, there was no call from the heart to the dark-eyed spirit rapper to whom he had pledged his "pure regard and love."

But then, all his life the impetuous Kane had blown hot and blown cold. If he was having second thoughts, it is not surprising; a less suitable alliance could scarcely have been imagined. His family was in a state of alarm to the point of attempting, unsuccessfully, to retrieve his letters to Margaret – and his family had always exerted a powerful influence upon him. Now he was torn between his love and respect for them and his curious, ambivalent attachment to her.

At last, forty-eight hours after his triumphant arrival, he came to her, and a vacillating relationship continued all that winter. On that initial visit, she was so distraught she wouldn't see him at first; then she was in his arms as he showered her with kisses. To her dismay he followed this moment of ardour with the declaration that any thought of marriage must be postponed because of his family's opposition – they would be as brother and sister, nothing more. He forced her to sign a document to that effect – for his mother, he claimed. She did so, in tears. Later he sent it back and she tore it up.

He feared she would return to the embarrassing séances; her mother and her sister Leah feared she would not. After all, Margaret had been their main source of income. When both families appeared to be against the marriage, Kane rebelled. He told Margaret his love was stronger than ever. But in the weeks that followed he gave little evidence that it was. He still indicated he could not entertain any idea of marriage because he was dependent on his family for support until his book was finished. That was too much. "I have seen you for the last time," she wrote. "I have been deceived."

Unpredictable as ever, Kane rushed to the weeping woman and acknowledged that he had betrayed her hopes. "The world shall not say that you, Maggie, are the discarded one!" he cried. "No! No – it is you who reject me! Dr. Kane is the discarded lover!" And with that, he threw himself on his knees, pleading, "Speak, Maggie! my destiny is in your hands!"

This scene and others come from Margaret's own account. It is probable that she or her editor exaggerated both the passion of those moments and the rift that followed. But the outline is undeniably true. The press was on to the story, asking questions, publishing rumours and details, and speculating about the possibility of a broken engagement. And certainly Margaret Fox's account of her turbulent relationship coincides with Kane's emotional character.

They continued to see each other during Kane's trips to New York until, in February, Mrs. Fox forbade him to visit or write to Maggie again – another ultimatum that had little effect. Meanwhile, the explorer was working furiously on his book, three hundred pages of which he had finished by Christmas.

In May 1856, with his two-volume tome almost complete – it would run to nine hundred pages with appendices – Kane received by proxy the coveted gold medal of the Geographical Society in Great Britain. He was also in correspondence with Lady Franklin, who was still stubbornly pursuing her crusade to find her missing husband. She appealed to Kane to take command of a ship to search for relics of her husband's lost expedition on King William Island. But Kane by this time was too ill to consider returning to the North.

The determined widow would not be put off. She needed Kane. If he couldn't command a ship at least he could bolster the campaign she was orchestrating behind the scenes to persuade the British Admiralty to send one last expedition to search for the lost party. Kane demurred. "*This dream must be over,*" he confessed in a letter to his father, " – my health is gone." And yet he was tempted: his prestige was such that he was certain he could convince the Admiralty to support Lady Franklin's cause. He was also certain that his withdrawal from the project would be "both a loss and a misfortune." She was prepared, she had said, to cross the Atlantic to persuade him. It wasn't necessary. He decided to go to her.

He would have been less than human if other considerations hadn't also tempted him. He was now an international figure; an effusive welcome awaited him on the other side. His book was about to be published. After basking briefly in the plaudits of the English he could go off to Switzerland to regain his health.

For Kane was indeed very ill. Grinnell told Lady Franklin that "he is but a skeleton or a shadow of one." He made plans to sail on the *Baltic* in October with his valet and servant, the faithful William Morton. Both explorers were given free passage.

He was still seeing Margaret Fox, squiring her about to the opera and the homes of friends in New York. At least that was her story. If she is to be believed, there was one last, final ceremony, a singular affair in which the pair entered into a sort of common-law marriage. Kane, she said, had spent an evening with her discussing his precarious health and the possibility that he might die. He feared she might not come to him if he called and asked if they might not plight their troth formally, in front of witnesses.

"Such a declaration," she quoted him as saying, "is sufficient to constitute a legal and binding marriage." She agreed. Four persons, including her mother, were present. Kane took her hand: "Maggie is my wife, and I am her husband. Wherever we are, she is mine, and I am hers. Do you understand and consent to this, Maggie?" She agreed that she did – or so she wrote years later. From that moment she called herself Mrs. Kane. It was, of course, in her interest to do so; when he died she claimed a widow's dower. The litigation lasted ten years.

Describing their one last evening together, she quoted him as crying, "Maggie, what if I should die away from you! Oh, my own Maggie, could I but die in your arms, I would ask no more."

It was a wish he could not be granted. He sailed for England on October 11. She never saw him again.

Chapter Eight

Leopold M'Clintock

The death of Franklin as envisioned by a contemporary artist

1

When Lady Franklin learned, in the spring of 1856, that John Rae had succeeded in his claim for the ten-thousand-pound reward offered for finding some clues to her husband's fate, she was irked and dismayed. She opposed the award; it was far too early, she insisted, to come to any conclusions as to what had happened. Rae's prize confirmed the government's belief that her husband was dead. She could not bring herself to accept that finality.

Certainly he had found circumstantial evidence of the fate of *some* of the Franklin party, but not of all. There was no evidence that her husband had been among the sorry crew the Eskimos had described to Rae. As for the tale of cannibalism, she did not believe that for an instant. That January (1856) she had a letter from James Anderson, the Hudson's Bay man, who had found some further relics, including part of a backgammon board she remembered putting aboard the *Erebus*. Anderson confirmed her belief in the need for another expedition when he told her he had done as much as he could. What was needed now was a ship with sledges to probe the unknown coasts of King William Island.

The Crimean War had ended in March. Why wouldn't the Navy now continue the search? Surely Rae's revelations were enough to goad it into a final solution of the mystery! But if not the government, then Jane Franklin was prepared once again to supply the means and the men to do the job.

"I am about to make a last effort to solve this mystery," she told Sherard Osborn in a spirited letter. Relics had been found, but no documents. And who was to say that Franklin himself or his men had not discovered the Passage well before McClure, forging, in John Richardson's loyal phrase, "the last link with their lives"?

She attacked the Admiralty once again with all the eloquence at her command: "Though it is my humble hope and fervent prayer that the Government of my country will themselves complete the work they have done and not leave it to a weak and helpless woman to attempt the doing that imperfectly which they themselves can do so easily and well, yet, if need be, such is my painful resolve, God helping me."

Of course she was anything but weak and helpless. She was iron willed and she had the support of some of the most powerful figures

311

in the country, not the least of whom was the Queen's consort. For the best part of a decade she had cajoled and threatened, pleaded and exhorted until the government and the Navy had undertaken a series of expeditions to the Arctic. She was herself a formidable public figure, having captured the imagination and appealed to the chivalry of the ordinary Briton who saw her, indeed, as "a weak and helpless woman" battling for her husband's life and her husband's honour. Almost singlehanded she had created a myth, turning John Franklin, a likeable but quite ordinary naval officer, into *the* Arctic hero.

He was scarcely that. His first command had been a human disaster; his second was worthy but uninspiring; his third ended in a dreadful tragedy, the worst the Arctic has ever seen. None of this mattered to the Victorians, who were captivated by noble failure, as Tennyson's paean to an extraordinary piece of military bungling had demonstrated. It didn't matter whether you won or lost, it was how you played the game; and Franklin, his memory kept alive and sanctified by his widow, was seen to have played it out according to the rules, dashing forward into the Arctic labyrinth, like the doomed cavaliers of the Light Brigade, an enthusiastic amateur to the last.

There is much that is admirable in nineteenth-century polar exploration and much that is misguided, but there is also a great deal that is obsessive. Yet no explorer – not Parry, not John Ross, not Kane – was as obsessed as Jane Franklin. She could not let go; her obsession sustained her, giving her life a meaning and a focal point. Her Pall Mall residence was nicknamed The Battery because she had battered the Admiralty with so many letters and memorials. And when she was not battering against the walls of officialdom, or writing to foreign powers, or penning letters to *The Times* thinly disguised under pseudonyms, she was manipulating events from behind the scenes.

It requires no special prescience to see Lady Franklin's hand behind the memorial that thirty-six of London's leading men of science, including all the major Arctic explorers, were persuaded to send to the Prime Minister, Lord Palmerston, in June. It urged another expedition "to satisfy the honor of our country, and clear up a mystery which has excited the sympathy of the civilized world." There was still a chance, the memorial insisted, that some of Franklin's men were still alive, existing among the Eskimos.

It quoted Elisha Kane: "I well know how glad I would have been, had my duties to others permitted me, to have taken refuge among the Esquimaux of Smith Strait and Etah Bay. Strange as it seems to you, we regarded the coarse life of these people with eyes of envy and did not doubt but that we could have lived in comfort upon their resources. It required all my powers, moral and physical, to prevent my men from deserting to the Walrus Settlements, and it was my final intention to have taken to Esquimaux life had Providence not carried us through in our hazardous escapade."

Perhaps without realizing it, the memorialists, by adopting Kane's views, were making a remarkable admission. Implicit in their petition to the British Prime Minister was acceptance of the truth that by adopting native methods, men could survive more easily in the Arctic. That was a revelation the Royal Navy was still unable to accept, then or for the remainder of the century.

The memorial ended with an appeal to honour. Were these men to be "abandoned at the very moment when an explanation . . . seems to be within our grasp?" Was another nation (the United States) going to be allowed to make the endeavour? Was the whole burden to fall upon the slender shoulders of "the noble minded widow of our lamented friend?"

It was. The noble-minded widow still had the steam yacht *Isabel* that Edward Inglefield had taken to Baffin Bay four years before. Goaded by no less a figure than the Prince Consort, the Admiralty agreed to put it into shape for another expedition. Now Lady Franklin searched about for a captain. There was no shortage of possibilities – M'Clintock, Collinson, and Osborn, to name three – but not Rae, that harbinger of unsavoury news whom Jane Franklin found equally unsavoury in appearance ("he has got off his odious beard but looks still hairy & disagreeable"). Osborn, whose health wouldn't allow him to go, recommended Kane, who refused for the same reason. Like the two ailing Arctic veterans, the little *Isabel*, too, was finally deemed unfit for further northern service.

Jane Franklin did not give up. By a freak of chance a ship had appeared out of the ice-bound Arctic the previous September with all the right qualifications for the kind of expedition she had planned. This was the *Resolute*, Kellett's old vessel, abandoned on Belcher's orders and discovered floating about in Davis Strait by an American whaler, a thousand miles from her original anchorage. At Lady Franklin's prompting, Kane and Henry Grinnell persuaded Congress to buy the ship and present her to Great Britain. This extraordinary gift, which cost the American taxpayer forty thousand

313

dollars, helped to cement the ties of friendship that had been sorely tried earlier in the century.

Nudged by Jane Franklin, Henry Grinnell suggested that the Admiralty use the vessel in the most appropriate manner – for another Franklin search. Strings were pulled on both sides of the Atlantic. The commander of the Kane relief expedition, Captain Henry Hartstene, was commissioned to bring the ship to England and present her to the Navy with the unspoken assumption she would go north once again. Lady Franklin's hand was again to be seen in the American ambassador's speech to the Geographical Society in which he referred to the *Resolute* as a "consecrated ship." This suggestion of a "sacred mission" – it was a phrase that Lady Franklin used more than once – drew a wave of applause. The *Resolute* was given a royal salute when she passed Cowes, and the Queen herself attended the ceremony of presentation. The events that followed – parties and gift-giving to honour the Americans – all bore Jane Franklin's touch. The suggestion was clear: the *Resolute* should be sent north to accomplish its holy enterprise; Hartstene even offered to command the expedition.

Meanwhile, the ailing Elisha Kane, his rheumatic heart now seriously weakened, had arrived in London, prepared to stay for only a few days and then seek a warmer climate, which he thought might aid his recovery. Lady Franklin hoped the English country air would restore him – she needed him badly to further her cause. She visited him daily, plied him with codliver oil, brought him books to read, and on each visit, in Kane's words, kissed "my pale forehead." To his dismay she continued to act as if he were in command of the search expedition. "The woman would use me, if she could, even now," he wrote to his father. When he considered visiting Madeira for his health, she offered to go with him, only, Kane believed, to ensure his return to England where she expected to enlist him in a scheme to push her case before Prince Albert. As Kane put it, "she has been skirmishing around this for some time." He was determined to put his foot down once and for all – to tell her that since he had withdrawn a year earlier from command, any representation he could make on her part would be an impertinence.

A series of dinners, ceremonies, presentations, and other honours kept him longer in England than he had planned. In the end he decided, on his doctor's advice, that Cuba was the best place for him.

He and Morton left on November 17. Three months later, with his mother and his two brothers at his side, Dr. Kane of the Arctic Seas, paralysed by two successive strokes, died quietly. The funeral journey that followed was the most spectacular the United States had ever known, exceeded in that century only by that of Abraham Lincoln. It took a month from Havana to New Orleans, up the Mississippi and Ohio to Cincinnati, and then by train to Philadelphia, the levees and wharfs of the great rivers black with people, the way stations of Ohio and Pennsylvania crowded with so many mourners that the tracks were jammed and the train repeatedly held up. Bands played, dirges droned, minute guns boomed, bells tolled, and the air was purple with elegiac oratory. At every major river port and whistle stop the casket came off the train and the body of the "Great Explorer, Ripe Scholar and Noble Philanthropist" lay in state. In Philadelphia seven of Kane's old comrades, including Hayes, Bonsall, Goodfellow, and even Godfrey, followed the bier to Independence Hall, where for three days thousands of mourners filed past. Kane's ceremonial sword lay on the coffin encircled by a garland of flowers. Only one other tribute lay beside it – a splendid wreath with an anonymous message: "To the Memory of Dr. Kane from Two Ladies." He was one with the spirits now; if from the dark reaches of the tomb – as frigid as the Arctic night – he rapped out a message for posterity, there was none to hear him.

2

It was 1857, the year of the bloody Sepoy Mutiny in India and a new book, *Tom Brown's School Days*, that Victorian panegyric to British sportsmanship and the stiff upper lip. The stiffest lip of all belonged to Jane Franklin, who kept up the public barrage for another search while her allies worked for her in parliament. She had appealed to the Prime Minister the previous December, relaying Captain Hartstene's offer. Now her lengthy epistle – it ran to more than three thousand words – was circulated in pamphlet form: if she could not sway Lord Palmerston, perhaps she could arouse the public. "This final and exhausting search is all I seek in behalf of the first and only martyrs to Arctic discovery in modern times," she wrote, "and it is all I ever

The cruise of the Fox

intend to ask." She was prepared to sacrifice her entire available fortune, she announced, and underwrite the cost of a private expedition if the government didn't budge.

At the same time she managed to arrange for a group of Americans to back her case with the Admiralty. Her methods here were byzantine. She persuaded Sir Roderick Murchison to send her a letter saying he approved of the idea of having Sir Francis Beaufort write another letter to Henry Grinnell, asking the American philanthropist to call a meeting in New York to send a proposal back to the British Admiralty pushing the idea of using the *Resolute* to search for her husband. She left nothing to chance, even choosing the wording for a suitable address that the gathering could use. She was a master of proper phrasing; Cobden said that she was better at it than any of the members who were pressing her case in parliament.

The New York meeting used her address almost word for word, whereupon she quoted it in another letter to Sir Charles Wood, the First Lord of the Admiralty. She sent a copy of that to the Prince Consort after persuading Murchison to write to Wood supporting her plea. All this circuitous campaigning had little effect. The Navy was adamant. Too many men had died, too many ships had been lost in the ten-year search. She could not have the *Resolute*.

She would not be stopped. She had her eye on a steam yacht in Aberdeen – the *Fox*. She bought it for two thousand pounds and persuaded Leopold M'Clintock to take it to the Arctic to King William Island, the one spot that nobody had yet searched and where she was now certain the secret of her husband's fate would be unravelled.

Fortunately, M'Clintock needed a job and the Navy hadn't given him one, perhaps because it was felt that he needed a rest after his harrowing sledge journeys. Lady Franklin, on James Ross's recommendation, had, in fact, offered him a similar command two years before. He'd turned it down then, partly because he didn't want to jeopardize his naval career if the Admiralty were opposed and also because he didn't want Jane Franklin put to further expense. Now, however, he saw that she was determined to go on.

The Admiralty offered some help in the form of provisions, but it would be no luxury cruise. With Captain Collinson supervising on her behalf, every penny was made to count. That seemed to invigorate M'Clintock. "The less the means, the more arduous I felt was

316

the achievement," he declared, "the more glorious would be the success, the more honourable defeat, even if defeat awaits us." Unconsciously, he had summed up the philosophy of Victorian derring-do: without striving against impossible odds, where was the victory?

The *Fox* was a small schooner-rigged steam yacht of 177 tons, half the size of one of Franklin's vessels. She had made one voyage only – to Norway. She was sheathed with stout planking, fortified by cross beams, her ladderways and skylights reduced to adapt her to the polar climate, her false keel removed, her slender brass propeller replaced by a sturdier one of iron, her boiler altered and enlarged. Her prow was encased in iron until, in M'Clintock's description, "it resembled a ponderous chisel."

Her quarters were incredibly cramped. The officers were "crammed into pigeon holes" to make room for provisions and stores. The room in which five persons messed was only eight feet square. A few small coal stoves replaced the standard heating apparatus.

M'Clintock wanted and got experienced men. Seventeen of the ship's company of twenty-five had taken part in previous Franklin searches. They included Carl Petersen from the Penny and Kane expeditions, dog driver, interpreter, and Arctic expert, who agreed to sign on when he learned who the captain was. "M'Clintock I know," he said. "With him will I serve."

M'Clintock had been moved by the wave of public sympathy that swept the country when the new expedition was announced. This last attempt to discover the fate of Franklin and his men "and rescue from oblivion their heroic deeds" seemed, he said, "the natural promptings of every honest English heart." It confirmed his impression that "the glorious mission intrusted to me was in reality *a great national duty*." (The emphasis was his.)

The chivalry that had prompted him to treat his sledgers as Round Table knights of old, with heraldic banners rippling in the Arctic breeze, extended now to his officers. He had refused to take a single penny from Lady Franklin; all the other commissioned men followed suit. Allen Young, his sailing master, a personable young Crimean War veteran from the merchant service, not only served without pay but also donated five hundred pounds to the public subscription that was rapidly approaching the three thousand mark. Jane Franklin would still have to dip into her own funds for an additional seven thousand. She insisted on a deed of indemnity freeing M'Clintock of all liabilities and also giving him the *Fox* as a reward. He was equally insistent on refusing it.

She was his captain and he deferred to her. He had asked for written instructions, but it was soon obvious that he needed none: their views were identical. On the last day of June, 1857, before the *Fox* sailed from the Orkneys for Greenland, she came down from Aberdeen to bid him good-bye. He could see how deeply agitated she was when she left the yacht, and he tried without success to prevent the crew from giving her the usual three lusty cheers; public demonstrations of that kind embarrassed her. They cheered anyway, and for that M'Clintock was grateful.

Once the ship was in the Atlantic he read to the crew a letter she had given him before they left, reminding him that the expedition had three purposes: first and most important was the rescue of the survivors; second, the recovery of "the unspeakably precious documents of the expedition"; and third, the confirmation of her own claims that "these martyrs in a noble cause achieved at their last extremity" the discovery of the North West Passage.

"My only fear," she wrote, "is that you may spend yourselves too much in the effort; and you must therefore let me tell you how much dearer to me even than any of them is the preservation of the valuable lives of the little band of heroes who are your companions and followers."

And so, twelve years after John Franklin set out to find the Passage, the final voyage of the long search to discover his fate had been dispatched. "I am doomed to trial & also struggle on to the end," his widow had written the year before. The struggle was continuing, but the end was at last in sight. This was her triumph. With a heart-rending desperation and a truly awesome resolve, this deceptively frail and wholly untypical Victorian lady – sometimes irritating, often engaging, ever constant – had inspired a loyalty that queens might envy and, through her persistence, added a footnote to history. As one newspaper put it: "What the nation would not do, a woman did."

The *Fox* reached Upernavik on August 6, 1857. It was her captain's hope that he could push his way westward straight through the main pack in Baffin Bay by what was known as the Middle Passage. The ice was too much for him. His only chance was to get past it by heading up the Greenland coast and circling round the northern end

318

of the pack before coming south again to enter Lancaster Sound. To do that he would have to cut directly across the shallow crescent of Melville Bay, the most feared stretch of open water on the Greenland coast. To his dismay he found that conditions here were the worst on record – and that record was appalling. In one bad year, 1830, nineteen ships had sunk in Melville Bay and twelve more had been seriously damaged.

The *Fox* managed to get three quarters of the way across before M'Clintock was faced with the "dreadful reality" of a winter in the pack. Fortunately he did not have Kane's excitability, McClure's bravado, or Collinson's excessive caution. In Sophia Cracroft's observation, he "never lost that equanimity which is his most remarkable characteristic." As the ice closed in, M'Clintock grew philosophical. To him, the great glacier that sprawled unbroken for fifty miles along the margin of the bay "serves to remind one at once of Time and of Eternity." If the *Fox* was beset, so be it. "I shall repeat the trial next year, and in the end, with God's aid, perform my sacred duty. . . ."

Yet the slow drift caused him some distress. The crew had, as yet, no suspicion of what was coming. But M'Clintock knew. Eight lonely winter months trapped in the pack would be bad enough for morale, but the danger of being crushed was worse. The *Fox*'s steam power wasn't enough to force the floes apart; all attempts to blast it free failed. By September, M'Clintock had lost control of his ship. He decided to make the best of it since his crew was healthy, well fed, "cheerful, willing and quiet – thoughtless, of course, as true sailors are."

A school was organized, an organ was unpacked, the men learned to build snow houses on the ice, and the two Eskimo hunters in the party brought in seals and the occasional bear as the ship drifted south, month after month, back toward the civilized world. By April 26, they had been beset for 250 days and had travelled 1,385 miles, most of it in the wrong direction.

A scene of terrifying confusion followed as the ice began to break up. Rolling wickedly in the heavy seas, bruised and buffeted by the rampaging floes, the *Fox* forced its way through the heaving pack. Outwardly stoical but inwardly trembling, M'Clintock realized that a single blow by one of the monstrous ice blocks could crush his ship in an instant. At times the vessel shuddered so violently that ship's bells rang and crewmen were almost knocked off their feet. What an ignominious end it would be if, after this long winter entrapment, the expedition was lost before it really began! "Such a battering . . . I hope not to see again," M'Clintock wrote, describing one eighteen-hour period of unrelenting torment. He knew then, he said, why a man's hair could turn grey in a few hours.

Suddenly it was over; the ice was gone; they were free. Sea birds wheeled around them and scudded over the waves. Whales and seals disported themselves in the open water. "All nature seemed alive," one officer recalled, "and we felt as if we had risen from the dead!"

M'Clintock might now, with honour, have gone south into the harbour at St. John's, Newfoundland, to repair his battered ship, take on extra provisions, and restore the spirits of his crew. He did no such thing. Back he went up the coast of Greenland and across Melville Bay, where after several anxious hours he found a way through the ice. At Cape York he encountered Eskimos from Etah who greeted Petersen, an old friend, and inquired after Kane. Hans Hendrik, they explained, was eking out a precarious existence with his new family in Whale Sound. Petersen sent him a message urging him to move farther south.

Early in July, 1858, M'Clintock steamed across the mouth of Smith Sound, following a hazy streak of water in the maze of ice, and reached the mouth of Lancaster Sound to find it barely open. It was July 14, exactly 242 years since Bylot and Baffin had sailed along the same coast without hindrance. Fighting its way through the floes, the *Fox* used up most of its coal. Happily, there was more in a depot that Belcher had left at Beechey Island. While there, M'Clintock raised a stone tablet to Franklin and his men. It had an interesting history. Made in New York at Lady Franklin's request and under Henry Grinnell's direction, it had been taken north on Hartstene's relief expedition to rescue Elisha Kane. Left at Upernavik, it was picked up by M'Clintock, who bore it at last to its intended destination.

From this point the real voyage began. It was obvious to M'Clintock that Franklin must have gone down Peel Sound, in spite of what earlier explorers had said about the ice. It was the only route that had not been thoroughly investigated. In the distance he could see the dim promontory of Cape Walker, guarding the sound's entrance on the west. Franklin had been ordered to go south of the cape. M'Clintock followed in his track "in a wild state of excitement – a mingling of anxious hopes and fears!"

320

After twenty-five miles a dike of ice barred his way. There wasn't a moment to lose. He turned about and chose another route. He would go down Prince Regent Inlet as far as Bellot Strait, then try to slip through that narrow passage back into Peel Sound. Steaming close under the imposing castellated cliffs of Cape Clarence, he entered the harbour of Port Leopold, where, ten years before, James Clark Ross had wintered and where William Kennedy had more recently been trapped. Ross's steam launch, badly damaged but reparable, was on the beach. The provisions he'd left, which had sustained Kennedy, were still in good condition. M'Clintock, who now had a secure fall-back position, didn't linger. On August 20, 1858, he was off to another historic stopping place: Fury Beach. He did not stop but kept on down the inlet and into Brentford Bay, whose northern margin masks the entrance to Bellot Strait. M'Clintock pushed the *Fox* westward until he realized he was actually halfway through the mysterious strait whose existence, ironically, young Bellot, the man for whom it was named, had questioned. William Kennedy had been right: here between lofty bluffs was a clear channel with only a few miles of heavy pack to bar his progress. M'Clintock was elated. He was sure the ice would quickly disperse and he could steam back into Peel Sound.

"A feeling of tranquility – of earnest, hearty satisfaction – has come over us. There is no appearance amongst us of anything boastful. We have all experienced too keenly the vicissitudes of Arctic voyaging to admit of such a feeling." All they had to do was wait at the mouth of the strait. They had no choice, as it turned out, for a stiff, seven-knot current drove them helplessly back, almost capsizing the yacht.

Bellot Strait, M'Clintock was convinced, was the link to the North West Passage. A slender channel, twenty miles long and scarcely a mile wide at its narrowest point, it was the aperture that separated the towering hills of Boothia Peninsula from the cliffs of Somerset Island. Once they were through, they would be within easy reach of King William Island, which held the answer to the Franklin mystery.

They waited. On August 25 they tried again and were driven back by the ice. They tried a total of six times without success. On September 6, in a final dash, they actually reached the strait's western outlet. Once again a belt of ice at the mouth blocked their way. They anchored for the winter in a sheltering inlet at the eastern end. M'Clintock named it for William Kennedy.

The fall and early winter were spent laying out depots for the three major sledge expeditions that M'Clintock was planning. Allen Young would take Prince of Wales Island. M'Clintock would scour the delta of the Great Fish and then move up the west coast of Boothia. Lieutenant William Hobson would search the north coast of King William Island. This last was a generous assignment on M'Clintock's part, for it was there, most probably, that the mystery would be solved. If so, Hobson would get the credit and a promotion.

By now M'Clintock had been partially converted to the advantages of using dogs. Twenty-two had sur-

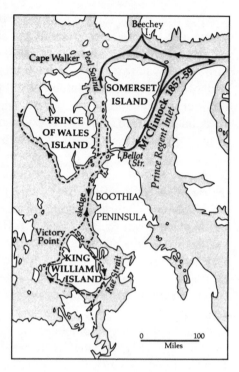

M'Clintock's expedition to King William Island, 1857-59

vived the trip from Greenland. But dogs are of no use without a trained driver, and he had brought only three – Petersen and two Eskimos. Each sledging party would therefore be mixed: four men hauling an eight-hundred-pound sledge accompanied by seven dogs hauling a seven-hundred-pound sledge. The advantages of a dogteam were demonstrated in March by Allen Young, who made a two-hundred-mile dash to Fury Beach to bring back eight hundred pounds of sugar. He took two dogsleds, two Eskimo drivers, and one seaman and, travelling light and running all the way, managed the return trip in just eight days.

M'Clintock was also prepared to save the extra weight of tents by building snow houses. Like dog driving, that required considerable skill. He set off on a scouting trip down the west coast of Boothia in February, taking only Petersen and one other man. They laboured two hours trying to build their nightly shelters until they encountered

322

a group of four Eskimos who, in return for a needle, did the job in half the time.

These were the first natives that the expedition had encountered. M'Clintock noticed that one was wearing a naval button. It had come, the Eskimos said, from some white men who had starved on an island in a river. One of the Eskimos had been to the island and brought back some wood and iron, but he had seen no white men. M'Clintock offered to trade presents for information and relics. A day or so later, an entire village of forty-five arrived – men, women, and children. M'Clintock was able to bring back to the *Fox* a quantity of silver cutlery, a medal, part of a gold chain, several buttons, and knives fashioned by the natives out of wood and iron obviously from a wrecked ship.

The old people remembered the arrival of John Ross's *Victory* in 1829 and even inquired after his newphew, James, using his Eskimo name, Agglugga. None had seen any of Franklin's crew, but one had seen the bones of a white man who had died on an island in the river many years before – probably Montreal Island in the delta of the Great Fish. One or two recalled a ship crushed by ice to the west of King William Island; the vessel had sunk, they said, but the crew had got off safely. Thus, in bits and pieces, did the vague outlines of the Franklin tragedy emerge.

By the time M'Clintock returned to his cheerless quarters on the *Fox*, he had covered 420 miles and had completed the discovery of the coastline of North America. He had added 140 miles to the charts. Equally important, he had discovered the practical route by way of Rae Strait that would lead eventually to the first water navigation of a North West Passage. But it would be another forty-five years before any vessel was able to make its way through that network of islands and ice-blocked channels.

On April 2, M'Clintock and Hobson set off for the south, with Carl Petersen driving M'Clintock's team. They encountered Eskimos who told them of two ships; one had sunk, the other had been forced ashore, badly broken. White men had been seen, they said, hauling boats south toward a large river on the mainland. At Cape Victoria on April 28, both teams separated. M'Clintock set off to the south, leaving Hobson to go west to explore the north shore of King William Island.

On a frozen channel between Boothia and King William Island,

M'Clintock came upon a village whose inhabitants had more Franklin relics, including silver plate bearing the crests of the explorer, his first officer, Crozier, and other members of the expedition. There were more hints of the lost party: tales of the wreck of a ship without masts, of books strewn across the Arctic terrain, of white men who dropped in their tracks on their way to the Great Fish River, some of whom were buried and some not. M'Clintock met an old woman and a boy who had been the last to visit the wrecked ship, apparently during the winter of 1857-58. But dates were vague and much of the information second-hand.

Moving south along the island's eastern coastline, M'Clintock encountered more Eskimos to whom, in that treeless land, wood was more precious than gold. They had made kayak paddles, snow shovels, spear handles, tent poles, and a variety of objects from wood they'd got from other Eskimos. Obviously, it had been scavenged from a ship, but none of these people knew anything about white men who had died on their shores.

M'Clintock's task would not be an easy one. The Eskimos had plundered everything they could find, throwing away what they didn't need – such as books, papers, and journals – and adapting the rest for their own use. And a spectral shroud of snow still covered the land, concealing the remains of the lost explorers as well as any artifacts not yet discovered by the natives.

It was all very tantalizing. Even to a man of M'Clintock's temperament, this early peripheral evidence of tragedy must have been both exciting and frustrating. He pressed on south to Montreal Island in the Great Fish delta, haunted by the shades of men long dead. Here Petersen found a bit of a preserved meat tin and some scraps of iron and copper, but these relics, too, were second-hand. A native stone marker made it clear that this was plunder taken earlier and set aside for later retrieval. In the eerie silence of the Arctic spring, M'Clintock circled the bleak and rugged coastline of Montreal Island by dogteam and found no evidence that any of Franklin's men had got that far.

He returned on May 24 to King William Island, the sledge travelling along the sea ice that overlapped the shore. Driving his own team, he kept a sharp lookout, frustrated again by the snow that shrouded the beach. At midnight, with the sun still bright in the sky, he trudged along a gravel ridge that had been swept clean and there, with dramatic suddenness, he came upon a human skeleton. This was

324

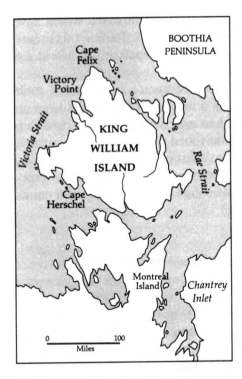

King William Island, c. 1859

a major find, the only first-hand evidence anybody had yet had of the Franklin disaster. There it lay, a grisly witness to history, the body face down as if its owner had stumbled forward and dropped, never to move again, the bones as white as chalk, a few rags clinging to the exposed limbs, which bore signs of having been gnawed at by animals.

He had been a young man, slightly built and probably, judging by the fragments left of his dress, a steward or an officer's servant. He had not been warmly clad; there was no evidence of any clothing other than the standard naval wool issue. A clothes brush and a pocket comb lay close by. Gazing down on his grim find, M'Clintock remembered what an old Eskimo woman had said to him: "They fell down and died as they walked along."

The party moved north along the gloomy and desolate west coast of the island. M'Clintock was certain that Franklin's men must have left some sort of record, but if they had, the Eskimos had long since scattered it to the winds; to them books and papers had no value or meaning. If the Navy had been quicker in its rescue operations, if the old Arctic hands had been less myopic, if Lady Franklin's own ships had persevered – in short, if the area he was now examining had been searched earlier – the full story of John Franklin's fate would undoubtedly have been discovered. At this late date, finding it seemed hopeless.

On the summit of Cape Herschel, 150 feet above the sea, M'Clintock came upon an old cairn left by Thomas Simpson in 1839. It had been badly broken down, undoubtedly by native looters, and it turned out to be empty. M'Clintock, who had been convinced that the dying men, retreating toward the Great Fish River, would have left some record here, was bitterly disappointed. To him, this dreary promontory was one of the most hallowed spots in the world for British seamen.

Then, twelve miles farther on, he came upon a smaller cairn, built by Hobson's party and containing a message. Hobson had been on the spot just six days earlier. He had seen nothing of a wrecked ship and had met no natives, but he *had* found a document! In a cairn at Victory Point, on the northwestern coast of King William Island, he had discovered the only record ever found of the lost Franklin expedition. It wasn't much, but it was enough to clear up the main points of the mystery.

3

The document at Victory Point The document found at Victory Point, maddening in its terseness, provided the only first-hand information ever uncovered regarding the progress and fate of the missing crews. Actually, it contained two separate messages – two cramped scribbles, written a year apart, in the margins of a regular printed Admiralty form. Hobson found it in the cairn that James Ross had built at Victory Point on the same journey that led to his discovery of the North Magnetic Pole on Boothia almost three decades before.

The first message, dated May 28, 1847, and signed by Lieutenant G.M. Gore, was determinedly cheerful. "All well," it read. It revealed that Franklin had certainly gone up Wellington Channel and had, in fact, circled round Cornwallis Island before settling down at Beechey Island for the winter of 1845-46. The second winter had found him beset in the ice stream just west of the northern tip of King William Island. Gore and a party of seven had left their message in Ross's cairn, fully confident that the two ships would shortly be freed and that the Passage would be breached that summer.

That was wishful thinking, as the second marginal message made clear. Written in a different hand and signed by Franklin's two deputies, Crozier and Fitzjames, it was dated April 27, 1848, and told a gloomier story. Franklin had died the previous June, only a month after Gore had scribbled his first message. At the time of the second message, the ships had been trapped in the ice for nineteen months, and no fewer than nine officers (including Gore) and fifteen men were dead. The remainder had abandoned their vessels and were trying to reach the Great Fish River.

Although no other written record has ever been found to illuminate the Franklin tragedy, there was enough here to piece together the probable story of his last expedition.

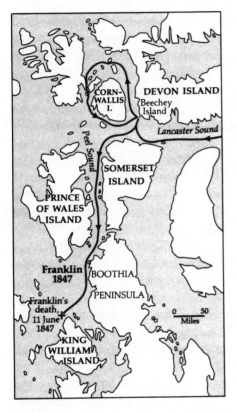

Franklin's last expedition, 1845-47

Racing to make time before the onset of autumn weather in 1845, Franklin apparently did not stop to build cairns or leave letters, as with sails full out he pressed confidently on through the open waters of Lancaster Sound. After all, the eternal optimist expected to be sailing into the North Pacific in less than a year.

He pushed on through Barrow Strait. Somewhere ahead loomed the precipices of Cape Walker, the last known point of land. To the southwest lay the Unknown, which his instructions had ordered him to explore. But now he found that direction blocked by ice. On the western shore of Devon Island he could see a stretch of clear water sparkling in the sunlight: this was Wellington

Channel. Following his instructions, he made for this alternative route and sailed north into unexplored territory. Was it a strait or merely a bay? No map could tell him.

The two ships headed north until the presence of the Grinnell Peninsula, as yet unnamed and unexplored, forced them to the northwest. At the very tip of the peninsula, Franklin once again found his

327

way barred by a wall of ice that (as later explorations would reveal) extended from the head of Wellington Channel for hundreds of miles to the west.

Forced to retreat south through a different channel, he realized that he had rounded Cornwallis Land, now seen to be an island. He re-entered Barrow Strait north of Cape Walker and was again frustrated in his attempt to push west. But directly to the south lay another channel. Somewhere beyond that, in the vicinity of King William Land, he knew from his earlier explorations and those of Back and Simpson that the way was clear to the western seas. More than once he had pointed out that area on the map and declared: "If I can get down there my work is done; thence it's plain sailing to the Westward."

It was obviously too late in the year to make the attempt. With the floes increasing in the strait, he would have to find a safe anchorage before the moving ice drove him out of Lancaster Sound. He had probably examined the harbour at Beechey before entering Wellington Channel. In the autumn of 1845 he made for it and spent the winter there, undoubtedly satisfied with his first year's accomplishments. Three of his men died of natural causes – not an unusual number – and were buried on the spot.

He was now within striking distance of his goal. King William Land was just 350 miles to the south. Once that gap was closed he would be near familiar waters leading to the west. Whether he could have completed the voyage through the narrow channels and treacherous shoals in his cumbersome ships is questionable. As Dr. King had tried to point out, in his irritating but sensible fashion, naval vessels such as the *Erebus* and the *Terror* were designed for the open ocean, not for coastal manoeuvring.

But why did he leave no record at Beechey Island? He spent the winter there, equipped for the usual activities – amateur theatricals, target practice, scientific observations, the collection of specimens. Yet no one, apparently, thought to leave a single scrap of paper outlining the expedition's plans for the following summer. This is the abiding mystery surrounding the tragedy, and the questions it raises cannot be answered. Was it because the optimistic explorer was so certain of getting through that year he didn't think it necessary? Was it because the two ships were driven involuntarily away from Beechey along with the ice in a sudden spring gale, before Franklin had time to prepare a record? Or was there a message left that has never been found? Each question is plausible, but each assumption has its own queries. Optimistic or not, Franklin always obeyed orders; why didn't he follow standard naval procedure this time? And again, why would this plodding but meticulous naval veteran, who had all winter to prepare a careful record, decide to wait until the last moment to build a cairn and leave a message? If he *did* leave a record, the place to leave it was on Beechey, for there were no natives in the vicinity (then or later) to loot its contents. No one knows the answer to this puzzle; no one will ever know.

What is known is that Franklin, following orders, would have set his course that spring for Cape Walker. He did not realize that he was sailing directly toward the great ice stream that pours down from the Beaufort Sea in an inexorable movement south. M'Clintock had seen the genesis of this slow-moving river of ice when he discovered Prince Patrick Island, seeing the great chunks breaking off the face of the permanent pack. Driven by the prevailing winds from the northwest, this ponderous frozen stream, awesome in its power, squeezes its way between the bleak islands, as it seeks warmer waters. Like a floating glacier up to one hundred feet thick, unbroken by any lane or channel, the moving pack is impenetrable.

The same ice stream that stopped Parry in 1819 and would halt McClure in 1851 was, in the summer of 1846, moving into a collision with Franklin's two vessels. Flowing down between Melville and Banks islands and through Melville Sound, it forced itself against the western shores of Prince of Wales Island, curved down the unexplored channel (later to be named for M'Clintock) on the eastern side of Victoria Island to block the narrows at King William Island. Here its southern edge encountered the warmer waters flowing from the continental rivers and began to break apart, leaving the channels to the south relatively clear.

Faced with the presence of this vast, slow-moving frozen mass, Franklin had to retreat. Another unknown channel, Peel Sound, lay to the south, beckoning in the direction of King William Land, and so he turned his ships south into untested waters. This course would have seemed unimpeded to him because he was sheltered from the inexorable ice stream by the bulk of Prince of Wales Island.

When he emerged from Peel Sound, he must have seen the northern tip of King William dead ahead, just one hundred miles away. But once he emerged from the shield of Prince of Wales Island, he would again have encountered the ice stream. To stay clear of it, he

329

would have had to cling to the west coast of Boothia, but that would have given him only temporary respite. Sooner or later he knew he would be forced to face the ice, for the only route to the known Passage shown in his charts led directly down the west coast of King William Land.

He had no way of knowing, in 1846, that King William Land was insular, unless he believed the theories of the eccentric Dr. King. He could have escaped the ice stream by cutting around the island's eastern side and slipping down the narrow strait that separates it from the mainland. But Franklin must have believed that route led to a dead end. Instead, he turned his ships into the ice stream just as King William Island was at hand. Winter closed in; on September 12, 1846, the *Erebus* and the *Terror* were beset – imprisoned in that frozen river that moved south at the frustratingly slow speed of one and a half miles a month.

Franklin's death the following June also remains an insoluble mystery. His burial place has never been found. Almost certainly he was buried at sea, but we do not know what caused his sudden death. All was well when Gore scribbled the first message in the cairn. A month later, as the second message made clear, Franklin was gone and Crozier was in command. All we know is that Franklin was infirm and in his sixtieth year – obviously too old to undertake such a quest – the victim of his friends' sentimentality, the Navy's rigidity, and his own dogged optimism.

The fate of his men is less mysterious. Over the years more skeletons or fragments of skeletons have been discovered. Modern research has shown evidence of cannibalism, scurvy, and lead poisoning from the poorly soldered tins of meat. The Eskimos' descriptions of the crews' final stages suggest that most of them succumbed to scurvy – the disease that haunted almost every Arctic expedition. Neither John Franklin nor the Royal Navy had learned much in spite of previous experience with the disease. *Erebus* and *Terror* were heavily stocked with salt meat. John Ross had been kept alive by fresh meat supplied by Eskimo hunters, but John Ross was not held in high repute by Franklin's generation of Arctic explorers. M'Clintock encountered no Eskimo who could remember that any native had been aboard the two ships while they were caught in the ice stream. Nor were Franklin and his men equipped to capture seals or walruses or to hunt big game.

Pieced together, the messages at Victory Point told a familiar

330

story. All was well one year; twenty-four men were dead the next. It is probable that Gore and his shore party moved far enough down the coast to discover for the first time the last link of the North West Passage. It is certain that with men dying daily the following winter, Franklin's successor, Crozier, knew his only hope lay in abandoning the ships before the entire company perished.

For the *Erebus* and the *Terror*, there was no way out of the floating trap. It had been the coldest winter in living memory. The ice had not melted; its progress was too slow. Crozier's mistake was to head south to the Great Fish River. Perhaps he thought that a relief party might have been sent there. If so, he underestimated the sluggishness of the Admiralty and the foolish optimism of the so-called Arctic Council of polar experts who exhibited little concern about Franklin and did not bestir themselves until the spring of 1848, when Franklin's surviving crews were already sledging to their deaths.

The Great Fish River with its myriad cataracts was trial enough for strong, healthy, well-fed voyageurs, as George Back had discovered. For Crozier's men, it would have been an impossibility to navigate, even if they had reached it. Ironically, a mountain of stores, not to mention several boats, lay at Fury Beach to the northeast, but again it is not easy to believe that in their debilitated condition they could have reached that Arctic oasis. They had neither dogs nor dog drivers, and the Navy sledges were unnecessarily heavy and cumbersome.

M'Clintock, moving along the shingle ridges of King William Island's ghostly northwest coast, came suddenly upon one of these sledges not far beyond the rugged cape he named for Captain Crozier. Hobson, it turned out, had been on the scene a few days before. What M'Clintock saw shocked him. The sledge itself was a monstrous contraption of iron and oak, weighing at least 650 pounds. On top of it was a twenty-eight-foot boat, rigged for river travel, weighing another 700 or 800 pounds. To M'Clintock, with his own sledging experience, this was madness. Seven healthy men would have had trouble hauling it any distance, even if it had not been loaded. But it *was* loaded, with an incredible accumulation of unnecessary articles: books (*The Vicar of Wakefield* was one), every kind of footgear from sea boots to strong shoes, towels and toothbrushes, gun covers and twine, soap and sheet lead, dinner knives, crested silver plate, pocket watches and tools, a bead purse, a cigar case – everything, in short, that civilized nineteenth-century travellers considered necessary for their comfort and well-being. In M'Clintock's guarded phrase, it was, for a sledge traveller of those times, "a mere accumulation of dead weight, but slightly useful, and very likely to break down the strength of the sledge-crews."

Inside the boat he found eerie evidence of this truth. Here were sprawled two skeletons, one of a slight young man, perhaps an officer, the other of an older and sturdier seaman. This far they had stumbled and no farther, while their comrades, abandoning most of their chattels, had struggled on. M'Clintock was convinced that the party had underestimated its needs as far as food went (and overestimated its other requirements) and was returning to the ship for more provisions. But the ships were at least sixty-five miles to the north. Unable to drag their boat farther, they had left the two weakest of their number with a little food (some tea and chocolate were all that remained), expecting perhaps to return with fresh stock. As M'Clintock put it, "they appear to have greatly overrated their strength and the distance they could travel in a given time." Scurvy, which debilitates the muscles, also clouds the mind, making its victims believe they can accomplish more than they are able.

Did they ever reach the ships? Certainly they never returned. The Eskimos reported they had searched the one ship that had foundered near the shore and found one body but no living man.

When M'Clintock reached the cairn that Hobson had found at Victory Point, he was faced with another extraordinary spectacle – further evidence that the men who abandoned the ships weren't aware of the extent to which they had been weakened. They had piled their sledges with ten tons of gear and abandoned most of it three days later when they reached Victory Point. The huge heap of discarded woollen clothing was four feet high. But by what weird caprice had they been persuaded to bring along button polish, heavy cookstoves, brass curtain rods, a lightning conductor, and a library of religious books? It had taken them three days to haul this ponderosity of non-essentials fifteen miles before they realized they were not equal to the task. Then, after Fitzjames had thawed out some ink and scribbled the second note, they lightened their sledges and headed south down the desolate western coastline of the island to their deaths.

M'Clintock left this gloomy scene on June 2, crossed the island, and made his way over James Ross Strait to Boothia. He reached the *Fox* on June 19 to find Hobson slowly recovering from scurvy and the ship's steward, Thomas Blackwell, dead of the disease. It turned out that Blackwell hated preserved meats and vegetables and had lived almost entirely on salt pork for the winter – as indeed Franklin's crews must have done.

Allen Young had returned to the ship on June 7. After two months of exploration, his health was so bad that the ship's doctor ordered him in writing not to go out again. Young ignored him and was away again after only three days' rest. M'Clintock set off at once by dog-team to find him and hustled him back to the ship on the twenty-eighth. Young and a companion recovered on a diet of venison, wild duck, homemade beer, lemon juice, and pickled whaleskin.

Young had, of course, found no trace of Franklin, but he had made some notable geographical discoveries. He had completed the exploration of Prince of Wales Island and the west coast of Somerset. He had also established the feasibility of a North West Passage through what was to be called the Franklin Strait. He had further demonstrated the impossibility of getting through the ponderous ice stream in the channel between Prince of Wales Island and Victoria Island, soon to be named for M'Clintock. Together, the three sledge expeditions under M'Clintock, Young, and Hobson had charted eight hundred miles of new coastline.

Indeed, almost all that part of the Arctic archipelago from the Parry Islands south to the continental shore had been unveiled as a result of the long, blundering search for Sir John Franklin. That was the supreme irony of the quest for the North West Passage. The Passage itself would have little commercial value even with the development of modern icebreakers in the century that followed. It had always been used as a symbol to gain public support for geographical and scientific investigation. And a symbol it remained.

If Franklin had somehow managed to make his way through it, further exploration would probably have been postponed, perhaps for decades. The continued bungling of the Navy and the other expeditions had kept the flame alive, prolonged the explorations, and furthered scientific observation in the North. The British government spent an estimated £675,000 trying to find Franklin. Lady Franklin spent an additional £35,000 – and to better effect. The United States government contributed $150,000 to the quest. Henry Grinnell, the president of the American Geographical Society, was out of pocket $100,000. The search was unnecessarily long and expensive, often magnificently inept, and at times farcical. But the money was not entirely wasted. By the time Leopold M'Clintock returned to England, near the end of September, 1859, most of the southern Arctic had been mapped.

4

Failed heroes The eleven-year search for the lost ships elevated Sir John Franklin to the pantheon of Arctic sainthood. To the *New York Times*, he was "one of the ablest, oldest and bravest men who had trodden that perilous path" (the Passage). The newspaper praised the Franklin expedition and the search that followed as being "as noble an epic as that which has immortalized the fall of Troy or the conquest of Jerusalem."

"There is hardly a man of this generation," the *Times* declared, "whom the noble story of Arctic exploration has not moved to the depths of his soul. . . ." It wrote of "unheard of fortitude," "religious heroism," "courageous endeavour," and "devotion to duty" in the face of "appalling perils" – typically Victorian phrases that were always brought out and dusted off whenever another quixotic adventurer went to his death attempting to plant his country's flag in one of the uncharted corners of the world.

It was the impossible quest that captured the imagination; and the Franklin debacle exactly fitted that ideal. "Our age," the *Times* wrote, "is the age of chivalry. The march of Christian civilization may have turned the fire which precipitates a murderous shock, but it has fed the calmer and nobler heroism, which, for duty's sake, supports the hardest strain, and the fiercest struggle, and the sorest trial, not for an hour, or for a day, but for weeks, and months, and years."

In its editorial, the American newspaper championed the English credo – that victory must not be achieved too easily. It was hard struggle that counted, not the final achievement. The spectacle of able seamen working like dray-horses to drag their heavy sledges across the frozen wastes was more appealing than that of a native dogteam threading its way through hummocks of ice. The British especially had a warm spot in their hearts for gallant losers; they preferred them to easy winners, as a bewildered Roald Amundsen would discover more than sixty years later, when he beat Robert Falcon Scott to the Pole and was shunned for it by Englishmen.

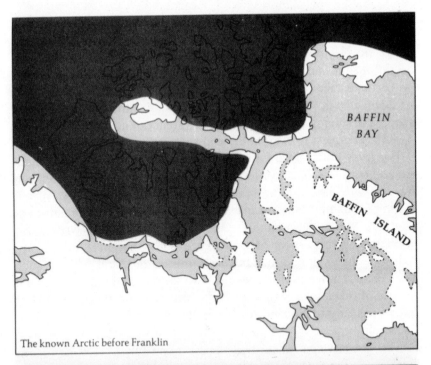

The known Arctic before Franklin

BAFFIN BAY

BAFFIN ISLAND

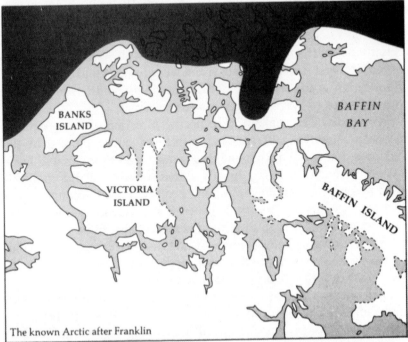

The known Arctic after Franklin

BANKS ISLAND

VICTORIA ISLAND

BAFFIN BAY

BAFFIN ISLAND

The known and unknown Arctic before and after the search

Scott, before his death, put into words the English sentiment that, for almost a century, governed the Royal Navy in its attitude to sledge travel: "No journey ever made with dogs can approach the height of that fine conception which is realized when a party of men go forth to face hardships, dangers and difficulties with their own unaided efforts, and by days and weeks of hard physical labour succeed in solving some problem of the great unknown. Surely in this case the conquest is more nobly and splendidly won."

For forty years, since Parry's triumphant return in 1820, the British had been fed a steady diet of published Arctic journals (seventeen dealing with the Franklin search alone), each featuring tales of appalling hardship, dreadful brushes with death, and hairbreadth encounters with wild animals. One cannot blame the writers for emphasizing this aspect of their expeditions: they *were* dangerous, many of the explorers' escapes *were* miraculous, and without such tales the published journals would have seemed dull indeed – in fact, several of them were. As for scientific observations, these were better left to the lengthy appendices the explorers confined to the back of each volume.

The greatest epic of all was the Franklin quest. Had he turned back when the ice blocked his way, he would have gone down as a minor figure in the history of Arctic exploration. If he and his men had been rescued alive and returned to England, he would be no better known than Simpson or Rae, and with less reason. If the expedition had managed to survive a winter sledge journey north to Fury Beach or to the Eskimo settlements in the south, it might have merited some of the overblown praise it received.

Why didn't they make it? The northern section of King William Island is a gloomy, infertile land, barren of game, shunned by the Eskimos. But as John Ross had discovered – and Franklin well knew – there were natives living directly across the water at Boothia who were to keep his own crew alive and healthy. Ross's account was in Franklin's shipboard library, but there is no evidence that any of his sledgers ventured over to Boothia. There were also Eskimos living on the south shore of King William Island, as M'Clintock discovered. Again there is no evidence that any sledge parties came to trade with these natives before that last fatal march south.

Gore's trip to the south seems to have been purely exploratory – to make sure the channel in which the ships were beset was truly the last link in the Passage. His cheery "all well" suggests that no one was worried about scurvy or starvation. After all, the ships were provisioned for another fourteen months, and that supply could easily be stretched (and almost certainly was) by careful rationing.

There is no shred of evidence of any contact with the natives until the dying men were dropping in their tracks. Nor is there any way of knowing whether or not the members of the expedition attempted to hunt big game. The evidence points against it. Years later, one native told the explorer-scientist Knud Rasmussen that his father, who had encountered three of the dying men, reported the strangers shot only wildfowl, though there were caribou aplenty. The only weapons found by Hobson were shotguns; the sailors followed the tradition of the English sportsmen back home who made a game of knocking down grouse and snipe on their vast estates. This lack of hunting skills had wrecked Franklin's first expedition. In nearly three decades he had learned nothing from that disaster.

Small game birds, even taken in quantity, would not sustain a crew of 126 men or protect them from scurvy. What was needed was deer, polar bear, or fresh seal meat, which only the Eskimos had the training, the knowledge, and the patience to supply. To hunt effectively, the members of the expedition would have had to rove a considerable distance from the island's barren northwest shore. They weren't equipped for it. Secure in their artificial environment, John Franklin and his officers dined in Victorian splendour, the brass buttons of their dress uniforms carefully polished by their servants, their tables set with linen, their salt meat carved with silver-plated, crested knives.

The most iconoclastic of the twentieth-century explorers, Vilhjalmur Stefansson, damned them with a bitter epitaph. They died, he wrote, because they brought their environment with them; they were not prepared and had not learned how to adapt to another.

In this, of course, they were the creatures of their age. All over the globe in the outposts of Empire, pukka sahibs were continuing to live as if the countryside of Wordsworth was at their back door, apparently oblivious to climate and culture, secure in their conviction that the English form of civilization was the only form. If, for instance, English wool was suitable for the fog-bound streets of London, it was equally suitable for the South Seas or the chill Arctic. Yet wool, as René Bellot had discovered, could not keep out the cold blasts of Boothia, while the sweat it absorbed froze in the clammiest fashion. Kennedy, the Canadian mixed-blood, taught Bellot, the inquiring

Frenchman, to wear deerskin – as John Rae did. Kane, steeped in the tradition of the American frontier, adopted the loose sealskin garb of the Eskimos, which allowed greater circulation of air and, with its fur-lined hood, prevented the disastrous heat loss from the exposed face and neck, the most vulnerable parts of the body. Few Englishmen anywhere in the world had the temerity to adopt native dress. The Royal Navy stuck to wool and flannel.

The *New York Times*, of course, in its paean to the Arctic searchers for their "deeper fortitude" and "holier enthusiasm," did not mention the natives, let alone give them credit for the part they played throughout the age of exploration in sustaining the polar heroes. In the famous painting of the so-called Arctic Council (which never met as a body), there is one face missing. Even Franklin is there, though Franklin was long dead when the faces of his contemporaries were immortalized in oils. But where is the symbolic Eskimo? Like the ghost at the banquet, he is unseen. Yet without him the painting is incomplete and the Arctic Council has no meaning.

These faceless natives are kin to those other dark menials who served their white masters in counterfeit English cottages in the Indian hill country or in classical colonial headquarters that might have been plucked brick by brick out of Whitehall. The English could not believe that any of these inferior people did not love to serve them and were bewildered by the dreadful realization of their misconception when the fires of rebellion exploded. The Sepoy Mutiny broke out just before M'Clintock left on his last voyage. The nation was still reeling from it when he sailed home.

In the same year that M'Clintock returned with the solution to the Franklin mystery, Richard Francis Burton and John Hanning Speke came back from another quest, as tantalizing in its own way as that for the key to the Passage. Their grail was the mysterious source of the Nile, and for the next thirty years, the nation would be caught up in the excitement and romance of the African discoveries. The engravings in the popular illustrated journals told the story: drawings of half-naked native bearers, each carrying white men's goods on his head; drawings of black men bearing white men on litters; drawings of yellow men pulling white women in rickshaws. Kipling would later write of the white man's burden, but the heaviest burdens in the Age of Exploration were borne by men of different colours who had mastered their environment and to whom the explorers turned time and again for protection and sustenance.

The picture of the last days of the Franklin expedition pieced together by M'Clintock and later investigators was bitterly ironic. It is a picture of inadequately clothed, badly nourished men, dragging unmanageable loads down the bleak coast of an Arctic island. As they stumble and drop in their tracks, other eyes watch them curiously. The Eskimos of King William Island were also hungry, and there were times when they too suffered from scurvy and even froze to death. But they were never wiped out. Meagre though their diet had been that winter, it kept them alive and warded off the disease.

Cold they certainly were, even in their superior sealskin, but they were hardened to cold and knew how to prepare for it. The Eskimos survived; the whites died to the last man. "They perished gloriously," to quote one of the letters to The *Times* after M'Clintock's revelations. That was the prevailing attitude. But if they and their contemporaries had paid more attention to the indigenous way of life, they need not have perished at all.

5

Lady Franklin had waited restlessly for M'Clintock's return. The *The ultimate* peripatetic widow could not stay still. Off she went with her niece *accolade* Sophia on another of those exhaustive journeys that marked her career. She did it, she said, to strengthen herself for the possible dénouement of the long drama, which she hoped and prayed M'Clintock would unveil.

What if he failed? How much longer could she continue the struggle to reclaim her husband's honour? How many more expeditions might be needed? And how many more could she afford to underwrite? There was so little time. On her sixtieth birthday she had scribbled: "I cannot write down all the feelings that press upon me now as I think how fast the sands of life are ebbing away."

Her forebodings were premature. In 1858, six years after she wrote those words, while her captain was enduring the freeze-up in Bellot Strait, she was determined to set off again – not on foot this time, for she was suffering from phlebitis, but by boat and train – through France, Greece, the Crimean battlefields, and North Africa. Everybody knew her; everybody met her. In Athens she had an audience with the Queen of Greece, in Tunis with the Bey himself and his prime minister in the privacy of his harem, which out of feminine curiosity she had asked to see.

She had not returned to London when M'Clintock arrived. She was on a mountain top in the Pyrenees, having been sent there ostensibly for her health and carried to the peak by porters. The news reached her in a terse telegram from Collinson relayed by the British consul at Bayonne, who had also received an equally terse letter from the taciturn M'Clintock, giving her details of his findings and adding, almost as an afterthought, that her husband could not have suffered long and had died with success in sight.

She hurried back to London to find herself the most admired woman in the realm. She had triumphed where the Navy had failed. Persistently, year after year, she had pointed in the right direction, secure in the belief that her husband, a stickler for orders, would follow his instructions to the letter, even at the risk of his life. He had been told to go south, and south he had gone; all along she had known he would. The relics of the expedition, sent to the Admiralty, went on display at the United Services Institution where the crowds were so thick it was necessary to issue tickets.

The press was urging that parliament reimburse her for the funds she had committed to the search. The spirited widow responded that she wouldn't accept a penny. But she did want to do something for M'Clintock and his crew, and she also wanted something more for her husband. She was determined that he and not McClure should be recognized as the man who first solved the puzzle of the Passage.

There were honours aplenty for the crew of the *Fox*. Those who had not previously received the Arctic Medal were granted it. Hobson was promoted to commander for his discovery of the cairn at Victory Point, a discovery made possible by M'Clintock's generosity. M'Clintock himself was toasted and fêted – with the freedom of the city of London, with honorary degrees from the three leading universities in Britain, with a fellowship and a medal from the Royal Geographical Society and a knighthood from the Queen.

In March 1860, Lady Franklin, working behind the scenes as usual, prompted a debate in parliament that resulted in an award of five thousand pounds to the crew of the *Fox*. Of that, M'Clintock received fifteen hundred. She herself was awarded the Patron's Medal of the Royal Geographical Society, becoming the first woman ever to receive that honour. It was no more than her due.

With this went the accolade she had sought for her husband – a memorial from the RGS testifying to the fact that his expedition had indeed been the first to discover a North West Passage. The indefinite article made it clear that there was no single channel through the Arctic labyrinth but several. Whether Franklin had actually seen the last link in the Passage before he died so mysteriously was never argued. Obviously, he hadn't. He must have been aware, of course, that Victoria Strait – the channel in which his ships were trapped – led inevitably to Queen Maud Gulf and then west to the Pacific. But to call him the discoverer of the Passage was stretching the known facts.

This sentimental decision downgraded McClure's later discovery of a Passage farther north. Unlike Franklin, McClure had actually traversed the Passage from west to east, though not entirely by water. But Franklin was the popular favourite. McClure's naked ambition had given him a brief moment of glory, but in the end it conspired to reduce him to the second rank of polar explorers.

For Franklin there would be other memorials: a tablet at Greenwich and a bust in Westminster Abbey, complete with a breathless couplet from Tennyson, exclaiming that "the white North has thy bones . . . Heroic sailor soul. . . ." But perhaps the greatest memorial of all was M'Clintock's own account of his search. His book, which went into seven editions, lacks the colour and introspection of a Kane or a Bellot narrative and the sensational disasters and hairbreadth escapes found in Sherard Osborn's overheated account of McClure. But it has something none of the other narratives of the Franklin search can equal, for it unfolds like a detective story, unravelling, bit by bit, in plain, unvarnished prose, the greatest mystery of its time.

Chapter Nine

Charles Francis Hall

Rescue of the Polaris *party by the* Ravenscraig

In mid-July 1859, as the world waited for the return of Leopold M'Clintock in the *Fox*, an obscure, half-educated printer in Cincinnati, Ohio, suddenly tossed aside his career, sold his business, left his wife and two children, and made plans to launch still another attempt to seek and rescue the survivors of the Franklin expedition.

It would be hard to imagine a more unlikely polar explorer than Charles Francis Hall, the proprietor of the little Cincinnati *News*. A former blacksmith and engraver, he was a high-school drop-out with no scientific background, no knowledge of navigation, and no training in any related skills. He was, however, obsessed with the Arctic, a quality that more and more seemed to be the prime requisite for would-be northern adventurers. He had read every available tome and article describing earlier explorations. He had studied the problems inherent in Arctic survival, including various theories about the relationship between diet and scurvy. The Eskimos fascinated him, though his attitude toward them was naïve in the extreme. When he visited New York City, he encountered on a crowded street the first Chinese he had ever seen. He stopped the stranger and asked if *he* was an Eskimo.

His hero was Elisha Kent Kane, whose two books captivated him as they had captivated most of America. Like Kane, he was an American romantic, as far removed in style from his tight-lipped British predecessors in the Arctic as the Italians are from the Scots. Like Kane, he had an iron will, a passionate nature, and an almost inexhaustible store of energy. His writing style was equally exclamatory.

Unlike his hero, he was robust. He was no more than five feet eight inches tall, but he weighed two hundred pounds; and little of that was fat. He was stocky and muscular, with big shoulders and a massive head. His features were masked by a brown beard, coarse and curly. His forehead was expansive, his close-set eyes a bright blue. He looked the part he had chosen for himself.

He was a genuine eccentric, single-minded, solitary, quick to take offence, with a capacity for suspicion and a propensity for nursing old hatreds. A captive of sudden enthusiasms, he could also be both tactless and intolerant. He did not work well with others, for he was essentially a loner; and it was as a loner that he did his best work in the Arctic.

He had learned that spring of 1859 that Dr. Isaac Hayes, Kane's former shipmate, was planning his own expedition to the Arctic to prove the existence of the Open Polar Sea and also to attempt to reach the North Pole. Hall's patriotism was aroused. In an enthusiastic editorial he urged the U.S. government to give liberal support to further Arctic exploration. His country, Hall declared, must be the first to plant the flag at the Pole. "Americans can do it – and *will*," he exclaimed.

Within a fortnight he had sold his paper and set out to organize an expedition of his own. It was a startling decision. What had caused this armchair explorer and romantic dreamer to throw everything aside to feed his obsession? Hall's explanation is the only plausible one: he had, he said later, received a call from Heaven; he was destined by God to go to the Arctic and search for John Franklin.

When M'Clintock returned with what seemed to be solid proof of the fate of Franklin's crews, Hall brushed it aside. There were still, he believed, unanswered questions, and the people who had those answers were the Eskimos of King William Island. Hall had convinced himself that there might still be survivors. England had abandoned the field; now, at last, here was an opportunity for a humble American to add some lustre to his country's reputation.

He had no real idea of what he faced, but then few newcomers to the Arctic did. His idea of hardening himself for the polar wastes was to camp out for a few days in a tent, which caused some merriment in Cincinnati. Yet such was his enthusiasm that he was able to persuade twenty-eight of the town's civic leaders to lend their names to a circular endorsing his proposed expedition.

In February 1860, he went to New York to meet one of Dr. Kane's brothers, Robert, and also Isaac Hayes and the philanthropic Henry Grinnell, who was helping to raise money for Hayes's proposed venture as well as contributing to it personally. Hall went on to the whaling port of New London, where he listened, open-mouthed, to the whalers' tales of life in the polar seas. There he was charmed by what he felt to be a semblance of Arctic weather. "As the snow came driving into my face – into my clothes – down into my busom [*sic*], I said, 'how beautiful you are. Thou wert created by the same hand that made the stars – Worlds – SYSTEMS!' " Hall's prose was heated enough to melt the ice itself.

In New York City, Hall was closeted with Henry Grinnell, who offered him encouragement and also wrote to Lady Franklin in England about Hall's plans. Her usual enthusiasm for any kind of search was dampened, however, by her Arctic friends, notably Leopold M'Clintock, who had no faith in the venture. But Grinnell offered the would-be explorer the use of his library and introduced him around town. To Hall, the philanthropist was the greatest man in the world, and when Grinnell actually deigned to visit him in his shabby hotel room, he was ecstatic: "Can it be possible that so poor a creature as I can be worthy [of] consideration of *so worthy a man as he*?" In truth, Hall must have had considerable charisma to attract Grinnell, who had already subsidized three Arctic expeditions and was now about to contribute to two more. But then, Grinnell was as obsessed with the Arctic as any explorer.

Hall had expected to take a ship to the Arctic and had settled on John Quayle, a whaling captain he had met in New London, as its navigator. But Hayes also was after Quayle and succeeded in hiring him for his own expedition, "a piece of double dealing" that drove Hall to a fury and turned his enthusiasm for Hayes's venture into bitter opposition. All the bile that lay dormant in his nature rose as he contemplated Hayes's "damnable work."

"I dare not put on paper . . . the rank inhumanity of Dr. I.I. Hayes & of Captain P.T. [*sic*] Quayle," he wrote, putting it all on paper. "Here I am, life devoted to rescuing of some lone survivor of Sir John Franklin's men and yet within their hearts *must lurk deep damnation*." In Hall's view, Hayes was beneath contempt. "I pity him, I pity his *cowardice & weakness*. I spurn his trickery – his DEVILRY!" But Hall had no intention of being put off by such setbacks. "Let the Curtain drop – I will go on, God willing, with my work."

As it turned out, he would have no need of a navigator because he would have no ship; he couldn't afford one. He had managed to raise only $980, of which Henry Grinnell supplied $343, plus some supplies. That did not deter him. He managed to wangle free passage on a whaler out of New London. It would drop him off on Baffin Island and return for him at the end of the season. He would spend the summer living with the Eskimos, perhaps learning their language, and pursuing his search for Franklin's men by sailing in a small boat to King William Island. It was an ambitious, even foolhardy adventure. No explorer, not even Rae, had attempted such a feat – to live alone in the Arctic, supported only by the natives.

He left New London on May 29, 1860, aboard the whaler *George*

Henry, his funds increased by Horace Greeley, who was happy to engage him to write his experiences for the New York *Tribune*. The little schooner *Rescue* accompanied the whaler as a tender. Hall saw her presence as a happy omen, for the *Rescue* had been one of the two American vessels seeking Franklin on the First Grinnell Expedition a decade earlier.

Hall not only felt that God had ordained his expedition but, like several other Arctic explorers, was also convinced that the Almighty was watching over him personally. That belief was confirmed in August when his revolver dropped on some rocks during a shore excursion and exploded so close to his face that he thought himself dangerously wounded. Fortunately, the ball just cleared his head. "THANKS BE TO GOD I STILL LIVE!" he exulted in his journal. "... No other arm but the Almighty's could have shielded me. . . ." He interpreted the event as a miracle and raised a small stone monument to the Deity.

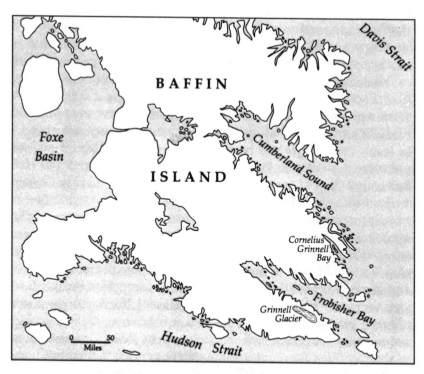

Hall's first expedition: Frobisher Bay, 1860-61

Although much of the coastline of Baffin Island had been explored, the interior, fringed by bays and inlets, was largely unknown. In mid-August, the *George Henry* anchored in the mouth of what was then known as Frobisher Strait, discovered 284 years earlier by the Elizabethan knight for whom it is named. Beyond lay the mysterious land that Elizabeth I had named *Meta Incognita*. Hall was ecstatic as he gazed into the distance through his telescope. "I saw its mountains," he wrote to Henry Grinnell, "like giants holding up the sky. My eyes felt charmed at what was before me. Never did I feel so spell bound to a spot as that whereon I stood. . . ."

He followed the northern horizon with his spyglass and noted that the mountains seemed to be joined to the land on which he stood. Was that possible? Could it be that this historic strait was actually a bay, with no exit that would lead to Foxe Basin and then on to King William Island? Very shortly, the Eskimos confirmed it; they had an astounding sense of geography and could draw maps of which few professional cartographers would be ashamed. This new information – that Frobisher Strait was actually a bay – threw Hall's plans into disarray.

As it turned out, he could not have reached King William Island anyway. A dreadful storm wrecked the schooner *Rescue* as well as another whaling brig, the *Georgiana*, both anchored in the bay. The crews were saved, but his own small boat was torn from its moorings and reduced to kindling. Only the *George Henry* escaped, to anchor farther north in Rescue Harbour off Cumberland Sound. In the face of his calamity, Hall did not flinch. "I was determined," he wrote later, "that, God willing, nothing should daunt me; I would persevere if there was the smallest chance to proceed. If one plan failed – if one disaster came, then another plan should be tried. . . ."

On November 2, while he was working in his cabin on his journal, he had an extraordinary encounter that was to affect the rest of his career. He heard, behind him, a "soft, sweet voice" – clearly feminine – "musical, lively and varied."

"Good morning, Sir!" the voice said; obviously, Hall thought, a lady of refinement. But here? On this whaling vessel anchored off Baffin Island? Could he be dreaming? His astonishment at the sound was nothing to the shock he received when he turned his head. There, in the doorway, backlit from the cabin's skylight and extending an ungloved hand, was a sturdy woman in crinolines and flounces, wearing a broad "kiss-me-quick" bonnet and a long, fringed cape of caribou hide. Peering up at her, Hall realized that this woman must be an Eskimo.

This was Tookolito – "Hannah" to the white men – who with her husband, "Joe" (Ebierbing), would become Hall's constant companions until the day of his death. In 1855, in the Repulse Bay area, the couple had come to the attention of British whalers who, impressed by their intelligence, had taken them to London. They spent two years there, created a sensation, were presented to the Queen, took tea with her and the Prince Consort, and learned something about the white man's world, which they much admired. On arriving in London, Joe's first act was to spend everything he had on an umbrella, which he considered the mark of a civilized man. Hannah and Joe took in the sights gravely and curiously – the hansom cabs and buggies, the narrow cobbled streets, the curiosity-seekers who stopped them continually – without a trace of culture shock. By the time they returned, at their own request, Joe spoke some English and Hannah was fluent. He took odd jobs piloting whaling vessels up the coast while she taught the Eskimo women how to knit wool.

Hall was charmed by the "exceeding gracefulness and modesty of her demeanour." There was, he declared, "a degree of calm and intellectual power about her that more and more astonished me." He was ecstatic at meeting a native he could converse with, since his entire plan had been to learn as much about the Eskimos as possible – to live with them, sleep in their snow houses, travel with them, and eat their food. He called them by their own name, *Inuit*, and was the first to use that term regularly in his writings.

He visited Hannah next day in her village and found her knitting socks for herself and her husband. She gave him tea – she had acquired the taste in England – and asked if he liked it strong or weak. He had given her a book at that first meeting, and she brought it out and asked for instructions. She had managed to spell words of two letters and to pronounce them properly; she felt triumphant at her success, for she was determined to learn to read.

The two Eskimos willingly agreed to work for Hall as guides and interpreters. They did not care greatly for the whalers, whom they considered coarse and unruly. "I feel very sorry to say that many of the whaling people are very bad," Hannah told Hall. ". . . They swear very much and make my people swear. I wish they would not do so. Americans swear a great deal – more and worse than the English. I wish no one would swear. It is a very bad practice, I believe." Hall was embarrassed at this stain on his country's reputation.

Yet, like almost every white explorer who entered the land of the Eskimos, Hall could not escape from the mind-set of his own culture. What he admired most about Ebierbing and Tookolito was the sheen of civilization they had acquired in England. If only all their people could knit socks, pour tea, talk in fluent English, and abhor swearing! "The Esquimaux," he wrote, "really deserve the attention of the philanthropist and Christian. Plant among them a colony of men and women having right-minded principles, and, after some patient toil, glorious fruits must follow." Hall did not live to observe the glorious fruits that eventually did follow, when Christians with right-minded principles helped to destroy the native culture, even banning the use of the Innuit language in the schools.

Nevertheless, Hall was the first white explorer to identify himself totally with the natives. He visited them frequently in their village, and they in turn came to see him on the ship. One night while writing in his journal, he counted seven Eskimos of both sexes asleep in his cabin, two of them in his own sleeping bag.

In January 1861, he decided to go with Joe and Hannah on a trip by dogsled to Cornelius Grinnell Bay. For the next forty-three days he lived as a native, sleeping on the frozen ledge of a snow house and eventually living on whale blubber. Hannah cut his hair and when his feet turned to lumps of ice, massaged them in the night with her own. (Hall tells the story so innocently in his memoirs that it is impossible to believe the encounter was in any way sexual.) When he returned to the ship on February 21, he found that after his nights in the native igloos, his cabin was too comfortable for sleep. Two of the crew were down with scurvy when he returned. Hall told them the best cure was to live with the natives.

He made two more sledge trips that spring. One night he found himself sleeping with eight adult Eskimos and a babe in arms, all jammed into a snow house no more than ten feet wide. But what really intrigued him was an interview with Joe's grandmother, a woman who must have been a hundred years old and who told him stories she had heard as a child about ships and white men who had arrived many years before her time and left behind supplies that Hall recognized as coal, brick, and iron.

The first arrivals, she said, had come in two ships. The following year, three ships came. The third year, many ships arrived. Hall was astounded, for he knew that Martin Frobisher had made trips in three successive years, first with two ships, then with three, and finally with fifteen. There were other details that fitted written history, including the tale of five seamen whom Frobisher had lost on one of the voyages. It dawned on Hall that the folk memory of Frobisher's expedition had been handed down orally for nine generations.

Other clues from Frobisher's day began to turn up. On one of his sledge journeys to an Eskimo village near Frobisher Bay, Hall came upon a piece of red brick. Joe told him that as a child he had played with many such bricks left by the white men years before. Hall was transfixed. He was holding in his hand a relic of an expedition that, just eighty-six years after Columbus's discovery of America, had visited these shores.

"This relic," he wrote, "was more precious to me than *the gold* which Frobisher sought there under the direct patronage of Queen Elizabeth." Until that moment no one had been sure that Frobisher had actually visited the so-called strait that bore his name. Now Hall was sure – and he was sure of something else: if these folk memories could extend down through time for almost three centuries, surely memories of Franklin's expedition would still be fresh in the minds of those who had heard the story of his tragedy.

Hall made plans at once to go by whaleboat to King William Island. Joe and Hannah were ready to accompany him. But the captain of the *George Henry* dashed his hopes when he made it clear that no whaleboat was equipped for so arduous a journey.

Hall took the setback in his stride. He would return home, mount a second expedition, build a boat strong enough to make the journey, and return to try again. That would cost a year. Meanwhile, he would try to discover more evidence of Frobisher's party.

The ice broke in the anchorage in mid-July 1861. At the end of the month, the *George Henry* headed off for the whaling grounds, leaving Hall alone with the Eskimos and a leaky old whaleboat, in which he hoped to make the trip to Frobisher Bay. As the whaler steamed off, he felt the strangeness of his position – "at last alone; the ship gone; all of my own people, my own blood, my own language, departed. . . ." Yet he was far from despondent. He felt exhilarated, for this was what he had planned. Here was real freedom: "Freedom dwells in the North – freedom to live as one pleases, act as one pleases, and go where and when one pleases. . . ." The fetters of

352

civilization, of family life, of the need to earn a living were off. He was on his own.

2

On July 6, 1860, about a month after Hall's departure, his despised *The Open* rival, Isaac Hayes, set off on his own expedition in search of the *Polar Sea* legendary Open Polar Sea – the pool of relatively warm water, ringed by ice, that Hayes, like so many others, was convinced circled the North Pole. His plan was to enter Smith Sound and then push his way into the ice belt, dragging a boat across it using Eskimo dogs, until he reached the open water and, perhaps, the Pole itself.

He had had some trouble raising money. The Franklin tragedy had caused some sober second thoughts about the romance of Arctic travel, and now, with Franklin's fate unravelled, Hayes knew it would be difficult to rouse enthusiasm for further polar exploration. To "instruct the public mind," as he put it, he had organized a lecture tour. This was the spark that had fired the imagination of Charles Francis Hall, Hayes's most ardent supporter at the outset and his bitterest enemy a few months later.

The young doctor's public relations campaign worked. His lectures to the American Geographical Society and the Smithsonian Institution and his tour through the United States brought in funds from scientific societies in America and Europe and from private individuals, the most generous of whom was the ever-dependable Henry Grinnell. Volunteers clamoured to join the expedition. Most had never been to sea, but all pronounced themselves eager to serve in any capacity, "a declaration," as Hayes remarked dryly, "which too often on this, as on other occasions, I have found to signify the absence of any capacity at all."

Like most other American undertakings, in contrast to those of the British Navy, this would be a compact one. Instead of two big ships there would be one smaller vessel, the schooner *United States*, especially strengthened for Arctic service and, at 133 tons, less than a third the tonnage of the British ships. She would be manned by fourteen officers and men – a fraction of Franklin's 133 followers.

Hayes was obsessed by the need for dogs. When he reached the Greenland coast, he was chagrined to find the Eskimos wouldn't sell

353

him their best teams. "They knew by bitter experience the risks of going into the long winter without an ample supply of dogs to carry them over the ice." Hayes knew them, too, from his days with Kane. "To part with their animals was to risk starvation." He finally managed to secure a handful of dogs, but not enough for his purposes. At Upernavik he bought a few more and also winter garments of reindeer and seal.

Only two other men in his party had had any previous Arctic experience. One, Gibson Carruthers, died before the party left Upernavik. That left August Sonntag, Hayes's former trailmate from the Kane expedition. Hayes strengthened his crew by adding three Eskimo hunters, an interpreter, and two Danish seamen, bringing his party to nineteen. Then he set off in his little ship through the transparent waters, crowded as always with great monoliths of ice, which "conjured up effigies both strange and wonderful." On deck were his thirty dogs, some tethered, some in cages along the bulwarks, others running free, all badly frightened, most fighting and making day and night hideous with their howls.

Surprisingly, the *United States* made the passage across the treacherous Melville Bay in just fifty-five hours – a startling contrast to M'Clintock's frustrating experience three years before and proof again of the capriciousness of the Arctic pack. At Cape York, Hayes kept a lookout for natives, for he had a feeling that Hans Hendrik, the youth who had been Kane's favourite, might be in the vicinity. Sure enough, as the schooner slid close to the shore, a group hailed the ship.

Hayes and Sonntag went ashore to find Hans himself with his wife, Merkut, whom he had married after leaving Kane, together with a new baby and a young mother-in-law. Hayes looked at Hans sceptically, noting that "six years' experience among the wild men of this barren coast had brought him to their level of filthy ugliness."

It turned out that Hans had been longing for some such encounter. Year after year, from a lookout 200 feet above the sea, he had searched in vain for a ship. Now he was eager to accompany his friends north again. He came aboard with his wife, baby, tent, and household goods, leaving behind his in-laws in spite of their cries and entreaties. Hayes, who had never cared much for Hans, suspected he would have been just as happy to leave his wife and child behind, too. The sailors gave them all red shirts to wear, which they loved. Then the crew did their best to scrub all three down with soap and water,

354

which they resisted. Was this the white man's religious rite? a baffled and outraged Merkut asked her husband as the sailors scoured away.

At ten o'clock on the evening of August 29, Hayes, warming himself beside a red-hot stove in the officers' cabin – a teakettle singing and bubbling in the background – looked out on a terrifying spectacle. Dead ahead loomed the lofty cliffs of Cape Alexander, guarding the entrance to Smith Sound, with its twin, Cape Isabella, just visible in the distance on the western side.

"The imagination," Hayes wrote in his journal, "cannot conceive of a scene so wild. . . ." Great sheets of drifting snow rolled down over the cliffs, pouring into every ravine and gorge like gigantic waterfalls. Whirlwinds shot skyward from the hilltops, spraying dense clouds of white through the air. A glacier tumbling into a valley was obscured by a vast cloak of revolving white. The sun was just setting on a black and ominous horizon. But the wildest scene was the sea itself. A solid mass of foam lashed the cape and was hurled through the air by the wind, breaking over the icebergs and fluttering across the sea like a thick fog, rising and falling with each gust.

"Earth and sea are charged with bellowing sounds," Hayes wrote, ". . . shrieks and wailings, loud and dismal as those of the infernal blast which, down in the second circle of the damned, appalled the Italian bard. . . ." He tried to capture the spectacle on the page of his journal and gave up. "My pen," he admitted, "is equally powerless."

Two days later, the schooner collided with an iceberg, losing a lifeboat, a jib boom, and two masts. Hayes realized he could go no farther. He found a wintering place in a small bay he named Port Foulke, about eight miles northeast of Cape Alexander and some twenty miles south of Kane's old wintering spot at Rensselaer Harbor. There the schooner remained until July 14 of the following year.

Fortunately, the neighbourhood teemed with game. The Eskimo hunters loaded the winterized vessel with reindeer, rabbit, and fox meat. The two Danish crewmen made dog harnesses, and Hayes set about the exacting business of learning how to drive a spirited team of twelve. Peter Jensen, the interpreter, took him out on a mad dash up the fiord "not calculated for weak nerves," as Hayes put it. The superiority of dogs over men was never better demonstrated than in one course of six measured miles, which the dogs covered in twenty-six minutes. Without stopping to rest, they turned about and made the return journey in thirty-three.

Hayes also received a practical demonstration of why so many of the earlier explorers had shunned dogsled travel. It took consummate skill and a great deal of experience to handle the animals. Hayes must have thought back ruefully to the time when he and his friends from the Kane expedition had tried to steal two teams to escape from the sleeping Eskimos. The natives had no trouble overtaking them as they blundered across the snow with tangled traces and overturned sleds.

These dogs were guided solely by voice and by a four-foot whip of strong sinew. As Hayes discovered, "your control over the team is exactly in proportion to your skill in the use of it." An experienced driver could touch any of his dozen dogs with a single crack of the whip. "You see dat beast?" Jensen asked, pointing to a recalcitrant animal that had exhausted his patience. "I takes a piece out of his ear." To Hayes's astonishment, he nipped off the tip of the ear with a single snap of the whip "as nicely as with a knife." Hayes did his best to learn the peculiar turn of the wrist necessary to handle the whip properly and decided that if he were ever obliged to turn driver in an emergency, he would be equal to the task. "But I fervently hope that emergency may not arise."

At last he decided he was ready to try his hand at a run around the harbour. Things went smoothly until he tried to turn the team back into the teeth of the wind. The dogs sensed his awkwardness. He brought them round in the end but was able to keep them on the trail only by the constant use of the lash, which, three times out of four, was blown back in his face. He knew he could not hold out for long. His face was freezing, his arm felt paralysed, and the whip trailed in the snow. The dogs, aware that something was wrong, looked back over their shoulders and found the whip no longer menaced them. They increased their speed, turned about, and dashed off on their own course, "as happy as a parcel of boys freed from the restraints of the school-room, and with the wild rush of a dozen wolves," yapping and rejoicing in their liberty. As the strength returned to Hayes's leaden arm he began to use the whip again. After a short struggle, in which the sled was overturned, the dogs meekly gave in. "I think they will remember the lesson," Hayes wrote triumphantly, but added, "and so shall I."

That month, October, Jensen, who, according to Hayes, looked on the Eskimos "as little better than the dogs which drag their sledges," discovered a couple of native graves and brought in two skin-robed

356

mummies, which he thought would make fine museum specimens. Almost immediately Hans's wife set up a terrible howl: she had recognized the clothing as belonging to one of her relatives. Hayes, "in respect to humanity if not to science," restored them to the piles of stone that were their tombs, "the mournful evidences of a fast dwindling race."

Hans Hendrik had been Kane's favourite. Hayes much preferred the other Eskimo hunter, Peter, who was "always eager to serve my wishes in everything." Peter's zeal was rewarded with a quantity of coveted red flannel shirts and even a suit of clothes made of pilot-cloth. Hans became jealous of Peter, sulking openly and coming home without any game from the hunt. To Hayes he was "a type of the worst phase of the Eskimau character."

Hayes found the natives interesting but not as useful as the dogs; *they* could be controlled with a whip, while the Eskimos could not be controlled at all. "They might properly be called a negative people in everything except their unreliability, which is entirely positive." Though they never denied help when asked, they ordinarily left to fend for themselves those who were sick, needy, or in other distress. Hayes wrote, "They are the most self-reliant people in the world. It does not appear ever to occur to them to expect assistance, and they never think of offering it . . . I cannot imagine any living thing so utterly callous as they. Why, even my Eskimo dogs exhibit more sympathetic interest in each other's welfare." This harsh assessment, from a man raised in a totally different culture, failed to take into account the pitiless Greenland environment. Without their flinty code for survival, which often required them to destroy their own offspring when they had more babies than they could support or to allow a sick parent to die alone in a snow house, the race would long since have vanished from the Arctic.

Hans, meanwhile, had pitched his tent on the schooner's upper deck and, with his wife and infant half buried in deerskins, was living "the life of a true native." Merkut, in Hayes's patronizing phrase, was, "for an Eskimau not ill-looking. In truth she is, I will not say the prettiest but the least ugly-looking thorough-breed that I have seen." The ten-month-old baby was "a lively specimen of unwashed humanity." The other two hunters, Marcus and Jacob, lived in a tent, too, but had grown fat and lazy aboard ship and lost their usefulness.

As the light began to fail, Hayes instituted a rule that all birthdays would be celebrated with a sumptuous banquet, each man so honoured being allowed to order the best that Hayes's own lockers and the steward's storeroom could furnish. He knew from bitter experience the winter gloom that was facing them and that "whether men live under the Polar Star or under the Equator they can be made happy if they can be made full." He had learned from Kane the value of fresh meat, whether it be venison or boiled rat, and so kept his hunters working daily bringing in every kind of provender from seals to dovekies. By the end of October, the carcasses of seventy-four reindeer were stowed aboard ship and thirty more were frozen in the snow. But on the sledge journeys a minimum weight would be carried – bread, meat, coffee, little else.

The winter moved on with small alarms and larger tragedies. Hans's wife had a mind of her own and refused point-blank to act as a servant for the crew, who wanted her to sew sealskins into coats, pantaloons, and boots. "The indolent creature persistently refuses to sew a stitch," Hayes exclaimed. "She is the most obstinate of her sex; feels perfectly independent of everything and of everybody."

After one domestic spat, Merkut announced that she would abandon her husband and return, with her baby, to her own people. Off she headed on foot toward Cape Alexander, while Hans complacently smoked his pipe and let her go. That worried Hayes.

"Where is she going, Hans?"

"She no go. She come back – all right."

"But she will freeze, Hans."

"She no freeze. She come back by by – you see."

He continued to smoke his pipe, chuckling quietly. Two hours later Merkut returned.

Meanwhile, the rivalry between Hans and Peter increased. In late November, Peter simply ran away, never to be seen again alive. Hans, when questioned, gave what Hayes called "vague and unsatisfactory answers." Hayes was sure that Hans had driven Peter off, but couldn't prove it. A search party found a small bag with Peter's possessions, but nothing more. It was Hayes's belief that Hans had convinced his rival, who spoke no English, that the crew was against him and thus engineered his flight.

As the winter approached its climax, Hayes was faced with another problem. The Eskimo dogs began to die, stricken by the same mysterious disease that had affected Kane's teams, perhaps a form of distemper. Each dog became restless, then started to dash about the ship as if in mortal dread of some imaginary object. The symptoms increased, the eyes became bloodshot, froth appeared on the mouth, the dog attempted to snap at anything that approached, until, weak and prostrate, it fell into a series of fits that ended in death.

By the third week in December, only nine dogs were alive. Hayes knew that without his teams he had no hope of discovering the Open Polar Sea. Hans had told him there were Eskimo villages in the vicinity. When the full moon rose on December 21, Hayes sent him off with Sonntag to drive a team of the surviving dogs in search of fresh animals. They took twelve days' provisions and no tent, for it appeared an easy task for Hans to reach the nearest community. But as the days went by with no word from the pair, Hayes began to worry.

Christmas passed and New Year's. Hayes recalled a disturbing dream he'd had the night they left that he could not shake from his mind. He had been standing, in the dream, with Sonntag on the frozen sea when a crack opened between him and his comrade, bearing Sonntag off to a distant horizon. Was this an omen?

On January 20, with no word yet from the missing pair, the first wan signs of light appeared on the horizon, nothing more than a faint flush but enough to signal the future return of the sun. In his concern, Hayes was moved to contemplate the mysteries of the Arctic night: the dreadful solitude that "oppresses the understanding, [and] the desolation, which everywhere reigns, haunts the imagination; the silence – dark, dreary and profound – becomes a terror."

It was the brooding silence, "an endless and fathomless quiet," that bore down on him. "Silence has ceased to be negative. . . . I seem to hear and see and feel it. It stands forth as a frightful spectre, filling the mind with the overpowering consciousness of universal death. . . . Its presence is unendurable . . . I plant my feet heavily in the snow to banish its awful presence – and the sound rolls through the night and drives away the phantom. I have seen no expression on the face of Nature so filled with terror as THE SILENCE OF THE ARCTIC NIGHT."

This gloomy introspection was accompanied by his growing dismay over the absence of Hans and Sonntag. On January 27, Hayes tried to send out a search party; a storm prevented it. The following morning two strange Eskimos appeared suddenly out of the darkness. Hayes sent Jensen to interpret, and a moment later, watching the Dane's face, he knew the worst. Sonntag was dead.

The natives, who had arrived on a single sled drawn by five dogs, were covered from head to foot in snow and frost. Hayes didn't get the full story until Hans arrived two days later with his wife's younger brother. He was in a bad state physically; his dogs had broken down and so had his wife's parents, who were travelling to the ship with him. He had been forced to leave the older people curled up in a cave in a snowbank near a glacier. A search party found them and brought them back to the ship. Only then was Hans able to tell Hayes what had happened to Sonntag.

The pair could not find the village they were seeking and so pushed on for Northumberland Island. Sonntag sprang off the sled to warm himself, got ahead of the dogs, wandered onto some thin ice, and was plunged into the freezing water. Hans rescued him and dashed for the snow house they'd abandoned that morning. But by the time they reached it, Sonntag was stiff and speechless. Hans put him in a sleeping bag and tried to warm him with brandy, but Sonntag never recovered and died the following day.

Hans went on to a village on Whale Sound where he distributed presents and sent some of the villagers to Cape York to get dogs. Hayes suspected Hans's real intention was to bring back his in-laws and take them to the ship.

The gloom caused by this sad news was softened when the sun finally reappeared on February 18. Hayes was determined to continue his explorations even if his men had to haul their own sledges. But with the sudden and welcome arrival of his old friend Kalutunah, this was not necessary. Kalutunah had become a chief since Elisha Kane's time, a title that had only an honorary meaning among the individualistic Arctic Highlanders. He reported that Sip-su, who had wanted to murder Hayes and his party, was long dead, having been stabbed one night by an enemy. Hayes, following Kane's example, negotiated a formal treaty of friendship with Kalutunah under which the natives would furnish dogs and Hayes would feed their families. To impress on the Eskimos that he was a great magician who could read their minds, Hayes produced a pack of cards and entertained them with some sleight-of-hand. Kalutunah also brought tragic news of the runaway, Peter; his body had been found in a hut in a deserted village.

On April 3, having established caches and depots, Hayes set off for the Open Polar Sea with twelve men, two dogsleds, and one manhauled sledge carrying the twenty-foot metal lifeboat in which he hoped to navigate the ice-choked waters of Smith Sound. That he soon abandoned; a hundred men, he said, couldn't have got it across those narrows. Only at this point did he realize the magnitude of the task that faced him. The great floes breaking from the glaciers and permanent pack to the north had been driven south by the winds into Kane Basin and were now being squeezed into the confines of Smith Sound, creating a traffic jam of terrifying proportions. Hayes measured one floe that covered twenty-four square miles, rose twenty feet above the sea, and reached an estimated depth of 160 feet. He guessed its weight at six thousand *million* tons – a floating glacier, growing and expanding year by year as the ancient ice, hundreds of years old, remained unmelted and fresh snow accumulated and congealed into new ice above it. Why did the sea not freeze solid to the ocean floor? Because, Hayes realized, the downward growth of the floating mass was arrested by a natural law: the ice itself was the sea's protection, acting as a blanket to prevent the waters below from losing their heat.

As the sledge crews worked their way through this appalling tangle, making no more than three miles a day, Hayes began to lose heart. By April 24, with the peaks of Grinnell Land (Ellesmere Island) still distant, with his men "completely used up, broken down, dejected," he was at the end of his rope. The following day a sledge broke down and he felt himself defeated. "I was never in all my life so disheartened." The entire expedition had been a series of disasters: the crippled ship driven into an early refuge, dogs lost, his closest assistant dead, and now, here in the middle of the sound, "stuck fast and powerless."

He made his decision. He would send all but three of his strongest men back to repair the ship. He and Jensen, with two others – Knorr and McDonald – would push on with fourteen dogs. "Away with despondency!" Hayes exclaimed. When the quartet set off on April 28, the men were too weak to cheer – "there was not a squeak left in them." That day they made a mile and a half of forward travel but actually covered twelve miles to achieve it.

Hayes realized that humans could not possibly have brought their sledge through it all. The dogs climbed the ice hummocks like mountain goats and, being lighter than the men, didn't break through the crusted snow. But the ravenous animals would eat their own harness if they weren't watched. One night Jensen forgot to cover his sled; the dogs tore it apart to consume the lashings.

The bold, mountainous coast of Grinnell Land lay ahead. To the north Hayes could see the immense bulk of Cape Louis Napoleon, rising fifteen hundred feet above the sea. Directly ahead was another gigantic rock "to which Gibraltar is a pygmy." He named it Cape Hawks. They reached it May 11; they had taken fourteen days to move forty miles.

Hayes's food was running out. The dogs were gobbling up spare shoes, socks, even a bar of soap. The sleds were falling apart. Jensen's legs gave out; he was forced to ride. The other three shouldered traces and joined the dogs as beasts of burden.

They moved into Kennedy Channel, a narrow strait where the ice pressure was even greater and every point of land was smothered under

Area of Hayes's explorations, 1860-61

thirty to sixty feet of ice blocks. Great cliffs of sandstone and limestone rose above them. Jensen, now groaning in pain, could go no farther. Hayes left him in McDonald's care and pushed on with Knorr. He *had* to find the Open Polar Sea, otherwise this dreadful journey would have been endured for nothing. He was convinced he had got farther north than Morton, but his calculations were faulty, the product perhaps of wishful thinking as much as mathematical error.

The two men set out through a winding gorge formed by a great wall of rock on their left and a ragged, fifty-foot ridge of crushed ice

362

on their right. In this realm of "boundless sterility" with no evidence of any creature, bird or animal, Hayes once again felt "how puny indeed are all men's works and efforts." It seemed to him "as if the Almighty had frowned upon the hills and seas."

On their third day out they found their passage permanently blocked by rotten ice on one side and by an 800-foot cliff on the other. Peering into the distance, Hayes could see the dim outline of a headland, the most northerly known land on the globe. He judged it to be some 450 miles from the North Pole; it was actually closer to a thousand.

The land in the distance veered off, or so he believed, leaving only the ocean, which would soon be clear of ice. Surely this was the Open Polar Sea! "All the evidences showed that I stood upon shores of the Polar Basin," he wrote exultantly. He built a cairn, left a message in a glass bottle, planted a flag, and reluctantly headed back, buoyed up by the thought that "these ice-girdled waters might lash the shores of distant islands where dwell human beings of an unknown race." He himself was determined to sail upon this mysterious sea, which generations of explorers had vainly sought. "I felt that I had within my grasp 'the great and notable thing' which had inspired the zeal of the sturdy Frobisher, and that I had achieved the hope of the matchless Parry."

In fact, Hayes had achieved nothing. His calculations were so inaccurate that they were never taken seriously. The Open Polar Sea, the one goal that would have justified his painful journey, was a myth. In later years he would be accused of faking his observations. At the very least, he fooled himself by the desperation of his ambition. But he fooled few others. He returned with Knorr to pick up Jensen and McDonald, and reached the ship on June 3 after an exhausting trip in which he had covered some 1,300 miles in two months, convinced that "a route to the Pole . . . free enough for steam navigation is open every summer."

He could not follow up the object of his desire. The ship had been so badly damaged that if she were to try to go farther into the ice, she would certainly sink. The ice broke in July, and Hayes set his course for home on the thirteenth. First, he made a final visit to his native friends without whose help he would never have crossed the sound. He shook hands for the last time with Kalutunah, whose eyes filled with tears at the parting, not only because he was seeing the last of the white men but also because he alone of the Eskimos realized that his people could not survive much longer under the harsh conditions of the North Greenland coast. The tribe now numbered no more than one hundred souls, a serious depletion since Kane's day.

"Come back and save us," Kalutunah implored, and Hayes promised that he would. There had been a time when he had seen Kalutunah as his enemy; now he realized that he was a "singular being – a mixture of seriousness, good nature and intelligence – seems truly to take pride in the traditions of his race, and to be really pained at the prospect of their downfall."

On August 12, the *United States* reached Upernavik. An old Dane dressed in sealskins climbed aboard. Knorr met him at the gangway and asked if there was any news from home.

"Oh! dere's plenty news."

"Out with it man! What is it?"

"Oh! de Sout' States dey go agin de Nort' States and dere's plenty fight."

Hayes dismissed this report as news of a war between two European states; civil war in America was unthinkable! Only when he received a package of mail from Copenhagen did Hayes learn the truth, and he did not get full details until he reached Halifax.

The news hung like a pall over the crew. When they reached Boston, nobody wanted to go ashore, each anticipating some personal misfortune and wishing to postpone the shock. Hayes had never seen a ship's company so lifeless.

Wending his way alone in the fog towards a friend's house, the doctor "felt like a stranger in a strange land." He turned back to the familiar surroundings of the ship, realizing now that he would not be going north again in the foreseeable future. "In the face of the duty which every man owes in his own person to his country when his country is in peril, I could not hesitate."

He joined the Union army and rose to the rank of brevet-colonel in command of an army hospital. He had one consolation: he was convinced that he had proved the existence of an Open Polar Sea, and nothing could dissuade him from that belief. He went to his death twenty years later, never knowing or understanding that in spite of all his exhausting efforts he was wrong.

On August 9, 1861, as Isaac Hayes was heading home down the *Frobisher Bay* Greenland coast, Charles Francis Hall left Cumberland Sound with six Eskimos to trace an Elizabethan expedition that had first explored the vicinity nine generations before. Thus Hall became the first white man to travel in the Arctic with only Eskimos as his companions.

Joe could not go; he was too ill. Hannah stayed behind to look after her husband. Hall told Joe that he prayed when he returned to find him well but added that it was possible they might never meet again. He might die; Joe might die. If so, he hoped they would meet in heaven. By the end of this gloomy recital the tears were streaming down the cheeks of all three.

Hall's objective was an island, Niountelik, in Frobisher's "Countess of Warwick Sound." It was there, Joe's grandmother had told him, that relics of a white man's voyage would be found. And relics there certainly were. "Great God!" Hall cried out to himself. "Thou hast rewarded me in my search!" For scattered before him on this bald and inhospitable islet was the sea coal that Frobisher had brought from England. It had lain there, furred a little with black moss, for almost three centuries. The three women who accompanied Hall confirmed that their people had used the black stones for cooking and that the coal was there because "a great many years ago, white men with big ship came here."

At these words Hall became ecstatic. He started to laugh, to leap up and down, to dance for joy. He even performed a somersault on a pile of old coal. He had confirmed for himself the value of oral testimony among the Eskimos. Frobisher's account of his landfall had remained in doubt for nearly three hundred years. The guesses as to its exact location had been mere approximations. Now Hall had identified historic ground.

As he moved along the shore, other Eskimos told him stories of coal, brick, even iron having been found from the old days. "I felt," he said, "as if suddenly taken back into ages that were past." In the days that followed, he reached the head of Frobisher Bay to prove with the evidence of his own eyes that it was not a strait. "*'Frobisher's Strait' is a myth*," he wrote, emphasizing the point. "It only exists in the minds of the civilized world – *not in fact*."

By this time he was ill and not as "free" as he had expected, for he realized that his life was in the hands of Koojeese, the leading Innuit, who stopped when he pleased and often ignored Hall's orders to examine a cove or an island. "You stop, I go," was Koojeese's curt, almost savage response to Hall's requests. The explorer smothered his anger and submitted "to the mortification of being obliged to yield to these untamed children of the icy north." He could not blame them; after all, they were born free with no one to check or control them, able to roam as they wished. "And while they have to find subsistence as best they can, it would be almost too much to expect any subservience from them to a stranger, especially when he is alone."

More relics turned up on a neighbouring island – pieces of tile, glass, and pottery, wood chips, excavations, foundations of lime and sand, a deep trench – all confirming, in Hall's view, the Eskimo folk memory of white men who had once tried to build a ship here to escape from the Arctic and failed, an account he felt squared with Frobisher's own reports of five crewmen who vanished, never to be seen again. On a tongue of land, Hall found more coal – five tons. Again the presence of old moss convinced him that this, too, was a relic of one of the Elizabethan expeditions. There was more scattered on adjacent islands and in coves, and there was also a large piece of iron that Hall was certain was a "gold proof" made by one of the miners brought by Frobisher, who thought, wrongly, that what he had discovered was real treasure, not iron pyrites.

On the island, which the natives called Kodlunarn ("White Men's Island"), Hall filled old stockings, mittens, hats, and everything that would hold relics and carefully labelled each article, which would eventually be presented to the British government. Then, with ice forming in the sea, he headed back to his starting point, Rescue Bay on Cumberland Sound.

He reached it on September 27 to find the *George Henry* at anchor. Her captain and crew had given him up for lost. When on the following day he visited his friends, Hannah was overcome, for she, too, had believed him dead. The tears coursed down her cheeks and her hands trembled as she embraced him. For days, she told him, she had regularly climbed a nearby hill, hoping and praying to see some sign of his boat. In the midst of this tearful greeting, Hall heard a tiny cry and turned to see a baby, only twenty-four days old, wrapped in furs. This was Joe and Hannah's first child, a son, Tuker-liktu, "Little Butterfly."

The captain of the *George Henry*, Sidney Budington, had planned to leave for the south on October 20. But the sound was full of ice by the seventeenth and the pack in Davis Strait was solid. "Our fate is sealed!" Budington told Hall. "Another winter here! We are already imprisoned!" By October 25, all chance of escape was gone. The effect on the crew, Hall noted, was painful. He himself was bitterly disappointed: another year lost! Yet he wrote: "I confidently believe *it is all for the best*."

Hall spent the early winter months visiting his Eskimo friends and questioning them further about the distant past. "I am convinced," he wrote in his journal on December 13, "that were I on King William's Land . . . I could gather facts relative to Sir John Frank-lin's expedition – gather facts from the Innuits – that would astonish the civilized world!"

As the dark, depressing winter dragged on, the men cooped up aboard ship grew testy. There were quarrels, fights, small pilferings. Hall felt estranged from the whalers who were treating him as a pariah, he thought, jealous of the food he was consuming. Well, he would show them! He would go on a hunger strike and, if necessary, starve himself to death! Budington reasoned with him and brought him round. Then, in hopes of shaking his men out of their apathy, the whaling captain sent them off to live with the Eskimos. It was not a successful experiment. Unlike Hall, they couldn't stand the native way of life and came traipsing back to the ship. "They all be same as small boys," was the way Joe Ebierbing put it to Hall.

In March, Hall began to prepare for a sledge trip to Frobisher Bay. He set off on April 1 with four of the whaling crew, four natives, and nineteen dogs, disappointed that Hannah hadn't turned up to see him off. He had travelled the best part of a mile when he was astonished to see another Eskimo far behind him in the distance, struggling to catch up. At first he thought he had left one of his party behind but realized, as she came nearer, that it was Hannah herself. He turned back and met her as she made her way laboriously across the ice hummocks, so exhausted that at first she could not speak.

"I wanted to see you before you left to bid you goodbye," she gasped. Hall asked what she had done with the baby. In answer, she rolled down the hood of her parka, and there, nestled at her back, was the sleeping child.

367

For the next fifty days Hall explored and mapped the country in the neighbourhood of Frobisher Bay. On May 1 he discovered and named the Grinnell Glacier, a vast wall of crystal that stretched for one hundred miles, sprawling down from 3,500-foot peaks to the water's edge. As he gazed with admiration and awe at this mountainous ice field he accosted it grandiloquently, as if it were a living monster: "Tell us, time-aged crystal mount, have you locked in your mirror chambers any image of white men's ships, that sailed up these waters near three centuries ago?" Then he climbed the ice field to its peak, following the natural steps cut into it by a polar bear, whose great weight had impacted a fresh fall of snow into depressions of solid ice.

By this time he was living entirely on native food, which few explorers to that time had been able to stomach. "One has to make up his mind, if he would live among that people, to submit to their customs, and to be entirely one of them," he later wrote. "When a white man for the first time enters one of their tupics [tents] or igloos, he is nauseated by everything he sees and smells – even disgusted with the looks of the innocent natives, who extend to him the best hospitality their means afford." A white newcomer first peering into an Eskimo dwelling would only see "a dirty set of human beings, mixed up among masses of nasty, uneatable flesh, skins, blood and bones scattered all about. . . . He would see, hanging over a long, low flame, the *oo-koo-sin* (stone kettle) black with soot and oil of great age, and filled to its utmost capacity with black meat, swimming in a thick, dark, smoking fluid, as if made by boiling down the dirty scrapings of a butcher's stall. He would see men, women, and children – my humble self included – engaged in devouring the contents of that kettle, and he would pity the human beings who could be reduced to such necessity as to eat the horrid stuff. The dishes out of which the soup is taken would turn his stomach especially when he should see dogs wash them out with their long pliant tongues previous to our using them." For Hall such conditions had long since become the norm.

The restless adventurer returned to the ship on May 21, paused for a few days, and was soon out again. In mid-June 1862, he made another two-month journey, living almost entirely off the land. Accompanied only by natives, including the faithful Joe, he resumed his quest for Frobisher relics. By the time he returned on August 9, he had assembled 136 parcels.

368

Hall invited Joe and Hannah to return with him to the United States – an invitation Hannah accepted with alacrity, for Joe's uncle, who had had twenty wives (three living at one time), was urging him to change spouses for the sake of his health! That she would not countenance. When Hall extended his invitation, Hannah was packed and ready to leave within an hour. Hall did not plan to linger long in civilization. His intention was a second expedition, this time to King William Island, taking the Eskimos with him.

The ship left its harbour on August 9, 1862, and reached St. John's, Newfoundland, on the twenty-second. When the pilot came aboard the following morning, Hall, who was starved for news, demanded to know who had been elected president in 1860. The Newfoundlander couldn't tell him, and it was some hours before Hall learned that civil war was raging in the United States. He was so shocked he refused at first to believe it. The joy he might have felt at coming home turned to gloom. He reached New York on September 7, with his country immersed in bloody conflict. The Second Battle of Bull Run had just ended in defeat for the Union.

Unlike Hayes, he had little taste for war. In a gesture to Salmon P. Chase, a member of Lincoln's Cabinet, he wrote, "I offer my heart's blood with a cheerful devotion to my country," and when that produced no reply, he all but ignored the conflict. He desperately needed money for a new expedition. Joe, Hannah, and little Tukerliktu appeared in native dress in P.T. Barnum's museum in New York for a two-week engagement and caused a sensation, from which Hall profited. Although he denied Barnum a second engagement on the grounds that further exposure would ruin the Eskimos' health, he had no compunction about including the couple on his own lecture tour that followed that winter.

The *New York Times*, reporting the appearance of the family of Ebierbing before the American Geographical Society, marvelled that "the bitter air . . . which made the teeth of all Gotham chatter last night, was a rather sultry sort of temperament for these children of the glaciers. . . ." The paper saw the pair as noble savages. It described Joe as looking "for all the world like a South Italian in North Pole uniform" and remarked on Hannah's "mild, amiable, and even ladylike expression. . . . When she turned her small but sparkling black eyes upon her Arctic flower – the baby on her breast – the beholder began to discover a very pretty and engaging woman, on whose clear, broad brow innocence and goodness sat enthroned. . . ."

The tour had a tragic conclusion. Joe and Hannah were exhausted; the baby grew ill, and on February 28, 1863, he died. Overwhelmed by her loss, Hannah remained unconscious for days. When she awoke, she cried piteously but vainly for her lost child.

Hall was too busy trying to raise funds for his next expedition to pay much attention to his own family. He spent two weeks with his wife, Mary, and the children, then returned to New York where his reception was cool. Washington was occupied with the war and Horace Greeley of the *Tribune*, when Hall approached him for help, was bluntly unsympathetic. There ought to be a law, the great editor declared, against Americans leaving their country in time of peril. "Away with politics," Hall wrote to Sidney Budington. He intended to go north in spite of them all, "where Peace reigns and noble people live."

Unfortunately, he was broke. When his old friend Budington decided to leave him and take Joe and Hannah with him, Hall was furious, and a bitter quarrel resulted. At the same time, Hall was working on a book about his expedition with the help of that curious adventurer William Parker Snow, who had been aboard Lady Franklin's *Prince Albert* in 1850. It was inevitable that the two men – eccentric, slightly paranoid, intolerant, tactless – would quarrel also, and quarrel they did. When the book was finally finished, Snow insisted that he had written most of it – an exaggeration, since it faithfully quoted Hall's journals. Meanwhile, Hall, with Joe and Hannah, managed to get free passage to the Arctic on another whaler, *Monticello*. Before he left, Hall had to face a lawsuit from Snow demanding money he claimed was owing him for his work on the book. The court threw it out and Hall embarked on July 1, 1864, intending to spend three years in the Arctic. It would be 1869 before he finally returned.

4

Execution The work that Hall contemplated might, he wrote to Henry Grinnell, "make some men shudder to undertake." He had planned to land at Repulse Bay – Rae's old wintering spot, off the Melville Peninsula. Unfortunately, by an error of the captain of the *Monticello*, he was dropped off in the wrong place, at Depot Island in Roes Welcome Sound, many miles to the south. Hall was plagued by this sort of bad luck; the delay cost him a year. The season was so late he could not hope to reach Repulse Bay that winter.

Although five whalers were wintering a few miles away from Depot Island, he seldom visited them. Instead, he spent his time in a cheerless snow house in an Eskimo village, living on putrid caribou meat and grasping at any rumour with which the natives regaled him. The elders remembered Parry from forty years back and also Crozier, who had been with him as a junior on that voyage to the Melville Peninsula. Their stories convinced Hall that Crozier and three others were still alive. The natives had a habit of telling white men what they wanted to hear. Hall, in his turn, was prepared to believe what he wanted to believe.

In February, Hall visited the whaling fleet, congratulating himself that he still knew how to use a knife and fork. He had been 135 days without any contact with civilization. But after a few days he returned to the snow house, where slices of frozen ink had to be chopped from their parent blocks and warmed over a tiny blubber stove before he could complete his nightly journal. By mid-March, with the blubber oil running low and the lamp wick reduced to a tiny point, he was writing in despair of the dismal gloom and the total darkness. But then he rallied: "Away, away thou fiend of DESPAIR! This is no home for you. We are the children of Hope, Prayer and Work. God is our father and better times will come." Unlike Kane and others before him, he cast no thoughts toward home; as far as his journal is concerned, his family had all but ceased to exist.

His ambitions were already taking flight. Hudson Bay was not enough for him; it was, in fact, old ground for any explorer. Once he had solved the Franklin mystery (for he still thought of it as that) he was determined to tackle farther fields. "Give me the means," he wrote, "and I will not only discover the North Pole, but survey all the land I might find between Kane's farthest and it, and have my own soul in the *work*." It was a subject he returned to more than once in his journal.

Yet the actual writing of that journal – the strain of committing his thoughts to paper in the dark of the igloo – "has been enough to kill many a man, and, has nearly killed me." He was suffering from agonizing pain in his left breast, brought on by the cramped position

371

he was forced to adopt before he could scrawl on the pages. None of his other work in the North, he said, had done him a hundredth part of the injury of this incessant scribbling.

The morals of the Eskimos and their superstitions began to offend his Christian sensibilities. The *angekos* – sorcerers or medicine men – caused him many frustrating moments. He could not openly oppose them. One went so far as to persuade Joe to trade wives – an arrangement that Hannah resisted and Hall was able to prevent. But, he said, it required the patience of Job to live with the natives.

On April 13, 1865, with thirteen Eskimo families, he set out at last for his original objective, Repulse Bay. He reached it on June 10. In August a whaling ship arrived with the news that the Civil War had ended and Lincoln had been assassinated. He settled down for the winter on the site of Rae's camp. All that remained from Rae's day was a stone oven. Hall used it for a cache. With the whalers gone he faced another winter alone with the natives. He would, he decided, follow Rae's tracks to the Boothia Peninsula the following spring.

That September, Hannah bore a second child. In spite of her thin veneer of Christianity, she insisted on obeying the taboos of her people. To Hall's fury, she chose to live as the *angeko* dictated, in total seclusion, sprinkling herself with cold water and existing on the stewed caribou meat she cooked.

Hall had, in fact, developed an ambivalent relationship with the natives. They were by turns friendly and sullen – and so was he. At one point he could write of "the noble soul" of Ouela, the Repulse Bay Eskimo who was his erstwhile friend, "a man that would command respect, honor & admiration in civilized lands for his truly eminent, genuine & inherent virtues." A week later, writing of the same Ouela, he declared that "should I live many, many years & should this party show me a thousand favors, he could not wipe out the stain that has been affected by his late wrongful acts."

All his former affection for the Innuit, all his zesty excitement at the idea of living as a native seemed to have been drained from him. "How terrible is my situation here, the only white man among a savage people!" he wrote; ". . . never again will I put myself in the power of an uncivilized race. . . . It is true that at times everything goes along smoothly: *but how unstable is the base!* A whisper, a tip of the finger is enough to throw all seeming order here into an *earthly hell*."

On March 31, 1866, he was ready to set out for King William

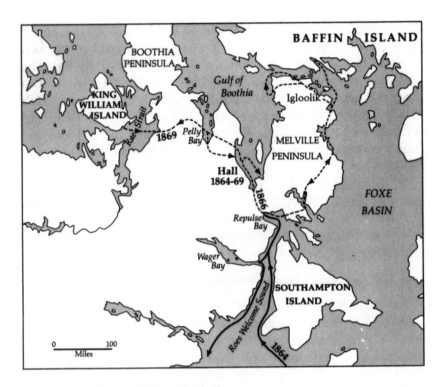

Hall's second expedition, 1864-69

Island, following Rae's tracks across the isthmus of the Melville Peninsula toward Committee Bay on the Gulf of Boothia. The party consisted of eight adult natives and six children, including Joe, Hannah, and their new baby, whom Hall had named Little King William. The start was not propitious, for they sledged into the teeth of a howling five-day blizzard. Fortunately, Hall had long since taken to wearing native fur garments exclusively, even discarding his regular undershirt and drawers. At the height of the gale, Hannah was reminded of a stiff-necked woman she'd met at the Brooklyn Fair who had declared that Eskimos ought to dress like ladies in the States. "I'd like to see her take a minute's walk over the hill," said Hannah. "She'd be glad to exchange her fine hat and hoop skirts for any of our rough dresses." The practical Hannah had long since used her own fashionable petticoat to line a snow house.

It was an ill-conceived and frustrating journey across the peninsula to Cape Weynton. The party, moving at a snail's pace, took twenty-eight days to cover the distance Rae had managed in five. When

Little King William grew ill, Hannah, to Hall's disgust, again placed herself in the care of an *angeko*. It did no good; the child grew sicker.

Now Hall encountered a group of Eskimos from Pelly Bay who had more relics of the Franklin expedition, including a spoon with Crozier's initials, a scissors, and a mahogany barometer case. They talked of ships sinking and dead white men, but they also mentioned a fierce native tribe on King William Island – a tale that so frightened Hall's people they refused to go farther and forced him to return to Repulse Bay.

In the meantime, Little King William died, and once again Hannah was bereft, clinging to the small corpse until it was taken from her to be wrapped for burial. Once again she reverted to the customs of her people, walking to the graveside with the body of her dead child dangling from a loop round her neck, refusing to dry her socks or repair her shoes, standing in the teeth of the gale, as ritual demanded, without the protection of her double jacket.

At the end of May, 1866, Hall was back where he started, at Repulse Bay. He determined to set out again the following spring, but this time he would take white men, not natives. His view of the Eskimos had continued to sink. Once he had believed them to be the freest people on earth. Now he realized that they were shackled by taboos generations old.

In August 1866, a boat from the whaler *Pioneer*, out of New London, reached his encampment, and Hall was moved to tears by the sight of the first white men he had seen in a year and a half. Other whalers brought news and letters, including one from Henry Grinnell, who enclosed a message from Lady Franklin urging that his "brave and adventurous protégé" send her all the information he was able to gather about the lost expedition, no matter how painful it might be. "It is our bounden duty," she wrote, "as it is an impetuous instinct, to rescue them if possible, even though we may feel shocked as at the sight of skeletons rising in their winding sheets from the tombs. . . ." She had offered a reward for her husband's journal, though she was certain that Hall himself was not motivated by any pecuniary interest. But if it should be found, then "nothing that reflects on the character of another should be published – nothing that would give sharp pain to any individual living." As for Hall's own expedition, she confessed ruefully that "when his first plan of going to Northumberland Inlet was brought before me in 1860, it was represented to me by all the Arctic people as the wildest and most foolhardy of

374

schemes, which must necessarily fail, and with which, for the poor man's own sake, I ought to have nothing to do." Now, she apologized for that lack of faith. "I believe Hall is now doing exactly what should have been done from the beginning, but which no government could *order* to be done." For she still entertained a hope that some of the members of the expedition might be alive. "It is painful to me that I should appear to have no heart for the rescue of others, because my own dear husband has long been beyond the reach of all rescue."

Thus encouraged, Hall hoped to recruit some white companions for his proposed expedition from the six whaling ships that were spending the winter of 1866-67 in Repulse Bay. He made a deal with the whaling captains, or thought he did, by which they would supply him with men the following spring while he, in turn, would arrange for Eskimos to hunt for them during the winter. All this time, he himself preferred to live in a snow hut though he might have had warm quarters aboard any of the ships in the harbour. He simply did not feel at ease in civilized surroundings.

For the spring journey he would need dogs. Since none were available at Repulse Bay, he set off in early February, 1867, with Ouela on a "hellish" trip (the adjective is his) to Igloolik to bargain for teams. It was a stormy journey, not only because of the weather. He quarrelled constantly with Ouela and more than once resisted the temptation to use violence on him. "I had great reason at times," he noted, "to shoot the savage down on the spot, and know not how long it may be before I shall have to do so terrible an act to save my own dear life" – a prescient remark, in the light of later events.

On Hall's return in March he discovered that the whalers had gone back on their word, or had, perhaps, misunderstood him. They could not spare a man to go with him to King William Island. He himself was too weakened by his recent journey to go alone. Once again, Charles Francis Hall faced another winter – his fourth – in the Arctic.

In the fall of 1867, however, he was at last able to persuade the whalers to allow him to contract for five men for a year. His appetite for the Franklin search was being whetted by more Eskimo tales. That same fall a group of natives from Igloolik claimed that some years before they had encountered two white men, one tall, one short, in the vicinity of their village. In January 1868, another group from Pelly Bay claimed they'd come across a stone monument on Simpson

Peninsula with a marker pointing east to Igloolik. That was enough for Hall, who promptly assumed that Crozier and another man must be alive and in the vicinity. He switched plans and in March sledged north with Hannah and Joe and one of his newly engaged seamen. At a village on the way, he met an Eskimo who told him of having seen a white man dressed in strange clothes about thirteen years earlier. Again Hall jumped to conclusions: it *must* be Crozier. It wasn't, of course. John Rae was convinced that it was he the Eskimos had seen, not in 1855, as they apparently thought, but in 1847. Later researches suggest it may have been James Clark Ross, at an even earlier date. Hall, however, was convinced that some of the missing men had headed east and were perhaps still living in the area of Fury and Hecla Strait.

He returned to Repulse Bay for the summer, without any further evidence. And there, on July 31, 1868, a tragic and inexplicable incident took place that would affect him for the rest of his life. After four years in the Arctic, he was understandably testy and temperamental. His nature was naturally suspicious and mercurial, as when he considered shooting his guide and former friend, Ouela. Now he became enraged because of what he considered unauthorized meddling by two of his contracted seamen, Peter Bayne and Patrick Coleman.

The two had taken it upon themselves to question a group of natives from Boothia Peninsula about a white man whose funeral they claimed to have witnessed some years previously. The white man, the natives said, had died aboard one of two ships buried in the ice near the village of Neitchille. The funeral was conducted with considerable ceremony, they said, and the dead man's body was covered with a substance that soon turned to stone. Both sailors were convinced that the Eskimos had watched the funeral of Sir John Franklin, whose body had apparently been encased in cement. But Hall was angered when they reported this remarkable story to him. *He* would do the interrogating – not common seamen! This breach widened when Hall caustically upbraided Coleman and another sailor for taking too long to bring in a cache of caribou meat. After his lecture "a burst of mutinous conduct" – to quote his own version – followed. The leader, Hall claimed, was Coleman. "I felt for my own safety that something must be done to meet so terrible a blow as seemed ready to fall."

The tension in the camp was indeed rising. At least four of Hall's

376

followers were in a state of near mutiny, or so he believed. Events moved quickly to a tragic climax. According to Hall, Coleman was "delivering himself of the most rebellious language possible." Trying to reason with him, Hall put a hand on his shoulder, but Coleman, a powerful, well-muscled man, squared off. Hall ordered Peter Bayne to hand him a rifle, then ran to his own tent where he replaced the rifle with a revolver. Brandishing it at the others, he demanded they end their insolent behaviour. But Coleman, in Hall's view, became even more threatening. Something in Hall snapped. Impulsively, he pulled the trigger. Coleman staggered and fell. At this Hall was nonplussed, like "a man then suddenly dreaming." He walked over to a group of frightened natives, handed the pistol to one, then turned back and helped the wounded man to his tent.

Hall's version of this incident, written months later, is the only account extant. It is transparently self-justificatory, explicable only in the wider context of the explorer's own paranoia and his four frustrating winters in the Arctic – four years in which he had accomplished virtually nothing. It is very improbable that the sailors were contemplating mutiny. The touchy explorer, goaded by their surliness, simply acted as he often did – on the spur of the moment – and was desperately sorry for what was clearly an instant of ungovernable rage.

Coleman did not die immediately. He lived on for a horrifying fortnight. Hall, remorseful and shaken, struggled vainly to save his life and prepared what became in his own mind a plausible defence. The following year he would write to Henry Grinnell, ". . . had I not taken this last 'dread alternative,' my fate would have been quite as sorrowful as that of Henry Hudson."

Hall was never brought to account for the death of Patrick Coleman, who died on August 14. No one was able to determine under whose jurisdiction that remote corner of the Arctic lay – and no one was particularly interested in finding out. The real mystery was the strange tale of the funeral and the cement tomb that Coleman's informants claimed they'd witnessed. Since those days, every corner of King William Island and the surrounding neighbourhood has been meticulously examined for Franklin relics, but no one has ever found that supposed cement coffin. The prevailing opinion – and the most plausible one – is that Franklin was buried at sea. Yet the graphic tale of a man who died aboard one of two ships caught in the ice and was buried after elaborate rites in a tomb made of a substance that turned to stone seems too complicated to be a figment of native imagination. It is one of the several mysteries of the frozen world that have plagued, befuddled, and fascinated Arctic historians.

When the whaling ships returned to Repulse Bay a few days after Patrick Coleman's death, the four remaining seamen deserted to them, leaving Hall to face a fifth winter in the North alone. He had no intention of returning to civilization until he had made the obsessive trek to King William Island.

The following March, accompanied by Ouela and the ever-faithful Joe and Hannah together with their newly adopted ten-year-old daughter and four other natives, he set off once more. Six weeks later he was on the shores of Rae Strait, directly across from his goal. Here, in an Eskimo village, he came upon another trove of relics: a silver spoon bearing Franklin's crest, a piece of a mahogany writing-desk, fragments of a handkerchief, a pickle jar, planking, and copper. The natives told him of a ship with a corpse in it, which they had plundered before it sank, and of a tent on the island's western shore, full of human bones, utensils, weapons, ammunition, and also books and paper. The latter, being of no value to them, they had left to the winds. There were other tales – of an igloo blown up by a youth who had found some gunpowder, and of other bodies, apparently cannibalized. Hall was impatient to spend the summer on the island searching for relics, but the Eskimos would have none of that. They would stay, they said, for one week only.

He did the best he could in the time available. On Todd Island off the coast of Boothia he found a human thigh bone. A day later on King William Island he found a skeleton, later identified as that of Lieutenant Le Vesconte of the *Erebus*. He learned more details from the Eskimos of the expedition's last days. Four families had encountered a tall man (Crozier?) and a party of some thirty white men dragging two sledges south. The starving men had pleaded for seal meat, and the natives had given them some. Then they packed up and fled, offering no further aid to the dying men. This story angered Hall, whose affection for the natives was sorely tried by this lack of humanity and by other tales of bodies disinterred and looted. But the Eskimos were nothing if not pragmatic. To feed such a large and hungry party was beyond their abilities and would have endangered their own existence. They themselves were subsisting on a minimum of food, and so they left the white men to their fate.

Now Hall was forced to face the truth – that there were no Franklin survivors; that many of the stories the Eskimos had told him did not square with the facts; that he himself had been too naïve and too gullible, a victim of his own wishful thinking. In his journal he no longer portrayed the natives as noble savages. Instead, he adopted the standard European recipe for their future: "*CIVILIZE, ENLIGHTEN, & CHRISTIANIZE* them & their race," he wrote, underlining the words in a bitter passage in his journal. "Then we shall have no more such sad history to hear & write."

He had spent five years in the Arctic with very little to show for his efforts. Vanquished and in despair, he set off for Repulse Bay, travelling through a country rich in game – the same realm that had once seen fivescore men die of scurvy and starvation. "O, that I could have met Crozier and his party twenty-one years ago," he exclaimed. "I am sure I could have saved the whole company. I say it with no egotistical feeling but with a confidence of what I know of the country."

Hall was remarkably resilient. By the time he reached Repulse Bay, he had regained his optimism and was ready for yet another Arctic adventure – the one that had been on his mind ever since he left New York. "How my soul longs for the time to come when I can be on my North Pole Expedition! I cannot, if I would, contained my zeal for making Arctic discoveries. . . . There is no use in man's saying, it cannot be done – that the North Pole is beyond our reach. . . ." He had no doubt that he could reach it in less time "and with far less mental anxieties" than had been involved in the journey to King William Island.

He indulged in the luxury of self-justification, persuading himself that his Arctic winters had not been a waste: it was all a preparation for his planned dash to the Pole. "I have always held the opinion that whoever would lead the way there should first have years of experience among the wild natives of the North: and this is one of my reasons for submitting to searching so long for the lost ones of Franklin's Expedition."

In the crowded pantheon of Arctic explorers, Hall is an original. There is nobody else remotely like him. A few others put up with the native way of life, but they can scarcely be said to have enjoyed it. Hall *revelled* in it. Always the loner, he preferred the squalid and cheerless snow houses to a comfortable berth aboard ship. He was the only one who genuinely delighted in native food, who wrote on his return of enjoying "a grand good feast" of the kind of meat he had been longing for – "the deer killed last fall, rotten, strong, and stinking, and for these qualities excellent for Innuit, and for the writer."

Few men could have endured five years living under the conditions that Hall suffered without wanting a change of scene. But Hall was obsessed by the Arctic. That obsession had sustained him – that and his own iron will and unbounded enthusiasm. When, on August 13, 1869, he and his faithful Innuit friends, Joe and Hannah, boarded the whaler *Ansell Gibbs* for New York, he had but one thought in mind – to return as soon as possible, to reach the environs of the Pole by the following fall, to live in a snow house until the spring of 1871, and in that year to "achieve the goal of my ambition" – the North Pole itself.

5

Death by By the time Charles Francis Hall emerged from his second Arctic
arsenic odyssey, Lady Franklin was seventy-seven years old and as active as ever. As long as she had breath left in her body, she was determined that the search for the records and relics of her husband's expedition would go on. To the indefatigable widow, and indeed to many Englishmen, they had taken on the same aura as the bones of the saints.

For more than two decades she had been preoccupied with her husband's fate. Other Victorian widows remarried, raised new families, and got on with life. Not she. Was she merely mourning for a lost love, as her Queen was mourning for her lost Albert? Perhaps; yet there is precious little evidence of the kind of ardour that, for instance, distinguished Edward Parry's correspondence with his Isabella. In fact, the Franklins' marriage was marked by long separations that do not appear to have bothered either one unduly. Was it then guilt, because she, above all, had insisted that he seize the opportunity for promotion and fame? If so, she kept it to herself. The answer surely lies in her own dominant personality. In life, her pliant husband had been an extension of herself; she controlled his destiny, as it were, from the wings. In death it was the same. Long before he vanished into the Arctic labyrinth and in the bleak but crowded years that followed, all her considerable energies had been channelled towards a single purpose: to make absolutely certain that he should be enshrined for posterity as the greatest of all Arctic explorers.

It was not in her make-up to sit still. No doubt she found, in her restless journeys round the world, some solace for a tragedy that for her had no apparent end. For all of the 1860s, while Hall trudged across the bald northern lands, seeking more clues to her husband's fate, she and her faithful niece, Sophia Cracroft, were traipsing from continent to continent, accepting the homage that the world felt was their due.

In the fall of 1860, at the invitation of Henry Grinnell, they set off for New York to cement the bonds of a friendship that had been launched by correspondence. They made a side trip to Canada, where Jane Franklin was presented to the touring Prince of Wales. A circuit of South America followed – by way of Brazil, Patagonia, and Chile. They continued on to California and British Columbia, still obsessed by gold fever. Up the turbulent Fraser the two ladies were borne in a canoe paddled by Indians – a faint reminder, perhaps, of Franklin's overland journeys four decades before.

Back in San Francisco, they embarked on the spur of the moment for Hawaii, where they were not only introduced to royalty but were also treated *as* royalty. Queen Emma was heard to remark that "with Lady Franklin I would go anywhere – even as a servant." And when the King, Kamehameha IV, gave a reception, it was noticed that those in the receiving line bowed and curtsied lower to the explorer's widow than they did to members of the royal family. The voyage took two years and also included stops at Japan, China, Singapore, Penang, and Calcutta.

The winter of 1864-65 found Lady Franklin in Spain. When Hall was still at Repulse Bay, she was crossing India in a bullock cart. She came home by way of the Isthmus of Suez, where huge cranes and dredges were at work on the half-finished canal. She remained in England long enough to see a national memorial to her husband erected at Waterloo Place; then she was off again to France, Switzerland, and Italy, where, in Sophia's phrase, the Pope "even paid her the striking compliment of advancing a few steps to meet her." She returned to England by way of Dalmatia and Germany (where a troop of bearers carried the pair up a six-thousand-foot mountain) and then, in the fall of 1867, was in Paris for the Exhibition.

The pace of travel continued. By the end of that year she was off to India again, where, among other feats, she rode in the howdah of a rajah's elephant, ten feet above the jostling crowd. After that it was

Spain, Portugal, the Canary Islands, and northwest Africa. It is exhausting to study Lady Franklin's itinerary for those years and equally exhausting to read the whirl of activity in which she involved herself on her return to England in August 1869.

There, on September 29, a paragraph in The *Times* leaped out at her: "Dr. Hall, the Arctic Explorer, arrived at New Bedford yesterday from Repulse Bay, after an absence of five years. He discovered the skeletons of several of Sir John Franklin's party at King William's Land, and he brings numerous relics of the Franklin expedition." But there was no mention of any journals or papers.

She got in touch with the Grinnells immediately, asking a series of explicit questions that she hoped would illuminate the explorer's rather vague reports of his expedition. Cornelius Grinnell replied, assuring her that Hall was "able, fearless, trustworthy and conscientious" – just the man to send north once again on an extended survey of King William Island.

But now Hall was more interested in going to the North Pole. Could Grinnell not persuade him to postpone his plans for a summer and join in "the so holy and noble cause as the rescue of those precious documents from eternal sepulture [*sic*] in oblivion?" In such a case she was sure that Hall would be prepared to forgo the command and serve under a British captain.

Hall was not prepared to serve under anyone. At best he might accept an equal position with somebody of the stature of Leopold M'Clintock, without pay – *if* he failed to get government or private aid for his expedition to the Pole. Only then would he be prepared to "do whatever I could to favor personally the noble aspirations of Lady Franklin." After that message she determined to go to the United States herself, to question Hall about his discoveries, and to try to persuade him to join her cause.

She took passage, with Sophia, in January 1870. That same month Hall wrote her a fevered letter promising to forward complete details of his discoveries and pledging that he would return to King William Island once his polar quest was completed. Optimistic as ever, he expected to achieve that goal by 1873.

He felt compelled to ask (and answer) some rhetorical questions: Why wasn't he immediately following up the search for Franklin? Was it over? Could any further information be gained? To these he said: ". . . the answer cannot be satisfactory, for I hardly know, myself, why I was led off from that almost holy mission to which I

382

have devoted about twelve years of my life, and well on to eight of these in the icy regions of the North. What burned within my soul like a living fire all the time, was the full faith that I should find some survivors . . . and that I would be the instrument in the hand of heaven, of their salvation. But when I heard the sad tale from living witnesses in the spring of 1869, how wickedly [they] . . . had been abandoned and suffered to die, my faith, till then so strong, was shaken and ultimately has extinguished. . . ."

Nonetheless, he felt there might still be records, and he would seek them – but only after his polar mission was accomplished.

He was a public figure by this time. Crowds flocked to his lectures, although, he said, "lecturing is a curse to my soul." He even found time to spend with his wife, whom he had virtually deserted during the previous decade. His son, Charles, was ten years old; Hall had been with him for hardly three months of those years. Mrs. Hall was nearly destitute but not so strapped for funds that she would accept charity. Egged on by Henry Grinnell, Lady Franklin sent her a cheque for fifteen pounds. Mrs. Hall sent it right back.

Her husband, meanwhile, was lobbying Congress for $100,000 to equip two ships to go to Jones Sound west from Baffin Bay – his choice as a jumping-off spot for the Pole. If the government didn't come through, he was prepared, he said, to have a naval ship drop him off at Ellesmere Island. From there he would proceed on foot, a lunatic scheme that would certainly have ended in disaster.

The lobbying eventually paid off – Hall even wangled an interview with President Grant – but though the House of Representatives voted the money in March, there were snags. Hall's old enemy, Isaac Hayes, came forward with his own plans, urging that he be given command of the expedition because of his scientific background. But Hayes, save for a brief foray into Baffin Bay with an artist friend, had done no exploring for a decade while Hall was fresh from his five-year stint in the Arctic. Hayes's scheme was finally rejected, but it delayed matters until July 1870. The Senate Appropriations Committee cut the grant in half, which meant that Hall would have to do with one ship. It was too late by then to mount an expedition. Once again, Charles Francis Hall had lost a year.

Later that same month, Lady Franklin arrived in Cincinnati with Sophia Cracroft "to cross examine him," as she put it. Hailed by the press as "the most distinguished woman of her time," she was closeted for several hours with "Captain Hall," as he was now called, even though he hadn't a shred of nautical experience. Presumably she tried to persuade him to cancel his polar plans in favour of her own, but if so, she failed; there is no record of their conversation.

Indeed, one is led to the conclusion that Lady Franklin was losing heart. She had certainly not pursued the Hall connection with her usual tenacity or dispatch. Since leaving London in January she had followed a leisurely course, visiting both California and Salt Lake City (where she showed a lively if disapproving curiosity about the Mormon faith) before arriving in Cincinnati in July. She was, perhaps, finally growing weary of her long quest. When Sherard Osborn, among others, had pressed her to support a British expedition to Repulse Bay, she had demurred, confessing to "a dread of future heart-rending revelations whether true or false." She met Hall once again in August 1870, at Henry Grinnell's house, where he repeated his desire to help her, but only after he had achieved the Pole.

The ship that would take Hall north again was the USS *Periwinkle*, a steam vessel of 387 tons. By the time the refitters were done with her in the winter of 1870-71, she was hardly the same craft, having been taken apart and rebuilt with thirteen extra tons of new timbers, bulkheads, spars, and rigging and given a new name – *Polaris*.

Hall would command the expedition, but Captain Sidney Budington would command the ship. Hall had made up with his old friend and mentor and even managed to hold his temper when Budington, dismayed by governmental delays, begged off and sailed north as captain of a whaler. The ice was so bad in Davis Strait that Budington returned and Hall took him on again. There was a snag, however. In the interim, Hall had offered the captaincy to another polar expert, Captain George Tyson, whom he had known since his Frobisher Bay days. Tyson had been unable to take the post because of whaling commitments, but when those fell through and Tyson suddenly became available, Hall persuaded the Navy to appoint him assistant navigator. In essence, that meant the *Polaris* had two captains.

Early in 1871, Hall was persuaded to accept Dr. Emil Bessels, a twenty-four-year-old German physician and naturalist, as his chief scientist. Hall was aware of his own deficiencies in the natural sciences, but Bessels was not his first choice. Tyson later noted "a want of mutual respect" between the two and suggested that Bessels was so discourteous that Hall would have been justified in replacing him before the ship left. Bessels was certainly described as "a sensitive man" by Joseph Henry, president of the National Academy of Scientists, who begged Hall to deal gently with him. Thus were sown the seeds of a later animosity. At the outset Hall made it clear that geographical discovery was to take precedence over scientific investigation. Bessels would be subordinate both to Hall and to Sidney Budington.

Meanwhile, the usual hordes of would-be adventurers were pleading to be part of the forthcoming expedition. These ranged from an aging seadog to a Broad Street broker. Swamped with applications, Hall had asked a reporter for the *New York Times* to outline some of the problems the tyro explorers would face, which he did with gusto, emphasizing the perils of century-old ice, the dank atmosphere aboard ship, plus "damp blankets, fetid woollens, odoriferous furs, filthy Esquimaux and myriads of unpleasant insects." He went on to describe the unbearable Arctic night and the explorers' "unhealthily fattened faces pale and dejected, worn out with long confinement, if not by the dread destroyer, scurvy." But he reserved his final warnings for what he considered the paramount horror. "Outside," he wrote, "he will be met by the repulsive features of the Esquimaux, their still more disgusting modes of life and the never ending line of ice and snow. . . ." What Hannah and Joe thought of this diatribe is not known.

Hall's first mate would be Hubbard Chester, whom he had known as mate of the whaling ship *Monticello*. His second mate would be Kane's former steward and trusted friend William Morton, the man who had been first to spy what he thought was an Open Polar Sea. The engineer was a German, Emil Schumann, and the crew included seven Germans. Two of the three-man scientific party were also Germans, which meant that there were as many Germans aboard as there were native-born Americans, a division that hinted at future trouble. In addition to all these, Joe and Hannah would come along, with their adopted daughter, Punny. Hall also expected to pick up Hans Hendrik, Kane's and Hayes's Eskimo companion, when he reached Greenland.

"I have chosen my own men," Hall told the American Geographical Society, "men who will stand by me through thick and thin. Though we may be surrounded by innumerable icebergs, and though our vessel may be crushed like an eggshell, I believe they will stand by me to the last."

In the light of the dismaying events that followed, Hall's view seems naïve in the extreme, though quite in keeping with his own optimism. As in his interrogation of the Repulse Bay Innuit, he believed what he wanted to believe. He had, as Rear Admiral C.H. Davis wrote, "either a lack of discrimination or a wonderful power of ignoring disagreeable facts when their recognition threatened to interfere with the progress of the expedition." Yet that could be written of almost all those cheerful optimists who plunged boldly into the Unknown, certain that they would capture their particular Grail after the briefest of trials. Admiral Davis, who edited Hall's journal for the U.S. Navy, also had a propensity for ignoring disagreeable facts (as so many other literary explorers did). He made a tension-filled voyage sound like a holiday romp. But he was right in his assessment of Hall's obsession to get to the Arctic without delay. "Every feeling and sentiment," he wrote, "seemed to be swallowed up in the absorbing desire to get north." That was Hall's downfall.

Davis likened Hall to an Arthurian knight, a not uncommon simile when describing Arctic explorers. He noted his dreamy expression and his romantic outlook, which was "not always a practical one." He speculated that a "skilled physiognomist would have descried too much of the poetic temperament in our Polar knight errant to have much faith in him as a successful discriminator or commander of men."

But, again, there was something of the romantic in even the most phlegmatic of Arctic knights. Some kept their feelings under a tighter rein than Hall or Kane, but it was scarcely possible to cross those green and dappled seas – the great bergs flashing in the sunlight, the brooding headlands looming from the mist – without feeling a catch in the throat and a tremor in the breast. To gaze on unknown ramparts, to enter mysterious channels, to touch bleak shorelines that no white man had trod before – this was the magic that had bewitched generation after generation of eager amateurs whose only credential was an obsessive desire to go a little farther than their predecessors.

Tyson, too, was a romantic. As a youth, he had worked in a New York iron foundry, but his heart belonged to the sea; he had been gripped by a desire to see something of the frozen world, for his imagination had been fed by accounts of the exploits of Parry, Ross, and Franklin. He longed to follow in their track, "to witness novel scenes, and to share in the dangers of Arctic travel." He was disgusted with shop labour, but at that time there were no northern expeditions he could join. The best thing to do was to sign on aboard a whaler. At the age of twenty-one, George Tyson did just that. By the time he joined the Hall expedition he'd had twenty years of experience in the Arctic seas.

For him it was a strange feeling to leave the navy yard on June 29, 1871, heading north once more. Since he was not, for once, in command of a ship, he had none of the usual responsibilities and so, for the first time, had the leisure to look about and contemplate the past and the future. His friends had told him he was off on a wild-goose chase. Would it prove to be one? Within a week he was noting a lack of harmony between the men whom Hall had declared would stand by him through thick and thin. The two Germans, Dr. Bessels and his scientific assistant, Frederick Meyer, were already refusing to obey Hall's orders. As for Captain Budington, he had been caught raiding the food supplies, had been given a dressing-down by Hall, and was already talking about quitting.

By the time the *Polaris* reached Disco Island off the Greenland coast, there were three warring factions aboard: Budington was at odds with both Hall and Tyson while the insubordinate Germans had closed ranks. Hall was forced to appeal to Captain Davenport, commander of the supply ship uss *Congress*, for help. Davenport threatened to put the German scientist Meyer in irons and send him home on the *Congress* for insolence. At that all the Germans threatened to quit on the spot. That would mean the end of the expedition.

"Was there ever a commander so beset by embarrassments. . . ?" Tyson wondered. Both Bessels and Meyer felt themselves superior to the half-educated Hall, while Budington felt he knew more about Arctic conditions and certainly more about navigation than his leader.

Davenport made it clear that everyone on the expedition was under naval discipline and that Hall was in charge. Before the ship left Disco he gathered the crew together and lectured them on the need to obey orders. After Davenport's tough speech, the Reverend Doctor Newman, who had been brought along on the supply ship to confer the Deity's blessing on the expedition, added a few words of his own to the usual benediction, urging that charity, pure emotions, noble thoughts, and generous sympathies reign during the long Arctic night. Meanwhile, Tyson discovered that Captain Budington was secretly raiding the liquor cabinet.

Hall ignored all this, avoiding any allusion to the troubles aboard.

In Tyson's opinion, he was able to "sink everything else in the one idea of pushing on to the far north." He dreaded any suggestion of delay, and the idea that he might be forced to return filled him with dismay. Yet he also seemed to have a premonition of coming disaster, for he suddenly left all the papers connected with his second expedition in the care of an official at Godhavn – an extraordinary step, as Tyson noted, because he had intended to while away the long Arctic night preparing them for publication on his return.

When the *Polaris* reached Upernavik, Hall sent Chester, the first mate, to find Hans Hendrik, who was fifty miles to the north. Chester returned with not only Hans but also his wife, Merkut, their three children, and a horde of puppies that Hans insisted on bringing with him. His boat was jammed with bags, boxes, skins, tents, cooking utensils, tools, and weapons, all of which would have to be accommodated. The grey-bearded William Morton, who remembered Hans from the Kane expedition almost twenty years before, strode forward to greet him. He had aged so greatly that Hans did not recognize him. But Morton pointed to the scars on the Eskimo's right hand and recalled the explosion on the shores of Smith Sound that had caused them. Then Hans remembered.

At this point Hall abandoned his plans to sail westward through Jones Sound. The news that the waters to the north were free of ice persuaded him to follow in Kane's wake through Smith Sound. They sailed out of Tesiussuq, the last of the Eskimo settlements, on August 24. "The *Polaris* bids adieu to the civilized world," Hall wrote in a dispatch that the governor of Greenland promised to deliver to the U.S. Embassy in Copenhagen. Three days later, having entered Smith Sound, and with a growing sense of excitement, they passed Kane's winter quarters. As Noah Hayes, an enthusiastic young seaman (no relation to Isaac), wrote, ". . . all are infatuated with the Open Polar Sea."

Now Budington began to display the want of confidence that widened the breach between him and both Hall and Tyson. He wanted to take the ship into winter quarters near Etah and let the expedition continue toward the Pole by sledge. To Tyson's relief, Hall refused. Budington, according to later testimony, was now behind Hall's back ridiculing him as a novice to members of the crew, a breach of both naval ethics and naval discipline. It was becoming clearer each day that he had little interest in reaching the Pole and that, in the words of Hubbard Chester, he thought the enterprise was all "damn nonsense."

On August 28, Chester reported impassable ice ahead. Budington, "in a fearful state of excitement at the thought of going forward," slowed the ship. Tyson spotted a dark streak of open water to the west, and Hall ordered the *Polaris* to proceed, skirting the pack. Tyson could not help sneering at Budington's timidity. "Out on such cowards, I say!" he wrote in his journal.

The *Polaris* was steaming through unknown waters, having gone farther north than any other known ship. Hall was lucky. Unlike Kane and Hayes, who had been stopped by the ice farther south, he had the weather on his side. The *Polaris* crossed Kane Basin and entered Kennedy Channel. But where was the Open Polar Sea that both Morton and Hayes had insisted they had seen years before? There was no sign of it. Instead, the ship entered another narrower basin. This was the water that Morton had spotted. Now they could see that the so-called open sea was landlocked. It would eventually be named for Hall himself.

Leading north beyond the basin was another channel, about eighteen miles wide and heavily obstructed by ice. Hall named it Robeson Channel after the U.S. Secretary of the Navy. The crew grew nervous; who knew what lay ahead? Like mariners of old venturing to the very lip of the known world, they were haunted by nameless terrors. "I believe," Tyson declared, "some of them think we are going over the edge of the world." The channel actually led to the Lincoln Sea, permanently frozen, but they were not to encounter that desert of rumpled ice. When they reached a latitude of 82°11'N, the pressure of the current pushed the ship back down the channel and into Hall Basin, where it was moored to a floe.

Hall convened a council of officers. Chester and Tyson were all for going forward. Budington was opposed and signalled his feelings by walking out of the cabin. Tyson, who rarely had a good word for anybody on the expedition, mocked "these puerile fears," which, he said, reminded him of Sir Edward Belcher during the Franklin search. He urged Hall to return north to add another two or three degrees to his record, but Hall, in Tyson's view, appeared afraid of offending Budington. In truth, there was little point in continuing. Winter was setting in; it would be foolhardy to risk lives for the sake of a few miles of geography.

Instead, Hall took the *Polaris* west to the northern tip of what he called Grant Land (now Ellesmere Island) and almost wrecked the ship in the process. Trapped in the pack and driven south, he finally found a small harbour on the Greenland shore. Here, on the most northerly patch of land on which any civilized flag had been planted, Hall raised the Stars and Stripes and named their refuge Thank God Harbor in honour of a deity who had thus far smiled on his expedition. On September 10, 1871, the expedition settled down for the winter.

Hall was determined to reach the Pole by sledge. He took Hubbard Chester, Joe Ebierbing, and Hans Hendrik. But he did not take Tyson, who later claimed that Hall, pointing to Budington, declared, "I cannot trust that man and I want you to go with me but don't know how to leave him on the ship." The quartet left on October 10 and returned two weeks later, having plotted a spring route to the Pole.

"Father Hall," as Hannah and Joe called him, looked fit enough on his return, although Chester later said he wasn't quite himself and some of the crew thought he seemed tired. Nonetheless, he insisted he'd had a good trip and declared, "I can go to the pole, I think, on this shore." He entered the ship – now being banked with snow like a gigantic igloo – and felt the interior heat at once, an eighty-degree contrast to the outdoor chill. He asked for a cup of coffee, a pot of which was brewed especially for him, and on drinking it almost immediately complained of nausea and vomited. No one took that too seriously. He had been subject to bilious attacks before, and some others had also drunk the same coffee without ill effects. Dr. Bessels advised against giving him an emetic. But in the morning Hall's condition was worse; in a few days he was delirious.

For the next week he was out of his head, apparently suffering from paranoia. He said there was poison in the coffee – that it had burned his stomach. He accused almost everybody of trying to murder him. He thought he saw blue smoke – poisonous vapours – emerging from Bessels's mouth. He refused to take any nourishment or medicine because he thought it might contain poison. He was especially suspicious of the doctor, "the little German dancing master," as he called him.

After a week he began to improve. His talk sounded rational. He was careful about his food, however. He insisted that it be prepared by the faithful Hannah and on occasion directed one of the seamen,

390

Joseph Mauch, who was acting as his secretary, to taste both food and drink before he would touch anything. On November 6, he was well enough to go out on deck. "I am as well as I ever was," he declared. Then, suddenly, he suffered a relapse.

Shortly after midnight, Chester aroused Budington to announce, "Captain Hall is dying." Budington found the explorer sitting on the edge of his bunk, feet dangling, eyes glassy and shifting furtively, "looking like a corpse – frightful to look at." He was trying to spell the word "murder." He died in the early morning of November 8, and was buried on the shore before a gloomy ship's company and a weeping Hannah.

The Arctic holds many mysteries, but the death of Charles Francis Hall is one of the most tantalizing. Was he murdered, and if so, by whom and for what reason? Certainly he suspected the worst; but then, Hall tended to be paranoiac at the best of times, and who can take seriously the suspicions of a man in a delirium? The board of inquiry set up by the Secretary of the Navy concluded that Hall died of apoplexy – a stroke. That accorded with the testimony of Dr. Bessels and also with many of Hall's symptoms – brief paralysis, slurred speech, erratic pulse, temporary coma – but not entirely with the high fever that Bessels had managed to control with quinine injections.

But was it only quinine that Bessels injected? In 1968, Chauncey Loomis, who was preparing a biography of Hall and who had read every available document about the expeditions, decided on some original research. He would get permission to exhume the body, go to Hall's grave on the shores of Thank God Harbor, and have an autopsy performed.

Loomis's party arrived in August. The dry Arctic cold had kept the corpse in a remarkable state of preservation. The hair, beard, and skin were all more or less intact and so, fortunately, were the finger-nails. Dr. Franklin Paddock, the medical man with the Loomis party, sent several slivers back to the Centre for Forensic Medicine in Toronto. After a careful examination, the centre issued a startling report: Hall in the last two weeks of his life had received toxic quantities of arsenic. He may have had a stroke, but it was not that that killed him. He had been poisoned.

Indeed, Hall's symptoms in those last two weeks were remarkably similar to those typical of arsenic poisoning. Arsenic can have a sweet taste: Hall had complained to Hannah of the sweet taste of the coffee. It also causes burning pains in the stomach – again, the very thing of which Hall had complained. Arsenic causes vomiting and dehydration, bringing on intense thirst: Hall had continually asked for water. It causes feeble pulse, vertigo, and in some cases stupor, even mania. Hall had suffered from all of these.

Three men were heard to express some relief after Hall's death. Several of the crew were to testify later that Budington had declared, "There's a stone off my heart." Budington denied that but didn't deny telling one seaman, Henry Hobby, "We are all right now . . . you shan't be starved to death now, I can tell you" – presumably meaning that all attempts to reach the Pole were over. Frederick Meyer of the scientific staff, who had complained that Hall was friendlier with the men than with the officers, was heard to suggest that the expedition would be better off with the officers back in charge. And Dr. Emil Bessels, according to Noah Hayes, declared that Hall's death was the best thing that could have happened to the expedition – and even laughed when he said it.

These three men were the ones who had in one way or another opposed Hall from the outset; all the evidence before the naval inquiry made it clear that he was liked and admired by the rest of the ship's company. But was any of this discordant trio capable of murder? Did any have the opportunity or the motive? The answer here seems to be no. Of the three, only Dr. Bessels was in constant attendance on Hall. The others who spent time with him – Joe, Hannah, Chester, and Morton – were his loyal friends. As Loomis has pointed out, it would have been possible for Bessels to administer arsenic, either in the quinine injections he gave Hall to keep his fever down or orally with some of the medicine. And certainly, when Hall refused all food and drink he did improve.

Yet it is equally possible that Hall in his delirium overdosed himself, either from his own considerable medical kit or from the doctor's. Arsenic was easily available. If Bessels did kill him – and Loomis rightly places him as the prime suspect – why did he do it? He had nothing to gain by Hall's death. In fact, unlike Budington, he was one of those who wanted to keep moving north. The naval inquiry cleared him. He was arrogant, certainly, and he was difficult to deal with. He considered himself a superior being and he looked down on Hall. But again, as Loomis has written, these are not rational motives for murder.

The operative word here is "rational." The history of Arctic exploration is riddled with irrational decisions and events. Hall's summary execution of Patrick Coleman was merely one in a long series of incidents that went back to the day when a nervous and irrational crew had cast Henry Hudson adrift. Quarrels, fancied slights, broken friendships, acts of mutiny or near mutiny, bitter dissension – these were the concomitants of life aboard a winterized vessel. The greatest hardship of all may not have been scurvy or starvation, cold or boredom, but the suppressed tensions gnawing away at men living too close together in cramped quarters in the gloom and solitude of the long Arctic night. The British managed to conceal much of this from the world. The Americans were more open, but even they tended to edit their journals for publication, as Kane had done, perhaps because on their return to civilization the bitterness and paranoia that marked those nightmare months vanished into the background. Noah Hayes, the least spiteful of all the *Polaris* crew, on rereading his journal after the voyage, regretted the hatred and selfish recrimination that had marked certain passages. "I am utterly disgusted with writing and with what I have written," he declared when he returned to the United States. He added, ". . . I believe that no man can retain the use of his faculties through one long night to such a degree as to be morally responsible . . . for all that he may say and do. . . ."

Every Arctic voyage was unique and each one had its secrets that can never be known. Hall's was no exception. The naval inquiry raised the curtain briefly, giving the audience a quick glimpse at the strengths and failings of the flawed heroes who attempted the impossible. Then the curtain dropped. Was Hall murdered? If so, why and by whom? No one will ever know. Perhaps the only sensible answer, as Chauncey Loomis suggested, is that his own obsession with the Arctic finally did him in.

6

After Hall's death, discipline on the *Polaris* fell apart. As Joe, Hall's faithful Eskimo companion, described it some years later, everybody was in charge, nobody was in charge: "No cap'n; nobody cap'n. Cap'n Budington, he cap'n. Captain Tyson, he cap'n. Doctor, he cap'n too. Mr. Chester, cap'n. Mr. Meyer, cap'n; me cap'n; everybody cap'n – no good."

George Tyson's remarkable drift

Nominally, Sidney Budington was in charge, but he exerted only minimal control. Unlike the officers of the British Navy, he didn't invent jobs to keep his men out of mischief, nor was there any attempt at regular periods of exercise or other forms of recreation. He put a stop to Hall's practice of daily religious services; once a week would be enough, he felt. Budington was now drinking regularly, raiding the scientific stores for the high-proof alcohol used to preserve specimens. Bessels, on one occasion, concealed himself and caught the captain in the act. A brief, inconclusive struggle followed.

The two despised each other. To Budington, Bessels was an arrogant elitist and a polar amateur. To Bessels, Budington was a half-educated bumpkin. The hypercritical Tyson disdained them both. As the winter dragged on and tensions grew, few of the officers were free of paranoia.

At the end of November, in a raging gale, the ship was almost crushed by the ice, which pushed up under her keel and raised her stern six feet. At this Hannah and Joe, still heartbroken over Hall's death, left the *Polaris* temporarily and built a snow house on the shore. Hans and Merkut followed with their children.

Budington had no interest in going farther north in the spring. All he wanted to do was to get home safely. "Whoever wants to go North, let them go, but I won't," he said. Tyson and Chester made an abortive attempt in June; one of their whaleboats was crushed in the ice, another abandoned. On August 12, 1872, the *Polaris* finally broke free of the ice, and that same morning Hans's wife, Merkut, gave birth to a baby boy. The incident – seen as a good omen – came as a complete surprise; her loose clothing had concealed her condition during the winter. The crew named the infant Charles Polaris.

Three days later, Budington, who had been drinking heavily, ran the ship into the pack; once again she was beset. For the next two months she drifted slowly south, tied to a floe. On October 12, with a strong wind from the north pushing them forward, they passed Kane's Rensselaer Harbor, but with the blizzard increasing and the sun failing, they had no real idea where the ship was heading. The pumps were operating day and night, gobbling fuel at a dismaying rate. As long as the ice held, cradling the vessel, she was in no danger. But if it should crumble in the narrow channel leading out of Kane Basin, the *Polaris*, drifting free, could be smashed against the nearest berg.

That night Tyson had a prophetic dream in which the ship was

394

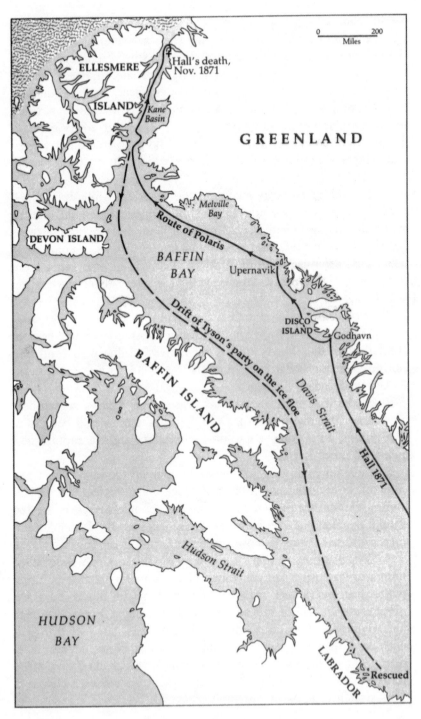

0   200
Miles

Hall's death,
Nov. 1871

ELLESMERE

ISLAND

Kane Basin

GREENLAND

Melville Bay

Route of Polaris

DEVON ISLAND

BAFFIN
BAY

Upernavik

Drift of Tyson's party on the ice floe

DISCO
ISLAND

Godhavn

BAFFIN
ISLAND

Davis Strait

Hall 1871

Hudson Strait

HUDSON

BAY

LABRADOR

Rescued

Hall sails north to his death, 1871; Tyson drifts south on an ice floe, 1872–73 hurled against a precipice. The following day, his nightmare was realized when the ice broke away and she was threatened by a huge berg. Cracking and groaning under the pressure of millions of tons of surrounding ice, trembling violently, alternately hoisted up and then dropped, she seemed doomed. The engineer, Emil Schumann, came rushing down the port alley screaming that the hull was staved in aft and the pumps couldn't keep up. According to Tyson's account, Budington was in a blue funk: "the poor trembling wretch stood there apparently oblivious to everything but his own coward thoughts."

Tyson said he would never forget the scenes that followed "while the heart beats or the brain throbs." Budington, in a panic, ordered everything thrown overboard. Barrels of flour and rice, tins of pemmican, boxes of preserved meats, and some five tons of coal, all of which had been gathered on deck for just such an emergency, were flung onto the ice below. Much of this was swept under the heaving vessel and lost.

Tyson and two or three others dropped onto the ice to save what they could. More followed in the raging storm. With the help of Hannah and Joe, Tyson loaded the natives' sledge with food and clothing and pushed it back onto the main floe to prevent it being sucked underneath the ship.

By eleven that night, the pressure ceased, and Tyson discovered to his disgust that the vessel wasn't in as bad shape as he'd been told. The pumps were doing their job. Schumann and the captain had panicked unnecessarily.

The men on deck were still flinging goods off the ship. Tyson, the only officer on the ice, felt it begin to crack under his feet. He warned Budington that the two whaleboats and the human beings on the floe should be taken back on board as quickly as possible. Instead, Budington ordered Tyson to move the boats farther from the ship.

As Tyson turned to obey, the floe to which the ship was tethered burst into fragments and the vessel parted from her fastenings. Some of the men on the ice vainly rushed to climb on board. In a few minutes the *Polaris* drifted off and was lost to sight, leaving nineteen men, women, and children alone on the ice.

Tyson with a few men was standing on one of the broken fragments. The others were trapped on a smaller piece. As Tyson made haste to haul up one of the boats to save them, he noticed a bundle of skins stretched across a widening crack. He retrieved it and found

396

Hans's four young children wrapped up inside. In another instant they would have been lost.

He managed to get everybody back onto the main floe, away from the crumbling edges. But he salvaged only a few sledge-loads of the goods that the indefatigable Hannah had helped haul well back onto the ice. The men had saved their guns, pistols, clothes bags, and ammunition. Tyson had only the clothes he stood in, a three-year-old pair of tattered sealskin breeches, an undershirt, overshirt, cotton jumper, and Russian cap. So, while the others slept, covered by a deepening blanket of snow, he walked the floe all night, watching the ice. As morning came the gale blew itself out; the snowfall diminished; a full moon revealed the snow-capped mountains and vast glaciers of Greenland in the distance. With the dawn, Tyson could look about and see that the floe on which they were huddled was enormous – a mile across and at least five miles in circumference. It was, as it turned out, to be their home for the next five months.

All next day they kept a sharp lookout for the *Polaris*. At last the ship appeared around a point of land eight or ten miles away. Tyson raised a mast with a piece of cloth fluttering from it but received no answering signal. The floe was already starting to drift south. Tyson climbed on a frozen hummock and saw to his dismay that the *Polaris* had anchored off an island in the sound. Surely, he reasoned, "this black mass of humans could have been seen at twice the distance." They had been abandoned! He blamed Budington, all of whose "villainous acts" flashed across his mind. But there was no sinister intent expressed in the explanations that the crew of the *Polaris* gave the naval inquiry months later. In truth, they had searched that vast expanse of ice for their missing comrades and found nothing.

Tyson's immediate plan was to take the two boats and try to reach land. But the men were exhausted and dejected. They made a half-hearted attempt to drag one boat across the floe, but when a gale burst upon them like a thunderbolt, filling the air with flying snow, they gave up. Tyson felt his command slipping away as several of the crew refused to haul the boat back to a secure spot. They slept, that night, exhausted, some crowded into the little canvas tent, the others under the second, upturned, boat. But their long ordeal had only begun.

It was mid-October, 1872. Now this ill-assorted group – nine white men, a black cook, four adult Eskimos, and five children – would make a voyage that has no parallel in polar history, drifting south for two thousand miles on windswept ice floes until the following April. Tyson was only nominally in command. He had no weapons. The crewmen, seven of whom were Germans, were armed with pistols. Tyson, in fact, had more in common with the Eskimos who built the snow hut in which he was sheltered. It was as well, perhaps, that he wasn't armed. There were times when he would almost certainly have murdered one of the men who opposed him.

His impotence was established at the outset. In the morning, a corner of the floe broke off, bearing away one of the boats and six precious bags of bread. Tyson pleaded with the men to launch the remaining boat and help retrieve the floe with its vital burden. Stupefied with exhaustion and horror, they refused.

Tyson realized that the fate of the party depended entirely on the natives, the only members of the group trained to hunt, especially for seals. To the irritation of both Joe and Hans, the sailors insisted on peppering away at the seals, hitting nothing but frightening them off. Tyson reckoned he had 1,900 pounds of food on the floe, since 500 pounds had been lost with the boat. He tried to ration it equally, but as soon as he turned to hand a portion to one man, another had his hand in the bread bag, stealing more than his share.

In her snow house, the loyal and dependable Hannah somehow managed to cook two hot meals a day for the entire party, using an Eskimo lamp and cooking pots made from discarded pemmican tins. Then, on October 23, as if by a miracle, the floe containing the lost boat and food drifted past and was rescued, together with a canvas hut and several half-starved dogs that had also drifted away. Within a few weeks the two Eskimo families had eaten all the animals.

But Tyson faced another problem. He could not convince the men that the ice had carried them to the west or Canadian side of Baffin Bay. Frederick Meyer, the German scientist, had persuaded them that they were on the east or Greenland side and would soon be within an easy haul of Disco Island. As a result they rejected Tyson's tight plan of conservation – to make a set of scales and ration everyone to an intake of eleven ounces a day.

Suspicious that Tyson might steal their food or give too much to his native companions, they appointed J.W.C. Kruger, the worst of the malcontents, as cook. In spite of the obvious need to conserve every ounce of supplies, they went on a wild orgy one night in early November, thawing and eating can after can of meat, most of which they vomited onto the snow. Tyson turned away in disgust. He and the two native families could easily have escaped by boat to land and thence, presumably, to the ship, but Tyson had refused to leave the others behind. And this, he thought bitterly, was the way they repaid him!

Without the Eskimos they were lost. The natives built them a new snow hut and every day were out on the ice seeking the seal, which supplied not only antiscorbutic sustenance but also blubber for the heating lamps. Yet the men whose lives they were sustaining begrudged them a share of their rations. Joe and Hans, the only hunters, felt they should have a larger share of the meat they shot, especially as they were exerting themselves, using up far more energy than anyone else. But as soon as they brought in a seal, the white men seized it, and there was nothing that Tyson could do.

He preferred to live with Joe and Hannah, both of whom, as well as the eldest child, Punny, spoke English. It was possible to converse with them, to communicate his plans intelligibly, and to listen to their ideas. The Germans, who lived separately, refused to speak anything but their own language, which Tyson did not understand.

The worst aspect of these long dark days was not hunger or cold; it was the sheer boredom that almost drove Tyson mad. There was nothing to do, nothing to read, and scarcely anybody to talk to. He could no longer write daily notes in his journal – it would take too much paper. Somebody had stolen the notes he had laid aside for future use. "Some of these men seize hold of anything they can lay hands on and secrete it. But no wonder; they were taught that on board the *Polaris*; they saw so much of pilfering going on there. It would have demoralized worse men than these."

On New Year's Day, 1873, he committed a wan note to his journal: "We cannot join in the glad shout at the birth of another year. I have dined today on about two feet of frozen seal's entrails and a small piece of congealed blubber. . . ."

He was the only man on the ice who had no change of clothes. The Eskimos were well off in their fur garments, the crew less so in their civilized attire. But at least they could change out of a wet and frozen suit, since many had three sets of shirts, drawers, and pants, and several had two coats. Tyson couldn't. The bag in which he had saved a few scraps of clothing had been stolen. He was condemned to wear the same clothes, wet or dry, day and night, month after month, while he waited for rescue.

Meanwhile, he had obtained a weapon. Joe let him have his pistol because, he said, he didn't like the look in the eyes of some of the men. He was terrified that in their hunger they might kill and eat the natives, especially the children. As Tyson remarked, it would be killing the goose that laid the golden egg, but he did not dismiss the possibility. The men, especially the Germans, were organized and determined to be in control. They swaggered about with their pistols and rifles, and Tyson knew he must be wary as well as firm. A quarrel would be fatal.

The crewmen's attitude to the Innuit was short-sighted. "They think the natives a burden . . . and they would gladly rid themselves of them. They think there would be fewer to consume the provisions, and if they moved closer to the shore there would not be children to lug. . . ." But without the two Eskimo hunters, Joe, and to a lesser extent Hans, there would have been precious little food and no fresh meat. Years later, Ebierbing was asked why he hadn't packed up his family and left on his own. He replied that he had promised Hall that he would hunt for the party. "Cap'n Hall good man; *good* man. If Cap'n Hall alive, *he* not run away. I not run away neither." For if he ran away, he knew the party could not survive. Joe brought in nine-tenths of the game that was shot; Hans Hendrik brought in the rest.

Since they confidently believed they would reach Disco early in February, the "poor deluded wretches," as Tyson called them, gave little thought to an extended stay on the floe. Their stock of prepared food was fast disappearing, since several crewmen were pilfering bread. Not deigning to adopt the native seal-blubber lamp, they broke up a sledge and one of the boats for fuel, thus lessening their chances of escape. Meanwhile, in Tyson's description, "some are continually crying out that they cannot exist on their present allowance."

In his journal on January 9, Tyson uttered a stifled lament: "I have nobody to cooperate with me. I am entirely alone." And so he was. Among that polyglot company, a black cook, an English steward, and seven recalcitrant Germans, his only trustworthy companions were the two native families.

Day after day, sometimes with the thermometer at fifty below, Joe went out to hunt, remaining for hours in the darkness and sometimes in a driving blizzard, waiting beside a hole in the ice for the appearance of a seal. Failure did not discourage him, nor the long hours of waiting. Nine times out of ten he returned empty-handed, but the following day he would set off again. On January 15 when he re-

400

turned with a seal, Tyson told the men to take it into Joe's snow hut, to skin and divide. But, led by Kruger, they seized the carcass and carried it off. At that moment, Tyson realized, if he'd had Joe's pistol in his hand, he would have murdered Kruger on the spot.

A few days later Kruger invaded Tyson's quarters to abuse him, and the two almost came to blows. Now some of the crew began to suspect Kruger of pilfering, and a new man, Frederick Jamka, was chosen as their cook. In the bitter January cold, the thinly clad Tyson could not venture outside. "The monotony," he wrote, "is fearfully wearisome." But he was trapped. He could not break it with either exercise or hunting.

"The German count," as the men were beginning to call Meyer, was still insisting that they were close to the eastern shore and an easy jump to Disco. Tyson, who was more familiar with that coastline, knew better. The rocky promontory could be spotted easily from a distance of eighty miles. But there was no sign of the village on the horizon.

If he could keep the Germans quiet until the temperature rose, he told himself, they might yet be saved. "But should they break camp in Feb, they are lost. No water to drink. Frozen skins to sleep upon. The party must perish."

"Oh, it is depressing in the extreme to sit crouched up all day with nothing to do but keep from freezing," Tyson wrote. There was no proper place to sit and absolutely nothing to read in the soft Arctic twilight. "It is now one hundred and seven days since I have seen printed words!"

Another problem faced them: Hans's six-year-old son, Tobias, took sick and couldn't eat his allowance of pemmican. There was nothing else for him but dry bread. "We are I fear all but surely starving, though slowly," Tyson noted on February 4. Hans's four-year-old, Succi, uttered "a chronic hunger wail." Tyson was terrified that the men, egged on by Meyer, who continued to believe the Disco shore was close by, would gobble all the provisions before the weather made sealing possible. At last it became clear that Disco had been passed – a realization that angered the men who had depended on the scientist.

Tyson continued to be a prisoner of the weather. He had now lived for four months in his original clothes, all stained and rendered filthy by greasy blubber. He had no handkerchief, could not even wash his hands. When he tried to clean a piece of deerskin in the hope of making a pair of socks, a horrified Hannah stopped him. She explained that her people had a tradition that if anyone tried to clean a deer on the ice, the ice would crumble. She herself was terrified the floe might split beneath them at any time; a number of cracks were already appearing in the old ice.

Hannah and Joe amused themselves by playing checkers, using buttons on a piece of ragged canvas that had been laid out with a pencil. Little Punny, wrapped in a muskox skin, cried out to her mother every few minutes, "I am *so* hungry!" In Hans's snow hut, Merkut tried to pick a few scraps of old blubber from the lamp to give to the wailing children. Augustina, her twelve-year-old, once naturally plump, looked peaked. The babies had no clothing of any kind, living in their mothers' hoods like kangaroos in pouches. Tyson, who must have felt almost as naked as the infants, was confined to a three-foot-square space of snow. His only surcease from the appalling boredom was his journal, in which he scrawled brief imprecations about "the treachery played by the villain Budington." It was as well that he had no mirror. One day Punny looked at him gravely and said, "You are nothing but bone."

He contemplated suicide but could not face what "God had forbid." By March, the group was down to one meal a day, subsisting entirely on the tiny dovekies the Eskimos were shooting. By the second, Hannah had blubber for the lamp for only two more days, Hans only enough for one. And then, at five in the afternoon, to the unspeakable joy of all, Joe shot a gigantic seal, the largest anyone had ever seen. It weighed more than six hundred pounds and required the strength of all hands to drag it to the hut. The men danced and sang for joy. "Praise the Lord," exclaimed Tyson, "for all his mercies." An orgy of gluttony followed, the men scooping up the warm blood in tin cans and drinking it like milk, others tearing at the raw flesh until their faces and hands were slathered with it. Several were sick, and the hut itself looked like a slaughterhouse, with meat, blood, entrails, and dirt covering the floor.

Now another peril faced the party. The ice beneath them was beginning to snap with the sound of distant thunder. On March 11, in the midst of a howling gale, a piece of the floe was torn away, no more than twenty yards from the Eskimo igloos. Three days of horror followed, then calm. These periods of relative quiet were interspersed by nights of crashing, grinding uproar, as great bergs pushed their way south with the current through a tangle of shattered floes.

Fortunately there were more seals available and, on March 28, a polar bear.

Two days later Tyson looked out from the filthy snow house and saw a gigantic berg towering above the floe that had been their home for five months. It was now no more than twenty yards across and separated from the rest of the pack, a flat, frozen slab drifting alone among hundreds of icebergs – slow-moving mountains of crystal ploughing through the glassy sea. On the western horizon, Tyson could see the white line of solid pack ice and knew that his party must try to reach it.

They set off on April 1 – towing Hans's skin kayak – nineteen souls crammed into a boat built to hold six or seven, so crowded that Tyson could scarcely move his arms to handle the tiller ropes without knocking over one of the frightened, crying children. Hans scarcely had room enough to bail – and bail he must, for even though they had jettisoned most of their meat, equipment, ammunition, and weapons, the boat was close to foundering.

Tyson could not leave the tiller, even to eat. Hannah fed him morsels of raw bear meat while the seamen moaned and complained. "The boat is sinking! The boat is sinking!" they cried over and over again as Hans bailed furiously with an old meat tin. But the boat did not sink. On April 3, Tyson gained the overnight safety of an old ice floe and the following morning embarked again. After a strenuous day, they reached the eastern fringe of the ice pack. By then everybody was soaked, freezing, and fighting a raging thirst.

They were too close to the edge of the pack. They set off westward again the following morning through a mass of seething ice until they reached a stronger floe. They scarcely had their tent up before the ice opened beneath it. They clung to a fragment as the gale increased and the frozen platform on which they were huddled pitched and tossed, rising and falling in the trough of the sea. They were scudding south before the gale at about three miles an hour when, at midnight on April 7, the ice split again, leaving Meyer marooned on a small floe with the boat and the kayak. The boat was too heavy for him to handle, and he had no experience with an Eskimo skin craft.

Joe and Hans immediately seized a paddle and worked their way across the floes until they reached the stricken man. Some of the others flung themselves on the ice, crying out "Oh, my God, boys, we are all goners!" and blaming Tyson for having got them into the predicament. Tyson ignored them, kept watch through the night, and

403

at first light called for volunteers to go with him across the half-frozen sea to pick up the three men on the other floe. Only the sullen Kruger volunteered. When he and Tyson joined the other three, the five men managed to lower the boat and steer it through the ice to the main party, but they were too weak to haul it onto the floe. At last a few others pitched in to help, and the entire company was reunited.

With great waves rolling over the tent, Tyson put the women and children in the boat for protection. The remainder, all huddled together, could only wait and hope. There was no fresh ice to suck on, no fuel to thaw it anyway. "We not only starve with hunger, freeze with cold, but we burn with thirst," Tyson wrote.

On April 11, they spotted their first raven, a sure sign that land was near. Tyson knew they must reach it soon. Hans's little boy was much improved, but Meyer was in a bad way, his toes and fingers frostbitten after his ordeal; he could not last more than a few days. Tyson had other fears: unless they got a seal soon he suspected again that some of the men might resort to cannibalism. On April 13, he recorded his suspicions: "The poor Esquimaux feel there [sic] situation dreadfully. They think the first to go will be the children. The white man will not starve they think, as long as there is a child to eat."

He impressed upon Joe and Hannah the need to keep their rifles loaded and handy. Having borrowed Hans's six-shooter, he was prepared to kill the first man who proposed cannibalism and took the two non-Germans – John Herron, the English steward, and William Jackson, the black cook – into his confidence. Herron had already caught Kruger stealing food, but there was nothing Tyson could do about it. Fortunately, on April 17 Joe shot another big seal, enough for three meals for the entire party.

The floe on which they were settled was becoming more and more unstable. Tyson wanted to move to a stronger one, but by the time the men had finished arguing about it, the opportunity was lost. They were now moving through a porridge of ice. Their own precarious platform, wearing away beneath them, was, Tyson knew, about to turn turtle.

On the night of April 20, a great wave rolled over the floe, swamping the tent and sweeping its contents into the sea. Tyson ordered the children into the boat. Even as they scrambled to safety, a second breaker knocked the tent over. The others clung to the boat to prevent it being washed into the ocean, then tried to haul it to the

404

weather edge of the floe. Then a third wave rolled over them, raising the boat waist high and flinging everything – boat, children, and adults, like so many shuttlecocks – fifty yards across the ice. All that night they clung to the boat and battled the ice-cold sea, as wave after wave washed them back and forth across the floe. By morning they were all exhausted.

Tyson spotted a more stable floe about twenty yards away and urged the men to push the boat into the water and make for it. The usual argument followed, and they almost missed their chance. Finally, they went for it. The cook, Jackson, missed the boat, tumbled into the water, but managed to grasp a gunwale. Tyson hauled him out. They rowed hard for their quarry and reached it. For the moment they were safe.

They were huddled now without food or shelter on an icy raft just six inches above the foaming sea. Tyson was driven to desperation by the German seamen, who clustered at some distance from the others. They continued moaning and grumbling that he was to blame for their predicament. Tyson found himself hoping that Kruger, the leader, would provoke him to the point where he'd have an excuse to shoot him.

They were reduced to gnawing on dried sealskin. If necessary, Tyson was prepared to eat the kayak, but fortunately, on April 22, with the help of Joe and Hans, he managed to track and kill a polar bear. Four days later the two native hunters shot three seals. The following day they quit the floe and moved to another, killing seals en route and slaking their thirst by drinking the blood. Then, later that day, they saw in the distance a column of smoke. *A ship!* Tyson had raised a small flag, which he had hoarded all these months for just such a moment. But the ship vanished.

Two days later, on April 28, 1873, they saw more smoke. The entire company fired pistols and rifles, trying to attract attention. Again it vanished, but then another ship appeared briefly and Tyson began to breathe more easily. They had reached the Labrador sealing grounds; the rock-ribbed coast could be seen emerging from the mist about thirty-five miles to the west.

That night they set seal-blubber fires as signals, but the fog closed in, blotting out all vision. Then, on the morning of April 30, at five o'clock, Tyson, rising from his sleep and throwing off the wet and tattered coat that was his only blanket, heard a cry: "There's a steamer!" A ship appeared out of the fog a scant five hundred yards from their floe. Everybody began to fire off weapons, and a moment later the vessel turned toward them.

Hans was in his kayak in an instant, paddling toward the ship. Tyson waved his old Russian cap. The entire company gave three weak cheers. A hundred throats aboard the steamer answered. The castaways replied with three more cheers and a tiger. Boats were lowered to the floe, and a few minutes later the bedraggled company of nineteen stood on the deck of the sealer *Tigress,* a barquentine out of Newfoundland.

A horde of curious whalers surrounded them uttering gasps of amazement when Tyson told them they'd been on the ice for six months. "And you on it night and day?" one of the Newfoundlanders asked. At this naïvety, Tyson could not suppress a laugh. It was his first in more than half a year. In Labrador Tyson was able to cable the first news of his rescue to the American consul at St. John's. The ship arrived at the Newfoundland capital on May 13, when a more complete story was wired to the New York press. At the outset, Tyson's statements were not believed. Words like "impossible" and "ridiculous" were used by more than one Arctic expert. But the wealth of detail reported at length in the New York papers made it obvious that the impossible had occurred: almost a score of men, women, and children had drifted from Smith Sound to Labrador without the loss of a single life.

In Tyson's account, which detailed the miracle of the six-month drift, scarcely any attention was paid to the role of the Eskimos in keeping the party alive. Not a word was written in the press about Joe, the hunter; indeed, neither he nor any of the others was named, except in the list of survivors. He was simply "one of the natives." A good deal of space was accorded to the building of snow huts and the shooting of seals, bears, and dovekies, but none of the credit for these accomplishments went to Joe or Hans. In fact, anyone reading the early New York newspaper accounts might have suspected that the natives, with their horde of children, were a drag on the party.

The American government immediately dispatched the USS *Frolic* to St. John's to bring the party to Washington. They arrived on June 5. Hall's widow left Cincinnati for the capital, hoping to get a first-hand account of her husband's death from Joe and Hannah. But in death he proved as elusive as in life. By the time she arrived, the Eskimo pair had already been sent to Maine. She herself had been subsisting on Hall's government pay of seventy-five dollars a month.

That would stop, the Secretary of the Navy announced, "as soon as the sad news of Captain Hall's death was confirmed." He found it necessary to add that the government would probably not try to seek a return from the widow of any overpayment.

Meanwhile, the *Tigress*, a Canadian vessel, was purchased and outfitted as a rescue ship. She left New York on July 14 for the Greenland coast to seek the rest of the missing *Polaris* party. The faithful Ebierbing joined Tyson in the rescue ship; so did Hans Hendrik and his family. Sympathetic Americans had given Hans's children a large supply of clothes; obviously delighted at the gift they insisted on wearing every shred. As the ship sailed away in the hot July weather, all were swathed in numberless dresses and shawls. That same month, Captain Budington and the rest of the *Polaris* survivors were plucked from the ice by the Dundee whaler, *Ravenscraig*.

Hannah remained behind with Punny. Joe, who had signed on as interpreter, was put to work on the *Tigress* as an ordinary seaman. Hans, who would not be returning from Greenland, was listed as a passenger. That didn't sit well with Joe, who took advantage of Hans's lack of English to turn him into his drudge, gravely informing him that both were expected to work.

In Greenland, the searchers learned that the *Polaris* had been abandoned the day after the Tyson party was carried away and that the crew had lived on land before the entire winter before taking to the ship's boats and eventual rescue. At the abandoned *Polaris* camp some of the logbooks and journals were found and retrieved. Perhaps significantly, the pages dealing with Hall's death and with the abandonment of the party on the ice floe had been torn out, a discovery that bears on the murder theory. Of Hall's personal papers there was no sign. Apparently they had been lost in the storm that drove the floe and its occupants away from the ship. It was fortunate that Hall had left the journals of his second voyage at Godhavn. These formed the basis of a published narrative.

Hans Hendrik and his family remained in Greenland, but Joe returned to the United States, where he and his family attempted to adapt themselves to civilized life. Joe worked as a farmer, a carpenter, and a fisherman. Hannah made fur clothing for purchasers in Groton and New London. Punny, whom Hannah re-christened Sylvia, after Sylvia Grinnell (Henry's daughter), attended school at Groton and showed herself to be an intelligent student.

But the family was not able to adapt. Joe went off to the Arctic again with Allen Young, M'Clintock's former officer. Sylvia died in 1875, followed a year later by Hannah, mourning her loss and her husband's absence, exhausted by her ordeal on the ice, and broken down with tuberculosis. "Come, Lord Jesus, and take thy poor creature home," she whispered on December 31, 1876. Before the New Year dawned, she was dead, at the age of thirty-nine.

Joe returned to visit her grave and weed away the tall grass. "Tookolito's gone, Punny's gone," he said. "I'm going back to King William Island." In 1878 he sailed with Frederick Schwatka's expedition to seek more relics. That they managed to do so was in large part due to Ebierbing's experience.

A long and tedious naval inquiry followed the rescue of the two *Polaris* parties. There, all the dissensions among the crew, the details of Charles Hall's death, and the heavy drinking among the officers – including George Tyson – before the division of the group were paraded before the public. The testimony was often conflicting, but it was clear that Budington had not intentionally left the nineteen castaways to their fate; he had simply been unable to find them in the storm and the following day had been forced to abandon his ship, which drifted off and eventually sank. But his lack of self-discipline and his uninspired leadership told against him. His career was over.

The naval board concluded that Hall had died of natural causes, probably apoplexy. That verdict held until Loomis disinterred the mummified body with the telltale signs of arsenic poisoning. By that time, there were graves of other explorers not far from Hall's last resting place. For the long search for the North Pole was by no means ended; it would continue for almost four decades.

Chapter Ten

George Nares

A SLEDGE PARTY FROM THE ALERT MAKING A PUSH FOR THE POLE

One of Nares's sledge crews

For all this time, while Hall was scouring King William Island and reconnoitring his proposed journey to the Pole, while Tyson and his surly companions were drifting slowly southward on their raft of ice, and while the U.S. Navy was examining the circumstances of Hall's death, two veterans of the Franklin search were agitating for another British scientific expedition to the Arctic. *"The navy needs some action"*

Clements Markham and Sherard Osborn spent nine years pursuing that unpopular cause. The public had turned against Arctic exploration after the Franklin tragedy was revealed and so had the government and the Admiralty, both of which were totally opposed to any further dangerous and expensive forays into the frozen world.

Markham and Osborn had once been shipmates. They served again in 1850-51 with Austin's squadron during the Great Search, Osborn as a lieutenant commanding the steam tender *Pioneer* and Markham as a midshipman on the *Assistance*. Both had literary pretensions; their baroque style had, in fact, helped turn several polar explorers into mythic figures.

Markham, who returned to civilian life, was made honorary secretary of the Royal Geographical Society in 1863. Osborn by then had risen to the rank of rear admiral. The two launched their campaign in January 1865, when Charles Francis Hall was in the first year of his five-year exile in the Arctic. It began with a speech by Osborn entitled "A Project of an Expedition to Reach the North Pole and Examine the Polar Regions." Osborn declared proudly that he and his fellow explorers did not belong to the new "rest-and-be-thankful school" and "were no more prepared to turn their backs on Arctic discovery because a Franklin had lost his life . . . than they would be to do so to an enemy's fleet because Nelson fell at Trafalgar."

Osborn was careful to stress the scientific aspects of such a venture, but he relied on the mystique of the Pole to catch the imagination of his listeners. He reinforced this by quoting a letter from John Ross's old adversary, Edward Sabine, now an army general and also president of the Royal Society. "To reach the Pole," Sabine had written, "is the greatest geographical achievement which can be attempted, and I own I should grieve if it should be first accomplished by any other than an Englishman."

Over the next several months, the proponents of a new polar expe-

411

dition were locked in an argument over the best possible route. Some, including both Markham and Osborn, favoured Smith Sound; others, including Edward Inglefield and Allen Young, opted for Spitzbergen. It all came to nothing. The public was not ready for any more Arctic ventures, and the press reflected that mood. *The Times* treated the proposal with what the RGS called "ribald buffoonery." The paper attacked Osborn's scheme as impolitic, sneered at "this bootless curiosity," which could produce no practical benefit, and declared, ". . . we must protest in the name of common sense and humanity. . . . We trust that not a single life may be adventured in another attempt to reach the North Pole."

For the next nine years, the two naval comrades struggled to turn public opinion around. By 1873, they had advanced to the point where Markham could publish the case for another polar effort in a popular book titled *The Threshold of the Unknown*. A best seller, it ran to four editions. In it, Markham quoted Osborn's original declaration that "the navy needs some action to wake it from the sloth of routine and save it from the canker of prolonged peace." He shrugged off the hazards of Arctic service, insisting that on eight expeditions only 32 men out of a total of 1,878 had died. But he omitted the Franklin expedition, a disaster that would have raised the death rate to close to 9 per cent.

"There is no undue danger in Arctic service," Markham wrote. All the Arctic experts, he said, were agreed on that, "provided that the expedition is under naval discipline and Government control" – a back-handed slap at the Americans. Scurvy he dismissed. It was, he said, "but little known now." In fact, he managed to suggest that scarcely any scurvy had occurred on previous expeditions, and then only in the third year. John Ross's fortunate 1829-33 experience – in a land where fresh meat was plentiful – had clouded the unhappy memory of other expeditions. Nonetheless, during the Franklin search, John Ross had commanded poorly equipped ships whose crews contracted scurvy within four months of leaving England, as Markham's friend Osborn well knew. For it had been Osborn who had helped battle the disease among Ross's crew by issuing them antiscorbutics.

Now Markham quoted Osborn on the subject of scurvy: "It is to the advanced state of knowledge in naval hygiene; to the attention paid to the cleanliness, warmth and ventilation of the ships, to the good quality of provisions, and especially to the preservation of

412

cheerfulness among the crews, that this immunity from scurvy is due and so rare has it become that the naval surgeons who possess any knowledge of this disease, derived from actual observation . . . may be counted upon one's fingers." In the light of what was to come, it is hard to imagine a more fatuous statement. Almost every Arctic expedition since the days of Parry had encountered scurvy. The sledge parties, which carried no lemon juice, were especially susceptible to it.

Markham apologized to his readers for dwelling so long on the supposed risks – "this disgraceful objection to Arctic exploration," as he called it. Were there really people in England who held these views? "To such men, if they really exist, the answer is, that even if the dangers were such as they describe, Englishmen have faced them before, and will do so again and again."

To shame the "danger mongers," as Markham called them, he published an old letter from Jane Franklin, now aged eighty-one and a living icon, a symbol of all that was gallant and *British* in the Arctic quest. In 1865 she had written to Sir Roderick Murchison that "for the credit and honour of England, the exploration of the North Pole should not be left to any other country. . . ."

It was this kind of patriotic appeal that helped to turn the tide of public opinion, spurred also by explorers from rival nations – Germans, Austrians, Scandinavians, Americans – who were poaching on Great Britain's frozen preserves. In 1873, a foreign flag, Austria's, was planted in the permafrost of Franz Josef Land. It would never do, in this age of exploration, to drop behind in the race for the Pole.

Since the days of the Great Search, the eyes of the nation had been turned towards Africa and the exploits of British explorers on the Dark Continent. Another geographical puzzle, the source of the White Nile, was on the verge of solution. By 1874, Henry Morton Stanley, Welsh-born in spite of his American residence, was about to set off for the mysterious Congo while Sir Samuel White Baker was back from his adventures in central Africa. The austere Prime Minister William Ewart Gladstone had been succeeded by an Imperial expansionist, Benjamin Disraeli. The compass needle of exploration was swinging back to the North. As Markham wrote: "A healthy interest in the glorious achievement of the Arctic worthies of former days was taking the place of sneering and indifference, and Englishmen were once more becoming alive to the importance of maritime enterprise."

A joint committee of the Royal Society and the Royal Geographical Society urged Disraeli to consider a new expedition. Most of the living "Arctic worthies" were represented – Back, Collinson, Rae, Osborn, and Markham. In November, Disraeli agreed that his government would organize an expedition not only for its scientific value but also to encourage "that spirit of maritime enterprise that has ever distinguished the English People." In those words, said The Times, reflecting the changed attitude of the country, "there is the true ring of national feeling."

The official emphasis had been entirely on scientific discoveries. The Arctic Committee of the Admiralty, which put its stamp on the enterprise, hadn't even mentioned the words "North Pole." But it was the Pole that caught the imagination of press and public. As far as the average Englishman was concerned, this was to be a polar expedition, and a successful one. The Union Jack was about to be planted at the top of the world! The Pole had replaced the Passage as the new British goal. As soon as the government gave its consent, the Committee appointed by the Admiralty to consider the purposes of the voyage made it clear that "the scope and primary object of the Expedition should be to attain the highest Northern latitude, and, if possible, to reach the North Pole. . . ." In the Admiralty's sailing orders, scientific matters were relegated to Paragraph 26.

No other English expedition – not even Franklin's – had been mounted with such an outpouring of national feeling. At that time the popular press was beginning to emerge. As the time for embarkation drew closer, the *Illustrated London News* and the *Graphic* devoted page after page to details of the forthcoming voyage. The new commander, George Nares, a veteran of the Franklin search, was front-page news. He and his officers were pictured in the engraved illustrations. Drawings of the two ships – the seventeen-gun steam sloop *Alert* and the steam whaler *Discovery* – were familiar to every literate Englishman. All the particulars of Arctic life were examined in detail. In more than one sense, the Nares expedition was to nineteenth-century England what the space program was to twentieth-century America. And, then as later, the public was oversold on the possibilities and undersold on the dangers.

If the Nares expedition proved anything it proved that the Royal Navy, after more than half a century of Arctic exploration, had learned very little. The crews that left Portsmouth on May 29, 1875, were no better equipped than those who had gone off to their deaths with John Franklin thirty years before. In almost every area, the Navy failed to profit from the experience of the North American travellers – men like Rae, Kennedy, Kane, Hall, and Hayes. Rae's advice, which was by far the best available, was generally ignored. Rae had, for instance, advised a friend who was going on the expedition, to take snowshoes. His friend reluctantly complied, although "he had been told by some of the great Arctic authorities they were no use." When the snowshoes were brought on board, there "was a shout of laughter and derision from the gallant but very inexperienced officers." But after the expedition returned, Rae's friend sought him out to express his gratitude "for many a long and pleasant walk." He told Rae that "without them, I should not have gone half a mile from the ship without much discomfort and labour."

Nor did the Navy profit from Rae's experience with snow houses. A skilled traveller, Rae found, could in one hour throw up a snow house big enough to hold five men. But the Navy wanted nothing to do with native techniques, although the advantages of the snow house should have been obvious. It meant that sledging parties would not have to carry and put up heavy tents or take them down and pack them each morning, stiff as they always were with condensed and frozen vapour. The snow house could be re-used on the return journey and was so warm that much less bedding was required. As Rae said, "When you use snow as a shelter your breath instead of condensing on your bedding gets condensed on the walls of the snow house, and therefore your bedding is relieved from nearly the whole of this."

Rae discounted Nares's excuse that the snow wasn't packed hard enough in the High Arctic to build an igloo. He himself had encountered all kinds of snow. In any snow, he said, a shelter could be built by digging out a three-foot basement, piling the snow into walls, and covering it with sheeting. On the other hand, there were no native peoples on Ellesmere Island, nobody to show Nares and his men – as Rae had been shown – how to construct a comfortable dwelling, or how to exist in a savage environment. Ellesmere was as barren of humankind as it was of trees.

Again, the cumbersome naval sledges with high runners were unsuitable for both heavy snow and hummocky ice. Rae had perfected a broader, lighter sledge with three runners, based on an Indian design, that ran equally well over snow or hard ice. It sank less than three-quarters of an inch in snow and did not get stuck when it came down off a hummock. But the Navy didn't listen to Rae. The major details were overseen by its own man, Leopold M'Clintock, the so-called master of Arctic sledging. Nares had been his sledgemate during the Franklin search.

Nares took along fifty-five Greenland dogs and several dog drivers including Hans Hendrik from the Kane, Hayes, and Hall expeditions. Astonishingly, he made no serious attempt to use them. The dogs were treated more as playthings than as beasts of burden by the Navy men, whose distaste for putting them in harness died hard. In the sledge journeys that followed, men, not dogs, would be in the traces. Nares, who clearly did not take dogteams seriously, described his crew of amateurs trying their hands at dog driving during an anchorage off Ellesmere Island: "With each dog pulling in a different direction, the starting was a ludicrous sight, and was seldom effected without the aid of a friend enticing the dogs on with a piece of meat. After struggling for about half a mile, they invariably obtained their own way, dragging their would-be guiders through many water pools in spite of the frequent application of the long whip, which, in inexperienced hands, was more frequently felt by the riders than the dogs."

As usual, the Navy paid no attention to the experience of the Eskimos. The natives, of course, wore the loosest possible clothing, usually made of doubled sealskin or other hide, with one side of the fur facing out, the other against the body. Nares's crew were issued tight woollen suits and flannel or duck overalls so clinging that the men had great difficulty stripping them off when wet. Nares felt that each man should have been separately fitted, but this was impossible because some of their clothing was still being sewn the day before they sailed. Nor was there enough emergency clothing to allow the men a change when their garments became soaked. Even worse was the lack of attached hoods. Again, the Navy never considered copying the hooded Eskimo parka, which protects the neck, the part of the body where the heat loss can be greatest.

The tents were more confining than on any previous Arctic expedition. Nares discovered too late that there had been "a steady & continuous reduction in space allotted since Arctic travelling was first undertaken." The Navy, in short, was continuing to pinch pennies. The nine-foot-long tents held eight men, each wedged into a space less than fourteen inches wide – or twenty-eight inches to a pair lying head to foot. On the last government expedition, each man had been

416

allotted sixteen and a half inches. Nares was forced to order an increase in the size of his tents, which meant adding an additional twelve-pound weight to each sledge.

The blanket bags in which the men slept were too short and open at the neck. That meant that each man had to wear his duffle coat as well. To Rae, who had adopted the Eskimos' sensible method of sleeping some thirty years before, all this made no sense. In his evidence before the committee that was eventually appointed to look into the problems faced by the Nares expedition, he had this to say:

"I consider also the mode of sleeping in the blanket bag a very bad one, because it separates the men from each other, and they cannot communicate the heat from one body to another . . . we never slept cold in the snow house, except once, although we only had one single blanket over us. Instead of putting on a coat to sleep in, we always took our coats off, simply for this reason, that if you have a great thick coat on, it keeps your arm from your body and you have not any heat communicated from the body to the arm. The Esquimau, who is a very knowing man, takes off both his coats and he has nothing on his upper parts at all, and therefore he lies with his arm close to his body, and as near his neighbour as possible, that the heat may communicate from one to the other. If you have got an immense duffle blanket separating you from your neighbour, and if you have got an immense duffle coat put on yourself, separating your arm from your body, and you lie with both coats impregnated with snow, the result must be most injurious. . . ."

In the ordeals they were about to face, Nares and his men would be forced to haul loads that were too heavy while subsisting on inadequate rations of three quarters of a pound of salt meat a day, which Nares later had to increase to one pound. Even that wasn't enough. Rae, a notoriously lean eater, consumed between three and four pounds a day while pulling sledges and carrying loads only half as heavy as the ones these inexperienced seamen would be forced to drag or tote. On the Saskatchewan, the regular daily ration was eight pounds of meat in addition to potatoes and other vegetables. Rae knew of some voyageurs who thought nothing of consuming ten or twelve pounds of meat a day. At Fort Confidence, Thomas Simpson had encountered one French Canadian who would eat sixteen pounds of meat a day "if he could get it."

Yet the sledge hauling required of naval men in the Arctic was harder and more debilitating than anything the Canadian fur-trading companies expected from tireless paddlers; nor were the sailors accustomed to the exertion, as the voyageurs were. Before leaving England, Nares did his best to prepare them for it. He warned his crew "that if they could ever imagine the hardest work they had ever been called upon to perform in their lives intensified to the utmost degree, it would only be as child's play in comparison with the work they would have to perform whilst sledging." Within a few months, the men of the *Alert* and the *Discovery* would learn that this was no overstatement.

As food and fuel were used up, the sledges would become lighter, but there was a basic weight – tents, bedding, equipment – that would never decrease. On the Nares expedition, where each man pulled more than two hundred pounds, the basic weight was eighty pounds. Rae, by using native techniques, had kept his basic weight to forty.

Again, as in previous British expeditions, the ships provided were too big and too cumbersome for men exhausted by hard work and disease to handle. Nares himself confided to his journal, "I always considered that our ships were too heavy for the crews and also for Arctic service. Now with our weakened men we find it very heavy work. Everything has to be done with the help of the capstan or windlass. Even the strong men appear to be weakened."

All of this might have been bearable – it had been bearable before – had it not been for one other problem: diet. A careful study of the journals of Arctic explorers, especially those of the Arctic veterans who were pushing so hard for a polar expedition, should have made it obvious that fresh meat and fresh vegetables were the best antiscorbutics. Yet Nares and his men were expected to survive almost entirely on salt meat. The Navy considered that the usual ration of lemon juice, plus the availability of muskoxen, would be enough to protect the crews against the disease. It forgot that men on sledging parties could not depend on the hunt for their food, even if game existed, and also that lemon juice freezes and so could not be carried on sledge trips. No one had yet thought of lacing the juice with rum or creating a lemon-juice lozenge. And, through one final ludicrous mistake, the Nares expedition was provisioned not with lemon juice but with lime juice. Because the Navy generally referred to lemon juice as "lime juice" (hence the nickname "Limey" for the British tar), someone substituted Caribbean limes for Mediterranean lemons, not realizing that the juice of the lemons was four times more effective in warding off scurvy.

Thus the Nares expedition set out under sentence of disaster. Over-publicized, it would never live up to the expectations of a nation convinced that these gallant young men would soon be planting a Union Jack on the Pole. Badly and hastily organized with a smugness and an arrogance that in hindsight seem almost criminal, this band of amateurs set off blithely, as so many had before it, without any real idea of what they were facing. None of Nares's officers had ever seen an iceberg, and as the leader was to complain in his journal, they didn't even know how to take care of their men. But England expected each of them to do his duty, trained or not, and to give them their due, they did it to the best of their ability.

2

At Portsmouth Harbour, May 29, 1875, the piers and foreshore were crammed with spectators, the masts of the harbour aflutter with flags. Cannons roared, bands played, soldiers in scarlet marched and wheeled. So great was the excitement in this spring month that the special trains from London had to be cancelled; the crowds climbing aboard the two Arctic ships were interfering with the work of the artificers. By the time the expedition was ready to sail, some 200,000 people were swarming around the harbour. *The seeds of scurvy*

It was one of those spontaneous moments of mass enthusiasm that marked the zenith of Empire. Disraeli was about to buy the Suez Canal and treat it as if it were the Queen's personal toy. ("You have it, Madame," he would tell Victoria). Her plump and popular heir, Bertie, Prince of Wales, was on the point of visiting India's coral strand, and she herself, on her birthday, had sent a warm and congratulatory message to the men planning to venture far beyond Greenland's icy mountains.

As the two ships left the harbour at four that afternoon, the *Telegraph*'s correspondent was already composing the fulsome phrases that would ornament the next morning's edition: "As we lose sight of the good ships and crews to whose despatch so many hopes, so much sympathy, and such careful preparations have gone, who is not conscious that the mere fact of their departure amid such testimonies of pride and love and enthusiasm does England great good? The feelings which were uttered in those ringing, repeated, hearty cheers along the Southsea shore and out into the dancing waves, are shared by all over the country and no man needs to know personally Captain Nares and his associates to call them 'friends.' Friends they are to every household. . . .

"The Admiralty could have filled twenty Arctic ships with volunteers . . . for the island realm is still rich in the old valorous breed, so little is it true that wealth and peace have corrupted English blood . . . the Government . . . has rightly interpreted the desire of the people not to see another flag other than that of England anticipate us in the crowning feat of maritime discovery. . . . England is not too rich to be bold, too luxurious to be simple, too cynical to be pious, too genteel to believe in honour and glory and the sweetness of self devotion. The England that History knows about . . . was down along the Channel shores on Saturday . . . watching her mariners set sail to plant the Jack on the top of the globe, if manhood and love of duty can find a way thither. . . ."

The explorer who was expected to plant the flag upon the Pole was a career naval officer in his forty-fifth year, unpretentious, matter-of-fact, and accustomed to following orders. George Strong Nares's forebears had served the realm in one war or another since his great-grandfather's day. The son of a naval commander, Nares had been in the service since the age of fourteen. His likeness in the National Portrait Gallery shows a handsome, clear-eyed man with a high, balding forehead and a full beard. His journal is devoid of passion but full of common sense, suggesting a man who took things as they came and accepted both triumphs and setbacks with an inner response that kept his temper in check and his enthusiasms suitably curtailed. He did not look on the polar quest with the romantic vision of a Kane (whose descriptions he considered highly coloured) or a Hall. He had no great longing to go north, as Franklin had had. Indeed, he once referred to the Arctic as "a wretched place but . . . still healthy," an even-handed description that suggests the temperament of the man.

He went north because he was told to go north and also because he knew, or at least hoped, that doing so would further his career. He was one of the last of the functioning officers who had taken part in the Franklin search, having served as second mate on the *Resolute*

420

under Kellett in 1852-54. He was a member of the sledging party that had discovered McClure's message on Melville Island. Where sledging was concerned, he was M'Clintock's disciple. He had served as a gunnery officer in the Crimean War and more recently as an accomplished oceanographer in the South Pacific. He had the reputation of being energetic, skilful, and thorough – in short, the best man the Navy could muster to preside over the latest attempt to reach the Pole.

Nares gave scant credence to the fantasy of an Open Polar Sea. As his two ships forced their way up the west coast of the Kennedy Channel, past the colourless world of Grinnell Land (black headlands riven by glacier-filled valleys), he was convinced that it was an illusion. And he was aware that Isaac Hayes's geographical calculations were so far off the mark as to be useless.

Nares left the *Discovery* under its captain, Henry Stephenson, to set up permanent winter quarters below the precipitous cliffs of Lady Franklin Bay off Hall Basin. Then, with the *Alert,* he entered the Robeson Channel, whose coastline was blocked by a jagged thirty-five-foot wall of ice floes. Only Nares had seen ice like this before – the ancient rock-ribbed ice of the Beaufort Sea, eight hundred miles to the west. These century-old blocks, tumbling down from the north, were eighty feet thick. When Nares reached the mouth of the channel at Lincoln Bay, he saw that they stretched off as far as the eye could see – a labyrinth of broken masses and hillocks unlike anything that had yet been faced. He searched about to find a suitable name for this ancient ice and hit on the adjective "paleocrystic." To Nares, it represented defeat.

He had taken his ship to the highest latitude that any sea-going vessel had so far attained. He knew he was on the rim of the polar sea. But he could not believe that the heavy naval sledges he had brought could ever manage to thread their way through the dreadful icescape that confronted him. The *Polaris* expedition had hinted at a land mass leading north, or perhaps an open-water channel. Nares now bluntly dismissed these suggestions as myths.

He managed to make his way to the northwest around Capes Union and Sheridan at the tip of Grant Land, as it was then known – all part of Ellesmere Island – until on August 31 he found a small bay in which the *Alert* could winter. Racing against time, he reached the shelter of the inlet just ahead of the advancing ice, then looked back in "wonder and awe" at the power exerted by the ice blocks, some of them weighing 30,000 tons, which congealed into a fifty-foot ram-

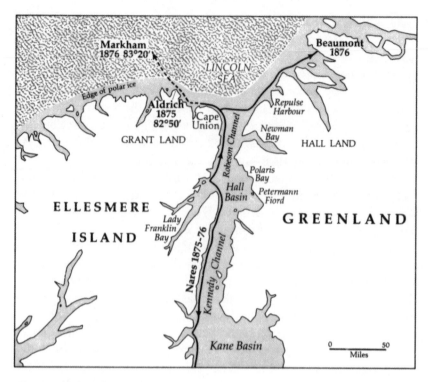

The Nares expedition, 1875-76

part, two hundred yards thick, locking in the ship but also protecting it from the danger of the pack beyond.

Nares's first mate, Albert Hastings Markham, a distant cousin of Sir Clements Markham, described the scene that September: "Nothing but ice, tight and impassable, was to be seen – a solid, impenetrable mass that no amount of imagination or theoretical belief could ever twist into an 'Open Polar Sea.'

"We were reluctantly compelled to come to the conclusion that we had in reality arrived on the shore of the Polar Ocean; a frozen sea of such a character as utterly to preclude the possibility of its being navigated by a ship; a wide expanse of ice and snow, whose impenetrable fastnesses seemed to defy the puny efforts of mortal men to invade and expose their hitherto sealed and hidden mysteries."

Their only hope – a slim one – was that a gale might open a channel that could lead to more land to the north, if, indeed, such land existed. Nares was more than sceptical; he was already convinced that his expedition could not reach the North Pole. He would

422

have preferred to devote his efforts to a sensible survey of the land that did exist; but his orders were to try to reach the Pole, and he was a man who conscientiously followed orders. The main object of his sledging parties, then, would be to try to seek land to the north. That September a series of depots must be laid out for such an effort the following spring.

These were man-killing trips. Lieutenant Pelham Aldrich, who commanded one sledge, set a new record by passing Parry's 1827 Farthest North – but only after a journey that left his men exhausted. The snow was the softest yet encountered; at each step they sank up to their knees. Without snowshoes, travel became a nightmare. Another sledge captain, Lieutenant William May, a future Admiral of the Fleet, later wrote, ". . . our sufferings from thirst . . . were almost beyond belief." He tried, with limited success, to dissuade his men from eating snow, which induced terrible cramps and heat loss. Markham, who took the largest party – twenty-one men and three officers – returned with a third of his crew incapacitated from frostbite. Three men suffered amputation of fingers or toes and were out of action for the winter. The lack of fresh food caused slow healing of their wounds; some of May's took five months to heal.

The sledgers faced another problem – one that Rae had predicted. The tents and bedding became moisture soaked and frozen so that the basic weight that had to be hauled, over and above that of fuel and food, increased, on Markham's journey, from 107 pounds to an impossible 216.

Nares planned several sledge trips for the spring. Aldrich, with another officer and fifteen men, would explore the coast of Grant Land. Markham, with a similar crew, would try to reach the Pole. Other sledge parties would go out from the *Discovery* in Lady Franklin Bay to explore the bay, which Nares thought might be an inlet leading into the Arctic Archipelago, and to examine Petermann Fiord on the Greenland shore opposite.

For safety's sake, each party would take a boat. That would raise the basic weight each man hauled to more than two hundred pounds – an impossibility if anything like two weeks' supply of food and fuel was also to be carried. The result was that the crews would have to drag the boat forward in stages and then go back for their sledge, so that the workload was doubled and the daily mileage halved.

The winter passed wearily, relieved by the usual lectures and entertainments in the naval tradition. (Nares reopened "The Royal Arctic

Theatre," after two decades.) The men built an observatory and several snow houses to hold equipment and meat and shot enough muskoxen to supply fresh meat twice every three weeks. By the time the light began to return in late January, the faces of the men were almost as white as the snow around them. "We were all in excellent spirits," Albert Markham recalled, "and supposed ourselves to be in perfect health. . . ." That supposition would be cruelly dashed within a few weeks, but even in March, when Nares told his men that they would be spending a second winter in the Arctic, there was no hint of trouble. Indeed, they seemed to receive that news with satisfaction.

Nares made two attempts that March to reach the *Discovery* by dogsled. The first was aborted when Niels Christian Petersen, his Danish dog driver and interpreter, developed stomach cramps. Petersen lingered for three months and then died. The second trip was more successful, but Nares became convinced that dogs were not effective on the kind of hummocky ice the teams had encountered on the two-week journey. This was directly contrary to Isaac Hayes's experience with dogs in similar ice conditions in Smith Sound, but given the nature of the Navy sledges and the inexperience of the drivers, the experiment with the teams was not repeated.

On the morning of April 3, 1876 (the year Bell introduced the telephone), the two sledging expeditions set out from the *Alert* – seven sledges and two boats, all drawn up in line, heraldic pennants flapping in the stiff Arctic breeze, and the entire ship's company of fifty-three men and officers singing the Church of England Doxology ("Praise God, from whom all blessings flow"). At eleven o'clock the sledge crews picked up the drag ropes and, to the traditional three hearty cheers, set off across the ice in different directions. The temperature stood at minus 33⁰ F. Thus began an ordeal whose arduousness few could have foreseen, in spite of the warnings that Nares himself had issued at the beginning of the voyage.

Nares was well aware of the toil involved, for he had endured it before. "Very few," he had written, "can possibly realize the utter wretchedness endured by young men in the utmost health & strength & full of life when imprisoned in a heavy gale of wind within a small light tent made of no thicker material than an ordinary cricketing tent."

It was bad enough to be confined for several days in a comfortable bed with plenty of kicking room but far worse to be "compelled to remain lying down at full length cramped up in a compacted space between 28 to 32 inches across for *yourself and companion* for one or two and even three consecutive days – packed in order to economize space, heads & tails alternating like preserved sardines . . . where, if your blanket bag allows you to kick it must necessarily be at the risk of striking your next neighbour's nose. Inside the tightly closed blanket bag it is too dark to read and woe betide anyone who leaves the mouth open. For the whole interior of the tent is filled with snow drift . . . so fine & light . . . as to be likened to the motes of a sunbeam . . . forever shifting gradually downwards and forming a thick & ever increasing deposit on the upper canvas covering stretched over the cramped men."

Struggling through soft snow sometimes up to their waists, hauling weights that in one case exceeded 240 pounds per man, the sledgers perspired in their tight clothing, which began to freeze until their duffle trousers could not be buttoned and their duffle coats became as stiff as strait jackets. These wet and freezing garments in turn dampened the interior of the tight-fitting blanket bags, which also froze, adding to the discomfort of the occupants and the weight that had to be dragged.

The combined sledge parties moved at a turtle's pace, west toward Cape Joseph Henry, hacking a road with pickaxes through hummocks as high as fifty feet. Then, on April 6, came the first hint of a more insidious factor to compound the stress of sledge travel. Two of Markham's men complained of feeling "seedy." At almost exactly the same time, two marines in Aldrich's party complained of illness. One, in fact, had to be sent back to the ship. This was hardly coincidence. The seeds of scurvy had been sown weeks before; now the disease was starting to take command. On April 10, at Cape Joseph Henry, the three supporting sledge crews returned to the ship and the two main parties separated, Aldrich moving west along the coast of Grant Land, Markham's two sledges heading due north.

On April 14, another of Markham's sledge crew, John Shirley, complained of pains and swelling in his ankles and knees. But scurvy was the last thing on Markham's mind. He had been told there was not the slightest chance of his crews being attacked. Like Aldrich, he attributed the symptoms to fatigue. Within three days, however, two of his men were so incapacitated they had to be carried on the sledges.

By April 19, Markham was forced to abandon the larger of his two boats to make up for the weight of the invalids. Already, however, another man had fallen sick. Markham suspected scurvy but kept his thoughts to himself in order not to panic his crews. On April 24, with more men complaining of stiffness in the joints, he knew his crew was in trouble. On that day the party reached the 83rd parallel of latitude – the farthest north that white men had ever gone. When within the next fortnight a third of the sledgers had fallen out of action, Markham had to concede that they were the victims of scurvy. He had reached a latitude of $83^0 20'$. The Pole was still four hundred nautical miles away. He allowed his crews two days' rest and then, bitterly disappointed, planted the Union Jack and prepared to retrace his steps.

Now began a race with scurvy as more and more men succumbed, leaving fewer and fewer to haul the sledges. By May 27, the situation was critical. Five men couldn't move; five more could only hobble behind the sledges, lying down in the snow to rest every thirty or forty yards. Three more were in the early stages of scurvy. Only two officers and two men could be considered effective. Markham was forced to abandon his remaining boat and cast off all superfluous weight. On June 5, to his great relief, he reached solid land. But he knew that at the speed he was making, he could not reach the ship for another three weeks. By then, he feared, all would be dead.

He realized that somebody would have to make for the ship, forty miles away, over floes covered with deep snow and heavy hummocks. The only man in the party strong enough for the ordeal was Lieutenant A.A.C. Parr, who volunteered for the task. Parr left on his rescue mission on June 7. The following day, George Porter, a Marine artilleryman, "one of the finest men we had in the crew," died of scurvy.

Parr's journey saved the others. Travelling light, stumbling over the loose rubble-ice and circling round the huge pressure ridges, he managed to reach the *Alert* in less than twenty-three hours, so exhausted that when he knocked on Nares's door, his captain at first failed to recognize him.

Nares at once sent an advance party out by dogteam. They reached Markham's crew on June 9. A larger rescue party arrived the following day. By the time the survivors reached the ship, only three of Markham's original fifteen men were still able to walk.

Aldrich, who had already sent one sledge back, was also facing a race with death; Nares realized that when he saw the condition of Markham's party. He shot off another team to the west, where they found only Aldrich and three others capable of working. Two men were hobbling along behind the sledges that carried the remaining four. The snow was so deep that the rescuers, without the assistance of snowshoes, were forced to crawl through it on their hands and knees.

The *Alert* itself had not escaped the disease. By late June, only nine of fifty-three crew members were fit for work. The rest were either coming down with scurvy or recovering from it. "How is it," Nares asked in his journal, "that the curse of the Arctic regions . . . has not been properly reported on by any captain on his return, and so by drawing the attention of the authorities to the fact, obtain a change of diet? No Arctic ships should have an ounce of salt meat on board."

He noticed that the officers suffered less from scurvy than the men, undoubtedly because the officers' mess was supplied with food they had bought privately – butter, milk, eggs, cheese, jams, rice, hams, tongues, and vegetables. Nares, realizing this, turned over his own personal supplies to the worst of the sufferers.

To the south, Lieutenant Lewis Beaumont's Greenland sledging party from the *Discovery* was suffering exactly the same fate as those of Aldrich and Markham. Beaumont had read something about scurvy in M'Clintock's account of Hobson's sufferings during the voyage of the *Fox*, and the diet aboard the Nares ships should have alerted him to the danger. During Nares's seventeen-month voyage, his crew would have only thirty-four days of fresh provisions; for one three-month period they had none. But even when one of his men, J.S. Hand, began to show serious symptoms of the disease a fortnight after the departure, Beaumont waited another three days before he was convinced that Hand was scorbutic – a truth that he too kept from his sledgemates.

Reluctantly, Beaumont sent Hand and half the party back to the ship. Hand died on June 3 before they reached it. By then, with the remaining crew members also in the throes of the disease, a "mournful and disappointed" Beaumont was already heading back, fearful that he would be unable to reach help in time.

Beaumont's journey was the most remarkable of all the sledging trips undertaken by the British Arctic Expedition that spring. The men became so exhausted that even Beaumont, the strongest of the group, was forced to throw away his belt and knife because he found them too heavy to carry. Forty-five years later, another Arctic ex-

427

plorer, the ethnologist Knud Rasmussen, was to write of Beaumont's secondary sledge party under Lieutenant Reginald Fulford, which trekked from Repulse Haven to Petermann Fiord: "How they managed to pull the sledges up Gap Valley . . . is a perfect riddle to all of us who have looked at the stony pass. . . . We others can only bow our heads to those who did it." Others who followed in Beaumont's tracks in later years were amazed at the Royal Navy's refusal to use dogs. Beaumont took thirty-two days to reach Sherard Osborn Fiord in Greenland from the tip of Ellesmere using manhauled sledges. Three decades later, George Borup, a young college graduate on the Peary North Pole expedition, made the same trip by dogteam in just eight days.

At the very last moment, on June 22, Beaumont was saved by a relief party that included the ship's doctor and Hans Hendrik. Beaumont credited Hans's skill as a dog driver with getting the invalids to Polaris Bay. Here, at Hall's old wintering spot (Thank God Harbor), a makeshift hospital had been set up, and here one more man died. Several of the others were close to death but recovered, again because of the fresh meat provided by Hans, the hunter.

Although he was expected to remain in the Arctic until 1877, Nares realized that his exhausted, scurvy-ridden crews couldn't survive another winter. At the end of July, he blasted a channel through the ice with torpedoes loaded with gunpowder and headed south to a rendezvous with the *Discovery*. There the wisdom of his decision to return to England was confirmed by news of more scurvy. As soon as Beaumont's crews returned, the two ships started south.

On September 9, at Cape Isabella, they discovered a cache of letters left by Sir Allen Young, who had made two attempts to communicate with them. Young's main purpose was to try to get through the North West Passage in his yacht *Pandora* by way of Peel Sound and also to find any overlooked relics of the Franklin expedition. His two journeys in 1875 and 1876, the first partially funded by Lady Franklin, were failures. In 1875, he was blocked, as so many others had been, by the ice in Peel Sound. The following year he was diverted from his goal by an Admiralty request to bring back news of the Nares expedition. He found one of Nares's records on the Cary Islands in 1875 and another at Littleton Island on his second trip. By the time the two expeditions came together on October 6, 1876, in Davis Strait, all three ships were headed for home, each having failed to accomplish its objective. No one had yet taken a ship through the

Passage, and no one had yet planted his country's flag on the North Pole.

3

The Nares Expedition reached England on November 2, 1876, to learn that Lady Franklin had died at the age of eighty-three, less than two months after its departure from Portsmouth. She had not lived to see the monument to her husband she had commissioned; it was unveiled in Westminster Abbey a fortnight after her death. It was, as the inscription said, "erected by Jane, his widow, who, after long waiting, and sending many in search of him, herself departed to seek and to find him in the realms of light. . . ."

It was truly the end of an era. Allen Young, the last British navigator to attempt the North West Passage, was back in England, and so was George Nares, the last of the Royal Navy's Arctic adventurers. Nares returned to what he described as "a warm and hearty reception . . . notwithstanding the somewhat natural disappointment that the North Pole had not been reached." The Queen herself sent the ship's company an immediate note of congratulation in which she extended sympathy for "the hardships and sufferings they have endured," and lamented "the loss of life which has occurred." The usual round of banquets followed. Nares was awarded the Founder's Gold Medal of the Royal Geographical Society and presented with a gold watch for achieving his farthest north. A special Arctic medal was struck for the crews. All the officers but one were promoted. Only the commander himself failed to receive the broad stripe of a flag officer. For in spite of all the shouts of approval, the expedition had been a disappointment. The public had been oversold on the North Pole – an indication that the world was entering an era when the power of the press to sense and then swing public opinion had become a fact of life. In England, the periodicals and newspapers had first echoed the general distaste for further polar adventures and then, when attitudes changed, had inflated the general desire for an Imperial triumph until the government was forced to act. Now it swung the other way. The Admiralty, the RGS, and the press were all at fault, but it was George Nares who got most of the blame.

The attitude of the magazine *Navy* was typical. In 1875 it had bubbled with enthusiasm for the venture: "As we hope, so we believe that they will end their northward advance only at the northernmost meeting of the meridians; that they will return in safety to receive well-won applause and reward for their achievements; and that they will have very much to tell of the circum-polar region, as well as of their hoisting the Union Jack upon the Pole."

In December 1876, the same journal launched a savage attack on both the Admiralty and George Nares: ". . . the nation has cause to blush at the manner in which the very best of opportunities of reaching the North Pole has been frittered away, and at the ridiculous figure which the First Lord of the Admiralty must cut in the eyes of foreign nations." In the magazine's view, the expedition was a glaring failure. It urged a searching inquiry "into the manner in which the management of the Expedition has been conducted," and it called for a court-martial of Nares himself for, among other misdeeds, an "absence of zeal and determination in abandoning the object of the Expedition," and for declaring the "Pole 'impracticable' without sufficient cause."

There was no court-martial, but there was a long and exhaustive public inquiry by the Admiralty into the causes of scurvy. The five-man committee included Richard Collinson and Edward Inglefield, both of whom by this time had achieved flag rank. The inquiry began on January 10, 1877, and continued until February 28. It subpoenaed fifty witnesses, twenty-one of whom had been members of the expedition. It was looking for a scapegoat, and it found one in Nares, who was censured for not providing his sledging crews with fresh lime juice. Yet the sworn evidence made it clear that Nares had never been ordered to make that provision; that sledging parties on previous expeditions, including M'Clintock's, hadn't carried lime (or lemon) juice; and that the director general of the Navy's own medical department, Sir Alexander Armstrong, hadn't recommended it. Armstrong had, in fact, declared at the outset that there would be no possibility of scurvy during the first winter and no widespread scurvy unless the expedition remained in the Arctic for a third winter. It was also made clear that there was no way to carry bottles of lime juice on an open sledge; it had never been done because in freezing, the juice expanded and broke the containers.

Then why had so many of the previous sledging expeditions been freer, apparently, of the disease? In Nares's view, they hadn't been; it was simply that the expedition leaders in those days confused the signs of scurvy with physical exhaustion. The expression used in the published journals was that the men were greatly "debilitated."

"I am certain," Nares told the committee, "that what is reported in the official papers as being an attack of debility was most decidedly the same as our attack by a more advanced form of scurvy, and had our men returned after about thirty days' travelling we should probably have officially reported that merely a slight attack of debility had been experienced." In 1854, for example, Kellett had reported to Belcher that only thirty of his ninety men were fit for service, together with only half his officers.

The great puzzle of the Nares fiasco is the dearth of knowledge about scurvy among the naval hierarchy. It is hard to believe that in a century that saw an explosion of scientific research and discovery, no one was inquisitive enough to sort through the mass of available information about the disease and come up with some useful findings. Scurvy had been known for centuries. The Laurentian Indians of Canada were familiar with it and had saved Jacques Cartier's life in 1536 with an infusion of white cedar bark. John Ross and others had testified before the middle of the century to the value of fresh meat, but the Royal Navy went on providing salt meat to its crews.

It was not then known, nor did it come out in the evidence, that the lime juice used as an antiscorbutic was far less effective than the lemon juice with which the earlier expeditions had been provided. As for potatoes, another known antiscorbutic, there had not been a proper storage room aboard ship for them. The officers' private stocks had delayed or prevented the affliction.

Modern research shows that scurvy is brought on by a lack of Vitamin C, which cannot be stored in the body but must be ingested regularly. The daily minimum needed to saturate the body and thus prevent or cure the disease runs between seventy and one hundred milligrams. If antiscorbutics are not taken regularly after the body is saturated, it will quickly lose its Vitamin C content, and the first symptoms of scurvy will appear in twenty-five to thirty weeks. On the *Alert* and the *Discovery*, the daily intake of Vitamin C per man is estimated at between 3.2 and 5.5 milligrams a day – an ineffectual dosage. Thus scurvy was present long before the sledge crews set out on journeys of seventy days or more. When no antiscorbutics were available and the workload was killing, the ravages quickly became apparent.

The committee looked into other aspects of the Nares fiasco. John

Rae's evidence on dogs, snow houses, snowshoes, and native clothing was especially revealing, although later events suggest it went unheeded.

The expedition was ultimately judged a failure because it did not do the impossible. One of the inquiry's chief findings was negative: the Smith Sound route, Nares claimed (wrongly, as it turned out), was not the best route to the Pole. Yet, unlike Hall and Kane, Nares had brought all his collections and notes safely home. His scientific observations – astronomical, geological, and botanical – were immensely valuable and resulted in no fewer than forty articles and published reports in the years that followed. Aldrich's charts of the northern Ellesmere coast were the only ones available for fifty years until aerial photography came into its own.

The Nares expedition established an abiding territorial claim, one that was to prove significant in a later century when two major powers would face each other across the polar wastes. Because of its explorations, British and ultimately Canadian sovereignty in the High Arctic was eventually established. In spite of later American and Scandinavian expeditions that built on Nares's discoveries, Ellesmere Island is part of Canada today. The British flag placed on the very tip of the island by scurvy-ridden men gave the mother country, and ultimately her dominion, unquestioned ownership of that forbidding and perilous terrain.

This was the last Royal Navy expedition to the Arctic. Not until the winter of 1934-35 did the British return to the High North. Instead, the Admiralty focused its attention on another frozen world – and with even more tragic results when "Scott of the Antarctic," ignoring the value of dogs, manhauled his sledges towards another Pole, only to be beaten by a thorough professional who survived in an environment where amateurs, no matter how enthusiastic, sicken and sometimes die.

Chapter Eleven

Adolphus W. Greely

Rescue of the Greely survivors in their collapsed tent

1

As the Nares expedition was setting off for Smith Sound in the *The polar* summer of 1875, a young Austrian scientist and naval lieutenant, *virus* Karl Weyprecht, fresh from his discovery of Franz Josef Land off northern Russia, began a campaign of his own. Simply put, Weyprecht's scheme was to strip the glamour and romance from polar exploration and concentrate exclusively on scientific matters.

It was, of course, an ingenuous idea. Explorers, almost by definition, are romantics; it is the very glamour of the quest that lures them on, not the laborious collection of geological or botanical data. The mass of scientific evidence collected since Parry's day was merely a byproduct of the ardent pursuit of the Unknown. Not only the explorers but even the hardest-headed of the scientists who accompanied the polar sorties were seduced by the spell of the Arctic and the need to move deeper and deeper into that mysterious and often magical realm. Weyprecht was right when he argued that the race for new discoveries – the search for the Passage and the Pole – had taken precedence over solid research.

His plan, which he proposed to a meeting of the German Scientific and Medical Association at Graz, was to forget matters of national prestige and personal ambition and to organize a carefully integrated international program of observation and analysis during the polar night of the Arctic and Antarctic that might lead to discoveries that would benefit mankind. This laudable proposal met with some opposition, but Weyprecht persisted over the next four years. He had history on his side, for this was, in a real sense, a golden age of applied scientific development. In those four years, the telephone, the typewriter, the electric light bulb, and the phonograph all came into their own. The world was dazzled by a burst of technical accomplishment – from the player piano to the carpet sweeper, from dryplate photography to the four-cycle gasoline engine. Science was seen to work; it was obvious now that it could improve the quality of life. Who could tell what new wonders might emerge from the laboratories of America or even from the makeshift observatories set up on the naked tundra of a remote Arctic island?

In 1879, Weyprecht's ideas were adopted by the International Polar Conference in Hamburg. That led, in 1882-83, to the establishment of the first International Polar Year, in which eleven nations were pledged to establish fifteen new observation stations in the Arctic and Antarctic.

The remotest station of all would be at Lady Franklin Bay, where George Nares's second ship, *Discovery,* had wintered in 1875-76. This would be the United States' contribution to the great international undertaking. On those barren shores, twenty-four men and two Eskimos, all under U.S. Army command, would carry out scientific observations for the good of humanity. There was, of course, another, less publicized purpose. In spite of Karl Weyprecht's high-minded pursuit of science, the expedition's task was to try to reach the Pole, or, at the very least, to beat the British record and plant the Stars and Stripes on a new Farthest North. Thus the stage was set for the most appalling tragedy since the loss of John Franklin and his men.

At the same time *another* polar tragedy was in the making. On July 8, 1879, the 420-ton barque-rigged coal burner, *Jeannette,* steamed out of San Francisco Bay under the command of a thirty-five-year-old naval veteran, Lieutenant George Washington De Long, who had taken part in the search for Charles Hall's *Polaris.* De Long was convinced that he could reach the North Pole by way of the Bering Sea. McClure's and Collinson's explorations should have convinced him that the permanent pack they had encountered off the Beaufort Sea would make such an excursion dubious. But De Long had been seduced by the theories of the noted German geographer August Petermann, the so-called "sage of Gotha," an armchair scientist who was convinced that a current of warm water from the Pacific led north through Bering Strait to a tepid basin – another version of the Open Polar Sea theory.

The expedition was under naval discipline but was financed by the flamboyant New York *Herald* publisher, James Gordon Bennett, who hoped that the impetuous De Long would do for him in the Arctic what an earlier explorer had done for him in Africa: De Long would become another Stanley; his Livingstone would be the Pole itself. As De Long's wife, Emma, put it, "the polar virus was in his blood and would not let him rest."

The *Jeannette* had last been seen by the homebound Pacific whaling fleet east of Wrangel Land – a mysterious realm that some thought stretched like a bridge to the Pole itself. (It was actually an island.) That was in September 1879. Now it was June 1881, and nothing had been heard or seen of the missing ship for twenty-two months. Some doubts, in fact, had been cast on her seaworthiness.

Before it left, the Lady Franklin Bay Expedition, as it was officially named, was given a secondary task – to search for any clues to the *Jeannette* in the ice-bound waters north of Ellesmere Island. There was an element of unofficial competition here: both the U.S. Navy and the U.S. Army had mounted expeditions to seek the Pole. Now the Army had been ordered to search out and perhaps rescue the missing naval vessel. The bluecoats of the senior service would have been less than human if that had not rankled.

The Army officer selected to take charge of this ambitious undertaking was a studious, straight-backed New England puritan named Adolphus Washington Greely, who, characteristically, preferred to use his initials "A.W." He was thirty-eight years old, a wiry, six-foot-one-inch veteran of the Civil War, bearded and bespectacled, well read but humourless, and a stickler for military discipline. Indeed, he was something of a martinet, an indication, perhaps, of an inner insecurity that would make itself felt in the ordeal to come. His creed was the work ethic. He did not countenance gambling for money; he allowed no frivolity on Sunday; he permitted no profane language among his men.

He was brave – he had shown that during his Civil War service; but he could also be irritable, and he didn't like to be crossed. He had a strong sense of his position as a commissioned officer and of the importance of maintaining a gap between himself and his enlisted men. Although he was not imaginative, he was ambitious. He wanted the Arctic posting badly, and he got it through the help of Captain Henry Howgate, a fellow officer in the Signal Corps, who had also been infected by the polar virus. Howgate, in fact, had tried unsuccessfully to mount an Arctic expedition of his own, with Greely's help. Neither man had ever been to the Arctic – nor had any of the officers and soldiers who would accompany Greely north – but Greely had devoured every book and journal he could find that dealt with the polar regions. He felt he had some useful experience, for he had survived a devastating three-day blizzard in the Sioux country of the American West. Clearly, the Army felt he was the best they could supply to establish a scientific station on Lady Franklin Bay. Of Greely's twenty-four followers, half were officers or non-commissioned officers, an indication of the importance the Army placed on the expedition.

The ship that would take this party north and deposit it on the inhospitable shores of Ellesmere Island was a 467-ton sealer, the *Proteus,* a rugged steamer built of oak and ironwood. Early in July, 1881, she reached St. John's, where the native Newfoundlanders, long since accustomed to polar parties shifting back and forth through their capital, showed a marked lack of interest in her departure. She crossed the treacherous Melville Bay in a record thirty-six hours – a remarkable feat – and reached her destination on August 11.

Greely had already written a last letter to his wife, Henrietta, which the *Proteus* would carry back: "I think of you always and most continually. I wonder what you and the darling babes are doing. I desire continually you and your society, our home and its comforts. I am content at being here only that I hope from and through it the future may be made brighter and happier for you and the children. Will it? We will so hope and trust. There seems so little outside of you and the babes that is of any real and true value to me. . . ."

Now here he was, as far from civilization as it was possible to get, almost a thousand miles north of the Arctic Circle, six hundred miles south of the Pole, living with two dozen followers in a barren hut named Fort Conger and facing, on that very first night, the same tensions that Hall and Kane had encountered and that the American government had hoped to forestall.

Both of his lieutenants, James B. Lockwood and Frederick Kislingbury, had been in the habit of lying in bed long after breakfast call when the enlisted men were up and about. Greely resented this and gave both men a dressing down. When Lockwood admitted his delinquency and promised to reform, Greely forgave him, although the promised reform took several weeks. But the other lie-abed, Kislingbury, took Greely's words in bad part, and that Greely couldn't abide. When Kislingbury continued to sleep in, Greely, nervous about his command, brought matters to a head in an acrimonious encounter that ended when Kislingbury asked to be recalled.

Obviously, there was more to it than that. Kislingbury, a veteran of fifteen years' Army service, eight on the frontier, had been the first to volunteer. He had lost two wives in three years and was now the single father of four small boys. The trip, he said, was "a Godsend . . . a wonderful chance to wear out my second terrible sorrow." Now he was throwing it all away. Obviously he felt he could not get along with his commander.

438

But Kislingbury had left his decision too late. The *Proteus* had unloaded her stores and was ready to leave as soon as the ice blocking the harbour cleared. On August 26, noticing that the way to the sea was open, the captain, in ignorance of Kislingbury's resignation, steamed off, leaving Kislingbury making his way across the ice toward the ship.

It was an unfortunate turn of events. Greely now had a supernumerary on his hands, a man who had resigned his command, who could be given no work of any kind, and who actively despised him. The feeling was mutual, aggravated by the close conditions under which all would suffer. It was one of those foolish standoffs that sometimes make grown men act like small boys. Greely needed Kislingbury. Kislingbury needed to be an active member of the company; all he had to do was swallow his pride and apply for reinstatement. Greely clearly expected this, but it didn't happen. All Greely had to do was *offer* reinstatement and Kislingbury would have jumped at it. Many months later, when both men were at the end of their tether, Greely relented. But for most of that long time of troubles, neither would unbend.

There were other problems. At Godhavn, Greenland, the expedition's remaining four men had been taken aboard – two Eskimo dog drivers, Jens Edward and Frederick Christiansen, and two civilian volunteers, Henry Clay (grandson of the great Kentucky orator) and a surgeon, Dr. Octave Pavy. Pavy was the problem. He and Clay quarrelled so viciously that one would have to go. Greely, who could not spare the doctor, agreed that Clay would return with the *Proteus*. Clay made the ship that Kislingbury missed.

Pavy was not an easy man to deal with. Mercurial, often moody, ambitious, this high-domed, pipe-smoking scientist felt himself superior to the others – as Dr. Bessels had on the Hall voyage. There was no doubt in his mind that he would make a better leader of the expedition than Greely. Technically, he was now a soldier, but he considered himself above military discipline; and there was little that Greely could do about that. As scientific leader of the expedition and its only doctor, Pavy was immune.

Except for his interest in polar exploration, which was obsessive, Pavy had very little in common with his commander. In fact, it would have been difficult to discover two more disparate characters. The strait-laced Greely didn't like him, was suspicious of his motives, and referred to him as a "Bohemian," a word that, in Greely's puritan lexicon, carried connotations of the devil.

Pavy's background was both romantic and bizarre. The son of a wealthy French plantation owner and cotton merchant in New Orleans, he had been educated in Paris, where he studied both science and medicine. He had travelled widely in Europe – French was his first language – and considered himself a connoisseur of painting and sculpture. But the virus was in him, too: the Arctic captivated him; the mystery of the Pole magnetized him. In his early twenties he had encountered the French explorer Gustav Lambert and planned with him a polar expedition that was aborted only by the onset of the Franco-Prussian War. Pavy fought with distinction as a captain in the Black Guerrillas. But his Arctic hopes were dashed when Lambert was killed.

Back in the United States, Pavy had fallen under the spell of Charles Francis Hall, with whom he held daily conversations. When Hall headed north on his government-sponsored expedition, Pavy sought to out-do him with a private one. Like De Long, he was convinced that the proper route to the Pole led through the Bering Sea, and so the "Pavy Expedition to the North Pole" was born in San Francisco. In a weird turn of fortune, the chief financial backer was murdered by his valet just before the expedition was to sail in the summer of 1872. Pavy was given the news while attending a fashionable ball. It changed his life.

For the next four years, sunk in despondency, the thwarted explorer became a vagabond, living along the banks of the Missouri River – a ragged, threadbare, and friendless wanderer, working at a series of menial jobs until he was taken up by two Missouri physicians. Suddenly, he was back in society, completing his medical studies, marrying into a well-to-do family, and lecturing at the St. Louis Academy of Science. In 1880 he headed for the Arctic. The following year, at Godhavn, he boarded the *Proteus* and became part of the Greely expedition.

There is something splendidly ironic about Pavy's connection with the International Polar Year. The Greely expedition, following Karl Weyprecht's philosophy, was supposed to be devoted entirely to scientific observation; the romantic idea of a "race to the Pole" had no part in its conception. Yet the scientist placed in charge at Lady Franklin Bay was less interested in meticulous observation than he

440

was in the adventure of polar discovery. Octave Pierre Pavy was determined to get as close to the Pole as possible – and to beat out any possible rival, including the members of his own expedition.

Greely was by no means immune to a similar ambition. At the very least, he wanted to push one party farther north than Markham of the Nares party had gone five years before. That fall he sent out two parties under Lockwood and Pavy to scout the land and set up depots for the spring sledging. He had already picked Lockwood – a tireless worker in spite of his problems at early morning rising – to try to beat the British record. But Pavy was determined to forestall him. That October, while on a sledging trip with Jens, the cheerful Eskimo dog driver, he revealed his plan to young Private William Whisler, his sledgemate. He promised he'd take Whisler with him in the spring to try to reach the highest northern latitude yet attained. He would manage this by having Whisler steal the expedition's only remaining dogteam. Without dogs, Lockwood wouldn't be able to travel as far, and Pavy would grab the glory. When Whisler refused, Pavy became abusive and angry. Whisler threatened him with a revolver, and there the matter ended. Whisler kept the plot to himself and didn't reveal it to Greely until both were on the point of death. Pavy and Whisler had attempted to reach Cape Joseph Henry on Ellesmere's northern coast but couldn't reach it. Nor did they find any traces of the missing *Jeannette*.

For 136 days, from mid-October 1881 to the end of February 1882, the twenty-five men closeted in the small hut they named Fort Conger were without the sun. Marooned on those bleak and treeless shores, hemmed in by sullen, wall-like cliffs that rose as high as a thousand feet, they did their best to pass the time playing Parcheesi and chess, backgammon and cards (but never for money), engaging in theatricals, taking classes in everything from grammar to meteorology, and publishing a newspaper, the *Arctic Moon*. Greely himself lectured on "the Arctic question," a euphemism for the North Pole discovery, which, as George Rice, the civilian photographer who had been given sergeant's rank, remarked, was "a subject especially absorbing to those present."

The four officers lived precariously, crammed together into a fifteen-by-seventeen-foot space and separated from the enlisted men by an entry alcove and a kitchen. The mordant Pavy, who felt confined "like a white bear in its cage," had gravitated toward the equally sarcastic Kislingbury; they shared a common distaste for Greely, whose "indomitable vanity" (Pavy's words) and rigid discipline continued to chafe.

To the restless young James Lockwood, eager to be off on his northern quest, the months seemed to stretch off endlessly. "Surely this is a happy quartet occupying this room!" he wrote sardonically in his journal that fall. "We often sit silent during the whole day and even a meal fails to elicit anything more than a chance remark or two. A charming prospect for four months of darkness penned up as we are. . . ."

Lockwood longed for relief, but there was none. They had arrived in the High Arctic to experience the coldest winter on record. The enlisted men became depressed, growling over the least imagined slight. Pavy noted sourly that "they say and express loudly that they came here only to make a stake. That they have no desire and interest to make discoveries and that if they could return next year, they will do so."

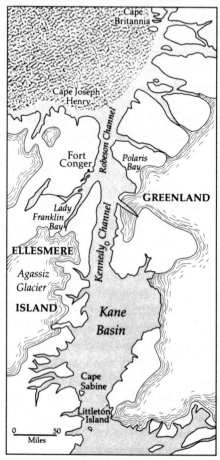

Greely at Fort Conger, 1881-83

On December 5, Jens, the Eskimo dog driver – a great favourite – ran away, apparently prepared to die from starvation or suicide. A search party found him, sullen and stubborn, and convinced him that no one had intended to wrong him. Two days later, his companion, Frederick, armed with a large wooden cross, presented himself to the officers, claiming that the men were going to shoot him. He announced that he was going away to die and was restrained only with

442

difficulty. Small wonder that Sergeant David Brainard, when he finally located Charles Hall's grave at Polaris Bay – an equally desolate prospect – sounded a wan note in his diary. "One scarcely wonders that Hall died," he wrote. "I think the gloom would drive me to suicide in a week." That night Brainard kept his spirits up with some of Lockwood's rum punch.

Late in April 1882, Greely dispatched his two main expeditions to try to better the British record of Farthest North. Pavy would take one party up the coast of Ellesmere Island, following it to Cape Joseph Henry, its northern tip, to try to beat Markham's record. Lockwood would take a second across Robeson Channel to the Greenland coast and then north in Beaumont's tracks.

Pavy had the bad luck to encounter open water. He returned empty handed and, if the letters Greely wrote to his wife in the expectation of a relief ship are to be believed, more surly than ever. Greely had already written that the doctor was "an arrant mischief maker." Now he described him to Henrietta Greely as a "tricky double-faced man, idle, unfit for any Arctic work except doctoring & sledge travel & not first class in the latter." Pavy and Kislingbury were now spending most of their time together, "united by the common wish and desire to break down the commander but not daring to openly act to that effect."

Greely's hope lay in Lockwood, who was facing harsh conditions in his attempts to better the British record. Within a week, four of his men had broken down and been sent back to Fort Conger. Brainard, his second-in-command, described the blowing snow as "like handfuls of gravel thrown in our faces." On April 29, on the northern coast of Greenland, with Cape Britannia in the distance, Lockwood sent all but two of his men back, three to wait at the *Polaris* boat camp, the others to return to the ship. Fred, the dog driver, was indispensable, and Brainard, in spite of snowblindness, was still the strongest and most steadfast of the group. This pair would accompany him on the final dash to break the record.

At twenty-four, Sergeant Brainard – blue-eyed, firm-jawed, and handsome – had already seen five years of service with the 2nd Cavalry. He had joined the Army at nineteen on an impulse, having left his home in Norway to visit the Philadelphia Centennial Exposition. Changing trains on the way back to New York, he found he'd lost the money he'd been keeping to buy a ticket home. He was too proud to write for help; instead, he took the free ferry to Governor's

Island and signed up. Wounded in the Indian wars in the West, he'd been ready to return to civilian life when the Arctic beckoned. Here he proved his mettle. Greely called him "my mainstay in many things," and so, in the dark days that followed, he would prove to be. David Brainard was all soldier. Others in that strangely assorted company might whine, grumble, and plot; not he.

In his own words, he "stumbled about all day like a blind man," his eyes smarting from the glare as if scoured by red-hot sand. In spite of that, the party made good time. On May 4, at four-thirty in the morning, the bulk of Cape Britannia loomed out of the haze. Beaumont had seen it, but, wracked by scurvy, had never reached it. The two Americans and their Eskimo driver, sucking on lemon-juice lozenges, arrived at its base at seven-thirty that evening and unfurled a small American flag to mark their triumph.

They pressed on for another ten days until their supplies ran out. At latitude 83^0 $24'$ N they built "a magnificent cairn which will endure for ages" and planted another Stars and Stripes on the spot. For the first time in three centuries, it was a non-British expedition that had reached the highest explored latitude on the globe, and Brainard was determined to mark it in a uniquely American way. Everywhere he had travelled, he noted, he had always seen a malt liquor called Plantation Bitters advertised conspicuously. Nothing would do but that he climb the face of a volcanic cliff and carve out the company's familiar trademark: *St 1860 X* ("Started trade in 1860 with ten dollars"). That done, it was time to head for home.

They had managed to get one hundred nautical miles farther north than Beaumont but only four miles farther than Markham. Nonetheless, the record stood for thirteen years. They had also charted eighty-five miles of unexplored Greenland coastline. On the return journey they came upon one of Beaumont's cairns containing a message detailing the onset of scurvy, from which, thanks to an improved diet and the lemon-juice lozenges, they were happily free. But two of the support party had been so badly blinded by the glare that they had to be led back by the hand to Fort Conger. They reached it on June 11.

Lockwood's victory did not sit well with the jealous Dr. Pavy, who was so persistently rude and hostile to him that Lockwood pleaded with Greely not to send the two out together the following spring. Greely refused. Scientific observations, he said, had to take precedence over personal failings. Greely himself set out that summer to explore the interior of Grinnell Land, as the mid-section of Ellesmere Island was called, seeking if possible to find a route through that fiord-riven domain to the "Western Sea" – in short another North West Passage. In this he was unsuccessful, but he did unlock many of the secrets of Ellesmere's mountainous interior – a country so rugged that when he and his men returned, their bleeding toes protruded from what was left of their tattered boots.

By August 1882, the party began to look forward to the arrival of the supply ship from the south, bringing new provisions, new personnel, and, far more important, mail and news from home. Days passed; nothing. Yet the harbour was relatively clear of ice, more open than it had been the previous year. Greely could not know that the ship, the *Neptune,* was two hundred miles to the south, vainly striving to force its way through a frozen barrier that could not be breached.

As hopes began to fade, the company was faced with the dismaying prospect of a second winter cut off from civilization. "The life we are leading now is somewhat similar to a prisoner in the Bastile [*sic*]," the impatient Lockwood wrote, "no amusements, no recreations, no event to break the monotony. . . . The others are as moody as I am – Greely sometimes, Kislingbury always, and as to the doctor, to say he is not congenial is to put it in a very mild way indeed." On the other hand, "the hilarity in the other room is in marked contrast to the gloom in this."

By late fall, with no hope of relief, the mood grew even darker. Sergeant William Cross, the glowering, black-bearded former machinist who had charge of the expedition's motor launch, *Lady Greely,* got drunk on spirit-lamp fuel pilfered from the little vessel and tumbled, senseless, into the icy waters of the harbour. Brainard pulled him out and because, like Pavy, he was indispensable, Greely treated him leniently. When Greely wasn't present Kislingbury and Pavy engaged in what Lockwood called "the most gloomy prognostications as to the future, and in adverse criticisms on the conduct of the expedition." Sometimes, Lockwood thought, the life of an exile in Siberia would be preferable. The only reading available consisted of novels and books on the Arctic. Lockwood, in studying these, became convinced, as did others, that Isaac Hayes had exaggerated his own exploits. He could not, for instance, have come anywhere near Cape Lieber as he claimed. To reach that farthest point he would have had to travel ninety-six miles in fourteen hours, a clear impossibility.

The monotonous winter dragged on. Because of the danger from polar bears the men were ordered to stay within five hundred feet of the hut, a restriction that made exercise boring. Brainard noticed the "state of nervousness our idleness has brought on all of us." The smallest things caused aggravation and annoyance. To combat lassitude Greely had forbidden the men to sleep in their bunks during the day. The Christmas celebration, Brainard noted, was a mockery. No other expedition had spent a second winter this far north; no other had experienced nights longer or darker than these. On New Year's Eve, there was barely enough spirit left to get up a dance. Fred, the Eskimo driver, was the star of the evening, dancing a hornpipe that at last brought a few chuckles from the downcast assembly.

Lockwood was in a frenzy to be off to reach the 84th parallel and set a new record. He left on March 2, 1883, with a party that again included Brainard and Frederick, his comrades on the previous journey. This time they failed. The polar pack, which the year before allowed the sledges to make shortcuts across the frozen inlets, was breaking up early. The party barely escaped drowning when the dogs crashed through the thin ice near Repulse Haven on Greenland's north shore. Lockwood wanted to keep on, but Greely's orders had been explicit: if the pack started to break up he was to return at once and not endanger human life. Brainard told him he had no choice. They arrived back at Fort Conger on April 11, 1883.

Lockwood was grievously disappointed. "Do I take up my pen to write the humiliating word *failed?*" he wrote. "I do, and bitter is the dose. . . ." He was eager to go out again – anything to get away from the morose Pavy and the gloomy Kislingbury – and so proposed a new scheme that, he insisted, would see him exceed his previous record and still be back within forty-four days. Greely quashed it; it wasn't prudent, he told Lockwood.

Lockwood promptly came up with an alternative plan – to go west along the north shore of Grinnell Land and then north to surpass the English again in new discoveries. This time Greely agreed. The romantic idea of an international race of discovery – the very kind of geographical contest that Karl Weyprecht had deprecated and this expedition was supposed to eschew – now seemed uppermost in everybody's mind. Lockwood took Brainard and Frederick with him

446

again; there was no more talk of Pavy travelling with him that spring. They set off on April 25, and this time their explorations bore fruit.

While the others continued with the ambitious scientific program the trio charted more of the interior of Grinnell Land. They discovered the vast Agassiz Glacier, which sprawls for eighty-five square miles over the heart of Ellesmere Island. They crossed the divide to the "Western Ocean" – a long fiord that led, not to the open sea, but to a tangle of islands off Ellesmere's western coast. On their return they came upon an unexpected sight: another of those strange fossil forests that are scattered across the face of the Arctic – trees nine inches thick, turned to stone, that hint at a temperate northern world before the ice ages.

Lockwood, Brainard, and Frederick had achieved for the Greely expedition three new records: a Farthest North, a Farthest East, and a Farthest West – records the British had held for three centuries. They had travelled by foot and dogsled a distance equal to one-eighth of the world's circumference at the eightieth parallel. Geographical exploration and national sentiment had again taken precedence over scientific observation. That became painfully clear when Greely discovered that Dr. Pavy's own collections were in a shambles. The doctor was far more interested in scoring geographical firsts than he was in keeping a systematic scientific record. He had deceived Greely, claiming that his specimens were properly preserved and that he'd kept careful notes. He had not. The "collection" was a vast jumble of artifacts, skins, pressed flowers, and rocks. Greely fired Pavy as scientific leader and appointed Lockwood, who had no training, to bring order out of chaos. In the end it didn't matter. The specimens, which Lockwood arranged, noted, and carefully packed, had to be abandoned.

Pavy's contract terminated on July 20. He announced he did not intend to renew it but would continue to attend to the men's medical needs free of charge until the expedition returned to the United States. Greely was outraged. He ordered the doctor to turn over all his official observations and memoranda to be sealed and kept for the Chief Signal Officer, as the original instructions provided. Pavy bluntly refused. He claimed his journal had no scientific value and contained only "personal and intimate thoughts . . . of an entirely private character." That wasn't entirely true, but there were some personal and intimate thoughts – those that criticized Greely and some of the others.

Greely put Pavy under arrest. Pavy blustered. Greely remained firm. He would not confine him, he said – the party needed a doctor – but he was determined to charge him with disobedience to orders and place him before a court-martial when the expedition returned.

He had a more pressing concern. What if the relief ship should again be blocked by ice? Before sailing, he had worked out a careful plan for that eventuality. If the relief ship didn't get through in 1882, she was to deposit supplies on the western shores of Kennedy Channel. These he could pick up if he was forced to retreat down the eastern coastline of Grinnell Land. He had laid out similarly detailed instructions for the failure of a second relief expedition in 1883, fully expecting that additional caches would be left at specific points both at Cape Sabine and farther north in the area of Cape Bache. In addition, the relief ship was to leave a depot of provisions at Littleton Island on the Greenland side, directly across the twenty-three-mile channel from Cape Sabine. Here a winter station would be established. Men with telescopes would search the shoreline of Ellesmere daily looking for the Greely party as it made its way south.

Greely had no real worries about supplies. With the depots he himself had established on the way north, he expected to find seven caches along the coastline. His orders were to leave Fort Conger by September 1, 1883, if the relief ship failed to appear. If necessary he could winter near the depot at Cape Sabine – a rock island 245 miles to the south, just off the Ellesmere coast at the head of Smith Sound. The relief party in winter quarters at Littleton Island would be able to cross the channel to help them, or, if the weather was right, his own party could make its way to the island by open boat and steam launch.

Greely didn't intend to wait until the September deadline. He had long since decided to leave for the south in early August if no ship appeared. He was convinced he would meet it somewhere along the Ellesmere coast, probably only a few miles south of Fort Conger.

Hindsight suggests that it would have been better to stay put. Game was plentiful in the area of Lady Franklin Bay, but conditions were quite different farther south. Adolphus Greely of course had no way of knowing the tragedy that was being forced on him by events over which he had no control. And so, on August 9, 1883, in two open boats and the steam launch, the party set off through the jostling ice pack on the second stage of its long ordeal.

2

The two attempts that were made to reach the Lady Franklin Bay *Abandoned*
Expedition in the summers of 1882 and 1883 were characterized by
bureaucratic bungling, vague and often contradictory orders, and
flawed planning.

The supply ship *Neptune* set off for the North in the summer of
1882, carrying more than eight tons of provisions for Greely and his
party. The man in charge of the expedition – but not of the ship –
was Private William Beebe, private secretary to General William
Babcock Hazen, the Chief Signal Officer and Greely's superior.
Beebe had asked for a promotion to sergeant "or better still . . .
lieutenant," but that request was denied. (He was later damned in the
press as a man that Hazen "knew to be an habitual drunkard.")

The *Neptune* deposited two small caches of 250 rations, one on the
Ellesmere coastline, the other at Littleton Island off Greenland. It
struggled for forty days to get through the pack at Kane Basin and
then returned to St. John's with a ton of canned meats, an equal
amount of fruit, and some six tons of seal meat, all of which might
have been left for the retreating Greely party. Poor Beebe could not
be blamed; he was following the general's orders to bring back the
rest of the supplies if the ship couldn't get through. A more experienced officer with a higher rank might have acted on his own. Private
Beebe did as he was told.

Henrietta Greely, the explorer's young wife, did her best to "simu-
late calmness," as she told James Lockwood's mother, after she
learned that the *Neptune* had failed to reach the party. After all, her
husband's expedition was provisioned for three years and, with the
fresh game available and with careful rationing, could probably hold
out for four. As far as she knew there would be no debilitating sledge
journeys toward the Pole; these men were to remain at Fort Conger
doing scientific work. All the same, with the help of the senior Lockwood – he was, after all, a general – she was doing some lobbying
behind the scenes in Washington for a better-equipped and better-led
expedition in 1883.

Mrs. Greely had long since come to terms with her husband's
obsession with the Arctic. It had been an obstacle to their marriage
in 1878, when Dolph Greely was trying vainly to help his friend

Howgate set up a North Pole expedition. "I could not think of going without you were my wife," he had written to her. "I should suffer untold agony while gone in thinking of you . . . I *could* not endure it! You must say that we will have a few months of happiness and of each other."

She had been torn, then. "Are not your ambition and pride guiding you to the exclusion of all other thought?" she asked him. She would rather be his wife than the widow of a dead hero, she declared. "I am *not* Lady Franklin. My spirit may be willing but my flesh is weak." Fortunately for her, the Howgate expedition came to nothing. They were married in June 1878. She bore him two children, made her peace with his ambitions, and, in the finest tradition of Arctic exploration, presented him when he left with a silk flag she had personally embroidered, to be placed on lands unknown.

Now, in the winter of 1882-83, she began to read the journals of Kane, Hayes, and other Arctic explorers until, like Lady Franklin, she became as knowledgeable about the frozen world as those who had dispatched her husband to examine it.

Her efforts and those of the Lockwood family bore fruit. They had chosen the *Proteus* as the best possible vessel to reach the expedition. Its skipper, Captain Pike, was a veteran of forty years in the sealing fields. Two years earlier he had taken the *Proteus* to Lady Franklin Bay. Now, under the same master, the sealer and its crew of New-foundlanders were the Army's ideal choice to repeat the voyage. The Navy supplied an escort vessel, the *Yantic,* to accompany her. The *Yantic* wasn't strong enough to invade the main pack, but she could act as a supply ship and, if necessary, an auxiliary rescue vessel.

The Secretary of War, Robert Todd Lincoln, son of the murdered president, wanted to clear up the whole embarrassing mess as quickly as possible. He had always been lukewarm to Arctic exploration. Now he was being harried by the press not only for the failure of the *Neptune* but also for his inability to bring Greely's old comrade, the would-be Arctic explorer Captain Henry Howgate, to justice. Shortly after Greely left for the North, Howgate was discovered to have embezzled $200,000 in Army funds, which he squandered on a paramour. Unfortunately, he had managed to escape custody and was now at large with a covey of Pinkerton detectives vainly trying to find him.

Even worse was the sobering news that trickled in from the *Jeannette* expedition, a tragic failure that had cost the lives of a

450

dozen men, including its commander, George De Long. Early in the fall of 1879, the vessel had been trapped and held in thrall by the ice pack beyond Wrangel Island, an experience that convinced De Long the theory of a warm gateway to the Arctic was "a delusion and a snare." For the next twenty-two months, the ship remained in the grip of the ice, which bore it slowly north and west along the Siberian coast until it was finally crushed and destroyed. The crew of thirty-three left the foundering vessel in three open boats and set off on a dreadful odyssey through the ice-choked Eastern Passage, the mainland several hundred miles away. After two months the boats became separated. One was lost in a gale; the other two landed at separate points in the bewildering maze of the Lena Delta in central Siberia. One party managed to find a native village and was eventually rescued. The other, led by De Long, perished on the tundra from starvation and exhaustion.

The subsequent naval inquiry in the winter and spring of 1882-83 (to be followed by a congressional inquiry) had turned up the usual stories of dissension, insubordination, rival cliques, plotted mutiny, and threats of court-martial – "a spirit of turmoil," one survivor called it – that were familiar to Arctic veterans but served to tarnish the glamour that had once captured the public. Small wonder, then, that Secretary Lincoln, and indeed the president himself, had little stomach for further Arctic adventure. All they wanted to do was get the whole imbroglio over as quickly as possible.

This time, the man in charge of the Greely relief expedition would be no office clerk but a career Army officer. Lieutenant Ernest A. Garlington was a thirty-year-old West Point graduate, "sober, persistent and able," in General Hazen's estimation. Hazen was positively ebullient about the success of the expedition. "Everything that the most careful study and close attention could devise has been attended to and will be availed of," he told the press. And to Henrietta Greely, he declared, "I am confident everything will go right."

Everything, in fact, went wrong. The *Proteus* was to be loaded with enough provisions to last forty men fifteen months, but Garlington and his crew were not on hand to supervise loading of these supplies onto the relief ship when she reached St. John's. Instead, they were shipped out of New York on the *Alhambra* on June 7 in charge of a young, newly married sergeant named Wall. Garlington and the rest of his men did not leave until four days later on the *Yantic*. Garlington had urged that they travel with the provisions, but that request was turned down on the grounds that discipline would be easier to maintain aboard a naval vessel.

When the *Alhambra* reached Halifax, Wall quit, having, it was said, been "injured by an accident"; a more believable suggestion was that he was eager to be back with his bride. Since no one from Garlington's crew was present when the supplies were unloaded from the *Alhambra* at St. John's and stowed aboard the *Proteus,* nobody knew exactly where anything was. To reach the meteorological instruments, for instance, the stores had to be broken into. The location of the guns and ammunition was never pinpointed, a delinquency that was to have serious consequences.

General Hazen appeared to harbour the belief that Greely was running short of supplies at Fort Conger. His orders to Garlington stressed haste. "Lieutenant Greely's supplies will be exhausted during the coming fall, and unless the relief ship can reach him he will be forced, with his party, to retreat southward by land before the winter sets in."

Actually, Greely had gone north with enough provisions to last three years and enough coffee, beans, sugar, and salt to last four and a half years. In addition he had, at the outset, three months' supply of fresh muskox meat, which could certainly be added to by the hunters in his party. The expedition could easily have remained at Fort Conger for another year in relative comfort and reasonably good health if Greely had not been ordered specifically to get out by September 1; and Greely was the kind of man who was a stickler for orders.

". . . no effort must be spared to push the vessel through to Lady Franklin Bay," was Hazen's written order to Garlington. He took this to mean that he shouldn't stop for anything – not for the slower *Yantic,* not to unload supplies at Littleton Island, not to pause on the way north to unload more supplies, not even to replenish existing caches on the coast of Ellesmere Island.

There was ambiguity here. For one thing, Garlington was told that the *Proteus* and the *Yantic* must stick together as far as Littleton Island, where the *Yantic* was to await his return – that would force him to wait for the slower vessel. And, though he wasn't told to stop on the way – the orders suggested the opposite – if he *did* stop, then he was to examine the depots for damage and, if necessary, replenish them. But the emphasis was on haste. If he couldn't get through, the orders read, he was to return to Littleton Island, unload his supplies, and search the opposite coastline for signs of Greely's party.

To add to the confusion, Garlington found included in the envelope that contained his orders a second memorandum that seemed to contradict Hazen's instructions. This one told him he *should* unload supplies at Littleton Island en route north and also at the various coastal depots. If the *Proteus* foundered, the *Yantic* was to bring the survivors back to Littleton Island. But the *Yantic* was given more leeway to go her own way if the ice conditions became too dangerous. This sensible memorandum, the result of some equally sensible afterthought – none of it officially approved – had been tacked onto Garlington's instructions as the result of a clerical error. Garlington questioned it: was it part of the official order? he asked. He was told it was not. That helped save Garlington's skin in the inquiry that followed.

He did not wait for the *Yantic*. He left St. John's on June 29 and pushed directly on to Godhavn on Disco Island off the Greenland coast. The *Yantic* limped along far in the wake of *Proteus* – as well adapted for the ice, in the words of one observer, "as a Brooklyn ferry boat" – and then, with her boilers giving out, stopped at Upernavik for a week of repairs.

Garlington, in the *Proteus,* blocked by the ice pack in Kane Basin, crossed Smith Sound and entered Payer Harbour off Cape Sabine on July 22. Here were two caches, one left by Beebe near the point of the cape the previous year and, on a small island about half a mile from the *Proteus*'s anchorage, another left by the Nares expedition in 1875. The Beebe cache was found and repaired, but in the four and a half hours that the *Proteus* stayed at Cape Sabine, no extra provisions were landed, even though these were easily available, having been stowed on board at Godhavn in separate packages especially for this purpose. Garlington's almost frantic insistence on getting under way frustrated any chance of leaving a substantial cache of food and fuel for the Greely party, which would, within a fortnight, begin its long struggle with the ice down the Ellesmere coastline.

From the shore, the impetuous Garlington thought he saw an open lane of water leading north. He hurried aboard the ship and ordered Captain Pike to get moving. Pike demurred. It was too early in the season, he insisted: what Garlington had seen was no more than the ice shifting with the tide. Garlington was stubborn. Unless the *Pro-

teus moved, he insisted, "he should not consider himself as performing his duty to the people at Lady Franklin Bay or the United States Government." And so a veteran of forty years of Arctic service was overruled by a thirty-year-old landlubber. The *Proteus* weighed anchor and headed out of the harbour. Fifteen minutes later she entered the loose pack.

She was a sturdy ship, built for the ice, but a decade in the sealing grounds had taken its toll. Her boilers were defective, two of her lifeboats unseaworthy, her rigging old, and her compass untrustworthy. The captain's twenty-one-year-old son was first mate; it was his first time in the Arctic. The second mate was the captain's cousin. The chief engineer had just been promoted to that post when the ship sailed. But even a new ship with an experienced crew could not have survived the beating the *Proteus* took the following afternoon.

She had tried to bull her way through a barrier of pack ice toward an open lane without success. Heavy floes, some ten feet thick, were pouring south through the narrow passage of Smith Sound. In the nip that followed at three o'clock, the sealer was in the worst possible position, headed east-west, so that the ice caught her amidships. Gripped in a hammer-lock between the pressure of the advancing ice and the unyielding barrier of the shore pack, she had no chance. Her starboard rail was crushed to matchwood at 4:30 p.m.

By this time Garlington and some of his men were desperately trying to untangle the jumble of stores in her hold. Another party at the forepeak was trying to save the parcels of prepared rations taken on in Greenland. These they hurled overboard onto the encroaching floes. A third of them tumbled into the sea and were lost.

Suddenly, the ship's sides burst open as a flood of ice and seawater poured into the bunkers and the hold. The ship stayed afloat, caught and held by the pressure of the ice against her, until 7:30, when the tide turned and she began to sink. By then the scene on the floes was chaotic.

Everything had to be abandoned, including the sledges and the dogs that were to have been used to succour the Greely party. There had been no boat drill; it was every man for himself. The Newfoundland sealers were interested only in saving themselves and their kits. With the ship foundering, their contracts came to an end, and they had no further responsibility to any but themselves. Now they began to plunder the relief expedition's supplies, rifling open boxes on the ice for clothing and food. There was nothing Garlington could do,

454

for his fourteen soldiers were weaponless. All the guns and ammunition had been stowed helter skelter in the hold in St. John's.

Pike could not control his own crew. "You've got a lot of *men*," he told Garlington ruefully. "But I've got a lot of dirty dogs who are too mean to live." All Garlington could do was to try to prevent a confrontation by keeping his group at a distance from the "pirates and scoundrels" on the ice.

A worse concern faced him. He realized that Greely would arrive at Cape Sabine to find that the promised provisions had not been placed in the cache. With Pike's help he persuaded four seamen to go with some of his men in a whaleboat and deposit five hundred individual rations on the nearest point of land, about three miles west of the Cape. These would last Greely's party of twenty-five no more than three weeks.

What was he to do? The previous spring, the young cavalry officer had been out in the Dakotas. Now here he was, a man with no experience at sea, caught in the centre of the ice-choked channel, responsible not only for the men under his immediate command but also for the beleaguered party threading its way down the Ellesmere coast.

He had several choices. He could stay at Cape Sabine and wait for Greely, meanwhile eating up the supplies. He could head north, looking for Greely, a foolhardy course that he immediately dismissed. Or he could seek out the *Yantic,* which had plenty of provisions, leave two or three men with the *Yantic*'s supplies at Littleton Island to maintain a lookout for the lost party, and hustle back to St. John's with the others to arrange for a new ship and more provisions.

He opted for the last course, but with apprehension. Although his orders were to rendezvous with the *Yantic* at Littleton Island, Garlington couldn't believe that the little ship could make it across Melville Bay, that notoriously dangerous stretch of water that had once cost Leopold M'Clintock a year's delay. It would make more sense, Garlington thought, to go in search of the *Yantic.* Thus was set in motion a series of mischances that might be called a comedy of errors had the results not been so tragic.

The shipwrecked party crossed Smith Sound – the *Proteus*'s crew in three of the ship's lifeboats, the soldiers in two whaleboats – and reached Littleton Island on the morning of July 26. The *Yantic* had not yet arrived, and Garlington didn't believe it would. With only his own rations saved from the *Proteus,* he could leave nothing for

Greely but a message. That done, he hurried south seeking his consort.

Contrary to Garlington's supposition, the *Yantic had* crossed the unpredictable Melville Bay without difficulty and was steaming steadily north. A series of rendezvous points had been arranged along the Greenland coast. One of these was the Cary Islands, some twenty miles west of the mainland. Garlington, who knew nothing of navigation, decided to by-pass this meeting place because he felt the approaches were too hazardous to make a safe landing. In doing so he overruled his more experienced second-in-command, Lieutenant J.C. Colwell. Thus he missed the *Yantic,* which that very day was putting in to the same rendezvous point. Not finding any message, her commander continued to steam north, passing Garlington's party in the fog. That mischance finally doomed the Greely party to a winter of starvation.

The near-misses continued. The *Yantic* reached Littleton Island where its commander, Frank Wildes, learned that Garlington had left for the south. He steamed after him, neglecting to leave any supplies or message for Greely. When he landed at the Cary Islands he found no trace of Garlington and so went back north again, still seeking his elusive quarry. At one point, the *Yantic* was within four hours' steaming distance of Garlington's five boats, but the two parties failed to meet.

At Northumberland Island, Wildes found the remains of Garlington's camp – the first clue as to his current whereabouts. He decided to turn south again to Cape York, another of the rendezvous points, but as his fuel was low and the situation looked treacherous, when he reached Cape York he decided not to land. The date was August 10; by a maddening coincidence, Garlington's party had just arrived at that meeting place. But even as they beached their boats and set up camp, the *Yantic* was heading south toward Upernavik. Wildes reached it on August 12, hoping that Garlington would soon turn up.

Garlington, however, with his shipwrecked crew of sailors and soldiers, was still at Cape York. On August 16, he decided to send the experienced Colwell and a few men in one of the whaleboats to attempt a dash south across the treacherous waters of Melville Bay. He and the others, in the remaining four boats, would creep around the shoreline.

In a remarkable feat of navigation, Colwell reached Upernavik on August 23, only to find that the *Yantic,* having waited for ten days,

456

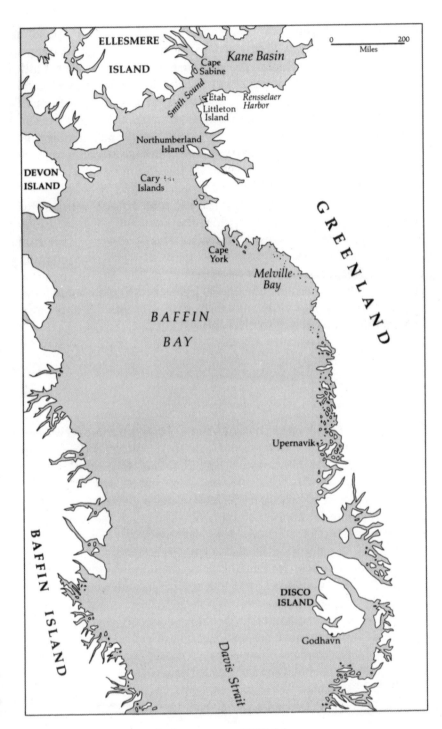

Area of the Greely relief attempts, 1882-84

had departed. Pausing only long enough to snatch some food and a few hours' sleep, Colwell borrowed an open launch from the governor and, with his exhausted men straining at the oars, headed south for Godhavn, the *Yantic*'s next port of call. He reached it and found the *Yantic* on August 31, having spent fifteen days in an open boat and covered close to nine hundred miles of some of the most treacherous water in the Arctic. Wildes took him and his men aboard the *Yantic* and returned to Upernavik, where Garlington's company and the crew of the *Proteus* were waiting. Thus, after more than a month of cat-and-mouse chase, the two search parties were reunited.

The survivors of the wrecked ship had come through without the loss of a man; but the relief mission that had brought them to the Kane Basin was a disaster. As General Hazen wrote to Henrietta Greely, it was too late in the season to mount another rescue attempt, but "no effort will be spared to set on foot another expedition at the earliest moment possible." Somehow Greely and his men would have to try to survive the winter on their own resources. "I hope," the general told Henrietta, "you will not be needlessly alarmed."

3

No turning On August 9, 1883, just as Garlington and his shipwrecked crew were
back vainly attempting a rendezvous at Cape York, Adolphus Greely and his men left the barren shores of Lady Franklin Bay and started on their long trek south. They left their dogs behind but did not kill them; they would be needed if the party were forced to return. They also left a winter's supply of food, albeit a meagre one. Each man was allowed to take no more than eight pounds of clothing and equipment, the officers sixteen. But Greely took more.

In addition to his scientific data, he insisted on bringing his dress uniform, sword, scabbard, and epaulettes, "an emblem of authority," as he told Lockwood. It was a significant remark, for had Greely been in firm command he would have needed no symbols. But in his attempts to hide his own uncertainties and irresolution he became a different man – imperious, irritable, unbalanced. On the second day out, he attacked the faithful Brainard with an undeserved tirade that astonished the stolid sergeant, who did not believe his commander capable of such profanity.

Like Garlington, Greely, the cavalryman and signal officer, had no idea of how to operate a boat in the ice, nor did any of his men. Only two had any sea training – Private Roderick Schneider, who had once been a seaman, and Sergeant Rice, the photographer, who had been raised on Cape Breton Island. Rice quickly became the hero of the journey. When the yacht, *Lady Greely*, steamed off into the ice-choked channel, towing three open boats, Rice, perched on the fore-deck of the jolly boat *Valorous*, developed an uncanny ability to spot lanes of open water. For his pains he suffered a series of duckings, which he took with good humour.

Even the gloomy Kislingbury thought the world of Rice, reserving his harshest condemnation for Greely. "Lt. G. controlling things," he wrote in his diary on August 13. "Poor man he knows nothing about the business, has not sense enough to put a good man like Rice as ice navigator . . . Lockwood could run things better than he does. We lose more distance, time and coal by his nonsense."

Kislingbury's comments might be taken as biased, but there were similar remarks in the diaries of others on that long journey. In order to establish authority, Greely tried to run things himself, refusing to listen to the counsel of others. Even Sergeant Joseph Elison, a more dispassionate observer, was vitriolic, referring to his commander as a "lunatic," a "miserable fool," "a fraud [and] a humbug."

Greely's temper did not improve when he discovered that Cross, the engineer aboard the yacht, was again getting blind drunk on fuel alcohol filched from the engine room. Greely's hands were tied: Cross, like Pavy, was essential to the expedition. Then, on August 15, he could stand it no longer; Cross was drunk again and insubordinate to the commander, whom he considered "a shirt tail navigator." In the bitter altercation that followed, Greely drew his pistol. "Shut up!" he shouted, "or else I put a bullet through you." At that Cross replied, "Go ahead!" Greely didn't shoot, but he suspended Cross and replaced him with Julius Frederick.

That same day an extraordinary incident took place that was not revealed until many years later. Everyone in the party was concerned because Greely was insisting on abandoning the launch, hoisting the boats onto an ice floe, and trying to drift nearly three hundred miles south to Littleton Island – an act that Brainard, for one, considered "little short of madness." On the day of the Cross incident, Pavy, Kislingbury, and Rice came to Brainard with a proposition. Pavy volunteered to examine Greely and pronounce him insane. It would

459

not be difficult, he explained, because the commander's frequent outbursts without provocation established a *prima facie* case of dementia.

Pavy said he was prepared to establish the legitimacy of his diagnosis before any later court of inquiry. Once Greely was shown to be incapable of maintaining leadership, he would be deposed and Kislingbury would assume control of the expedition. The party would at once turn about and go back to Fort Conger, spend the winter there, and then sledge south in the spring. If Lockwood refused to acknowledge Kislingbury's authority, he was to be placed under arrest. But the plotters had to have Brainard on their side. The men respected the senior sergeant and would follow his lead. Without him the plan was doomed.

Brainard was, by this time, almost certain that disaster was inevitable. He, too, thought the party's best chance was to return to Fort Conger. But Brainard was all Army, and this was mutiny. He was having no part of it. In fact, he said, he would resist any such attempt with his life. Nonetheless, he did not tell Greely, for he knew his obstinate nature and was convinced the commander would immediately put into practice the very plan they were resisting – to drift helplessly south with the polar pack. Brainard disclosed the plot only in 1890 and in doing so made it clear that he was not in any way condemning the plotters, who, he felt, were "impelled by a spirit of devotion to the expedition." Indeed, he wrote that had the plan been consummated, "it is not at all improbable that every man would have escaped with his life."

But the plan was abandoned. By August 22, the party had reached the halfway point between Fort Conger and Littleton Island. Now there was no turning back. By August 26, when they arrived at a depot that Nares had left at Cape Hawks, they had only sixty days of provisions left, augmented by 250 pounds of mouldy bread and 165 pounds of potatoes left by the English.

Greely could not understand why there was no sign of the relief vessel. More and more he despaired of reaching Littleton Island. If Cross and Kislingbury are to be believed, he had become benumbed, spending more and more time in his sleeping bag. The flotilla, now trapped in the ice, was drifting helplessly with the pack – a perilous position in which the boats could be crushed or destroyed at any moment. When he overheard Kislingbury discussing this with the men and publicly chafing at the inactivity of his superior, Greely upbraided him for undermining his authority. But on September 9 he did call a council of his officers and senior sergeants and turned the navigation over to Rice.

Their progress had been maddeningly slow. Beset in the ice for fifteen days, they had moved only twenty-two miles. The council decided to abandon the yacht and the jolly boat and haul the other boats and supplies across the ice to the Ellesmere shore, eleven miles to the west. Remarkably, the men unanimously agreed not to jettison the hundred-pound pendulum whose observations, taken at Fort Conger, would have no value unless they could be subsequently repeated with the same instrument. Off the party went – twenty-five men hauling sixty-five hundred pounds across the broken surface of the frozen sea. It was more than they could handle. Two days later the whaleboat also was abandoned.

To move everything one mile the men had to haul for five, shuttling the supplies forward bit by bit. The situation grew more dangerous. Even Brainard was shaken by the roar of the grinding pack to the east, "so terrible that even the bravest cannot appear unconcerned." The floe they were crossing was not connected to land but drifted helplessly about in the basin. When the wind suddenly shifted, the weary men realized they were being blown back north. By the afternoon of September 15, they had lost fifteen miles and were down to forty days' rations, together with whatever seal meat the two Eskimo hunters could shoot for them.

In order to prevent a further decline in morale, Greely forbade his meteorologist, young Sergeant Edward Israel, to disclose to the others any observations of latitude. Pavy, meanwhile, was bitterly denouncing his commander, claiming that had his advice been taken the party would have remained safely at Fort Conger. A nasty row ensued, but since the doctor was irreplaceable Greely again could take no action.

The wind changed. The floe spun about and began to drift south again. On September 19, land was spotted no more than three miles away. But where was the relief ship? There was no sign of human movement on the Ellesmere shore.

Again the wind shifted. The floe was driven back into the Kane Basin until they were farther north and east of land than before – a good twenty miles. Brainard was heartsick. "Misfortune and calamity, hand in hand, have clung to us along the entire line of this retreat. . . . To cross the floes over this distance seems a hopeless undertaking when we can average only about a mile and a quarter per day. And

461

now we have been shown what child's play the wind can make of our struggles. How can we put our heart and strength into hauling the sledges!" That night the wind abated and Greely called a council, urging that an attempt be made to cross to the Greenland shore by abandoning everything except twenty days' provisions, records, boat, and sledge. To Brainard that was madness.

The floe had become their prison. As long as it whirled about precariously in the moving pack – the ice grinding, crumbling, and piling up about the edges – there was no opportunity to reach land. The pressure on it increased until on September 25 the floe broke apart and the corner on which the party was camped fell away, leaving them marooned on a tiny chunk, the plaything of the winds, tides, and current. That afternoon the wind shifted again. To their dismay, they found that after thirty-two days adrift, they had passed Cape Sabine, where the food caches were supposedly waiting for them, and also the first point on the Ellesmere coast where the relief ship would have stopped.

Following another wild night the floe broke again, leaving them scarcely room enough to stand beside the boats. They were moving farther and farther south of their original destination at alarming speed in a violent ocean that seethed and foamed and could swamp them at any moment. "I see nothing but starvation and death," Lieutenant Lockwood wrote in his journal.

Two days later the floe slammed against a grounded iceberg, "an act of Providence," in Brainard's grateful words, that saved them from being driven into Baffin Bay. Now two lanes of water opened up through which they ferried the sledges and provisions to the Ellesmere shore, four miles away. By this time a third of the party was ill and Cross, the engineer, so hopelessly drunk on alcohol that he couldn't work the drag ropes on the sledges. But at least, after more than six weeks of exposure, hardship, and terror, they were on solid ground.

They realized they could not possibly cross the strait to Littleton Island. They would have to winter at this spot. The indefatigable Rice volunteered to trek north to Cape Sabine to find the cache. He and Jens, the Eskimo hunter, set off on October 1 with four days' rations while the others built three hovels on the barren, snow-covered rocks at the base of a conical hill, using the debris from some old Eskimo huts and the oars from the two boats.

Greely estimated the party had enough food to last thirty-five

462

days; in a pinch, that could be stretched to fifty. He showed that he intended to maintain discipline when he broke Sergeant Maurice Connell to private for complaining about his leadership and reprimanded the normally mild Edward Israel for flaring up at Brainard. Israel's outburst suggests the strained nerves among the company. At twenty-one, the meteorologist was the youngest member of the expedition and the only Jew, a great favourite with everyone – cheerful, good humoured, innocent. He had accused Brainard of grabbing the best material for his hut but quickly regretted that outburst, apologizing profusely to Brainard, charging that others in the party had goaded him into it.

By the time Rice and Jens returned from Cape Sabine on October 9, Greely and his men were worn ragged from digging the heavy stones out of the ice with their bare hands. Greely's own hands were torn and bleeding, his joints stiff and sore, his clothing tattered, his footgear full of holes, and his back so lame he could not stand erect. "The work," he wrote, "has taxed to the utmost limit my physical powers, already worn by mental anxiety and responsibility."

Rice brought terrible news. He had found Garlington's note reporting the loss of the *Proteus* but discovered that the three caches in the area – Nares's, Beebe's, and Garlington's – contained only enough rations to last for forty or fifty days.

Garlington's note had suggested that the *Yantic* would leave more rations at Littleton Island, just twenty-three miles across the strait from these caches. At this, some of the party, Greely included, cheered up. Surely a rescue party in sledges could make its way there from Cape Sabine once the sea froze! Hadn't Garlington written that "everything within the power of man" would be done to rescue them? Even Lockwood brightened at the prospect. "We all feel now in excellent spirits by the news," he wrote.

Greely decided to move north to Cape Sabine at once. Garlington's note, he thought, made their fate "seem somewhat brighter." Privately, however, he expected to see to "privation, partial starvation, and possible death for a few of the weakest." Brainard was even gloomier. Rice's news, he noted, had brought them "face to face with our situation as it really is. It could hardly be much worse."

Here they were, six hundred miles north of the Arctic Circle, on a rocky, windswept islet off Ellesmere – a spot rarely visited by ships, a land that had scarcely been mapped – subjected to the intense cold and deathly blizzards of the High Arctic, without shelter or fuel and with very little food. With the long Arctic night about to close in, the only glimmer of light was the hope that men were waiting across the strait to rescue and feed them. It was this belief, and this alone, that sustained them. Had they known they had been abandoned, Greely said later, he would have attempted to cross the ice-choked channel to Littleton Island, a foolhardy act that would certainly have doomed them all.

4

Starvation The move to Cape Sabine began on October 12, 1883, and for the
winter next several weeks Greely and his men shuffled back and forth, hauling supplies to the new camp. The weather was dreadful; October 15 was, in Brainard's words, "the worst night of our lives." That same day Greely examined the cache left by Garlington and discovered to his bitter disappointment that it held much less than he had anticipated. Instead of five hundred rations of meat, for instance, there were only one hundred. Meanwhile, Rice, who had been sent to examine the Nares cache, returned to report that it contained only 144 pounds of preserved meat.

Starvation faced them, but the party was in more immediate danger of freezing to death. In spite of the cold they laboured to build a hut with stone walls and a roof made of the whaleboat supported by spars made from oars. It was soon buried in snow and so cramped, being but three feet high, that even in a sitting position the taller men found their heads scraping the ceiling. They named it Camp Clay, after their erstwhile shipmate who had left the expedition because of the quarrel with Pavy.

Clay's name turned up in some scraps of old newspapers, used for wrapping lemons, that were found in the *Proteus* cache. In the dim light of an Eskimo lamp, the marooned company devoured the few fragments of news from the outside world. The president, James Garfield, had been shot and replaced by Chester Arthur. And an article by Clay, written the previous May, condemned as inadequate a government plan for relief. Clay had urged that two ships be sent north; otherwise, he predicted disaster for the Greely party if it was forced to exist entirely on the provisions left by Beebe at Cape Sabine.

"The cache of 240 rations," Clay had written, "if it can be found, will prolong their misery for a few days. When that is exhausted they will be past all earthly succor. Like poor De Long, they will then lie down on the cold ground, under the quiet stars."

Obviously Clay's letter had had some effect. But it was also clear that the *Jeannette* expedition, for which Greely had been ordered to search, had ended in tragedy. Now at last he learned that De Long had perished. It was not a cheerful piece of news.

By the end of October everybody was ravenous. When a hundred pounds of dog biscuits were opened, Greely was dismayed to discover that all were mouldy and half had been reduced to a filthy green slime. At the doctor's urging, these were thrown away as inedible. Later, he discovered that some of his people had searched for them and gobbled them up. Lockwood was one who found himself "scratching like a dog in the place where moldy dog biscuit [*sic*] were emptied." He found a few crumbs and devoured them, mould and all.

The party was already subsisting on reduced rations. Now Greely realized he must reduce rations again if they were to survive the winter. Over Dr. Pavy's objections he cut the total daily quantities to a lean fourteen ounces per man. That, he figured, would make supplies last until March 1, when they could cross the strait with the few ounces of pemmican, bread, and tea left.

"Whether we can live on such a driblet of food remains to be seen," Lockwood wrote. "We are now constantly hungry and the constant thought and talk run on food, dishes of all kinds, and what we have eaten, and what we hope to eat when we reach civilization. I have a constant longing for food. Anything to fill me up. God! what a life. A few crumbs of hard bread taste delicious."

In spite of the bad weather and the darkness, Greely knew he would have to send a party to Cape Isabella to bring back the 144 pounds of preserved meat from the Nares cache. He chose Rice to lead a party of four: Private Julius Frederick, Sergeant Joseph Elison, and David Linn, the latter newly promoted to sergeant to fill the demoted Connell's position. The party, having been fed extra rations for several days, left on November 2. They took with them additional clothing borrowed from other members of the party.

A week passed with no word. Then at two o'clock on the morning of November 10, Rice stumbled into the hut, broken, exhausted, unable to speak. At last he managed to blurt out a single sentence: "Elison is dying at Ross Bay."

As Greely made hasty plans for a rescue attempt, Rice recovered enough to give a few details of the party's ordeal. In the third day, Elison's thirst was so great that in spite of all warnings he was reduced to eating snow. In doing so he froze both hands and his nose. Worse, his body heat was drained off, as the snow he had devoured melted. By the time the party reached the cache on November 7, he was in a bad way. By the morning of the ninth, during the return trip, with both his hands and his feet frozen, he had to be carried on Frederick's back. At that point the party was forced to abandon its precious supply of meat.

The nights were a horror. The four-man sleeping bag was frozen stiff because Elison, in dreadful pain, had become incontinent, and his urine froze. In order to thaw Elison's limbs, Rice cut up Nares's abandoned ice boat for fuel. The results, for Elison, were excruciating. In spite of that, his feet were so solidly frozen that by the time the group reached Ross Bay, he could no longer stand. Rice grabbed a chunk of frozen beef and set off at once for the main camp, sixteen miles away. He had already walked nine miles that day; by the time he reached the hut he had been on the trail without rest and scarcely any food for sixteen hours.

At 4:30 that morning, Brainard and Fred, the Eskimo hunter, set off as an advance party. A six-man sledge, under Lockwood, followed behind. Brainard reached the Ross Bay camp at noon to find Elison and his two comrades frozen into their sleeping bag. Brainard no longer had the strength to free them. All he could do was force some brandy down their throats. Elison uttered a strangled cry: "Please kill me, will you?" Linn was not much better; Elison's nightly screams had unhinged his mind, and it was with difficulty that Frederick had prevented Linn from leaving the sleeping bag to encounter certain death.

Brainard immediately turned back into the howling gale to find Lockwood and hurry his party along. When he reached it, he took his place in the drag ropes, and the group reached the sufferers at 5:30 that afternoon. Exposed to the storm, the three men were still frozen into their sleeping bag. The bag was chopped apart and Elison, delirious from pain, was wrapped in a dogskin coverlet and placed on the sledge. The party then set off for Camp Clay, a sixteen-mile trek that Greely was to call "the most remarkable in the annals of Arctic sledging." Seventeen hours later they reached their destination.

Elison's condition was pitiful. His feet were shrunken, black, and lifeless, his ankle bones protruding through the emaciated flesh. Private Henry Biederbeck, the medical orderly, who spoon fed him, changed his bandages, and helped with his bodily functions, did not leave his side for sixteen waking hours.

Meanwhile, there were thefts. Somebody had broken into the commissary and stolen hard bread. Schneider was suspected, especially when it was found that a milk tin had been broken into with a knife that was traced to him. Schneider denied it; he had lent the knife to Private Charles B. Henry. Nobody then knew that Charles B. Henry was actually Charles Henry Buck, a convicted forger and thief who had once killed a Chinese in a barroom brawl in Deadwood and had served a prison term for the crime. He had been dishonourably discharged from the cavalry but re-enlisted under an assumed name. Greely had his suspicions about Henry, whom he had caught in several lies. But at this point the evidence against him was inconclusive.

On land, Greely was a better commander than he had been at sea. With nine of his men under Pavy's care, suffering from a variety of ailments – rupture, frostbite, rheumatism, infections, and incipient scurvy – he organized a series of two-hour morale-building lectures on the geography of the United States, covering one state at a time. Meanwhile, the two Eskimo hunters with Sergeant Francis Long set out to hunt for meat. They brought in an occasional fox or seal, but game was not as plentiful as Greely had supposed. By mid-November, he was again forced to reduce the daily ration to four ounces of meat and six of bread. The ravenous men grew more irritable, each eyeing and mentally weighing in his mind the rations doled out to the others. When the scanty meals were cooked, the entire hut was filled with the dense, choking smoke from the damp wood. Half suffocated, the men crawled into their sleeping bags. But the cooks could not protect themselves, suffering "such misery and discomfort," in Brainard's description, "as can scarcely be appreciated by others."

"We are all more or less unreasonable, and I can only wonder that we are not all insane," Brainard wrote. "All, including myself, are sullen, and at times very surly. If we are not mad, it should be a matter of surprise."

To these burdens, another was added. One night in early December, Greely realized that Dr. Pavy was stealing from Elison's bread can. What could he do? A confrontation would provoke a bitter fight. The doctor was the one indispensable man in camp. Greely confided in Lockwood and Brainard but took no further action.

The conversation at night centred exclusively on food. Each man made lists of the delicacies he intended to order on his return to civilization. Lockwood, who by December was obsessed by food to the point of dementia, listed a series of repasts he intended to organize with his fellows after relief came. He took to writing memoranda to himself as if the very act of committing the names of dishes to paper could somehow assuage his hunger. The result was a veritable lexicon of American regional cooking: Virginia Indian corn pone, turkey stuffed with oysters, chives with scrambled eggs, pumpkin butter, corn fritters, bacon in cornmeal, oatmeal muffins, sugar-house molasses, fig pie, coffee cake, apricot paste, Maryland biscuit, Boston pilot bread, smoked goose, spiced oysters, leaf dough biscuit, hot porter with nutmeg and sugar, hog's marrow, blood pudding, cracked wheat with honey and milk, cranberry pie, corn pudding, bannock cake, green tomato pie, macaroni pudding, charlotte of apples – the list went on, day after day.

"Chewed up a foot of a fox this evening raw," he wrote on November 23. "It was altogether bone and gristle." He followed that sentence with another memorandum to himself: "Pie of orange and coconut." Two days later in another obsessive entry he listed all the food he intended to keep in his room in Washington for midnight snacks. There were thirty-five items in all, enough to provision a medium-sized restaurant, ranging from smoked goose and eel to Virginia seedling wine and Maryland biscuit.

Christmas came. In the interests of morale Greely briefly relaxed his Spartan rationing. The men devoured a meal of seal stew with preserved potatoes and bread, followed by rice pudding, a little chocolate, and rum punch. They talked, laughed, cheered, sang songs, and exchanged with each other fanciful menus from happier Christmas days.

Elison was worse. The demarcation lines between his useless fingers and his hands, the feet and the ankles, became more pronounced each day. His fingers began to drop off. On January 2, the doctor severed the small piece of skin holding his left foot to his ankle, without Elison realizing what was happening. The following day he amputated another finger. Two days later Elison's other foot dropped off.

468

By January both Lockwood and Cross were failing. Lockwood's mind was wandering and he could not rise from his sleeping bag. It was discovered that he had hoarded his bread allowance and then eaten it all at once – twenty-four ounces. In his half-starved condition that orgy of gluttony caused him dreadful distress. He began to see double, but when Greely offered to let him have his own ration of beef, he gamely refused. Everyone was suffering from thirst by this time, chewing on old tea leaves to help fill their stomachs. Greely put some ice in a rubber bag and took it to bed with him; it melted and was used to help slake Lockwood's raging thirst. In addition, he raised the bread ration by half an ounce a day. That was too late to save Cross, who died on January 18, a victim of both scurvy and starvation. Greely hid these causes from the others, though they no doubt understood the symptoms. Cross was buried in a gunny sack; Greely could not spare wood for a coffin.

Tempers continued to fray. Private William Whisler kept offering to take people outside to fight them, an invitation subject to fits of passion and insubordination. Kislingbury and Pavy came close to blows. "Better this than mental apathy," Greely wrote philosophically.

On February 1, Rice and Jens attempted to cross Smith Sound to reach Littleton Island. Their passage was blocked by a lead of open water and they returned a week later, exhausted and frustrated. To counter the loss of morale Greely raised the rations for a week. He was struggling now to keep his party alive, doling out an extra ounce of meat here, an extra gill of rum there, whenever it became necessary. Brainard had told him that the party could hold out until April 1 if they could exist on four ounces of meat and eight ounces of bread a day. But the lack of game was distressing. This dismal land appeared to be destitute of life.

A kind of torpor was setting in. Sergeant Winfield Jewell spent twenty-two hours a day in his sleeping bag. Linn was gradually losing his mind. Schneider was so debilitated he refused to cook. Private William Ellis became fearful of his fellows and talked of cannibalism; later it was discovered he was stealing Israel's tobacco. Henry, whose profanity increased each day, gloomily predicted all would be dead within five weeks. Lockwood was so obsessed with hunger he could talk of nothing but food. He complained bitterly of the meagreness of his rations, called Biederbeck "a miserable spy," and quarrelled with Greely. Biederbeck himself was ill with fatigue brought on by caring for Lockwood and Elison. Greely doubled Elison's rations; he could only hope to retain his own mental powers after his physical powers failed. "I am troubled by the many little matters as well as by our situation, that my temper is not as good perhaps as it should be," he confided to his journal.

In mid-March the sun was back, but there was no sign of game. Francis Long and Fred Christiansen travelled for seventy-five miles and saw not so much as a track in the snow. Had they stayed at Fort Conger, they realized, they would now be feasting on muskox meat. As Greely put it, "we have been lured here to our destruction." How could they attempt to cross Smith Sound – twenty-four weakened men, two unable to walk, half a dozen others incapacitated? "It drives me almost insane to face the future. It is not the end that afrights any one, but the road to be travelled to reach that goal. To die is easy . . . it is only hard to strive, to endure, to live."

A freakish accident almost finished them. Fumes from the alcohol cooking lamp escaped into the hut, and the men began to topple. Biederbeck, acting as cook, succumbed first, then young Israel. Sergeant Hampden Gardiner got the door open and the others began to crawl from the hut, some fainting on the way. Greely saw Brainard stretched out on the snow. Whisler tottered in front of him, but before the commander could reach him he too lost all his strength and fell to the ground. Gardiner tried to get to him to put mittens on his fingers, but before he could do so, Gardiner himself succumbed. Nobody died, but many suffered frostbite. Greely could not use his hands to eat with for a week.

It was noticed that during the confusion one man, Private Charles B. Henry, had not tried to help anybody but himself. Little Jens reported that he had seen Henry hide half a pound of bacon in his shirt. Later that night, the culprit vomited up most of it. Greely relieved him of duty and confined him to his sleeping bag. There was little else he could do.

Meanwhile, the energetic Sergeant Rice was fishing for shrimps. He expected, he said, to rake in about a quart a day. It was little enough. The crustaceans were no bigger than a grain of wheat, and three quarters of their bulk was hard shell. Seven hundred shrimps were needed to produce an ounce of meat. But it was nourishment of a sort, and so were the tiny dovekies that began to appear at the end of March.

Although Elison's sufferings were truly terrible, he was remark-

470

ably patient. "My toes are burning dreadfully and the soles of my feet itch," he told Dr. Pavy. "Can't you do something for me?" But he had neither toes nor feet, a condition that had been kept from him since January. Pavy continued to steal his bread, as Israel reported to Greely, but Greely was impotent to act.

On April 4, Fred Christiansen, the Eskimo hunter, became delirious. By morning, he was dead. The following day Linn pleaded for water; there was none to give him and he died almost immediately. Rice and a fellow Signal Corps sergeant, David Ralston, slept soundly in the same sleeping bag with the corpse, preparing for the exertion of the following day's burial. As Brainard wrote, death "has ceased to arouse our emotions."

For some days, Rice had been pleading with Greely to be allowed to return to Cape Baird, where the Nares beef had been jettisoned the previous November during the Elison fiasco. Greely refused, not wishing to endanger his men further. Now, with two more of the party dead, he changed his mind. Rice had been ill, but he insisted on going. At midnight, April 6, he and Private Julius Frederick set off.

Three days later, the emaciated Lockwood died. Greely restored Kislingbury to duty as his second-in-command and eulogized him for his hard work during the desperate winter days. Young Sergeant Israel broke down the following day, and Sergeant Winfield Jewell lapsed into a delirium from which he did not recover in spite of the extra rations Greely allowed him. Only the fortunate capture of a bear prevented the others from starving to death. Had it not been for this miraculous supply of fresh meat, Brainard noted grimly, most would have died within a fortnight. Greely allowed Brainard and the other shrimp fishermen two ounces extra rations a day. It was scarcely enough.

The day after Jewell's death, Frederick returned alone with a terrible tale. He and Rice had jettisoned their sleeping bag and most of their rations at Eskimo Point in a final dash to find the English beef on the floe of Baird Inlet. To their bitter disappointment, there was no sign of it in the swirling snow. Rice was weakening badly, his feet frozen solid from trudging through pools of ice water. Dragging their light sledge, the pair started back to the point empty-handed, but Rice was soon too weak to continue. Frederick removed his own outer clothing to wrap around Rice's feet and there, seated on the sledge, cradling the sergeant in his arms, he watched his partner die.

He described his situation in a report to the War Department:

"Here I was left alone with the body of my friend in an ice-bound region, out of reach of help. . . . The death of my companion . . . made a deeper impression on my mind than any experience in my whole life. As here I stood, completely exhausted, by the remains of poor Rice, shivering with the cold, unable to bury the remains, hardly able to move, I knew that my chances to reach Eskimo Point . . . were very small indeed. I was completely disheartened; I felt more like remaining here and perishing by the side of my companion than to make another effort, but the sense of the duty which I owed my country and my companions and to my dead comrade to bear back the sad tidings of the disaster, sustained me in this trial."

Frederick realized that if he didn't return, another party would risk their lives trying to find him. He kissed Rice's freezing face and, after seven hours of hard travel, reached his abandoned sleeping bag. It was frozen so hard he couldn't unroll it, but he sustained himself by sniffing at a phial of ammonia. That revived him to the point where he could force his way into the bag. The following morning he went back to bury Rice's body. Without a shovel or an axe, he was reduced to scraping away the loose ice with his hands and there, on a paleocrystic floe, he laid the dead sergeant in an icy grave. When he stumbled at last into the hut at Camp Clay, terribly worn down, he returned to Greely all of Rice's unused rations. Despite his condition, the dedicated young cavalryman had refused to eat more than his share.

In spite of a small increase in rations – partly the result of Long's capture of a sixty-pound seal – the state of the survivors continued to deteriorate. Kislingbury's mind was wandering. "He talks at times like an infant," Greely wrote. He was now concerned about the line of succession if he, the commander, expired. After some discussion with Biederbeck he agreed to increase his own ration slightly; Elison was already being allowed extra meat and so were the hunters, Brainard, Long, and Jens. Biederbeck was relieved. "Lt. G. has shown himself to be a man of more force of character & in every way greater than I believed him to be," he wrote, "that I think it better that he & our records be saved than all of us together. I am very sorry not to have sooner found out his full worth & done him while at Conger & coming down, on the retreat, so often injustice in my thoughts."

Greely, the martinet and arrogant amateur navigator had, under stress, become a patient and caring father-figure, sometimes even denying himself while secretly doling out extra rations to men so proud they would often refuse them. He himself was suffering from heart palpitations, convinced that his own end was near. But when Schneider broke down and refused to cook dinner, Greely left his bag and, in spite of the men's entreaties, did the job himself.

Everyone was in poor spirits, in spite of a welcome increase in rations. Pavy had been caught by Long stealing Schneider's rum ration. A day or two later he was found stealing Elison's bacon. Yet in spite of these individual lapses, the party's long trial was marked by other moments of selflessness. When Schneider spilled his tea and Ralston his stew, the others offered the two men part of their own meagre portions.

The strongest men were the two hunters, Long and Jens. Kislingbury's mind was almost gone, and he was no longer fit to command. Brainard, who would take over if Greely and Kislingbury died, was too weak to cut up the frozen meat. When Henry stole some fuel alcohol and drank himself into intoxication, Gardiner wanted to throttle him, but was too frail to crawl toward the culprit's sleeping bag.

Then, on April 29, Long came back from hunting with terrible news. Jens, the cheerful Eskimo, had ripped his kayak chasing a seal and drowned. Both the kayak and Jens's Springfield rifle, the best weapon in the party, were also gone – a triple loss that cast everyone into further gloom. "I think that I am near my end," Greely confessed to Brainard a few days later. That same morning – May 3, 1884 – Private Jacob Bender and Henry forced open the commissary door to steal rations. Whisler could not resist the temptation to seize a piece of bacon, whereupon the other two raised a cry, putting all the blame on Whisler. Whisler was contrite and offered to accept any punishment inflicted upon him, but no action was taken.

The glue of comradeship and discipline that had held the company together was coming unstuck. Pavy, ever the troublemaker, quarrelled with Greely over the distribution of rations. "If you were not the surgeon of this expedition I would shoot you!" Greely cried. When Bender tried to take the doctor's side, Greely threatened to shoot him too. He seized Long's rifle, but Brainard quietly took it from him and ordered Bender into his sleeping bag.

In the days that followed, Greely scribbled to Henrietta on a narrow slip of paper some final words that he expected would be found on his body: May 10: "Our chances are going fast – no game now in 27 days & only 3 days food remaining. I have cut off some hair for you . . ." May 12: "The whole party are prepared to die and I feel certain that they will face death quietly and decently . . ." May 16: "Our last regular rations . . . given out today . . . I think but one or two have any confidence in surviving. My heart troubles me & grows worse so my chances are very slim. . . ."

In a shaky hand he wrote some last instructions to his wife. He suggested she remain in their home in Newburyport, which "has many advantages. Cheap, good society, excellent schools, widows house not taxed, etc. etc." His watch, he said, should go on loan to one of his daughters "with the understanding that it goes on his twenty-first birthday in perfect condition to the first male born of either daughter." He knew a man in New York who could make excellent carbon pictures on a stretched canvas, and he urged his wife to have a dozen of his most striking photographs reproduced in that manner. It would, he scribbled weakly, be a good investment. "You can finish them off, and sell for from $50 to $100 or more according to your talent. . . ." A few more lines and he could write no more. He scrawled his initials "AWG" and put down his pencil.

He had already divided up the last of the rations to prevent further theft. On the seventeenth he distributed the last of the lard, which had been saved for medicinal purposes. Elison, in spite of his amputations, continued to live and even to thrive on his extra rations, while Dr. Pavy, in an unexpected burst of energy, paid several visits to the lake behind the ridge to chop ice for fresh water. But the weakest men began to die: Ellis first, on the nineteenth, followed by Ralston, four days later. And then Whisler, still begging forgiveness for stealing the bacon. According to Pavy he succumbed from fright. On May 27, Sergeant Israel, Greely's bag companion and favourite, also died. His "cheerful and hopeful words during the long months," Greely wrote, ". . . did much to . . . relieve my overtaxed brain."

Those who were left existed on shreds of saxifrage, the occasional dovekie shot by Long, and the shrimp that Brainard continued to bring in. Bender, spotting a caterpillar, swallowed it whole, exclaiming, "This is too much meat to lose." The fourteen survivors had to abandon the hut when melt water made it uninhabitable. They were now crowded into a tent pitched on a knoll 150 yards away. Brainard, returning exhausted from a shrimping trip on May 27, was forced to sleep outside in a storm because Pavy and Corporal Nicholas Salor, who shared his sleeping bag, refused to make room for him. Brainard was too weak to remonstrate. On June 1, Kislingbury

474

died. Salor followed two days later. No one had the strength to bury the corpse, which was simply hidden behind a projection of ice.

That same day Long shot a dovekie and Greely ordered that it be given to the hunters to maintain their strength. Bender pleaded for a portion; Greely reluctantly allowed it, and that caused further trouble. Shortly afterward Henry was again caught stealing from the supply of shrimps. Bender and Schneider were also suspected of theft. "It will be necessary," Greely confided to his journal, "to take some severe action, or the whole party will perish."

The following day, June 5, Greely issued an order to his three sergeants, Brainard, Frederick, and Long. If Henry was again caught stealing, they were to shoot him at once. "Any other course would be a fatal leniency, the man being able to overpower any two of our present force."

Next day, Frederick caught Henry stealing shrimp again. He had also taken part of the dovekie set aside for the hunters and had stolen and eaten sealskin lashings and boots taken from the expedition's stores. Greely did not hesitate: "Private Henry will be shot today. . . . Decide the manner of his death by two ball and one blank cartridge. This order is *imperative*, and *absolutely necessary* for *any chance* of life."

There was only one rifle left, however. The three sergeants drew lots and agreed never to reveal who fired the fatal shot. A brief struggle followed as Henry tried to fight with his executioners. He died with a bullet in his chest, another in his head. When his bag was opened it was found to contain various articles stolen from the stores.

A few hours later, unnerved, perhaps, by his comrade's execution, Bender succumbed. Dr. Pavy died almost immediately after. That was a surprise, for he had seemed remarkably healthy. But he had been secretly dosing himself with the drug ergot, which, in his deranged state, he believed to be iron. In the pockets of both Bender and Pavy the survivors found stolen sealskin and thongs, which, in Schneider's phrase, "showed how dishonest they was."

The remaining nine men were reduced to eating lichens. On June 12, Gardiner died, a blow to the others because, as Greely put it, "he has appeared to live mainly by will power for the past two months," an inspiration to all after the doctor had predicted his imminent death the previous April. He had been determined to return to his family and in the moments before his death had clutched an ambrotype of his wife and mother. "Mother! Wife!" he cried, and then expired.

By Sunday, June 15, the party was gnawing at the oilskin covers from Greely's and Long's sleeping bags. Schneider pleaded for opium pills to put him out of his misery. The shrimps had all but disappeared. Brainard worked for five hours in a high wind and got only two or three ounces. It was all he could do to crawl home with them. On June 19, Schneider died. The following day, Greely scribbled a gloomy note in his journal: "Six years ago today I was married and three years ago I left my wife for this Expedition. What contrast! When will this life in death end?"

For nearly eleven months none had washed or changed his clothes. Elison, ironically, was perhaps the strongest man in the tent. Biederbeck, who rarely left his side, strapped a spoon to one of his stumps so he could feed himself with stewed sealskin if the others perished before him.

By June 21, 1884 – the summer solstice – neither Greely nor Brainard was strong enough to hold a pencil to keep up their journals. Connell was close to death. Greely was too weak to read from his Bible. And so the seven survivors of the Lady Franklin Bay Expedition composed themselves for the end, paying only scant attention to an odd sound blowing faintly through the gale just before midnight on June 22. What had produced that mournful note? Was it the wind . . . or was it something else?

Greely, who could barely speak, asked whether Brainard or Long had the strength to investigate. Brainard crept out of the tent, crawled up a small knoll, and returned to report he could see nothing; it was only the wind howling across the barren rocks. He got back into his sleeping bag, resigned to death. But Long stayed out to raise the distress flag that had been blown down. A fruitless discussion followed as to the source of the sound. Suddenly, Greely sat bolt upright, his heart racing. Outside the tent he heard strange voices, calling his name.

5

The eleventh hour In his annual report for 1883, Secretary of War Lincoln did his best to mask the mounting public anxiety about the Lady Franklin Bay Expedition. There would, he said, "be no reasonable apprehension for their safety" if it were known that they had remained at Lady

Franklin Bay. It was possible, of course, that they had left Lady Franklin Bay. It was, in fact, more than "possible," since Greely's orders required him to do that very thing – and by September of that year. Lincoln made a clumsy attempt to explain away the probability that Greely would follow orders, go south, and find the caches all but empty. "Even in this case his condition would be by no means desperate," he declared, for "it is thought that it would not be impossible for him to retrace his steps." But old Arctic hands like Henry Clay and new Arctic experts, of whom Henrietta Greely was now one, knew that a trek north to Fort Conger in the winter of 1883-84 was quite impossible. Lincoln's smooth words, however, served to allay concern. When the president, Chester A. Arthur, delivered his annual address to Congress in December, there was no hint of any money being set aside to rescue Greely.

Meanwhile, a lengthy inquiry into the *Proteus* disaster was still taking evidence. In January, after ten weeks of hearings, it lightly rapped the knuckles of Lieutenant Garlington and Commander Wildes. Garlington had "erred" in leaving Littleton Island without waiting for the *Yantic,* while it was "greatly to be regretted that in his earnest desire to succor the crew and party of the *Proteus"* Wildes had not delayed a few hours to unload his own supplies. The inquiry reserved a harsher criticism for General Hazen for his failure to organize a proper expedition and for his muddy instructions to Garlington. The *New York Times* had been baying all the fall of 1883 for Hazen's resignation, but by the time the 575-page printed report was issued, the general was already sitting on a joint Army and Navy board contemplating another relief expedition. Nobody was court-martialled as a result of the summer's botched mission.

On January 17, 1884, the Army and Navy board recommended to the president that up to three sturdy vessels – Dundee whalers or Newfoundland sealers – be purchased, fitted out, and provisioned for two years to seek out Greely. Every moment counted. The relief ships should be at Upernavik by May 15 at the latest if they were to get across Melville Bay and Smith Sound in time.

This sense of urgency did not communicate itself to the legislators in the House and Senate, who argued over the bill for weeks. The board had asked for unlimited funds; the politicians wanted to put a ceiling on the cost. Was this really a relief expedition, some asked, or was it yet another disastrous attempt to reach the North Pole? Congress, still investigating the *Jeannette* disaster, had had quite enough of the North Pole, and its members wanted to make sure that there would be no more publicly financed attempts to reach it.

Some worried about the dangers and tried to insist on a clause that would limit the expedition to volunteers. Several insisted that only American-built ships be sent north. (It turned out there were none suitable.) Others wrangled over procedural points and technical errors. There were discussions and behind-the-scenes conferences. General Lockwood himself was closeted with the president, on whom he made little impression. At one point, the senator in charge of the relief bill, Eugene Hale of Maine, was moved to cry out that "if Lieutenant Greely is to be left to perish with his followers, I hope they may die in a parliamentary manner, so that it shall be satisfactory, so that no question may be raised as to their violating any rule!"

At last, on February 13, the resolution was approved. It was very late in the day. Most available ships were spoken for as early as December. Fortunately, the two secretaries – War and Navy – acting on their own, took a chance. Before the congressional wrangling ended they bought the *Proteus*'s sister ship, *Bear,* considered the best vessel in the St. John's fishing fleet, for $100,000. She arrived in New York harbour just two days after the appropriation was passed. By then the shortage of suitable vessels had bumped up the price. A second ship, the *Thetis,* purchased in Dundee, cost the government $140,000. She reached New York on March 23.

Now, however, the bread cast upon the Atlantic waters many years before returned to save the American taxpayers further expense. The Admiralty had not forgotten the generosity of the United States in salvaging the *Resolute* and presenting her to Britain. The British government had the opportunity of replying in kind. It gave the United States Nares's old vessel, the *Alert,* which had been lying dismantled at Chatham, England, and fitted her out in the country's best shipyard, with Nares himself and some of his officers acting as advisers. She arrived in New York on April 22. Two days later, the *Bear* left for the Arctic. The *Thetis* followed a week afterward.

This was entirely a Navy show. The crews were made up of naval volunteers, and the overall command was in the hands of a naval officer, Winfield Scott Schley. This time there would be no ambiguous instructions. One man and one man only would be responsible for everything – from the recruiting of the crews and the strengthening of the ships to the sailing orders.

"I leave the dearest home ties in the earnest hope & with the sincerest purpose to return to you the noblest of husbands," Schley wrote to Mrs. Greely just before he sailed. "May God bless our efforts and help you to be patient in the long hours between our sailing and return."

The two whaling ships reached Upernavik at the end of May after a difficult passage. The *Alert* arrived a fortnight later. Melville Bay lay ahead. Greely had crossed it in thirty-six hours, Beebe in eighty, Garlington in seventy-six. But this was June, not July, and it took the two leading relief ships twenty days to reach Cape York. Beside them and behind them, strung out through the shifting ice, were eight commercial whalers, spurred on by the U.S. government's promise of a reward of $25,000 to any private vessel that should save the Greely party.

The *Thetis* reached Littleton Island on June 21. Schley immediately set his men combing the terrain. They found a pile of coal. They found a cache left by Beebe. They found traces of the Nares expedition. But there was no sign of Greely or his men.

When the *Bear* arrived the following day, Schley decided to cross Smith Sound at once and search the Cape Sabine area just in case Greely might be in the vicinity. He felt reasonably certain that the party had returned to Lady Franklin Bay. On the other hand, Greely might have reached the southern tip of Ellesmere. He knew it was a long shot: Greely simply didn't have enough supplies to sustain him on that bleak promontory, but he had to make sure. The least he could do would be to examine the cairns there, leave a new cache of four thousand rations to fall back on, and then push on north.

The cape lay twenty-three miles away, hidden in the murk of an Arctic storm. Driven with the wind, the two ships reached it in just four hours. They anchored off the shore ice in Payer Harbour – a notch cut into the tip of the peninsula. Schley sent out four parties: one would search the Nares cairn, which could be seen plainly on Stalnecht Island, a low strip of land connected at low tide with the shore. One would try to find the cairn that Beebe had left in 1882 on nearby Brevoort Island. A third would take the steam tender *Cub* and look for the cairn that Garlington had left some three miles to the northwest after the *Proteus* wreck. A fourth would comb the shoreline of the harbour. No one expected to find living men.

But even as the *Bear* was lowering the *Cub* to seek out Garlington's cache, a sailor was spotted returning from the Beebe cairn, carrying a bundle of papers and crying out that Greely was at Cape Sabine after all. Schley seized the papers and found that they gave details of the expedition and also the position of Greely's camp. Then, to his dismay, he realized that they were dated October 21, 1883. How could these lightly clad men possibly have survived for eight months on this wind-swept promontory, with only forty days' rations in the caches and very little fuel?

Even as Schley was pondering this news, a signal came from Stalnecht Island that more papers had been found in the Nares cairn. These consisted of the original records of the expedition together with Lockwood's journals, a set of photographic records, and again the position of the expedition's camp at Cape Sabine.

Schley at once dispatched Lieutenant Colwell, the veteran navigator of Garlington's ill-fated relief attempt, in the *Cub*. Colwell, on an impulse, called for a flag, which he attached to a boat-hook. The *Thetis* sounded her steam whistle above the storm, recalling all shore parties, while Schley, in the *Bear,* set off behind Colwell's launch, dreading what he would find.

Colwell's cutter rounded the point of the cape that evening and moved up the rocky coast, which Colwell recognized from his previous visit. He found the site of the *Proteus* wreck cache and searched the shore with his spyglass but saw no sign of human habitation. The cutter moved on in the tossing sea and rounded another rocky point. As Colwell scanned the ridge above, he suddenly saw a figure limned against the grey sky. He called for his flag and waved it furiously. The man on the ridge stooped down painfully, picked up a flag lying on the rocks, and waved it back. Then he made his way slowly down the rocks, falling twice, and walked feebly toward Colwell, who was standing on the prow of the *Cub*.

"Who all are there left?" Colwell asked.

"Seven left," said Sergeant Long.

Colwell jumped onto the shore, shocked at the scarecrow figure who approached him – hollow-cheeked, wild-eyed, ragged and filthy, hair and beard matted and straggly. Long mumbled something, twitching as he tried to speak. Then, on an impulse, he removed his tattered glove and shook Colwell's hand.

"Where are they?" Colwell asked.

"In the tent. Over the hill. The tent is down."

"Is Mr. Greely alive?"

"Yes, Greely's alive."

480

"Any other officers?"

"No. The tent is down."

Colwell was already striding up the hill, his pockets bulging with bread and pemmican. He gained the crest and looked about him on a scene of desolation – a long expanse of rock sloping to the shore ice, a low range of hills behind, its steep face broken by a gorge through which the wind howled, and a small elevation in front of which lay the collapsed tent. Colwell, with his ice pilot, James Norman, and another seaman crossed the hollow just as a man emerged from the tent. It was Brainard.

The sergeant drew himself up at once and raised a hand to salute, but Colwell forestalled him and grasped it instead. Within the tent he heard a weak voice ask, "Who's there?"

"It's Norman – Norman who was in the *Proteus*," the ice pilot answered. A feeble cheer followed.

One of the relief party began to weep as Colwell, calling for a knife, slit the cover of the fallen tent and looked in on a scene of horror.

One man, apparently dead, his eyes glassy, his jaw slack, lay close to the opening. Another, without hands or feet, a spoon tied to the stump of his right arm, lay opposite. Two others, seated in the middle, were trying to pour some liquid from a rubber bottle into a tin can. Directly across, on his hands and knees, was a pathetic figure with a long, matted beard, wearing a skullcap and a tattered dressing gown. His body was skeletal, his hands and face black with filth, his joints swollen, his eyes sunken and feverish. He stared at Colwell and then put on a pair of eyeglasses.

"Who are you?" Colwell asked.

Greely was unable to answer, but one of the others, in a weak voice, identified him.

Colwell crawled into the toppled tent and took him by the hand.

"Greely, is this you?"

"Yes," Greely croaked. His voice was faint and hesitant as he managed a few faltering phrases: "Yes – seven of us left – here we are – dying – like men. Did what I came to do – beat the best record." Thus did the commander of the Lady Franklin Bay Expedition reveal the true and secret purpose of the so-called scientific survey. He had got closer to the Pole than any other expedition; that was what mattered and, with what had been almost his dying breath, he made it clear. Having said that, he fell back, exhausted.

481

Colwell looked about him – at the filthy piles of cast-off clothing, at the ragged sleeping bags in which these men had spent most of their time for several months, at the tins of disgusting jelly made from boiling strips cut from sealskin clothing, and at the remnants of a bottle of brandy the men had been sharing when he entered.

Connell was close to death, unable to speak, his body cold, his heartbeat weak, all sensation gone. Biederbeck and Frederick were too weak to walk. Greely could not stand upright. Long and Brainard, both men of iron constitution, were in slightly better shape. Colwell sent a man to the *Bear* for a doctor and fed the survivors, bit by bit, from the biscuits and pemmican he'd brought in his pockets. When they cried and pleaded for more, he sensibly refused. Greely seized one of the tins of sealskin jelly, saying it was his and he had a right to eat it. Colwell took it away from him, but while he was trying to raise the tent, the others grabbed a half-empty pemmican tin, clawed out the contents with their hands, and devoured it. When Colwell told them rescue was at hand, they refused to believe it.

The doctor arrived, and little by little Greely and his comrades revived on small amounts of milk punch and beef tea. Even Connell began to recover; his rescue had come not one minute too soon. Six of the starving men were placed on stretchers and taken in the driving rain to the two rescue ships. Frederick insisted on trying to walk but had to be supported in this act of braggadocio by two seamen.

All of the bodies were exhumed, over Greely's protests, identified, and brought to the ships. Schneider's four-day-old corpse lay at the foot of the ridge facing the sea; his comrades had not had the strength even to cover it with a few shovelfuls of sand. Some distance away, Henry's corpse was found, with the two bullet holes clearly visible. Schley's men carefully sifted through the scattered piles of old clothing, notebooks, diaries, empty tins, cooking utensils, and rubbish that lay scattered everywhere. Anything of value – including a fat roll of banknotes – was to be brought home, along with the scientific records and Greely's precious pendulum. The following afternoon, both vessels were back at Littleton Island. They left for the south on the morning of June 24.

In sick bay, the survivors began to mend. On June 28, Greely, who, next to Connell, was the weakest, was able to dress and sit up briefly. He appeared on deck for the first time on July 1. But Elison's condition began to deteriorate. When the relief vessels arrived at Disco Island on July 5, it was clear that the stumps of his ankles would have to be amputated or he would die of blood poisoning. His strength was so badly depleted that he did not survive the effects of the operation. He died on July 8.

Six men out of twenty-five had survived. When Greely learned of the bungled efforts to relieve him the previous summer, he was bitter. In his memoirs, he blamed Garlington for "taking every ounce of food he could carry when he turned southward," and Wildes for his long delay in the Greenland ports and "his precipitate retreat" from Smith Sound. Nor could he understand why the government hadn't sent another ship north immediately it received the news of the *Proteus* disaster. If a stout sealer had left St. John's within ten days of the *Yantic*'s return, he believed, the entire company would have been saved.

Meanwhile, on July 18, 1884, the first news of the rescue hit the American newspapers and the country went wild. There was no room for any other news on the front page of the *New York Times* that morning. When the rescue ships arrived at Portsmouth, New Hampshire, on August 1, they were greeted by a screaming mob who waved and shouted from the shores and from hundreds of pleasure craft. But nobody – not even Schley's wife – was allowed on the *Thetis* until Henrietta Greely had been taken aboard for a quiet reunion with her husband, alone and unobserved in the commander's cabin.

Fifteen thousand people poured into town that weekend for the parade on Monday, August 4. On doctor's orders, the six survivors did not attend the welcome-home rally held that night in the Portsmouth Music Hall, when fifteen hundred of Greely's New Hampshire neighbours lauded him to the skies. Only the Secretary of War was missing. He sent along a tepid telegram which contrasted starkly with the ebullience of the moment.

The ebullience *was* momentary. The press soon turned from celebrating the rescue of six men to ferreting out the most melodramatic details of the deaths of nineteen others. General Hazen had tried to contain the account of Henry's execution within Army circles. He relieved Greely's mind by reporting that Secretary Lincoln had agreed that his act in putting down a mutiny was "thoroughly legal and proper." But the *New York Times* was busily investigating rumours flying around the hospital where some of the survivors were still patients. On August 12, the paper's front page carried a sensational scoop. It disclosed not only the story of the bullet holes in Henry's body but something much more horrifying – cannibalism.

The government, it charged, was covering up the fact that "many of the seventeen men who are said to have perished by starvation had been eaten by their famished comrades." (As usual, the *Times* appeared to ignore the existence of two Eskimos in the party.)

Based on gossip and innuendo, garbled and exaggerated in the telling, the *Times* story could scarcely be denied. Schley's party had exhumed the bodies and discovered that six – Kislingbury, Jewell, Ralston, Henry, Whisler, and Ellis – had been mutilated. Strips of flesh had been cut from their limbs after their deaths. Because of this discovery, Schley had sent an urgent wire as soon as he reached St. John's, asking permission to have the corpses sealed in metal caskets.

The story caused an uproar as other newspapers scrambled to catch up to the *Times*. The reports grew wilder and woollier, but no one could dispute the findings of the Rochester *Post-Express*, which persuaded Kislingbury's three brothers to allow it to exhume the body and examine it medically. The medical finding was that large strips had been cut from the trunk and the thigh.

Greely was shocked. He issued an immediate statement denying any knowledge of cannibalism at Camp Clay. If it had occurred, he said, it had been done in secrecy. Each of the survivors had come to him to swear that they knew nothing about it. Schley helped to dampen the most outlandish rumours in the press by confirming, on August 22, that only six of the corpses had been mutilated.

The *Times,* in its interview with the Kislingbury brothers, reported that the flesh had been removed "by a hand skilled in dissection." The flesh was not hacked but neatly cut in a systematic manner by a sharp knife or scalpel, with the flaps of the skin used to conceal the wounds. That and other evidence seemed to point to Dr. Pavy as one of the culprits, perhaps the only one. The deaths of the six men in question took place between April 12 and June 6 – the latter the day Henry was shot. Pavy himself expired a few hours later, somewhat to Greely's surprise because he had appeared to be in better condition than the others. It was recalled that in May, he had frequently gone to the lake near Cemetery Ridge (as the survivors called it) to chop ice for fresh water, an exertion that was for him unusual. At that time he could easily have taken flesh from five of the bodies. But the doctor had died only a few hours after Henry. Did he have the strength in that extremity to crawl from the tent and mutilate the body of the executed private? Perhaps; it was, apparently, the doses of ergot that killed him, not the lack of food. But it may also be that someone else was a party to cannibalism. No one will ever know.

The furore died down eventually. A remarkably large number of people took Greely's side in what the *Times* insisted on calling The Shame of the Nation. Thirty years had passed since an earlier generation had rejected the suggestion that Franklin's men could have engaged in cannibalism. Now, the attitude of Americans and Britons alike seemed to be that starving men on the brink of death could be excused for wanting to stay alive.

More significant than these disclosures was a new trend in the American press, which reflected public disillusion by excoriating what the Philadelphia *Inquirer* called "the monstrous and murderous folly of so-called Arctic expeditions." The president himself concurred. "The scientific information secured," he declared, "could not compensate for the loss of human life."

Reasonable as it was, this reaction overlooked Greely's genuine accomplishments. He had triumphed over scurvy, thanks to his use of fresh muskox meat and pemmican treated with lemon juice. Although the medical secrets of the disease had not yet been unlocked, it was now clear that an expedition could exist in the High Arctic without danger from scurvy if it adopted the proper diet. And Greely's voyage to the top of the world had amassed more than two years' worth of systematic scientific and geographical records. His official two-volume report ran to thirteen hundred pages. It covered everything from the tide patterns of Arctic waters to the question of the insularity of Greenland. In every scientific field, from meteorology and astronomy to oceanography and biology, Greely's facts, figures, charts, and photographs became the basis for future Arctic studies. But this substantial contribution was long overshadowed by the disclosure of cannibalism, the rigid temperament that prevented Greely from becoming a popular hero, and above all public revulsion against expeditions that sacrificed human lives to personal ambition and government goals. The *New York Times* thundered, "Let there be an end to this folly."

Did Greely's scientific discoveries justify the agony that his own misjudgements and rigid adherence to orders inflicted on his men? Like his admirable sergeant, David Brainard, he eventually rose to general's rank, having long since subdued, at least publicly, any doubts about the worth of his expedition. By the time of his death, at ninety-one, he had become an authentic American hero not only because of his Arctic ordeal but also because of his work in organizing relief for the victims of the San Francisco earthquake. His published memoirs, written shortly after his return from Ellesmere Island, summed up his own blunt view of that ghastly winter of 1883-84. "I know of no law, human or divine," he declared, "which was broken at Sabine, and do not feel called on as an officer or as a man to dwell longer on such a painful topic."

Chapter Twelve

Roald Amundsen

Fridtjof Nansen

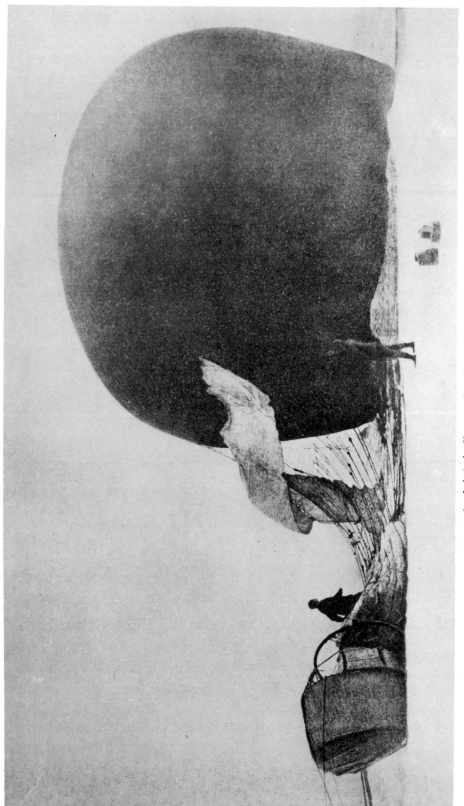

Andrée's balloon after foundering

By the mid-1890s, Brigadier General Adolphus Washington Greely *Nansen's drift* had come to the conclusion that his Scandinavian counterparts were demented. One, a Swede named Salomon Andrée, was proposing to fly off to the North Pole in a balloon, of all things. Another, a Norwegian named Fridtjof Nansen, had already set out in a tub of a boat and was planning to get himself purposely stuck in the ice and drift – yes, *drift* – across the polar basin.

In 1890, when Nansen first unveiled his mad project, Greely had had his say. "It is doubtful," he declared, "if any hydrographer would treat seriously his theory of polar currents, or if any Arctic travellers would endorse the whole scheme. . . . Arctic exploration is sufficiently credited with rashness and danger in its legitimate and sanctioned methods, without bearing the burden of Dr. Nansen's illogical scheme of self destruction."

By the summer of 1895, when Greely was turning his guns on Andrée, the balloonist, these words seemed to have been more than prescient. At that point Nansen had been out of touch with the world for almost two years; if he was not dead, he might as well be dead. But Greely was wrong. Nansen was very much alive in a kayak off Franz Josef Land, having made a daring if unsuccessful assault on the North Pole and reached a higher latitude than any explorer in history – 200 statute miles farther than Greely's own expedition.

Thirty-five months after his departure, Nansen returned to civilization like a ghost rising from the grave, to be hailed as the greatest explorer of his day – greater by far than any of his detractors – and the founder of a new school of Viking explorers whose crowning ornament would be Roald Amundsen, the future conquerer of both the North West Passage and the South Pole.

The Scandinavian explorers were a different breed from the hide-bound British and the impetuous Americans. They were, after all, a subarctic people, used to cold weather and high winds, familiar with skis, sledges, and dogs. They were also immensely practical. Nansen was daring but never rash; bold but never impulsive; fatalistic but never foolhardy; poetic but never naïve. A cool professional, he admired the British explorers for their grit, but he also learned from their mistakes and lack of experience. He believed in careful preparation. He watched every detail himself, leaving nothing to chance. He scorned men like Kane, whose polar expedition he called a "reckless, unjustifiable proceeding." Nansen was the first explorer to take a ship into the Arctic that was custom-built to his own specifications – neither a whaler nor a naval bomb vessel. This was the *Fram,* perhaps the most famous vessel in Arctic history and certainly the most practical.

Nansen was thirty-one when he set off on his extraordinary journey – a Norse demi-god, tall, fair, blue-eyed, and physically tough. He had become an explorer by design. As a young science graduate he had, at twenty-one, shipped aboard a Greenland sealer to gain experience in zoology. At that point the Arctic captivated him. By 1888, after completing his scientific studies, he was prepared for his first adventure – nothing less than an attempt to ski across the unexplored Greenland ice cap, from coast to coast.

Skis had never before been used for such a journey. Nansen was later to write that "most people considered it simple madness . . . and were convinced that I was either not quite right in the head or was simply tired of life." His hero, Baron A.E. Nordenskiöld, who had failed in his attempt to cross the ice sheet in 1866, was one of the early sceptics. Nansen's enthusiasm and confidence won him over. The risk, Nordenskiöld finally decided, was worth it. But the Norwegian government thought differently and refused to fund the venture.

Nansen was determined to keep the risks to a minimum. He designed his own equipment, ranging from a new kind of portable cooker to flexible new sledges, running on skis and equipped with sails. He took lessons in the Eskimo language. An expert skier himself, he recruited five other experts, the toughest he could find, including Otto Sverdrup, the future master of the *Fram* and later a notable Arctic explorer. The party landed on the bleak, unpeopled east coast of Greenland both because Nansen wanted the prevailing wind behind him as he moved west across the great ice cap and because he wanted to cut off all lines of retreat. Behind was nothing but rock and ice; ahead lay the inhabited coastal strip on the shores of Baffin Bay. There could be no turning back.

The zigzag journey through this lifeless land covered four hundred miles over highlands that exceeded eight thousand feet. The conditions were so severe that one of Nansen's companions, a Laplander, teetered on the verge of madness. Nansen, a born leader, managed to calm him down, and the party confounded the experts by succeeding. Unable to get a ship for home out of Disco Bay that fall, the industrious young man spent the winter in Greenland studying the Eskimos. When he returned to Norway he was famous – a popular hero. In the welcoming crowd that day, "with beating heart" stood a young seventeen-year-old student, Roald Amundsen. "All the dreams of my boyhood woke to storming life," Amundsen was later to recall. "And for the first time I heard, in my secret thoughts, the whisper clear and insistent: 'If *you* could do the North-West Passage!'"

For all of this time, a second adventure had been percolating through Nansen's brain. The catalyst was an odd throwback to the past – to 1875, when Allen Young, M'Clintock's sledgemate on the Franklin search, had set off in his little ship *Pandora* to try to force his way through Peel Sound and complete the Passage. Young had failed, and eventually the *Pandora* was sold to James Gordon Bennett of the New York *Herald* to be refitted and renamed the *Jeannette,* the vessel that took the ill-fated De Long expedition north to the Bering Sea to try to reach the Pole. The *Jeannette* foundered off the coast of Siberia, but in 1884 pieces of the wreckage began turning up on the coast of Greenland. This suggested the presence of an Arctic current leading from Siberia around the Pole toward North America. There were other clues: Nansen, on his own expedition, had collected traces of sediment from the drift ice east of the island that, on examination, proved to have come from Siberian rivers. Eskimo throwing sticks, peculiar to Alaskan natives along the Bering Strait, and driftwood from Siberian trees had also been found along Greenland's east coast. Why not, then, put a ship into the floes off east Siberia and let the ice carry her westward across the unknown polar basin toward Greenland – perhaps across the Pole itself?

In short, instead of fighting the ice as other explorers had done, Nansen proposed to use the moving ice stream as a propellant, albeit a sluggish one. For that he would require a special kind of craft with straight sides, like a tub, which the ice could not grip or crush, and with a reasonably flat bottom – a ship that, in his words, could "slip like an eel out of the embraces of the ice."

He would also require a special breed of explorer – men who could withstand three or four years of sheer monotony without going mad or resorting to violence. Only Norwegians, he felt, were equal to that ordeal. As he put it, with dry humour, two Norwegians, alone of all other nationals, could sit face to face on a cake of ice for three years without hating each other. Nansen had learned the art of patience from the Eskimos. He liked to tell the story of one group of natives who had travelled up a fiord seeking grass for hay. When they arrived at the field and found the grass too short to cut, they simply sat down and waited for it to grow.

Greely was not the only critic of the Norwegian's scheme. When Nansen addressed the Royal Geographical Society in London in 1892, he found many old Arctic hands highly sceptical. George Nares, "in a friendly spirit," indicated that he didn't think there was such a thing as polar drift. Allen Young, knighted in 1877, believed there was land around the Pole that would frustrate Nansen's plans. Sir Joseph Hooker, who had been to the Antarctic with James Clark Ross, thought the risks not worth taking. Another naval veteran, Admiral Sir George Richards, called it "an amateur nautical expedition." Leopold M'Clintock, on the other hand, praised Nansen and called the project "the most adventurous programme ever brought under the notice of the Royal Geographical Society."

Nansen himself was supremely confident. This time he got the financing he needed, most of it from his government but some from private subscribers who included the king himself. On June 24, 1893, from Christiania, Norway, to the cheers of the multitudes on shore, the little *Fram* set off. Everything about this tightly organized, carefully streamlined journey was in sharp contrast to the cumbersome expeditions of the British Navy. The *Fram* carried only thirteen men, each hand-picked by Nansen himself. There would be no feeling of rank or hierarchy. The work was to be apportioned evenly among Nansen, his captain, Otto Sverdrup, and the others.

The day was dull and gloomy, and Nansen's own feelings matched the weather as he left his home and took the little launch out to the ship. He knew he faced years of exile in the frozen world. "Behind me lay all I held dear in life. And what before me? How many years should pass ere I should see it all again? What would I not have given at that moment to be able to turn back!" He could see his little daughter, Liv, framed in the window of his home, clapping her hands. How long would it be before he saw her again?

But in Nansen's journal there are no entreaties to a protecting Deity, no fevered calls to ambition or even to national sentiment. "If, after all, we are on the wrong track, what then?" he wrote. "Only disappointed human hopes, nothing more. And even if we perish, what will it matter in the endless cycles of eternity?"

After coasting around Europe and Asia, the *Fram,* loaded with

492

dogs, provisions, and equipment, entered the ice off the northeast coast of Siberia and was frozen into the pack on September 25, 1893. There followed two and a half years of monotony, uninterrupted by any of the hardships associated with so many earlier Arctic journeys, as the little vessel slowly drifted in a zigzag course for four hundred miles across the polar sea. The crew grew fat "like prize pigs," in Nansen's phrase. He was, he said, almost ashamed of the easy life "with none of the darkly painted sufferings of the long winter night, which are indispensable to a properly exciting Arctic expedition."

The main worry, he wrote in a bantering aside, was that they would have nothing to write about when they got home. In spite of the hours spent in scientific study – soundings and temperatures to be taken, magnetic observations to be recorded – there was a sense of lassitude that Nansen found hard to shake. "Here I am whining like an old woman," he wrote. "Did I not know all this before I started?" At one point he dreamed that he had got to the Pole – but had taken no accurate observations! To Nansen, a dedicated scientist, the dream was close to being a nightmare.

To while away the time, he read Darwin, Schopenhauer, and the published journals of the earlier explorers, and edited a weekly journal, *Framjaa*. He agreed with David Hume, the English philosopher, that "he is more excellent who can suit his temperament to any circumstances"; that, he wrote, was the philosophy he was practising at the moment. It wasn't always easy: "I long to return to life. . . . The years are passing here. . . . Oh! at times this inactivity crushes one's very soul; one's life seems as dark as the winter night outside; there is sunlight on no other part of it except the past and the far, far distant future. I feel I *must* break through this deadness, this inertia and find some outlet for my energies."

How ironic that Nansen, in the indestructible *Fram,* almost hoped for something close to a catastrophe to break the monotony in the same way that the earlier explorers had prayed for a break from the grinding ice and screaming storms that threatened to wreck their vessels! "Can't something happen?" he asked. "Could not a hurricane come and tear up this ice, and set it to rolling in high waves like the open sea?" But no untoward incident marred the voyage. The ice could not nip or crush the round-sided vessel. When the pressure built up around her she was simply squeezed upward to ride easily over the surrounding floes.

One thing was becoming clear: she would not pass over the Pole.

With that knowledge Nansen found the excuse he needed to shake himself free of inaction. Scientific considerations were thrown aside as he prepared for another audacious exploit. He could no more resist the lure of the Pole than could his predecessors. In January 1895, he made plans for a dash by dogteam to the top of the world. Nansen, the pragmatic scientist, had been replaced by Nansen, the romantic adventurer.

The "exulting feeling of triumph deep in the soul" that swept over him when he realized his ship had reached a record latitude was tempered by "a wave of sadness . . . like bidding farewell to a dear friend" – the *Fram*. Never again, he wrote, "shall I tread this snow-clad deck . . . never again sit in this friendly circle." Nor would he be on hand when the ship burst the bonds of ice and turned her prow homeward.

He well knew the danger he faced in setting off across that ravaged and frozen sea with a single companion. He wrote that a chill crept over him every time he gazed upon the map of the polar world. "The distance before us seems so long and the obstacles in our path may be many." Yet he remained both optimistic and philosophical. In the immensity of the polar night, under the glittering vault of stars, bathed in the light of the flaming aurora, he felt his own insignificance. "Toiling ant," he wrote, "what matters it, whether you reach your goal . . . or not!" On the other hand, he reassured himself that "everything is too carefully prepared to fail now."

He fashioned his own snowshoes: "smooth, tough and light . . . they shall be well rubbed with tar, stearine and tallow, and there shall be speed in them." He had no doubt his legs were up to the test. His companion would be Hjalmar Johansen, "a plucky fellow [who] never gives in." They would take three light sledges, twenty-eight dogs, three kayaks, and food for one hundred days. On March 14, after a couple of false starts, they set off across a hummocky desert that no man had trodden before.

By early April, the going was so hard that Nansen began to have doubts about continuing. He had already recognized that they couldn't reach the Pole. As Parry had discovered almost seventy years before, the ice was moving south as Nansen and Johansen struggled north. Yet he hated to give up. On the verge of despair, he almost turned back, but something impelled him to go on. He gave himself one more day – and then another. He had already gone

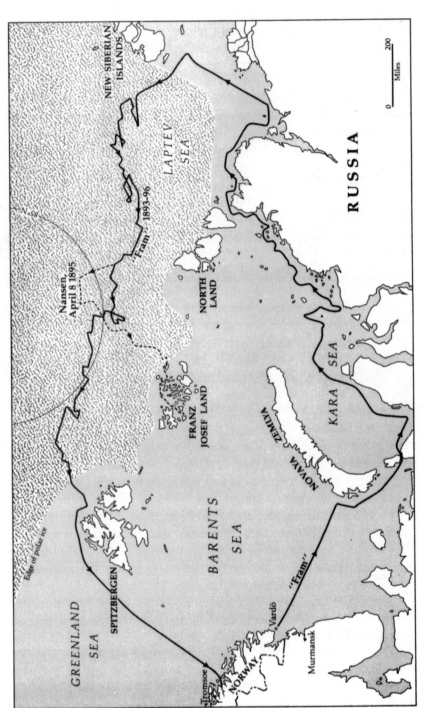

Nansen's Arctic drift and polar attempt, 1893–96

farther north than any previous explorer, but he wanted to squeeze out the last possible mile for his record. At last, on April 8, 1895, he quit. He had reached 86⁰ 13′ N.

Now began a race with time. The closest wintering point would be Franz Josef Land, more than four hundred miles to the southwest. Could they make it before they starved or dropped from exhaustion? The prospect was horrifying, for there was no straight or positive path to their goal. Lanes of water known to the whalers as "leads" opened up before them, making it impossible to reckon the length of a day's march. "What would I not give," Nansen wrote, "to have a certain way before me . . . and be free from this never ending anxiety and uncertainty. . . . I am so tired that I stagger on my snowshoes, and when I fall down, only wish to lie there to save myself the trouble of getting up again. . . ."

He was forced to kill his dogs, one by one, as food for both men and beasts, using a knife to save precious bullets. Yet there was no use for bullets; for almost three months they saw no living creature – only an endless expanse of drift ice. In May they began to scan the horizon longingly, seeking land. A fortnight passed; nothing.

Nansen couldn't understand it: they should have reached Franz Josef Land by this time. Perhaps they were farther east than they had thought. "We do not know where we are and we do not know when this will end," he wrote on June 11. And later: "Shall we reach land while yet we have food . . . ? A quarter of a year we have been wandering in this desert of ice, and here we are still. When we shall see the end of it. I can no longer form any idea. . . ."

The snow turned wet and "as soft and loose as scum," clinging like glue to the sledge runners and to their boots, slowing their march to a crawl and exhausting the dogs. By June 16 there were only three animals left. More leads of water barred their way. That meant that the two men were forced to launch their kayaks, unload the sledges and place them across the little boats, and repeat the process in reverse when they reached the far side. On the last day of June, Nansen grimly surveyed their position: "Here we lie far up in the north: two grim, black soot-stained barbarians, stirring up a mess of soup in a kettle and surrounded on all sides by ice; by ice and nothing else – shining and white, possessed of all the purity we ourselves lack. . . ."

For days they were immobilized by the stickiness of the snow.

Then, in mid-July, when the temperature rose, they began to push forward again, climbing pressure ridges that seemed as high as mountains with clefts between, splashing through ponds and puddles, and paddling across the dark, jagged leads in their kayaks. At last, on July 24, Johansen remarked on a curious black stripe on the horizon. At first he thought it was a cloud, but as they drew closer Nansen thought he saw something rising above the never-ending white line on the horizon. Could it be land?

As they approached, they realized that for the first time in almost two years they were seeing something other than the endless ice-choked sea. To Nansen it was like a vision, a fairyland. "Drift white, it arches above the horizon like distant clouds, which one is afraid will disappear every minute." But it took the pair another month to reach it in their kayaks. It was some time before they realized they had reached one of the islands north of Franz Josef Land.

Their ordeal was not over. The island was uninhabited; winter was closing in. They dug a three-foot hollow in the ground, piled stones above it, roofed it over with walrus skins, and, in this hovel, prepared to sit out the winter.

Since the land was teeming with walrus and polar bear they had plenty to eat. But the monotony was maddening. There was nothing to read but Nansen's navigation table and pocket almanac: ". . . the sight of the printed letters gave one the feeling that there was, after all, a little bit of civilized man left." They had exhausted all conversation and were reduced to playing fantasy games, talking of life at home and how they would spend the following winter. Most of the time they slept. Formal to the end, in the Norwegian manner they did not address each other by their Christian names.

On May 19, 1896, they headed south, hoping somehow to reach Spitzbergen. A month later they had crossed a frozen sound and reached one of the southern islands of Franz Josef Land. There, on the early morning of June 17, Nansen, having set a pot on the fire for breakfast, was about to creep back into his sleeping bag when he heard a sound from out of the mist above the screeching of auks and kittiwakes, a sound that reminded him of a barking dog. He dismissed it, but then he heard it again – a succession of barks. He woke Johansen, who didn't believe him. Nansen, however, set off in the direction of the sound, finding what looked like dog tracks in the snow. Soon, he heard a series of canine yelps. For a moment, he thought he was in a dream, but then the sound of a human voice and a series of halloos caused his heart to pound and the blood to rush to his brain.

He stumbled forward through the ice ridges and saw in the distance, picking his way between the hummocks, the dark figure of a man approaching. This apparition wore an English checked suit and a pair of high rubber boots. The contrast was startling as the two raised their hats and greeted one another. The Englishman, shaved and well groomed, brought with him, in Nansen's description, "a perfume of scented soap, perceptible to the wild man's sharpened senses." The wild man, clad in dirty rags, black with oil and soot, with long, uncombed hair and a shaggy beard, was unrecognizable.

But Nansen recognized the Englishman as Frederick Jackson, who had been commissioned by Alfred Harmsworth, the future Lord Northcliffe, to seek a land route to the North Pole by way of Franz Josef Land. During the brief conversation that followed Nansen took it for granted that Jackson knew who he was and was quite taken aback when the Englishman finally asked, "Aren't you Nansen?"

Nansen acknowledged that he was, whereupon Jackson cried out, "By Jove, I am glad to see you!"

This unexpected and miraculous meeting was not without its ironies. For Nansen, in proving that the North Pole was surrounded by frozen ocean, had dashed all his rescuer's hopes for a land expedition. The two Norwegians returned to Norway on Jackson's ship to a hero's welcome. The *Fram* arrived a week later in almost perfect condition. By drifting from Siberia to Spitzbergen she had proved Nansen right and his detractors dead wrong. En route home, Sverdrup in the *Fram* had stopped at Spitzbergen, where Salomon Andrée, the Swedish balloonist, was making his first attempt to reach the Pole by air. That winter, Nansen, who now knew more about ice conditions in the polar sea than any living man, tried to dissuade him from that mad project. But like so many others before him, Andrée had gone too far on his personal quest to be deterred by cold reason.

2

Andrée's folly On July 29, 1895, while Nansen and Johansen were paddling desperately toward land, a solemn-looking man with a vast walrus moustache rose to his feet in the Great Hall of the Royal Colonial Institute in London to propose to the Sixth International Geographical Congress his audacious scheme to reach the North Pole by air.

Salomon Andrée's audience, which included some of the most distinguished geographers and Arctic experts of the day, was mesmerized by his contagious enthusiasm, his mastery of scientific facts, and his bluntness. When a French scientist asked what Andrée would do if his balloon collapsed in the water before he had time to assemble his boat, Andrée replied with one word: "Drown." But there was considerable scepticism. A.H. Markham, the veteran of the Nares

The Polar ice cap

expedition, now an admiral, opened the discussion on Andrée's paper to point out that in a balloon nobody knew exactly where he was or what was under him. Even if he returned safely and *said* he had reached the Pole, he wouldn't be able to say exactly where he'd been travelling. And what would happen if the balloon came down? How would he survive?

Adolphus Greely, now a general, engaged in a spirited debate with "our ballooning friend," as he called him (just the slightest hint of condescension there), and tried to appeal to Andrée's common sense, urging him to explore something more important. Greely was sceptical of the ability of any balloon to reach the Pole. He pointed out that the escaping gas – a perennial problem with all balloons at that time – would cause the canopy to lose half its carrying power before the voyage was over.

Andrée listened carefully to his critics and, when they were finished, met them head on. Staring down at the old Arctic hands, he asked, "When something happened to your ships, how did you get back? I risk three lives in what you call a foolhardy attempt and you risked how many? A shipload?"

Having thus twisted the knife in General Greely, Andrée now proceeded to extract, like a rabbit from a hat, his answer to a patronizing hint from Greely that he would have trouble raising funds for such a venture.

"*He* hopes I may succeed in *trying* to raise the money and at least make the attempt."

He paused and gestured triumphantly with a swing of his arm.

"*Well, I haf got the money!*"

This dramatic statement brought cheers from the assembly. Foolhardy or not, Andrée had convinced them that he would carry his scheme to completion.

Salomon Andrée was forty-one years old; he had been obsessed by aeronautics for most of his life. As a boy of ten he built a paper airship, which he set off by means of a percussion cap from a hill above his home town of Grenna. That was a mixed success. The balloon soared beautifully over the community, but when it landed it almost set fire to a neighbour's house.

A prize-winning scholar with a degree from the Royal Institute in Stockholm and two years' experience as a draughtsman, the prodigy, aged twenty-two, "bold, proud and just a little cocky," went off to North America to the great Centennial Exposition in Philadelphia. In his spare hours he learned aeronautics from John E. Wise, an experienced aeronaut with four hundred balloon ascents to his credit.

Andrée was very much a child of his time – a dedicated believer in the scientific method, an optimist who had a burning faith in the future of science as the saviour of mankind, which, he wrote, "is still only half awake." He wanted no truck with the supernatural; science, he was convinced, could explain everything. Back in Sweden, he was appointed to help staff his country's polar station at Spitzbergen during the International Polar Year of 1882 – the year that saw Adolphus Greely stationed at Lady Franklin Bay.

Here the industrious young Swede investigated everything from the mysteries of electromagnetism to the properties of whirling snow. The tiniest problems fascinated him; nothing would do but that he try to solve them empirically. Was it, for instance, the polar darkness that affected the colour of the face after a long winter cooped up in a sunless realm? Or was the yellow tint that seemed to suffuse the features due simply to the fact that the investigators themselves were dazzled by the light? To prove his point, after the sun emerged, Andrée shut himself up indoors during the daylight hours for an entire month. "Dangerous? Perhaps; but what am I worth?" he asked. At the end of the period he came out to discover that his face really was a yellowish green, while those of his companions had begun to take on their normal hue.

On another occasion he decided to see how many eggs he could eat at a sitting. He ordered twoscore, boiled, along with bread, butter, and milk. "And now," the waitress asked, deadpan, as she served this monstrous repast, "would you like something else to eat?"

This restless curiosity, this determination to demonstrate the truth or falsity of a theory by personal experimentation, lay behind Andrée's obsession with a balloon voyage to the North Pole. One suspects that unlike his fellow explorers, he wasn't driven so much by the dream of reaching the Pole as by his own curiosity. He wanted to find out if such a trip was possible.

He was a supreme optimist – anybody who thought a balloon would soar over the North Pole would have to have been – but there wasn't a sentimental bone in his body. A cool rationalist, he was also a social reformer, not because his heart bled for the less fortunate but because he believed that technology would make the world a better and more efficient place. He lost his brief appointment to the municipal council of Stockholm because he advocated a reduction of the twelve-hour day to ten hours for men and eight for women. He was convinced that the new technology could and would eventually reduce the length of the work week, and he was right.

A rationalist, he was anti-war, anti-conservative, anti-organized religion. He was also strong willed, ruthlessly self-critical, and a thorough individualist who spoke of egoism as a principle of life and wrote that "to be one's self is, according to my experience, one of the chief conditions for a relatively happy life."

He was both energetic and imaginative, if humourless, but he was never impulsive. Everything must be carefully investigated, each step meticulously worked out. His drives were never sexual. He had a horror of romantic entanglement, ruthlessly stifling the smallest twinges of affection. He abhorred the idea of marriage because it involved "factors which cannot be arranged according to plan." When he felt a "few heart leaves sprouting," he said, "I resolutely pull them up by the roots. . . . I know that if I once let such a feeling live, it would become so strong that I dare not give in to it." He channelled his affections toward his mother, who had been widowed when he was ten. A queer fish indeed – but then only a queer fish of Andrée's boundless curiosity, self-confidence, iron will, and single-minded drive would have mounted such an expedition as took off from Spitzbergen in August of 1897.

In hindsight, Andrée's balloon trip seems the most romantic and madcap of all Arctic adventures – romantic, because balloons were about to become all but obsolete and so are seen today as part of the nostalgia of a vanished era; madcap, because the expedition was clearly doomed from the start. Greely and Markham were right; but as the months wore on and Andrée prevailed, enthusiasm mounted and the world began to think them wrong. In the nineties, Andrée's voyage was not seen as romantic but as futuristic. Then, the balloon represented the cutting edge of technological advance, along with the automobile, the wireless, the X-ray machine, and the bicycle. Sailing ships were already outmoded in this age of steam. But the balloon! Soaring majestically above the crowd, its canopy bulging with hydrogen gas, it heralded the dawn of a new age of flight. Ships had failed to reach the Pole; now science would take over.

Andrée spent three years between 1893 and 1896 testing himself by making nine balloon ascents. His craft, which he bought through a grant from a Swedish foundation, was named *Svea* for his native land. In it, he rose as high as three miles and, on a record trip,

502

travelled for 240 miles. None of this, for Andrée, was sport. While other balloonists floated about, swilling champagne and enjoying the view, Salomon Andrée was taking observations – four hundred in all – on weather, air currents, humidity, and temperature while applying himself to the problem of steering. If he was to seek the Pole, he must learn to direct his vessel, a feat he solved in part through experiments with sails and trailing guide lines.

His polar project was born in March 1894, following a discussion with the great polar explorer Baron Nordenskiöld. The following year, he broached it to the Swedish Academy. The balloon, he announced confidently, would replace the sledge as the main method of Arctic travel. He followed that statement with a formidable set of statistics. He had worked out the principle of dirigibility; he knew exactly how his balloon should be made and what its volume should be (212,000 cubic feet), its construction (varnished double silk), the point of departure (Spitzbergen), the month (July), the exact route to the Pole, and the time required for the balloon to stay in the sky (thirty days). Andrée also had a careful budget: the journey could be made, he reckoned, for $34,500 – and that included the cost of his scientific instruments.

He pooh-poohed critics who were concerned that the weight of the snow or rain that would fall on the canopy would force the balloon to land. He had studied these conditions with his usual thoroughness and was convinced that they presented no problem. The weather was relatively warm in July; the precipitation was light; snow, if it fell at all, would quickly melt; rain would evaporate in the high altitudes.

Andrée finished his speech by appealing to the national honour of his audience – a device that so many previous explorers had used with effect. "Who, I ask, are better qualified to make such an attempt than we Swedes?" The world, he said, expected it of his country, which "must maintain the best traditions in the field of natural science in general, and, not least, in that of polar research in particular."

He did not yet have the money, but he had the backing of Nordenskiöld and other scientists. Soon there appeared at his door an unexpected but welcome visitor in the person of Alfred Nobel, the inventor of dynamite, who contributed half the cost – an example that soon promoted the rest of the sum, including a handsome personal gift of eight thousand dollars from King Oscar himself. Thus Andrée was able to inform the sceptical General Greely the following year, "I haf the money!"

He reached Spitzbergen in the summer of 1896. The canopy of the great balloon, named the *Eagle,* was spread out on June 23. It took four days to inflate it with hydrogen gas, produced on the spot from sulphuric acid and zinc. Now it towered seventy-five feet above the heads of the small group of men who had come to help. When the observation platform and wicker gondola were added, the total height was just under one hundred feet.

Andrée and his two companions were ready to leave. But the wind was wrong, and as the days went by gales sprang up. He began to despair of taking off. Suddenly, on August 14, to the astonishment of all, a strange ship arrived out of the fog. This was the *Fram.* From Otto Sverdrup, Andrée learned that Nansen was somewhere to the north, heading for the Pole by dogteam. It was clearly too late, at this point, to attempt the journey by balloon. The *Eagle* was deflated and the party returned to Stockholm, later to learn that Nansen had been unsuccessful. The prize still remained to be gained.

That winter Andrée sought out Nansen for meteorological advice. Nansen told him bluntly that the prevailing winds were not favourable nor were the weather conditions. He wrote a subtle letter to his fellow explorer, praising him for his courage in abandoning the project and suggesting that he display the same courage again "to await the favorable moment and not start until you are sure it has come."

Nansen, in fact, thought the project foolhardy and was trying to tell Andrée that he should have the guts to quit, but Andrée was now trapped in the momentum of his own enthusiasm. He told Nansen that he would not be able to show the same courage a second time; people were calling him a coward for abandoning the flight in 1896 – or at least he thought they were. Now he was determined to press on. Ballooning was very much in vogue, as the stampede to the new Klondike gold fields would soon demonstrate. All sorts of imaginative schemes would be hatched in 1897 to reach the gold fields by air. In New York, one Leo Stevens, Jr. (who called himself Don Carlos Stevens), was planning to build the largest balloon in the world. In Kalamazoo, another entrepreneur would announce a regular fortnightly balloon route to Dawson City. In Dublin, an Irish gold seeker claimed to be building a balloon big enough to take fifty passengers to the Klondike. In the long run nothing came of any of these schemes – but ballooning, as a practical method of travel, was very much in the public mind. How could Andrée call it quits?

He arrived in Spitzbergen in May 1897, much earlier than the

504

previous year. It did not help that one of his crew from the year before – Nils Ekholm, his former boss on the International Polar Year Expedition – had declined to sign on again. Ekholm didn't think the *Eagle* would retain enough of its gas to complete the journey; recently married, he was also reluctant to leave his wife. But Nils Strindberg, a twenty-five-year-old physicist from an old Stockholm family, stayed with the expedition even though he too was engaged to be married immediately on his return. Ekholm's place was taken by Knut Frankel, a twenty-seven-year-old sportsman, gymnast, and civil engineer.

The *Eagle* was inflated early in July. Forty tons of iron filings, thirty-nine tons of sulphuric acid, and seventy-five tons of water were required to produce enough hydrogen to inflate the canopy. By July 11, everything was ready. A stiff wind from the east was rattling the slats of the wooden structure in which the balloon was held captive. Andrée and his two associates were eager to be off. When the wind changed direction at last, Andrée gave the word to prepare for take-off.

The balloon was ready in a few hours. Thirty-two carrier pigeons, which would relay messages to civilization, were taken on board. Twelve cork buoys with Swedish flags that could be dropped into the sea were also loaded. The scientific instruments hung from a wooden ring three feet above the observation platform. Three hundred canvas pockets in the netting held enough provisions for four months as well as a collapsible boat, a sled, and a cookstove that could be lowered into the gondola.

In the words of his French assistant, Alexis Machuron, Andrée remained, as always, "calm, cold, and impassible, not a trace of emotion . . . visible on his countenance, nothing but an expression of firm resolution and an indomitable will." Andrée's enthusiastic young companions could not know that for some time the explorer had been assailed by doubts and forebodings. He had prepared his will, the preamble to which was uncharacteristically gloomy. "I have a premonition," he wrote, "that this terrible journey will lead to my death." Otto Sverdrup, who was on hand that day, was one of the few who sensed Andrée's uncertainty. It seemed to Sverdrup that the balloonist had little faith in the success of the expedition.

But the die was cast. Andrée was the prisoner of his own publicity. As Sverdrup put it, "he felt he ought to start as he and his companions had made all preparations." He could not in honour turn back.

505

The absolute certainty with which he had planned and expounded on his aerial odyssey had convinced the lay world, if not the scientists, that he could bring it off. "The departure is decided upon," he said, and that was that.

There were a few last farewells. Strindberg was suddenly overcome with emotion as he consigned to a friend his last letter to his fiancée, whose photograph he carried next to his heart. Andrée dispatched some hasty telegrams. Then he tore himself away from the embraces of his comrades, took his position on the wicker bridge of the gondola, and shouted, "Let's go."

The group on the ground watched as the three men cut away the ballast bags. A few minutes later, all ties were severed and the great vessel soared into the sky. Dragged by the wind a mere hundred metres above the sea, it suddenly dipped in the onslaught of the air currents pouring down from the mountains behind. The onlookers watched with horror as the gondola touched the water; then, to their relief, the balloon slowly began to rise. There was one unfortunate portent: the guidelines that had been designed to help the vessel tack in the wind caught on some rocks and were torn away. But to this the ground party paid little attention as they waved handkerchiefs at the disappearing sphere, travelling straight north. Machuron, the balloon expert, was sure that if the balloon kept that direction it would reach the Pole in two days.

The *Eagle* travelled on, its size diminishing to that of an egg in the eyes of the onlookers, until it cleared a low ridge of hills where it stood out clearly for several minutes against the frost blue of the northern sky. Then it was gone, never to be seen again.

Andrée and his two companions were swallowed by the Arctic. Apart from a single pigeon, which returned with a brief message of his position on July 13, no hint of their fate was revealed for another thirty-three years, in spite of a series of relief expeditions. Then, in the summer of 1930, a whaling ship discovered a trio of skeletons on an ice-sheathed rock known as White Island, just off the main island of the Spitzbergen archipelago. From Andrée's diary and other records, members of the Swedish Society for Anthropology and Geography were able to piece together and publish most of the story of what happened to Salomon August Andrée and his two companions.

Balloon travel is one of the most peaceful of all pursuits. When the three explorers set off from Spitzbergen they must have felt the sense of elation that comes over every balloonist as he slides silently

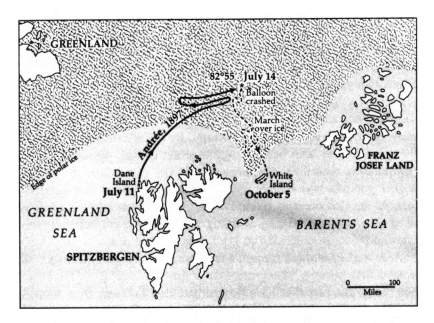

Andrée's ill-fated balloon expedition, 1897

through the skies. Because the balloon is moving with the wind, there *is* no wind, not even the sound of the wind. Andrée once remarked that from the distance of a mile in the sky he could easily hear the barking of a dog on the ground below.

But he had not reckoned on the sensitivity of the *Eagle* – indeed of all balloons – to changes in temperature and to the moisture content of the surrounding air. In the sunlight, when the inflating gas heated and expanded, the balloon rose half a mile. But when the *Eagle* entered clouds and mist began to gather on the canopy, the weight of the water and the change in the temperature caused it to drop to a point where the broken guidelines touched the sea – a circumstance that would doom the expedition within three days.

By early morning on July 12, the *Eagle* had taken on a character of its own. It dropped; it rose; it stood still; it gathered speed, slowed down, moved on, changed direction. The lack of guidelines made it difficult to steer. The only real control that Andrée and his comrades had was when they jettisoned some ballast to cause a temporary rise. Before the flight ended, they had thrown out 680 pounds.

At one point when they were caught in the dead centre of a cyclonic disturbance (the so-called "eye" of the cyclone) the balloon

507

didn't move at all. When it dropped and the shortened guidelines touched the ground, the weight was automatically decreased by that portion of the lines dragging on the ice. That caused the balloon to rise again briefly. It also meant that the period of free flight was over. From this point on the *Eagle* was bumping along above the ice, dragging the lines below it.

As the journey progressed through fog and cloud, both water and snow began to weigh down the canopy. By the afternoon of July 12, the gondola was also being dragged along the ice. By dinnertime, Andrée was recording eight touches in thirty minutes. Soon the wicker gondola was leaving its mark on the ice every five hundred feet. At ten that evening, the heavily weighted-down *Eagle* came to a dead stop, with everything dripping wet. At midnight her three exhausted passengers decided to grab some blessed rest.

Now Andrée allowed himself a few rare philosophical musings. "Is it not a little strange," he wrote, "to be floating here above the Polar Sea. To be the first that have floated here in a balloon. How soon, I wonder, shall we have successors? Shall we be thought mad or will our example be followed? I cannot deny that all three of us are dominated by a feeling of pride. We think we can well face death, having done what we have done. Isn't it all, perhaps, the expression of an extremely strong sense of individuality which cannot bear the thought of living and dying like a man in the ranks, forgotten by coming generations? Is this ambition?"

For thirteen hours, the balloon hung motionless, anchored by a guide rope hooked under a block of ice. Here was irony. The wind had changed direction during the night. Had the guide rope not been caught, the *Eagle* would almost certainly have been blown back to northern Spitzbergen. But at 10:55 on the morning of July 13, the wind reversed again; the balloon loosed itself with a jerk and resumed its northerly flight. The latitude at that moment was 82° N.

The fog increased. Heavy with hoarfrost, the balloon dragged its car along the ice hummocks. The concussions were so frequent that Strindberg became seasick. More ballast went over the side, and the balloon rose. With the fog growing thicker, the car was again pounded violently against an endless expanse of ice, veined by dark channels and pocked by pools of melt water.

Andrée realized that this desperate journey could not continue. He began to search about for a place to land, but it was past seven on the

508

morning of the fourteenth before he found one. His diary entries, which were becoming increasingly brief, simply reported: "We jumped out of the balloon."

Exhausted, they could not afford to rest for another seven hours. There was packing to be done; a camp must be set up; careful scientific records had to be kept. They had reached latitude 82⁰ 56' N. Two hundred miles from the nearest land, they were precariously camped on a sea filled with drifting ice. From the roof of the car of the fallen *Eagle,* Andrée looked out on a fearful expanse of white. Peering through the mist, in all directions he could see only a chaos of twisting, moving, shifting ice blocks, connected into vast fields, each one honeycombed with dark channels and small lakes. The balloon would have to be abandoned.

By evening, the fog had closed in so tightly they were marooned for a week. They had packed each of the three sledges with four hundred pounds of provisions and equipment, and there was also the collapsible boat. When the fog lifted on July 22, 1897, they set off, hoping to reach Cape Flora on the Franz Josef Land archipelago, some two hundred and ten miles to the southeast. There, where Nansen had wintered successfully, was a large supply depot. On July 25, the birthday of his fiancée, Anna, Strindberg wrote an optimistic letter. His only worry, he told her, was that they would not reach home by autumn and then *she* would worry. "You can imagine how I am tortured by the thought of it, too, but not for my own sake, for now I do not mind if I have hardships, as long as I can come home at last."

The going was dreadful, the fog sometimes so thick they could scarcely spot the dark leads that blocked their passage. On July 31, in one six-hour period they were forced to ferry the sledges over ten such channels. Even on solid ice they were often floundering through snow up to their knees. By that time they had jettisoned part of their load. Five days later they realized that the intervening sea current made it impossible to continue eastward toward Cape Flora. The ice drift was taking them west faster than they had been able to march toward the east. On August 4, Andrée decided to abandon the attempt to reach Franz Josef Land and change direction in hopes of reaching Seven Island off the north coast of Spitzbergen, where, he knew, a smaller depot was available. The journey westward, he figured, would take six or seven weeks.

Their meals were spartan, even when they shot an occasional gull and, on one memorable day, a fat bear cub. Before them, the frozen world stretched endlessly to the blurred line of the horizon. Here were mile-wide leads that took four hours to cross. Here were vast jungles of ice hillocks, separated by frozen pools, stretching for miles. And then, by contrast, a webbing of melt-water ponds, so shallow that the boat could not be launched. The travellers, suffering now from dysentery, hunger, and lameness, were forced to splash their way through.

The early August days had been so warm that Andrée wished he could remove his jumper. But as the month dragged on the temperature dropped. Frankel injured his left foot and couldn't haul his sledge; the others took turns shuttling it forward. Worst of all, the sea currents refused to co-operate. By September 9 the drift had again taken them eighteen miles in the wrong direction. They had lost all hope of reaching their goal.

Worn out and ill, their sledges broken down, their inadequate clothing in tatters, they decided to seek out a level floe, make camp, and let the drift take them south. Strindberg found a hollowed-out piece of ice, which he converted into a hut by building a ramp of ice blocks. There, fortified at last by fresh seal and bear meat, some of which they devoured raw, they rested.

On September 17, they spotted land – a low, whalebacked island, almost completely smothered by a vast glacier. As the weather grew worse and the Fahrenheit thermometer registered eighteen degrees of frost, the drifting floe took them round to the island's south side. On the night of October 4, in the bitter cold, their precarious raft broke into splinters not far from shore.

From the fragmentary and almost illegible notes left by Andrée and Strindberg, the investigators pieced together a brief account of the expedition's last days. Somehow they made it to shore. They put up a tent on a rocky hill above the beach and crouched in it, half protected from the howling wind, snow, and sleet that whirled about them. They tried to build a snow house and managed to pull some driftwood up near the tent. But after October 7 there was only silence.

In 1930, when the skeletons of the missing men were discovered on White Island, it was clear that none had had the strength to build a proper shelter or to unload the boat, which was found, with one of the sledges, drawn up on the beach. Cold and exhaustion had done for all three. Strindberg had apparently died first; his body was found, buried by his surviving comrades in Arctic fashion between two rocks. The other skeletons were found not far from the beached boat. The investigators guessed that Andrée had been the last to die. He had, apparently, sat down quietly in the snow, leaned back against a rocky projection, and, impassive and unemotional to the end, quietly and perhaps gratefully awaited death.

3

Early in October the following year – 1898 – Otto Sverdrup, still the captain of the *Fram,* had a chilly and oddly revealing encounter on the shores of a fiord in the east coast of Ellesmere Island.

Peary's obsession

Sverdrup was a dedicated explorer. The race to reach the North Pole was growing in intensity, but to Sverdrup it was little more than an international sporting event. He had a more positive program in mind. With Nansen's blessing, he had set off in the *Fram* to chart the maze of unknown islands west of Ellesmere – an undertaking that would occupy four years, unlock the secrets of 100,000 square miles of unexplored territory, enshrine his name on the map of the High Arctic, and make his reputation as one of the greatest explorers of his era.

On this cold, clear October day, Sverdrup and his companions were preparing a meal in a tent pitched on the bank of the fiord. The *Fram* was nearby, not far from the entrance to the frozen waters of Kane Basin. Suddenly, in the distance, somebody spotted two fur-clad figures seated on an Eskimo sledge drawn by eight dogs. Who could they be? No natives lived on this inhospitable island. Sverdrup guessed at once that this must be Robert Peary, the American explorer, whose name was already becoming a legend in the North.

A few moments later Peary and his native companion drew up. It was not a propitious encounter.

"Are you Sverdrup?" Peary asked, curtly.

Sverdrup acknowledged that he was.

"My ship is frozen in at Cape Hawks," said Peary. "There is no way of getting through Robeson Channel. It has frozen fast." Peary, who was obsessively jealous and secretive, volunteered no further information. He was planning to go north to Fort Conger, Greely's old headquarters, to use it as a base for an assault on the North Pole, but he had no intention of telling anything to Sverdrup. Peary wrote to his wife that the meeting between the two was short "but not effusive." The lack of cordiality was all on Peary's part. The genial Sverdrup would have been astonished to know that the American considered him a rival in his drive to the Pole. He offered Peary a cup of coffee. One of his own men was already grinding the beans. Peary refused, and a moment later he was off. The meeting was so short that Sverdrup later said he'd hardly had time to take off his mittens.

Later, aboard his ship, the *Windward,* pacing angrily up and down his cabin, Peary turned to his black servant, Matthew Henson, and cried, "Sverdrup may at this minute be planning to beat me to Fort Conger! . . . I can't let him do it! I'll get to Conger before Sverdrup if it kills me!" It almost did.

No other explorer in Arctic history was ever as single-minded in the pursuit of his goal as Robert Edwin Peary, no other as paranoid in his suspicion and even hatred of those he considered rivals and interlopers, no other as ruthless, as arrogant, as insensitive, or as self-serving. Of all the bizarre and eccentric human creatures who sought the Arctic Grail, Peary is the least lovable. He toadied to his superiors and rode roughshod over those beneath him, some of whom – as even an admiring biographer has admitted – reached the finish of an expedition with murder in their hearts. Yet it may be that these very qualities were the key to Peary's success. Relentless ambition drove him on where others might have faltered. Even aside from the North Pole, he must be given his due as one of the greatest explorers of the period.

But it was the Pole that had obsessed him since early manhood and perhaps even before that. He was not really concerned about scientific discoveries or in charting the unknown. He had little interest in flora and fauna. His prime purpose was to reach this single goal before anybody could "forestall" him – a much-used Peary word that, with its suggestion of underhanded tactics, hints at his paranoia. And even the conquest of the Pole was not, in Peary's view, an end in itself but only a means to an end. Peary hungered for fame and fortune; he made no bones about that. The Pole, he knew, would give him both.

When Sverdrup encountered him in October 1898, Peary was far from attaining his life's ambition. At forty-two he was a formidable figure, six feet tall, erect and strapping, big chested and hard muscled. There was an animal fierceness about him – the shaggy red

512

beard, the tangled mat of hair, the steely grey eyes, the flared nostrils and strong, almost wolfish teeth – enhanced by the furs that enveloped him. He loved to be photographed in those furs, glowering fiercely into the camera, the quintessential Arctic explorer. These were studio portraits, carefully posed often in the heat of summer; but there was nothing phony about them, for they caught the real Peary – implacable, relentless, savagely ambitious.

As a child he had been inspired by Elisha Kane and the tales of the polar regions in Kane's "wonderful book." In those early years he had spoken with a lisp; he fought hard to rid himself of this seemingly effeminate affliction and almost succeeded, so that in his manhood he was able to conceal it by speaking slowly and distinctly. Only in his rages did the impediment betray him. It was one of many examples of his drive toward self-improvement.

He joined the U.S. Navy as a civil engineer. In spite of the fact that he would later be called "Commander Peary," and finally "Rear Admiral Peary," he was never a line officer. His proper title was always "Civil Engineer Peary," but he didn't care for that.

From the beginning of his career he knew what he wanted. At twenty-four, he wrote: "I would like to acquire a name which could be an open sesame to circles of culture and refinement." At twenty-five he told his mother, "I must be the peer or superior of those about me to be comfortable. . . ." Peary was not a team player; he, and he alone, must always get the credit.

In 1886, after a stint in Nicaragua, Peary the civil engineer obtained a summer's leave from the Navy and some funds from his mother, set aside his plans for an advantageous marriage, and attempted the first crossing of the Greenland ice cap at its widest point.

It was a failure. After twenty-six days he had managed to travel less than one hundred nautical miles and was forced to return. But it was not in his nature to countenance failure. In all of Peary's Arctic adventures, he always managed to emerge with some trophy, real or imagined, that would carry with it the aura of success. He was later to downplay this first effort by calling it merely a "reconnaissance." But he also claimed that he had penetrated the ice cap "a greater distance than any white man previously." That was a shaky boast and a mean-spirited one. Baron Adolph Erik Nordenskiöld had attempted the crossing three years before Peary. Two of his Laplanders had gone farther than the American. Peary, who hated giving credit to anyone else, no doubt felt they were not "white men."

When he returned, Peary boasted in a letter to his mother that the trip had "brought my name before the world." He explained: "I will next winter be one of the foremost in the highest circles in the capital, and make powerful friends with whom I can shape my future." And then he added the phrase so often quoted by admirers and detractors alike: "Remember, Mother, I *must* have fame."

He would have it at anyone's expense. In 1889, when he learned that Nansen had made the Greenland crossing at a narrower point farther south, he minimized the Norwegian's achievement and tried to claim publicly that Nansen had, in effect, stolen his plan, which he had published in 1886. Nansen, however, had published his own theories about the crossing as early as 1882 and in more detail in 1883. Nansen's achievement, Peary wrote to a friend, "in forestalling my work was a serious blow to me." As for Nansen's book, Peary dismissed it as a pretentious affair. The original material it contained, he said, "was hardly greater than I obtained . . . Nansen profited much by my experience."

Peary married his fiancée, Josephine Diebitsch, the daughter of a Smithsonian savant, and immediately set about planning a more ambitious expedition. He would cross northwest Greenland over the ice cap and continue into unknown territory to the north. It was not known for certain at that time that Greenland was an island. For all anybody knew, that mysterious realm might extend all the way to the Pole. Peary meant to find out and in the process scout a possible polar route.

He had immersed himself in Arctic lore. He had read all the journals of the explorers and was prepared to learn from them. He had already concluded that the time had arrived for an organizational change in polar exploration. "The old method of large parties and several ships has been run into the ground. . . . The English, with true John Bull obstinacy, still stick to the old plan." Peary was more struck by the example of Frederick Schwatka of the U.S. Cavalry, who in 1878 had found further Franklin relics on King William Island and had adopted the idea of a small party depending largely on native techniques. (One of those natives was Ebierbing, Charles Hall's old companion Joe.) That, Peary wrote, "deserves to be recorded as the American plan." It was, of course, not new. Rae, Kennedy, and Hall, among others, had helped to pioneer it. But Peary, with his meticulous preparation and his use of hand-picked and personally trained natives, took it several steps farther.

514

By June 1891, he was ready to go north again. He had spent the intervening years raising ten thousand dollars for the venture – not an easy task after the twin tragedies of the Greely and the *Jeannette* expeditions. He sailed on June 21 with seven companions, including Matthew Henson, his black body-servant, John Verkoeff, a young geologist who contributed two thousand dollars to the venture, Eivend Astrup, an enthusiastic young Norwegian who hero-worshipped his leader, and a genial Brooklyn doctor, Frederick Albert Cook, whose name would forever be intertwined with Peary's. The most controversial member of the party was Josephine Peary, the explorer's tall, attractive, and strong-willed wife, the first white woman ever to venture into the Arctic. Many disapproved of a woman accompanying a dangerous expedition, but Peary believed, as the Eskimos did, that women were an important source of morale on any journey. Indeed, he advocated that his men take native women with them whenever possible.

The party wintered on the Greenland coast. On April 30, 1892, Peary set off on a sledge journey that more than equalled any earlier one. With only Astrup as his companion for most of the way, he cut across the northwest corner of the great island – a distance of some five hundred miles – to reach what he believed to be its northernmost point. In doing so he established its insularity – or so he thought. He reached a large indentation in the coast, which he named Independence Bay, and climbed an escarpment he called Navy Cliff. From here, he claimed, he saw a channel marking Greenland's most northerly boundary and beyond that a vast new land. He named the channel Peary Channel and the new land Peary Land. Astrup, in his own account of the arrival at Independence Bay and the scaling of Navy Cliff, made no mention of the Peary Channel – and with good reason: it did not exist. But a generation passed before Peary's error was discovered. Greenland actually continued on for some distance. Peary, in spite of his claim, had not crossed the island.

These phantom discoveries may have been the results of wishful thinking, a weakness that dogged more than one Arctic explorer. Even without them, Peary had made a remarkable trek. In a singular feat of endurance he and Astrup had managed the longest sledge journey of its kind – more than 1,100 miles over a period of eighty-five days. Nansen, by contrast, had gone 235 miles in forty days, and Peary's speeds were double those of Nansen. With this one feat, Peary had vaulted into the ranks of the world's leading explorers.

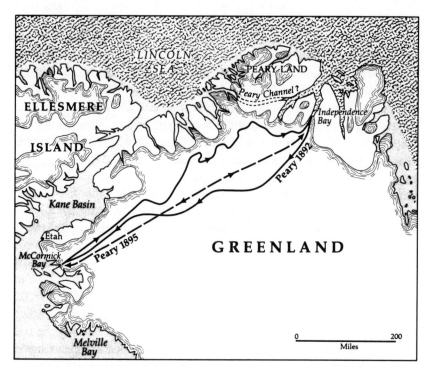

Peary's two expeditions across Greenland, 1892 and 1895

The excursion had not been without its tensions. The independent-minded John Verkoeff had chafed under Peary's authoritarian command and even more under Mrs. Peary's domination. "I will never go home in the same ship with that man and that woman," he told Dr. Cook. That was to be his undoing. During a winter trip around Inglefield Gulf, he left the main party, never to be seen again.

Peary reached the United States determined to return to the Arctic as soon as feasible. He set himself a gruelling pace on the lecture circuit, giving 165 speeches in 103 days. The sizable fees – as much as two thousand dollars a day – augmented by additional contributions from wealthy supporters funded the expedition that left for Greenland in the summer of 1893. This time the amiable Dr. Cook declined to be a member of the Peary party; he had asked his leader's permission to publish a report on his ethno-biological studies, but Peary, who wanted no rival for the public's attention, turned him down. So Cook quit. Like all members of all of Peary's expeditions, Cook's

516

contract was specific: Peary, he had agreed, would be sole commander, his instructions and directions would be law, no one but Peary would write or lecture or give out any information about the expedition, and all journals and diaries were his property and must be turned over to him.

Peary's ship, the *Falcon*, slipped across the treacherous Melville Bay in an astonishing twenty-four hours and dropped the party off at Bowdoin Bay in Inglefield Gulf on the Greenland coast. There Peary set up his headquarters, which he named Anniversary Lodge; and there, on September 12, Jo Peary gave birth to a blue-eyed baby girl, Marie Ahnighito, a curiosity for the Eskimos, who travelled for miles to see the "Snow Baby," as they called her.

These were the same Etah Eskimos that John Ross in 1818 had named the Arctic Highlanders and who had, over the best part of a century, aided and succoured so many exploring parties. Peary called them the Polar Eskimos and adopted a proprietary attitude toward them. They were "my Eskimos" or sometimes "my children." He boasted that he had trained them in what became known as the Peary System. But if Peary trained the Eskimos, it was also true that the Eskimos trained Peary.

Peary's attitude toward these natives was ambivalent. He liked and admired them. He did not believe, as the early explorers had believed, that they should be Christianized or civilized – quite the opposite. Nor was he in the least offended, as others had been, by their morals. In fact, he took an Eskimo mistress. She bore him a child, and he even published a nude photograph of her in one of his books, horrifying several of his wealthy benefactors.

On the other hand, Peary always thought them an inferior race. Like the dogs who pulled his sledges, they were a means to an end. "I have often been asked," he wrote, " 'Of what use are the Eskimos to the world?' They are too far removed to be of any value for commercial enterprises; and furthermore they lack ambition. They have no literature, nor, properly speaking, any art. They value life only as does a fox, or a bear, purely by instinct. But let us not forget that these people, trustworthy and hardy, will yet prove their value to mankind. With their help, the world shall discover the Pole."

Like Matthew Henson, his black servant, whom he once upbraided for failing to call him "Sir," the Eskimos, to Peary, were no more than tools. Henson had learned to speak their tongue, even though he was paid less than his white companions (forty dollars a

517

month in contrast to eighty or one hundred). But Peary, in all his years in the Arctic, never learned the language of "his" Eskimos, although from time to time some of his supporters hinted that he was fluent. Nor did he produce a single useful ethnographical or archaeological study.

On the other hand, Peary must be credited with adapting native methods to modern sledging parties to a remarkable degree. More than any previous explorer, he understood the value of dogs. Others had been forced on occasion to eat their animals; Peary *planned* to eat his, thus extending the range of his light, flexible sledges. Like Rae, he carried no tents, relying entirely on snow houses. He didn't pack a sleeping bag, either; he *wore* it, as the fur-clad natives did. He lived off the land wherever possible, with the help of experienced native hunters. And he even improved the quality and the flavour of the pemmican that was still the staple food in polar exploration.

None of these techniques, however, was very effective in March 1894, when he tried and failed to cross the Greenland ice cap. He managed 128 miles and then was forced to give up with nothing to show for his efforts. But he refused to admit defeat. The others might return gratefully to America when the ship arrived, but he, Peary, insisted on staying another winter to try again – alone, if necessary. He had a brief reunion with his wife when he returned to the Greenland coast and then bid her and all his crew good-bye, save for the faithful Henson and a young man named Hugh Lee, who volunteered to remain.

It is impossible not to admire Peary's strength of will during these last moments of leave-taking. It could not have been an easy parting. On that melancholy morning of August 26, when the ship left, he wrote that he had "eyes only for the white handkerchief fluttering from the port of Jo's cabin." But those last good-byes were to him no sadder than his recent failure. "So ends with the vanishing ship the ill-omened first half of my expedition. . . ." he declared. That night he found he could not bear to sleep in the room that the two had shared; instead, he rolled himself up in a couple of deerskins in the dining room.

On April 1, 1895, Peary set off again for the northwest tip of Greenland, again seeking a possible route to the North Pole. "The winter has been a nightmare to me," he wrote to Jo before taking off, ". . . the cold, damp, frost-lined room has made me think of the tomb. The only bright moments have been when I was thinking of

518

you. . . . I have kissed the place where your head rested, have kissed my blue-eyed baby's socks, and I carry with me next my heart your last letter. . . ."

The struggle would be gruelling. Almost at the outset he discovered that the caches he had laid out for the journey could not be found. At the foot of the great ice cap he sent his four native companions back to the coast. With Henson, Lee, and forty-two dogs, he would attempt the main journey alone. When the trio reached the crest, five hundred miles from Anniversary Lodge, they had eleven animals left and not enough food to ensure a return journey. Peary determined to continue towards Independence Bay. Lee was forced to drop out; the other two pushed on. At last, fortified by a kill of muskoxen, they reached Independence Bay and climbed Navy Cliff, which Peary and Astrup had first climbed in 1892. In the distance, Peary declared later, he could see a line of black, precipitous cliffs and a towering mountain, seventy-five miles due north, which he named Mount Wishtar.

But where was Peary Channel, which he claimed to have seen on that previous expedition? He made no mention of it in his later reports, although, he said, the day was clear – clearer, in fact, than it had been on that previous occasion. Later explorations would confirm that there was no Peary Channel. Was Peary confused by another mirage? Was it a figment of his imagination? It is hardly possible that he could have made the same mistake twice, but if he realized that it was a mistake he kept quiet about it. The territory occupied by the "Peary Channel," which in his words "marked the northern boundary of the mainland of Greenland," was later found to contain high land. On two separate trips Peary didn't mention seeing that. Instead, he again insisted that he had confirmed the insularity of Greenland and for that the world had only his word. Henson, who was "as loyal and responsive to my will as the fingers of my right hand," could not read instruments. Was Peary actually where he claimed to be on two occasions? If so, was he indulging in a form of wishful thinking? Or, realizing his previous error, did he now gloss over it rather than admit failure? Whatever the answer, he was dead wrong.

A race to the west coast followed – a literal race with death in which they made incredible speeds, travelling more than twenty miles a day. Lee, whom they picked up on the return journey, found it difficult to keep up the pace. He urged Peary to leave him to die, but

519

Peary would have none of that. "We will all get home or none of us will," he declared. It was a close thing; they stumbled into camp half starved and demented, with just one dog left alive. Lee later said he thought Peary seemed to want to avoid having to go home a failure; he had been strangely reckless about the great crevasses that could easily have swallowed him.

For he had failed. His only real discovery was negative. This was obviously not the route to the North Pole. Peary's mind seemed to have been affected: he actually toyed with the suspicion that Henson was trying to poison him. He rid himself of that fantasy, but his shattered dreams could not be dismissed so easily.

He *must* bring back some sort of trophy to show that these two years had not been in vain. In the summer of 1894 he had set out to find the mysterious "iron mountain" that had been a legend among explorers since John Ross's day. Ross, in 1818, had discovered that of all the Greenland Eskimos he encountered, only his "Arctic High-landers" were using implements made of iron. The iron came from a "mountain" some twenty-five miles from his anchorage, but although Ross learned the exact latitude and longitude of the find, he was unable to take the time to seek it out. A piece of this iron, brought back to England and analysed, proved to have come from a meteorite.

There was, in fact, very little real mystery and no "mountain," in spite of the legends. Peary, too, was convinced that the iron was meteoric. There appeared to be three sources, shaped, according to the natives, like a woman, a dog, and a tent, and all hurled from the sky by a supernatural power. The Eskimos were reluctant to take Peary to the site; it was to them a sacred spot and, until traders arrived, had been their only source of metal. In the end, however, they revealed the secret. Digging in the snow, Peary found the "woman," a shapeless mass of brown ore. He scrawled his initials on it and, with his polar route attempt a failure, was able in the summer of 1895 to raise both the three-ton "woman" and the three-hundred-pound "dog" meteorites and take them back to the United States.

These prizes were not enough for Peary. The only real purpose of his two-year absence from civilization, the route to the Pole, still eluded him, and he was now forty years old. "I shall never see the North Pole unless some one brings it here," the dispirited explorer told the press on his return. "In my judgement such work requires a far far younger man than I."

Nonetheless he went back to Greenland on two summer journeys in 1896 and 1897 and in the second year managed to bring back the largest meteorite of all, the one the Eskimos called "the tent." It weighed 37.5 tons. Peary explained away his apparent theft of three priceless relics by pointing out that the natives no longer needed the iron, thanks to the presence of white traders (of whom he was the leading figure). Besides, he explained, he had rewarded "my faithful Eskimos" with biscuits, guns, knives, and ammunition. It was certainly a profitable bargain. Some time later Jo Peary sold all three meteorites to the American Museum of Natural History for forty thousand dollars.

Nor were these Peary's only trophies. Dr. Franz Boas, the famous anthropologist, then assistant curator of the museum, had suggested that Peary also bring an Eskimo back for study. Peary, who in 1896 had thought nothing of digging up the graves of newly dead natives (some of whom were his friends) and selling the bodies to the museum for profit, obliged in 1897 with no fewer than six. These included Nuktaq, son of the great Kalutunah (Hayes's friend), and Qisuk, whom Peary called the Smiler, two of his best hunters and dog drivers, together with Nuktaq's wife, Atanga, his twelve-year-old daughter, Aviak, Qisuk's son, Minnik, and a sixth youngster, Usaakassak.

As Minnik was later to describe it, "they promised us nice warm houses in the sunshine land, and guns and knives and needles and many other things." These promises were not kept. The six Eskimos were housed in the basement of the museum, where they soon developed colds that turned into pneumonia. By May 1898, Nuktaq, Qisuk, Atanga, and Aviak were dead and their bodies had been turned over to the museum for examination and study. To keep this knowledge from young Minnik, the museum's scientists held a bizarre "funeral," using a log in place of a corpse, in Boas's words "to appease the boy, and keep him from discovering that his father's body had been chopped up and the bones placed in the collection of the institution." Peary appears to have paid very little attention to these tragedies. Certainly in the book he published about his two-year stint in Greenland there is no mention of the incident; on the contrary, he referred to his two male hunters as if they were still alive in the Arctic.

Usaakassak managed to get home, but it was years before Minnik returned. At first he didn't want to go; later, Peary refused to take him in the belief that it was too late for him to acclimate himself to Eskimo life after the long term in New York. Certainly when Minnik finally reached Greenland, some years after the New York *World* broke his story, he found he could not fit in. He went back to the United States in 1916, drifted from one job to another, and died of influenza in the fall of 1918.

While his Eskimo friends were dying in Bellevue Hospital, Peary was preparing for another onslaught on the Pole. The gloom he had expressed to the press on his return from Greenland in 1895 had been at least partially dissipated when the American Geographical Society in January 1897 awarded him its first Cullom Gold Medal for establishing the insularity of Greenland. The Royal Geographical Society followed in 1898, awarding him its Patron's Gold Medal. Thus inspired, Peary prepared for a new assault on the Pole. His plan was to sail as far north as possible and establish a base from which he could make spring drives to his objective.

As early as 1897 he had tried for a five-year leave from the Navy, a delicate proposition in the light of the threat of war with Spain. Active naval officers were jealous of Peary's political wire-pulling, but it got him what he wanted – not only leave but also funds for the venture (in spite of the war that was declared in April 1898). His chief supporter was Morris K. Jesup, a philanthropist who had made a fortune in banking and railroad supplies. One of the founders of the American Museum of Natural History and also president of the American Geographical Society, Jesup through his support of Peary would soon have his name stamped on the northernmost point of land in the world.

Jesup persuaded a group of prominent businessmen to back Peary's newest attempt to reach the Pole. In London, Alfred Harmsworth, the London newspaper magnate, offered his steam yacht, *Windward*, the same vessel that had rescued Nansen in Franz Josef Land.

Shortly thereafter, Peary learned that Otto Sverdrup was planning to take the *Fram* into the same area of Smith Sound and Kane Basin. Peary was furious. This was *his* territory and Sverdrup was poaching on it! He could not believe that Sverdrup had no interest in the Pole. The proposed expedition, he told Jesup, was "an unprincipled attempt . . . to appropriate my route, my plans and my objects. . . ." Accordingly, he accelerated his own plans to go north.

The captain of the *Windward* would be John Bartlett, an experi-

522

enced Newfoundland skipper. Bartlett offered the post of first mate to his nephew, Bob.

"What sort of a man is Peary?" young Bartlett asked his uncle.

"He's like a T-square, Bob. He thinks in a straight line. And you can't bend him any more than you can bend steel."

"Does he know his business?"

"He's the kind that doesn't make it his business unless he does know it."

"Is he a rough handler?"

"Not by our way of thinking. He doesn't ask a man to go where he wouldn't go himself."

Bob Bartlett took the post, and for the next decade his career was inextricably bound up with Peary's.

In the spring of 1898, the nucleus of what would soon be called the Peary Arctic Club was forming around Jesup. This powerful organization, which would finance, protect, and defend Peary in the turbulent years to come, included among its members Herbert L. Bridgman, part-owner of the Brooklyn *Standard Union,* Henry W. Cannon, president of the Chase National Bank, and James J. Hill, the man who built the Great Northern Railway. The name was not adopted officially until January 1899, when Peary was in the Arctic. The club was incorporated in 1904, and by then it numbered among its members company directors, presidents of insurance companies and banks, manufacturers and transportation magnates (from the founder of the Remington Typewriter Company to the chairman of the Erie Railroad).

Why would a group of millionaires band together to finance and support a decade of polar exploration by one man? A letter that Peary sent out in 1900 soliciting further funds supplies one answer: ". . . if I win out in this work, the names of those who made the work possible will be kept through the coming centuries floating forever above the forgotten and submerged debris of our time and day. The one thing we remember about Ferdinand of Spain is that he sent Columbus to his life work." In short, Peary was offering these self-made men something that money usually could not buy – a chance at immortality. And there was one more appeal to the pocketbook. Sverdrup, a foreigner, was apparently after the same prize as Peary. The "race to the Pole," as it was called, was on. It was imperative that an American should win.

Peary rushed his plans forward and left hurriedly on July 4, 1898, in order to forestall Sverdrup, whose four-year plan had nothing to do with any kind of race. Sverdrup's view – that an attempt on the Pole was a useless adventure – was echoed by other explorers including the veteran Sir Clements Markham, who declared that "since Nansen's discovery that the Pole is in an ice-covered sea there is no longer any special object to be attained in going there."

But to Peary and the men who backed him, the Pole was the one great geographical prize remaining in northern exploration. The *Windward* forced its way through Smith Sound, past Cape Sabine, and into Kane Basin as far as Princess Marie Bay. It was blocked by ice off Cape Hawks, and there, on a scouting trip, Peary encountered the man he considered his rival. In his published account of the expedition, Peary made no mention of the meeting, though Otto Sverdrup did in his. Peary's only reference to the Norwegian explorer appeared indirectly in his preface when he referred to "the introduction of a disturbing factor in the appropriation by another of my plan and field of work. . . ."

With Sverdrup already on Ellesmere, Peary was frantic to get as far north as possible. From Fort Conger, Greely's old headquarters on Lady Franklin Bay, he had two possible routes to the Pole: either from the tip of Ellesmere Island on the west or from the tip of Greenland on the east.

Convinced that Sverdrup had the same idea, he refused to wait for better weather. It was a foolhardy undertaking, as Matt Henson realized: "But, Lieutenant, this is the dead of winter. It's stormy and damned cold on the trail. Wouldn't it be better to wait until spring?"

Peary was adamant. "No! I can't possibly afford to lose my one chance of a northern base to a competitor. . . ."

In December, the worst possible month, he set out on the twentieth with Henson, Dr. Tom Dedrick, four Eskimos, and thirty-six dogs. The thermometer dropped below –60⁰ F. Most of the journey was made in utter darkness. The nightmare ended in the early hours of January 7, when the party stumbled into the barn-sized hut that the Greely party had left. By then Peary was close to collapse.

Now, in the gloom of an Arctic morning, he gazed by candlelight on a scene that had been frozen in time for almost two decades. The floor was littered with boxes, pieces of fur, cast-off clothing, and rubbish of every description – just as the departing Greely expedition had left it. Partially consumed tins of provisions, tea, and coffee were scattered on the table and floor. Dishes set out for a final meal remained as they had been when Greely left the fort. Biscuits were strewn about in every direction. Peary found them tough but edible. Even the coffee was drinkable.

While he was sipping Greely's coffee, Peary became aware of a wooden feeling in his feet. When Henson ripped off the sealskin boots he saw that the explorer's legs were bloodless white to the knee. As he tore off the undershoes, two or three toes from each foot clung to the hide and snapped off at the joint.

"My god, Lieutenant!" he cried. "Why didn't you tell me your feet were frozen?"

"There's no time to pamper sick men on the trail," Peary told him, and added, "besides, a few toes aren't much to give to achieve the Pole."

Peary's almost maniacal urge to beat Sverdrup to Fort Conger had crippled him permanently. Dr. Dedrick was forced to amputate seven of his toes. For a month Peary couldn't move; then the others strapped him onto one of the sledges and dragged him back on a winding 250-mile trip to the *Windward,* a journey they completed in a remarkable eleven days. All this time Peary suffered excruciating pain but uttered not a whimper. On the walls of Fort Conger he had scrawled a quotation from Seneca: *Find a way or make one.* The adjective "indomitable" has been used to describe more than one polar hero, but it fits no other so neatly as it does this single-minded and desperately driven forty-two-year-old American, who would for the rest of his life hobble on the stumps of his feet, yet feel it a small price to pay for the fulfilment of a dream.

After he reached the ship, Peary underwent a second operation that left only his little toes. He still couldn't believe the Norwegians weren't seeking the Pole, even when, on March 13, Victor Baumann, Sverdrup's second-in-command, paid him a visit. Baumann explained that Sverdrup wanted to avoid unnecessary duplication of effort with Peary, but Peary, ever suspicious, hid from him the fact that he'd already been to Fort Conger. When Baumann sympathized over the condition of Peary's feet, he received a laconic answer. "You must take your chances up here, you know," said Peary. Baumann returned to report to Sverdrup, who set off across Ellesmere to investigate the unknown land to the west – the archipelago that would be called the Sverdrup Islands.

The *Windward* crossed over to Etah on the Greenland coast in August 1899. There Peary encountered the relief ship *Diana,* financed and sent north by the newly formed Peary Arctic Club. And there a letter told him that the previous January, while he was at Fort Conger, his wife had given birth to another baby girl, Francine. Life, Jo Peary wrote, was slipping away; he had been absent for a year and was planning to be gone for three more.

Peary agreed glumly, but there was nothing he felt he could do. "You are right, dear, life is slipping away. That cannot come to you more forcibly than it has repeatedly to me in times of darkness and inaction the past year. More than once I have taken myself to task for my folly in leaving such a wife and baby (babies now) for this work. But there is something beyond me, something outside of me, which impels me irresistibly to the work. . . ."

He returned to Fort Conger, decrying the folly of Greely for abandoning such a base – "a blot upon the record of Arctic exploration," he later called it – a remark that, when it reached the general, caused a breach between them that was never healed.

The following spring – 1900 – he set off on another extraordinary journey across Greenland, hobbling and shuffling on his mangled feet or riding in one of the sledges. On May 8 he reached Lockwood's farthest point and picked up from a cairn the record that Lockwood and Brainard had left eighteen years before, still in prime condition. The two men had reported sighting in the distance to the northeast a headland that they called Cape Washington. Would this turn out to be the most northerly point of land on the globe? If so, Peary would be robbed of a first. To his immense relief when he reached it, he saw farther on another headland surrounded by twin glaciers. "It would have been a great disappointment to me," he wrote, "after coming so far to find that another's eyes had forestalled mine in looking first upon the coveted northern point."

Five days later he did reach the top of Greenland. He named it for his benefactor – Cape Morris Jesup – one of several landmarks that would bear the names of his backers. And now, for the first time, Peary set his eyes on the awesome polar sea – a forbidding realm of broken ice and open water. He ventured out for a few miles, enough to convince him that this was not a good route to the Pole.

He had yet to achieve a Farthest North. Unknown to him then, Umberto Cagni, an Italian naval officer with the Duke of Abruzzi's North Pole expedition operating out of Franz Josef Land in 1899, had already exceeded Nansen's record by twenty-three miles, losing

526

three men to starvation in the process. But the ultimate prize eluded the Italians as it had everybody else. Cagni stopped 237 miles short of the Pole.

Peary made the 400-mile trip back to Fort Conger in nineteen days. He spent the following winter at Greely's old headquarters not knowing that his wife and daughter were only about 200 miles to the south and that his second child had died in infancy. The *Windward* had returned to the United States and brought the pair back to Etah in August 1900. Jo Peary had no way of communicating with her husband – had no idea, indeed, where he was. The Eskimos thought he had gone to Payer Harbour off Cape Sabine, and so the *Windward* fought its way across Smith Sound, only to find there was no sign of him. Worse, the ship was driven against the rocks and imprisoned in the ice. Mrs. Peary was condemned to a winter in the Arctic.

She was also faced with an embarrassing situation. A comely young Eskimo woman, Allakassingwah – "Ally" for short – was also aboard the ship. She made no secret of the fact that she was Peary's mistress and that he had fathered the baby she carried with her. It did not, of course, occur to her that this intelligence might have a devastating effect on Josephine Peary; the natives had a different set of morals. Now the two were destined to spend an entire winter together. Peary's strong-willed wife was clearly aghast at the revelation, even though she was aware of her husband's earlier declaration that he considered "the presence of women an absolute necessity to keep men contented." A letter that she wrote at the time – it would not reach him until the following spring – merely hints at the depth of her despair: "Today I feel as though I should not see you this year. . . . You will have been surprised, perhaps annoyed, when you hear I came up on a ship . . . but believe me had I known how things were with you I should not have come."

Peary was still at Fort Conger, faced with problems of his own. Dr. Dedrick was jealous of Matthew Henson and was demanding that Peary make it clear both to him and to Henson that he, Dedrick, was the party's second-in-command. Peary prepared a set of notes for a heart-to-heart talk with his black servant:

> *. . . you have been in my service long enough to*
> *show me respect in small things.*
> *Have a right to expect you will say sir to me always.*

*That you will pay attention when I am talking to you
and show that you hear directions I give you by saying yes
sir, or all right sir. . . .*

That April of 1901, while moving down the Ellesmere coast from
Fort Conger, Peary encountered a group of natives who were sledging north to meet him and there, for the first time, he learned that his
wife and daughter were at Payer Harbour, cooped up with his friend
Ally and the baby. If there was a breach with his wife when he
reached the ship, it was papered over; she was not one to show her
feelings to strangers. The two women had got on reasonably well
during the winter, and Peary's extramarital arrangements in the
Arctic (and those of Henson, who also fathered a child) remained a
secret for years.

In August, another relief ship, the *Erik,* financed again by the
Peary Arctic Club, arrived with devastating news. Peary's mother –
his friend and closest confidante – was dead. This blow drove him
further into a state of melancholia. Also aboard the *Erik* was Dr.
Frederick Cook, who had been persuaded by the explorer's backers
to come north in the belief that another doctor might be needed.
Cook examined the despondent Peary, told him he was suffering
from anemia, and urged him to return to New York. "You are
through as a traveler on snow on foot," Cook told him, "for without
toes and a painful stub you can never wear snowshoes or ski." Peary
ignored him.

He had, meanwhile, fired his own doctor, Dedrick, who was, in his
view, becoming a nuisance. Dedrick refused to leave. Cook, by no
means an unbiased witness, was later to declare that Dedrick stayed
with the Eskimos over the winter of 1901 at Etah, "living in under-
ground holes as wild men do," because he felt the natives would be
needing him. When an epidemic sprang up at Cape Sabine, Dedrick
crossed the sound to help out. According to Cook, Peary sent him
back. Cook, who saw the unburied bones of the victims in 1908,
called this "one of the darkest unprinted pages of Arctic history." By
the time that was written (a decade later) Cook and Peary were bitter
enemies. Peary never mentioned that summer nor did his official
biographer, who wrote simply that the natives died of dysentery and
that Peary did his best to nurse them, giving no thought to summon-
ing Dedrick, to whom he was to refer as his "crazy doctor."

Peary, meanwhile, was preparing to make one more attempt to

528

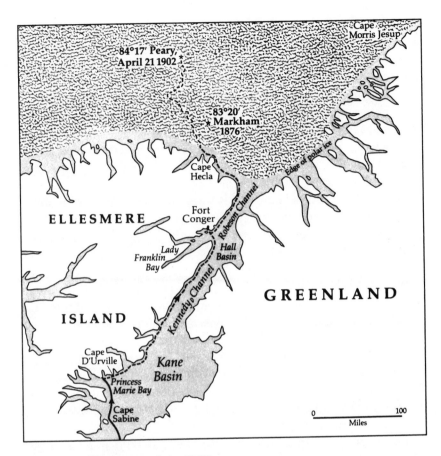

Peary's Farthest North in 1902

reach the Pole. In March 1902, he started up the Ellesmere coast with Henson and a few natives. He reached Cape Hecla, the northernmost point of the island, in early April. On the sixth they set off across the frozen surface of the Lincoln Sea, heading for the Pole.

It was a nightmare journey. He had already endured a month of travel before he took to the ice and had come four hundred miles. But the Pole was more than that distance to the north. The ice was often impassable. The exhausted party was forced to follow a wavering course over the hummocks and around open water, to hack a roadway using pickaxes through frozen barriers, to hoist their sledges over walls of broken blocks. Finally, a vast open lead barred their way – a semi-permanent channel in the ice, marking the edge of the continental shelf, to which Peary gave a variety of descriptive names:

the Big Lead, the Hudson River, the Grand Canal, the Styx. They were forced to wait for it to freeze, but as their daily mileage continued to decrease they had no choice but to give up on April 21. The Pole was still 395 statute miles to the north. Moreover, when Peary determined his latitude and longitude, he discovered that, in spite of his compass readings, he had not been travelling due north. The ice drift had taken him twelve degrees to the west.

Peary was disconsolate. "The game is off," he wrote in his diary. "My dream of sixteen years is over. . . . I have made a good fight but I cannot accomplish the impossible." He was back at Fort Conger on May 3 and three days later, on his forty-sixth birthday, wrote finish to his Arctic adventures: "I close the book and turn to others less interesting but better suited for my years. . . . I accept the result calmly. . . . The goal still remains for a better man than I, or more favourable conditions, or both."

In spite of these fatalistic words, he was merely at a low ebb. Later he described himself as "a maimed old man, unsuccessful after the most arduous work, away from wife and child, mother dead, one baby dead," and asked, "Has the game been worth the candle?" In his secret heart, of course, he knew that, for him, it had been. "I could not have done otherwise than stick to it . . . [but] when I think of the last four years, and what I have been through as I think of all the petty details, it all seems so small, so little worth the while that I could cry out in anguish of spirit."

The anguish of spirit did not last. Peary would not have been Peary if he had not contemplated another try at the Pole. There was still one bitter moment to come. On August 5, 1902, the *Windward* returned to Payer Harbour to take him home. His wife and daughter were aboard, and then he learned for the first time that Captain Cagni of the Italian Navy had established a new Farthest North ("We have conquered! We have surpassed the greatest explorer of the century," his men had exulted, meaning Nansen.).

Matt Henson, who was present when Peary got that news, saw him wince as he learned that Cagni had beaten him by 158 miles. Then he saw Peary's jaw tighten and listened as he spoke with something very close to a snarl. "Next time I'll smash that all to bits," said Robert Edwin Peary. "Next time!"

When the seventeen-year-old Roald Amundsen stood in the crowd *Amundsen's*
on that sunny summer's morning in 1889, cheering Fridtjof Nansen, *triumph*
he had felt again the revival of a childhood ambition – to become the
first man to navigate the North West Passage.

Now, in June of 1903, the year following Peary's return from the
Arctic, Amundsen set out to do just that and succeeded brilliantly –
succeeded where all of those predecessors whom he worshipped so
enthusiastically – Parry, Franklin, Collinson – had failed. In the
same environment where others suffered hardships and death,
Amundsen survived and thrived. It was no picnic, of course, but next
to the accounts of earlier struggles it *sounds* like a picnic. None of the
afflictions that had bedevilled earlier explorers – scurvy, starvation,
exhaustion, semi-madness – were visited upon him and his comrades.
He knew what he was facing and prepared for it. Because he made it
look so easy, because he suffered few of the privations that plagued
the ponderous British school of navigators, history has tended to
downgrade Amundsen.

It has been said of him, quite unjustly, that he merely climbed a
ladder set in place by others. Yet the errors of his predecessors,
manifest long before he came on the scene, were still unacknowledged
by the Royal Navy, for one. In 1889, Sir Clements Markham was still
championing the outmoded practice of manhauled sledges. The use
of dogs "was a very cruel system," Markham told the International
Geographical Congress in Berlin that year, to which Nansen responded tartly, "It is also cruel to overload a human being with
work." It was no accident that the better-trained and better-equipped
Norwegian beat Markham's protégé, Scott, to the South Pole. Scott
was always an amateur. Amundsen, like Nansen and Peary, was a
professional.

He had prepared himself for the task since childhood. Long before
he heard that secret voice urging him to conquer the Passage, he had
been devouring the works of the explorers. John Franklin was his
first hero. Franklin's account of starvation on the Barren Grounds of
northern Canada "thrilled me as nothing I had ever read before." He
credited this single volume, which he had read at fifteen, with shap-
ing the course of his life. At that point he decided, irretrievably, to
become an explorer. Oddly, in view of Amundsen's later unblem-

ished record, it was Franklin's account of his sufferings that appealed most to the fifteen-year-old. "The idealism of youth, which often takes a turn toward martyrdom, found its crusade in me in the form of Arctic exploration."

But Amundsen's admiration of Franklin didn't extend to emulation. When Amundsen set out in 1903 to conquer the Passage, he had no intention of suffering the way Franklin had. He had spent half his life preparing for just such a journey. He had, by then, read every word of every journal published by every Arctic explorer, and he had talked to several face to face. He knew the vicissitudes that awaited him; he also knew how to cope.

As a teenager he hardened his muscles by playing football (which he didn't like) and skiing (which he adored). He went on ski trips and clambered up the mountains around Christiania (Oslo) to toughen himself. In order to acclimatize himself to the chill blasts of winter, he insisted on leaving his bedroom window open in the otherwise hermetically sealed house. Eight years of conscientious exercise developed him so well that when he took his medical for compulsory army service, the doctor ignored his myopia and called in his colleagues to exclaim over his muscles.

His mother refused to allow him to volunteer to go with Nansen on the *Fram;* she wanted him to be a doctor. That same year – his twenty-first – she died, and he was free to follow his chosen profession. In his study of the various Arctic journals, he had been struck by two fatal weaknesses common to many expeditions, especially the American ones. First, he noted, the commander often had no navigational experience and had to defer to the advice of others. Thus each expedition had, in effect, more than one leader – Charles Hall's case was the extreme example – and that led to tension, disagreement, lowered morale, and indecision. Secondly, there had often been friction between the scientific staff on one hand and the captain and crew on the other. That had been apparent on the Kane, Hall, and Greely expeditions and to a lesser extent on earlier ones. Armstrong, the doctor and scientist on board the *Investigator,* had never got on well with McClure, for instance. To these twin problems, Amundsen had an indisputable solution. He would study navigation and science until he had mastered both. On his expedition there would be no divided command.

His first task was to get a skipper's licence, a lengthy and difficult procedure. For two summers he shipped as an ordinary seaman aboard an Arctic sealing vessel. Then, in 1897, he became first mate aboard the *Belgica*, carrying a Belgian expedition seeking the South Magnetic Pole. The Belgians were not prepared for polar travel. Their clothes, equipment, and food were all inadequate. The captain's aversion to fresh meat amounted to a mania. He not only refused to eat it, he also kept it from the crew until everybody came down with scurvy, the captain and commander so ill they took to their beds and made their wills.

Here Amundsen developed a lifelong admiration for the ship's doctor, the same Frederick Cook who had been on an earlier expedition with Peary. With Amundsen's help, Cook saved the day, digging in the snow around the ship for carcasses of seals, sewing warm clothing into blankets, and goading the emaciated men into sawing a channel through the ice that had trapped them. At one point, the ingenious Dr. Cook carefully collected a cache of specimen penguin skins, which he sewed into a mattress to use as a buffer to protect the ship's sides from the pressure of the ice.

Amundsen returned from the Antarctic after two years with the practical experience he would need to get his skipper's papers. He was still studying both navigation and the work of the Arctic explorers, notably that of Frederick Jackson, the man who had rescued Nansen, and James Clark Ross, who had discovered the North Magnetic Pole. In the Antarctic, Amundsen had listened to his scientific colleagues arguing whether or not the magnetic poles were fixed or whether they moved. He was fired then by a new idea: if he could discover the secret of the North Magnetic Pole, that would be a coup almost equal to the conquest of the Passage. More, it would give him a scientific cover for his main objective, providing a guise of respectability to cloak the raw romance of exploration.

Scientists who cared not a whit for the Passage tended to brighten when the young Norwegian mentioned the North Magnetic Pole. Amundsen had no intention of taking along experts in magnetism when he made his voyage. Instead, *he* would become a scientist; he would make himself proficient in taking magnetic observations. He approached the British for aid; when they refused his request, he turned to the Germans.

And so, late in 1900, Amundsen, virtually penniless, took a cheap room in a poor quarter of Hamburg. Armed with an introduction from an Oslo scientist, he rapped unannounced on the door of the acknowledged authority on terrestrial magnetism, Professor George

Neumayer, director of the German Marine Observatory. He explained his mission. To justify further explorations, he told the professor, he must acquire scientific knowledge. Neumayer, who reminded Amundsen of the Hungarian composer Franz Liszt, stared hard at the lanky young Norwegian with the long, morose face. "Young man," he said, "you have something more on your mind than this! Tell me what it is."

Amundsen mentioned the Passage. That did not satisfy the professor. "Ah," he said, "there is still more." At last Amundsen mentioned studying the North Magnetic Pole. At that Neumayer flung his arms around him, crying, "If you do that you will be the benefactor of mankind for ages to come. *That* is the great adventure." He took Amundsen under his wing. The precise young man calculated that in the forty days that followed, he had spent two hundred and fifty hours studying the theory and practice of magnetic observation.

His next move, in Norway, was to secure Nansen's backing for his proposed expedition. With more than a little trepidation, he went out to his hero's villa at Lysaker and knocked on the door of his study, humbled by his own insignificance in the presence of the greatest Norwegian of his day – a man who to him seemed almost superhuman. Nansen, as a result of the journey of the *Fram,* had acquired a towering reputation, fuelled by a burgeoning Norwegian nationalism that in five years would cause a permanent break with Sweden. The Norwegian independence movement required a pantheon of heroes, and Nansen stood on the pinnacle. In Amundsen's eyes, he was as terrifyingly austere as the Arctic itself. But now he was happy to lend his support and prestige to the venture, for he saw the younger man as the British and Americans had seen their polar adventurers – as a future hero who could give his country a new sense of pride by carrying its flag through uncharted channels. Amundsen said later that he dated the actual realization of his expedition from that moment.

That winter of 1900-1901, he went off to Tromsoe, the headquarters of the whaling captains. There, with funds borrowed from his brother, he bought a little wooden square-sterned sloop, the *Gjöa.* Compared to the three-hundred- and four-hundred-ton British ships that had butted vainly against the Arctic ice, it was a cockleshell. But Amundsen was an advocate of smallness. The Arctic archipelago was a skein of shoals, channels, and ice barriers. Only a small ship, Amundsen believed, could thread her way through this maze. "What has not been accomplished by large vessels and main force," he said, "I will attempt with a small vessel and patience."

His crew too would be small, all handpicked and prepared to live off the land. There might not be game enough for 129 men, as Franklin's officers had discovered; but there would be enough, Amundsen was convinced, for seven. That would be the total complement of the *Gjöa*. They would all go native, wearing native clothing, sleeping in native snow houses. Rae had done it, he reminded the Norwegian Geographical Society, and at trifling cost.

For the next two years, Roald Amundsen was caught up in a flurry of fund-raising and preparation. He learned from everyone – from the whalers at Tromsoe and also from the Lapps, who taught him the insulating properties of sennegras. He took the *Gjöa* on a training cruise. He got his master's certificate. He had long sessions with Otto Sverdrup, from whom he learned the mystique of Eskimo dogs and dog driving: how to treat dogs as equals, how to use dogs in concert with skis, why Greenland huskies were better than the Siberian breed. Nothing escaped him; he even rejected commercial pemmican in favour of his own recipe. Late in 1902 he went off to England to talk to other Arctic explorers – Sir Clements Markham, Sir Allen Young, and the aging Sir Leopold M'Clintock, who was still in bed the morning Amundsen knocked on his door – and then on to Potsdam for more work on terrestrial magnetism.

At last he was ready. He had everything he needed, except money. On June 16, 1903, with the thirty-one-year-old herring boat loaded with five years' provisions and equipment, all tightly sealed in large, oddly built provision boxes, he and his crew of six cast off from the docks at Christiania in a torrential downpour. Underfunded and in debt, he left on the stroke of midnight, it was said, to escape his creditors. As a scientific explorer Amundsen had no peer; in financial matters he was always a child.

Within two months the *Gjöa* had pierced the heart of the Arctic archipelago. On the evening of August 22 she arrived at Franklin's last safe wintering place, Beechey Island. For the explorer, this was hallowed ground. Standing on the deck of the little schooner, he tried to picture the scene: the splendidly equipped ships with the British colours flying at the mastheads, all abustle; the officers in their dazzling uniforms; the boatswains with their pipes; the blue-clad sailors scrambling ashore; and the commander himself, his round face beaming with gentle amiability. At least, that is what Amundsen

535

says he thought. But he wrote those words in 1908 when international hero-worship of Franklin was at its height and every writer, whether English, American, or Scandinavian, paid lip-service to the mythic stature of the commander of the *Erebus* and the *Terror*. No one interested in raising funds for a new expedition, as Amundsen then was, would have dared to puncture the Franklin legend. By his own actions, however, Amundsen showed that he was totally at odds with the Franklin school of exploration, though he had no intention of being ungracious. "Let us raise a monument to them, more enduring than stone," he was to write, "that they were the first discoverers of the Passage."

Which route should he now follow? To the northwest the hunting fields of Melville and Prince Patrick islands, with their vast herds of muskoxen, beckoned invitingly. But Amundsen was not a slave to personal sentiment. When he took his magnetic observations, the needle pointed stubbornly south, so south he determined to go. He left Beechey Island, with its three grave markers, its ruined depots, and its monuments to faded glories – Lady Franklin's marble slab, Belcher's memorial column, and the little plaque in memory of young Bellot – and with "the heaviness and sadness of death" hanging over that lifeless, fog-shrouded shore, he headed into "waters never sailed in . . . hoping to reach still farther where no keel had ever ploughed."

He moved down Peel Sound and into Franklin Strait. Here, in the vicinity of the North Magnetic Pole, the compass was useless. Like the Vikings of old he steered by the stars. He passed the point where Allen Young had been forced to turn back by the ice. Would this be his fate, too? M'Clintock had once said that in his opinion, the sound was navigable no more than once in every four or five years. Pacing nervously back and forth along the deck, Amundsen tried to hide his inward agitation from his comrades. The ship lurched under his feet, increasing his concern. But the sea was calm; he felt irritated by his own skittishness. Again he felt movement beneath him and again he looked over the rail at a glassy sea. The irregular motion continued until he realized at last what it was. He would not, he said later, have sold that slight motion for any amount of money! What he was receiving was a message from the open ocean – a swell that told him there was no wall of ice to block his way to the south. Fortune, which had defeated Allen Young, was on his side.

On August 31, after he had passed Bellot Strait, where M'Clintock had been trapped, the engine room caught fire. Disaster faced the

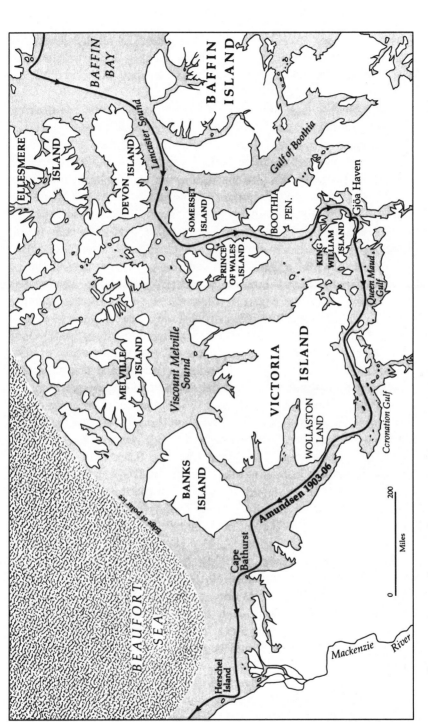

Amundsen navigates the North West Passage, 1903–1906

Gjöa's company. Twenty-two hundred gallons of oil lay directly in the path of the flames. At any moment the ship might be blown to bits. But the crew worked smoothly and without panic to quell the blaze before it reached the oil.

The following day, the sloop ran aground on a reef. Amundsen and his men pitched ten thousand pounds of dogfood overboard in a vain attempt to free her. A gale sprang up, flung the *Gjöa* against a rock, and splintered her false keel. Holding fast with all his strength to prevent being thrown into the boiling sea, Amundsen cursed himself for not keeping watch in the crow's-nest. As the vessel blundered ahead under full sail (Amundsen's decision), dancing from rock to rock (Amundsen's description), he wondered whether she might break up. Should they lower a boat and escape with a few necessities? Or should they take a chance and drive on to possible destruction?

He ordered the small boats to be cleared and loaded. As that was being done, the others began to throw the rest of the deck cargo into the sea. The schooner was being driven toward the shallowest part of the reef when suddenly she was hurled upward and flung bodily onto the rocks with a series of thumps that caused Amundsen to pray to his Maker for succour. One final thump occurred, and then, to everyone's amazement and relief, she slid off the reef into deep water.

Amundsen had learned his lesson. From that moment on he would keep one man always aloft and another at the prow testing the depths with a lead. They were moving down the east coast of King William Island through James Ross Strait and into Rae Strait – the route Franklin had not known existed. Suddenly, Godfred Hansen cried out from aloft, "I see the finest little harbour in the world." Here, on the southeast corner of King William Island, they anchored. Amundsen christened it Gjöa Haven. It would be their home for the next two years.

The Passage beckoned invitingly. Simpson Strait was open; the way seemed clear to the west. But Amundsen was mindful of his scientific responsibilities. He must build an observatory, explore the unmapped neighbourhood, and locate the North Magnetic Pole, which he figured was some ninety miles to the northeast. When that was accomplished there would be time to follow the channels westward.

He had developed an ingenious form of prefabrication by using the big packing boxes as building materials. With these boxes, filled with sand, he constructed two buildings for magnetic observation (using copper nails to prevent magnetic interference), a supply hut, an astronomical observatory, and another small hut in which two of the crew lived for two winters. The rest bunked down on the *Gjöa.*

The buildings were scarcely completed before a band of Netsilik Eskimos arrived. These were pure aborigines, untainted by recent white contact. Seventy-five years before, their grandparents had briefly encountered James Clark Ross on his trip to the site of the North Magnetic Pole, and this folk memory remained with them as clearly as if the meeting had taken place that month. To the Netsiliks, the arrival of the legendary white men was like the coming of supernatural beings. When, in November, Amundsen visited one of their camps, there was pandemonium: men, women, and children rushed forward to grab at his clothing, to stroke his face, and to feel the contours of his body. An affectionate bond developed between the explorers and these primitive people – the merriest human beings that the sombre Norwegians had ever encountered. A gregarious lot, they moved to Gjöa Haven in a body. At one point Amundsen discovered there were eighty women and children camped there.

This eighteen-month contact with the Netsiliks had profound effects. Amundsen was not a trained anthropologist, but he was on the ground and able to study their lifestyle before civilization changed them. The results, when published, were invaluable. He approached them with humility in the belief that they had a great deal to teach him. Commander Robert Scott and his men were in the Antarctic on their first expedition at this same time, stubbornly manhauling 240-pound loads on heavy sledges in the old British naval tradition, starving and freezing because of improper clothing and inadequate food. Amundsen, meanwhile, was flourishing in a similar environment. Here on King William Island, where Franklin's followers had perished, he was honing the techniques that would make it possible for him to conquer the South Pole and live to tell about it.

The Eskimos became his teachers, and Amundsen and his comrades were willing pupils. A jocular old man, Teraiu, whom Amundsen befriended and gave a berth aboard the *Gjöa,* showed them all how to build snow houses, using a long-handled knife and a forty-inch caribou horn. In his memoirs, Amundsen cheerfully described one of these earlier attempts: "They, no doubt, hardly thought that a 'Kabluna' (foreigner) could manage a piece of work, which was their own specialty. But they did not wait very long before very audibly expressing their views on the point. Hansen and I did something or other they were not used to, and in a trice the whole crowd burst into noisy exultation. Their laughter was uncontrollable; the tears ran down their cheeks; they writhed with laughter, gasped for breath, and positively shrieked. At last . . . they took the whole work in hand, but had to stop now and then to have another laugh at the thought of our stupidity. . . ."

But the Norwegians persevered because, as Rae had discovered before them, and Peary too, the snow houses they could build on the trail were vastly more comfortable than any tent. There were other discoveries: the Netsiliks scoffed at the white man's attempt to stop frostbite by rubbing the skin with snow. Snow against frost? It was nonsense. The right way, the white men learned, was to remove a warm hand from a glove and rub it vigorously against the affected spot.

These were no ordinary gloves; these were Eskimo gloves, with long cuffs tied tightly to prevent snow creeping up the arm. Three weeks after his arrival, Amundsen was wearing a full set of deerskin clothing and for the next twenty months continued to dress as a native. The secret, which was still eluding the British Navy, was air circulation. Tight wool clothing caused men to sweat. The native parkas and trousers were loose, fast drying, and windproof. It was essential, too, that the undergarments be made of deerskin. Unlike wool, deerskin sheds dirt; unlike wool, it is warm to the touch when it is put on. As Amundsen remarked, "in woollen things you have to jump and dance about like a madman before you can get warm."

The Netsiliks taught Amundsen the value of deerskin stockings, with the fur turned inward, and deerskin footgear stuffed with sedge grass, which absorbed moisture and dried out quickly at night. Again, as Peary had learned, this added to the flexibility of polar travel. Amundsen noted how quickly an Eskimo could leap out from under the covering of his sleeping bench in the morning and jump into his loose clothing; it took but an instant. It was the same at bedtime. Amundsen published all this detail in his book *The North West Passage,* which was available in English in London by 1908. More than three years later, Apsley Cherry-Garrard recounted in *The Worst Journey in the World* – the story of the second Scott expedition – that British naval officers required half an hour to *thaw* themselves into their frozen sleeping bags each evening.

There was more to learn, ranging from the secret of operating a kayak (Amundsen took a chilly ducking on his first try) to the native

540

system of coating the sledge runners with a film of ice, which Amundsen found allowed them to "slide like butter" over any kind of snow. The Netsiliks also helped the Norwegians grasp the art of dog driving – a technique that requires humility, for this is in no sense a master-servant relationship; there must be a rapport between man and beast.

Finally, from the Eskimos Amundsen, like Nansen, learned the value of patience in the Arctic. Earlier explorers, reckless to achieve record mileages, had derided the natives for their sloth. But the natives understood the value of maintaining proper pace. Sweat in the Arctic can kill. To overtax one's strength can be fatal, for that leaves the human body with no resources for an emergency. M'Clintock's sledgers had exhausted and crippled themselves, sometimes permanently, for no other reason than vanity, as their published boasts make clear. The Eskimos arrived at their destinations more slowly but with minds and bodies unimpaired – able to move forward, day by day, without collapsing. For this, they were often reviled for "laziness."

Certainly, two winters at Gjöa Haven required monumental patience. The North West Passage continued to beckon. Who knew whether Simpson Strait would be free of ice when the scientific work was finally done? Amundsen "burned at the thought of the time when we should show our Norwegian flag to the first vessel on the other side. . . ." But having clothed his plans in the garment of science, he was determined to fulfil his pledge. He knew that idleness, especially under these conditions, could be demoralizing; he had read the works of the earlier explorers. That was one reason why he had kept his numbers small: as he said "there can always be work found for a few." Actually, he found his comrades prepared to make their own work. He had brought along no fewer than seventy-five games to play; significantly, they were never used except by the Eskimos, who didn't understand them but played them anyway – and with great enthusiasm.

In the spring and summer all seven were occupied with expeditions to map the northwest coastline of Victoria Land and also to find the site of the North Magnetic Pole. When Amundsen reached the spot where James Clark Ross had located the pole, he discovered that it had moved some thirty miles. He did not reach that site, but that didn't matter. Science would recognize his discovery that the pole was not fixed as his major achievement.

He came to another realization: the unnavigated portion of the North West Passage was no more than one hundred and fifty miles as the crow flies. It lay between Cape Crozier, the most westerly point of King William Island, and Cambridge Bay, where Collinson had wintered. One old man with whom Amundsen had developed a close friendship confided to him that one of Franklin's ships had drifted to Cape Crozier where he and his friends looted it before it was crushed by the ice.

The time for departure was rapidly approaching. In May, 1905 the first mail in two years arrived by native dogsled from the west. On June 1, the self-regulating instruments that had been operating for nineteen months were stopped. The houses were taken down and the ship was painted. By the end of June, with the last of the exploring parties back at Gjöa Haven, the channels were beginning to open. But it was August 12 before the coast of King William Island was free of ice.

It was time to leave. They had spent two years in relative comfort, growing fat on game and fish. To pass the time, Amundsen had founded a society to taste all the products of the land – from fox steaks to caribou tripe. "Thanks to my comrades," he wrote, "I left Gjöa Havn with nothing but happy memories. We never had a misunderstanding or a dispute of any kind." Few other Arctic explorers could have made that statement. But few other expeditions had operated as Amundsen's had – with no social or disciplinary gap between the members. Amundsen treated his six crew members as equals and shared their labours. It was the same with the Eskimos; if anything, he treated them as his superiors, unlike Peary, who saw them as chattels.

But like Peary, he held no brief for the popular notion that by Christianizing or "civilizing" them, they would somehow become better human beings. Quite the contrary: "During the voyage of the '*Gjöa*' we came into contact with ten different Eskimo tribes in all, and we had good opportunities of observing the influence of civilization on them, as we were able to compare those Eskimo who had come into contact with civilisation with those who had not. And I must state it as my firm conviction that the latter, the Eskimo living absolutely isolated from civilisation of any kind, are undoubtedly the happiest, healthiest, and most honourable and most contented among them."

542

Amundsen urged (vainly, as it turned out) that the natives be guarded from "the many perils and evils of civilisation" by strict laws, thus following the example of Denmark. "My sincerest wish for our friends the Nechilli Eskimos is, that civilisation may *never* reach them," he declared.

On their part, the Eskimos had been studying the illustrated papers and magazines that Amundsen had brought along, many of them depicting terrifying battle scenes from the Boer War. Understandably, they showed no interest in emigrating to the land of the white man – a realm they visualized as one of unlimited violence. "Good-da! Good-da! (Good-day)," they shouted cheerfully as the sloop cast off into the thick fog and left them behind. In truth, Amundsen said, they had learned his language more easily than he and his comrades had learned the Netsilik tongue.

The *Gjöa* groped its way through the fog into the shallow, island-dotted strait named for Thomas Simpson guided by some of the natives in their kayaks, who seemed to know exactly where they were heading in spite of the murk. These were totally unknown, totally unpredictable waters; no white man had sailed through them before. The soundings jumped from seventeen fathoms to five, then back again. Sandy bottoms suddenly turned ragged and stony. They were in the midst of what Amundsen called "disconcerting chaos." Sharp stones faced them on every side. Low-lying rocks loomed up just above the surface of the channel. "We bungled through zigzag as if we were drunk," he said. The lead continued to fly up and down in dismaying fashion. Standing at the helm, Amundsen found that he was shuffling his feet out of sheer nervousness while the lookout in the crow's-nest flung his arms about like a maniac indicating sudden shifts to port and starboard. There were so many rocks ahead that "it was just like sailing through an uncleared field."

Somehow the *Gjöa* got through, then slipped between the ice floes in Victoria Strait to reach the flat, monotonous coastline of Victoria Land, and anchored at last in Cambridge Bay. The date was a historic one: August 17, 1905. Roald Amundsen and his crew had managed to bring their ship through the hitherto unnavigated link in the North West Passage.

What Amundsen had shown was that there was no practical passage here for large ships. Nor could any vessel of his time, no matter what its size, force its way through the ice stream that swept round

Banks and Prince Patrick islands from the Beaufort Sea. And only a tiny craft of shallow draft, such as the *Gjöa,* could hope to make it through Simpson Strait.

The truth was now revealed: even if Sir John Franklin had known that King William Land was insular, even if he had been able to slip past its east coast by Rae Strait, he would certainly have foundered among the rocks and shoals that almost did for Amundsen's little ship. The *Erebus* and the *Terror* were too big and too awkward, and it is more than probable that the expedition's fate would have differed only in degree from the tragedy of 1848.

For Amundsen, the rest of the journey was comparatively easy. He had Collinson's charts and descriptions to guide him. Every fibre urged him to press on, now that he was on the threshold of success; but the waters were shallow and hazardous, and he knew that it was better to sacrifice a few hours rather than jeopardize his vessel. Once again the Norwegian practised patience.

One last set of rocks and shoals barred the entrance to Dolphin and Union Strait. Once through that hazard, Amundsen found himself breathing more easily. In spite of a devouring hunger, he had not been able to swallow a morsel of food or snatch a moment's sleep during this critical passage. Now, having regained his calm, he had "a most rapacious hunger" to satisfy.

At eight on the morning of August 26 he was awakened by his second-in-command, Hansen, crying "Vessel in sight!" These were memorable words, for Amundsen realized that the ship in question must have come from the Pacific. His childhood dream had been fulfilled; the North West Passage had been conquered at last.

He was not an emotional man, but now he experienced a peculiar sensation in his throat and felt unexpected tears starting in his eyes. "I suppose it was a weakness on my part," he wrote later – always the phlegmatic Scandinavian. He dressed himself quickly and before going out on deck paused for a moment to look at Nansen's picture on the wall of his cabin. For a moment he thought that it had winked at him. Then, smiling broadly, he strode out to meet the strange sail from the west.

She was a two-masted schooner, the *Charles Nansen* of San Francisco, her decks jammed with a cosmopolitan group of well-wishers – Eskimo women in red dresses and black American seamen in variegated costumes, all "mingling together just as in a land of fable."

Out of this throng stepped a corpulent and jovial figure with

544

wrinkled, copper-coloured features – Captain James McKenna, the ship's master and an old Arctic trader. "Are you Captain Amundsen?" he asked. The explorer was surprised that he was known. When he answered, McKenna seized his hand and asked if his was the first ship he had encountered. He brightened when Amundsen told him she was. "I am exceedingly pleased," he said, "to be the first one to welcome you on getting through the North West Passage."

Amundsen was hungry for news. The only newspapers on board were old. One carried a dismaying headline suggesting that Norway was about to go to war with Sweden, an eventuality that was happily averted. But he was delighted to find that McKenna had a set of up-to-date charts and plenty of information about ice conditions to the west.

Amundsen's goal was Bering Strait, but as the *Gjöa* moved west and the ice grew thicker, her passage became more sluggish. She passed the mouth of the Mackenzie, tried to make Herschel Island, but was blocked by ice on September 9. She was not alone; some dozen ships were in the vicinity, all stuck fast. On the shore, at King Point, the schooner *Bonanza* was grounded and beached, and here a little colony had sprung up – sailors from the wreck and Eskimo families building huts. Here the crew of the *Gjöa*, too, was destined to spend a third winter – ten more months – in the Arctic.

Amundsen was eager to get the news of his triumph to the civilized world. That would not be easy. The nearest telegraph post was at Eagle, Alaska, on the Yukon River, five hundred miles to the south on the far side of the nine-thousand-foot Ogilvie range. Captain William Mogg of the *Bonanza* was also anxious to get to San Francisco to outfit another ship and get back to the Arctic before losing another whaling season. Both men knew that the mail run from Herschel Island was due to leave for the Yukon by way of Fort McPherson in late October. They decided to go with it.

There was a problem: Amundsen, who had left Christiania one jump ahead of his creditors, didn't have a cent. That meant that Mogg, with no experience of Arctic land travel, would be in charge. He was short and he was fat and he couldn't run with the dogs, so he would have to ride on one of the sledges – a dead weight for the entire trip. Moreover, he positively refused to take any pemmican – the ideal nourishment for such a journey – because he considered it dog meat. Amundsen had no choice but to eat Mogg's beans, cooked, dried, and packed in sacks – beans for breakfast, lunch, and dinner, day after day, a daunting and unpalatable prospect. But there was no help for it. Equipped with two sledges, twelve dogs, and two Eskimo mail carriers, they set off from Herschel Island on October 24, 1905, growing hungrier and thinner on their bean diet.

The Eskimos left them at Fort Yukon. Amundsen trotted ahead of the single dogsled bearing Mogg, who was now so eager to reach Eagle that he refused to stop for lunch. Amundsen hungrily protested; Mogg was obdurate; after all, he pointed out, he had the money and he was in charge. The trail along the Yukon River was dotted with roadhouses, each a day's travel apart – a legacy of the Klondike gold rush. Amundsen took advantage of this to bring Captain Mogg to his senses. He stopped the team at the exact halfway point between two roadhouses. Then he turned back to Mogg and told him he could keep the team and the provisions. He, Amundsen, would trudge on alone.

Mogg was terrified. He

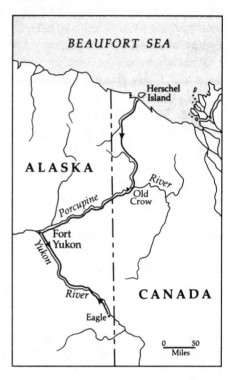

Amundsen's overland trek to reach the telegraph at Eagle, Alaska, in the late fall of 1905

cried out that he knew nothing of northern travel; Amundsen was leaving him to certain death. The explorer replied that he could not continue without three meals a day; if Mogg didn't feed him properly, he would abandon him. At that Mogg surrendered. The pair reached Eagle on December 5, 1905, with the Fahrenheit thermometer reading –60⁰. At the U.S. Army telegraph station Amundsen dispatched a one-thousand-word message to Nansen, whose letter to the Norwegian Consul at San Francisco had helped publicize the expedition. Since Amundsen had no money, he was forced to send the telegram collect, a circumstance that caused so many complications that the story reached the press before it reached Nansen, thus frustrating his chance to sell it as an exclusive for Amundsen's benefit.

The following March, 1906, Amundsen arrived back at King Point to discover that his second engineer, Gustav Wiik, was dangerously ill, apparently from pleurisy. He died a few days later before help could reach him from Herschel Island. In Amundsen's absence, his men had constructed a crude observatory to continue their magnetic studies. In July, the instruments were taken down and placed on board, ready for departure. The mail from Edmonton arrived on August 9, bringing news of the great San Francisco fire and the massive relief arrangements organized by General Greely. The following day, the *Gjöa* slipped through a channel in the bay ice and resumed her passage westward.

There was one last struggle with two large masses of ice off Point Barrow. The six Norwegians attacked the great blocks with ice hooks, and the vessel charged through. With that barrier breached, the *Gjöa* moved on to meet that portion of the whaling fleet that had not been frozen in and had come up from San Francisco for the summer season. With it came Captain William Mogg and a large packet of mail.

At Nome, early in September, a huge celebration awaited them. An enormous searchlight played on the little vessel as she came in sight and a roar of welcome issued from a thousand throats, followed by a sound that brought tears to Amundsen's eyes. It was the national air of his country.

For more than three centuries, since Martin Frobisher's day, the North West Passage had defied the efforts of the world's best seamen, to become a graveyard of broken ships. John Barrow had once thought it could easily be conquered in two seasons. But eighty-eight years had gone by since John Ross, glimpsing a phantom range of mountains, had failed to penetrate the mysterious archipelago at the top of the world. Parry had almost made it in 1819 – only to be blocked by an implacable wall of ice. Franklin's men had actually located the Passage, only to die before they could *reach* it. McClure had managed to get through – but only by sledge. For three decades, since Allen Young's last failed attempt in 1875, the Arctic had been silent and the Passage remained unchallenged. Now, through careful planning, some luck, great common sense, and, perhaps most important, the example of the Eskimos, Roald Amundsen had snatched the prize of centuries from the greatest navy in the world. But another thirty-four years would pass before another little ship – the *St. Roch* – would be able to repeat Amundsen's triumph.

Chapter Thirteen

Robert Peary

Frederick Cook

Peary's North Pole expedition crossing pressure ridges

In July of 1905, as Roald Amundsen was preparing to leave Gjöa *Nearest the* Haven on the final leg of his long voyage through the North West *Pole* Passage, Robert Edwin Peary was about to set off from New York to make what he thought would be a final successful assault on the North Pole.

The shaggy American and the solemn Norwegian shared certain similarities. Both were fiercely ambitious; both were meticulous planners; both had mastered the techniques of the Eskimos. But the contrasts between the two ran deeper. As a leader, Amundsen was the first among equals; his crew was a team. Peary, on the other hand, was a dictator. One cannot imagine Amundsen forcing his fellow Norwegians to sign the kind of feudal agreement that bound Henson and the others to Peary. On the other hand, it's not possible to imagine Peary remaining two seasons at Gjöa Haven to perform scientific observations while the Passage beckoned. Amundsen saw himself as a scientist as well as an explorer; Peary had little interest in anything but reaching his goal; his own observations, when he took them at all, were appallingly slipshod. To him, the polar expedition was a sporting event, not a scientific exercise.

His previous four years of exploration in the High Arctic had made Peary a national figure, yet that wasn't enough for him. He had rounded the northern coast of Greenland, covered fifteen hundred miles of Ellesmere Island by sledge, climbed to the peak of the vast Agassiz Glacier, and gone farther north by way of the so-called American route to the Pole than any other man. While Amundsen and his comrades were lost from sight on King William Island, Peary was making his plans for another expedition to the frozen world. His considerable accomplishments would have satisfied an ordinary explorer (if any explorer can be called ordinary), but Peary craved some more conspicuous feat that would be forever identified with his name.

He had already made a stab at immortality – or thought he had. In June of 1899, while Amundsen was still studying navigation, Peary, standing on an ice-sheathed peak on Ellesmere's great inland glacier, thought he saw a mountainous land off to the northwest. What he probably saw were the Blue Mountains of Ellesmere's west coast, just to the north of Greely Fiord. But Peary, in his eagerness to discover something, transformed this misty vision into a distinct geographical feature, which he named for his chief supporter, Morris K. Jesup.

Clearly unsure of his ground, Peary didn't even mention "Jesup Land" in his report a year later to the Peary Arctic Club. It wasn't until 1903, when Otto Sverdrup reported that he had circled and charted a vast new island, which he named Axel Heiberg, that Peary announced he'd seen it first. It was a flimsy claim. He'd seen some mountains in the misty distance from the top of a peak. Sverdrup had circumnavigated Axel Heiberg and charted it so carefully that modern maps differ little from his original. Peary's "discovery" and Sverdrup's were not identical either in shape or in geographical position. Whatever Peary saw, it wasn't Sverdrup's island. Even the National Geographic Society, always an ardent Peary supporter, rejected his claim.

Was this phantom sighting another innocent mistake, like the ephemeral Peary Channel? The most charitable explanation is that the explorer was engaging once more in an act of self-deception, fuelled by an inner need to produce some tangible trophy on his return to civilization. If it couldn't be the Pole, it must be *something* that could bear his stamp – a body of water, a mysterious meteorite, a new island.

There is, as well, a darker possibility – that Peary was manufacturing evidence to support his claims. A recent modern critic, Dennis Rawlins, has pointed out that Peary in 1903 apparently reshaped and moved Jesup Land on his map to conform to Sverdrup's original drawing. Yet, writing in 1906, Peary brazenly insisted he *had* seen it and named it "though Sverdrup has later given it the name of Heiberger [*sic*] land."

Jesup Land had not yet been discredited in 1903 when Peary was elected president of the American Geographical Society after a behind-the-scenes struggle with Adolphus Greely. The following year he again bested Greely to become president of the Eighth International Geographical Congress. These considerable honours failed to satisfy him; he wanted the Pole, and he wanted it desperately, in spite of the pleas of his family. His wife, Jo, had urged Herbert Bridgman, secretary of the Peary Arctic Club, to "let me keep my old man at home." His eleven-year-old daughter, Marie, begged the father she hardly knew to stay with the family. She was tired of seeing him only in press photographs, she said. "I want to see my father. I don't want people to think me an orphan."

But the call of family could not keep the forty-seven-year-old explorer from completing his life's ambition. Others were seeking the prize. In June 1903, an American businessman, William Ziegler, who longed to have his name associated with Arctic discovery, had dispatched another expedition to try to reach the Pole by way of Franz Josef Land. This determinedly patriotic effort (the all-American crew included Sergeant Francis Long, one of Greely's survivors) was the second Ziegler had funded; an earlier attempt had failed. By the time the Peary Arctic Club was incorporated in 1904, the Ziegler Polar Expedition was already in trouble. When its ship, the *America*, was crushed in the ice and sank, the crew was forced to spend two winters in the open. Anthony Fiala, the leader, made a bold attempt in 1905 to get to the Pole but didn't manage to get beyond the 82nd parallel. That confirmed Peary's belief that the only feasible way to the Pole was the so-called American Route – a misnomer, for it hugged the Ellesmere coast and was therefore thoroughly Canadian.

Since his return from the Arctic in 1902, Peary had spent three years raising money and planning his new expedition. He went at it with his usual thoroughness; not for him the slapdash impetuosity of a Kane or a Hall or the obstinacy of the Royal Navy. Peary learned from his mistakes. He was convinced that he must devise a different approach. He would, first of all, have to eliminate the ghastly sledge trips up Ellesmere's ragged coast from Kane Basin that had exhausted him and his companions long before they reached their jumping-off point. His remedy was to build a special ship that could force its way through the narrow, ice-locked channels between Greenland and Ellesmere and deposit his party on the very rim of the permanently frozen sea.

Second, he would need a larger company than he had once thought necessary. He would divide it into three sections: a pioneer party to break trail and build igloos; support groups to follow behind, shuttling caches of supplies forward; and, finally, the polar party, which would bring up the rear so that rested, refreshed, and lightly equipped it could make the final dash to the objective.

This was the essence of what, with his usual flair for self-promotion, he called the Peary System. It might as easily have been called the M'Clintock System, for it had been used half a century before when Leopold M'Clintock's satellite sledges had crossed Melville Island. But Peary did improve on M'Clintock: he would use dogs, not manpower; his followers would be dressed in native garb, and they would live in snow houses that could be used on the return journey.

Peary knew that the ship that would take him through Kennedy and Robeson channels would need to be specially designed. For that alone he would need $100,000. The construction of the *Roosevelt*, as she was to be called, actually began before all the money for the venture was raised. In the end Peary got $50,000 from the ailing Morris K. Jesup, another $50,000 from George Crocker, a director of the Southern Pacific Railroad, and $20,000 more from General Thomas Hubbard, vice-president of the Peary Arctic Club. Peary made up the rest from his own funds, mortgaging himself to the point of bankruptcy.

The vessel that steamed out of New York harbour on July 16, 1905, was the most practical ship yet to invade Arctic waters and, apart from the *Fram*, the only one especially constructed for the task. Like the *Fram*, she was designed to ride up on the ice. Her egg-shaped sides were both elastic and strong – as much as thirty inches thick. She was narrower than Nansen's ship – 185 feet long with a thirty-five-foot beam – and her prow was flared to let her cut into the floes. Her hull was braced by massive crossbeams, her engine was powerful, her shaft and propellers were oversize. Unlike the *Fram*, which moved with the ice, the *Roosevelt* was designed to attack the pack by brute force.

To command this battering ram of a ship, Peary chose the thirty-year-old Bob Bartlett, who had been first mate under his uncle on the previous expedition. Bartlett came from a long line of rugged New-foundland sealers and whaling masters and looked the part: stocky, powerful, and barrel-chested, with close-cropped hair and a weather-beaten face. Peary was convinced that Bartlett could get him to the top of the world if any man could. When he approached him at the end of the previous voyage and offered him the command of a new vessel, Bartlett had accepted, under one condition: he wanted to accompany Peary on the final dash to the Pole itself. "On the next voyage I'm going to the North Pole," he told his father. It was a wistful hope that never came true.

Other members of the twelve-man company included Bartlett's grizzled, six-foot cousin, Moses Bartlett, as first mate; Professor Ross Marvin, late of Cornell University, a willowy, earnest academic; and, of course, Peary's faithful black servant, Matthew Henson, who had

554

been with him since the days of Nicaragua and was now in his fortieth year.

But as usual, it was the Eskimos who would make Peary's polar journey possible. In Etah he planned to recruit twenty families – the men to build sledges and supply him with fresh meat (not to mention furs and ivory to sell in the South), the women to sew Arctic clothing. They were happy to work for him, for he had been their chief source of wealth over the years. In return for the weapons and ammunition, wood for sledges, metal for harpoons, knives, hatchets, saws, and cooking utensils he provided, they were prepared to take part in a quest that baffled them. To the natives, the Pole seemed tangible; its name suggested a perpendicular object projecting from the ice. They called it the Big Nail, after a useful trade article with which they could identify. But why would anybody wish to go there, across a treacherous desert of heaving ice? No Eskimo really wanted to go far beyond the sight of land, but by threats, cajolery, and bribes Peary managed to subdue their natural fear.

The *Roosevelt* reached Etah in mid-August and, after taking on supplies and native families, nosed her way up Kane Basin and then into the narrow passageways leading to the Lincoln Sea. "We are beyond the world's highways now," Peary wrote, "and we shall see no sail or smoke except our own until our return."

Under the explorer's urging, Bartlett drove the ship full speed into the ice. Sometimes she wrenched a passage through; sometimes Bartlett was forced to detour. He was spending almost all his time in the crow's-nest, conning the ship as she hammered, squeezed, and twisted her way northward at the agonizing speed of half a knot (six-tenths of a mile) an hour, "vibrating like a violin," in Peary's description. Bartlett recalled that every day of that tortuous journey seemed to him likely to be his last until, on September 5, they reached the tip of Ellesmere and put in at a small cove off Cape Sheridan on the rim of the permanently frozen Lincoln Sea. "I do not believe," Peary declared (forgetting Nares's voyage on the *Alert* thirty years before), "there is another ship afloat that would have survived the ordeal."

The expedition spent a comfortable winter at Cape Sheridan, living sumptuously on the vast quantities of muskoxen and caribou brought in by the Eskimo hunters. The party's surgeon, Dr. Louie J. Wolf of San Francisco, who whiled away the time reading Isaac Hayes's published accounts of his hardships, was impressed and surprised at the contrast between the two expeditions.

On February 9, Peary began to dispatch his supporting parties to Point Moss, twenty miles to the west of Cape Hecla at 83⁰ N. From this point they would leave solid land and move out onto the rough sea ice toward the Pole, almost five hundred miles due north, setting up caches some fifty miles apart all along the route.

He himself reached the jumping-off point at midnight on March 5, a brilliant moonlit night. He was exhausted after his journey but elated, for he was launching his expedition a month earlier than he had in 1902. On that last trip he had reached a north latitude of 84⁰ 17′. Surely this time he could attain 90⁰! "If I can do as well this time we shall win," he exclaimed in his journal. "God and all good angels grant it, and let me seize this great trophy for the Flag."

The additional distance would be 343 nautical miles. Peary used the nautical measurement – one mile to one minute of latitude. The nautical mile is about 800 feet longer than the statute mile, which means that by the more familiar measurement Peary had about 394 miles farther to go beyond his previous record. Peary's critics always charged that he preferred citing the longer mile because his claimed distances, which were astonishing in any case, would not seem quite so incredible to the layman. All naval explorers used nautical miles.

When Peary set off the following day, March 6, 1906, Henson and his team of Eskimos were far in the lead, hacking a trail through the pressure ridges and building snow houses. The other support parties followed behind Henson. Peary brought up the rear. Soon the entire polar expedition – six white men, one black, twenty-one Eskimos, and 120 dogs – were strung out for a hundred miles across the frozen sea.

It was heavy going. Broad leads, old floes, broken blocks, young, treacherous ice, and the inevitable pressure ridges barred the way, forcing lengthy detours. Howling winds conspired to slow the advancing parties. Stumbling impatiently forward on his crippled feet, Peary was the captive of a single resolve – to get to the Pole. The time wasted stopping to rest at the igloos that had been built for him drove him to quiet desperation. He could hardly sleep waiting for the dogs to be rested to the point where they could move on. He was plagued by the possibility that some insuperable obstacle might bar his way. That he could scarcely bear to contemplate. "Will it break my heart," he asked himself, "or will it simply numb me into insensibility?"

556

He alternately froze and sweated as the temperature dropped to −50⁰ F at night and then soared as high as 65⁰ when the sun shone. Once again, he found himself in the grip of conflicting passions. He longed for home, but he was obsessed by his need to fulfil what he thought of as his destiny. He knew that in two months at the most, "the agony will be over and I shall know one way or the other." He was comforted by the knowledge that however it turned out, he would be back at his home on Eagle Island before the leaves of autumn fell, "going over the well-known places with Jo and the children, and listening to the birds, and the wind in the trees, and the sound of lapping waves." Did such things really exist on this frozen planet? he asked himself. Here, when the curtain of whirling snow lifted, it revealed a lifeless terrain, stark white, unending, pitiless.

On March 26, he reached the Big Lead – apparently the same "Hudson River" that had blocked his passage in 1902. At this point, where the "fast ice" (ice frozen fast to the land) met the moving pack, an immense, semi-permanent gap of black water, as much as two miles wide and only partly frozen, halted the parties and forced them to bunch up. In twenty days, Peary had moved north by 124 statute miles from Point Moss – an average of six miles a day. His actual travel mileage was greater; astonishingly, he did not take a longitude reading until he reached the Big Lead. That meant he had no real idea where he was. When he got out his instruments, he found he had strayed eighty miles off course to the west.

For a man of Peary's temperament, the wait that followed must have been maddening. The weather was almost perfect for Arctic travel – crisp and clear – but he could not move as long as open water barred his way. An agonizing week crawled slowly by. Peary sent his support parties back to Point Moss for more supplies. And then, on April 2, before they had had time to return, the temperature dropped, allowing enough young ice to form on the water to permit a hazardous crossing. He sent a spare man back with a message for the others to follow him if and when they could. Then he, Henson, and six Eskimos crossed the new ice and headed north.

He had lost a precious week of superb weather. The Pole was still 360 statute miles away. At the rate he was travelling, barring unforeseen holdups, it would take almost two months to reach it and even longer to get back to land.

After just three days of hard travel, he was faced with another setback. The wind sprang up; a blizzard followed. The floe on which they had made their camp broke open, demolishing Henson's igloo. For the next week Peary was pinned down at "Storm Camp," as he called it, his ears assaulted day and night by the "hell-born music" of the howling wind. That seven days, he wrote later, felt more like a month. In his desperation, Peary sought an outlet for his nervous energy by pacing back and forth, often on his hands and knees, for three hours a day, across the small floe on which they were trapped.

He must have realized by this time that he could not reach the Pole. Yet he could not return empty-handed, for that would mean the end of his life's work and all his ambitions. He craved wealth and fame, but this expedition had beggared him; and he knew that the fat lecture fees, book royalties, and testimonials – not to mention his own name and photograph on the front pages of the world's newspapers – would not be forthcoming. "Unless I win *here*," he wrote, "all these things fall through. Success is what will give them existence."

He needed some trophy to present to the men who had pledged more than one hundred thousand dollars to his cause. At the very least, he knew, he must try to set a new record by getting closer to the Pole than any other explorer. His journal entries began to dwell on Nansen's Farthest, and Cagni's, sure evidence that Peary had given up his assault on the Big Nail.

On April 13, the wind dropped at last and the weather cleared, the sky a brilliant blue flecked with "mare's tail" clouds. Now he made a rash decision. He would jettison all unnecessary baggage and make a run, if not for the Pole, at least for a record. The speeds he claimed from this point on were little short of miraculous. On the first two days out of Storm Camp he said that he travelled at least sixty miles in spite of crossing eleven leads. Between April 14, when he left Storm Camp, and April 21, when he claimed to have beaten the Italian record by thirty-six miles, he travelled by his own reckoning 130 statute miles due north – an average speed of nineteen northerly miles a day with nobody to break trail for him and no allowance for ice drift or detours; all this was based on a single position line, which Peary listed as 87° 6′ N. (In fact, he had covered more than 130 miles, for his own map showed that he believed he had also come forty miles east.) Yet his earlier average speed between Point Moss and the Big Lead – a distance of at least 147 miles, taking into account his westerly drift – had been little more than seven miles a day. In short, in his final dash north, Peary had claimed three times his normal speed.

For this astonishing feat the world had only Peary's word. There were no reliable witnesses, since neither Henson nor the Eskimos could make astronomical calculations. Peary's critics have emphasized his failure to document his achievements by taking the other usual observations. He was still about two hundred miles from the Pole, but there is no evidence that when he reached that point he took a longitudinal reading; nor did he check his compass variations as he had on earlier occasions. That documentation would have established that he was where he said he was. Yet he didn't bother with it.

Exhausted or not, he did not stop to camp. "When I looked at the drawn faces of my comrades," he wrote later, "at the skeleton figures of my few remaining dogs, at my nearly empty sledges . . . I felt I had cut the margin as narrow as could reasonably be expected." He turned about to follow the half-obliterated trail back to Storm Camp and then on to the Big Lead, knowing that if he could not get across that dark gash in the frozen sea he and the others would starve to death. Later he would claim that he made a beeline down the 50th meridian to the Big Lead, apparently without a single deviation, but that is hard to believe.

To his dismay, when he reached his "river Styx," he found half a mile of black water stretched before him. The party moved east seeking a safe crossing. A day later, they found a kind of bridge formed by ice rubble that appeared just strong enough to bear their weight. They were wrong. The ice began to bend beneath them as they scrambled back to safety. By this time Peary was killing his dogs and roasting them over a fire built from abandoned sledges.

His own account of this return trip is remarkably vague, with scarcely a date or a mileage figure to serve as a signpost to the reader. Words like "one day" and "later" so fuzz the narrative that it's difficult to know exactly where Peary, Henson, and the natives actually were during their thirty-seven-day journey back to the ship at Cape Sheridan, or how many days he was held up at the Big Lead. For this period, apparently Peary did not keep a diary.

The later description of his eventual crossing, however, is graphic enough. His Eskimo companions discovered a film of young ice, barely enough to bear a man's weight, some miles to the east. The members of the party fastened on their snowshoes and then advanced gingerly in extended line across this filament, each man fifty feet from his neighbour, none daring to raise his feet, so that they glided rather than walked.

Without the snowshoes, the venture would have been impossible; a slip or a stumble would have been fatal. Once they started they could not stop. Peary was later to admit that this was the first and only time in all his Arctic work that he'd felt doubtful about the outcome. At one point he heard a cry from somewhere down the line as the toe of someone's snowshoe broke through the ice. "This is the finish," he thought. But he could not look up or take his eyes for an instant from the steady, even gliding of his feet. To his relief they made it – but without a moment to spare. Even while they were removing their snowshoes they saw a jagged gap appear in the ice as the lead opened up again.

The coast of Greenland lay 113 miles to the south. Again Peary's account of the journey is confused and contradictory. He insisted that his party moved south in a straight line, apparently avoiding the drift and deviation that had pulled them sideways on the way north. Yet he also admitted that after crossing the Big Lead, they encountered "a hell of shattered ice" such as he had never seen before. He described the spectacle: some blocks the size of paving stones, others ranging to enormous heights as high as the dome of the Washington capitol – almost certainly an exaggeration inserted by one of his ghost writers. Peary also declared that "it did not seem as if anything not possessing wings could negotiate it." Yet he insisted that he did not deviate as much as a mile from his straight-line course.

There is no reason to doubt Peary's description of the hardships on this return journey. Henson was a reliable witness to these conditions, even if he couldn't read a sextant. The trip south must have been a nightmare, with men stumbling painfully across the ice – and none in more pain than their leader, whose stumps of feet were especially vulnerable. Peary wrote that at the end of the day, his jaws ached from the continual grinding of his teeth – his only way of subduing his torment.

Just before reaching the raw and lifeless Greenland shore on May 9, the party encountered one of the supporting divisions, led by Charles Clark, a fireman from the *Roosevelt*. Clark had reached the Big Lead on his way north one day behind Peary but was unable to cross. He had then turned south and, like Peary, was pinned down by a week-long storm. Again, like Peary, he had been pushed east by the ice drift.

Here was a mystery. If Peary had gone on north to 87° 6′, how

560

could he and Clark both have arrived at Cape Neumayer on the Greenland coast at the same time? Clark had less than half the distance to travel on the return trip from the Big Lead. On April 14, Peary left Storm Camp and headed north. On the same day, Clark left the Big Lead and headed south. Theon Wright is one of several critics who have analysed Peary's mileage. His calculations have shown that Clark travelled about 180 statute miles from the Big Lead while Peary travelled 414 miles in the same period – a rate of sixteen statute miles a day if no allowance is made for detours and ice drift. Clark was travelling at less than half that speed – about seven miles a day.

Was Clark a slowpoke? Certainly he didn't have Peary's sledging experience, but he did have Peary's trained Eskimos. Clark's sledging speeds were credible; on the first twenty days out of Point Moss under the same conditions and including his westerly drift Peary hadn't made much better time. What is remarkable – perhaps incredible – is Peary's claimed speed when only he, Henson, and the Eskimos, exhausted men driving tired dogs, were allegedly bettering the Italian record. Wright has speculated that he may not have gone north at all after the storm but turned directly east to the 50th meridian and then headed due south across the Big Lead to the Greenland coast. The distance was about 150 miles, which would have given Peary an average daily speed of about six miles. Wright's theory is certainly as plausible as Peary's account – indeed, more plausible; but when Peary returned to civilization, nobody was ungentlemanly enough to challenge his figures.

Nevertheless, it would be unjust not to recognize Peary's remarkable feat of sledge travel in the spring of 1906. He had spent sixty-four days out on the polar ice, far from land, never changing his clothes, enduring appalling physical pain and hardship, and surviving several brushes with death. Having reached the windswept shores of Cape Neumayer, he faced another seventeen days of hard travel west to the north coast of Ellesmere, where the *Roosevelt* was anchored. Fortunately, on this final stretch of the journey, there was plenty of game to sustain the party.

At first, when he reached the ship, he was too weary to put pencil to paper. Then he wrote: "To think that I have failed once more; that I shall never have the chance to win again." The key word here is "win." What others might have considered a triumph, Peary saw as a failure.

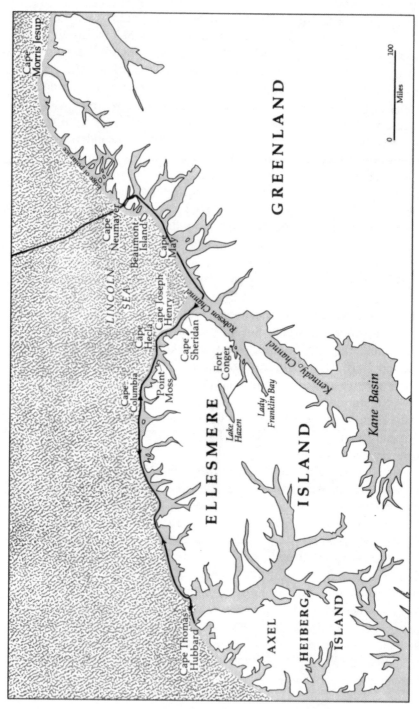

Peary's exploration of Ellesmere Island, June 1906

He was still seeking some sort of prize to bring back to his supporters at the Peary Club. One week after reaching the ship he was off again, intent on exploring the hundred uncharted miles of Ellesmere's north coast that lay to the west. The least he could do would be to name the unknown capes and bays for his wealthy supporters, a time-honoured method of rewarding financial backers that went back to the days of John Ross and Felix Booth.

He left on June 2, this time without Henson. On the sixteenth, he passed Aldrich's Farthest, a record made during the Nares expedition. Ahead lay uncharted territory. Peary was exultant, and in his book *Nearest the Pole*, he made no attempt to hide from his readers his own naked ambition. Rather, he revelled in it: ". . . what I saw before me in all its splendid, sunlit savagery, was *mine*, mine by right of discovery, to be credited to me, and associated with my name, generations after I ceased to be."

Peary pushed on westward, alone except for his Eskimo companions. To protect the stumps of his feet he had fashioned metal insoles from pemmican tins. Before the trip was over they had been worn down to the thickness of silver dollars. On June 24, he reached Cape Colgate, and from this vantage point he was later to write that "now it was with a thrill that my glasses revealed the faint white summits of a distant land which my Eskimos claimed to have seen as we came along from the last camp." Four days later, having crossed the frozen channel to Axel Heiberg Island, he climbed to the top of a promontory that he named for General Thomas Hubbard. From there he saw once more, or thought he saw, "snow clad summits of the distant land in the northwest, above the ice horizon. My heart leaped the intervening miles of ice, as I looked longingly at this land, and in fancy I trod its shores and climbed its summits. . . ."

These words were written by Peary months later in *Nearest the Pole*. Yet there isn't a single mention of any mysterious land in his journal for those two days. There is no journal entry at all for June 24, the day of his first "sighting." There is a voluminous and detailed entry for June 28, but no mention of any sighting on that day. He did not mention the sighting of any new land northwest of Ellesmere in either of the telegrams he sent to the government in November 1906. He did not even mention his discovery to Bob Bartlett or the others when he returned to the ship. He left behind messages in three cairns: one on June 28, the day he climbed Cape Thomas Hubbard, another on June 30, and a third on July 5. All were recovered by later explorers; none made reference to any new land seen by Peary. In fact, Peary's cairn memorandum describing the view from Cape Hubbard on June 30, two days after his second sighting of the "snow clad summits of a distant land," merely reported that June 27 and June 28 were "fine clear days giving a good view of the northern horizon from the summit of the cape."

Like his 1899 location of "Jesup Land," Peary's memory of what he saw seems to have come as an afterthought. The first public reference appeared in an article he wrote for *Harper's* in February 1907 – more than six months later. At that point he named the new land for his benefactor George Crocker, and Crocker Land it became on the map until 1914, when one of his old associates, Donald Mac-Millan, led an expedition to seek it, only to discover that it didn't exist. Like Jesup Land, it had been seen in the misty distance by Peary without any other witness except the natives.

The most charitable explanation for this lapse is that Peary was misled by an Arctic mirage – the same phenomenon that had caused John Ross's downfall when he, too, hoped to gain support from a powerful figure – Croker, not Crocker, in that case. If Peary did see anything, he must have dismissed it at the time as illusive. Only months later, when he was pushed by the need to raise more funds for another try at the Pole, did he "discover that he had discovered it," in Dennis Rawlins's phrase.

Again, there is another, harsher possibility – that Peary's discovery of Crocker Land was a naked fraud, coldly designed to butter up a rich backer. Unlike Jesup Land, which did not remain long on the maps, Crocker Land was accepted as genuine for seven years after Peary announced his find. Nobody questioned Peary. No scientific body, including the one that sent Donald MacMillan in search of Crocker Land, ever checked Peary's field notes before they were lost. Nor did Peary produce a scintilla of scientific data to locate the position of his supposed discovery.

The *Roosevelt*, meanwhile, had broken free of the bay ice and had moved twenty miles down the Ellesmere coast. Peary had three hundred miles of hard travel through the summer slush to reach her. By this time she was a badly crippled ship, having suffered a series of damaging blows that wrecked her rudder, tore off two of her four propeller blades, ripped open a hole in her bottom "almost big enough for a small boy to crawl through" (Bartlett's phrase), and damaged her sides. Bartlett and his crew patched her up as best they

564

could with a jury-rigged rudder, stuffing the rips in her sides and bottom with a cubic yard of oakum and rags mixed with a barrel of cement. Then, with the pumps working continuously, they pushed off for Etah.

They arrived on September 16 after a desperate seventy-five-day struggle with the ice. Bartlett in his log described the *Roosevelt* as "a complete wreck," but he had no intention of abandoning her. After a six-day pause she limped out to sea again. This journey from the top of Ellesmere Island to the Port of New York stands as one of the most remarkable on record and testifies to Bartlett's stubbornness and brilliant seamanship. When the *Roosevelt* ran out of fuel, he used green spruce, whale blubber, and seal oil to stoke her furnaces, together with frozen coal salvaged and sometimes dynamited from old caches. The crippled ship went through four rudders; at one point she was reduced to half a propeller; and the boiler leaked continually. She fought her way through ice, gales, and shoals. At Battle Harbour, Labrador, she was pinned down by a ten-day gale that snapped her lines and broke her main anchor. Bartlett managed to save the ship by mooring her to some rocks with chains. But when he tried to get his rudderless craft into the locks at St. Peter's Canal, Cape Breton Island, she ran up onto a mudbank, crashed into a fence, and headed straight for a milkmaid, who fled screaming up a hill with her cow scrambling after her. "The poor old *Roosevelt*, as well as ourselves, was ready for the insane asylum or the dump heap," Bartlett later recalled.

At last, on Christmas Eve, 1906, the *Roosevelt* staggered into New York harbour. By then, Peary was home; he had taken the train from Sydney, Nova Scotia. Bartlett could have beached his ship there and waited until spring to repair her, but that was not his way. "We have got to get her back, Captain," Peary had told him. "We are going to come again next year." For that project he would again need the *Roosevelt*, not to mention her tough and plucky captain.

2

Peary reached the United States in the fall of 1906 fully intending to return to the Arctic the following summer. Although he claimed to have been farther north than any other man and to have discovered a

"Mine at last!"

565

vast new island, he thought of himself as a failure. The Pole – and only the Pole – could wipe out the acrid taste of defeat. Its discovery was something "which must be done for the honor and credit of this country," he told the National Geographic Society when it awarded him its first Hubbard Medal that December – at the hands of Theodore Roosevelt.

Like so many other explorers before him, Peary continued to harp on the patriotic theme; it was, after all, the surest way to the pocketbooks of the nation. As he told the *New York Times* the following spring, when he officially announced his newest plan, "the attainment of the Pole spells National prestige." It was, he added (dismissing the whole of the Antarctic), "the last great geographical prize which the world has to offer to adventurous men."

Through the efforts of the president, now his most ardent supporter, Peary again obtained leave from the Navy – three years this time. Roosevelt, the Rough Rider who had led the charge on San Juan Hill in the Spanish-American War, was also an explorer as well as a writer, conservationist, and big-game hunter who had unwittingly given his name to the teddy bear during an outing in the American West. The bluff and forthright president was captivated by the equally bluff and forthright Peary, who sent him narwhal horns from the Arctic and cultivated his patronage to the point of naming a ship after him. Peary's public image as a dedicated and unselfish explorer, sacrificing a comfortable family life in his effort to carry the Stars and Stripes to the farthest corner of the earth, fitted the Roosevelt style.

But his leave at first came to nothing, for his ship was so badly damaged she could not be repaired in the time available. In August, 1907, Peary was forced into a rueful announcement. The project, for that year, would have to be abandoned.

There was another reason. Peary did not have the funds to mount an expedition. He was broke and in debt. He had expected to make one hundred thousand dollars in royalties from his new book, *Nearest the Pole*, but it was a flop. In 1907 it sold only 2,230 copies – a meagre return that didn't even cover the five-thousand-dollar advance. The world didn't want to hear about another failed attempt to reach the Pole. It wanted a success story, and Peary could not provide that.

With Bob Bartlett, Peary had stumped the country trying to raise funds, knocking on the doors of millionaires and politicians and

566

giving public lectures. It didn't work. "I was rebuffed, laughed at, offered jobs, sympathized with and in a hundred ways resisted," Bartlett recalled. "It was a glorious fight but we failed. . . ." Bartlett returned to the Newfoundland seal hunt only to be shipwrecked off the east coast, his vessel a total loss, his hoped-for profits wiped out.

Meanwhile, Peary learned that his former associate, the amiable Brooklyn surgeon Frederick Cook, had sailed for Etah aboard a yacht owned by John R. Bradley, a wealthy sportsman. Officially, Cook was Bradley's guest on a hunting trip. But rumour said that Cook, fresh from his reported conquest of Mount McKinley, North America's highest peak, was planning an attempt on the Pole.

Peary at first dismissed this talk and refused to believe other rumours – that Cook had faked the Mount McKinley climb. "Cook is an honourable man," he told Vilhjalmur Stefansson. And to a friend who predicted that Cook intended to fake the polar journey, Peary replied, "Oh, no. I do not believe Cook would do that."

But when Bradley returned to the United States that fall and announced that Cook intended to try for the North Pole in 1908 by a new route, taking dogs and Eskimos from the Etah area, Peary was outraged. Cook was about to steal *his* route to the North Pole – the route he had been exploring and surveying for the best part of twenty years. More, Cook was planning to steal *his* Eskimos, the very ones he had painstakingly trained in the Peary System. Peary made no bones about his title to that part of the Arctic and its people. It was, he once wrote, "as much a part of his [the explorer's] capital as the gold and silver in the vault of a bank." Until an explorer abandoned the route he had pioneered, "no one else, without his consent, has any more right to take it and use it, than a stranger has to enter the vaults of the bank, and take its treasure."

Even before Bradley returned, Peary was alerting his long-time sponsor, the National Geographic Society, to the facts about what he considered Cook's infamy and Bradley's dubious credentials. He sent documents to Gilbert Grosvenor, the editor of the *National Geographic*, for his private information: "Dr. Cook's backer . . . is known in certain New York circles as 'Gambler Jim.' I have been informed that he was at one time a card sharp on the Mississippi River until turned out. It is a well known fact that he is the owner of a gambling hell at Palm Beach, in which I am told women, as well as men, gamble. I feel the whole spirit and method of execution of this last move of Dr. Cook is of a nature that should receive, as a matter of principle, the distinct dis-approval of all reputable Geographic and scientific organizations and individuals." Thus did Peary begin to lay the groundwork for the controversy that followed.

Peary's plan for a new start in 1908 suffered another blow when his chief financial supporter, Morris K. Jesup, died. Nonetheless, his widow provided five thousand dollars, and General Thomas Hubbard, who succeeded as president of the Peary Arctic Club, provided a good deal more. The ever-helpful President Theodore Roosevelt, at Peary's prodding, persuaded the Navy to put him back on full pay on the excuse that he would carry out tidal observations along the northern coasts of Greenland and Ellesmere Island. But Peary needed another twenty-five thousand dollars before the *Roosevelt* could sail. There was considerable jealousy among senior naval officers over the ease with which Civil Engineer Peary got what he wanted, especially when he continued to allow himself to be called "Commander." When that title appeared in an advertisement announcing his lecture at Washington's Belasco Theatre, he received a stiff letter from the Navy Department, pointing out the title was "unauthorized and contrary to naval regulations" and demanding an explanation. Peary curtly replied to the Secretary of the Navy that he wasn't responsible for the advertising. The press continued to use the improper title.

In June 1908, he took a gamble. With his ship not yet ready and the full sum required for the voyage still unavailable, he boldly announced that he would sail north that season. At the same time he was shooting off letters to every possible supporter, seeking financial help. When Zenas Crane, vice-president of the Peary Arctic Club, donated five thousand dollars to the expedition, Peary was quick to use the gift as a lure to other possible donors.

In a typical letter to A.W. Douglass, vice-president of the Simmons Hardware Company in St. Louis, he explained the value to a commercial firm of associating its name with the polar attempt. "Mr. Crane's generous gift was made on Friday," Peary wrote. "Saturday his name and the fact of his gift was known in every state and city and town in this country, and was wired to the principal papers in Europe. Incidentally the papers have noted that Mr. Crane is a partner in a great paper manufacturing concern in Massachusetts. . . ." A gift from Douglass or his boss, Simmons, "would carry your name to every city in the country and incidentally that you were members of the great firm of Simmons Hardware Company, and the papers of your city and state would take it up as a matter of state pride." Shades of Sir John Ross and Felix Booth's gin!

The age of hype was dawning, and Peary was one of its early practitioners. "Of course you know," he wrote to Douglass, "that thousands of people today are using Lipton's Tea who had never heard of Lipton's Tea until they knew of Sir Thomas, through his interest and association with the International Yacht races."

The Simmons company responded not with cash but with kind – five sets of their Keen Kutter tools "for distribution among your favourite Eskimos." All Douglass wanted in return was some sort of native testimonial. "See if you can teach them in English to call them KEEN KUTTER goods," he asked Peary, "or tell me what the equivalent would be in Eskimo language."

Throughout June, Peary was bombarded with various offers, some impractical, some financially attractive. Turned down by his former backer, the New York *Herald* (which thought, mistakenly, that its readers had had enough Arctic tales), he got a four-thousand-dollar advance from the *New York Times* – conditional on his actually reaching the Pole. He was offered free a variety of commercial products, from Horlick's Malted Milk to Huyler's Chocolate Dipped Triscuits. The Twentieth Century Globe company agreed to pay him a fifty-cent royalty on every globe it sold in return for a testimonial letter; and the American Mutuoscope and Biograph film company, which lent him a movie camera, agreed to pay a two-cent royalty on every foot of processed film of his Arctic venture that it was able to sell.

One private citizen even sent a thousand-dollar cheque with "no strings" for "Peary the Man, and not necessarily the Explorer – in other words to make any use you wish of the cheque, without feeling under obligation to devote it to the expeditionary fund." That must have been a cheering note. In the midst of the letters urging Peary to use or plug every kind of product, from dehydrated food to piano rolls, were less welcome letters dunning him for money. "We regret very much indeed," one merchant wrote, "that you do not see fit to even answer our letters regarding our account which is long overdue. . . . We have written you pleasantly about the matter a number of times, and really see no way now but to place the matter in the hands of our attorneys. . . ."

The matter, apparently, was settled. General Hubbard came up with another substantial contribution, Crane with an additional ten thousand. Peary had his money at last and on July 6, 1908, the *Roosevelt* got away to the usual accompaniment of cheers and tug-boat whistles. One hundred guests of the Peary Arctic Club accompanied the ship down the East River as far as the Stepping Stone Light. The following morning at Oyster Bay on Long Island, the president himself climbed aboard, wearing a white duck suit and booming out his favourite adjective. "*Bully!*" cried Theodore Roosevelt, or so it was reported. After an hour's inspection he left, having peered into every cranny on the ship, shaken hands with all the crew, and even examined Peary's Eskimo dogs. "I believe in you, Peary!" he roared as he went over the rail.

At Sydney, Nova Scotia, Peary once again said good-bye to his wife and family. "Another farewell," he was later to recall. "And there had been so many! Brave, noble little woman! You have borne with me all the brunt of my Arctic work." Or at least that was the way his ghost writer, the dedicated but effusive Elsa Barker, was to phrase it. ("The divine fire that produces literature cannot be hired by the week, nor does it come at call" is the way she described her work to Peary.) Nonetheless the leave-taking was not as wrenching as it had been on previous ventures. Both Peary and his wife realized that this must be his last expedition.

Peary's crew included some old hands from previous polar attempts: Bob Bartlett and Matt Henson, of course, the earnest, quiet Professor Marvin, and Charles Percy, his steward. Three newcomers were added to the expedition – "tenderfeet" as Peary called them: Donald MacMillan, a mathematics and physical training instructor at a small Massachusetts college; Dr. John Goodsell, a massive, swarthy surgeon; and an enthusiastic twenty-one-year-old college athlete, George Borup.

Peary's plan differed from that of 1906 only in detail. This time, he would jump off from Cape Columbia, about forty miles west of Point Moss, to try to compensate for the drift of the ice. He would keep his support divisions much closer together and he would establish his base camp well north of the Big Lead, about 170 miles from the Pole. He would keep the best dogs, the best supplies, and the best men for the final dash. Meanwhile, the supporting parties would keep the homeward trail open to speed the polar party on its return.

The *Roosevelt*, accompanied by the sealer *Erik*, loaded with eight hundred tons of coal, reached Etah on August 12; Bartlett had no intention this time of running out of fuel. And there, in Henson's

570

description, they encountered "the most hopelessly dirty, unkempt, filthy-littered human being any of us had ever seen." This was Rudolph Franke, a twenty-nine-year-old German, who had been left behind at the neighbouring village of Anoatok by Dr. Frederick Cook to guard his supplies during his absence.

Cook, with two young Eskimos, was heading for the Pole. Nothing had been heard of him since March 1908, when he had sent back a note from Cape Thomas Hubbard, at the tip of Axel Heiberg Island, reporting that he was starting out onto the polar ice.

Franke was in a bad way, suffering from scurvy and an injured leg. Dr. Goodsell pronounced him unfit to remain in the North, and since Cook had given him permission to leave if necessary, Peary grudgingly offered him a berth on the *Erik* – for which he was later billed one hundred dollars – and a loan of fifty dollars, which Mrs. Cook eventually repaid. Cook had left a quantity of supplies, furs, and narwhal and walrus tusks at his hut in Anoatok. Peary assigned his illiterate and surly bosun, John Murphy, and his young cabin boy, Billy Pritchard, to guard them.

In the later controversy that erupted between the two explorers, much was made of Peary's "seizure" of Cook's supplies. The record is muddied by rumours and countercharges. On the one hand, Cook had been given up for dead and his man, Franke, was unable to stay at Anoatok to guard his cabin against looters. Peary gave Murphy that job. On the other, the ailing Franke was persuaded to turn over all of Cook's supplies – under duress, as he later claimed. In Peary's view, Cook no longer had any claim on them.

Murphy's main task was not to guard the Cook hut but to trade with the natives for furs, hides, and narwhal tusks, all of which Peary planned to sell for profit. Harry Whitney, a wealthy sportsman who had come up on the *Erik* to hunt for game, decided to stay over the winter and was also given permission to use Cook's hut at Anoatok. Peary was later attacked by Cook's supporters for refusing to let Franke take any of Cook's goods home on the supply ship *Erik*. Franke, who valued them at ten thousand dollars, later declared, "I had to hand over the furs, just as the enemy has to hand over their arms to the victorious party." But that was after the controversy reached its height. A letter Franke wrote to Peary at Etah on August 13, 1908, is genial enough. It authorizes Peary to take Cook's property into his care and to receive a narwhal horn as a present "for your kindness and hospitality."

On August 18, the *Erik* returned south and the *Roosevelt* turned its prow north again through the narrow channels that led to the top of Ellesmere, "fighting for every foot of the way against the almost impossible ice," in Henson's words. It was, according to Peary's account, "a theatre of action which for diabolic and Titanic struggle makes Dante's frozen circle of the Inferno seem like a skating pond." The description owes more to Elsa Barker's literary ornamentation than it does to the matter-of-fact explorer's own blunt style.

The trip certainly was a horror. Crammed aboard a vessel no bigger than a Hudson River tug were Peary's party of twenty, plus sixty-nine Eskimos, 550 tons of coal, seventy tons of whale meat, the blubber of fifty walruses, and 246 dogs, all fighting and howling. "To my dying day," Bartlett wrote, "I shall never forget the frightful noise, the choking stench and the terrible confusion that reigned aboard. . . ." On the first night out, as the stubby little ship nosed its way into Kane Basin, they tried to eat some canned peaches for supper. "But the odor about us was so powerful that the peaches simply felt wet and cold on one's tongue, having no fruit flavor whatsoever."

For the next thirteen days, neither Peary nor Bartlett was able to change clothes as the *Roosevelt* bored and twisted her way through 350 miles of almost solid ice. With Bartlett in the crow's-nest scouting the frozen desert ahead, Peary, on the bridge, exhorted his chief engineer not to let the engines fail, for the slightest hesitation would have meant loss of the ship. "Chief," Peary shouted through the speaking tube, "you've got to keep her moving until I give you the word, no matter what happens." On more than one occasion, with the vessel stuck between the corners of two converging floes, Peary told the engineer, Wardwell, "to jump her now . . . fifty yards." He could feel the ship shake beneath him as she seemed to take a flying leap forward under the pressure of live steam poured directly from the boilers into the cylinder.

The *Roosevelt* arrived at Cape Sheridan on September 5. The Pole lay five hundred statute miles to the North. Cape Columbia, Peary's jumping-off point, was ninety miles north and west – 475 miles from the Pole. For much of the winter Peary's support parties sledged provisions and equipment to "Crane City," a huddle of snow houses at the foot of the steep cliff that Peary named for his benefactor, the Peary Arctic Club's vice-president.

By the last day of February, 1909, the entire company was assembled at Crane City, in the -50^0 cold, ready to set off for the Pole. Bartlett was the first to go; he and his Eskimos were to break trail, using pickaxes if necessary. In a romantic gesture, the husky captain had jettisoned his precious supply of chewing tobacco in favour of a copy of the Rubaiyat of Omar Khayyam. Borup, the college athlete, followed with his team two hours later. His instructions were to travel for three marches, drop his supplies, return for a second load, and then catch up with the main party.

The next day, March 1, the other divisions left at one-hour intervals – Henson first, with his dogs and Eskimos, and then the remaining teams under Dr. Goodsell, Professor Marvin, and Donald MacMillan. Peary brought up the rear, like a general commanding his troops from behind the lines, following the well-beaten trail and the chain of igloos and caches that formed the life line between Crane City and the forward party. In this way, Peary was able to check on stragglers, keep in touch with the returning parties, and save his energies for the final run to the Pole.

As he set off on this, his last odyssey, Robert Peary knew that for him it was now or never. He *had* to reach the Pole. It represented everything he had struggled for since childhood. If achieved, it would make him the most famous explorer in the world, perhaps in history. It would bring him untold wealth – a newspaper series, a magazine series, a lucrative lecture series, a best-selling book, fat fees for testimonials – and, most important of all, perhaps, the adulation and friendship of presidents and kings, the gold medals of geographical societies, and his name enshrined in the encyclopaedias and the history books.

Failure was unthinkable. Peary was already on the verge of bankruptcy. The *New York Times* contract explicitly stated that if he did not reach the Pole, he must return the advance the paper had paid him for his story. Nobody wanted to read about another Farthest North; no magazine, no book publisher would print that tale again. The merchants who had supplied him with piano rolls and cameras would have no interest in his endorsements. Worse, his most powerful friends, who had raised hundreds of thousands of dollars for his several ventures, would drop away like the leaves of autumn. In the history books he would be just another explorer, one who had tried but failed, a minor paragraph in the reference works, nothing more.

There were, at this point, twenty-four men, nineteen sledges, and 133 dogs on the ice. Up ahead, Bartlett was breaking trail, hard put to make ten miles a day. The other divisions, travelling in his wake, made better time, although the trail was often half obliterated by blowing snow. Henson and the supply parties also had to use pick-axes to hack their way through. Only the back-and-forth shuffling of each relay division kept the route open at all.

The farther they went, the harder the going. For the first few miles the fast ice attached to the Ellesmere coast was fairly smooth, but the outer edge of this icy fringe rose and fell with the tides. When it came into contact with the moving pack, pressure ridges formed parallel with the shore, barring the way north. Some of these ridges were only a few feet high; some were fifty feet. Some were only a few feet wide; others extended for a quarter of a mile. Through these heaped-up ice masses – the larger ones as big as a two-storey house – Bartlett's party had to chop its way.

As far as he could see into the mists and blowing snow, Bartlett faced a rumpled, tangled world. Between each ridge was a broken expanse of fragmented ice made up of sheets and chunks, all in constant motion, driven this way and that by the wind. Connecting this moving jumble were thin strips of newly frozen sea ice, forming a corrugated pattern of "unimaginable unevenness and roughness" (Peary's description) that stretched all the way to the Pole. But that pattern was broken by open lanes of water, some mere cracks in the ice floes, others as straight as canals and as wide as meandering rivers.

The trail from Crane City, laid by Bartlett and repaired by Henson, became harder and harder to follow. The ice drift was not constant. The general drift was from east to west, as Nansen knew, but it could also reverse itself. Sometimes, as Edward Parry had discovered to his chagrin, it moved north and south. Borup, returning to Crane City for supplies, found that the drifting ice had moved the trail fifteen miles to the west. At some points it was almost wiped out. Marvin, who went back for fuel and joined Borup, encountered similar conditions.

There was a worse setback, albeit a familiar one. On March 5, when no more than fifty miles from land, the forward parties were halted by a broad channel, apparently that same Big Lead that had held them up on the previous expedition. There it lay, blocking Peary's route to the Pole, a malevolent expanse of inky water, its sinister appearance enhanced by the clouds of vapour that rose from its surface, misting the yellow orb of the noon sun that moved low across the southern horizon.

574

For Peary, the five-day wait that followed was intolerable. Once again, as in 1906, the meticulous planner found his way blocked by forces over which he had no control. Plagued by "the gnawing torment of those days of forced inaction," he paced impatiently back and forth in front of the group of igloos built by the forward party. He scarcely spoke. Every little while he climbed a pinnacle of ice to peer through the dim light, hoping to find a way across. He slept fitfully, waking every few hours to catch the slightest noise and often rising to go outside and listen for the sound of approaching dogs. Where were Marvin and Borup with the supplies and fuel he needed for his march to the Pole?

Both men had been held up by a similar lane of open water. "There may be a HELL in the next world," Borup wrote, "but nothing worse could be devised by fiends than the gnawing agony of that long wait beside that black lead which wouldn't close, and, ever widening, would not let itself be frozen over."

To add to Peary's frustration, the weather was splendid for travelling. "Seven precious days of fine weather lost," Henson recorded, adding that "fine weather is the exception, not the rule, in the Arctic." To Peary, history was repeating itself.

On March 11, ice formed on the water and he and the others scurried to get over. Crossing such leads, Peary later remarked, was rather like crossing a river on a succession of gigantic shingles, all afloat and moving. He scribbled a note for Marvin and left it in his igloo: "It is *vital* you overtake us and give us fuel." Marvin and Borup caught up with him three and a half days later. At that point they were 370 statute miles from the Pole.

The supporting parties had already began to turn back, first Dr. Goodsell, then, on March 15, Donald MacMillan. The following day, Henson, breaking trail up ahead, was facing terrifying conditions. The ice began to break with a deafening roar. Another open lead barred his way. Although the floes were scarcely big enough to hold a dog, Henson chanced a crossing, knowing that a single awkward step could mean the end. He made it, only to find the far side even more treacherous, so unstable that three sledges were smashed. He managed to fashion two sound ones from the wreckage. With Peary delayed by more open water, the party was not reunited until March 17.

Now Peary sent Marvin ahead to plot a route through the chaos while the others rested. They started off next morning in -40^0

weather through a wilderness of hummocks that damaged two more sledges. The following day they fought their way through pressure ridges sixty feet high, breaking trail over mountains of ice and shuttling back to haul up their sledges, "pushing from our very toes, straining every muscle, urging the dogs with voice and whip," in Henson's description.

Sometimes the dogs gave up and the men would have to struggle to prevent the sledges from sliding back until the dogs could be started again. The descent on the far side was even more hazardous. Coming down a pressure ridge, one sledge broke away, tumbling thirty feet and terrifying both animals and men.

Peary caught up again on March 19 and told Henson to choose the best dogs for the remainder of the journey. The others would be taken back to land the following day by Borup, who took the order philosophically, although as he said, "I would have given my immortal soul to have gone on." Borup, who enlivened the journey with college yells and songs and sprinkled his later narrative (*A Tenderfoot with Peary*) with "gee whizzes" and "Holy Smokes," wrote that "when the Captain of your eleven orders you to go to the sidelines, there's no use making a gallery play by frenzied pleas to be allowed to go on."

Peary arranged to shuttle the remainder of the expedition forward in two groups. While the main party slept, Bartlett and his Eskimos would break trail with Henson and his natives acting as scouts. Then the trail-breaking party would rest while the main party moved forward on the route prepared for it. Borup, who travelled back at a speed of twenty-two miles a day, was directed to set up a cache of supplies at Cape Fanshaw Martin, eighty miles to the west of Cape Columbia, in case of westward drift. Six days later, Ross Marvin took his final sighting and prepared to turn back with his team. The expedition had now reached 86⁰ 38′ – about 230 statute miles from the Pole.

But Ross Marvin never returned to land. On the way back, one member of his team, Kudlukto, got into an argument because Marvin, who tended to be overbearing, had refused to allow one of the young Eskimo boys – Kudlukto's cousin – to ride on the sledge. The boy was exhausted and pleaded to be given a chance to rest; when Marvin refused, Kudlukto shot him and pushed his body through the thin ice of an open lead. The party moved on with the boy riding on the sledge. Kudlukto reported that Marvin had accidentally drowned. The true story didn't emerge until fifteen years later, when Kudlukto became a Christian and confessed. He was not punished because no one could be certain under what jurisdiction the murder had occurred.

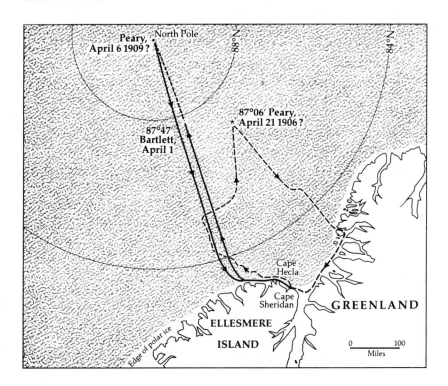

Peary's polar records, 1906 and 1909

Oblivious of this tragedy, Peary, Bartlett, Henson, and the Eskimos continued north. On March 31, Bartlett's calculations showed that they had reached a latitude of 87° 47' – the farthest north ever recorded. For the last fortnight, they had been travelling at a rate of about twelve miles a day. Since the Pole was still about one hundred and fifty miles ahead, at that rate it would take them close to thirteen days to reach it. Bartlett, who had noted a speed-up during the previous week, thought it might be done in eight days.

Peary now prepared for the polar dash. He told Bartlett that he was to go back on the following day, April 1, 1909, to help prepare the return trail for the polar party, which would be made up of Peary, Henson, and four natives – Egingwah, Seeglo, Ootah, and

577

Ooqueah. Almost certainly, Bartlett felt that this was a betrayal. In 1905, he had agreed to captain the *Roosevelt* only if Peary allowed him to accompany the polar party, a promise Peary apparently re-affirmed before this voyage. In his memoirs, written years after the event, he was philosophical about the decision, insisting that Peary's reasoning was sound, that Henson was a better dog driver, and that he had "never held it against him." But that September, when he returned to civilization, he was still smarting over the incident and blurted out to the New York *Herald* that "it was a bitter disappoint-ment. I got up early the next morning while the rest were asleep and started north alone. I don't know, perhaps I cried a little. I guess perhaps I was a little crazy then. I thought I could walk on the rest of the way alone. It seemed so near."

His account may well have been exaggerated by the journalistic licence of the time. On the other hand, both Peary and Henson recorded that Bartlett *did* walk several miles out of the camp. The reason, they said, was that he wanted to be able to say that he had reached the 88th parallel before turning back. But, as Bartlett well knew, that was more than a dozen miles away. Why didn't he take a sledge and team?

Peary's jettisoning of Bartlett at this crucial moment forecast the furious controversy that would erupt after the expedition's return. Once again, as in the case of Jesup Land, Crocker Land, and his own Farthest North, Peary was setting off into the unknown without a reliable witness, since neither Henson nor the Eskimos knew how to calculate observations.

Peary later gave several explanations for his decision, some of them distasteful. If he had sent Henson south instead of Bartlett, he said, Henson might not have reached land. "While faithful to me, and when *with me* more effective in covering distance with a sledge than any of the others, he had not as a racial inheritance the daring and initiative of my Anglo-Saxon friends. I owed it to him not to subject him to dangers and responsibilities with which he was temperamentally unable to cope."

At another point, Peary gave an entirely different explanation, which was certainly in keeping with his character: "The pole was something to which I had devoted my life; it was a thing on which I had concentrated everything, on which I had expended some of myself, for which I had gone through such hell and suffering as I hope no man . . . may ever experience, and in which I have put

578

money, time, and everything else, and I did not feel under those circumstances I was called upon to divide with a man who, no matter how able and deserving he might be, was a young man and had only put in a few years in that kind of work, and who had, frankly, as I believed, not the right that I had to it. . . ." If he took Henson and not Bartlett, and reached the Pole, Peary could claim that he was the only white man to capture that honour. The black man and the Eskimos did not count.

Bartlett and his Eskimos left on April 1. Peary, Henson, and the four natives started for the Pole early the following morning and achieved phenomenal – one might say unbelievable – speeds. They did not need twelve or thirteen days to reach final camp, or even eight days, as Bartlett had figured. According to Peary's own claims, he made it in five, an average speed of twenty-nine statute miles a day. Although he always insisted that he made a beeline for the Pole, it is hard to believe that suddenly there were no obstacles that would force him into detours. Peary's average speed to the Pole without educated witnesses is almost three times faster than his average speed from Crane City with such witnesses.

There is a remarkable similarity between Peary's story of his journey to the Pole and back in 1909 and his earlier account of his Farthest North in 1906. In each case he lists phenomenal speeds; in each case he claims the going suddenly got easier; in each case he insists he returned straight down the meridian without detours. In each case he had no one with him who could confirm his observations.

His account of the last five days of his 1909 journey to the Pole does differ from Henson's, however. Henson may not have been able to work out astronomical observations, but he knew a pressure ridge when he saw one. In his own account, which was also ghost-written, he told of open water that necessitated "detours east and west" (Peary claimed the leads all ran north and south), of the men repeatedly falling down in their tracks, and of pressure ridges that had to be attacked with pickaxes. Later explorers confirm Henson's version – that there is little difference between ice conditions close to the Pole and those farther south. Aerial research in the mid-1930s, for example, revealed two pressure ridges to the mile in the same area. Polar explorers in the 1960s and 1980s reported a devastated world of broken ice blocks and a wilderness of hummocks.

On April 6 at 10 a.m. (Peary's account; Henson says it was that evening), Peary stopped and, while his Eskimos built a snow house, opened a parcel, withdrew a small taffeta flag, fastened it to a staff, and placed it firmly on the igloo. Henson figured the camp must be an important one and asked Peary what he would call it.

"This, my boy, is to be Camp Morris K. Jesup," Peary replied, "the last and most northerly camp on the earth." But he did not say he had reached the Pole.

He consulted his chronometer. If he was still on the same meridian on which he had left Cape Columbia, it must be approaching noon local time. He took an observation with his sextant but did not show the results to Henson, as he usually did. (Henson could use a sextant but could not do the calculations.) It was usual for Henson to note such positions in his diary, but this time he was not invited to do so or to sign Peary's sheet of calculations, as Borup and Marvin had always done. Thus Peary's observations at Camp Jesup were the only ones that no one else looked at.

This is inexplicable. By getting Henson to record the results independently, Peary could have copper-plated his claim to achieving the Pole. Why didn't he? Here was a meticulous planner who likened his attainment of the Pole to winning a game of chess – all the moves planned in advance, every earlier defeat analysed as to its causes "until it became possible to believe that those causes could in future be guarded against . . . and the losing game . . . turned into one final, complete success." He had designed an assault on the North Pole that would impress any modern military commander. Why, then, did he fail to take the final step to pin down the certainty of his victory? There can be only two explanations: either he didn't expect that another person would also claim the Pole and therefore believed his own feat would not be questioned (as had been the case in the past), or he simply faked the whole story.

According to Peary, his latitude at Camp Jesup showed he was about five statute miles from the Pole. Henson, sensing this, removed a glove and extended a hand in congratulation. Peary didn't see it. "I was actually too exhausted to realize at the moment that my life's purpose had been achieved." He rubbed his eyes, stumbled into his igloo, and slept for four hours.

Oddly, his diary contains no references for April 7, when Peary was at the Pole, or the day following. In that journal, which may well be a copy of his original, since it is clean and not stained with oil or soot, there is a loose sheet of a different kind of paper, undated, which reads: "The Pole at last!!! The prize of 3 centuries, my dream and ambition for 23 years MINE at last. I cannot bring myself to realize it. It all seems so simple and commonplace, as Bartlett said 'just like every day.' I wish Jo could be here with me to share my feelings. I have drunk her health and that of the kids from the Benedictine flask she sent me.

"3 years ago today, the storm began at Storm camp. 7 years ago today, I started north from Cape Hecla."

The blanks in the diary, the loose, undated sheet – almost an afterthought – pose unanswerable questions.

Peary took a series of observations, thirteen in all, "at two different stations, in three different directions at four different times. . . ." There was a brief gathering for a photograph and the inevitable three cheers. Then, at 4 p.m. on April 7, thirty hours after arriving at their goal, the party turned and headed south.

Peary had taken leave of Bartlett around midnight, April 1; he arrived back at the same camp at midnight, April 9. It is these eight days that are in question. The distance from the camp to the Pole and back was three hundred miles. Deducting the thirty hours he claimed to have spent there, Peary must have travelled at an average daily speed of at least forty-three miles to cover that three-hundred-mile distance; and that makes no allowance for detours, which, before 1906, Peary had always estimated at 25 per cent.

In the fortnight before Peary left Bartlett, his best daily speed was twelve miles, not counting detours. A smaller party should have been able to go faster. But even if Peary had travelled an average of fifteen miles a day, he could not have got closer to his goal than ninety miles before turning back.

Peary's account simply doesn't ring true. He was, according to Henson, so exhausted and lame that he was forced to ride all the way back on a sledge, a dead weight that had to be dragged over pressure ridges and around open water. No other explorer had achieved such a record and none has achieved it since. Nansen averaged no more than 14 miles a day and never exceeded 23. Cagni's speed over 600 miles of polar ice was 6.3 miles a day. Ralph Plaisted, who reached the Pole by snowmobile in 1968, averaged about 11 miles. In 1986, Will Steger averaged about 8.5 miles a day by dogteam, and Jean-Louis Etienne achieved the same rate that year on skis. All but Steger were supplied by air, and none made the return trip; all were flown out.

Peary's method of making observations was as casual as it had been in 1906. There is no evidence that he ever knew his longitude. Although he insisted he had headed straight to the Pole and back again, he had no way of knowing whether he had strayed off course or not. Sextant readings for latitude are taken at noon. But when *was* "noon"? Without having his longitude, Peary couldn't know the local time.

After he left Bartlett he took only one latitude reading at what he thought was noon, Cape Columbia meridian time. He made no observations for variations as other explorers had done. "When I was sledging north," Albert Markham said, ". . . I was very careful to check my course by constant observations for the variation of the compass, thus enabling me to shape my course along the same meridian of longitude." But Peary, who could only guess at his mileage, travelled by dead reckoning, a method made unreliable by zigzagging.

All the evidence suggests that a beeline journey to the Pole, such as Peary described, would have been impossible. Henson said they "followed the lines of least resistance . . . frequently . . . going due east or west in order to detour around pressure ridges, floebergs and leads." Borup earlier recalled that "we guessed and groped with many a twist and turn." Yet Peary claimed that his course "was nearly as the crow flies, due north, across floe after floe, pressure ridge after pressure ridge, headed straight for some hummock or pinnacle of ice which I had lined in with my compass." Plaisted found that through detours and ice drift he had travelled an additional three hundred miles in his five-hundred-mile snowmobile journey to the Pole; Steger, in 1986, found that detours added an extra four hundred miles.

Other members of the Peary expedition encountered ice drift. Henson wrote that "the way to the Pole lay across the ever moving and drifting ice of the Arctic ocean. . . . Continuously the steady drift of the ice carried us back on the course we had come." Borup and Marvin, returning north to join Peary, noticed on March 7 a steady easterly drift – the floebergs moving so swiftly that one they had marked vanished from sight within two hours. Yet Peary insisted that the drift had ceased as he neared the Pole, allowing him to travel in a straight line.

Why these discrepancies? Why would Peary, a seasoned Arctic hand, with more experience than any other explorer in polar travel – a man who had more than once vividly described to his readers and to his lecture audiences the treacherous nature of the ice pack – why would he continue to insist that he had never veered from his course? The only plausible explanation is that he didn't want to add any extra mileages to his claimed speeds, which were already suspiciously high.

Even before parting with Bartlett, Peary was meticulously considering the benefits his discovery would bring him: adulation from his peers, public applause, social standing, and, not least, hard cash. On March 26, the day Marvin turned back, he began to jot down in the margins of his diary the various methods he might use to exploit his triumph for its maximum rewards. These notations to himself, which continued for three weeks, confirm that Peary was not primarily interested in geographical or scientific discovery. He coveted the Pole as a prize that would guarantee not only international recognition but also commercial benefits.

It was his intention to cash in on his discovery by patenting and selling everything from special North Pole clothing to ivory-mounted snowshoes. If Elisha Kent Kane could get seventy-five thousand dollars in book royalties, Peary intended to try for one hundred thousand. If Nares could be knighted and Schley and George Melville (of the ill-fated *Jeannette* expedition) made admirals, if Parry could receive one hundred and twenty-five thousand dollars from a grateful government, then why not Peary? These marginal notations are so astonishing, so revealing, and (some would say) so crass that they deserve to be quoted in detail:

March 26: Have set of ivory mounted sledge implements made. . . . Ivory mounted snowshoes? Think up some ivory articles to be made for the home folks. . . .

Present sextant . . . to Navy Museum (Annapolis?). Have my eye glasses gold mounted for constant use. Have extra pair ditto as a present to someone. . . .

March 28: Suggest sending piece of fringe to each local or state division D.A.R. . . . piece of N.P. bearskin fringe for souvenirs to women. The N.P. flag with white bar. This as a stamp on all N.P. articles?

April 4: Have special pair of "Peary North Pole" snowshoes made. Raised toe and heel, curved body, lacquered bows, ebony crossbars, silver keel & name plate white gut lacing. . . .

Have Henson make pattern "Peary North Pole sledges". . . . For miners, prospectors, lumbermen, explorers, children.

April 5: North Pole coats, suits, tents, cookers at Sportsmens Show with male & female attendants in Eskimo costume....

Jewel for Order of the North Pole. Have Borup take a 5" x 7" 3 1/2 to 4 pl. focus portrait of me in deer or sheep coat with bear roll (face unshaven), & keep on till satisfactory one obtained. Have Foster color in a special print of this to bring out the gray eyes, the red sunburned skin, the bleached eyebrows & beard, frosted eyebrows, eye glasses, beard.

April 6: Have Harpers take entire matter, book, magazine articles, pictures & stories (100). Kane got 75 from his books, Nansen 50 for his.

... flag with diagonal white bar to be my personal flag. Fly a fine one at Eagle I.

April 9: ... send photo Pres. & self shaking hands to him ... send R a Pole Peary sledge....

April 10: U.S. made Melville & Schley Admirals and Greely Brigadier General for their arctic work. England knighted James & John Ross, Parry, Franklin, Nares, McClintock, Richards (?), Beaumont etc. etc. Paid Parry $125,000....

April 19: ... have aluminum case Harvard watches repaired by makers & put gold hunting cases for presents. One properly engraved to be given to Bridgman This watch carried by me to the North Pole, is given to my friend H.L. Bridgman as a slight token of my appreciation of his invaluable assistance and loyal devotion to the cause for years, R.E. Peary.

Peary reached Cape Columbia on April 23, 1909 – only five days behind Bartlett. "My life work is accomplished," he wrote in his diary. "The thing which it was intended from the beginning that I should do, the thing which I believed could be done and that I could do, I have done. I have got the North Pole out of my system. After 23 years of effort, hard work, disappointments, hardships, privations, more or less suffering, and some risks, I have won the last great geographical prize ... for the credit of the United States, the Service to which I belong, myself and my family. My work is the finish, the cap and climax, of 300 years of effort, loss of life and expenditure of millions, by some of the best men of the civilized nations of the world, and it has been accomplished with a clean cut dash, spirit, and I believe, thoroughness characteristically American. I am content."

Two days later he was aboard the *Roosevelt*, where Bartlett, without waiting for Peary to greet him, came up to shake his leader's hand. "I congratulate you, sir," he said, "on the discovery of the Pole."

Oddly, Peary made no reply. In his first few days aboard the *Roosevelt*, he showed none of the elation to be found in his diary entries. Indeed, he forbore to mention the crowning achievement of his life to anyone aboard ship. He appeared to avoid Henson, who wrote that for three weeks after their arrival, he caught no more than a fleeting glimpse of his commander. "Not once in all that time did he speak a word to me. . . . Not a word about the North Pole or anything connected with it."

To the others he was surprisingly coy. One might have expected him to send an exultant message to MacMillan, who was across the Robeson Channel on the Greenland side. But he didn't mention either the Pole or the date on which he claimed to have reached it. "Northern trip entirely satisfactory," was all he wrote. And when Dr. Goodsell put the question to him directly, he received an oblique response: "I have not been altogether unsuccessful."

Why this enigmatic silence? Even though the news of Marvin's death must have dampened his natural jubilance, Peary's reticence is out of character. Was he still unsure whether he should claim the Pole? Or was he simply trying to keep it a secret from his associates so that the word would not get out before he could proclaim his success to the public? His sledgemates certainly believed he had reached the Pole, and when they discussed it at the dinner table, Peary did not correct them. Henson mentioned to Dr. Goodsell that the sun appeared to have made a uniform circle of the horizon, as it would at 90° N, but hurriedly added that it "might have dipped a little to the south."

On June 12, Borup and a party of natives erected at Cape Columbia the standard cairn that contained the details of the expedition – something Peary himself had neglected to do. That was the first specific public record of his success. This apparent indecision is reminiscent of his so-called discovery of "Jesup Land," which he had delayed reporting officially for three years, and "Crocker Land," which he claimed to have seen in June of 1906 but didn't mention publicly until February of 1907.

The *Roosevelt* broke out of her harbour at Cape Sheridan on July 17. A month later, after a long and stormy struggle with the ice, she reached Etah, where the descendants of John Ross's Arctic Highlanders rushed to greet her. In the crowd was Peary's boatswain,

Murphy, and his cabin boy, Pritchard, who had been guarding Peary's own supplies at Etah and Frederick Cook's at neighbouring Anoatok. And there, too, looking more like an Eskimo than the natives themselves, was Harry Whitney, the sportsman, who had spent the winter with the other two.

Here Peary got confirmation of what some Eskimos had told him on one of his stops down the Greenland coast: Dr. Cook had returned from Ellesmere Island alive, with two native companions. Where had he been? What had he done? Peary was intent on finding out; but that wasn't easy, because Cook, before he left for the south, had sworn both Whitney and the Eskimos to silence. Peary called young Billy Pritchard into his cabin and subjected him to what the cabin boy later described as a "third degree." Pritchard broke down and confessed that he had heard Cook tell Whitney, "I've been to the Pole," after which Cook swore both men to secrecy. "He said he didn't want Mr. Peary or anyone else to know anything about it."

There is nothing in Peary's own account to hint at his feelings at this disturbing revelation. Henson, too, glosses over it, simply writing that the idea of Cook making such an astounding claim "was so ludicrous that after our laugh, we dropped the matter altogether."

But, of course, they did not drop the matter. It is not difficult to guess at Peary's bitterness and fury. Here was an upstart claiming to have beaten him to his prize in the most casual fashion, without any of the meticulous planning and the military precision of the Peary System! It was too much. Once again it seemed another had "forestalled" Peary and turned his triumph to gall. From that moment on, Robert Peary's purpose, to which he devoted all his considerable talents, was to expose his rival as a fraud. He and his supporters would not be content until Cook was demolished, flattened, ridiculed, and driven from the society of his peers.

3

Dr. Cook's It was impossible not to like Frederick Cook. He belonged to that
strange human subspecies whose members seem forever courteous, gentle,
odyssey and apparently open. In 1907, when he set off on his polar journey,
he had few antagonists apart from Peary. Even Peary, on first acquaintance some years before, had called him "a thoroughly decent

fellow." Roald Amundsen, who spent a winter with him in the Antarctic, went further. He was, Amundsen recalled, "loved and respected by all, a man of unfailing courage, unfailing hope, endless cheerfulness, unwearied kindness." He was genial, inventive, eager to help out, and incurably optimistic. People took to Cook on first meeting: he was so ingenuous, so direct, with his clear blue eyes and his shock of ash blond hair that hinted at his German ancestry.

This affability concealed certain flaws in the Cook character. When the full record is examined, he emerges as a remarkably careless human being – careless with the truth, careless with his financial obligations, careless of the consequences of his actions. The world is full of Cooks – charming, child-like people who rarely look ahead but leap from one of life's pinnacles to the next, hoping always to land unharmed.

The contrast between the two remarkable explorers, each of whom claimed the North Pole, could not have been more extreme. Cook was later to write of his polar quest that he had "a personal ambition, a crazy hunger I had to satisfy." It was, of course, the popular thing to say; it fitted the public's concept of what an explorer should be – a man who sacrificed everything for a dream. But there is little suggestion of any "crazy hunger" in Cook's actions before or after his attempt on the Pole – none of the fierce, obsessive will to succeed that drove Peary. On the contrary, Cook was remarkably casual. He had none of Peary's superb organizational skills, and it wasn't in his nature to indulge in the kind of military precision that Peary brought to his long-range planning. Cook's various ventures seem to have been entered upon almost by chance, or as an afterthought, or as the result of a sudden spur-of-the-moment decision. That was certainly true of his much-trumpeted conquest of Mount McKinley in 1906. It was also true of his first trip to the Arctic with Peary in 1891. He spotted an advertisement in the Brooklyn *Standard-Union* asking for volunteers to join Peary in his first North Greenland expedition. Cook, who had been enthralled by Kane's accounts of the Arctic just as Peary had been, answered the ad and was surprised to find himself accepted. His assault on the Pole was equally impulsive. Though he had certainly talked with John Bradley about his hopes before leaving New York, he didn't make up his mind until he reached Anoatok and found weather conditions favourable.

In 1907, when he was heading north once again, he was forty-two years old and already one of the best-known explorers in the world.

One of five children born to a German immigrant (Cook was originally "Koch"), he had had his share of vicissitudes and hardships. His widowed mother supported her family by working in a sweatshop. Cook put himself through medical school by delivering milk door to door at three in the morning. His first wife died of peritonitis. His first attempts at a practice in Brooklyn were a failure. But in 1907 he was a public figure, respected by his fellow explorers. He had been four times to the Arctic, once to the Antarctic, had written two best-selling books on his adventures, had succeeded Adolphus Greely as president of the Explorers' Club (the third – Peary would be the fourth), was founder and first president of the Arctic Club of America and the recipient of honours and medals from both sides of the Atlantic. Standing five feet nine inches in his Eskimo furs, a stocky, rugged figure with weather-beaten features, he looked the very model of a modern American explorer.

Cook's voyage to Greenland with "Gambler Jim" Bradley was planned as a hunting expedition. Cook had no fixed or definite intentions, apart from furthering his studies of Eskimo culture, but the idea of a polar attempt lurked somewhere in the back of his mind. Bradley was happy to have such a noted explorer with him, while Cook, as he told Cyrus Adams of the American Geographical Society, "half hoped" that he might "make the expedition a jumping-off point for the Pole." Bradley told Cook that if he did decide to go, he was prepared to underwrite the cost.

When the yacht reached the Greenland coast, the pair set off for the Eskimo hunting grounds at Anoatok, thirty miles north of Etah. There they found a bear hunt in progress. The best dogs in the area and the most capable natives (many of them doubtless trained by Peary) were assembled in a region abounding with game. In Cook's mind every essential for Arctic exploration was present. He decided on the spot to make an attempt on the Pole the following spring. What Anoatok could not supply, Bradley certainly would.

Cook, like Peary, saw the so-called "dash" as a kind of sporting event without scientific value. It was a challenge – like the ascent of Mount McKinley – nothing more. But Cook's attitude was far more casual than that of his rival. "The attaining of this mystical spot," he wrote later, "did not then, and does not now, seem in itself to mean anything; I did not then, and do not now, consider it the treasure house of any great scientific secrets. The only thing to be gained from reaching the Pole, the triumph of it, the lesson in accomplishment, is

588

that man, by brain power and muscle energy, can subdue the most terrific forces of a blind nature if he is determined enough, courageous enough, and undauntedly persistent despite failure."

When winter approached, Bradley returned to New York on his yacht. One volunteer stayed behind with Cook – the yacht's twenty-nine-year-old steward, Rudolph Franke. The two men spent five months in a gloomy stone hut at Anoatok, "a land of sorrowful dead," in Cook's phrase. Rewarded with Bradley's supply of weapons, tools, and trade goods, the entire band of 250 natives gathered from the surrounding villages cheerfully set about to outfit him for the coming venture – sewing clothes of hides, building light, flexible sledges, gathering grass to insulate boots, and preparing food and other supplies.

In the dimly lit igloos, the women of the tribe worked industriously, as they had for Peary, drying skins and cutting and sewing them into serviceable garments. Cook moved from igloo to igloo "with an interest that verged on anxiety" because he knew that his life and that of his companions depended on the warmth and durability of the clothing. He was soon reassured, for the skill of these primitive tailors was remarkable. They took his measurements by roughly sizing up his old garments and measuring him by sight. After a preliminary fitting they adjusted the clothes by cutting out and inserting patches of fur. They made their own thread by drying and stripping caribou and narwhal sinews; the white man's steel needles were so precious to them that if a point or eye was broken, they heated and flattened the appropriate end and shaped a new point or with a bow drill bored a new eye. In the gloom of the snow houses, their vision was extraordinary. They could see objects no white man could have spotted and perform tedious feats that an outsider would have bungled.

Cook's plan was to head for the Pole by crossing Kane Basin to Ellesmere Island, sledge over its frozen midriff to the west coast, and follow the fiords north to the tip of Axel Heiberg Island. This remarkable journey would not have been possible without Cook's Eskimo companions, who repeatedly saved the party from starvation by seeking out and killing muskoxen and bear. Cold was an even worse enemy. Cook claimed that the temperature dropped as low as -83^0F – a record that, if true, was never exceeded in the years that followed. At one point, the air was so heavy with frost that Cook realized he could not long breathe it and survive. The Eskimos buried

589

him in a snow bank to prevent him from freezing and then proceeded to build a large igloo – checking on his condition every few minutes to make sure he was still alive. A little more than two hours later, the igloo was completed and all the party crammed inside, so tightly that Cook found that he was actually perspiring.

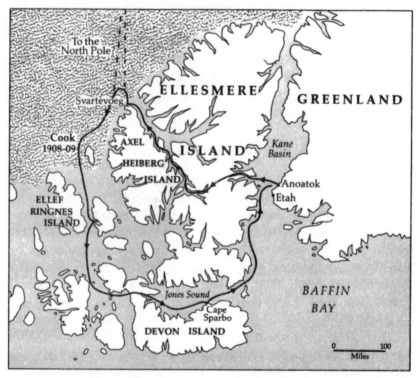

Cook's route from Anoatok to Axel Heiberg and return, 1908-09

On March 8, Cook's party of ten reached the tip of Axel Heiberg Island and camped beneath the monstrous, black-scarred cliff that Sverdrup had named Svartevoeg. Here Cook prepared to launch himself at the Pole, some six hundred miles to the north. On March 18, with two sledges, twenty-six dogs, and half a ton of food, he set off. Franke and seven of the natives were sent back shortly afterwards. Cook chose two young Eskimos, Ahwelahtea and Etukishook (the spelling is Cook's) as his sole companions.

From this point until his return to land, the world has only Cook's account of what occurred. There's no doubt that he crossed Ellesmere and reached Axel Heiberg Island. Franke was with him – an

590

educated witness – and Cook's own photographs and descriptions confirm that he made the journey. But for the details of what Cook achieved on his trip across the polar ice, there is no corroboration.

His story of that journey repeats the usual tribulations that every polar explorer faced: back-breaking work hacking through pressure ridges, storms that smothered igloos, leads of waters that yawned before them and threatened to engulf them, forced marches to make up lost mileage "until dogs languished or legs failed," together with hunger, thirst, exhaustion, and despair. At one point, Cook wrote, with half the food gone and the Pole still 160 statute miles away, Ahwelahtea lost all hope. "It is well to die," he cried, tears streaming down his face. "Beyond is impossible." But Cook urged him on.

Cook's descriptions of the polar scape, that "swirling, moving scene of dull white and nebulous gray," always vivid and often lurid in the acceptably fevered style of that time, have a mystical quality, enhanced, perhaps, by his editor, T. Everett Harré of *Hampton's Magazine*, whom Cook praised for relieving him of "much of the routine editorial work." The land ice, he wrote, "ran in waves of undulating blue shimmering with streams of gold . . . the last vestiges of jagged land rose and fell like marionettes dancing a wild farewell." The Big Lead, which Peary had encountered far to the east, was "a long river winding between pallisades of blue crystal . . . mottled and tawny colored, like the skin of a great constrictor." The northern mirages "wove a web of . . . marvellous cities with fairy-tale castles. . . . Huge creatures, misshapen and grotesque, writhed along the horizon. . . ." The midnight sun was "pressed into a basin flaming with magical fires, burning behind a mystic curtain of opalescent frosts. Blue at other times, it appeared like a huge vase of luminous crystal, such as might be evoked by the weird genii of the Orient."

Cook's most controversial discovery was of a huge new island to the west, which he named Bradley Land after his patron. "I think," he wrote, "I felt a thrill such as Columbus must have felt when the first green vision of America loomed before his eye." But Cook was no Columbus, and Bradley Land was as illusory as Peary's Jesup Land and Crocker Land. It has been suggested that what both Cook and Peary saw may have been one of the mysterious "ice islands" – great floating masses that weren't discovered until forty years later. But Cook's description of Bradley Land doesn't fit with modern photographs and descriptions of the ice islands T-1, T-2, or T-3.

Cook said he saw two distinct land masses, separated by a gap of fifteen to twenty miles. The southern mass had an irregular, mountainous skyline, with peaks as high as eighteen hundred feet; the more northerly land had a flat, ice-capped surface with steep cliffs rising to twelve hundred feet. The ice islands of the Arctic rise no more than sixteen feet from the pack. At Cook's distance – he was fifty miles away – it would have been almost impossible to spot one of these low masses.

By April 11, Cook wrote, he found he had used up half his food supply, which meant that with the Pole still two hundred miles away, the party would have to go on short rations. Ten days later, half starved and wholly played out, they reached "the spot toward which men have striven for more than three centuries."

"In my own achievement," Cook wrote, "I felt that dizzy moment that all the heroic souls who had braved the rigors of the Arctic region found their own hopes' fulfilment. I had realized their dream. I had culminated with success the efforts of all the brave men who had failed before me. I had finally justified their sacrifices, their very death; I had proved to humanity humanity's supreme triumph over a hostile death-dealing Nature. It seemed that the souls of the dead exulted with me, and that in some substrata of air, in notes more subtle than the softest notes of music, they sang a paean in the spirit with me."

He pinned a Stars and Stripes to a tent pole and, according to his book, took a series of observations that established his presence at the very top of the globe. He and his two companions had come six hundred miles in thirty-two days – a rate of nineteen miles a day. Now they had to cover an equal distance to get back to their starting point. Cook said he did not intend to follow their outward track, which would be half obliterated by snow. Instead he took a new course to the west, hoping to explore Bradley Land. But Bradley Land was not to be found.

They were lost. "The route before us was unknown. We were in the fateful clutch of a drifting sea of ice. I could not guess whither we were bound. At times I even lost hope of reaching land. Our bodies were tired. Our legs were numb. We were almost insensible to the mad craving hunger of our stomach. We were living on a half ration of food and daily becoming weaker."

On May 24, Cook reckoned his position as well to the west of Axel Heiberg. "The following days were days of desperation. The food for man and dog was reduced . . . we traveled twenty days without knowing our position. A gray mystery enshrouded us. Terror followed in our wake."

Cook's account of this period is sketchy. He says they made their way south through Hassel Sound, which separates Ellef Ringnes from Amund Ringnes, the two islands Sverdrup named for a couple of hometown beer merchants. About the middle of June, Cook wrote, they heard their first animal cry – the call of the snow bunting – and shortly after landed on a rocky coastline where they successfully hunted for bear and small birds. For the last ten weeks, according to Cook's own figures, the three men and all their animals together had been forced to subsist on little more than six pounds of food a day plus whatever meat they could scrape from the carcasses of those overworked and emaciated dogs that died or were slaughtered.

With fresh game sustaining them, they pushed on south. Soon they entered historic country – the maze of islands discovered during the search for Franklin. They travelled down Penny Strait between Bathurst Island and the Grinnell Peninsula of Devon Island. Cook's first plan had been to continue down Wellington Channel and then on to the whaling grounds of the Atlantic by way of Lancaster Sound. But the lack of game in the area and the known presence of wildlife on the shores of Jones Sound changed his mind.

They climbed the gaunt, dun-coloured scarps of North Devon and crossed over to Jones Sound, where they released their remaining dogs, jettisoned much of their equipment, and embarked in the portable boat that they had taken with them but had never used. There followed a perilous two months on Jones Sound. By early September they had reached the huge granite cliffs of Cape Sparbo on its south shore. They could go no farther; this would be their winter camp.

They were destitute. All they had left were four rounds of ammunition, half a sled, the canvas boat, a torn silk tent, a few camp kettles, tin plates, knives, and matches – nothing else save for the tattered clothing on their backs. Thus equipped, they prepared to settle down for the winter on the site of an abandoned Eskimo village in a little bay surrounded by gloomy walls of granite.

This three-man trek from the vicinity of Axel Heiberg to Anoatok on the Greenland coast by way of the Cape Sparbo wintering place stands as the most remarkable saga in the history of Arctic exploration. Even Cook's severest critics, who tore his tale of polar discovery to shreds, allowed him that. For the next five months, the trio reverted to the stone age, living in a cave hollowed from the earth by tribesmen long dead. As Cook grubbed in the black soil, trying to expand this hovel, he experienced a "heart depressing chill." There, half hidden in the muck, a hollow-eyed skull stared up at him, and he realized that he and his companions were making their home in a primitive tomb.

With no food and no proper tools for capturing game, they were forced to live by their wits. They tried at first to kill muskoxen by hurling stones. When that failed they fashioned bows out of hickory torn from the sledge and arrows tipped with metal from the Eskimos' pocket penknives. They managed with these primitive weapons to kill a duck and a hare, but the arrows could not penetrate the muskoxen's tough hides.

They used more sledge hickory to make harpoons and lances, the harder points carved from fragments of whalebone and muskox horn found scattered on the beach, and tried again without success. They tore the metal points off their sledge shoes and the rivets from their cookbox to tip more weapons. But the most practical hunting device was the lasso, made from sledge thongs twisted together. With one of these they managed, at last, to corral and kill one of the beasts. For the rest of the season, using lassos and lances, they hunted muskoxen whose carcasses sustained them. From the bones they made harpoons and arrowheads, knife handles, fox traps, and sledge mountings. The skins they fashioned into coats, hoods, stockings, mitts, lashings, and boots. The fat they used for lamp oil, with wicks made from peat moss. The meat became their staple food, supplemented occasionally by a hare, ptarmigan, or fox.

The bears that prowled about the cave were a double menace: they not only tried to steal the trio's food but were also prepared to make a meal out of the humans. Cook and his two companions were like prisoners in their cave, with the bears as warders, prowling so close that it was not possible to move more than a hundred feet from the narrow entrance without "every dull rock rising as a bear ghost." At night, they set fires at the mouth and stood six-hour watches to scare off the beasts. But by day the bears crowded up to the portal and snatched the blocks of blubber used for fuel. Sometimes they made a leap for the door, which, fortunately, was not large enough for them to enter. The Eskimos shot arrows through this tiny entrance, without much effect. Occasionally, when a bear's head appeared in the silk-covered window near the roof, they were able to wield a knife at close range with what Cook called "sweet vengeance." As a last resort they made a hole through the top of the den; when the head of a bear appeared, they thrust a flaming torch through the opening. It illuminated the snow for acres around with such a ghostly whiteness that it startled the humans more than it did the animals. The bears took advantage of the light to seize another piece of precious blubber.

The sun vanished on November 3. It would not return for 110 days. On November 17, they heard the last cry of the ravens. Etukishook looked into the sky and called to one of the birds, "Go and take the tears from Annadoa's eyes. Tell her that I am alive and well and will come to take her soon. . . . Bring us some powder to blacken the bear's snout. . . ."

"Dry the tears of my mother's cheeks," cried Ahwelah to the raven. "Then go to Serwah; tell her not to marry that lazy gull, Tatamb; tell her that Ahwelah's skin is still flushed with thoughts of her, that he is well, and will return to claim her in the first moon after sunrise."

"Ka-ah, ka-ah, ka-ah!" replied the raven, or so it seemed to the two homesick and love-stricken natives in whose language the word *ka-ah* means "yes." Alas, when they finally reached home, all the young women in the village were spoken for.

With the bears in hibernation, Cook, in the flickering light of the crude oil lamp, began to set down his account of the polar journey and its aftermath. He was painfully short of writing material; all he had was a small pad of prescription blanks, two miniature memo books, four pencils, and an eraser. He scribbled away in a tiny, almost microscopic hand, keeping the points of his pencils needle sharp and employing a self-invented form of shorthand. In this way he managed, he said, to get 150,000 words on paper. Thus "absolute despair, which in idleness opens the door to madness, was averted."

Anoatok was more than three hundred miles away on the far side of Kane Basin. Cook was counting on finding a cache that Etukishook had asked his father to leave at Cape Sabine, near the site of Greely's misfortune. On February 18, with the Fahrenheit thermometer registering –40°, the three men set off down Jones Sound toward Baffin Bay, hauling the little sledge they had repaired with muskox bones and sinew. They reached the mouth of the sound and turned north, following the sea ice along the Ellesmere coast. The deep, drifting snow, huge pressure ridges, and protruding glaciers kept them far from land.

At last on March 25, with their food gone, they reached land –

Cape Faraday, near Smith Sound. They fended off starvation by chewing on bits of skin, old walrus hides, and even a piece of candle. Four days later they managed to lasso a polar bear. Cook produced one of the four bullets he had squirreled away and handed the rifle to Ahwelahtea, who shot the bear, saving their lives.

By the time they reached Cape Sabine they were again out of food. Luckily, Etukishook's father had cached an old seal, so rotten now that it smelled like limburger cheese. They ate it greedily, along with a pound of salt left in the cache, which, Cook said, tasted like sugar to them, "for no salt had passed our withered tongues for over a year." In the cache Cook found a crude drawing, "spotted with sooty tears," that told the story of a bereft father searching for his lost son.

The Greenland coast was only about thirty miles away on the far side of the sound, but the sound was open. Cook and his two companions were forced to make a seventy-mile detour on the shore ice as far as Cape Louis Napoleon before they could cross on the ice of Kane Basin. The only food they had was the rotten seal meat. When that was gone they were reduced to gnawing at their sealskin boots and lashings. "Life," Cook recalled, "no longer seemed worth living." But they kept on until, clambering up a tall iceberg, they spotted in the distance the village of Anoatok.

Harry Whitney, who went out to meet Cook, found a gaunt spectre of a man, his hair falling to his shoulders, his bones protruding from his stretched skin – "the dirtiest white man I had ever seen," Whitney called him. His two companions collapsed on one of the sledges, but Cook, in an act of bravado, tried to walk to the village. He didn't make it.

Now he found that Peary had put his bosun, the illiterate John Murphy – "a rough Newfoundland bruiser" – in charge of his hut. Cook's version of what had happened is diametrically opposed to Peary's. In his memoirs he charged Peary with theft of his furs, ivory, and supplies. Although Cook had left a native friend, Koolooting-wah, in charge, Peary wrote that he had given the job to his own followers "to prevent the Eskimos from looting the supplies and equipment left there by Dr. Cook." Cook took umbrage at that. "It was," he said, "a mean, petty and unworthy slur upon a brave, loyal people, among whom thievery is a thing unknown."

Meanwhile, he had told Whitney that he had reached the Pole and pledged him to silence. He wanted to be the first to let the world know of his achievement. But Cook himself does not appear to have grasped the full significance of his feat. ". . . to me the Polar experience was not in the least remarkable, considered with our later adventures," he wrote.

Pole or no Pole, Cook's assessment of his other accomplishments was eminently reasonable. His long journey to Axel Heiberg Island and then back through the Sverdrup Islands to Devon Island and Jones Sound *was* remarkable. No other white man had spent fourteen consecutive months in the High Arctic (Hall's experiences were more than two hundred miles farther south) living much of the time like a prehistoric savage.

At this point, the spring of 1909, Cook set out on another extraordinary trek. He wanted to reach civilization as quickly as possible to announce his news. The fastest route, he felt, was to go south from Etah to the Danish settlement of Upernavik and from there by native mail boat and later by steamer to Europe, then back to North America. Upernavik was more than five hundred miles as the crow flies to the south – and more than half again as far by a winding route that would involve the climbing of mountains and glaciers, the crossing of open lanes of water with the ice already in motion, and the dragging of heavy sledges through slush.

Before he set off, Cook, according to his own account, made a very strange decision. He decided, he explained later, to leave his original notes, calculations, and instruments in a box in the care of Harry Whitney, who promised to bring it out later that year. Apparently Cook was quite prepared to separate himself from the proofs of his discoveries. In the annals of exploration, that was almost unheard of.

But what exactly did he leave with Whitney? Did he leave all the calculations and observations he had made at the Pole, assuming there were any? Did he leave his journals? What about the 150,000 words he claimed to have written in a minuscule shorthand at Cape Sparbo – did he leave that too? Or did these pages exist? It passes credibility that Cook, no matter how sharp his pencils, how microscopic his shorthand, could possibly have got a book-length narrative onto a small pad of prescription blanks and a couple of memo booklets. Cook's published account, *My Attainment of the Pole*, is only 10 per cent longer than the one he said he wrote in pencil, yet it occupies 566 pages of printed text.

Cook would later downplay the importance of this material. "The instruments . . . had served their purpose," he wrote. "The corrections, notes and other data were also no longer needed; all my observations had been reduced and the corrections were valuable only for a future re-examination."

Clearly, he did not expect a "future re-examination" any more than Peary did. In fact, if it hadn't been for Peary there probably wouldn't have been one. An explorer's word was not questioned by members of the scientific establishment. If some harboured doubts – as was certainly the case when Isaac Hayes claimed he had reached Cape Hawks – they kept such doubts to themselves. If Cook said he'd climbed Mount McKinley, if Peary announced he'd found a new island, no one came forward to dispute those claims. There's little question that had Peary not returned from the Arctic determined to discredit his rival, Cook would have been hailed in perpetuity as the first man to reach the North Pole. And if Cook hadn't been in Peary's way, then Peary's unsupported word would have been accepted, as, indeed, in many quarters it was.

No one was ever to know exactly what was in the packages that Cook left in Whitney's care; Cook himself would change his story about what he took with him and what he didn't take. There *were* instruments left with Whitney – that much is certain – and also clothing, supplies, geological specimens, and furs. When Peary arrived, Whitney took passage aboard the *Roosevelt* but didn't bring Cook's box because Peary wouldn't let him. To be fair to Peary, he didn't want to be charged with losing or damaging anything belonging to his rival.

Whitney cached all Cook's belongings at Etah, leaving them, in Cook's phrase, to "the mercy of the weather and the natives" – a strange remark from a man who, in the same memoir, had castigated Peary for thinking the Eskimos thieves. The story is blurred because Whitney himself was remarkably tight-lipped about the matter when it finally became public. But if Cook left any documents behind, no trace of them has ever been found.

Cook left Etah in the third week of April, accompanied by a throng of cheerful natives who spread the news of his feat from village to village on the way to Upernavik. According to his own account, Cook gave very little thought to the sensation that his discovery would cause. Uppermost in his thoughts was "an intense longing for home." He insisted in his memoirs that "in the wildest flights of my imagination I never dreamed of any world wide interest in the Pole. . . . I regarded my entire experience as purely personal. I supposed that the newspapers would announce my return, and that

598

there would be a three days' breath of attention, and that would be all. . . ."

Those words do not ring true. Cook was either extraordinarily naïve or his remarks were hypocritical. He knew very well that other attempts on the Pole had caused a series of public sensations. Kane, Nansen, and Peary had become legendary heroes just by *trying* to get there. All had benefited financially. Surely Cook must have known what awaited him. After the controversy over his polar claims, he wrote, "I desire to emphasize the fact that every movement I had made disproves the allegation that I planned to perpetuate a gigantic fraud upon the world." But it can just as easily be said that by affecting such a casual attitude to his apparent triumph, Cook was disarming his critics.

In late May he reached Upernavik, the home of some three hundred Eskimos living in box-shaped huts built of turf. He spent a month there, at the home of the Danish governor. Then, on June 20, he took a ship as far as Unanak, where he enjoyed an enthusiastic reception, and boarded a second vessel bound for Denmark. En route, he stopped off at Lerwick, in the Shetland Islands, where he sent a cable to James Gordon Bennett of the New York *Herald*, announcing that he had left a two-thousand-word message with the Danish consul there. "If you want it, send for it," the telegram read. He expected three thousand dollars, a trifling sum considering the import of his news. The *Herald*, which had turned down Peary, grabbed at the offer.

From this point on Cook could scarcely deny the impact of his story. Off the Skaw, at the northernmost tip of Denmark, half a dozen seasick reporters, "looking like wet cats," climbed over the rail and told him that all of Fleet Street had moved to Copenhagen. But here Cook encountered some scepticism. He declined to answer reporters' questions, insisting that he could not elaborate because of prior commitments to a newspaper syndicate.

At Elsinore, a blizzard of cables and letters engulfed him. "I became a helpless leaf on a whirlwind of excitement," he recalled. He was, he wrote, utterly bewildered by the clamour of the ovation that followed when he docked at Copenhagen. The Danish cabinet had met and decided that, as he was a reputable public figure, they had no option but to accept his word that he had reached the Pole and tender him a reception that would be headed by the Crown Prince himself.

599

The great English editor W.T. Stead was one of those in the dense crowd that pressed forward to greet Cook when he arrived on Saturday morning, September 4. Stead noticed that the explorer looked a little dazed. As the multitude cheered, a woman thrust a bunch of red roses into his hand. Then, unrestrained by the police, the mob swept forward, forcing Cook back. Stead, standing directly behind him, and seeing that Cook was unprepared for the onslaught, flung his arms around him under his armpits and pressed backward with all his weight to ease the pressure of the crowd. Three or four others came to the rescue and, struggling and staggering, bore the explorer through the throng. The roses had long since vanished, and before Cook could reach the safety of his carriage one of his cuffs had been torn off by a souvenir hunter.

In the days that followed, Stead had a chance to assess the explorer. "I think that almost all of us who went to Copenhagen would agree . . . that he does not strike us as a man, but rather as a child – a naive, inexperienced child, who sorely needed someone to look after him," Stead wrote in the American *Review of Reviews*. ". . . his inability to protect his own interests, even in matters of pounds, shillings and pence, it was almost pitiful." Stead's comments appear to support Cook's later insistence that he had no idea of the importance of his polar revelations. "Everything a clever rogue would do instinctively, if he wished to hoax the public, Dr. Cook did not do," said Stead. But it can also be argued that Cook, having casually tossed off a comment about reaching the Pole, had at that time no idea of the furore he would cause. He seemed unaware that every statement he made would be questioned, and every apparent contradiction submitted to meticulous examination.

One experienced journalist certainly had doubts. Philip Gibbs of the London *Daily Chronicle*, then on the threshold of a brilliant career that would, after his Great War reporting, lead to a knighthood, interviewed Cook and was profoundly disturbed. The explorer did not look him in the eye, and Gibbs thought his answers to his questions both contradictory and hesitant. He was shocked when, on asking to see Cook's diary, Cook gave him "a strange defensive look" and replied that he had none; everything was at Etah with Whitney.

Gibbs had difficulty swallowing this. "But surely you have brought your journal with you? The essential papers?" Cook replied that he

600

had brought nothing and then turned on Gibbs with a sudden violence that startled him. "You believed Nansen and Amundsen and Sverdrup," he rasped. "They had only their story to tell. Why don't you believe me?" (Cook glossed over the fact that all three had been accompanied by witnesses.)

"This man protests too much," Gibbs told himself. He pressed Cook again and again. Surely he wasn't coming to Europe to announce the greatest prize of exploration without a scrap of his notes or any of his observations? Cook grew more and more angry, Gibbs more and more sceptical.

Cook claimed that Sverdrup had heard his story and "pledged his own honour in proof of his achievements." Gibbs promptly interviewed Sverdrup and learned that Cook had provided the explorer with no proof of any kind. Cook intimated to reporters that he had handed a written narrative and astronomical observations to the University of Copenhagen. Gibbs dragged a reluctant statement from the head of the university (which was about to grant the explorer an honorary degree) that Cook had submitted nothing.

With Peter Freuchen, another Arctic traveller and journalistic sceptic, Gibbs analysed Cook's statements regarding distances, sledge weights, timetable, and food carried. These he and Freuchen found to be absurd and contradictory. But the public was on Cook's side, and when Gibbs's reports were published, the journalist found himself vilified in public and even challenged to a duel. As for Freuchen, his own editor at the Danish periodical *Politiken* refused to publish his case against Cook. "We cannot wine and dine a man one day and call him a fraud the next," was the way he put it.

For Cook was the man of the hour, caught up in a whirl of banquets and receptions. There were presentations, speeches, medals, royal congratulations, and, of course, the honorary degree. It was during a banquet for journalists at the Tivoli that the real sensation evolved. Suddenly attendants appeared carrying sheafs of cables, which were placed under the plates of all the journalists in the room. Cook received one too. As he opened it, he sensed a lull falling over the assembly. Stead, the senior journalist present, stood up and read his copy. It contained a single, blunt sentence: "In a wire from Indian Harbour, Labrador, dated September 6, 1909, Peary says: Stars and Stripes nailed to the Pole."

Cook's expression gave no hint of any inner turbulence as he rose to his feet to congratulate Peary. "There is glory enough for us all," he declared; and at that the affair broke up as the journalists rushed off to duty.

4

Cook took passage from Copenhagen for New York that week, but not before a second cable arrived from Peary. This claimed that Cook's two Eskimo companions, under cross-examination by Borup and MacMillan, had revealed that Cook hadn't got out of sight of land after leaving Axel Heiberg Island. Cook's response seemed plausible enough. He said that because all Eskimos were fearful of leaving the sight of land and venturing into the unknown, he had repeatedly encouraged "the delusion that mirages and low lying clouds which appeared almost daily were signs of land. In their ignorance and their eagerness to be near land they believed this, and by this innocent deception I prevented the panic which seizes nearly every Arctic savage when he finds himself upon the circumpolar sea. . . ."

Peary's own Eskimos, in fact, had on reaching the Big Lead shown a similar panic, which Peary stifled only by threatening to abandon them on the ice. Cook's critics were to use this interview as proof that the explorer didn't get near the Pole. On the other hand, the natives often told white men what they wanted to hear, and Cook had instructed his two companions to tell Peary and his men nothing about the trip. As evidence, the natives' denial under pressure was inconclusive.

Peary, meanwhile, had wired the *New York Times*: "Do not trouble about Cook's story. I have him nailed." This provoked a newspaper battle between the *Times* and its bitter rival, the *Herald*, which had scooped it neatly by splashing Cook's account of his adventures day after day across its front page.

The *Times* could only struggle to stay even until Peary's exclusive tale of his own triumphs exploded in its September 7 edition. The paper, which had shown some scepticism about Cook's revelations, boldly declared that day that "no other proof of his [Peary's] verified statement from Indian Harbour, Labrador . . . will be required by the scientific world." Sir George Nares, now an admiral, sent a message to Peary through the *Times* the following day: "Owing to your well known veracity, all will accept your statement that you have reached the north pole."

But a majority of the scientific world was at least outwardly on Cook's side. While Admiral George Melville branded Cook's statement a fake, most leading explorers, no matter what their private opinions, held their tongues or issued non-committal congratulations to both men. In fact, Peary was seen as mean-spirited for his attacks on Cook's integrity, especially his claim that Cook had gone north "*sub rosa* for the admitted purpose of forestalling me."

There was considerable eyebrow-raising over Cook's statement that he had averaged fifteen nautical miles (seventeen statute miles) a day on his polar journey. Ernest Shackleton, the British Antarctic explorer, pointed out that "no other expedition has been able to do anything near this." Peary's supporters insisted that such speeds were impossible. Cyrus Adams of the American Geographical Society declared that "four miles a day is considered a fair average over polar ice." This carping ended when Peary's own story in the *Times* claimed *twenty-five* nautical miles a day.

Once the *Times* had Peary's story locked up – it threatened court action against any other paper that appropriated its copy – it leaned heavily toward Peary. The *Herald* took the other tack:

DR COOK WINS FRIENDS
  BY HERALD STORY

DR. COOK'S NARRATIVE
  PLEASED SCIENTISTS

SUSPECT DEEP PLOT
  TO DISCREDIT DR. COOK

WASHINGTON PRAISES
  DR. COOK'S STORY

GERMAN PRESS LEANS
  TOWARD DR. COOK

Cook arrived in New York on September 21 to be greeted by a cheering crowd of either fifty thousand (*Times*) or "hundreds of thousands" (*Herald*). The reception both amazed him and filled him with dismay, he said later. From that moment on "my life was a kaleidoscopic whirl of excitement for which I found no reason." He likened it to a child's first ride on a carousel. The world, he said, "seemed engaged in some frantic revel." He needed a secretary to deal with the letters and invitations, which all but swamped him, and persuaded Walter Lonsdale, who had been on the staff of the American consul in Copenhagen, to handle that task.

Peary and his supporters continued to demand that Cook produce proofs of his feat. Cook hedged. He would engage in no controversy, he said, until Peary reached New York. But he then announced that he had "brought irrefutable proof of his right to the title of discoverer of the North Pole." This was the kind of rash statement that would help, in the long run, to doom him. In Copenhagen he had impulsively announced that he would go north and bring back his two Eskimo companions to prove that he'd been to the Pole. Hours later he retracted the statement. It was too late in the season to go north again, he told the press. Besides, what would be the use? These lame evasions did little to help his cause and would be remembered later when the controversy grew warmer.

But if Cook was required to produce proofs, then surely, he argued, so must Peary: "Commander Peary has as yet given to the world no proof of his own case. My claim has been fully recognized by Denmark and by the King of Sweden. . . . A specific record of my journey is accessible to all, and everyone who reads can decide for himself. When Peary publishes a similar report then our cases are parallel. Why should Peary be allowed to make himself a self appointed dictator of my affairs?"

But, of course, Peary *had* published a report in the *Times* comparable to Cook's in the *Herald*. Both were "accessible to all," both were narratives of adventure, neither constituted proof that its hero had been to the North Pole. Indeed, Peary and his supporters, in urging that Cook produce proofs, had, perhaps unwittingly, sparked an unwelcome spirit of inquiry. Nobody had ever demanded proofs from Peary before; now they would.

Cook, now in New York, made another rash statement in which he insisted that "the Danish Government and the University of Copenhagen as well as the Danish Geographical Society, have . . . taken over the virtual guarantee for the sincerity and authenticity of my records. They have stood up for them, so to speak, before the world.

604

They do not ask me to furnish any further proof or evidence of any kind, but in justice to Denmark it is my intention to place the first completed record of my polar journey at the disposal of the University of Copenhagen."

The university, of course, had not "stood up" for Cook. It had simply, in the long tradition of exploration, accepted his unsupported word that he had reached the Pole.

Cook played down the importance of the records and instruments he said he had left at Etah. "The impression seems to prevail that Mr. Harry Whitney has records of importance with him. He may not know that he has them, for they are packed with my instruments which I left in his care. These instruments he will probably bring here in October. None of the records . . . are absolutely essential for I have duplicates of them. . . ."

After these assertions, Cook refused to produce proofs of his attainment of the Pole, arguing that the University of Copenhagen was entitled to see them first. After that, he said, he would be happy to make them public. At that point, he shut himself up in his hotel suite and refused to see the press. "Dr. Cook," said Walter Lonsdale, "does not care to go into any discussion on the point of his discovery of the pole."

Yet the explorer remained the man of the hour. A series of newspaper straw polls showed that the public was on his side in the mounting controversy. The Toledo *Blade*, for instance, polled its readers and found that 550 believed Cook had reached the Pole while only 10 believed Peary. A copy of Cook's *Herald* series was sealed in the cornerstone of a Long Island church; New York moved to give him the freedom of the city; the Arctic Club tendered him a banquet at the Waldorf Astoria, where twelve hundred guests roared their approval. It was urged, in Brooklyn, that a statue be erected to him as a local hero; Harlem illuminated its streets in his honour.

It was agreed he would need time to work on his proofs. But Cook didn't take the time. Instead, on September 24, three days after his return, he launched at Carnegie Hall a national lecture tour so lucrative that one city – St. Louis – was said to have offered him ten thousand dollars to appear.

The following day, a *Times* reporter collared Harry Whitney, who had arrived in St. John's, Newfoundland, aboard Peary's ship. Whitney revealed that the box Cook had left with him, presumably containing records and instruments, was still cached at Etah.

Cook, "considerably agitated" in the *Times*'s view, now contradicted his earliest statements that he had brought nothing with him. "I gave Mr. Whitney some of my original proofs and some duplicates . . . I took a copy of these and brought it back with me. The duplicates I gave him were not proofs that were all right – that had not been blurred. The originals of these proofs I brought with me. I have them now."

This baffling statement suggested that, at best, Cook had been incredibly careless in dealing with a precious and irreplaceable set of documents. His explanation was as badly blurred as the records he said he'd left behind. Peary flatly refused to believe that Cook had left anything of significance at Etah. "I cannot conceive it possible for a man, under the circumstances, to have left such priceless things out of his sight for an instant," he said. As for Harry Whitney, he said he didn't know what was in Cook's box or boxes.

Cook continued to insist he had copies of all the essential records. "The presentation of the matter to the proper authorities will not in any way be affected," he declared. It would take him some months, he added, to prepare his report and proofs. He was sure the missing instruments were safe and promised he would mount and personally finance an expedition to go north in the spring and retrieve everything. But he never did.

Meanwhile, with Peary due to arrive home in a few days, his supporters in the Peary Arctic Club, led by its president, General Thomas Hubbard, and its secretary, Herbert Bridgman, were working to discredit Cook. Bridgman's paper, the Brooklyn *Standard-Union*, revealed that two of the polar photographs published with Cook's *Herald* series were actually taken on a previous Arctic expedition. The *Herald* admitted that but explained it away as "an inadvertence." The captions had identified the photographs as taken by Cook "on his North Pole trip." But Cook was forced to admit that they had been taken seven years before.

There was worse to come. For some time, rumours had been flying around Alaska that Cook had faked his Mount McKinley climb. The matter had come up before the Explorers' Club and had been dismissed after Cook threatened a libel suit. Bridgman was in touch with Ralph Stockman Tarr, a professor of geography and geology at Cornell University, who had just returned from Alaska and who told Bridgman that it was "the almost unanimous verdict of Alaskans knowing that country that the feat was impossible." Tarr said that

Edward "Big Ed" Barrill, the guide who accompanied Cook on the trip and who was still owed money by the explorer, had himself stated that the pair had not climbed above five thousand feet. Barrill would probably talk, Tarr wrote Bridgman, "if he could be sure of his pay." Bridgman leaked the story to the *Times*, which put it on the front page.

Cook, well launched on his popular lecture tour, denied everything. Peary meanwhile arrived in New York to a reception the *Herald* termed "cheerless" and the *Times* called "triumphal." The press and public were still on Cook's side. (The Peary Club did their best to get Peary to tone down his anti-Cook comments because they did not sit well with the public.) But Gilbert Grosvenor of the *National Geographic* wrote to Peary from Washington on October 5 assuring him that sentiment was changing rapidly and predicting that he would soon be overwhelmed by a flood of appreciation. "Don't let Mrs. Peary be disturbed," he wrote. "I went to the Cook lecture here Sunday and want to tell you that his reception was tremendously exaggerated by the press. . . . The effect on the majority of the audience was very unpleasant and the applause at the end very little. . . ."

"We feel for you and Mrs. Peary in such a trying experience," Grosvenor added, "but the end is very near; greater honors and rewards than you would otherwise have experienced I am confident will be showered upon you presently, from every quarter of the Globe."

Thus did the National Geographic Society, which had seen no proofs from either Peary or Cook, make it unequivocally clear where it stood in the controversy. Meanwhile, one of Bridgman's agents was approaching the Pinkerton detective agency to find out what it would cost to delve into the Mount McKinley affair. If the public attitude could be changed – if the country could be led to believe that Cook, already lacking credibility, hadn't got to the Pole – then, by some curious inversion of logic, it would follow that Peary *must* have reached it.

In mid-October, George Kennan, a distinguished Arctic traveller (whose son became a distinguished American diplomat), published in *Outlook* magazine the second of three devastating articles analysing Cook's food consumption on his polar journey. Cook's original estimate of a pound of pemmican a day for each man and each dog, supplemented by 13.8 ounces of other staples, was meagre enough –

Rae, M'Clintock, Schwatka, and Peary had all consumed a larger ration. But, even assuming Cook killed some of his dogs, Kennan's analysis showed, his food would have lasted only forty-two days. To stretch it over the eighty-four days of his journey Cook would have to halve his daily per capita ration to eight ounces of pemmican.

"No man and no dog ever lived and worked for twelve weeks under polar conditions on eight ounces of pemmican or its equivalent a day," Kennan wrote. He himself had sledged for three years between the Arctic Ocean and the Okhotsk Sea; if his diet had been restricted to eight ounces of pemmican, he declared, "I should have expected to perish on the ice in less than thirty days."

At the same time, Cook was coming under increased criticism for the delay in preparing his proofs for the University of Copenhagen, whose rector was plaintively asking "why Dr. Cook cannot send us before two months have elapsed the observations he made at the North Pole?" Cook, unwilling to interrupt his lucrative lecture tour, claimed it would take *three* months to prepare his observations, "not a situation," said the New York *Evening Post*, "in which a man of a delicate sense of personal honor would be willing to place himself."

Then, on October 14, a worse blow fell. The Peary Arctic Club had finally located Big Ed Barrill, Cook's sole companion on the Mount McKinley climb. General Hubbard's New York *Globe* published an affidavit by Barrill, which Cook's supporters charged, probably correctly, was purchased. In it Barrill swore unequivocally that Cook had faked the claim by persuading him to doctor his diary to make it appear they'd reached the summit. Barrill also swore that a photograph appearing in Cook's book about the climb, showing Barrill waving a flag on the peak, had in fact been taken at another Alaskan peak, at an altitude of only eight thousand feet.

Cook denied it all, charging that the Peary Arctic Club had bribed Barrill. That may well have been true, since Barrill complained that Cook hadn't paid him for his work. But when Cook was asked to produce his original diary of the climb, he equivocated. "I do not see that it is material," he told reporters who asked for it, adding that it was hidden away in one of his trunks and difficult to get at. Instead, he referred them to his published account of the climb. Thus, as on his North Pole trip, Cook had no original details or observations to support his claim. He did announce, however, that he would organize and lead an expedition to climb the mountain and retrieve the brass cylinder he said he'd left on the summit as evidence he had been there. Like the other verifying expeditions he had promised – to interview his Eskimo companions and retrieve his lost records in Greenland – nothing ever came of it.

Up to this point a majority of public and press had taken Cook's side, resenting Peary's attacks on his rival. The Mount McKinley revelations turned public opinion around. The Peary Arctic Club was pressuring the American Geographical Society to force Cook to prove his story and Peary was telling Bridgman that "Cook should be handled without gloves." Cook promptly announced that he was cancelling his lecture tour to present "the complete proofs of my trip to the north pole."

Now the New York *Herald* all but abandoned Dr. Cook. Its reportage grew slimmer, its stories less frequent. The *Times* continued in full cry:

COOK WILL NOW TRY
   TO PUNISH BARRILL

SCIENTISTS CALL FOR
   MT. MCKINLEY REVIEW

PEARY SATISFIES
   BOARD OF EXPERTS

Peary had indeed satisfied a three-man subcommittee of the friendly National Geographic Society, which, after a few hours of casual discussion, reported it was convinced that he had reached the Pole. The society responded with a gold medal and *Hampton's Magazine* followed with a record forty-thousand-dollar fee for his ghost-written story. On Cook's side, the scientist Knud Rasmussen, who spoke the Eskimo tongue and had interviewed several friends of Cook's native companions, announced publicly that he now believed Cook had reached the Pole.

By this time, Cook was in seclusion, apparently working on his proofs. Actually, he was suffering from a nervous breakdown, brought on by the mental strain under which he had laboured and an unpleasant confrontation with his former associate Barrill during a lecture in Montana on October 28.

Walter Lonsdale, Cook's secretary, who acted as his spokesman and who almost certainly prepared most of Cook's data, announced that his employer would not be going to Copenhagen. In view of the voluminous details being dispatched to Denmark, Lonsdale said, Cook didn't think his presence would be required. That was poppycock. Cook was in no shape to go anywhere – especially to face a probing academic committee and a swarm of curious newsmen. Lonsdale's own role in the Cook affair was almost certainly based on an expected financial windfall. Aboard the ship that took them to America, the pair had figured that Cook might easily reap a profit of $1,500,000 from his polar venture in the shape of books, articles, lectures, and testimonials. Now, with his meal ticket fraying at the edges, Lonsdale continued to keep up a bold front.

On November 24, Lonsdale helped Cook cut his hair and shave off his moustache. With a black slouch hat half concealing his features, the embattled explorer left by train to take refuge in Toronto from the expected storm. The following day Lonsdale announced that he would take "the original records [!] just as they were made by Dr. Cook in the Arctic regions," together with a fifty-thousand-word manuscript, to Copenhagen on the steamer *United States* of the Scandinavian Line, sealed in a strongbox, padlocked and guarded against interlopers. Later Lonsdale revealed that this package was merely "a dummy to trap conspirators who have resorted to every means to gain possession of Dr. Cook's data." The real documents, he said, had already been dispatched on a faster steamer. Lonsdale was bluffing – an indication of the paranoia of that time; the records presented at Copenhagen were the ones he took with him. There is no shred of evidence that anyone in the Peary camp had the slightest interest in appropriating them.

By this time the press was alive with rumours. Cook had disappeared – nobody knew where. Reporters tried to find him; one claimed he was at Billy Muldoon's sanitarium in White Plains. Cook's lawyer, a man with the imposing if slightly bizarre name of H. Wellington Wack, claimed he had sailed for Naples. A close personal friend of Cook's, Charles Wake, denied it. An irrepressible deskman at the usually sober *Times* couldn't resist that:

COOK OFF SAYS WACK;
SAYS WAKE NOT SO

By November 27, the affair had taken on a dime-novel quality. Wack announced that he had evidence from "absolutely reliable sources" of "one of the most diabolical plots that had been hatched against an explorer or any other man." The lawyer claimed that "some persons hostile to Cook" had hired three agents, a woman and two men, to poison Lonsdale. They had boarded the *United States* in New York, he said; the woman was to attempt to flirt with the young man while the others drugged his champagne. With Cook's secretary out of action, they would ransack his cabin for the explorer's data and make away with it.

Carefully skirting the laws of libel, Wack, with many a wink and nudge, made it clear who was behind the alleged conspiracy. The "opposition," he said, had hired three detectives to spy on Cook. The opposition, of course, could only be the Peary Arctic Club. "We hired detectives to watch their detectives," Wack declared, explaining how the plot had been discovered. This preposterous tale, which was quickly exploded, was only the most outlandish example of the unfounded suspicions that swirled about the Cook camp. The strongest card the explorer's supporters had to play was to present their hero as a lone underdog, battling single-handedly against the power, money, and influence of an entrenched Arctic establishment.

But young Lonsdale arrived in Copenhagen unscathed, with his iron box containing Cook's documents. He took the box to the university, accompanied by two detectives, and formally turned it over. In New York, meanwhile, the *Times*, which was not above seeing diabolical plots on its own, had a new anti-Cook scoop on its front page. Two men, also with Dickensian names – Loose and Dunkle – swore that Cook had hired them to fake his astronomical observations. George Dunkle was an insurance man, Captain A.M. Loose an expert navigator. They had certainly approached Cook with an offer of help, but whatever work they may or may not have done for him (and for which they too said they'd not been paid) never appeared in the documents that went to Copenhagen. But their accusations, however irrelevant, contributed to the public's disillusionment with Frederick Cook.

The real blow fell three days before Christmas, 1909. The University of Copenhagen issued a report announcing that Cook's submissions constituted no proof that he had reached the Pole. All that Walter Lonsdale had brought in his padlocked strongbox was a sixty-one-page typewritten report that he himself had prepared and a sixteen-page typewritten transcript made from what Cook claimed were copies of his original notebooks.

Lonsdale, who was about to return to his post in Copenhagen, had clearly fallen under Cook's spell. The sixty-one-page report turned out to be virtually identical with the story the New York *Herald* had published under Cook's by-line more than two months earlier. The second document, based on the copies of Cook's notebooks, contained no original astronomical data – no calculations arrived at from readings of sextant, compass, and chronometer that should have been scribbled down on the spot and entered in the appropriate place in a journal. Such a journal – greasy, smudged, and often tattered – with its day-by-day chronology supported by regular observations in the explorer's own cramped hand would have supplied convincing evidence that Cook had been where he claimed he was. But Cook's papers provided no evidence that he'd been anywhere.

To produce these two typewritten documents, neither of which differed greatly from what was already known, Cook and Lonsdale had laboured for the best part of two months! For these they had padlocked a strongbox, indulged in an apparent deception, and engaged detectives as guards – all, presumably, in the belief that the public would swallow the myth that Cook was dispatching to Copenhagen records so secret, so valuable, and so persuasive that a mysterious Peary-inspired cabal would stop at nothing to lay hands on them.

The Copenhagen committee issued a curt statement declaring that the two documents were "inexcusably lacking" in information that would prove that any astronomical observations had actually been made; nor did they contain any details describing the practical work of the expedition that might enable the committee to determine their reliability.

Cook did not respond. But in his book, published in 1911, he affected to believe that the committee had simply returned a mild verdict of "not proven," a claim echoed by his supporters through the years. Cook wrote that "they never said, mind, that I had not found the Pole; they merely said my . . . [proof] was not absolutely positive."

In fact, the committee was indignant. There was lacking "to an outrageously inadmissible degree" proof that would suggest Cook had performed any astronomical observations at all. One committee member, Commander Gustav Holm, a noted explorer, declared that Cook's papers "convict him of being a swindler." Knud Rasmussen, who also signed the report and who had been a Cook supporter, called the matter "a scandal." The papers submitted, he said, were "most impudent . . . no schoolboy could make such calculations. It is a most childish attempt at cheating." Other Danish experts chimed in. Commander Horgaard, another explorer, declared, "I can only regard Cook now as an impostor." The secretary of the Danish Geographical Society said it was the saddest event of his life. "As an explorer there seems to be no doubt that Cook is absolutely unreliable." The Danes, who had wined and dined their hero, now turned on him. Peter Freuchen's editor asked to have the anti-Cook article back; he was now prepared to publish it.

Suddenly, Cook was anathema. In New York on December 24, the big Christmas shopping day, the stores reported that Cook toys had suddenly gone out of vogue. Dolls dressed in white furs and bearing some resemblance to the explorer, small sledges carrying a fur-clad figure and labelled "Dr. Cook on his dash to the Pole," and a series of mechanical devices bearing Cook's name had become a glut in the market.

The affair was further confused by Walter Lonsdale's announcement that Mrs. Cook would arrive shortly in Copenhagen with the "original" notebooks that Cook had once claimed he hadn't brought with him from Etah. These, Lonsdale declared, had been sent separately in case of foul play. Cook's casual attitude to his own documents had long since been replaced by a paranoiac obsession to preserve them, even when it turned out they weren't worth preserving. The so-called original notebook – the only one Mrs. Cook turned over to the university committee – was found to contain nothing new. In fact, the university announced that it appeared that "important parts of it are manufactured."

This was too much even for H. Wellington Wack, the exposer of dark and sinister plots, who was forced to face the truth that Cook's "proofs" weren't worth stealing and never had been. The flexible Mr. Wack tried to salvage some scraps of integrity by confessing, belatedly, to a certain scepticism. He revealed that he had seen the diary in question before it was sent and thought the handwriting remarkably even, especially as Cook was supposed to have been wearing two pairs of mittens when he held the pencil.

Wack, Wake, and Lonsdale scrambled to dissociate themselves from the discredited explorer, now travelling incognito in Europe. So did the Arctic Club, which Cook had helped found, and the Explorers' Club of New York, which had once elected him president. Both summarily kicked Cook out. In just eight months he had made the dizzy descent from hero to pariah.

As Cook tumbled, Peary soared. He was the hero of the hour, enriched by *Hampton's* record-breaking fee, engulfed by lecture offers (he wouldn't speak for less than a thousand dollars), honoured by testimonials, elevated to honorary membership in the New York Chamber of Commerce and, shortly after, given a triumphal welcome in England followed by an extraordinary reception by the Royal Geographical Society.

The reasoning was flawed, but, given the circumstances, understandable. If Frederick Cook hadn't got to the Pole, then, surely Robert Peary must have.

But had he?

5

The end of The quest for the Arctic Grail, which had occupied most of the
the quest nineteenth century, ended early in the twentieth, not with a bang but with a long, distasteful, and often farcical whimper. That is not the way knightly quests are supposed to finish. The canons of romance dictate neat and noble endings – high sacrifice (Scott, in the Antarctic); gallant rescue (Stanley, in Livingstone's Africa); brilliant triumph (Burton, at the source of the Nile). When Cook reached Denmark in May of 1909 he seemed to have capped the long search with a stunning climax. That was what the world wanted but didn't get. From the moment Peary reached Labrador, both stories began to unravel, like a frayed sledge thong. The process has continued until this day.

Cook and Peary were opposites in almost every way, but they had one thing in common – a desire to win at any cost, fair or foul. In this obsession, they were the harbingers of the new century – the American century – in which winning is everything and it matters not how you play the game. The nineteenth-century explorers, British and American, who ventured into the frozen world were of a different breed. They were ambitious, certainly; they wanted the prize of Passage or Pole; but their enthusiasms were those of the amateur. They stopped along the way, as the modern song has it, to pick the flowers. The phrase is more than a metaphor, as anyone who has read the long appendices to their journals – jammed with Latin names for new species – will understand. They were explorers in the true sense in that they *explored* in a way that Cook and Peary failed to do. Peering at new life forms, scribbling down names for unknown plants and lichens, chipping away at chunks of gneiss and feldspar, recording water temperatures, ocean depths, and tidal movements, they added to the world's store of useful knowledge. The new Grail was as impossible to reach in the Victorian Age as the old one had been in Arthurian days, but it acted as the lure that caused the mysterious archipelago of bald and forbidding islands to be exposed. In turn, it made saints and heroes out of flawed but courageous human beings, from the ambitious Parry and the incautious McClure to the passionate Kane and the eccentric Hall.

But the American public wanted something more than a hero. It demanded a winner, and the only one available was Robert Edwin Peary. The National Geographic Society had given him its seal of approval just a few weeks before the Copenhagen revelations. That was good enough for the public; at the time, it was good enough for the world.

The world was not aware at this juncture of the flaws in the Peary record, as it was of Cook's. His sighting of a non-existent Peary Channel (twice!) and also of Crocker Land would be believed for years. Nor would the superficiality of the National Geographic's investigation of his claims be known.

Cook's reputation, on the other hand, continued its downward slide. In 1910, two separate alpine investigations confirmed that his claim to the ascent of Mount McKinley was a fraud. Two experienced mountaineers, Belmore Brown and Herschel Parker, discovered that the photograph Cook published in *Harper's*, purporting to show Ed Barrill standing on the peak, had been retouched to remove a mountain in the background that might have identified the spot. The pair travelled to the area and, using the un-retouched photo as a guide, found the place from which it had been taken. That was twenty miles from Mount McKinley and no more than five thousand feet above sea level.

That same summer, a group of Cook's supporters from the Mazama Club of Oregon followed his route hoping to prove him right and ended up proving him wrong. At a point ten miles southeast of the summit, his 1907 map "abruptly departed from reasonable accuracy into complete fantasy."

615

In August, Peter Freuchen reported that he had found the box Cook left with Whitney at Etah. Cook's former companion Etukishook had taken it in lieu of the pay Cook had promised but never delivered. (All the two Eskimos got for their work was a penknife and some matches.) The box contained a sextant, four burning glasses, a pocket barometer, and a Fahrenheit thermometer. Freuchen, who spoke the language and knew Etukishook well, asked him several times about books and papers. Had the children taken them as toys? Etukishook insisted there were no papers. "He always wrote in two little books and those he took along when he left us," he explained, adding that Cook had done his writing during the winter at Cape Sparbo. As for the so-called polar journey, the Eskimo said they had never been out of sight of the mountains of Axel Heiberg.

With Cook out of the picture in the late fall of 1909, Peary began to push furiously for a promotion, employing a professional lobbyist to plead his case in Washington. He wanted, before retirement, to be advanced to the status of rear admiral, a rank generally reserved for officers of the line; it would mean an annual pension of $6,500. But Congress would have to approve, and that meant hearings before the House Naval Affairs Committee. It was these hearings that were to cast the first cloud over Peary's claim to have reached the Pole. The explorer had enemies in the Navy, jealous of his repeated leaves and his celebrity, contemptuous of his appropriation of a rank to which he was not entitled and his furious efforts to be raised to flag rank. The Navy also knew how to lobby, and there's little doubt that this disgruntled attitude prompted the hard questioning that Peary faced from some members of the congressional committee.

The hearings began in March 1910, were adjourned for nine months, and then resumed in January 1911. The long delay was caused by Peary's refusal to produce his original records – the same kind of "proofs" that had been required of Cook – on the grounds that to make them public would be breaking faith with the publishers of his forthcoming book. This was patent nonsense – a delaying tactic. No narrative intended for the lay public was going to stand or fall on the basis of astronomical computations. Nor did Peary's contract contain any pledge of secrecy. He could easily have submitted the material the congressmen asked for without any protest from his publishers. Indeed, since he was on the naval payroll, these computations could be considered public property. He chose not to submit them, and the committee didn't press him. Instead, it adjourned the

616

session until the book appeared. By then another year had passed, and Peary had solidified his position in the public's esteem by producing a best seller of adventure and hardship on the frozen polar sea. The delay worked for Peary. With press and public weary of the dispute, the testimony received less attention than it would have at the height of the controversy.

Nonetheless, the seven-member congressional committee placed on the record evidence that later critics would examine in the re-evaluation of Peary that has since taken place. The chief revelation was the slipshod nature of the investigation carried out by the subcommittee of the National Geographic Society in October 1909.

After his return from the Arctic, Peary was reluctant to let anybody but his friends in the NGS examine his records. He was careful not to submit them to Copenhagen, perhaps because, as Dennis Rawlins has pointed out, he realized that some of the university committee's sarcastic references to Cook's failure to check his compass variations applied equally to him. Indeed, many of the charges against Cook – his lack of scientific proof, his reported excessive speeds over the ice, his reluctance to release his observations, the absence of any corroborative witnesses – applied also to Peary, who brought back nothing of scientific value from his final polar dash. He made no scientific report to the Navy, which paid his salary, and he ignored repeated requests from the Coast and Geodetic Survey for data that it could add to its Arctic charts. At best, he was high-handed and evasive; at worst, he was a charlatan.

None of this seemed to have bothered the three men who examined the Peary record for the National Geographic Society. They could scarcely be called dispassionate observers. All were partial to Peary. Two, Henry Gannett, the NGS's vice-president (soon to be president), and Admiral Colby E. Chester, were close friends. Chester, in fact, was a member of the Peary Arctic Club and had already publicly denounced Cook as a fraud. The third committee member, Otto H. Tittman, was supervisor of the Coast and Geodetic Survey, which, at Roosevelt's request, had sponsored Peary and kept him on naval pay. Both Gannett and Tittman admitted they believed in Peary long before they looked at his records. As Gannett put it, "everybody who knows Peary's reputation, knows he would not lie." All three sat on the dinner committee for the NGS award ceremony for Peary in 1906. All three were on the NGS committee that voted a thousand dollars to support Peary's final North Pole expedition. Thus, the society was committed to Peary. Gilbert Grosvenor, a past president and editor of its magazine, was a close personal friend who had already assured Peary that his wife and family "have been confident from the first how this affair will end." At that point – before the NGS made up its official mind – he had been making arrangements for a paid lecture that Peary was to give before the society.

In spite of this cosy arrangement, Peary was still reluctant to come to Washington, perhaps because he too had suffered a nervous breakdown. Certainly he had to be nudged by the committee. At last his lawyer turned up, bringing a document that fell far short of adequate evidence. It was, in fact, very similar to the report that Cook had submitted to Copenhagen: nothing more than a general account of the expedition – and only up to the time that Bartlett had turned back. There was nothing to cover the final polar attempt. The NGS committee demanded more.

About two weeks later, on November 1, Peary finally arrived. He lunched with the three committee members and then repaired to Admiral Chester's home, where the most cursory examination took place. As Gannett later testified, "We simply sat down with him and read his journal from his original records; he had an original record made in a little book, a notebook you know, at that time, and it had all the earmarks of being the original." It's not easy to tell from the later testimony exactly what it was the three men examined or how much time they spent examining it. Tittman admitted he read very little because he "was very much occupied with other matters." Gannett, in spite of seeing Peary's notebooks, was so badly informed that he got the explorer's travel statistics on the polar dash wrong and had to be prompted by Gilbert Grosvenor.

Fifteen months after this meeting, when the explorer finally appeared before the Naval Affairs Committee, he was remarkably vague and uncertain about the events of that day – events that should have stood out in his mind since they were designed to settle the question of his having attained the Pole. He wasn't able to remember, for instance, how detailed the scrutiny of his notebook had been. "I will not say they read all of it carefully," he testified. "It was passed around. I cannot say how much of it they read."

After the NGS's three appointees looked at the written record, they went to the Union Station to examine the instruments that Peary had left there in a trunk. In his later testimony Peary refused to say whether or not any of the NGS examining trio checked the instruments to see whether or not they were accurate. But dusk had fallen and "I should imagine that it would not be possible to make tests there." As one of the congressmen, Ernest W. Roberts, later wrote in a minority report, "the fact that the incidents of the day made no sharper impression on his mind than is shown by his testimony is very conclusive evidence that the examination of his records was anything but minute, careful or rigorous."

The National Geographic Society did its best to make it appear that the tests *were* rigorous. The society's president, Willis L. Moore, another friend of the explorer, announced that it was "absolutely conclusive." In fact, the entire examination had occupied no more than the time between lunch and dinner.

The title "National Geographic Society" impressed the public, as it impressed many foreign organizations, all but one of which accepted its findings without further investigation. But the NGS, which sounded so official, had no official status. It was, in reality, a private publishing company, interested in promoting magazine circulation. The only *official* organization to examine Peary's records was Britain's Royal Geographical Society. At its request, Peary sent it copies of his journal and some of his observations. When his submission was considered, only seventeen members of the RGS board of thirty-five were present. Eight voted for Peary, seven were against, two abstained. The narrow margin indicates that the issue was in doubt.

Yet Peary couldn't lose. In spite of his equivocations before the naval committee, most of the politicians (including the ex-president) were on his side. Congressman Robert Macon denounced him as "a fake pure and simple," but neither the congress nor the country was in a mood for any more fakers. The naval committee approved him, and congress in 1911 retired him with the pension of a rear admiral and gave him an official vote of thanks. For the rest of his life, Civil Engineer Peary would be known to press and laymen as Admiral Peary, a spurious title that nobody bothered to dispute.

He was now listed in the history books and the encyclopaedias as the discoverer of the North Pole. At last he had what he wanted – the laurel wreath of recognition for which he had struggled with so much pain and so much personal sacrifice for most of his adult life. "I *must* have fame!" he had told his mother; now he had it, but it wasn't quite what he had expected, for fame came accompanied by its disreputable cousin, notoriety. The unseemly controversy with Cook had left the nation with a sour aftertaste. The sudden dazzling triumph that should have been his had been clouded by doubt, postponed, and in the end watered down. Cook was still very much in the public eye. His name, popping up on the front pages from time to time (usually to his discredit), only served to remind the public that there was some argument about the quest for the Pole.

The embattled doctor continued to insist that his story was true. He returned to New York in December 1910, after a year-long absence in Europe and South America, in order to promote a four-part series in *Hampton's Magazine* giving his side of the story. Characteristically, when he signed the contract, he had given no more than casual attention to the fine print in which he agreed that the publisher was making "no editorial guarantees whatsoever." In short, they could tamper with his story; and tamper they did. The galleys were cut apart and certain subtle changes made. Cook, after noting the torments of Arctic travel, had explained that he couldn't pinpoint the position of the Pole absolutely – no explorer could. But *Hampton's* doctored that passage to read: "No one should discredit me until he knows what I endured during two and a half years of Arctic experience. . . . Not until then can he understand my mental condition at the time and appreciate just what I feel now and what I believe to be true. Did I get to the North Pole? Perhaps I made a mistake in thinking that I did; perhaps I did not make a mistake. After mature thought I confess that I do not know absolutely whether I reached the Pole or not. . . ."

That was damning enough. The promotion department of *Hampton's* made it worse. On December 1, about a fortnight before the issue was due to appear on the stands, the magazine held a press conference in which it doled out a few tidbits from what would be billed as "DR. COOK'S CONFESSION." The following day, readers of the *Times*'s front page were told that "in these articles Dr. Cook will admit frankly that he doesn't know whether he reached the north pole. He now says that his privations during his travels toward the pole put him in a 'mental condition,' which the American public has not been able to 'understand.' "

Poor Cook! Whatever his failings, he scarcely deserved this kind of shameless distortion or the damning headlines that pursued him: "DR. COOK ADMITS FAKE! . . . DR. COOK MAKES PLEA OF INSANITY." When Cook's book, *My Attainment of the Pole*, appeared in 1911, giving his version of the story, the *Times* damned it with a sarcastic headline: "DR. COOK CONFESSES HE DIDN'T CONFESS." Four more years would pass before another confession, by a former *Hampton's* sub-editor, would reveal the truth.

Cook's book did not restore his reputation; it was too late for that. In it, he toned down some of the more expansive statements he had blurted out on his arrival in Denmark before he learned that Peary was also claiming the Pole and thus before he realized that he would be forced to provide irrefutable data for his claims. His descriptions of Bradley Land were less specific; he no longer pinpointed his positions to the last second of latitude – impossibly precise calculations that caused the scientific community to scoff; and he tried, not too successfully, to explain his first rash and confusing statement to the *Herald* that "a triangle of 30,000 square miles has been cut out of the terrestrial unknown." (If, as he tried to explain to Philip Gibbs, that was what he had been able to see for fifteen miles on each side of his route, he would have had to be plodding along a ridge 150 feet above the general ground level.)

Cook's fierce attempts to restore his own credibility – he tried, vainly, to sue anyone (including his rival) who questioned his veracity – continued to irritate Peary and rob him of the peace that might otherwise have accompanied his retirement. The full report of the naval committee, with its embarrassing testimony, lay like an unexploded bomb in a congressional archive. It had never been made public – was, indeed, guarded from distribution – and was almost impossible to find. But in 1916 Congressman Henry Hegelsen of North Dakota located a copy and read the most devastating portions into the *Congressional Record*. Hegelsen's analysis of the evidence took up 120 columns of small print and would provide much of the underpinning for the anti-Peary books that followed.

For this Peary had no one but himself to blame. He had lobbied hard in congress for a rear admiral's pay and pension. Now the results of that lobbying were coming back to haunt him. Hegelsen followed up his attack in July of 1916 with a second blast, tearing apart Peary's book *The North Pole* and urging (vainly) that Peary be removed from the retired list and his pension stopped because the explorer's "claims to discoveries in the Arctic regions have been proven to rest on fiction and not on geographical facts. . . ." But Hegelsen got nowhere. Four years later, Robert Edwin Peary was dead at the age of sixty-four.

Cook outlived him by twenty years, but these could not have been happy. In 1923 he was convicted of stock fraud in Fort Worth. In the judge's remarks, there is a broad hint at earlier deceptions: "Now, Cook, you may stand up. . . . This is one of those times when your peculiar and persuasive personality fails you, doesn't it? You have at last got to the point where you can't bunco anybody. You have come to the mountain and you can't reach the latitude; it's beyond you. . . . Oh, God, Cook, haven't you any sense of decency at all. . . ?" On and on he went, attacking Cook's "monumental" vanity and nerve. Then he sentenced Cook to fourteen years and nine months in prison and fined him fourteen thousand dollars.

Peary's ghost continued to haunt Cook. When he became eligible for parole in March 1930, one of his rival's chief supporters, Professor William Hobbs, author of an uncritical biography of Peary, tried to organize a protest to keep him behind bars. It failed and Cook was free.

In the years that followed, the discredited explorer tried to sue a variety of writers for claiming that he had faked the polar trip. He lost every case. In 1940, Franklin Roosevelt pardoned him as an act of mercy towards a dying man. Cook had just finished another book about his adventures, *Return from the Pole*, when he suffered the stroke that killed him. The book was published posthumously.

One can feel compassion for Cook, the Prince of Losers – so casual that he left his precious instruments and records behind, so inattentive that he didn't read the promotional letters his agents were dispatching (even though one of them had already been convicted of fraud), so naïve that he didn't understand the implications of *Hampton's* "no editorial guarantees." He has been seen by some as an anti-establishment hero (the establishment being represented by Peary and his powerful friends) – a sympathetic albeit a tragic figure. But he is also a maddening one, and it must be said that most of the tragedy was of his own making. There are some significant parallels between the Mount McKinley charade and the polar venture. Cook's attempt to climb the mountain – his second in two years – was a spur-of-the-moment decision; so, to a considerable degree, was his attempt on the Pole. In both cases he returned without bringing corroborative evidence. In both cases he announced that he would provide positive proof – a new attempt on the mountain to support his case, another expedition to Etah to interview his native companions and retrieve his records. In each instance, it was pure bluff.

Cook, in fact, lived a day-to-day Micawber-like existence, putting off the inevitable with pledges he couldn't fulfil, promises he couldn't keep, statements he couldn't back up – hoping, perhaps, that something might turn up to postpone the fateful moment when he would be found out, then fleeing when he was unmasked, as he had done in 1909. Indeed, it is more than possible that he set off on the cruise with Bradley in order to escape the inevitable showdown that was building up at the Explorers' Club among those members, including Parker and Brown, who were openly disputing his claims to the McKinley record.

It is difficult to escape the conclusion that Cook, like so many con-men, was his own worst victim. He conned himself into believing he wouldn't be found out. He blurted out his remarkable stories without realizing what the consequences might be. He had the con-man's easy geniality and bluff composure. In the fiercest moments of the controversy he remained outwardly calm, answering the reporters' toughest questions with a disarming smile. It was hard not to like him – he seemed so ingenuous. Peter Freuchen, who thought him a liar, also thought him a gentleman – Peary, said Freuchen, was neither!

Yet Peary's claim to have reached the Pole rests on no firmer ground than Cook's – a fact that was glossed over in the days when Cook was being vilified. He did not present a shred of scientific evidence to show that he had got closer than 150 miles, while the circumstantial evidence against him is damning. The best that can be said of him is that he got closer than any explorer to that time; Bartlett's independent sextant readings confirm it. The best that can be said of Cook is that he reached the tip of Axel Heiberg Island and probably wintered there before making the return journey south.

For most explorers that might have been enough. Cook's incredible trek across Ellesmere to Axel Heiberg Island and then south through Jones Sound has no parallel in polar annals. His winter at Cape Sparbo, where he lived like a caveman with only two companions, was a masterpiece of Arctic survival for which he would have been lauded and honoured, had it not been for his claim on the Pole.

Peary's system of trail-breaking and support parties carried him farther north than any man up to his time. His methods are still used by mountaineers; they helped Hillary and Tenzing reach the peak of Everest. His meticulous planning and adaptation of native methods broke new ground. Peary had many failings, but he cannot be faulted for lack of intelligence, industry, or executive ability.

The tragedy is that neither man was satisfied with those genuine and considerable achievements. It was the Pole that obsessed them, as it had obsessed so many others, and the Pole that, in the end, tarnished both their reputations. Although Peary was for years hailed in the textbooks and reference works as "discoverer" of the North Pole, his claims have not stood the intensive scrutiny of such modern critics as Dennis Rawlins. A leading American astronomer and professor of physics, with at least one significant celestial discovery to his credit, Rawlins in 1973 published a detailed critique of the Peary record. The book was titled *Peary at the Pole: Fact or Fiction?* Unlike so many of Peary's critics, Rawlins also dismissed Cook as a charlatan. In his book he made no bones about his conviction that Peary's account of his discovery of the Pole was more fiction than fact. The following year, the *Encyclopaedia Britannica*, in its Fifteenth Edition, rephrased its previously unequivocal entry about Peary to say that he is "usually credited" with the discovery.

It would diminish the story of the long quest for the Arctic Grail to leave it on such a low note; nor would it be fair. In all the argument about who did what and who got where, one remarkable record has been overlooked. Pole or no pole, Robert Edwin Peary did something that no explorer before him was able to do, and that none has managed to do since. Without mechanical aid he got farther north than had any human being before him – *and he got back*. It is one thing to get within striking distance of 90⁰ North by dogteam; it is quite another to make the return trip. No one has yet managed that feat overland. In Peary's day, every scrap of food had to be hauled north over the ice, with enough left to sustain life on the route back to land. And since fuel was needed to melt snow as well as to warm the body, every ounce of that had to be carried both ways. Peary came closest to solving the problem of weight by his system of support parties. But his claimed speeds – which pass all comprehension – suggest that he was in fact forced to shave about two hundred miles off his intended journey in order to make it back before he died of starvation or thirst.

Since Peary's time a number of attempts have been made on the Pole by dogteam, motorcycle, skis, and snowmobile. All have been one-way trips, the participants airlifted out when they reached their goal. All but one expedition have been supplied en route by air, and that one – Will Steger's 1986 dash by dogsled – reached its destination only after jettisoning most of its equipment and with only a few pounds of food to spare.

624

Thus, unless somebody in the future manages to go over the Arctic ice to the Pole and back again without re-supply, an almost impossible feat, Peary's record remains. In spite of his carefully designed sleds, his team of picked dogs, his methodically trained retainers, he could not complete his quest. But then, neither could the knights of Camelot with their palfreys, their squires, and their suits of shining armour. The sacred chalice the Arthurians sought was always just beyond reach. That, after all, was the secret of its lure.

Afterword:
The chart of immortality

"There is nothing worth living for but to have one's name inscribed on the Arctic chart," Tennyson wrote during the search for Franklin. For those who sought to live forever, the poet was right. In his day it was the certain way to ensure immortality. The chart itself makes that obvious; the place names provide a roster of those who might otherwise have been forgotten.

If one wonders why gin-makers and merchant princes would want to throw away thousands of pounds or dollars on shaky investments in implausible expeditions, one has only to examine the map. Their names are emblazoned on land masses north of the Circle. Henry Grinnell has his peninsula jutting from the forlorn expanse of Devon Island; Morris Jesup and Thomas Hubbard have their names inscribed in perpetuity on capes at the very top of the world. John Ross's name may be missing (though that of Sabine, who quarrelled with him, is not), but that of his sponsor appears boldly on a gulf, a peninsula, and a harbour.

Ross was an exception; none of his colleagues, apparently, wanted to honour that crusty and difficult seadog. But almost every other major explorer, and a good many minor ones, had his name so enshrined. Parry's name dominates, as no doubt it should, since he was the first white explorer to pierce the mysterious Arctic archipelago. Today, all the unknown lands that loomed up on his starboard bow, from Devon to Melville, are known as the Parry Islands. Parry's subordinates, Lyon and Liddon, are there by name in smaller type, and even his ships, *Hecla*, *Griper*, and *Fury*, are rendered forever familiar by a strait, a bay, and that wan and chilly beach where more than one expedition was restored by the provisions taken from the foundering *Fury*.

Whose Arctic is it? The question, which is raised intermittently when Canada's sovereignty over the frozen waters comes into dispute, is answered by the map. It is obvious who got there first. British place names abound – Devon, Somerset, Kent, and Cornwall islands – and so do the names of British heroes (Wellington Channel, Cornwallis Island), British institutions (Admiralty and Navy Board inlets), and British statesmen (Melville Island and Peel Sound).

The British royal family is represented from the Prince Regent to King William, from the Princess Royal to Princess Adelaide, from Prince Leopold of Saxe-Cobourg to his nephew, the Consort, who has both a sound and a peninsula named for him – both appropriately part of that vaster and more formidable island that bears the name of his Queen. As for Albert Edward, the plump and much abused "Bertie," Prince of Wales, his name is commemorated by a strait, an island, and a bay all quite properly in the periphery of Victoria Land.

But the Arctic chart memorializes more than men of rank, power, blood, or property. The real immortals, whose names are sprinkled throughout the Arctic on bays and bights, capes and channels, are those who dared and sometimes died so that the map might take form.

The name of Franklin, the man who wouldn't hurt a fly but caused more deaths than all the others combined, is everywhere. That is only proper. Since the search to discover his fate filled up the blank spaces on the map, it is just that an entire Canadian territorial district should honour him. There is more: a deep bay on the Arctic coast recalls his first disaster; a point on King William Island takes note of his last. George Back, whom he didn't much care for, named a lake for him at the mouth of the Great Fish River. The name of the river was changed, in turn, to honour Back.

Back's partner, the waspish Dr. King, is ignored by cartographers, but two other overland explorers, the easy-going Dease and the doomed and bitter Simpson, both have straits to commemorate their explorations. So does that consummate traveller, the knowledgeable John Rae. The isthmus that he crossed to prove that Boothia Felix was a peninsula bears his name, as it should; so does a small river not far from the Coppermine's mouth, which parallels a similar stream that pays tribute to Rae's travelling companion, John Richardson.

The area of the Great Search is studded with the names of the searchers. The unspeakable Belcher has a channel, the bluff whaler Penny a strait. The most literary of all the explorers rejoices in several memorials: Cape Osborn, Cape Sherard, and Point Sherard Osborn. Kellett, who was a gentleman, has his name in small type on a cape and a river; McClure, who was not, has his in large type on the strait that he discovered leading to a North West Passage.

628

M'Clintock, the prince of sledgers and captain of the *Fox*, is memorialized by the great channel that leads south to the island where he found the Franklin relics. The cautious Richard Collinson's name can be found in the same area – a rounded cape to the north and, more to the point, the very peninsula across from King William Island from which he might have launched a search to discover the missing explorer's fate.

Amundsen's track is to be found everywhere – in Rasmussen Basin, in the Nordenskiöld Islands, and in the great gulf itself that commemorates his conquest of the Passage in 1905.

Farther to the north, American names abound – Kane and Hall basins, Greely Fiord, and Peary Channel (the real Peary Channel, west of Axel Heiberg Island, not the mirage off Greenland's tip). The Scandinavians, too, have left their memories. The archipelago west of Ellesmere is named for Sverdrup, who first explored it.* There is also a Danish Strait, a Nansen Sound, and a Prince Gustav Adolf Sea.

Could the Americans and the Scandinavians, then, lay claim to this bleak land of crags and glaciers? Scarcely, for the British were here first, and the names remind us of their presence in 1875, at the very top of Ellesmere. Alert, Canada's farthest north weather station, is named for George Nares's ship that spent the winter there. Fifty miles to the south lies the historic bay, the most prominent of four, named for Lady Franklin. How odd that that most impressive of Englishwomen, who did so much to erect memorials to her husband, should have her own so far from his final resting place!

The story of the Nares expedition is told in the place names at the top of the world. Clements Markham, who lobbied so hard for another attempt at the Pole, is remembered by an inlet, his cousin, Albert, whose men almost died of scurvy, by a fiord. Nares's name is on a cape, a minor tribute to that doughty captain who took an unfair share of the blame for the disaster.

They are all on the Arctic chart, with Tennyson – amateurs and professionals, knaves and heroes, opportunists and idealists. That enthusiastic and attractive French naval officer "little Bellot," as Sophia Cracroft fondly called him, has the littlest of straits named for him. An islet off the coast of Ellesmere honours Bedford Pim, the

---

*On November 11, 1930, Canada paid Otto Sverdrup $67,000 "for services rendered" in exploring the islands that bear his name. On the same day, Norway formally recognized Canada's title to the islands.

man who saved McClure. Another, in Coronation Gulf, pays its tribute to John Hepburn, the seaman who survived the first Franklin tragedy, near the headwaters of the Coppermine.

But what of the man who saved him? What of Akaitcho, the chief of the Copper Indians, without whose presence all would have perished? One searches the map in vain to find his name. And where are the Eskimos, without whom no white explorer, from Parry to Peary, could have conquered the frozen world? Where is the name of Tookolito, known to the white men as Hannah? Or Ebierbing, whom everybody called Joe? Their names are not writ large on the chart of the Arctic; you will not find them in an ordinary atlas. Hall's name is there in bold type – but could he have found the Frobisher relics without them? And where is Kalutunah, Hayes's companion, or Hans Hendrik? No type at all for them.

Peary made sure his wealthy backers received their due on cape and headland. Every school atlas records their names. But only the large-scale charts show the tiny features named for Egingwah and Henson, the men who struggled with him toward the Pole. When the National Geographic Society gave gold medals to Peary and Bartlett, it ignored the black man who had gone farther north than the white sea captain. Like the Eskimos, he was the wrong colour.

This saga of the double quest for the Pole and the Passage began with Ross and Parry in their cocked hats and buckled shoes greeting the Etah Eskimos in their furs and mukluks – strangers from different worlds, baffled by one another. In the ninety years that passed before Peary and Cook set off on their missions, the gap between the two worlds had certainly narrowed. To the *Innuee*, the *kabloonas* were no longer superhuman beings who came from the sun or the moon but men like themselves with human weaknesses and failings. To the *kabloonas*, the *Innuee* were no longer disgusting savages, indolent and ignorant, desperately in need of a Christian civilized upbringing. But the gap still needed to be closed, as the map shows, for the haunts of the original people continued to bear the names of the strangers – and still do today.

This didn't bother the originals. The squat little men who fed John Ross's company in the Gulf of Boothia, who cheerfully extended their hospitality to Parry and Lyon at Repulse Bay and Igloolik, who taught Rae, Hall, and Peary how to exist under polar conditions, gave no thought to such white concepts as fame, ambition, or immortality. These abstract ideas had no meaning; the future to them was

630

no farther away than the next fat seal; beyond that, they did not care to consider its rewards or its terrors. Nor would it concern them for an instant that their names should be left off the maps of the Arctic; after all, they had their own names for the snowy peaks and the frozen inlets that formed their world. It is not their loss that the map ignores them; it is our own.

Author's Note

The bibliography of the Arctic quest is interminable. Scores of books deal with the search for the North West Passage; scores more deal with the fate of Sir John Franklin; an entire library concentrates on the quest for the North Pole. Most major explorers published their own accounts. Almost every one has had his biographer; some have had several.

Apart from Lawrence Kirwan's short work, *The White Road*, I know of no other study that treats the entire period, from Parry to Peary, as a single narrative. This I have tried to do in some detail for it seems to me the stories of the search for the Passage, the Pole, and for Sir John Franklin, are so intertwined that it is difficult to unravel them. They form the three acts of a seamless drama that has fascinated the world for the best part of two centuries.

Readers who have come this far will know that this is a book as much about *explorers* as it is about *exploring*. I have done my best to rescue the men who sought this Grail from the dead hands of adulatory biographers and the must of history, to examine their characters and personalities, their strengths and their weaknesses and restore them as human beings with human flaws and human ambitions.

This is also a book about the Inuit, those much neglected native people (whom I have called Eskimos, the name used almost exclusively during the period, to avoid confusion). Too many historians have given them short shrift; but without the presence of these cheerful and accommodating people the story would not be complete.

The Arctic Grail is based very largely on original documents – the letters, journals, and personal papers of the leading characters and their associates. I have, whenever possible, examined the handwritten accounts, which in many cases differ substantially from the published ones. Elisha Kane, for instance, emerges as a different personality when one compares his original journal with his published work. The contemporary newspapers and periodicals and government documents – especially reports of investigating committees – have also been extremely useful.

A work of this complexity would not be possible without the dedicated spadework of a good many predecessors. I stand in awe of Frances J. Woodward, whose diligence in ploughing through the voluminous correspondence of Lady Franklin produced her remarkable *Portrait of Jane*, a work that no student of the period can neglect. Mrs. Gell's *John Franklin's Bride* (Eleanor Anne Porden) and Kathleen Fitzpatrick's *Sir John Franklin in Tasmania* were also invaluable secondary sources. Richard Cyriax's scholarly and definitive *Sir John Franklin's Last Arctic Expedition* is another essential secondary source for the Franklin era.

Other works which I found especially valuable were Ernest S. Dodge's *The Polar Rosses*, Alexander Simpson's *Life and Travels of Thomas Simpson*, George W. Corner's *Doctor Kane of the Arctic Seas*, Chauncey Loomis's *Weird and Tragic Shores* (Hall), A.L. Todd's *Abandoned* (Greely), John Weems's *Peary*, and Dennis Rawlins's *Peary at the Pole: Fact or Fiction?*

Once again I have had the invaluable assistance of a team of dedicated people without whom this book would not have been possible. Barbara Sears, my indefatigable research assistant, tracked down and dug out the various works described in the bibliography. Janice Tyrwhitt, my editor, forced me to rewrite several sections of the book and provided a shrewd overview of the entire work. Janet Craig, my copy editor, acted as a remarkable backstop; without her meticulous and painstaking blue pencil, this would be a flawed work. Geoffrey Matthews again drew the maps; Walter Stefoff was responsible for the design; Tom McNeely did the drawings and endpapers; Elsa Franklin provided useful advice. My wife, Janet, not only read the manuscript for grammatical errors but also bore with me when my efforts at concentration sometimes rendered me deaf, dumb, and blind.

Miss Sears and I would like to thank a number of people and institutions in Canada, England, and the United States for their help. These include:

Alison Wilson, archivist, in charge of the Polar Records at the National Archives, Washington, D.C., particularly for her help well above and beyond the call of duty. She would suggest things for us to look at (she drew the John Wall Wilson diary to my attention, for example), and she went out of her way to make sure that it was a pleasure to work at the Archives.

Robert Headland, archivist at the Scott Polar Research Institute.

Leonard F. Guttridge, who generously shared suggestions and

leads on the Adolphus Greely story at a time when he was working on the same subject.

Dr. Owen Beattie, at the University of Alberta, for providing copies of his papers on his latest research on the fate of the Franklin expedition; and Dr. James Savelle, for providing information on his work with the Franklin relics.

Captain T.C. Pullen, for reading the chapter on Peary and Cook.

And the following institutions:

The staff of the Baldwin Room, Metropolitan Toronto Central Library, unfailingly courteous and helpful with a constant stream of requests; the Thomas Fisher Rare Book Library at the University of Toronto; the National Archives of Canada; the Historical Society of Pennsylvania, for making the Elisha Kent Kane journal available; Stanford University Library, for making the other half of Kane's journal available; the National Maritime Museum, London, England; the Royal Geographical Society, for allowing us to examine the William Hooper Journals; and the Mercer County Historical Society.

Chronology

1837-1839	Hudson's Bay Company expedition by land, led by Peter Dease and Thomas Simpson, surveys most of the remaining unknown areas of the North West Passage.
1845-1847	Sir John Franklin's expedition aboard the vessels *Erebus* and *Terror* in search of the North West Passage.
1848-1849	James Clark Ross expedition in search of Sir John Franklin with vessels *Investigator* and *Enterprise*.
1848-1851	John Richardson, accompanied by Dr. John Rae, leads land expedition to the Mackenzie River, Wollaston Peninsula, and elsewhere on Victoria Island in search of Franklin.
1848-1851	*Plover* and *Herald* reach Bering Strait; Lieutenant W.J.S. Pullen leads expedition by boat in search of Franklin, exploring the Arctic coastline to the Mackenzie delta.
1850-1854	Robert McClure leads expedition in *Investigator* through the Bering Strait in search of Franklin. He establishes the last link in one route of the North West Passage and claims the parliamentary award for its discovery.
1850-1855	Richard Collinson commands the *Enterprise*, part of the expedition through the Bering Strait in search of Franklin.
1850-1851	William Penny expedition with the *Lady Franklin* and *Sophia* to the eastern Arctic in search of Franklin.
1850-1851	Horatio T. Austin commands official four-ship Admiralty expedition to the eastern Arctic in search of Franklin.
1850-1851	Sir John Ross, aged seventy-three, leads private expedition in search of Franklin.
1850	Charles Codrington Forsyth leads Lady Franklin's privately financed expedition in search of her husband on the *Prince Albert*.
1850-1851	Edwin J. De Haven leads the first U.S. (Grinnell) expedition to the Arctic in search of Franklin. Elisha Kent Kane is surgeon on one of De Haven's two vessels.

Chronology

1817	William Scoresby's Greenland voyage, in which he observes unusually open ice conditions.
1818	John Ross's first expedition in search of the North West Passage; he turns back at Lancaster Sound.
1818	David Buchan's expedition in search of the North Pole via Spitzbergen; John Franklin second in command.
1819-1820	William Edward Parry's first voyage in search of the North West Passage reaches Melville Island.
1819-1822	John Franklin's first overland expedition to Point Turnagain, in search of the North West Passage in conjunction with the Parry voyage, ends disastrously with eleven members of the expedition losing their lives.
1821-1823	Parry's second voyage in search of the North West Passage reaches Fury and Hecla Strait.
1824-1825	Parry's third and final voyage to the Canadian Arctic, again in search of the North West Passage, ends with the wreck of one of his vessels on Fury Beach, Somerset Island.
1825-1827	John Franklin's second land expedition to the mouth of the Coppermine River; with John Richardson he explores and maps more than a thousand miles of coastline from Coronation Gulf to Icy Cape, Alaska.
1827	Parry's expedition attempting to reach the North Pole via Spitzbergen; he reaches 82° 45′N and establishes a Farthest North that will stand for fifty years.
1829-1833	John Ross's second expedition in search of the North West Passage, privately sponsored by gin merchant Felix Booth. With the help of Eskimos, Ross and his crew survive through four Arctic winters.
1833	George Back, with Richard King, leads an expedition to the Great Fish River in search of John Ross.

637

1837-1839	Hudson's Bay Company expedition by land, led by Peter Dease and Thomas Simpson, surveys most of the remaining unknown areas of the North West Passage.
1845-1847	Sir John Franklin's expedition aboard the vessels *Erebus* and *Terror* in search of the North West Passage.
1848-1849	James Clark Ross expedition in search of Sir John Franklin with vessels *Investigator* and *Enterprise*.
1848-1851	John Richardson, accompanied by Dr. John Rae, leads land expedition to the Mackenzie River, Wollaston Peninsula, and elsewhere on Victoria Island in search of Franklin.
1848-1851	*Plover* and *Herald* reach Bering Strait; Lieutenant W.J.S. Pullen leads expedition by boat in search of Franklin, exploring the Arctic coastline to the Mackenzie delta.
1850-1854	Robert McClure leads expedition in *Investigator* through the Bering Strait in search of Franklin. He establishes the last link in one route of the North West Passage and claims the parliamentary award for its discovery.
1850-1855	Richard Collinson commands the *Enterprise*, part of the expedition through the Bering Strait in search of Franklin.
1850-1851	William Penny expedition with the *Lady Franklin* and *Sophia* to the eastern Arctic in search of Franklin.
1850-1851	Horatio T. Austin commands official four-ship Admiralty expedition to the eastern Arctic in search of Franklin.
1850-1851	Sir John Ross, aged seventy-three, leads private expedition in search of Franklin.
1850	Charles Codrington Forsyth leads Lady Franklin's privately financed expedition in search of her husband on the *Prince Albert*.
1850-1851	Edwin J. De Haven leads the first U.S. (Grinnell) expedition to the Arctic in search of Franklin. Elisha Kent Kane is surgeon on one of De Haven's two vessels.

1851-1852	William Kennedy, accompanied by Joseph-René Bellot, leads another expedition privately financed by Lady Franklin in search of her husband.
1852-1854	Sir Edward Belcher leads a five-ship Admiralty expedition in search of Franklin. Robert McClure rescued.
1852	Edward A. Inglefield explores Smith and Jones sounds, returning to England with the (false) story that Franklin had been murdered by Greenland Eskimos.
1853-1855	Elisha Kent Kane leads the second U.S. expedition in search of Sir John Franklin, choosing a Smith Sound route.
1853-1854	Dr. John Rae, sent by the Hudson's Bay Company to complete a coastal survey in the area of King William Land and Boothia, discovers relics of the Franklin Expedition in the possession of the Eskimos. British authorities give him the $10,000 reward for establishing the fate of the expedition.
1857-1859	Francis Leopold M'Clintock leads the *Fox* expedition, financed by Lady Franklin, that confirms Rae's report of Franklin's fate.
1860-1861	Isaac Hayes leads a U.S. expedition in search of the Open Polar Sea.
1860-1863	American Charles Hall makes his first Arctic journey in search of Franklin survivors; finds Frobisher relics.
1864-1869	Hall's second expedition reaches King William Island.
1871-1873	Charles Hall's third expedition, in search of the North Pole, aboard the *Polaris*; Hall dies under mysterious circumstances in November 1871. On the return voyage, half the *Polaris*'s crew are stranded on the ice in a storm and drift for six months before being rescued by whalers.
1875-1876	George Nares leads the British Navy's last attempt at Arctic exploration in search of the North Pole.
1879-1882	Lieutenant George Washington De Long of the U.S. Navy commands the ill-fated *Jeannette* expedition, searching for the North Pole from Siberia.

1881-1884	Adolphus Greely leads an American expedition to Ellesmere Island as part of the First International Polar Year. His junior officer Lieutenant Lockwood establishes a Farthest North, taking from the British a record they have held for three centuries. Only six of twenty-four expedition members survive.
1886	Robert Peary attempts and fails to cross Greenland.
1888	Fridtjof Nansen makes the first crossing of Greenland.
1891-1892	Peary's first large Arctic expedition to Greenland.
1893-1895	Peary's second Greenland expedition.
1893-1895	Fridtjof Nansen, with Otto Sverdrup, in the *Fram* drifts across the Arctic Ocean and establishes a new Farthest North.
1897	Salomon Andrée attempts unsuccessfully to reach the North Pole in his balloon, the *Eagle*.
1898-1902	Peary's third Arctic expedition fails in its attempt to reach the North Pole.
1899-1900	The Duke of Abruzzi leads an expedition in search of the Pole from Franz Josef Land; Lieutenant Cagni establishes a Farthest North twenty-two miles beyond Nansen's.
1901-1902	First Ziegler expedition, led by Evelyn Baldwin, attempts to reach the Pole from northern Norway but returns unsuccessful.
1903-1905	Second Ziegler expedition, commanded by Anthony Fiala, attempts the Pole from Trondheim, Norway; expedition ends in disaster with the loss of the vessel *America*.
1903-1905	Roald Amundsen completes first successful navigation of the North West Passage.
1905-1906	Peary's fourth Arctic expedition fails in attempt at the Pole but establishes a new Farthest North.
1907-1909	Frederick Cook expedition in search of the North Pole.
1908-1909	Peary's final expedition in search of the North Pole.

Bibliography

Note: Full titles are given in the first citation; second and subsequent citations are by short-form reference.

CHAPTER ONE
Unpublished Manuscripts

Royal Geographical Society
William H. Hooper Journals, 1818-1825
Scott Polar Research Institute
MS438 William Edward Parry Papers
MS647 Joseph Nias Papers
MS862 Edward Sabine Journal and Papers
MS486 John Ross Papers
MS271/25 Private journal of William Mogg
MS655 John Ross Memoirs
MS1059 John Ross Journal
MS1021 Douglas Clavering Letters
MS1199/1/1 Private journal of W.E. Parry, HMS *Alexander*, 1818.

Published Sources

Anon. "A Voyage of Discovery Made under the Order of the Admiralty, in His Majesty's Ships *Isabella* and *Alexander*. . . ," *Quarterly Review*, January, 1819.

Barrow, John. *Voyages of Discovery and Research within the Arctic Regions*. . . . London: John Murray, 1846

Beechey, F.W. *A Voyage of Discovery towards the North Pole*. . . . London: Richard Bentley, 1843.

Claustre, Daniel. "The Northwest Passage or Voyage Finished: a Polar Play and Musical Entertainment," *Polar Record* 21, No. 131, 1982.

Cyriax, Richard J. "Arctic Sledge Travelling by Officers of the Royal Navy, 1819-1849," *Mariner's Mirror* 49, No. 2, 1963.

Damas, David. *Handbook of North American Indians*, Vol. 5. Washington: Smithsonian Institution, 1984.

Dawson, Warren R. *The Banks Letters*. London: Trustees of the British Museum, 1958.

Dodge, Ernest. *The Polar Rosses: John and James Clark Ross and Their Explorations*. London: Faber & Faber, 1973.

Fisher, Alexander. *A Journal of a Voyage of Discovery to the Arctic Regions in His*

Majesty's Ships Hecla *and* Griper. London: Longman, Hurst, Rees, Orme & Brown, 1821.

Jones, A.G.E. "Rear-Admiral Sir William Edward Parry: A Different View," *Musk-Ox*, Vol. 21, 1978.

———. "Sir John Ross and Sir John Barrow," *Notes and Queries*, new ser. 19, No. 8, 1972.

Lloyd, Christopher. *Mr. Barrow of the Admiralty: A Life of Sir John Barrow, 1764-1848*. London: Collins, 1970.

Lewis, Michael. *The Navy in Transition, 1814-1864: A Social History*. London: Hodder & Stoughton, 1965.

Lyon, George F. *The Private Journal of Captain George F. Lyon of* HMS Hecla *During the Recent Voyage of Discovery under Captain Parry. . . .* Boston: Wells and Lilly, 1824.

Mackinnon, C.S. "The Wintering Over of Royal Navy Ships in the Canadian Arctic, 1819-1876," *Beaver*, Outfit 315, No. 3, 1984/85.

Mitford, Nancy (ed.). *The Ladies of Alderley*. London: Chapman & Hall, 1938.

———. *The Stanleys of Alderley*. London: Chapman & Hall, 1939.

Parry, Ann. *Parry of the Arctic: The Life Story of Admiral Sir Edward Parry, 1790-1855*. London: Chatto & Windus, 1963.

Parry, Edward. *Memoirs of Rear-Admiral Sir W. Edward Parry*. London: Longman, Brown, Green, Longmans & Roberts, 1858.

Parry, William Edward. *British Seamen*. N.p., Religious Tract Society, 1853.

———. *Journal of a Second Voyage for the Discovery of a North-West Passage from the Atlantic to the Pacific. . . .* London: John Murray, 1824.

———. *Journal of a Voyage for the Discovery of a North-West Passage from the Atlantic to the Pacific Performed in the Years 1819-20 in His Majesty's Ships* Hecla *and* Griper. *. . .* London: John Murray, 1821.

———. *Thoughts on the Parental Character of God*. Privately printed, 1841.

Rice, A.L. "The Oceanography of John Ross's Arctic Expedition of 1818: A Reappraisal," *Institute of Oceanographic Sciences*, collected reprints, 1975, No. 1098.

Ross, John. *A Voyage of Discovery Made under the Orders of the Admiralty in His Majesty's Ships* Isabella *and* Alexander. *. . . .* London: Longman, Hurst, Rees, Orme and Brown, 1819.

Ross, W. Gillies. "Parry's Second Voyage," *History Today* 10, No. 2, 1960

Rowley, Graham. "Rear-Admiral Sir John Ross, R.N., 1777-1856: Archival Material in the Scott Polar Research Institute," *Polar Record* 15, No. 94, 1970.

Sabine, Edward. *Remarks on the Account of the Late Voyage of Discovery to Baffin's Bay*. London: John Booth, 1819.

Scoresby, William. *The Polar Ice*. Whitby: Caedmon, 1980 (reprint).

Stamp, Tom and Cordelia. *William Scoresby, Arctic Scientist*. Whitby: Caedmon, [1976].

Stone, Ian R. "Profile: Edward Sabine, Polar Scientist, 1788-1883," *Polar Record* 22, No. 138, 1984.

Taverner, L.E. "William Mogg," *Nautical Magazine*, Vol. 170, 1953.

CHAPTER TWO
Unpublished Manuscripts

Royal Geographical Society
Hooper Journals, 1818-1825
Scott Polar Research Institute
MS438/26 William Edward Parry Letters
MS438/10 William Edward Parry list of visitors on board HMS "Hecla"
MS438/4/1-4 Journal of Isabella Louisa Parry

Published Sources

Anon. "The Late Sir Edward Parry," *Shipwrecked Mariner*, No. 9, January, 1856.

Barrow, *Voyages of Discovery and Research*.

Cyriax, "Arctic Sledge Travelling by Officers of the Royal Navy."

Franklin, Sir John. *Narrative of a Journey to the Shores of the Polar Sea in the Years 1819, 20, 21 and 22*. London: John Murray, 1823.

———. *Narrative of a Second Expedition to the Shores of the Polar Sea in the Years 1825, 1826 and 1827*. London: John Murray, 1828.

Gell, Edith Mary. *John Franklin's Bride*. London: John Murray, 1930.

Houston, C. Stuart. *Arctic Ordeal: The Journal of John Richardson. . . .* Kingston, Ont.: McGill-Queen's University Press, 1984.

———. *To the Arctic by Canoe, 1819-1821: The Journal and Paintings of Robert Hood*. Montreal & London: McGill-Queen's University Press, 1974.

Johnson, Robert E. *Sir John Richardson: Arctic Explorer, Natural Historian, Naval Surgeon*. London: Taylor & Francis Ltd., 1976.

Jones, "Rear-Admiral Sir William Edward Parry."

MacLeod, Margaret, and Glover, Richard. "Franklin's First Expedition as Seen by the Fur Traders," *Polar Record* 15, No. 98, 1971.

Mitford, *Ladies of Alderley*.

———, *Stanleys of Alderley*.

Mogg, William. "The Arctic Wintering of HMS *Hecla* and *Fury* in Prince Regent Inlet 1824-25," *Polar Record* 12, No. 76, 1964.

Nanton, Paul. *Arctic Breakthrough: Franklin's Expeditions, 1819-1847*. Toronto and Vancouver: Clarke Irwin, 1970.

Parry, E. *Memoirs of Rear-Admiral Sir W. Edward Parry*.

Parry, William Edward. *Journal of a Third Voyage for the Discovery of a North-West Passage from the Atlantic to the Pacific in the Years 1824-25 in His Majes-*

ty's Ships Hecla *and* Fury. . . . London: John Murray, 1826.

―――― . *Narrative of an Attempt to Reach the North Pole.* . . . London: John Murray, 1828.

Scoresby, William. *Remarks on the Probability of Reaching the North Pole.* . . . Whitby: Caedmon, 1980 (reprint).

Simpson, George. *Journal of Occurrences in the Athabasca Department.* Toronto: Champlain Society, 1938.

Stefansson, Vilhjalmur. *Unsolved Mysteries of the Arctic.* New York: Macmillan, 1939.

Traill, Henry Duff. *The Life of Sir John Franklin, R.N.* London: John Murray, 1896.

Weekes, Mary. "Akaitcho, A Link with Franklin," *Beaver*, Outfit 270, No. 1, 1939.

Woodward, Frances J. *Portrait of Jane: A Life of Lady Franklin.* London: Hodder & Stoughton, 1951.

CHAPTER THREE
Unpublished Manuscripts

Scott Polar Research Institute

MS116 William Penny Papers

MS395/63 John Ross, letter to George Back

MS486/4 James Clark Ross Letters

MS486/6/1-22, John Ross, phrenological deductions

MS651/1 John Ross, letter to Captain Humphreys

MS655/3 John Ross Journal, second expedition

MS1059 John Ross Journal

MS248/56 Jane Franklin Journal

MS248/298 John Franklin, letters to his sister

MS248/303 John Franklin, letters to his wife Jane

MS248/316 John Franklin, letters to James Clark Ross

MS248/363 Lieutenant Couch to his parents

MS248/364 Francis Crozier, letters to James C. Ross

MS248/380 John Barrow Sr., letters to John Barrow Jr., annotated by Lady Franklin

MS248/449 Charles Osmer, letter to his wife

MS248/476 Stephen Stanley, letter to John Richardson

MS312/3 Alexander McDonald Letters

MS824/1 John Gregory, letter to his wife

MS1021 Douglas Clavering, letters to James Smith

MS1372 Francis Crozier, letters to his sister

National Maritime Museum

FRN/1 Franklin Papers

Newspapers, Magazines

Athenaeum, 11 Jan., 11 Feb., 15 Mar. 1845

Government Documents

Report from Select Committee on the Expedition to the Arctic Seas Commanded by Captain John Ross, R.N. [London]: House of Commons, 1834.

Published Sources

Anon. "Two Franklin Documents," *Beaver*, Outfit 278, September, 1947.

Anon. Review of "Narrative of a Second Voyage in Search of a Northwest Passage . . . by John Ross," *Edinburgh Review*, July, 1835.

Anon. Review of "Narrative of a Second Voyage in Search of a Northwest Passage . . . by John Ross," *Quarterly Review*, July, 1835.

Amy, Roger; Bhatnagar, Rakesh; Damkjar, Eric; and Beattie, Owen. "The Last Franklin Expedition: Report of a Postmortem Examination of a Crew Member," *Canadian Medical Association Journal*, Vol. 135, 15 July 1986.

Back, George. *Narrative of an Expedition in HMS Terror Undertaken with a View to Geographical Discovery on the Arctic Shores. . . .* London: John Murray, 1838.

_____ . *Narrative of the Arctic Land Expedition to the Mouth of the Great Fish River. . . .* Edmonton: Hurtig, 1970 (reprint; originally published 1836).

Beattie, Owen, and Savelle, James. "Discovery of Human Remains from Sir John Franklin's Last Expedition," *Historical Archeology* 17, No. 2

_____ . "A Report on Newly Discovered Human Skeletal Remains from the Last Sir John Franklin Expedition," *Musk-Ox*, No. 33, Winter, 1983.

_____ , and Geiger, John. *Frozen in Time: The Fate of the Franklin Expedition.* London: Bloomsbury, 1987.

Bell, Benjamin. *Lt. John Irving R.N. of HMS Terror.* Edinburgh: David Douglas, 1881.

Braithwaite, John. *Supplement to Captain Sir John Ross's Narrative of a Second Voyage in the Victory. . . .* London: Chapman & Hall, 1835.

Coningham, William (ed). *The Last Journals of Captain Fitzjames R.N. of the Lost Polar Expedition.* Brighton: W. Pearce, n.d.

Cooke, Alan, and Holland, Clive. "Chronological List of Expeditions and Historical Events in Northern Canada VII, 1846-54," *Polar Record* 16, No. 101, 1972.

Cyriax, "Arctic Sledge Travelling by Officers of the Royal Navy."

_____ . *Sir John Franklin's Last Arctic Expedition; A Chapter in the History of the Royal Navy.* London: Methuen, 1939.

_____ . "The Two Franklin Expedition Records Found on King William Island," *Mariner's Mirror* 44, No. 3, 1958.

Dodge, *The Polar Rosses.*

L'Estrange, Rev. A.G. *Lady Belcher and Her Friends*. London: Hurst and Blackett, 1891.

Fitzpatrick, Kathleen. *Sir John Franklin in Tasmania, 1837-1843*. Melbourne: Melbourne University Press, 1949.

[Franklin, John]. "An Unpublished Letter of Sir John Franklin," *Polar Record* 5, No. 33/34, 1949.

Galaburri, Richard. "The Franklin Records: A Problem for Further Investigation," *Musk-Ox*, No. 32, Summer, 1983.

Gibson, William. "Sir John Franklin's Last Voyage," *Beaver*, Outfit 268, No. 1, 1937.

————. "Some Further Traces of the Franklin Retreat," *Geographical Journal* 79, No. 5, 1932.

Holland, Clive. "Captain Ross's Welcome Back," *Polar Record* 17, No. 106, 1974.

Huish, Robert. *The Last Expedition of Captain Sir John Ross R.N. for the Discovery of a North-west Passage....* London: George Virtue, n.d.

Jones, "Sir John Ross and Sir John Barrow."

King, Richard. *The Franklin Expedition from First to Last*. London: John Churchill, 1855.

————. *Narrative of a Journey to the Shores of the Arctic Ocean in 1833, 1834 and 1835 under the Command of Captain Back R.N.* London: Richard Bentley, 1836.

Lloyd, *Mr. Barrow of the Admiralty*.

MacKay, Douglas, and Lamb, W. Kaye. "More Light on Thomas Simpson," *Beaver*, Outfit 269, No. 2, 1938.

Markham, Clements. *Lands of Silence*. Cambridge: Cambridge University Press, 1921.

McArthur, Alex. "A Tragedy of the Plains: The Fate of Thomas Simpson," *Historical & Scientific Society of Manitoba*, Trans. No. 26, 1887.

McKenzie, W.G. "A Further Clue to the Franklin Mystery," *Beaver*, Outfit 299, Spring, 1969.

Nanton, *Arctic Breakthrough*.

Neatby, Leslie. *The Search for Franklin*. London: Arthur Barker, 1970.

Notman, Derek; Anderson, Lawrence; Beattie, Owen; and Amy, Roger. "Arctic Paleoradiology: Portable Radiographic Examination of Two Frozen Sailors from the Franklin Expedition," *American Journal of Roentgenology*, Vol. 149, 1987.

Owen, Roderic. *The Fate of Franklin*. London: Hutchinson, 1978.

Ross, John. *Explanation and Answer to Mr. John Braithwaite's Supplement to Captain Sir John Ross's Narrative....* [London: A.W. Webster, 1835]

————. *Narrative of a Second Voyage in Search of a North-West Passage and of a Residence in the Arctic Regions during the Years 1829, 1830, 1831, 1832, 1833.* London: A.W. Webster, 1835.

————. *Rear-Admiral Sir John Franklin, a Narrative....* London: Longman, Green, Brown and Longmans, 1855.

Rowley, Graham. "Rear-Admiral Sir John Ross R.N., 1777-1856: Archival Material in the Scott Polar Research Institute," *Polar Record* 15, No. 94, 1970.

Savours, Ann. "Sir James Clark Ross, 1800-1862," *Geographical Journal* 128, Pt. 3, 1962.

Simpson, Alexander. *The Life and Travels of Thomas Simpson, the Arctic Discoverer*. Toronto: Baxter Publishing Co., 1963 (reprint; originally published 1845).

Simpson, Thomas. *Narrative of the Discoveries on the North Coast of America Effected by the Officers of the Hudson's Bay during the Years 1836-39*. London: Richard Bentley, 1843.

Skewes, Joseph Henry. *Sir John Franklin: The True Secret of the Discovery of His Fate*. London: Bemrose & Sons, 1889.

Stefansson, *Unsolved Mysteries of the Arctic*.

Stevenson, John A. "The Unsolved Death of Thomas Simpson, Explorer," *Beaver*, Outfit 266, No. 1, 1935.

Sutherland, Patricia D. *The Franklin Era in Canadian Arctic History, 1845-1859*. Ottawa: National Museums of Canada, 1985.

Traill, *The Life of Sir John Franklin*.

Wallace, Hugh N. *The Navy, the Company and Richard King: British Exploration in the Canadian Arctic, 1829-1860*. Montreal: McGill-Queen's University Press, [1980].

Woodward, *Portrait of Jane*.

Wright, Noel. *Quest for Franklin*. London: Heinemann, 1959.

CHAPTER FOUR
Unpublished Manuscripts

National Archives of Canada
MG24 H27 Sir Francis Leopold McClintock Papers
Scott Polar Research Institute
MS116 Penny Papers
MS1503 Richardson-Voss Collection
MS248/112, 115, 161 Jane Franklin Journal
MS248/229 Sophia Cracroft Journal
MS248/247 Sophia Cracroft, letters to her mother and sisters
MS787/1 John Rae Autobiography

Newspapers

Athenaeum 11 Jan., 11 Feb., 15 Mar. 1845
Illustrated London News, 1847-1859
The Times, 1847-1859

Published Sources

Bellot, Joseph-René. *Memoirs.* . . . London: Hurst and Blackett, 1855.

Cooke, Alan. "The Autobiography of Dr. John Rae (1813-1893): A Preliminary Note," *Polar Record* 14, No. 89, 1968.

———— and Holland, "Chronological List of Expeditions and Historical Events in Northern Canada."

Corner, George. *Doctor Kane of the Arctic Seas.* Philadelphia: Temple University Press, 1972.

Cyriax, "Arctic Sledge Travelling by Officers of the Royal Navy."

————, *Sir John Franklin's Last Expedition.*

Dodge, *The Polar Rosses.*

Elder, William. *Biography of Elisha Kent Kane.* Philadelphia: Childs & Peterson, 1858.

Goodsir, Robert Anstruther. *An Arctic Voyage to Baffin's Bay and Lancaster Sound in Search of Friends with Sir John Franklin.* . . . London: John Van Voorst, 1850.

Hodgson, Maurice. "Bellot and Kennedy: A Contrast in Personalities," *Beaver*, Outfit 305, No. 1, 1974.

Holland, Clive. "The Arctic Committee of 1851: A Background Study, Part 1," *Polar Record* 20, No. 124, 1980.

———— . "The Arctic Committee of 1851: A Background Study, Part 2," *Polar Record* 20, No. 125, 1980.

Johnson, *Sir John Richardson.*

Kane, Elisha Kent. *The U.S. Grinnell Expedition in Search of Sir John Franklin: A Personal Narrative.* New York: Harper & Bros., 1854.

Kennedy, Mary. "Lt. Joseph-René Bellot," *Beaver*, Outfit 269, No. 1, 1938.

Kennedy, William. *A Short Narrative of the Second Voyage of the* Prince Albert *in Search of Sir John Franklin.* London: W.H. Dalton, 1853.

King, *The Franklin Expedition from First to Last.*

M'Dougall, George F. *The Eventful Voyage of H.M. Discovery Ship 'Resolute' to the Arctic Regions.* . . . London: Longman, Brown, Green, Longmans & Roberts, 1857.

Neatby, *The Search for Franklin.*

Osborn, Sherard (ed.). *The Discovery of the North-West Passage.* . . . Edmonton: Hurtig, 1969 (reprint; originally published 1856).

———— . *Stray Leaves from an Arctic Journal.* . . . New York: George P. Putnam, 1852.

Owen, *The Fate of Franklin.*

Pullen, W.J.S. "Pullen in Search of Franklin, Part 1," *Beaver*, Outfit 277, March, 1947.

———— . "Pullen in Search of Franklin, Part 2," *Beaver*, Outfit 278, June, 1947.

Rae, John. *Narrative of an Expedition to the Shores of the Arctic Sea in 1846 and 1847.* Toronto: Canadiana House, 1970 (reprint).

Rich, E.E. *John Rae's Correspondence with the Hudson's Bay Company on Arctic Exploration, 1844-1855*. London: Hudson's Bay Record Society, 1953.

Richards, Robert L. *Dr. John Rae*. Whitby: Caedmon, 1985.

Richardson, John. *Arctic Searching Expedition: Journal of a Boat Voyage through Rupert's Land and the Arctic Sea in Search of the Discovery Ships under the Command of Sir John Franklin*. London: Longman, Brown, Green and Longmans, 1851.

Ross, John, *Rear-Admiral Sir John Franklin*.

Savours, "Sir James Clark Ross."

Shaw, Edward. "Captain William Kennedy," *Historical and Scientific Society of Manitoba Papers*, Ser. III, No. 27, 1970-71.

Snow, William Parker. *Voyage of the* Prince Albert *in Search of Sir John Franklin*. London: Longman, Brown, Green and Longmans, 1851.

Stefansson, Vilhjalmur. "Rae's Arctic Correspondence," *Beaver*, Outfit 284, March, 1954.

Sutherland, Peter. *Journal of a Voyage in Baffin's Bay and Barrow Straits in the Years 1850-51.* . . . London: Longman, Brown, Green and Longmans, 1852.

Wallace, H.N., *The Navy, the Company and Richard King*.

Wallace, R.C. "Rae of the Arctic," *Beaver*, Outfit 284, March, 1954.

Woodward, Frances J. "The Franklin Search in 1850," *Polar Record* 5, No. 40, 1950.

———. "Joseph-René Bellot, 1826-53," *Polar Record* 5, No. 39, 1950.

———, *Portrait of Jane*.

Wright, Noel, *Quest for Franklin*.

CHAPTER FIVE
Unpublished Manuscripts

National Archives of Canada
MG24 H30 McClure Papers
National Maritime Museum
JOD/102 Henry Piers Journal

Newspapers

Illustrated London News, 1847-1859
The Times, 1847-1859

Published Sources

Armstrong, Alexander. *A Personal Narrative of the Discovery of the North-West Passage.* . . . London: Hurst and Blackett, 1857.

Bellot, *Memoirs*.

Kennedy, Mary, "Lt. Joseph-René Bellot."

Kennedy, William, *A Short Narrative*.

Jones, A.G.E. "Captain Robert Martin: A Peterhead Whaling Master in the 19th Century," *Scottish Geographical Magazine* 85, No. 3, 1969.

Neatby, L.H. (ed.). *Frozen Ships: The Arctic Diary of Johann Miertsching, 1850-54*. Toronto: Macmillan of Canada, 1967.

———, *The Search for Franklin*.

Nelson, J.H. "The Last Voyage of H.M.S. *Investigator*, 1850-53 and the Discovery of the North West Passage," *Polar Record* 13, No. 87, 1967.

Osborn, *The Discovery of the North-West Passage*.

———, *Stray Leaves from an Arctic Journal*.

Owen, *The Fate of Franklin*.

Shaw, "Captain William Kennedy."

Sutherland, Patricia, *The Franklin Era in Canadian Arctic History*.

Woodward, "Joseph-René Bellot."

———, *Portrait of Jane*.

Wright, Noel, *Quest for Franklin*.

CHAPTER SIX
Unpublished Manuscripts

Historical Society of Pennsylvania
Dreer Collection: Elisha Kent Kane Journal

National Archives of Canada
MG24 H27 Sir Francis Leopold McClintock Papers
MG24 H31 W. May Papers

Scott Polar Research Institute
MS116 Penny Papers

Stanford University Libraries, Dept. of Special Collections
Elisha Kent Kane Journal

United States National Archives
RG401 John Wall Wilson Journal

Government Documents

House of Commons, *Sessional Papers*, Reports from Committees, Vol. 7, session 12, Dec. 1854–14 Aug. 1855.

Newspapers

Illustrated London News, 1847-1859

Published Sources

Belcher, Edward. *The Last of the Arctic Voyages.* . . . London: Lovell Reeve, 1855.

Burns, Flora Hamilton. "H.M.S. *Herald* in Search of Franklin," *Beaver*, Outfit 294, Autumn, 1963.

Corner, *Doctor Kane of the Arctic Seas*.

Cullum, George W. "Doctor Isaac I. Hayes," *American Geographical Society Bulletin*, Vol. 13, 1881.

Elder, *Biography of Elisha Kent Kane*.

[Fox, Margaret]. *The Love-Life of Dr. Kane, Containing the Correspondence and a History of the Acquaintance, Engagement and Secret Marriage between Elisha Kent Kane and Margaret Fox*. New York: Carleton, 1865.

Godfrey, William C. *Godfrey's Narrative of the Last Grinnell Arctic Exploring Expedition.* . . . Philadelphia: J.T. Lloyd & Co., 1857.

[Hans Hendrik]. *Memoirs of Hans Hendrik, the Arctic Traveller Serving under Kane, Hayes, Hall and Nares . . . 1853-1876*. London: Trubner & Co., 1876.

Hayes, Isaac Israel. *An Arctic Boat-Journey in the Autumn of 1854*. London: Richard Bentley, 1860.

Inglefield, E.A. *A Summer Search for Sir John Franklin.* . . . London: Thomas Harrison, 1853.

Kane, Elisha Kent. *Arctic Explorations: The Second Grinnell Expedition in Search of Sir John Franklin, 1853, '54, '55*. 2 vols. Philadelphia: Childs & Peterson, 1856.

Kennedy, Mary, "Lt. Joseph-René Bellot."

Kerr, Howard. *Mediums and Spirit-rappers and Roaring Radicals: Spiritualism in American Literature, 1850-1900*. Urbana: University of Illinois Press, 1972.

————, and Crow, Charles (eds.). *The Occult in America: New Historical Perspectives*. Urbana and Chicago: University of Illinois Press, 1983.

L'Estrange, *Lady Belcher and Her Friends*.

Markham, Sir Clements R. "Admiral Sir Leopold M'Clintock, K.C.B.," *Geographical Journal* 31, No. 1, 1908.

————. *The Life of Sir Leopold McClintock*. London: John Murray, 1909.

M'Dougall, *Eventful Voyage of H.M. Discovery Ship 'Resolute.'*

Neatby, Leslie. *Conquest of the Last Frontier*. Toronto: Longmans Canada, 1966.

————, *Frozen Ships*.

————, *The Search for Franklin*.

Nelson, "The Last Voyage of H.M.S. *Investigator*."

Osborn, *The Discovery of the North-West Passage*.

Owen, *The Fate of Franklin*.

Rich, *John Rae's Correspondence with the Hudson's Bay Company*.

Richards, *Dr. John Rae*.

Stefansson, "Rae's Arctic Correspondence."

_____ , *Unsolved Mysteries of the Arctic*.

Sutherland, Patricia, *The Franklin Era*.

Traill, *The Life of Sir John Franklin*.

Villarejo, Oscar (ed.). *Dr. Kane's Voyage to the Polar Lands*. Philadelphia: University of Pennsylvania Press, 1965.

Wallace, Hugh, *The Navy, the Company and Richard King*.

Wallace, R.C., "Rae of the Arctic."

Woodward, Frances J. "Edward Augustus Inglefield," *Polar Record* 5, Nos. 35/36, Jan.-July, 1948.

_____ , *Portrait of Jane*.

Wright, Noel, *Quest for Franklin*.

CHAPTER SEVEN
Unpublished Manuscripts

Historical Society of Pennsylvania
Dreer Collection: Kane Journal
National Maritime Museum (London)
Philip Sharpe Papers
Scott Polar Research Institute
MS1161 Private journal of Francis T. Skead
Stanford University Libraries, Dept. of Special Collections
Elisha Kent Kane Journal
United States National Archives
RG401 John Wall Wilson Journal

Newspapers

Illustrated London News, 1847-1859
The Times, 1847-1859

Published Sources

Collinson, Richard. *Journal of H.M.S.* Enterprise, *on the Expedition in Search of Sir John Franklin's Ships by Behring Strait, 1850-55* (ed. Thomas Collinson). London: Sampson Low, Marston, Searle & Rivington, 1889.

Corner, *Doctor Kane of the Arctic Seas*.

Cullum, "Doctor Isaac I. Hayes."

Elder, *Biography of Elisha Kent Kane*.

[Fox], *The Love-Life of Dr. Kane*.

Godfrey, *Godfrey's Narrative of the Last Grinnell Arctic Exploring Expedition*.

[Hans Hendrik], *Memoirs*.

652

Hayes, *An Arctic Boat-Journey*.

Kane, *Arctic Explorations*.

Neatby, *Conquest of the Last Frontier*.

———, *The Search for Franklin*.

Sutherland, Patricia, *The Franklin Era*.

Villarejo, *Dr. Kane's Voyage*.

Wright, Noel, *Quest for Franklin*.

CHAPTER EIGHT
Unpublished Manuscripts

National Maritime Museum
Philip Sharpe Papers
National Archives of Canada
MG24 H27 McClintock Papers

Newspapers

Illustrated London News, 1847-1859
The Times, 1847-1859

Published Sources

Amy, Bhatnagar, Damkjar, and Beattie, "The Last Franklin Expedition."

Anderson, James. "Extracts from Chief Factor James Anderson's Arctic Journal," *Journal of the Royal Geographical Society*, Vol. 27.

Beattie, "A Report on Newly Discovered Human Skeletal Remains."

——— and Geiger, *Frozen in Time*.

——— and Savelle, "Discovery of Human Remains from Franklin's Last Expedition."

Corner, *Doctor Kane of the Arctic Seas*.

Cyriax, *Sir John Franklin's Last Arctic Expedition*.

———, "The Two Franklin Expedition Records."

Elder, *Biography of Elisha Kent Kane*.

Galaburri, "The Franklin Records."

Gibson, "Sir John Franklin's Last Voyage."

———, "Some Further Traces of the Franklin Retreat."

Markham, "Admiral Sir Leopold McClintock."

———, *The Life of Sir Leopold McClintock*.

M'Clintock, Capt. F.L. *The Voyage of the* Fox *in the Arctic Seas: A Narrative of the Fate of Sir John Franklin and His Companions*. Edmonton: Hurtig, 1972 (reprint).

653

Neatby, *The Search for Franklin.*

Notman, Anderson, Beattie, and Amy, "Arctic Paleoradiology."

Owen, *The Fate of Franklin.*

Skewes, *Sir John Franklin.*

Stefansson, *Unsolved Mysteries of the Arctic.*

Traill, *The Life of Sir John Franklin.*

Wallace, Hugh, *The Navy, the Company and Richard King.*

Woodward, *Portrait of Jane.*

Wright, Noel, *Quest for Franklin.*

CHAPTER NINE
Unpublished Manuscripts

United States National Archives

RG401/33 Tyson Papers: expedition notes and diaries, fair copy 1872-73, nos. 1-6

RG45-D136 Noah Hayes Journal

Government Documents

43rd Congress, 1st session, executive document 1, part 3. Report of the Secretary of the Navy, transcript of the Board of Inquiry into the *Polaris.*

Newspapers

New York *Herald*, September/October, 1873.

New York Times, 1860-1873

The Times, 1873

Published Sources

Anon. "Report of the Reception by the American Geographical Society of Captain Hall and His Officers Previous to Their Departure for the Arctic Regions, Held 26th June 1871," *Journal of the American Geographical Society*, 1870-71.

Blake, Euphemia Vale (ed.). *Arctic Experiences, Containing Capt. George E. Tyson's Wonderful Drift on the Ice Floe....* New York: Harper Bros., 1874.

Burgess, Helen. "Tookoolito of Cumberland Sound," *North* 15, No. 1, 1968.

Cullum, "Doctor Isaac I. Hayes."

Cyriax, Richard J. "Captain Hall and the So-called Survivors of the Franklin Expedition," *Polar Record* 4, No. 28, 1944.

Davis, Rear-Admiral C.H. *Narrative of the North Polar Expedition U.S. Ship Polaris....* Washington: Government Printing Office, 1876.

Hall, Charles Francis. *Life with the Esquimaux....* Edmonton: Hurtig, 1970 (reprint).

[Hans Hendrik], *Memoirs*.

Hayes, Isaac Israel. *The Open Polar Sea: A Narrative of a Voyage of Discovery towards the North Pole*. New York: Hurd & Houghton, 1867.

Loomis, Chauncey, and Wilson, M.A. "The Polaris Expedition, 1871-73: A Newly Found Graphic Record," *Prologue, Journal of the National Archives*, Spring, 1970.

_____. *Weird and Tragic Shores: The Story of Charles Francis Hall, Explorer*. New York: Alfred Knopf, 1971.

Neatby, *Conquest of the Last Frontier*.

_____. "Joe and Hannah," *Beaver*, Autumn, 1969.

Nourse, J.E. (ed.). *Narrative of the Second Arctic Expedition Made by Charles F. Hall. . . .* Washington: Government Printing Office, 1879.

Ross, W. Gillies. *Arctic Whalers, Icy Seas: Narratives of the Davis Strait Whale Fishery*. Toronto: Irwin Publishing, 1985.

CHAPTER TEN
Unpublished Manuscripts

National Archives of Canada
MG29 B12 George Strong Nares Papers
National Maritime Museum
Wm. May Papers MAY 11/2; MAY 13
Albert Markham Papers, MRK13, MRK45, pts. 2 and 3

Government Documents

House of Commons, Parliamentary Papers:
   1875, Vol. XLV, p. 523. Papers and correspondence as to equipment and fitting out of expedition of 1875, including report of Admiralty Arctic Committee.
   1876, Vol. XLV, p. 463. Further Papers and Correspondence.
   1877, Vol. LVI, p. 1. Journals and Proceedings of Expedition 1875-76, under command of Captain Sir George Nares.
   1877, Vol. LVI, p. 1137. Letter addressed by Admiralty to Sir George S. Nares on outbreak of scurvy.
   1878, Vol. LII, p. 791. Medical report on Eskimo dog disease by fleet surgeon Belgrave Ninnis, M.D.

Newspapers

The Graphic, 1875-1876
Illustrated London News, 1875-1876

The Spectator, 4 Nov. 1876
The Times, 1874-1877

Published Sources

Caswell, John. "The RGS and the British Arctic Expedition, 1875-76," *Geographical Journal* 143, Pt. 2, 1977.

Chick, Harriette; Hume, E. Margaret; Skelton, Ruth F.; Smith, Alice Henderson. "The Relative Content of Antiscorbutic Principle in Limes and Lemons," *Lancet*, 30 November 1918.

Deacon, Margaret, and Savours, Ann. "Sir George Strong Nares (1831-1915)," *Polar Record* 18, No. 113, 1976.

[Hans Hendrik], *Memoirs*.

Hattersley-Smith, Geoffrey. "The British Arctic Expedition, 1875-76," *Polar Record* 18, No. 113, 1976.

Kendall, Dr. E.J.C. "Scurvy during Some British Polar Expeditions, 1875-1917," *Polar Record* 7, No. 51, 1955.

MacKinnon, C.S. "The Wintering Over of Royal Navy Ships in the Canadian Arctic, 1819-1876," *Beaver*, Outfit 315, No. 3, Winter, 1984/85.

Markham, Albert Hastings. *A Whaling Cruise to Baffin's Bay and the Gulf of Boothia. . . .* London: Sampson Low, Marston, Low and Searle, 1875.

Markham, Clements. "The Arctic Expedition of 1875-76," *Royal Geographical Proceedings* 21, No. 6, 1877.

———. *The Threshold of the Unknown Region.* London: Sampson Low, Marston, Low and Searle, 1873.

Markham, M.E., and Markham, F.A. *The Life of Sir Albert Hastings Markham.* Cambridge: The University Press, 1927.

May, W.H. *The Life of a Sailor.* London: William Clowes & Sons, n.d.

Nares, Capt. George Strong. *Narrative of a Voyage to the Polar Sea during 1875-76 in H.M. Ships 'Alert' and 'Discovery'. . . .* 2 vols. London: Sampson Low, Marston, Searle and Rivington, 1878.

Neatby, *Conquest of the Last Frontier*.

CHAPTER ELEVEN
Unpublished Manuscripts

Library of Congress
Adolphus Greely Papers, Boxes 3, 69, 70, 71
United States National Archives
RG27 Records of Lady Franklin Bay Expedition
RG200 David L. Brainard Papers

Newspapers, Magazines

New York Times, 1881-1888

Published Sources

Barr, William. "Geographical Aspects of the First International Polar Year, 1882-1883," *Annals of the Association of American Geographers* 73, No. 4, 1984.

Greely, Adolphus W. *Report on the Proceedings of the United States Expedition to Lady Franklin Bay. . . .* Vols. 1 and 2. Washington: Government Printing Office, 1888.

_____ . *Three Years of Arctic Service. . . .* New York: Charles Scribner's Sons, 1886.

Guttridge, Leonard F. *Icebound.* Annapolis: Naval Institute Press, 1986.

Hoehling, A.A. *The Jeannette Expedition.* London: Abelard-Schuman, 1967.

James, Bessie Rowland (ed.). *Six Came Back: The Arctic Adventure of David L. Brainard.* Indianapolis/New York: Bobbs-Merrill, 1940.

Kersting, Rudolf (ed.). *The White World. . . .* New York: Lewis Scribner Co., 1902.

Lanman, Charles. *Farthest North, or the Life and Explorations of Lieutenant James B. Lockwood of the Greely Arctic Expedition.* New York: D. Appleton & Co., 1889.

Neatby, *Conquest of the Last Frontier.*

Schley, Comm. W.S., and Soley, J.R. *The Rescue of Greely.* London: Sampson Low, Marston, Searle and Rivington, 1885.

Todd, Alden. *Abandoned: The Story of the Greely Arctic Expedition, 1881-1884.* New York: McGraw-Hill, 1961.

CHAPTER TWELVE
Newspapers

New York Times, 1897, 1903-6, 1930
The Times, 1897, 1930

Published Sources

Amundsen, Roald. *My Life as an Explorer.* New York: Doubleday, Page & Co., 1927.

_____ . *The North West Passage. . . .* 2 vols. London: Archibald Constable & Co., 1908.

_____ . "To the North Magnetic Pole and Through the North-West Passage," *Geographical Journal* 29, No. 5, 1907.

Bartlett, Robert A. *The Log of "Bob" Bartlett.* New York: Blue Ribbon Books, 1928.

Eames, Hugh. *Winner Lose All: Dr. Cook and the Theft of the North Pole.* Boston:

Little, Brown & Co., 1973.

Gibson, William. "Amundsen in King William Land," *Beaver*, Outfit 271, June, 1940.

Guttridge, *Icebound*.

Harper, Kenn. *Give Me My Father's Body: The Life of Minik the New York Eskimo*. Frobisher Bay: Blacklead Books, 1986.

Hayes, James Gordon. *R bert Edwin Peary: A Record of His Explorations, 1886-1909*. London: Grant Richards & Humphrey Toulmin, [1929].

Hobbs, William Herbert. *Peary*. New York: Macmillan Co., 1936.

Hoehling, *The Jeannette Expedition*.

Horwood, Harold. *Bartlett, the Great Canadian Explorer*. Toronto: Doubleday & Co. Inc., 1977.

Hunt, William R. *To Stand at the Pole*. New York: Stein and Day, 1981.

Huntford, Roland. *Scott and Amundsen*. London: Hodder & Stoughton, 1979.

Jackson, Frederick G. *A Thousand Days in the Arctic*. London and New York: Harper & Bros., 1899.

Lachambre, Henri, and Machuron, Alexis. *Andrée's Balloon Expedition in Search of the North Pole*. New York: Frederick Stokes Co., 1898.

Nansen, Fridtjof. *Farthest North*. London: Archibald Constable & Company, 1897.

Neatby, *Conquest of the Last Frontier*.

Peary, Robert Edwin. *Nearest the Pole: A Narrative of the Polar Expedition of the Peary Arctic Club*. London: Hutchinson, 1907.

Putnam, George Taylor. *Andrée: The Record of a Tragic Adventure*. New York: Brewer & Warren Inc., 1930.

Sverdrup, Otto. *New Land: Four Years in the Arctic Regions*. New York: Longmans, Green & Co., 1904.

[Swedish Society for Anthropology and Geography]. *Andrée's Story: The Complete Record of His Polar Flight*. New York: Viking Press, 1930.

Weems, John. *Peary, the Explorer and the Man*. Boston: Houghton, Mifflin Co., 1967.

Whitehouse, J. Howard. *Nansen: A Book of Homage*. London: Hodder & Stoughton, 1930.

Wordie, J.M. "The Andrée Diaries," *Polar Record* 1, No. 1, 1931.

Wright, Theon. *The Big Nail: The Story of the Cook-Peary Feud*. New York: John Day & Co., 1970.

CHAPTER THIRTEEN
Unpublished Manuscripts

United States National Archives
RG 401 Peary Papers
Papers relating to Arctic Expeditions, North Pole Boxes 1-3
Correspondence, 1908-1909

Kuhne, Marie Peary, "Memoranda re Henshaw Ward article, American Mercury September, 1934"

Government Documents

Congressional Record, 61st Congress, 3rd session, Vol. 46, Pt. 3
Congressional Record, 64th Congress, 1st session, Vol. 53, Pt. 13 and Pt. 14

Newspapers

New York *Herald*, September-December, 1909
New York Times, 1907-1911
New York *World*, September-October, 1909

Published Sources

Anon. "Peary's Journey to the Pole," *Geographical Journal* 89, No. 3, 1937.
Bartlett, *The Log of "Bob" Bartlett*.
Borup, George. *A Tenderfoot with Peary*. New York: Frederick A. Stokes Co., 1911.
Bradley, John R. "My Knowledge of Dr. Cook's Polar Expedition," *The Independent*, 16 Sept. 1909.
Bridgman, Herbert. "Commander Peary," *The Independent*, 16 Sept. 1909.
Cook, Frederick. "Dr. Cook's Own Story," *Hampton's Magazine*, January-April, 1911.
_____. *My Attainment of the Pole*. New York: Polar Publishing Co., 1911.
Dunbar, Moira. "Historical References to Ice Islands," *Arctic* 5, No. 2, July, 1952.
Eames, *Winner Lose All*.
Etienne, Jean-Louis. "Skiing alone to the Pole," *National Geographic*, September, 1986.
Euller, John. "The Centenary of the Birth of Frederick A. Cook," *Arctic* 17, No. 4, 1964.
Fiala, Anthony. *Fighting the Polar Ice*. New York: Doubleday, Page & Co., 1907.
Freeman, Andrew. *The Case for Doctor Cook*. New York: Coward-McCann, 1961.
Gibbons, Russell. "Frederick Albert Cook: An Enigma in Polar History," *Polar Notes*, No. 8, June, 1968.
_____. "Frederick Cook and the North Pole: The Unmaking of a Discoverer," *Arctic Circular* 25, No. 1.
Gibbs, Philip. *Adventures in Journalism*. New York: Harper & Bros., 1923.
Goodsell, John. *On Polar Trails: the Peary Expedition to the North Pole 1908-09*. Austin: Eakin Press, 1983.

Greely, A.W. "Dr. Cook's North Polar Discoveries," *The Independent*, 16 Sept. 1909.

Greenaway, K.R. "Additional Information from Flights and Air Photographs in the Canadian Arctic," *Arctic* 5, No. 2, 1952.

Harper, *Give Me My Father's Body*.

Hattersley-Smith, Geoffrey. "Comments on the Origin of Ice Islands," *Arctic* 5, No. 2, 1952.

Hayes, *Robert Edwin Peary*.

Henson, Matthew. *A Black Explorer at the North Pole* . . . . New York: Walker and Co., 1969 (reprint).

———. "The Negro at the North Pole," *World's Work*, April, 1910.

Herbert, Wally. *Across the Top of the World*. London: Longmans, 1969.

Hinks, Arthur R. "Notes on the Determination of Position near the Poles," *Geographical Journal* 35, No. 3, 1910.

Hobbs, *Peary*.

Horwood, *Bartlett*.

Hunt, *To Stand at the Pole*.

Kennan, George. "Arctic Work and Arctic Food," *Outlook*, 16 Oct., 20 Nov. 1909.

Koenig, L.S. "Discovery of Ice Islands on USAF Flights over the Arctic Ocean," *Arctic* 5, No. 2, 1952.

Moore, Terris. *Mount McKinley: The Pioneer Climbs*. Anchorage: University of Alaska Press, 1975.

Neatby, *Conquest of the Last Frontier*.

Peary, Robert. "The Discovery of the North Pole," *Hampton's Magazine*, January, 1910–September, 1910.

———. *The North Pole: Its Discovery under the Auspices of the Peary Arctic Club*. Toronto: Copp, Clark Co., 1910.

Plaisted, Ralph. "How I Reached the North Pole on a Snowmobile," *Popular Science*, September, 1968.

Rawlins, Dennis. "Peary and the North Pole: The Lingering Doubt," *U.S. Naval Institute Proceedings*, June, 1970.

———. *Peary at the Pole: Fact or Fiction?* Washington/New York: Robert Luce, 1973.

Stanton, Theodore. "Dr. Cook at Copenhagen," *The Independent*, 7 Oct. 1909.

Stead, W.T. "Dr. Cook, the Man and the Deed," *Review of Reviews*, October, 1909.

Steger, Will. "North to the Pole," *National Geographic*, September, 1986.

Ward, Henshaw. "Peary Did Not Reach the Pole," *American Mercury*, September, 1934.

Weems, *Peary*.

———. *Race for the Pole*. New York: Henry Holt Co., 1960.

Whyte, Frederic. *The Life of W.T. Stead*. London: Jonathan Cape, 1925.

Wright, Theon, *The Big Nail*.

Index

664

665

attempt, 573-82 *passim*
Hepburn, John, 65, 68, 71, 73, 75, 196, 630; *quoted*, 90
Herald (HMS), 163, 215, 232, 246, 297
Herron, John, 404
Herschel I., 545, 546
Hiccles (sailor), 248
Hickey, "Irish Tom," 274, 278
Hill, James J., 523
Hillary, Sir Edmund, 623
Hobbs, Prof. William, 622
Hobby, Henry, 392
Hobson, Lieut. William, 322, 323, 326, 331, 332-33, 337, 340
Holm, Comm. Gustav, 612
Hong Kong, 211, 298, 302
Honolulu, Hawaii, 213, 214-15, 296-97
Hood, Robert, 65, 68, 71, 72, 73, 74, 90
Hooker, Sir Joseph, 492
Hooper, William, 31, 38, 39
Hope, Sir George, 23
Hope, 292
Hoppner, Lieut. Henry Parkyns, 85-86, 87
Horgaard, Commander, *quoted*, 613
Howgate, Capt. Henry, 437, 449-50
Hubbard, Gen. Thomas, 554, 563, 568, 569, 606, 627
Hudson, Henry, 17, 35, 46, 393
Hudson Bay, 17, 18, 46, 47, 59, 65
Hudson's Bay Co., 64, 66, 67, 81, 91, 126-27, 131, 133, 136, 148, 153, 158, 159-60, 162, 163, 169, 172, 194, 209, 218, 265
Hudson Strait, 17, 47, 55
Huish, Robert, 114
Humboldt Glacier (Greenland), 256-57, 290
Hume, David, *quoted*, 493

Igloolik, 51, 52, 58, 63, 375-76, 630
Illustrated London News, 414; *quoted*, 236
Independence Bay (Greenland), 515, 519
Indians, 65, 69, 70, 73-74, 90, 91, 94, 148, 158, 431; Coppermine, 66, 68; Cree, 68, 209
Inglefield, Comm. Edward, 241, 249, 412, 430; and Franklin search, 205-6, 235-36, 250, 252
Inglefield Gulf (Greenland), 516, 517
Inglis, Sir Robert, 167
In-nook-poo-zhee-jook, 266
Innuit (word), 350
International Geographical Congress, 499, 531, 552
International Polar Conference, 435
International Polar Year, First, 435-36, 440, 501
Intrepid (HMS), 179, 244, 245, 263
Investigator (HMS), 164, 169, 202, 204-5, 211, 213-14, 215-28 *passim*, 247, 248, 249, 259, 260, 299, 532
Isabel, 205, 235, 236, 250, 313
Isabella, 16, 26, 119
Israel, Sgt. Edward, 461, 463, 470, 471, 474

Jackson, Frederick, 498, 533
Jackson, William, 404, 405
Jacob (hunter), 357
Jago, Lieut. Charles, 302

James Ross Strait, 173, 332, 538
Jamka, Frederick, 401
Jeannette, 436-37, 441, 450-51, 465, 477, 491, 515
Jens, Edward, 439, 441, 442, 462-63, 470, 473
Jensen, Peter, 355-56, 359, 361, 362-63
Jesup, Morris K., 522, 523, 552, 568, 627
Jesup Land, 552, 554, 564, 585, 591
Jewell, Sgt. Winfield, 469, 471, 484
Joe (Ebierbing), 350-51, 352, 367-80 *passim*, 385, 390-408 *passim*, 514, 630
Johansen, Hjalmar, 494, 496-97
Jones, Alderman, 17
Jones Sound, 17, 37, 173, 178, 180, 191, 205, 236, 383, 388, 593, 595, 597, 623

Kalutunah, 280, 281-86, 360, 363-64, 521, 630
Kamchatka Peninsula, 37, 215
Kamehameha IV, King of Hawaii, 381
Kane, Elisha Kent, 175, 197, 306, 313, 314-15, 320, 338, 358, 490, 583, 584; *quoted*, 22, 177-78, 185, 258, 276, 278-79, 287-88; influence of, 175-76, 304, 306, 345, 513, 587; character and back-ground, 176-77; on first Grinnell expedition (Franklin search), 175, 176, 177-85, 302-3; and second Grinnell expedition (Franklin search), 237, 241-43, 250-59 *passim*, 273-95 *passim*, 532; and Margaret Fox, 237-42, 304-7; as hero, 302-4, 599
Kane, John, 303
Kane, Robert, 346
Kane, Thomas, 279
Kane Basin, 257, 361, 389, 449, 453, 461, 522, 553, 555, 572, 589, 596, 629
Kangara, 55
Kellett, Capt. Henry, 232, 260, 262, 263, 269, 297-98, 431, 628; *quoted*, 188; and Franklin search, 215-16, 244, 245, 249; and McClure rescue, 246-48, 249
Kennan, George, *quoted*, 607-8
Kennedy, Capt. William, 185, 228-29, 321, 337-38, 514; character and background, 193-94, 196, 209-10; and Franklin search, 193, 197-98, 206, 209, 210-11, 235, 250
Kennedy Channel, 258, 362, 389, 421, 448, 554
Kent I., 627
Kent Peninsula, 70, 94
King, Dr. Richard, 330, 628; and Back expedition, 127, 128, 130, 131; and search for Passage, 147-48; and Franklin search, 153-54, 157, 170, 268, 328
Kingiktok, 284
King Point, Yukon, 545, 547
King William Land (King William I.), 113, 128, 134-36, 147, 165, 173, 201, 265-66, 295, 296, 299, 305, 311, 316, 321-30 *passim*, 336, 347, 349, 352, 372-73, 408, 514, 538, 539, 542, 544
Kislingbury, Lieut. Frederick, 438-39, 442, 443, 445, 459-60, 469-75 *passim*, 484
Klondike gold rush, 504, 546
Knorr (sailor), 360, 362-63
Kodlunarn I., 366
Koojeese, 366
Koolootingwah, 596
Kotzebue Sound, Alaska, 89, 94, 215

Parry Is., 627

Pavy, Dr. Octave, 439-41, 443-48 *passim*, 459-75 *passim*, 484-85; *quoted*, 442

Payer Harbour (Ellesmere I.), 453, 479, 527, 528, 530

Peary, Francine, 526, 527

Peary, Josephine Diebitsch, 514, 515, 516, 518, 521, 526, 527, 530, 552

Peary, Marie Ahnighito, 517, 527, 530, 552

Peary, Robert Edwin, 49, 175-76, 511-12, 516, 527-28, 565-69, 630; character and background, 512-13, 551, 614-15; Greenland expedition, 513-21, 526, 587; and Eskimos, 517-18, 520-22; polar expeditions, 528-30, 551, 553-61, 570-86; Ellesmere expedition, 563-64; and Cook, 586-87, 596, 598, 602-3, 606-7; as hero, 599, 615; and polar claim, 601, 609, 614-20, 621, 623-25

Peary Arctic Club, 523, 526, 528, 553, 568, 570, 606, 607, 608, 609, 611, 617

Peary at the Pole: Fact or Fiction?, 624

Peary Channel, 515, 519, 552, 615, 629

Peary Land, 515

Peary System, 517, 553, 567, 586, 623

Peel, Robert, 82

Peel Sound, 164, 165, 189, 210, 243, 320, 321, 329, 428, 491, 536, 628

Pelly Bay (Boothia Peninsula), 266

Peltier, Joseph, 73

Penetanguishene, U.C., 89

Penny, William, 170-71, 181, 187, 192, 252, 628; and Franklin search, 171-72, 173, 178, 180, 185, 189-90, 201, 202, 204

Penny Strait, 593, 628

Percy, Charles, 57

Periwinkle (USS), *see Polaris*

Peter (hunter), 357, 358, 360

Petermann, August, 436

Petermann Fiord, 423, 428

Petersen, Carl, 192, 251, 252, 254, 255, 258, 275, 276, 280, 282-84, 287, 289, 293-94, 317, 320, 322, 323, 324

Petersen, Niels Christian, 424

Phayer, Lieut. George, 298

Philadelphia, Pa., 176, 177, 238, 240, 315; Centennial Exposition, 443, 500

Philadelphia *Inquirer*, 485

Phoenix (ship), 249, 250

Phrenology, 23

Pike, Captain, 450, 453-54, 455

Pim, Lieut. Bedford, 202, 232, 246-47, 629

Pinkerton agency, 450, 607

Pioneer, 203, 411

Plaisted, Ralph, 581, 582

Plover (HMS), 163, 214, 215, 296, 297

Point Back (Banks I.), 228

Point Barrow, Alaska, 131, 132-33, 161, 216, 297, 298, 547

Point Hope, Alaska, 297

Point Moss (Ellesmere I.), 556, 557, 570

Point Sherard Osborn, 628

Point Turnagain, 70, 95, 107, 114, 133, 161

Polaris (USS), 384, 387-90, 393, 394-97, 399, 407, 421, 436

Polaris Bay, 428, 443

Politiken, 601

Poowutyuk, 116-17

Porden, Eleanor Anne, 76-81. *See also* Franklin, Eleanor Anne Porden

Port Clarence, Alaska, 301

Porter, George, 426

Port Foulke, Greenland, 355

Port Leopold (Somerset I.), 164, 178, 179, 197-98, 206-7, 208-9, 210, 231, 321

Portsmouth, Eng., 419

Portsmouth, N.H., 483

Prince Albert, 174, 179, 185, 191, 193, 194, 197-98, 206, 208, 209, 211, 229, 235

Prince Albert Land (Victoria I.), 222, 224, 225, 299

Prince Gustav Adolf Sea, 629

Prince of Wales, 77

Prince of Wales Land (Prince of Wales I.), 189, 210, 322, 329, 333

Prince of Wales Strait, 222-23, 224, 226, 228, 231, 260, 299

Prince Patrick I., 248, 329, 536

Prince Regent Inlet, 39, 59, 81, 84, 85, 86, 107, 109-10, 113, 118, 127, 143, 174, 179, 193, 197, 198, 206, 210, 321

Princess Marie Bay (Ellesmere I.), 524

Princess Royal Is., 221, 224, 226, 231, 262, 299

Pritchard, Billy, 571, 586

Proteus (sealer), 438, 439, 450-54; inquiry, 477

Prudhoe Bay, Alaska, 131

Pullen, Lieut. W.J.S., 163-64, 169

Punch, 150

Punny (Sylvia), 385, 399, 402, 407, 408

Qisuk, 521

Quarterly Review, 33, 88, 98, 120

Quayle, John, 347

Queen Maud Gulf, 134, 341

Rae, Dr. John, 161, 169, 189, 201, 294, 301, 302, 311, 313, 338, 347, 372-73, 376, 415, 423, 431-32, 514, 535, 628, 630; *quoted*, 102, 417; background and character, 158-61, 163; and Franklin search, 158, 161-63, 170; and fate of Franklin expedition, 265-68

Rae Strait, 134, 323, 378, 538, 544, 628

Ralston, Sgt. David, 471, 473, 474, 484

Rasmussen, Knud, 337, 428, 609; *quoted*, 612-13

Rasmussen Basin, 629

Rattlesnake, 301

Ravenscraig (whaler), 407

Rawlins, Dennis, 552, 617, 624; *quoted*, 564

Red Eric, 293

Red River, 131-32

Rensselaer Harbor, Greenland, 253, 355, 394

Repulse Bay (Melville Peninsula), 18, 46, 47, 48, 65, 95, 130, 159, 160, 212, 265, 267, 350, 370, 372, 374, 375, 376, 378, 379, 384, 630

Repulse Haven, Greenland, 428, 446

Rescue, 175, 178, 181, 182, 184, 348, 349

Resolute (HMS), 182, 232, 243, 245, 263, 282, 313-14, 316, 420-21, 478

Resolute Passage, 185

Return from the Pole, 622

671

Matthew Henson

Robert Peary

Roald Amundsen

Hans Hend

Fridtjof Nansen